STATA LONGITUDINAL/PANEL-DATA REFERENCE MANUAL
RELEASE 10

A Stata Press Publication
StataCorp LP
College Station, Texas

Stata Press, 4905 Lakeway Drive, College Station, Texas 77845

The suggested citation for this software is

StataCorp. 2007. *Stata Statistical Software: Release 10*. College Station, TX: StataCorp LP.

Table of Contents

Cross-Referencing the Documentation

When reading this manual, you will find references to other Stata manuals. For example,

[U] **26 Overview of Stata estimation commands**
[R] **regress**
[D] **reshape**

The first is a reference to chapter 26, *Overview of Stata estimation commands* in the *Stata User's Guide*, the second is a reference to the `regress` entry in the *Base Reference Manual*, and the third is a reference to the `reshape` entry in the *Data Management Reference Manual*.

All the manuals in the Stata Documentation have a shorthand notation:

[GSM]	*Getting Started with Stata for Macintosh*
[GSU]	*Getting Started with Stata for Unix*
[GSW]	*Getting Started with Stata for Windows*
[U]	*Stata User's Guide*
[R]	*Stata Base Reference Manual*
[D]	*Stata Data Management Reference Manual*
[G]	*Stata Graphics Reference Manual*
[P]	*Stata Programming Reference Manual*
[XT]	*Stata Longitudinal/Panel-Data Reference Manual*
[MV]	*Stata Multivariate Statistics Reference Manual*
[SVY]	*Stata Survey Data Reference Manual*
[ST]	*Stata Survival Analysis and Epidemiological Tables Reference Manual*
[TS]	*Stata Time-Series Reference Manual*
[I]	*Stata Quick Reference and Index*
[M]	*Mata Reference Manual*

Detailed information about each of these manuals may be found online at

http://www.stata-press.com/manuals/

Title

> **intro** — Introduction to longitudinal/panel-data manual

Description

This entry describes this manual and what has changed since Stata 9.

Remarks

This manual documents the `xt` commands and is referred to as [XT] in cross-references.

Following this entry, [XT] **xt** provides an overview of the `xt` commands. The other parts of this manual are arranged alphabetically. If you are new to Stata's `xt` commands, we recommend that you read the following sections first:

[XT] **xt**	Introduction to xt commands	
[XT] **xtset**	Declare a dataset to be panel data	
[XT] **xtreg**	Fixed-, between-, and random-effects, and population-averaged linear models	

Stata is continually being updated, and Stata users are always writing new commands. To find out about the latest cross-sectional time-series features, type `search panel data` after installing the latest official updates; see [R] **update**.

What's new

This section is intended for previous Stata users. If you are new to Stata, you may as well skip it.

1. New command `xtset` declares a dataset to be panel data and designates the variable that identifies the panels. In previous versions of Stata, you specified options `i(`*groupvar*`)` and sometimes `t(`*timevar*`)` to identify the panels. You specified the `i()` and `t()` options on the `xt` command you wanted to use. Now you "`xtset` *groupvar*" or "`xtset` *groupvar timevar*" first. The values you set will be remembered from one session to the next if you save your dataset.

   `xtset` also provides a new feature. `xtset` allows option `delta()` to specify the frequency of the time-series data, something you will need to do if you are using Stata's new date/time variables.

   Finally, you can still specify old options `i()` and `t()`, but they are no longer documented. Similarly, old commands `iis` and `tis` continue to work but are no longer documented. See [XT] **xtset**.

2. New estimation commands `xtmelogit` and `xtmepoisson` fit nested, hierarchical, and mixed models with binary and count responses; i.e., you can fit logistic and Poisson models with complex, nested error components. Syntax is the same as for Stata's linear mixed-model estimator, `xtmixed`. To fit a model of graduation with a fixed coefficient on x1 and random coefficient on x2 at the school level, and with random intercepts at both the school and class-within-school level, you type

   ```
   . xtmelogit graduate x1 x2 || school: x2 || class:
   ```

   `predict` after `xtmelogit` and `xtmepoisson` will calculate predicted random effects. See [XT] **xtmelogit**, [XT] **xtmelogit postestimation**, [XT] **xtmepoisson**, and [XT] **xtmepoisson postestimation**.

1

3. New estimation commands are available for fitting dynamic panel-data models:

   a. Existing estimation command xtabond fits dynamic panel-data models by using the Arellano–Bond estimator but now reports results in levels rather than differences. Also, xtabond will now compute the Windmeijer biased-corrected two-step robust VCE. See [XT] **xtabond**.

   b. New estimation command xtdpdsys fits dynamic panel-data models by using the Arellano–Bover/Blundell–Bond system estimator. xtpdsys is an extension of xtabond and produces estimates with smaller bias when the AR process is too persistent. xtpdsys is also more efficient than xtabond. Whereas xtabond uses moment conditions based on the differenced errors in producing results, xtpdsys uses moment conditions based on differences and levels. See [XT] **xtdpdsys**.

   c. New estimation command xtdpd fits dynamic panel-data models extending the Arellano–Bond or the Arellano–Bover/Blundell–Bond system estimator and allows a richer syntax for specifying models and so will fit a broader class of models then either xtabond or xtdpdsys. xtdpd can be used to fit models with serially correlated idiosyncratic errors, whereas xtdpdsys and xtabond assume no serial correlation. xtdpd can be used with models where the structure of the predetermined variables is more complicated than that assumed by xtdpdsys or xtabond. See [XT] **xtdpd**.

   d. New postestimation command estat abond tests for serial correlation in the first-differenced errors. See [XT] **xtabond postestimation**, [XT] **xtdpdsys postestimation**, and [XT] **xtdpd postestimation**.

   e. New postestimation command estat sargan performs the Sargan test of overidentifying restrictions. See [XT] **xtabond postestimation**, [XT] **xtdpdsys postestimation**, and [XT] **xtdpd postestimation**.

4. Existing estimation command xtreg, fe now accepts aweights, fweights, and pweights. Also, new option dfadj specifies that the cluster–robust VCE be adjusted for the within transform. This was previously the default behavior. See [XT] **xtreg**.

5. Existing estimation commands xtreg, fe and xtreg, re used to be willing to produce cluster–robust VCEs when the panels were not nested within the clusters. Sometimes this VCE is consistent and other times it is not. You must now specify the new nonest option to obtain a cluster–robust VCE when the panels are not nested within the clusters.

6. The numerical method used to evaluate distributions, known as quadrature, has been improved. This method is used by the xt random-effects estimation commands xtlogit, xtprobit, xtcloglog, xtintreg, xttobit, and xtpoisson, re normal.

   a. For the estimation commands, the default method is now intmethod(mvaghermite). The old default was intmethod(aghermite).

   b. Option intpoints(#) for the commands now allows up to 195 quadrature points. The default is 12, and the old upper limit was 30. (Models with large random effects often require more quadrature points.)

   c. The estimation commands may now be used with constraints regardless of the quadrature method chosen.

   d. Command quadchk, for use after estimation to verify that the quadrature approximation was sufficiently accurate, now produces a more informative comparison table. Before, four fewer and four more quadrature points were used, and that was reasonable if the number of quadrature points was, say, $n_q = 12$. Now you may specify significantly larger n_q and the ± 4 is not useful. Now quadchk uses $n_q - \text{int}(n_q/3)$ and $n_q + \text{int}(n_q/3)$.

    e. `quadchk` has new option `nofrom` that forces refitted models to start from scratch rather than starting from the previous estimation results. This is important if you use the old `intmethod(aghermite)`, which is sensitive to starting values, but not important if you are using the new default `intmethod(mvaghermite)`.

    See [XT] **quadchk**.

7. All `xt` estimation commands now accept option `vce(`*vcetype*`)`. As mentioned in the [U] **1.3.3 What's new in statistics (general)**, `vce(robust)` and `vce(cluster `*varname*`)` are the right ways to specify the old `robust` and `cluster()` options, and option `vce()` allows other VCE calculations as well.

8. Existing estimation command `xtcloglog` has new option `eform` that requests exponentiated coefficients be reported; see [XT] **xtcloglog**.

9. Existing estimation command `xthtaylor` now allows users to specify only endogenous time-invariant variables, only endogenous time-varying variables, or both. Previously, both were required. See [XT] **xthtaylor**.

10. Most `xt` estimation commands have new option `collinear`, which specifies that collinear variables are not to be removed. Typically, you do not want to specify this option. It is for use when you specify constraints on the coefficients such that, even though the variables are collinear, the model is fully identified. See [XT] **estimation options**.

11. Existing command `xtdes` has been renamed to `xtdescribe`. `xtdes` continues to work as a synonym for `xtdescribe`. See [XT] **xtdescribe**.

12. The [XT] manual has an expanded glossary.

For a complete list of all new features in Stata 10, see [U] **1.3 What's new**.

Also See

[U] **1.3 What's new**

[R] **intro** — Introduction to base reference manual

Title

> **xt** — Introduction to xt commands

Syntax

> xt*cmd* ...

Description

The xt series of commands provide tools for analyzing panel data (also known as longitudinal data or in some disciplines as cross-sectional time series when there is an explicit time component). Panel datasets have the form $\mathbf{x}_{it}$, where $\mathbf{x}_{it}$ is a vector of observations for unit i and time t. The particular commands (such as xtdescribe, xtsum, and xtreg) are documented in the entries that follow this entry. This entry deals with concepts that are common across commands.

The xtset command sets the panel variable and the time variable; see [XT] **xtset**. Most xt commands require that the panel variable be specified, and some require that the time variable also be specified. Once you xtset your data, you need not do it again. The xtset information is stored with your data.

If you have previously tsset your data by using both a panel and a time variable, these settings will be recognized by xtset, and you need not xtset your data.

If your interest is in general time-series analysis, see [U] **26.14 Models with time-series data** and the *Stata Time-Series Reference Manual*.

Remarks

Consider having data on n units—individuals, firms, countries, or whatever—over T periods. The data might be income and other characteristics of n persons surveyed each of T years, the output and costs of n firms collected over T months, or the health and behavioral characteristics of n patients collected over T years. In panel datasets, we write x_{it} for the value of x for unit i at time t. The xt commands assume that such datasets are stored as a sequence of observations on (i, t, x).

For a discussion of panel-data models, see Baltagi (2005), Greene (2003), Hsiao (2003), or Wooldridge (2002).

▷ Example 1

If we had data on pulmonary function (measured by forced expiratory volume, or FEV) along with smoking behavior, age, sex, and height, a piece of the data might be

```
. list in 1/6, separator(0) divider
```

	pid	yr_visit	fev	age	sex	height	smokes
1.	1071	1991	1.21	25	1	69	0
2.	1071	1992	1.52	26	1	69	0
3.	1071	1993	1.32	28	1	68	0
4.	1072	1991	1.33	18	1	71	1
5.	1072	1992	1.18	20	1	71	1
6.	1072	1993	1.19	21	1	71	0

The xt commands need to know the identity of the variable identifying patient, and some of the xt commands also need to know the identity of the variable identifying time. With these data, we would type

```
. xtset pid yr_visit
```

If we resaved the data, we need not respecify xtset.

◁

❑ Technical Note

Panel data stored as shown above are said to be in the long form. Perhaps the data are in the wide form with 1 observation per unit and multiple variables for the value in each year. For instance, a piece of the pulmonary function data might be

```
pid   sex   fev91   fev92   fev93   age91   age92   age93
1071    1    1.21    1.52    1.32     25      26      28
1072    1    1.33    1.18    1.19     18      20      21
```

Data in this form can be converted to the long form by using reshape; see [D] **reshape**.

❑

▷ Example 2

Data for some of the periods might be missing. That is, we have panel data on $i = 1, \ldots, n$ and $t = 1, \ldots, T$, but only T_i of those observations are defined. With such missing periods—called unbalanced data—a piece of our pulmonary function data might be

```
. list in 1/6, separator(0) divider
```

	pid	yr_visit	fev	age	sex	height	smokes
1.	1071	1991	1.21	25	1	69	0
2.	1071	1992	1.52	26	1	69	0
3.	1071	1993	1.32	28	1	68	0
4.	1072	1991	1.33	18	1	71	1
5.	1072	1993	1.19	21	1	71	0
6.	1073	1991	1.47	24	0	64	0

Patient ID 1072 is not observed in 1992. The xt commands are robust to this problem.

◁

❑ Technical Note

In many of the [XT] **xt** entries, we will use data from a subsample of the NLSY data (Center for Human Resource Research 1989) on young women aged 14–26 years in 1968. Women were surveyed in each of the 21 years 1968–1988, except for the six years 1974, 1976, 1979, 1981, 1984, and 1986. We use two different subsets: nlswork.dta and union.dta.

For nlswork.dta, our subsample is of 4,711 women in years when employed, not enrolled in school and evidently having completed their education, and with wages in excess of $1/hour but less than $700/hour.

```
. use http://www.stata-press.com/data/r10/nlswork
(National Longitudinal Survey.  Young Women 14-26 years of age in 1968)
```

```
. describe
Contains data from http://www.stata-press.com/data/r10/nlswork.dta
  obs:         28,534                         National Longitudinal Survey.
                                              Young Women 14-26 years of age
                                              in 1968
  vars:            21                         7 Dec 2006 17:02
  size:     1,055,758 (89.9% of memory free)
```

variable name	storage type	display format	value label	variable label
idcode	int	%8.0g		NLS ID
year	byte	%8.0g		interview year
birth_yr	byte	%8.0g		birth year
age	byte	%8.0g		age in current year
race	byte	%8.0g		1=white, 2=black, 3=other
msp	byte	%8.0g		1 if married, spouse present
nev_mar	byte	%8.0g		1 if never married
grade	byte	%8.0g		current grade completed
collgrad	byte	%8.0g		1 if college graduate
not_smsa	byte	%8.0g		1 if not SMSA
c_city	byte	%8.0g		1 if central city
south	byte	%8.0g		1 if south
ind_code	byte	%8.0g		industry of employment
occ_code	byte	%8.0g		occupation
union	byte	%8.0g		1 if union
wks_ue	byte	%8.0g		weeks unemployed last year
ttl_exp	float	%9.0g		total work experience
tenure	float	%9.0g		job tenure, in years
hours	int	%8.0g		usual hours worked
wks_work	int	%8.0g		weeks worked last year
ln_wage	float	%9.0g		ln(wage/GNP deflator)

```
Sorted by:  idcode   year
. summarize
```

Variable	Obs	Mean	Std. Dev.	Min	Max
idcode	28534	2601.284	1487.359	1	5159
year	28534	77.95865	6.383879	68	88
birth_yr	28534	48.08509	3.012837	41	54
age	28510	29.04511	6.700584	14	46
race	28534	1.303392	.4822773	1	3
msp	28518	.6029175	.4893019	0	1
nev_mar	28518	.2296795	.4206341	0	1
grade	28532	12.53259	2.323905	0	18
collgrad	28534	.1680451	.3739129	0	1
not_smsa	28526	.2824441	.4501961	0	1
c_city	28526	.357218	.4791882	0	1
south	28526	.4095562	.4917605	0	1
ind_code	28193	7.692973	2.994025	1	12
occ_code	28413	4.777672	3.065435	1	13
union	19238	.2344319	.4236542	0	1
wks_ue	22830	2.548095	7.294463	0	76
ttl_exp	28534	6.215316	4.652117	0	28.88461
tenure	28101	3.123836	3.751409	0	25.91667
hours	28467	36.55956	9.869623	1	168
wks_work	27831	53.98933	29.03232	0	104
ln_wage	28534	1.674907	.4780935	0	5.263916

For `union.dta`, our subset was sampled only from those with union membership information from 1970 to 1988. Our subsample is of 4,434 women. The important variables are `age` (16–46), `grade` (years of schooling completed, ranging from 0 to 18), `not_smsa` (28% of the person-time was spent living outside an SMSA—standard metropolitan statistical area), `south` (41% of the person-time was in the South), and `southXt` (`south` interacted with year, treating 1970 as year 0). The dataset also has variable `union`. Overall, 22% of the person-time is marked as time under union membership, and 44% of these women have belonged to a union.

```
. use http://www.stata-press.com/data/r10/union
(NLS Women 14-24 in 1968)

. describe

Contains data from http://www.stata-press.com/data/r10/union.dta
  obs:          26,200                          NLS Women 14-24 in 1968
 vars:              10                          27 Oct 2006 13:51
 size:         393,000  (96.3% of memory free)
```

variable name	storage type	display format	value label	variable label
idcode	int	%8.0g		NLS ID
year	byte	%8.0g		interview year
age	byte	%8.0g		age in current year
grade	byte	%8.0g		current grade completed
not_smsa	byte	%8.0g		1 if not SMSA
south	byte	%8.0g		1 if south
union	byte	%8.0g		1 if union
t0	byte	%9.0g		
southXt	byte	%9.0g		
black	byte	%8.0g		race black

```
Sorted by:

. summarize
```

Variable	Obs	Mean	Std. Dev.	Min	Max
idcode	26200	2611.582	1484.994	1	5159
year	26200	79.47137	5.965499	70	88
age	26200	30.43221	6.489056	16	46
grade	26200	12.76145	2.411715	0	18
not_smsa	26200	.2837023	.4508027	0	1
south	26200	.4130153	.4923849	0	1
union	26200	.2217939	.4154611	0	1
t0	26200	9.471374	5.965499	0	18
southXt	26200	3.96874	6.057208	0	18
black	26200	.274542	.4462917	0	1

With both datasets, we have typed

```
. xtset idcode year
```

❑

❑ Technical Note

The `xtset` command sets the t and i index for xt data by declaring them as characteristics of the data; see [P] **char**. The panel variable is stored in `_dta[iis]` and the time variable is stored in `_dta[tis]`.

❑

❏ Technical Note

xtmixed, xtmelogit, and xtmepoisson do not use the information pertaining to i and t that is stored by xtset. Unlike the other xt commands, these can handle multiple nested levels of groups and thus use their own syntax for specifying the group structure of the data.

❏

❏ Technical Note

Throughout the xt entries, when random-effects models are fitted, a likelihood-ratio test that the variance of the random effects is zero is included. These tests occur on the boundary of the parameter space, invalidating the usual theory associated with such tests. However, these likelihood-ratio tests have been modified to be valid on the boundary. In particular, the null distribution of the likelihood-ratio test statistic is not the usual χ_1^2 but is rather a 50:50 mixture of a χ_0^2 (point mass at zero) and a χ_1^2, denoted as $\overline{\chi}_{01}^2$. See Gutierrez, Carter, and Drukker (2001) for a full discussion, and see [XT] **xtmixed** for a generalization of the concept as applied to variance-component estimation in mixed models.

❏

References

Baltagi, B. H. 2005. *Econometric Analysis of Panel Data*. 3rd ed. New York: Wiley.

Center for Human Resource Research. 1989. *National Longitudinal Survey of Labor Market Experience, Young Women 14–26 years of age in 1968*. Columbus, OH: Ohio State University Press.

Greene, W. H. 2003. *Econometric Analysis*. 5th ed. Upper Saddle River, NJ: Prentice Hall.

Gutierrez, R. G., S. L. Carter, and D. M. Drukker. 2001. sg160: On boundary-value likelihood-ratio tests. *Stata Technical Bulletin* 60: 15–18. Reprinted in *Stata Technical Bulletin Reprints*, vol. 10, pp. 269–273.

Hsiao, C. 2003. *Analysis of Panel Data*. 2nd ed. New York: Cambridge University Press.

Wooldridge, J. M. 2002. *Econometric Analysis of Cross Section and Panel Data*. Cambridge, MA: MIT Press.

Also See

[XT] **xtset** — Declare data to be panel data

Title

> **estimation options** — Estimation options

Description

This entry describes the options common to many estimation commands. Not all the options documented below work with all estimation commands; see the documentation for the particular estimation command. If an option is listed there, it is applicable.

Options

Model

noconstant suppresses the constant term (intercept) in the model.

offset(*varname*) specifies that *varname* be included in the model with the coefficient constrained to be 1.

exposure(*varname*) specifies a variable that reflects the amount of exposure over which the *depvar* events were observed for each observation; ln(*varname*) with coefficient constrained to be 1 is entered into the log-link function.

constraints(*numlist* | *matname*) specifies the linear constraints to be applied during estimation. The default is to perform unconstrained estimation. See [R] **reg3** for the use of constraints in multiple-equation contexts.

> constraints(*numlist*) specifies the constraints by number after they have been defined by using the constraint command; see [R] **constraint**.

> constraints(*matname*) specifies a matrix containing the constraints; see [P] **makecns**.

collinear specifies that the estimation command not remove collinear variables. Usually there is no reason to leave collinear variables in place and in fact doing so usually causes the estimation to fail because of the matrix singularity caused by the collinearity. However, with certain models, the variables may be collinear, yet the model is fully identified because of constraints or other features of the model. In such cases, using option collinear allows the estimation to take place, leaving the equations with collinear variables intact. This option is seldom used.

force specifies that estimation be forced even though the time variable is not equally spaced. This is relevant only for correlation structures that require knowledge of the time variable. These correlation structures require that observations be equally spaced so that calculations based on lags correspond to a constant time change. If you specify a time variable indicating that observations are not equally spaced, the (time dependent) model will not be fitted. If you also specify force, the model will be fitted, and it will be assumed that the lags based on the data ordered by the time variable are appropriate.

Correlation

corr(*correlation*) specifies the within-group correlation structure; the default corresponds to the equal-correlation model, corr(exchangeable).

When you specify a correlation structure that requires a lag, you indicate the lag after the structure's name with or without a blank; e.g., corr(ar 1) or corr(ar1).

If you specify the fixed correlation structure, you specify the name of the matrix containing the assumed correlations following the word `fixed`, e.g., `corr(fixed myr)`.

─────┐ Reporting ├──

`level(#)` specifies the confidence level, as a percentage, for confidence intervals. The default is `level(95)` or as set by `set level`; see [U] **20.7 Specifying the width of confidence intervals**.

`noskip` specifies that a full maximum-likelihood model with only a constant for the regression equation be fitted. This model is not displayed but is used as the base model to compute a likelihood-ratio test for the model test statistic displayed in the estimation header. By default, the overall model test statistic is an asymptotically equivalent Wald test of all the parameters in the regression equation being zero (except the constant). For many models, this option can substantially increase estimation time.

─────┐ Int opts (RE) ├──

`intmethod(intmethod)` specifies the integration method to be used for the random-effects model. It accepts one of three arguments: `mvaghermite`, the default, performs mean and variance adaptive Gauss–Hermite quadrature first on every and then on alternate iterations; `aghermite` performs mode and curvature adaptive Gauss–Hermite quadrature on the first iteration only; `ghermite` performs nonadaptive Gauss–Hermite quadrature.

`intpoints(#)` specifies the number of integration points to use for integration by quadrature. The default is `intpoints(12)`; the maximum is `intpoints(195)`. Increasing this value slightly improves the accuracy but also increases computation time. Computation time is roughly proportional to its value.

Also See

[R] **estimation options** — Estimation options

[U] **20 Estimation and postestimation commands**

Title

quadchk — Check sensitivity of quadrature approximation

Syntax

quadchk $[\#_1 \ \#_2]$ $[$, nooutput nofrom $]$

Description

quadchk checks the quadrature approximation used in the random-effects estimators of the following commands:

    xtcloglog
    xtintreg
    xtlogit
    xtpoisson, re with the normal option
    xtprobit
    xttobit

quadchk refits the model for different numbers of quadrature points and then compares the different solutions.

$\#_1$ and $\#_2$ specify the number of quadrature points to use in the comparison runs of the previous model. The default is to use (roughly) $2n_q/3$ and $4n_q/3$ points, where n_q is the number of quadrature points used in the original estimation.

Most options supplied to the original model are respected by quadchk, but some are not. These are or, vce(), and the *maximize_options*.

Options

nooutput suppresses the iteration log and output of the refitted models.

nofrom forces the refitted models to start from scratch rather than starting from the previous estimation results. Adaptive quadrature with intmethod(aghermite) is more sensitive to starting values than nonadaptive quadrature, intmethod(ghermite), or the default method of adaptive quadrature, intmethod(mvaghermite). Specifying the nofrom option can level the playing field in testing estimation results.

Remarks

Remarks are presented under the following headings:

> *What makes a good random-effects model fit?*
> *How do I know whether I have a good quadrature approximation?*
> *What can I do to improve my results?*

11

What makes a good random-effects model fit?

Some random-effects estimators in Stata use adaptive or nonadaptive Gauss–Hermite quadrature to compute the log likelihood and its derivatives. As a rule, adaptive quadrature, which is the default integration method, is much more accurate. The quadchk command provides a means to look at the numerical accuracy of either quadrature approximation. A good random-effects model fit depends on both the goodness of the quadrature approximation and the goodness of the data.

The accuracy of the quadrature approximation depends on three factors. The first and second are how many quadrature points are used and where the quadrature points fall. These two factors directly influence the accuracy of the quadrature approximation. The number of quadrature points may be specified with the intpoints() option. However, once the number of points is specified, their abscissas (locations) and corresponding weights are completely determined. Increasing the number of points expands the range of the abscissas and, to a lesser extent, increases the density of the abscissas. For this reason, a function that undulates between the abscissas can be difficult to approximate.

Third, the smoothness of the function being approximated influences the accuracy of the quadrature approximation. Gauss–Hermite quadrature estimates integrals of the type

$$\int_{-\infty}^{\infty} e^{-x^2} f(x)\, dx,$$

and the approximation is exact if $f(x)$ is a polynomial of degree less than the number of integration points. Therefore, $f(x)$ that are well approximated by polynomials of a given degree have integrals that are well approximated by Gauss–Hermite quadrature with that given number of integration points. Both large panel sizes and high ρ can reduce the accuracy of the quadrature approximation.

A final factor affects the goodness of the random-effects model: the data themselves. For high ρ, for example, there is high intrapanel correlation, and panels look like observations. The model becomes unidentified. Here, even with exact quadrature, fitting the model would be difficult.

How do I know whether I have a good quadrature approximation?

quadchk is intended as a tool to help you know whether you have a good quadrature approximation. As a rule of thumb, if the coefficients do not change by more than a relative difference of 10^{-4} (0.01%), the choice of quadrature points does not significantly affect the outcome, and the results may be confidently interpreted. However, if the results do change appreciably—greater than a relative difference of 10^{-2} (1%)—then quadrature is not reliably approximating the likelihood.

What can I do to improve my results?

If the quadchk command indicates that the estimation results are sensitive to the number of quadrature points, there are several things you can do. First, if you are not using adaptive quadrature, switch to adaptive quadrature.

Adaptive quadrature can improve the approximation by transforming the integrand so that the abscissas and weights sample the function on a more suitable range. Details of this transformation are in *Methods and Formulas* for the given commands; for example, see [XT] **xtprobit**.

If the model still shows sensitivity to the number of quadrature points, increase the number of quadrature points with the intpoints() option. This option will increase the range and density of the sampling used for the quadrature approximation.

If neither of these works, you may then want to consider an alternative model, such as a fixed-effects, pooled, or population-averaged model. Alternatively, a different random-effects model whose likelihood is not approximated via quadrature (e.g., xtpoisson, re) may be a better choice.

▷ Example 1

Here we synthesize data according to the model

$$E(y) = 0.05\,x_1 + 0.08\,x_2 + 0.08\,x_3 + 0.1\,x_4 + 0.1\,x_5 + 0.1\,x_6 + 0.1\epsilon$$

$$z = \begin{cases} 1 & \text{if } y \geq 0 \\ 0 & \text{if } y < 0 \end{cases}$$

where the intrapanel correlation is 0.5 and the x1 variable is constant within panels. We first fit a random-effects probit model, and then we check the stability of the quadrature calculation:

```
. use http://www.stata-press.com/data/r10/quad1

. xtset id
        panel variable:  id (balanced)

. xtprobit z x1-x6
  (output omitted )
```

```
Random-effects probit regression            Number of obs      =        6000
Group variable: id                          Number of groups   =         300

Random effects u_1 ~ Gaussian               Obs per group: min =          20
                                                           avg =        20.0
                                                           max =          20

                                            Wald chi2(6)       =       29.24
Log likelihood  = -3347.1097                Prob > chi2        =      0.0001
```

z	Coef.	Std. Err.	z	P>|z|	[95% Conf. Interval]	
x1	.0043068	.0607058	0.07	0.943	-.1146743	.1232879
x2	.1000742	.066331	1.51	0.131	-.0299323	.2300806
x3	.1503539	.0662503	2.27	0.023	.0205057	.2802021
x4	.123015	.0377089	3.26	0.001	.0491069	.196923
x5	.1342988	.0657222	2.04	0.041	.0054856	.263112
x6	.0879933	.0455753	1.93	0.054	-.0013325	.1773192
_cons	.0757067	.060359	1.25	0.210	-.0425948	.1940083
/lnsig2u	-.0329916	.1026847			-.23425	.1682667
sigma_u	.9836395	.0505024			.889474	1.087774
rho	.4917528	.0256642			.4417038	.5419677

```
Likelihood-ratio test of rho=0: chibar2(01) =  1582.67 Prob >= chibar2 = 0.000

. quadchk

Refitting model intpoints() =  8
  (output omitted )

Refitting model intpoints() = 16
  (output omitted )
```

	Quadrature check		
	Fitted quadrature 12 points	Comparison quadrature 8 points	Comparison quadrature 16 points
Log likelihood	-3347.1097	-3347.1153 -.00561484 1.678e-06	-3347.1099 -.00014288 4.269e-08	Difference Relative difference
z: x1	.0043068	.0043068 2.875e-13 6.675e-11	.00430541 -1.388e-06 -.00032222	Difference Relative difference
z: x2	.10007418	.10007418 8.142e-14 8.136e-13	.10007431 1.362e-07 1.361e-06	Difference Relative difference
z: x3	.15035391	.15035391 2.031e-13 1.351e-12	.15035406 1.520e-07 1.011e-06	Difference Relative difference
z: x4	.12301495	.12301495 1.324e-13 1.076e-12	.12301506 1.099e-07 8.931e-07	Difference Relative difference
z: x5	.13429881	.13429881 1.572e-13 1.170e-12	.13429896 1.471e-07 1.096e-06	Difference Relative difference
z: x6	.08799332	.08799332 1.072e-13 1.218e-12	.08799346 1.363e-07 1.549e-06	Difference Relative difference
z: _cons	.07570675	.07570675 6.280e-13 8.295e-12	.07570423 -2.516e-06 -.00003323	Difference Relative difference
lnsig2u: _cons	-.03299164	-.03299164 2.326e-12 -7.049e-11	-.03298184 9.798e-06 -.00029699	Difference Relative difference

We see that the largest difference is in the x1 variable with a relative difference of 0.03% between the model with 12 integration points and 16. This example is somewhat rare in that the differences between eight quadrature points and 12 are smaller than those between 12 and 16. Usually the opposite occurs: the model results converge as you add quadrature points. Here we have an indication that perhaps some minor feature of the model was missed with eight points and 12 but seen with 16. Since all differences are very small, we could accept this model as is. We'd like to have a largest relative difference of about 0.01%, and this is close. The differences and relative differences are small, indicating that refitting the random-effects probit model with a few more integration points will yield a satisfactory result. Indeed, refitting the model with the intpoints(20) option yields completely satisfactory results when checked with quadchk.

Nonadaptive Gauss–Hermite quadrature does not yield such robust results.

```
. xtprobit z x1-x6, intmethod(ghermite) nolog
```

Random-effects probit regression

Group variable: id

Random effects u_i ~ Gaussian

Number of obs = 6000

Number of groups = 300

Obs per group: min = 20

avg = 20.0

max = 20

Wald chi2(6) = 36.15

Log likelihood = -3349.6926

Prob > chi2 = 0.0000

z	Coef.	Std. Err.	z	P>|z|	[95% Conf. Interval]
x1	.1156763	.0554925	2.08	0.037	.0069131	.2244396
x2	.1005555	.066227	1.52	0.129	-.0292469	.230358
x3	.1542187	.0660852	2.33	0.020	.0246941	.2837433
x4	.1257616	.0375776	3.35	0.001	.0521108	.1994123
x5	.1366003	.0654696	2.09	0.037	.0082823	.2649182
x6	.0870325	.0453489	1.92	0.055	-.0018497	.1759147
_cons	.1098393	.0500514	2.19	0.028	.0117404	.2079382
/lnsig2u	-.0791821	.0971063			-.2695071	.1111428
sigma_u	.9611824	.0466685			.8739313	1.057145
rho	.4802148	.0242386			.4330281	.5277571

Likelihood-ratio test of rho=0: chibar2(01) = 1577.50 Prob >= chibar2 = 0.000

```
. quadchk, nooutput
```

Refitting model intpoints() = 8

Refitting model intpoints() = 16

Quadrature check

	Fitted quadrature 12 points	Comparison quadrature 8 points	Comparison quadrature 16 points	
Log likelihood	-3349.6926	-3354.6372	-3348.3881	
		-4.9446636	1.3045063	Difference
		.00147615	-.00038944	Relative difference
z:	.11567633	.16153998	.07007833	
x1		.04586365	-.045598	Difference
		.39648262	-.39418608	Relative difference
z:	.10055552	.10317831	.09937417	
x2		.00262279	-.00118135	Difference
		.02608297	-.01174825	Relative difference
z:	.1542187	.15465369	.15150516	
x3		.00043499	-.00271354	Difference
		.00282062	-.0175954	Relative difference
z:	.12576159	.12880254	.1243974	
x4		.00304096	-.00136418	Difference
		.02418032	-.01084739	Relative difference
z:	.13660028	.13475211	.13707075	
x5		-.00184817	.00047047	Difference
		-.01352978	.00344411	Relative difference
z:	.08703252	.08568342	.08738135	
x6		-.0013491	.00034883	Difference
		-.0155011	.00400809	Relative difference

```
z:                .10983928      .11031299      .09654975
    _cons                        .00047371     -.01328953   Difference
                                 .00431274     -.12099067   Relative difference

lnsig2u:         -.07918212     -.18133821     -.05815644
    _cons                       -.10215609      .02102568   Difference
                                1.2901408      -.26553572   Relative difference
```

Here we see that the x1 variable (the one that was constant within panel) changed with a relative difference of nearly 40%! This example clearly demonstrates the benefit of adaptive quadrature methods.

◁

▷ Example 2

Here we rerun the previous nonadaptive quadrature model, but using the intpoints(120) option to increase the number of integration points to 120. We get results close to those from adaptive quadrature and an acceptable quadchk. This example demonstrates the efficacy of increasing the number of integration points to improve the quadrature approximation.

```
. xtprobit z x1-x6, intmethod(ghermite) intpoints(120) nolog
Random-effects probit regression               Number of obs     =      6000
Group variable: id                             Number of groups  =       300

Random effects u_i ~ Gaussian                  Obs per group: min =        20
                                                              avg =      20.0
                                                              max =        20

                                               Wald chi2(6)       =     29.24
Log likelihood  = -3347.1099                   Prob > chi2        =    0.0001
```

z	Coef.	Std. Err.	z	P>|z|	[95% Conf. Interval]	
x1	.0043059	.0607087	0.07	0.943	-.114681	.1232929
x2	.1000743	.0663311	1.51	0.131	-.0299322	.2300808
x3	.1503541	.0662503	2.27	0.023	.0205058	.2802023
x4	.1230151	.0377089	3.26	0.001	.049107	.1969232
x5	.134299	.0657223	2.04	0.041	.0054856	.2631123
x6	.0879935	.0455753	1.93	0.054	-.0013325	.1773194
_cons	.0757054	.0603621	1.25	0.210	-.0426021	.1940128
/lnsig2u	-.0329832	.1026863			-.2342446	.1682783
sigma_u	.9836437	.0505034			.8894764	1.08778
rho	.491755	.0256646			.4417052	.5419706

```
Likelihood-ratio test of rho=0: chibar2(01) =  1582.67 Prob >= chibar2 = 0.000
```

```
. quadchk, nooutput
```

```
Refitting model intpoints() = 80
Refitting model intpoints() = 160
```

Quadrature check

	Fitted quadrature 120 points	Comparison quadrature 80 points	Comparison quadrature 160 points	
Log likelihood	-3347.1099	-3347.1099 -.00007138 2.133e-08	-3347.1099 2.440e-07 -7.289e-11	Difference Relative difference
z: x1	.00430592	.00431318 7.259e-06 .00168592	.00430553 -3.871e-07 -.00008991	Difference Relative difference
z: x2	.10007431	.10007415 -1.519e-07 -1.517e-06	.10007431 5.585e-09 5.580e-08	Difference Relative difference
z: x3	.15035406	.15035407 1.699e-08 1.130e-07	.15035406 7.636e-09 5.078e-08	Difference Relative difference
z: x4	.12301506	.12301512 6.036e-08 4.907e-07	.12301506 5.353e-09 4.352e-08	Difference Relative difference
z: x5	.13429895	.13429962 6.646e-07 4.949e-06	.13429896 4.785e-09 3.563e-08	Difference Relative difference
z: x6	.08799345	.08799334 -1.123e-07 -1.276e-06	.08799346 3.049e-09 3.465e-08	Difference Relative difference
z: _cons	.07570536	.07570205 -3.305e-06 -.00004365	.07570442 -9.405e-07 -.00001242	Difference Relative difference
lnsig2u: _cons	-.03298317	-.03298909 -5.919e-06 .00017945	-.03298186 1.304e-06 -.00003952	Difference Relative difference

◁

▷ Example 3

Here we synthesize data the same way as in the previous example, but we make the intrapanel correlation equal to 0.1 instead of 0.5. We again fit a random-effects probit model and check the quadrature:

```
. use http://www.stata-press.com/data/r10/quad2
. xtset id
       panel variable:  id (balanced)
. xtprobit z x1-x6
Fitting comparison model:
Iteration 0:   log likelihood = -4142.2915
Iteration 1:   log likelihood = -4120.4109
Iteration 2:   log likelihood = -4120.4099
Fitting full model:
rho =  0.0    log likelihood = -4120.4099
rho =  0.1    log likelihood = -4065.7986
rho =  0.2    log likelihood = -4087.7703
Iteration 0:   log likelihood = -4065.7986
Iteration 1:   log likelihood = -4065.3157
Iteration 2:   log likelihood = -4065.3144
Iteration 3:   log likelihood = -4065.3144
```

Random-effects probit regression					Number of obs	=	6000
Group variable: id					Number of groups	=	300

Random effects u_i ~ Gaussian			Obs per group: min =	20
			avg =	20.0
			max =	20
			Wald chi2(6) =	39.43
Log likelihood = -4065.3144			Prob > chi2 =	0.0000

z	Coef.	Std. Err.	z	P>|z|	[95% Conf. Interval]	
x1	.0246943	.025112	0.98	0.325	-.0245243	.0739129
x2	.1300123	.0587906	2.21	0.027	.0147847	.2452398
x3	.1190409	.0579539	2.05	0.040	.0054533	.2326284
x4	.139197	.0331817	4.19	0.000	.0741621	.2042319
x5	.077364	.0578454	1.34	0.181	-.036011	.1907389
x6	.0862028	.0401185	2.15	0.032	.007572	.1648336
_cons	.0922653	.0244392	3.78	0.000	.0443653	.1401652
/lnsig2u	-2.343939	.1575275			-2.652687	-2.035191
sigma_u	.3097563	.0243976			.2654461	.3614631
rho	.0875487	.0125839			.0658236	.1155574

Likelihood-ratio test of rho=0: chibar2(01) =   110.19 Prob >= chibar2 = 0.000

```
. quadchk, nooutput
Refitting model intpoints() =  8
Refitting model intpoints() = 16
```

```
                             Quadrature check
                   Fitted        Comparison     Comparison
                   quadrature    quadrature     quadrature
                   12 points     8 points       16 points
```

	Fitted quadrature 12 points	Comparison quadrature 8 points	Comparison quadrature 16 points	
Log likelihood	-4065.3144	-4065.3144	-4065.3144	
		-2.268e-08	5.457e-12	Difference
		5.578e-12	-1.342e-15	Relative difference
z: x1	.02469427	.02469427	.02469427	
		-3.645e-12	-8.007e-12	Difference
		-1.476e-10	-3.242e-10	Relative difference
z: x2	.13001229	.13001229	.13001229	
		-1.566e-11	-6.879e-13	Difference
		-1.204e-10	-5.291e-12	Relative difference
z: x3	.11904089	.11904089	.11904089	
		-6.457e-12	-3.030e-13	Difference
		-5.425e-11	-2.545e-12	Relative difference
z: x4	.13919697	.13919697	.13919697	
		1.442e-12	1.693e-13	Difference
		1.036e-11	1.216e-12	Relative difference
z: x5	.07736398	.07736398	.07736398	
		-5.801e-12	-4.556e-13	Difference
		-7.499e-11	-5.890e-12	Relative difference
z: x6	.08620282	.08620282	.08620282	
		5.903e-12	3.191e-13	Difference
		6.848e-11	3.702e-12	Relative difference
z: _cons	.09226527	.09226527	.09226527	
		-2.850e-12	-1.837e-11	Difference
		-3.089e-11	-1.991e-10	Relative difference
lnsig2u: _cons	-2.3439389	-2.3439389	-2.3439389	
		-2.946e-09	-2.172e-10	Difference
		1.257e-09	9.267e-11	Relative difference

Here we see that the quadrature approximation is stable. With this result, we can confidently interpret the results. Satisfactory results are also obtained in this case with nonadaptive quadrature.

◁

Methods and Formulas

quadchk is implemented as an ado-file.

Title

> *vce_options* — Variance estimators

Syntax

> *estimation_cmd* ... $\left[\,,\ vce\_options\ ...\right]$

vce_options	description
vce(oim)	observed information matrix (OIM)
vce(opg)	outer product of the gradient (OPG) vectors
vce(<u>r</u>obust)	Huber/White/sandwich estimator
vce(<u>cl</u>uster *clustvar*)	clustered sandwich estimator
vce(<u>boot</u>strap $\left[\,,\ bootstrap\_options\right]$)	bootstrap estimation
vce(<u>jack</u>knife $\left[\,,\ jackknife\_options\right]$)	jackknife estimation
nmp	use divisor $N - P$ instead of the default N
<u>s</u>cale(x2 | dev | phi | #)	override the default scale parameter; available only with population-averaged models

Description

This entry describes the *vce_options*, which are common to most xt estimation commands. Not all the options documented below work with all xt estimation commands; see the documentation for the particular estimation command. If an option is listed there, it is applicable.

The vce() option specifies how to estimate the variance–covariance matrix (VCE) corresponding to the parameter estimates. The standard errors reported in the table of parameter estimates are the square root of the variances (diagonal elements) of the VCE.

Options

⌐ SE/Robust ⌐

vce(oim) is usually the default for models fitted using maximum likelihood. vce(oim) uses the observed information matrix (OIM); see [R] **ml**.

vce(opg) uses the sum of the outer product of the gradient (OPG) vectors; see [R] **ml**. This is the default VCE when the technique(bhhh) option is specified; see [R] **maximize**.

vce(robust) uses the robust or sandwich estimator of variance. This estimator is robust to some types of misspecification so long as the observations are independent; see [U] **20.15 Obtaining robust variance estimates**.

If the command allows pweights and you specify them, vce(robust) is implied; see [U] **20.17.3 Sampling weights**.

vce(cluster *clustvar*) specifies that the standard errors allow for intragroup correlation, relaxing the usual requirement that the observations be independent. That is to say, the observations are independent across groups (clusters) but not necessarily within groups. *clustvar* specifies to which group each observation belongs, e.g., vce(cluster personid) in data with repeated observations on individuals. vce(cluster *clustvar*) affects the standard errors and variance–covariance matrix of the estimators but not the estimated coefficients; see [U] **20.15 Obtaining robust variance estimates**.

vce(bootstrap [, *bootstrap_options*]) uses a bootstrap; see [R] **bootstrap**. After estimation with vce(bootstrap), see [R] **bootstrap postestimation** to obtain percentile-based or bias-corrected confidence intervals.

vce(jackknife [, *jackknife_options*]) uses the delete-one jackknife; see [R] **jackknife**.

nmp specifies that the divisor $N - P$ be used instead of the default N, where N is the total number of observations and P is the number of coefficients estimated.

scale(x2 | dev | phi | #) overrides the default scale parameter. By default, scale(1) is assumed for the discrete distributions (binomial, negative binomial, and Poisson), and scale(x2) is assumed for the continuous distributions (gamma, Gaussian, and inverse Gaussian).

scale(x2) specifies that the scale parameter be set to the Pearson chi-squared (or generalized chi-squared) statistic divided by the residual degrees of freedom, which is recommended by McCullagh and Nelder (1989) as a good general choice for continuous distributions.

scale(dev) sets the scale parameter to the deviance divided by the residual degrees of freedom. This option provides an alternative to scale(x2) for continuous distributions and for over- or underdispersed discrete distributions.

scale(phi) specifies that the scale parameter be estimated from the data. xtgee's default scaling makes results agree with other estimators and has been recommended by McCullagh and Nelder (1989) in the context of GLM. When comparing results with calculations made by other software, you may find that the other packages do not offer this feature. In such cases, specifying scale(phi) should match their results.

scale(#) sets the scale parameter to #. For example, using scale(1) in family(gamma) models results in exponential-errors regression (if you assume independent correlation structure).

Remarks

When you are working with panel-data models, we strongly encourage you to use the vce(bootstrap) or vce(jackknife) option instead of the corresponding prefix command. For example, to obtain jackknife standard errors with xtlogit, type

(*Continued on next page*)

```
. use http://www.stata-press.com/data/r10/clogitid

. xtlogit y x1 x2, fe vce(jackknife)
(running xtlogit on estimation sample)

Jackknife replications (66)
————+——— 1 ——+——— 2 ——+——— 3 ——+——— 4 ——+——— 5
..................................................  50
...............
```

Conditional fixed-effects logistic regression	Number of obs	=	369
Group variable: id	Number of groups	=	66

	Obs per group: min =	2
	avg =	5.6
	max =	10

	F(2, 65) =	4.58
Log likelihood = -123.41386	Prob > F =	0.0137

(Replications based on 66 clusters in id)

y	Coef.	Jackknife Std. Err.	t	P>|t|	[95% Conf. Interval]
x1	.653363	.3010608	2.17	0.034	.052103	1.254623
x2	.0659169	.0487858	1.35	0.181	-.0315151	.1633489

If you wish to specify more options to the bootstrap or jackknife estimation, you can include them within the vce() option. Below we refit our model requesting bootstrap standard errors based on 300 replications, we set the random number seed so that our results can be reproduced, and we suppress the display of the replication dots.

```
. xtlogit y x1 x2, fe vce(bootstrap, reps(300) seed(123) nodots)
```

Conditional fixed-effects logistic regression	Number of obs	=	369
Group variable: id	Number of groups	=	66

	Obs per group: min =	2
	avg =	5.6
	max =	10

	Wald chi2(2) =	8.52
Log likelihood = -123.41386	Prob > chi2 =	0.0141

(Replications based on 66 clusters in id)

y	Observed Coef.	Bootstrap Std. Err.	z	P>|z|	Normal-based [95% Conf. Interval]
x1	.653363	.3015317	2.17	0.030	.0623717	1.244354
x2	.0659169	.0512331	1.29	0.198	-.0344981	.1663319

❏ Technical Note

To perform jackknife estimation on panel data, you must omit entire panels rather than individual observations. To replicate the output above using the jackknife prefix command, you would have to type

```
. jackknife, cluster(id): xtlogit y x1 x2, fe
  (output omitted )
```

Similarly, bootstrap estimation on panel data requires you to resample entire panels rather than individual observations. The vce(bootstrap) and vce(jackknife) options handle this for you automatically.

❏

Methods and Formulas

By default, Stata's maximum likelihood estimators display standard errors based on variance estimates given by the inverse of the negative Hessian (second derivative) matrix. If vce(robust), vce(cluster *clustvar*), or pweights are specified, standard errors are based on the robust variance estimator (see [U] **20.15 Obtaining robust variance estimates**); likelihood-ratio tests are not appropriate here (see [SVY] **survey**), and the model χ^2 is from a Wald test. If vce(opg) is specified, the standard errors are based on the outer product of the gradients; this option has no effect on likelihood-ratio tests, though it does affect Wald tests.

If vce(bootstrap) or vce(jackknife) is specified, the standard errors are based on the chosen replication method; here the model χ^2 or F statistic is from a Wald test using the respective replication-based covariance matrix. The t distribution is used in the coefficient table when the vce(jackknife) option is specified. vce(bootstrap) and vce(jackknife) are also available with some commands that are not maximum likelihood estimators.

Reference

McCullagh, P., and J. A. Nelder. 1989. *Generalized Linear Models*. 2nd ed. London: Chapman & Hall/CRC.

Also See

[R] **bootstrap** — Bootstrap sampling and estimation

[R] **jackknife** — Jackknife estimation

[R] **ml** — Maximum likelihood estimation

[U] **20 Estimation and postestimation commands**

Title

> **xtabond** — Arellano–Bond linear dynamic panel-data estimation

Syntax

> xtabond *depvar* [*indepvars*] [*if*] [*in*] [, *options*]

options	description
Model	
<u>noconstant</u>	suppress constant term
<u>lags</u>(#)	use # lags of dependent variable as covariates; default is lags(1)
<u>maxldep</u>(#)	maximum lags of dependent variable for use as instruments
<u>maxlags</u>(#)	maximum lags of predetermined and endogenous variables for use as instruments
<u>twostep</u>	compute the two-step estimator instead of the one-step estimator
<u>diff</u>vars(*varlist*)	already-differenced exogenous variables
inst(*varlist*)	additional instrument variables
Predetermined	
<u>pre</u>(*varlist* [...])	predetermined variables; can be specified more than once
Endogenous	
<u>endo</u>genous(*varlist* [...])	endogenous variables; can be specified more than once
SE/Robust	
vce(*vcetype*)	*vcetype* may be gmm or <u>r</u>obust
Reporting	
<u>l</u>evel(#)	set confidence level; default is level(95)
<u>ar</u>tests(#)	use # as maximum order for AR tests; default is artests(2)

A panel variable and a time variable must be specified; use xtset; see [XT] **xtset**.

indepvars and all *varlists*, except pre(*varlist*[...]) and endogenous(*varlist*[...]), may contain time-series operators; see [U] **11.4.3 Time-series varlists**. The specification of *depvar*, however, may not contain time-series operators.

by, statsby, and xi are allowed; see [U] **11.1.10 Prefix commands**.

See [U] **20 Estimation and postestimation commands** for more capabilities of estimation commands.

Description

Linear dynamic panel-data models include p lags of the dependent variable as covariates and contain unobserved panel-level effects, fixed or random. By construction, the unobserved panel-level effects are correlated with the lagged dependent variables, making standard estimators inconsistent. Arellano and Bond (1991) derived a consistent generalized method-of-moments (GMM) estimator for the parameters of this model; xtabond implements this estimator.

This estimator is designed for datasets with many panels and few periods, and it requires that there be no autocorrelation in the idiosyncratic errors. For a related estimator that uses additional moment conditions, but still requires no autocorrelation in the idiosyncratic errors, see [XT] **xtdpdsys**. For estimators that allow for some autocorrelation in the idiosyncratic errors, at the cost of a more complicated syntax, see [XT] **xtdpd**.

Options

Model

noconstant; see [XT] **estimation options**.

lags(#) sets p, the number of lags of the dependent variable to be included in the model. The default is $p = 1$.

maxldep(#) sets the maximum number of lags of the dependent variable that can be used as instruments. The default is to use all $T_i - p - 2$ lags.

maxlags(#) sets the maximum number of lags of the predetermined and endogenous variables that can be used as instruments. For predetermined variables, the default is to use all $T_i - p - 1$ lags. For endogenous variables, the default is to use all $T_i - p - 2$ lags.

twostep specifies that the two-step estimator be calculated.

diffvars(*varlist*) specifies a set of variables that already have been differenced to be included as strictly exogenous covariates.

inst(*varlist*) specifies a set of variables to be used as additional instruments. These instruments are not differenced by xtabond before including them in the instrument matrix.

Predetermined

pre(*varlist* [, lagstruct(*prelags*, *premaxlags*)]) specifies that a set of predetermined variables be included in the model. Optionally, you may specify that *prelags* lags of the specified variables also be included. The default for *prelags* is 0. Specifying *premaxlags* sets the maximum number of further lags of the predetermined variables that can be used as instruments. The default is to include $T_i - p - 1$ lagged levels as instruments for predetermined variables. You may specify as many sets of predetermined variables as you need within the standard Stata limits on matrix size. Each set of predetermined variables may have its own number of *prelags* and *premaxlags*.

Endogenous

endogenous(*varlist* [, lagstruct(*endlags*, *endmaxlags*)]) specifies that a set of endogenous variables be included in the model. Optionally, you may specify that *endlags* lags of the specified variables also be included. The default for *endlags* is 0. Specifying *endmaxlags* sets the maximum number of further lags of the endogenous variables that can be used as instruments. The default is to include $T_i - p - 2$ lagged levels as instruments for endogenous variables. You may specify as many sets of endogenous variables as you need within the standard Stata limits on matrix size. Each set of endogenous variables may have its own number of *endlags* and *endmaxlags*.

SE/Robust

vce(*vcetype*) specifies the type of standard error reported, which includes types that are derived from asymptotic theory and that are robust to some kinds of misspecification; see *Remarks* below.

vce(gmm), the default, uses the conventionally derived variance estimator for generalized method-of-moments estimation.

vce(robust) uses the robust estimator. After one-step estimation, this is the Arellano–Bond robust VCE estimator. After two-step estimation, this is the Windmeijer (2005) WC-robust estimator.

⌐ Reporting ⌐

level(#); see [XT] **estimation options**.

artests(#) specifies the maximum order of the autocorrelation test to be calculated. The tests are reported by estat abond; see [XT] **xtabond postestimation**. Specifying the order of the highest test at estimation time is more efficient than specifying it to estat abond, because estat abond must refit the model to obtain the test statistics. The maximum order must be less than or equal to the number of periods in the longest panel. The default is artests(2).

Remarks

Anderson and Hsiao (1981, 1982) propose using further lags of the level or the difference of the dependent variable to instrument the lagged dependent variables that are included in a dynamic panel-data model after the panel-level effects have been removed by first-differencing. A version of this estimator can be obtained from xtivreg (see [XT] **xtivreg**). Arellano and Bond (1991) build upon this idea by noting that, in general, there are many more instruments available. Building on Holtz-Eakin, Newey, and Rosen (1988) and using the GMM framework developed by Hansen (1982), they identify how many lags of the dependent variable, the predetermined variables, and the endogenous variables are valid instruments and how to combine these lagged levels with first differences of the strictly exogenous variables into a potentially large instrument matrix. Using this instrument matrix, Arellano and Bond (1991) derive the corresponding one-step and two-step GMM estimators, as well as the robust VCE estimator for the one-step model. They also found that the robust two-step VCE was seriously biased. Windmeijer (2005) worked out a bias-corrected (WC) robust estimator for VCEs of two-step GMM estimators, which is implemented in xtabond. The test of autocorrelation of order m and the Sargan test of overidentifying restrictions derived by Arellano and Bond (1991) can be obtained with estat abond and estat sargan, respectively; see [XT] **xtabond postestimation**.

▷ Example 1

Arellano and Bond (1991) apply their new estimators and test statistics to a model of dynamic labor demand that had previously been considered by Layard and Nickell (1986) using data from an unbalanced panel of firms from the United Kingdom. All variables are indexed over the firm i and time t. In this dataset, n_{it} is the log of employment in firm i at time t, w_{it} is the natural log of the real product wage, k_{it} is the natural log of the gross capital stock, and ys_{it} is the natural log of industry output. The model also includes time dummies yr1980, yr1981, yr1982, yr1983, and yr1984. In table 4 of Arellano and Bond (1991), the authors present the results they obtained from several specifications.

In column a1 of table 4, Arellano and Bond report the coefficients and their standard errors from the robust one-step estimators of a dynamic model of labor demand in which n_{it} is the dependent variable and its first two lags are included as regressors. To clarify some important issues, we will begin with the homoskedastic one-step version of this model and then consider the robust case. Here is the command using xtabond and the subsequent output for the homoskedastic case:

```
. use http://www.stata-press.com/data/r10/abdata

 xtabond n l(0/1).w l(0/2).(k ys) yr1980-yr1984 year, lags(2) noconstant
```

```
Arellano-Bond dynamic panel-data estimation   Number of obs       =        611
Group variable: id                            Number of groups    =        140
Time variable: year
                                              Obs per group:   min =          4
                                                               avg =   4.364286
                                                               max =          6

Number of instruments =      41               Wald chi2(16)       =    1757.07
                                              Prob > chi2         =     0.0000
One-step results
```

n	Coef.	Std. Err.	z	P>|z|	[95% Conf. Interval]	
n						
L1.	.6862261	.1486163	4.62	0.000	.3949435	.9775088
L2.	-.0853582	.0444365	-1.92	0.055	-.1724523	.0017358
w						
--.	-.6078208	.0657694	-9.24	0.000	-.7367265	-.4789151
L1.	.3926237	.1092374	3.59	0.000	.1785222	.6067251
k						
--.	.3568456	.0370314	9.64	0.000	.2842653	.4294259
L1.	-.0580012	.0583051	-0.99	0.320	-.172277	.0562747
L2.	-.0199475	.0416274	-0.48	0.632	-.1015357	.0616408
ys						
--.	.6085073	.1345412	4.52	0.000	.3448115	.8722031
L1.	-.7111651	.1844599	-3.86	0.000	-1.0727	-.3496304
L2.	.1057969	.1428568	0.74	0.459	-.1741974	.3857912
yr1980	.0029062	.0212705	0.14	0.891	-.0387832	.0445957
yr1981	-.0404378	.0354707	-1.14	0.254	-.1099591	.0290836
yr1982	-.0652767	.048209	-1.35	0.176	-.1597646	.0292111
yr1983	-.0690928	.0627354	-1.10	0.271	-.1920521	.0538664
yr1984	-.0650302	.0781322	-0.83	0.405	-.2181665	.0881061
year	.0095545	.0142073	0.67	0.501	-.0182912	.0374002

```
Instruments for differenced equation
     GMM-type: L(2/.).n
     Standard: D.w LD.w D.k LD.k L2D.k D.ys LD.ys L2D.ys D.yr1980
               D.yr1981 D.yr1982 D.yr1983 D.yr1984 D.year
```

The coefficients are identical to those reported in column a1 of table 4, as they should be. Of course, the standard errors are different because we are considering the homoskedastic case. Although the moment conditions use first-differenced errors, xtabond estimates the coefficients of the level model and reports them accordingly.

The footer in the output reports the instruments used. The first line indicates that xtabond used lags from 2 on back to create the GMM-type instruments described in Arellano and Bond (1991) and Holtz-Eakin, Newey, and Rosen (1988); also see *Methods and Formulas* in [XT] **xtdpd**. The second and third lines indicate that the first difference of all the exogenous variables were used as standard instruments. GMM-type instruments use the lags of a variable to contribute multiple columns to the instrument matrix, whereas each standard instrument contributes one column to the instrument matrix. The notation L(2/.).n indicates that GMM-type instruments were created using lag 2 of n from on back. (L(2/4).n would indicate that GMM-type instruments were created using only lags 2, 3, and 4 of n.)

After `xtabond`, `estat sargan` reports the Sargan test of overidentifying restrictions.

```
. estat sargan
Sargan test of overidentifying restrictions
        H0: overidentifying restrictions are valid
        chi2(25)    =   65.81806
        Prob > chi2 =    0.0000
```

Only for a homoskedastic error term does the Sargan test have an asymptotic chi-squared distribution. In fact, Arellano and Bond (1991) show that the one-step Sargan test overrejects in the presence of heteroskedasticity. Since its asymptotic distribution is not known under the assumptions of the `vce(robust)` model, `xtabond` does not compute it when `vce(robust)` is specified. The Sargan test, reported by Arellano and Bond (1991, table 4, column a1), comes from the one-step homoskedastic estimator and is the same as the one reported here. The output above presents strong evidence against the null hypothesis that the overidentifying restrictions are valid. Rejecting this null hypothesis implies that we need to reconsider our model or our instruments, unless we attribute the rejection to heteroskedasticity in the data-generating process. Although performing the Sargan test after the two-step estimator is an alternative, Arellano and Bond (1991) found a tendency for this test to underreject in the presence of heteroskedasticity. (See [XT] **xtdpd** for an example indicating that this rejection may be due to misspecification.)

By default, `xtabond` calculates the Arellano–Bond test for first- and second-order autocorrelation in the first-differenced errors. (Use `artests()` to compute tests for higher orders.) There are versions of this test for both the homoskedastic and the robust cases, although their values are different. Use `estat abond` to report the test results.

```
. estat abond
Arellano-Bond test for zero autocorrelation in first-differenced errors
```

Order	z	Prob > z
1	-3.9394	0.0001
2	-.54239	0.5876

```
H0: no autocorrelation
```

When the idiosyncratic errors are independently and identically distributed (i.i.d.), the first-differenced errors are first-order serially correlated. So, as expected, the output above presents strong evidence against the null hypothesis of zero autocorrelation in the first-differenced errors at order 1. Serial correlation in the first-differenced errors at an order higher than 1 implies that the moment conditions used by `xtabond` are not valid; see [XT] **xtdpd** for an example of an alternative estimation method. The output above presents no significant evidence of serial correlation in the first-differenced errors at order 2.

◁

▷ Example 2

Consider the output from the one-step robust estimator of the same model:

```
. xtabond n l(0/1).w l(0/2).(k ys) yr1980-yr1984 year, lags(2) vce(robust)
> noconstant
Arellano-Bond dynamic panel-data estimation   Number of obs      =       611
Group variable: id                            Number of groups   =       140
Time variable: year
                                              Obs per group: min =         4
                                                             avg =  4.364286
                                                             max =         6
Number of instruments =      41               Wald chi2(16)      =   1727.45
                                              Prob > chi2        =    0.0000
One-step results
```

n	Coef.	Robust Std. Err.	z	P>|z|	[95% Conf. Interval]	
n						
L1.	.6862261	.1445943	4.75	0.000	.4028266	.9696257
L2.	-.0853582	.0560155	-1.52	0.128	-.1951467	.0244302
w						
--.	-.6078208	.1782055	-3.41	0.001	-.9570972	-.2585445
L1.	.3926237	.1679931	2.34	0.019	.0633632	.7218842
k						
--.	.3568456	.0590203	6.05	0.000	.241168	.4725233
L1.	-.0580012	.0731797	-0.79	0.428	-.2014308	.0854284
L2.	-.0199475	.0327126	-0.61	0.542	-.0840631	.0441681
ys						
--.	.6085073	.1725313	3.53	0.000	.2703522	.9466624
L1.	-.7111651	.2317163	-3.07	0.002	-1.165321	-.2570095
L2.	.1057969	.1412021	0.75	0.454	-.1709542	.382548
yr1980	.0029062	.0158028	0.18	0.854	-.0280667	.0338791
yr1981	-.0404378	.0280582	-1.44	0.150	-.0954307	.0145552
yr1982	-.0652767	.0365451	-1.79	0.074	-.1369038	.0063503
yr1983	-.0690928	.047413	-1.46	0.145	-.1620205	.0238348
yr1984	-.0650302	.0576305	-1.13	0.259	-.1779839	.0479235
year	.0095545	.0102896	0.93	0.353	-.0106127	.0297217

```
Instruments for differenced equation
        GMM-type: L(2/.).n
        Standard: D.w LD.w D.k LD.k L2D.k D.ys LD.ys L2D.ys D.yr1980
                  D.yr1981 D.yr1982 D.yr1983 D.yr1984 D.year
```

The coefficients are the same, but now the standard errors match that reported in Arellano and Bond (1991, table 4, column a1). Most of the robust standard errors are higher than those that assume a homoskedastic error term.

(Continued on next page)

The Sargan statistic cannot be calculated after requesting a robust VCE, but robust tests for serial correlation are available.

```
. estat abond

Arellano-Bond test for zero autocorrelation in first-differenced errors
```

Order	z	Prob > z
1	-3.5996	0.0003
2	-.51603	0.6058

```
H0: no autocorrelation
```

The value of the test for second-order autocorrelation matches those reported in Arellano and Bond (1991, table 4, column a1) and presents no evidence of model misspecification.

◁

▷ Example 3

xtabond reports the Wald statistic of the null hypothesis that all the coefficients except the constant are zero. Here the null hypothesis is that all the coefficients are zero, because there is no constant in the model. In our previous example, the null hypothesis is soundly rejected. In column a1 of table 4, Arellano and Bond report a chi-squared test of the null hypothesis that all the coefficients are zero, except the time trend and the time dummies. Here is this test in Stata:

```
. test l.n l2.n w l.w k l.k l2.k ys l.ys l2.ys

 ( 1)   L.n = 0
 ( 2)   L2.n = 0
 ( 3)   w = 0
 ( 4)   L.w = 0
 ( 5)   k = 0
 ( 6)   L.k = 0
 ( 7)   L2.k = 0
 ( 8)   ys = 0
 ( 9)   L.ys = 0
 (10)   L2.ys = 0

           chi2( 10) =   408.29
         Prob > chi2 =    0.0000
```

◁

▷ Example 4

The two-step estimator with the Windmeijer bias-corrected robust VCE of the same model produces the following output:

```
. xtabond n l(0/1).w l(0/2).(k ys) yr1980-yr1984 year, lags(2) twostep
> vce(robust) noconstant
```

```
Arellano-Bond dynamic panel-data estimation   Number of obs      =       611
Group variable: id                            Number of groups   =       140
Time variable: year
                                              Obs per group:  min =         4
                                                              avg =  4.364286
                                                              max =         6

Number of instruments =      41               Wald chi2(16)      =   1104.72
                                              Prob > chi2        =    0.0000
Two-step results
```

n	Coef.	WC-Robust Std. Err.	z	P>|z|	[95% Conf. Interval]
n					
L1.	.6287089	.1934138	3.25	0.001	.2496248 1.007793
L2.	-.0651882	.0450501	-1.45	0.148	-.1534847 .0231084
w					
--.	-.5257597	.1546107	-3.40	0.001	-.828791 -.2227284
L1.	.3112899	.2030006	1.53	0.125	-.086584 .7091638
k					
--.	.2783619	.0728019	3.82	0.000	.1356728 .4210511
L1.	.0140994	.0924575	0.15	0.879	-.167114 .1953129
L2.	-.0402484	.0432745	-0.93	0.352	-.1250649 .0445681
ys					
--.	.5919243	.1730916	3.42	0.001	.252671 .9311776
L1.	-.5659863	.2611008	-2.17	0.030	1.077731 .0512381
L2.	.1005433	.1610987	0.62	0.533	-.2152043 .4162908
yr1980	.0006378	.0168042	0.04	0.970	-.0322978 .0335734
yr1981	-.0550044	.0313389	-1.76	0.079	-.1164275 .0064187
yr1982	-.075978	.0419276	-1.81	0.070	-.1581545 .0061986
yr1983	-.0740708	.0528381	-1.40	0.161	-.1776315 .02949
yr1984	-.0906606	.0642615	-1.41	0.158	-.2166108 .0352896
year	.0112155	.0116783	0.96	0.337	-.0116735 .0341045

```
Instruments for differenced equation
        GMM-type: L(2/.).n
        Standard: D.w LD.w D.k LD.k L2D.k D.ys LD.ys L2D.ys D.yr1980
                  D.yr1981 D.yr1982 D.yr1983 D.yr1984 D.year
```

Arellano and Bond recommend against using the two-step nonrobust results for inference on the coefficients because the standard errors tend to be biased downward. (See Arellano and Bond 1991 for details.) The output above uses the Windmeijer bias-corrected (WC) robust VCE, which Windmeijer (2005) showed to work well. The magnitudes of several of the coefficient estimates have changed, and one even switched its sign.

The test for autocorrelation presents no evidence of model misspecification:

```
. estat abond
```

```
Arellano-Bond test for zero autocorrelation in first-differenced errors
```

Order	z	Prob > z
1	-2.1255	0.0335
2	-.35166	0.7251

```
H0: no autocorrelation
```

◁

▷ Example 5

Thus far we have been specifying the noconstant option to keep to the standard Arellano–Bond estimator, which uses instruments only for the differenced equation. The constant estimated by xtabond is a constant in the level equation, and it is estimated from the level errors. The output below illustrates that including a constant in the model does not affect the other parameter estimates.

```
. xtabond n l(0/1).w l(0/2).(k ys) yr1980-yr1984 year, lags(2) twostep
> vce(robust)
```

Arellano-Bond dynamic panel-data estimation Number of obs   =   611
Group variable: id   Number of groups   =   140
Time variable: year
                                             Obs per group: min =   4
                                                              avg =   4.364286
                                                              max =   6

Number of instruments =   42   Wald chi2(16)   =   1104.72
                                             Prob > chi2   =   0.0000
Two-step results

n	Coef.	WC-Robust Std. Err.	z	P>|z|	[95% Conf.	Interval]
n						
L1.	.6287089	.1934138	3.25	0.001	.2496248	1.007793
L2.	-.0651882	.0450501	-1.45	0.148	-.1534847	.0231084
w						
--.	-.5257597	.1546107	-3.40	0.001	-.828791	-.2227284
L1.	.3112899	.2030006	1.53	0.125	-.086584	.7091638
k						
--.	.2783619	.0728019	3.82	0.000	.1356728	.4210511
L1.	.0140994	.0924575	0.15	0.879	-.167114	.1953129
L2.	-.0402484	.0432745	-0.93	0.352	-.1250649	.0445681
ys						
--.	.5919243	.1730916	3.42	0.001	.252671	.9311776
L1.	-.5659863	.2611008	-2.17	0.030	-1.077734	-.0542381
L2.	.1005433	.1610987	0.62	0.533	-.2152043	.4162908
yr1980	.0006378	.0168042	0.04	0.970	-.0322978	.0335734
yr1981	-.0550044	.0313389	-1.76	0.079	-.1164275	.0064187
yr1982	-.075978	.0419276	-1.81	0.070	-.1581545	.0061986
yr1983	-.0740708	.0528381	-1.40	0.161	-.1776315	.02949
yr1984	-.0906606	.0642615	-1.41	0.158	-.2166108	.0352896
year	.0112155	.0116783	0.96	0.337	-.0116735	.0341045
_cons	-21.53725	23.23138	-0.93	0.354	-67.06992	23.99542

Instruments for differenced equation
        GMM-type: L(2/.).n
        Standard: D.w LD.w D.k LD.k L2D.k D.ys LD.ys L2D.ys D.yr1980
                  D.yr1981 D.yr1982 D.yr1983 D.yr1984 D.year
Instruments for level equation
        Standard: _cons

Including the constant does not affect the other parameter estimates because it is identified only by the level errors; see [XT] **xtdpd** for details.

◁

▷ Example 6

Sometimes we cannot assume strict exogeneity. Recall that a variable x_{it} is said to be strictly exogenous if $E[x_{it}\epsilon_{is}] = 0$ for all t and s. If $E[x_{it}\epsilon_{is}] \neq 0$ for $s < t$ but $E[x_{it}\epsilon_{is}] = 0$ for all $s \geq t$, the variable is said to be predetermined. Intuitively, if the error term at time t has some feedback on the subsequent realizations of x_{it}, x_{it} is a predetermined variable. Because unforecastable errors today might affect future changes in the real wage and in the capital stock, we might suspect that the log of the real product wage and the log of the gross capital stock are predetermined instead of strictly exogenous. In this example, we treat w and k as predetermined and use lagged levels as instruments.

```
. xtabond n l(0/1).ys yr1980-yr1984 year, lags(2) twostep pre(w, lag(1,.))
> pre(k, lag(2,.)) noconstant vce(robust)
Arellano-Bond dynamic panel-data estimation  Number of obs      =       611
Group variable: id                           Number of groups   =       140
Time variable: year
                                             Obs per group:  min =         4
                                                             avg =  4.364286
                                                             max =         6

Number of instruments =      83              Wald chi2(15)      =    958.30
                                             Prob > chi2        =    0.0000
Two-step results
```

n	Coef.	WC-Robust Std. Err.	z	P>|z|	[95% Conf. Interval]	
n						
L1.	.8580958	.1265515	6.78	0.000	.6100594	1.106132
L2.	-.081207	.0760703	-1.07	0.286	-.2303022	.0678881
w						
--.	-.6910855	.1387684	-4.98	0.000	-.9630666	-.4191044
L1.	.5961712	.1497338	3.98	0.000	.3026982	.8896441
k						
--.	.4140654	.1382788	2.99	0.003	.1430439	.6850868
L1.	-.1537048	.1220244	-1.26	0.208	-.3928681	.0854586
L2.	-.1025833	.0710886	-1.44	0.149	-.2419143	.0367477
ys						
--.	.6936392	.1728623	4.01	0.000	.3548354	1.032443
L1.	-.8773678	.2183085	-4.02	0.000	-1.305245	-.449491
yr1980	-.0072451	.017163	-0.42	0.673	-.0408839	.0263938
yr1981	-.0609608	.030207	-2.02	0.044	-.1201655	-.0017561
yr1982	-.1130369	.0454826	-2.49	0.013	-.2021812	-.0238926
yr1983	-.1335249	.0600213	-2.22	0.026	-.2511645	-.0158853
yr1984	-.1623177	.0725434	-2.24	0.025	-.3045001	-.0201352
year	.0264501	.0119329	2.22	0.027	.003062	.0498381

```
Instruments for differenced equation
    GMM-type: L(2/.).n L(1/.).L.w L(1/.).L2.k
    Standard: D.ys LD.ys D.yr1980 D.yr1981 D.yr1982 D.yr1983 D.yr1984
             D.year
```

The footer informs us that we are now including GMM-type instruments from the first lag of L.w on back and from the first lag of L2.k on back.

◁

❑ Technical Note

The above example illustrates that xtabond understands pre(w, lag(1, .)) to mean that L.w is a predetermined variable and pre(k, lag(2, .)) to mean that L2.k is a predetermined variable. This is a stricter definition than the alternative that pre(w, lag(1, .)) means only that w is predetermined but include a lag of w in the model and that pre(k, lag(2, .)) means only that k is predetermined but include first and second lags of k in the model. If you prefer the weaker definition, xtabond still gives you consistent estimates, but it is not using all possible instruments; see [XT] **xtdpd** for an example of how to include all possible instruments.

❑

▷ Example 7

We might instead suspect that w and k are endogenous in that $E[x_{it}\epsilon_{is}] \neq 0$ for $s \leq t$ but $E[x_{it}\epsilon_{is}] = 0$ for all $s > t$. By this definition, endogenous variables differ from predetermined variables only in that the former allow for correlation between the x_{it} and the ϵ_{it} at time t, whereas the latter do not. Endogenous variables are treated similarly to the lagged dependent variable. Levels of the endogenous variables lagged two or more periods can serve as instruments. In this example, we treat w and k as endogenous variables.

> Manuel Arellano (1957–) was born in Elda in Alicante, Spain. He earned degrees in economics from the University of Barcelona and the London School of Economics. After various posts in Oxford and London, he returned to Spain as professor of econometrics at Madrid in 1991. He is a leading expert on panel-data econometrics.
>
> Stephen Roy Bond (1963–) earned degrees in economics from Cambridge and Oxford. Following various posts at Oxford, he now works mainly at the Institute for Fiscal Studies in London. His research interests include company taxation, dividends, and the links between financial markets, corporate control, and investment.

```
. xtabond n l(0/1).ys yr1980-yr1984 year, lags(2) twostep endogenous(w, lag(1,.))
> endogenous(k, lag(2,.)) noconstant vce(robust)
```

```
Arellano-Bond dynamic panel-data estimation    Number of obs       =        611
Group variable: id                             Number of groups    =        140
Time variable: year
                                               Obs per group:  min =          4
                                                               avg =   4.364286
                                                               max =          6

Number of instruments =       71              Wald chi2(15)        =     967.61
                                              Prob > chi2          =     0.0000
Two-step results
```

n	Coef.	WC-Robust Std. Err.	z	P>|z|	[95% Conf. Interval]	
n						
L1.	.6640937	.1278908	5.19	0.000	.4134323	.914755
L2.	-.041283	.081801	-0.50	0.614	-.2016101	.1190441
w						
--.	-.7143942	.13083	-5.46	0.000	-.9708162	-.4579721
L1.	.3644198	.184758	1.97	0.049	.0023008	.7265388
k						
--.	.5028874	.1205419	4.17	0.000	.2666296	.7391452
L1.	-.2160842	.0972855	-2.22	0.026	-.4067603	-.025408
L2.	-.0549654	.0793673	-0.69	0.489	-.2105225	.1005917
ys						
--.	.5989356	.1779731	3.37	0.001	.2501148	.9477564
L1.	-.6770367	.1961166	-3.45	0.001	-1.061418	-.2926553
yr1980	-.0061122	.0155287	-0.39	0.694	-.0365478	.0243235
yr1981	-.04715	.0298348	-1.58	0.114	-.1056252	.0113251
yr1982	-.0817646	.0486049	-1.68	0.093	-.1770285	.0134993
yr1983	-.0939251	.0675804	-1.39	0.165	-.2263802	.0385299
yr1984	-.117228	.0804716	-1.46	0.145	-.2749493	.0404934
year	.0208857	.0103485	2.02	0.044	.0006031	.0411684

```
Instruments for differenced equation
        GMM-type: L(2/.).n L(2/.).L.w L(2/.).L2.k
        Standard: D.ys LD.ys D.yr1980 D.yr1981 D.yr1982 D.yr1983 D.yr1984
                  D.year
```

Although some estimated coefficients changed in magnitude, none changed in sign, and these results are similar to those obtained by treating w and k as predetermined.

◁

The Arellano–Bond estimator is for datasets with many panels and few periods. (Technically, the large-sample properties are derived with the number of panels going to infinity and the number of periods held fixed.) The number of instruments increases quadratically in the number of periods. If your dataset is better described by a framework in which both the number of panels and the number of periods is large, then you should consider other estimators such as those in [XT] **xtivreg** or xtreg, fe in [XT] **xtreg**; see Arellano and Alvarez (2003) for a discussion of this case.

▷ Example 8

Treating variables as predetermined or endogenous quickly increases the size of the instrument matrix. (See [XT] **xtdpd** *Methods and Formulas* for a discussion of how this matrix is created and what determines its size.) GMM estimators with too many overidentifying restrictions may perform poorly in small samples. (See Kiviet 1995 for a discussion of the dynamic panel-data case.)

To handle these problems, you can set a maximum number of lagged levels to be included as instruments for lagged-dependent or the predetermined variables. Here is an example in which a maximum of three lagged levels of the predetermined variables are included as instruments:

```
. xtabond n l(0/1).ys yr1980-yr1984 year, lags(2) twostep
> pre(w, lag(1,3)) pre(k, lag(2,3)) noconstant vce(robust)
```

```
Arellano-Bond dynamic panel-data estimation   Number of obs      =       611
Group variable: id                            Number of groups   =       140
Time variable: year
                                              Obs per group:   min =         4
                                                               avg =  4.364286
                                                               max =         6

Number of instruments =      67               Wald chi2(15)      =   1116.89
                                              Prob > chi2        =    0.0000
Two-step results
```

n	Coef.	WC-Robust Std. Err.	z	P>|z|	[95% Conf. Interval]	
n						
L1.	.931121	.1456964	6.39	0.000	.6455612	1.216681
L2.	-.0759918	.0854356	-0.89	0.374	-.2434425	.0914589
w						
--.	-.6475372	.1687931	-3.84	0.000	-.9783656	-.3167089
L1.	.6906238	.1789698	3.86	0.000	.3398493	1.041398
k						
--.	.3788106	.1848137	2.05	0.040	.0165824	.7410389
L1.	-.2158533	.1446198	-1.49	0.136	-.4993028	.0675962
L2.	-.0914584	.0852267	-1.07	0.283	-.2584997	.0755829
ys						
--.	.7324964	.176748	4.14	0.000	.3860766	1.078916
L1.	-.9428141	.2735472	-3.45	0.001	-1.478957	-.4066715
yr1980	-.0102389	.0172473	-0.59	0.553	-.0440431	.0235652
yr1981	-.0763495	.0296992	-2.57	0.010	-.1345589	-.0181402
yr1982	-.1373829	.0441833	-3.11	0.002	-.2239806	-.0507853
yr1983	-.1825149	.0613674	-2.97	0.003	-.3027928	-.0622369
yr1984	-.2314023	.0753669	-3.07	0.002	-.3791186	-.083686
year	.0310012	.0119167	2.60	0.009	.0076448	.0543576

```
Instruments for differenced equation
    GMM-type: L(2/.).n L(1/3).L.w L(1/3).L2.k
    Standard: D.ys LD.ys D.yr1980 D.yr1981 D.yr1982 D.yr1983 D.yr1984
             D.year
```

◁

▷ Example 9

xtabond handles data in which there are missing observations in the middle of the panels. In the following example, we deliberately set the dependent variable to missing in the year 1980:

```
. replace n=. if year==1980
(140 real changes made, 140 to missing)
. xtabond n l(0/1).w l(0/2).(k ys) yr1980-yr1984 year, lags(2) noconstant
> vce(robust)
note: yr1980 dropped from div() because of collinearity
note: yr1981 dropped from div() because of collinearity
note: yr1982 dropped from div() because of collinearity
note: yr1980 dropped because of collinearity
note: yr1981 dropped because of collinearity
note: yr1982 dropped because of collinearity
```

```
Arellano-Bond dynamic panel-data estimation   Number of obs      =        115
Group variable: id                            Number of groups   =        101
Time variable: year
                                              Obs per group:  min =          1
                                                              avg =   1.138614
                                                              max =          2
Number of instruments =        18             Wald chi2(12)      =      44.48
                                              Prob > chi2        =     0.0000
One-step results
```

n	Coef.	Robust Std. Err.	z	P>|z|	[95% Conf.	Interval]
n						
L1.	.1790577	.2204682	0.81	0.417	-.253052	.6111674
L2.	.0214253	.0488476	0.44	0.661	-.0743143	.1171649
w						
--.	-.2513405	.1402114	-1.79	0.073	-.5261498	.0234689
L1.	.1983952	.1445875	1.37	0.170	-.0849912	.4817815
k						
--.	.3983149	.0883352	4.51	0.000	.2251811	.5714488
L1.	-.025125	.0909236	-0.28	0.782	-.203332	.1530821
L2.	-.0359338	.0623382	-0.58	0.564	-.1581144	.0862468
ys						
--.	.3663201	.3824893	0.96	0.338	-.3833451	1.115985
L1.	-.6319976	.4823958	-1.31	0.190	-1.577476	.3134807
L2.	.5318404	.4105269	1.30	0.195	-.2727775	1.336458
yr1983	-.0047543	.024855	-0.19	0.848	-.0534692	.0439606
yr1984	(dropped)					
year	.0014465	.010355	0.14	0.889	-.0188489	.0217419

```
Instruments for differenced equation
        GMM-type: L(2/.).n
        Standard: D.w LD.w D.k LD.k L2D.k D.ys LD.ys L2D.ys D.yr1983
                  D.yr1984 D.year
```

There are two important aspects to this example. First, xtabond reports that variables have been dropped from the model and from the div() instrument list. For xtabond, the div() instrument list is the list of instruments created from the strictly exogenous variables; see [XT] **xtdpd** for more about the div() instrument list. Second, because xtabond uses time-series operators in its computations, if statements and missing values are not equivalent. An if statement causes the false observations to be excluded from the sample, but it computes the time-series operators wherever possible. In contrast, missing data prevent evaluation of the time-series operators that involve missing observations. Thus the example above is not equivalent to the following one:

```
. use http://www.stata-press.com/data/r10/abdata, clear

. xtabond n l(0/1).w l(0/2).(k ys) yr1980-yr1984 year if year!=1980,
> lags(2) noconstant vce(robust)
note: yr1980 dropped from div() because of collinearity
note: yr1980 dropped because of collinearity
```

```
Arellano-Bond dynamic panel-data estimation    Number of obs      =        473
Group variable: id                             Number of groups   =        140
Time variable: year
                                               Obs per group:    min =          3
                                                                 avg =   3.378571
                                                                 max =          5

Number of instruments =       37               Wald chi2(15)      =    1041.61
                                               Prob > chi2        =     0.0000
One-step results
```

n	Coef.	Robust Std. Err.	z	P>|z|	[95% Conf. Interval]	
n						
L1.	.7210062	.1321214	5.46	0.000	.4620531	.9799593
L2.	-.0960646	.0570547	-1.68	0.092	-.2078898	.0157606
w						
--.	-.6684175	.1739484	-3.84	0.000	-1.00935	-.3274849
L1.	.482322	.1647185	2.93	0.003	.1594797	.8051642
k						
--.	.3802777	.0728546	5.22	0.000	.2374853	.5230701
L1.	-.104598	.088597	-1.18	0.238	-.278245	.069049
L2.	-.0272055	.0379994	-0.72	0.474	-.101683	.0472721
ys						
--.	.4655989	.1864368	2.50	0.013	.1001895	.8310082
L1.	-.8562492	.2187886	-3.91	0.000	-1.285067	-.4274315
L2.	.0896556	.1440035	0.62	0.534	-.192586	.3718972
yr1981	-.0711626	.0205299	-3.47	0.001	-.1114005	-.0309247
yr1982	-.1212749	.0334659	-3.62	0.000	-.1868669	-.0556829
yr1983	-.1470248	.0461714	-3.18	0.001	-.2375191	-.0565305
yr1984	-.1519021	.0543904	-2.79	0.005	-.2585054	-.0452988
year	.0203277	.0108732	1.87	0.062	-.0009833	.0416387

```
Instruments for differenced equation
        GMM-type: L(2/.).n
        Standard: D.w LD.w D.k LD.k L2D.k D.ys LD.ys L2D.ys D.yr1981
                  D.yr1982 D.yr1983 D.yr1984 D.year
```

The year 1980 is dropped from the sample, but when the value of a variable from 1980 is required because a lag or difference is required, the 1980 value is used.

◁

Saved Results

xtabond saves the following in e():

Scalars

e(N)	number of observations
e(N_g)	number of groups
e(df_m)	model degrees of freedom
e(g_max)	largest group size
e(g_min)	smallest group size
e(g_avg)	average group size
e(t_max)	maximum time in sample
e(t_min)	minimum time in sample
e(chi2)	model χ^2 statistic
e(arm#)	test for autocorrelation of order #
e(artests)	number of AR tests computed
e(sig2)	estimate of σ_ϵ^2
e(rss)	sum squared differenced residuals
e(artests)	number of AR tests performed
e(sargan)	Sargan test statistic
e(zrank)	rank of instrument matrix

Macros

e(cmd)	xtabond
e(cmdline)	command as typed
e(depvar)	name of dependent variable
e(twostep)	twostep, if specified
e(ivar)	variable denoting groups
e(tvar)	time variable
e(vce)	*vcetype* specified in vce()
e(vcetype)	title used to label Std. Err.
e(system)	system, if system estimator
e(hascons)	hascons, if specified
e(transform)	specified transform
e(datasignature)	checksum from datasignature
e(engine)	xtdpd
e(div_odvars)	differenced variables used as standard instruments for differenced equation and not for level equation
e(div_olvars)	level variables used as standard instruments for differenced equation and not for level equation
e(liv_olvars)	level variables used as standard instruments for level equation and not for differenced equation
e(div_dvars)	differenced variables used as standard instruments for differenced equation
e(div_lvars)	level variables used as standard instruments for differenced equation
e(liv_lvars)	level variables used as standard instruments for level equation
e(dgmmiv_vars)	variables used to create GMM-type instruments for differenced equation
e(dgmmiv_flag)	first lags of variables used to create GMM-type instruments for differenced equation
e(dgmmiv_llag)	last lags of variables used to create GMM-type instruments for differenced equation
e(lgmmiv_vars)	variables used to create GMM-type instruments for level equation
e(lgmmiv_flag)	first lags used to create GMM-type instruments for level equation
e(properties)	b V
e(estat_cmd)	program used to implement estat
e(predict)	program used to implement predict

Matrices

    e(b)   coefficient vector

    e(V)   variance–covariance matrix of the estimators

Functions

    e(sample) marks estimation sample

Results e(div_odvars), e(div_olvars), e(liv_olvars), e(div_dvars), e(div_lvars), e(liv_lvars), e(dgmmiv_vars), e(dgmmiv_flag), e(dgmmiv_llag), e(lgmmiv_vars), and e(lgmmiv_flag) describe the instruments used by xtabond. These results are rarely of interest; see the options of xtdpd for more details.

Methods and Formulas

xtabond is implemented as an ado-file.

A dynamic panel-data model has the form

$$y_{it} = \sum_{j=1}^{p} \alpha_j y_{i,t-j} + \mathbf{x}_{it}\boldsymbol{\beta}_1 + \mathbf{w}_{it}\boldsymbol{\beta}_2 + \nu_i + \epsilon_{it} \quad i = 1,\ldots,N \quad t = 1,\ldots,T_i \qquad (1)$$

where

the α_j are p parameters to be estimated,

$\mathbf{x}_{it}$ is a $1 \times k_1$ vector of strictly exogenous covariates,

$\boldsymbol{\beta}_1$ is a $k_1 \times 1$ vector of parameters to be estimated,

$\mathbf{w}_{it}$ is a $1 \times k_2$ vector of predetermined and endogenous covariates,

$\boldsymbol{\beta}_2$ is a $k_2 \times 1$ vector of parameters to be estimated,

ν_i are the panel-level effects (which may be correlated with the covariates), and

ϵ_{it} are i.i.d. over the whole sample with variance σ_ϵ^2.

The ν_i and the ϵ_{it} are assumed to be independent for each i over all t.

By construction, the lagged dependent variables are correlated with the unobserved panel-level effects, making standard estimators inconsistent. With many panels and few periods, estimators are constructed by first-differencing to remove the panel-level effects and using instruments to form moment conditions.

xtabond uses a generalized method of moments (GMM) estimator to estimate $\alpha_1, \ldots, \alpha_p, \boldsymbol{\beta}_1$, and $\boldsymbol{\beta}_2$. The moment conditions are formed from the first-differenced errors from equation (1) and instruments. Lagged levels of the dependent variable, the predetermined variables, and the endogenous variables are used to form GMM-type instruments. See Arellano and Bond (1991) and Holtz-Eakin, Newey, and Rosen (1988) for discussions of GMM-type instruments. First differences of the strictly exogenous variables are used as standard instruments.

xtabond uses xtdpd to perform its computations, so the formulas are given in *Methods and Formulas* of [XT] **xtdpd**.

References

Alvarez, J., and M. Arellano. 2003. The time series and cross-section asymptotics of dynamic panel-data estimators. *Econometrica* 71: 1121–1160.

Anderson, T. W., and C. Hsiao. 1981. Estimation of dynamic models with error components. *Journal of the American Statistical Association* 76: 598–606.

——. 1982. Formulation and estimation of dynamic models using panel data. *Journal of Econometrics* 18: 47–82.

Arellano, M., and S. Bond. 1991. Some tests of specification for panel data: Monte Carlo evidence and an application to employment equations. *Review of Economic Studies* 58: 277–297.

Baltagi, B. H. 2005. *Econometric Analysis of Panel Data*. 3rd ed. New York: Wiley.

Bruno, G. S. F. 2005. Estimation and inference in dynamic unbalanced panel-data models with a small number of individuals. *Stata Journal* 5: 473–500.

Hansen, L. P. 1982. Large sample properties of generalized method of moments estimators. *Econometrica* 50: 1029–1054.

Holtz-Eakin, D., W. Newey, and H. S. Rosen. 1988. Estimating vector autoregressions with panel data. *Econometrica* 56: 1371–1395.

Kiviet, J. 1995. On bias, inconsistency, and efficiency of various estimators in dynamic panel data models. *Journal of Econometrics* 68: 53–78.

Layard, R., and S. J. Nickell. 1986. Unemployment in Britain. *Economica* 53: S121–S169.

Windmeijer, F. 2005. A finite sample correction for the variance of linear efficient two-step GMM estimators. *Journal of Econometrics* 126: 25–52.

Also See

Title

> **xtabond postestimation** — Postestimation tools for xtabond

Description

The following postestimation commands are of special interest after `xtabond`:

command	description
estat abond	test for autocorrelation
estat sargan	Sargan test of overidentifying restrictions

The following standard postestimation commands are also available:

command	description
estat	VCE and estimation sample summary
estimates	cataloging estimation results
lincom	point estimates, standard errors, testing, and inference for linear combinations of coefficients
mfx	marginal effects or elasticities
nlcom	point estimates, standard errors, testing, and inference for nonlinear combinations of coefficients
predict	predictions, residuals, influence statistics, and other diagnostic measures
predictnl	point estimates, standard errors, testing, and inference for generalized predictions
test	Wald tests for simple and composite linear hypotheses
testnl	Wald tests of nonlinear hypotheses

See the corresponding entries in the *Stata Base Reference Manual* for details.

Special-interest postestimation commands

`estat abond` reports the Arellano–Bond tests for serial correlation in the first-differenced errors.

`estat sargan` reports the Sargan test of the overidentifying restrictions.

Syntax for predict

predict [*type*] *newvar* [*if*] [*in*] [, xb e stdp <u>diff</u>erence]

Options for predict

   ⌐ Main ⌐

xb, the default, calculates the linear prediction.

e calculates the residual error.

stdp calculates the standard error of the prediction, which can be thought of as the standard error of the predicted expected value or mean for the observation's covariate pattern. The standard error of the prediction is also referred to as the standard error of the fitted value. stdp may not be combined with difference.

difference specifies that the statistic be calculated for the first differences instead of the levels, the default.

Syntax for estat abond

> estat abond [, artests(#)]

Option for estat abond

artests(#) specifies the highest order of serial correlation to be tested. By default, the tests computed during estimation are reported. The model will be refitted when artests(#) specifies a higher order than that computed during the original estimation. The model can be refitted only if the data have not changed.

Syntax for estat sargan

> estat sargan

Remarks

Remarks are presented under the following headings:

> *estat abond*
> *estat sargan*

estat abond

estat abond reports the Arellano–Bond test for serial correlation in the first-differenced errors at order m. Rejecting the null hypothesis of no serial correlation in the first-differenced errors at order zero does not imply model misspecification because the first-differenced errors are serially correlated if the idiosyncratic errors are independent and identically distributed. Rejecting the null hypothesis of no serial correlation in the first-differenced errors at an order greater than one implies model misspecification; see [XT] **xtdpd** for an example of the alternative estimator.

After the one-step system estimator, the test can be computed only when vce(robust) has been specified. (The system estimator is used to estimate the constant in xtabond.)

See *Remarks* in [XT] **xtabond** for more remarks about estat abond that are made in the context of the examples analyzed therein.

estat sargan

The distribution of the Sargan test is known only when the errors are independently and identically distributed. For this reason, `estat sargan` does not produce a test statistic when `vce(robust)` was specified in the call to `xtabond`.

See *Remarks* in [XT] **xtabond** for more remarks about `estat sargan` that are made in the context of the examples analyzed therein.

Methods and Formulas

All postestimation commands listed above are implemented as ado-files.

See [XT] **xtdpd postestimation** for the formulas.

Also See

[XT] **xtabond** — Arellano–Bond linear dynamic panel-data estimation

[U] **20 Estimation and postestimation commands**

Title

> **xtcloglog** — Random-effects and population-averaged cloglog models

Syntax

Random-effects (RE) model

> xtcloglog *depvar* [*indepvars*] [*if*] [*in*] [*weight*] [, re *RE_options*]

Population-averaged (PA) model

> xtcloglog *depvar* [*indepvars*] [*if*] [*in*] [*weight*] , pa [*PA_options*]

RE_options	description
Model	
<u>nocon</u>stant	suppress constant term
re	use random-effects estimator; the default
<u>off</u>set(*varname*)	include *varname* in model with coefficient constrained to 1
<u>constraints</u>(*constraints*)	apply specified linear constraints
<u>collin</u>ear	keep collinear variables
SE	
vce(*vcetype*)	*vcetype* may be oim, <u>boot</u>strap, or <u>jack</u>knife
Reporting	
<u>level</u>(#)	set confidence level; default is level(95)
noskip	perform overall model test as a likelihood-ratio test
<u>ef</u>orm	report exponentiated coefficients
Int opts (RE)	
<u>intmethod</u>(*intmethod*)	integration method; *intmethod* may be <u>mvaghermite</u>, <u>ag</u>hermite, or <u>g</u>hermite; default is intmethod(mvaghermite)
<u>intpoints</u>(#)	use # quadrature points; default is intpoints(12)
Max options	
maximize_options	control the maximization process; seldom used

(*Continued on next page*)

PA_options	description
Model	
<u>nocon</u>stant	suppress constant term
pa	use population-averaged estimator
<u>off</u>set(*varname*)	include *varname* in model with coefficient constrained to 1
Correlation	
corr(*correlation*)	within-group correlation structure; see table below
force	estimate even if observations unequally spaced in time
SE/Robust	
vce(*vcetype*)	*vcetype* may be conventional, <u>r</u>obust, <u>boot</u>strap, or <u>jack</u>knife
nmp	use divisor $N - P$ instead of the default N
<u>s</u>cale(*parm*)	overrides the default scale parameter; *parm* may be x2, dev, phi, or #
Reporting	
<u>l</u>evel(#)	set confidence level; default is level(95)
<u>ef</u>orm	report exponentiated coefficients
Opt options	
optimize_options	control the optimization process; seldom used

correlation	description
<u>exc</u>hangeable	exchangeable; the default
<u>ind</u>ependent	independent
<u>uns</u>tructured	unstructured
<u>fix</u>ed *matname*	user-specified
ar #	autoregressive of order #
<u>stat</u>ionary #	stationary of order #
<u>non</u>stationary #	nonstationary of order #

A panel variable must be specified. For xtcloglog, pa, correlation structures other than exchangeable and independent require that a time variable also be specified. Use xtset; see [XT] **xtset**.

depvar and *indepvars* may contain time-series operators; see [U] **11.4.3 Time-series varlists**.

by, statsby, and xi are allowed; see [U] **11.1.10 Prefix commands**.

iweights, fweights, and pweights are allowed for the population-averaged model, and iweights are allowed for the random-effects model; see [U] **11.1.6 weight**. Weights must be constant within panel.

See [U] **20 Estimation and postestimation commands** for more capabilities of estimation commands.

Description

xtcloglog fits population-averaged and random-effects complementary log-log (cloglog) models. There is no command for a conditional fixed-effects model, as there does not exist a sufficient statistic allowing the fixed effects to be conditioned out of the likelihood. Unconditional fixed-effects cloglog models may be fitted with cloglog with indicator variables for the panels. The appropriate indicator variables can be generated using tabulate or xi. However, unconditional fixed-effects estimates are biased.

By default, the population-averaged model is an equal-correlation model; that is, xtcloglog, pa assumes corr(exchangeable). See [XT] **xtgee** for details on fitting other population-averaged models.

xtcloglog, re, the default, is slow because the likelihood function is calculated by adaptive Gauss–Hermite quadrature; see *Methods and Formulas*. Computation time is roughly proportional to the number of points used for the quadrature. The default is intpoints(12). Increasing the number of quadrature points can improve the quadrature approximation. See [XT] **quadchk**.

See [R] **logistic** for a list of related estimation commands.

Options for RE model

    ⌐ Model ⌐

noconstant; see [XT] **estimation options**.

re requests the random-effects estimator, which is the default.

offset(*varname*), constraints(*constraints*), collinear; see [XT] **estimation options**.

    ⌐ SE ⌐

vce(*vcetype*) specifies the type of standard error reported, which includes types that are derived from asymptotic theory and that use bootstrap or jackknife methods; see [XT] **vce_options**.

    ⌐ Reporting ⌐

level(*#*), noskip; see [XT] **estimation options**.

eform displays the exponentiated coefficients and corresponding standard errors and confidence intervals.

    ⌐ Int opts (RE) ⌐

intmethod(*intmethod*), intpoints(*#*); see [XT] **estimation options**.

    ⌐ Max options ⌐

maximize_options: difficult, technique(*algorithm_spec*), iterate(*#*), [no]log, trace, gradient, showstep, hessian, shownrtolerance, tolerance(*#*), ltolerance(*#*), gtolerance(*#*), nrtolerance(*#*), nonrtolerance, from(*init_specs*); see [R] **maximize**. These options are seldom used.

Options for PA model

    ⌐ Model ⌐

noconstant; see [XT] **estimation options**.

pa requests the population-averaged estimator.

offset(*varname*); see [XT] **estimation options**

    ⌐ Correlation ⌐

corr(*correlation*), force; see [XT] **estimation options**.

vce(*vcetype*) specifies the type of standard error reported, which includes types that are derived from asymptotic theory, that are robust to some kinds of misspecification, and that use bootstrap or jackknife methods; see [XT] *vce_options*.

vce(conventional), the default, uses the conventionally derived variance estimator for generalized least-squares regression.

nmp, scale(x2 | dev | phi | #); see [XT] *vce_options*.

level(#); see [XT] **estimation options**.

eform displays the exponentiated coefficients and corresponding standard errors and confidence intervals.

optimize_options control the iterative optimization process. These options are seldom used.

iterate(#) specifies the maximum number of iterations. When the number of iterations equals #, the optimization stops and presents the current results, even if convergence has not been reached. The default is iterate(100).

tolerance(#) specifies the tolerance for the coefficient vector. When the relative change in the coefficient vector from one iteration to the next is less than or equal to #, the optimization process is stopped. tolerance(1e-6) is the default.

nolog suppresses display of the iteration log.

trace specifies that the current estimates be printed at each iteration.

Remarks

xtcloglog, pa is a shortcut command for fitting the population-averaged model. Typing

```
. xtcloglog ..., pa ...
```

is equivalent to typing

```
. xtgee ..., ... family(binomial) link(cloglog) corr(exchangeable)
```

Also see [XT] **xtgee** for information about xtcloglog.

By default or when re is specified, xtcloglog fits, via maximum likelihood, the random-effects model

$$\Pr(y_{it} \neq 0 | \mathbf{x}_{it}) = P(\mathbf{x}_{it}\boldsymbol{\beta} + \nu_i)$$

for $i = 1, \ldots, n$ panels, where $t = 1, \ldots, n_i$, ν_i are i.i.d., $N(0, \sigma_\nu^2)$, and $P(z) = 1 - \exp\{-\exp(z)\}$.

Underlying this model is the variance-components model

$$y_{it} \neq 0 \iff \mathbf{x}_{it}\boldsymbol{\beta} + \nu_i + \epsilon_{it} > 0$$

where ϵ_{it} are i.i.d. extreme-value (Gumbel) distributed with the mean equal to Euler's constant and variance $\sigma_\epsilon^2 = \pi^2/6$, independently of ν_i. The nonsymmetric error distribution is an alternative to logit and probit analysis and is typically used when the positive (or negative) outcome is rare.

▷ Example 1

Suppose that we are studying unionization of women in the United States and are using the union dataset; see [XT] **xt**. We wish to fit a random-effects model of union membership:

```
. use http://www.stata-press.com/data/r10/union
(NLS Women 14-24 in 1968)

. xtcloglog union age grade not_smsa south southXt
```
  (output omitted)

```
Random-effects complementary log-log model     Number of obs      =      26200
Group variable: idcode                          Number of groups   =       4434

Random effects u_i ~ Gaussian                   Obs per group: min =          1
                                                               avg =        5.9
                                                               max =         12

                                                Wald chi2(5)       =     248.59
Log likelihood  = -10535.929                    Prob > chi2        =     0.0000
```

union	Coef.	Std. Err.	z	P>|z|	[95% Conf. Interval]	
age	.0122702	.0032675	3.76	0.000	.0058659	.0186744
grade	.0698218	.0138027	5.06	0.000	.042769	.0968747
not_smsa	-.1984773	.0647835	-3.06	0.002	-.3254506	-.071504
south	-.897343	.0869064	-10.33	0.000	-1.067676	-.7270095
southXt	.0163768	.0059911	2.73	0.006	.0046345	.0281192
_cons	-3.301838	.2001433	-16.50	0.000	-3.694112	-2.909564
/lnsig2u	1.241305	.0461661			1.150822	1.331789
sigma_u	1.860142	.0429378			1.777861	1.946231
rho	.6777837	.0100824			.6577135	.6972188

```
Likelihood-ratio test of rho=0: chibar2(01) =  6016.55 Prob >= chibar2 = 0.000
```

The output includes the additional panel-level variance component, which is parameterized as the log of the standard deviation, $\ln\sigma_\nu$ (labeled `lnsig2u` in the output). The standard deviation σ_ν is also included in the output, labeled **sigma_u**, together with ρ (labeled **rho**),

$$\rho = \frac{\sigma_\nu^2}{\sigma_\nu^2 + \sigma_\epsilon^2}$$

which is the proportion of the total variance contributed by the panel-level variance component.

When **rho** is zero, the panel-level variance component is not important, and the panel estimator is no different from the pooled estimator (`cloglog`). A likelihood-ratio test of this is included at the bottom of the output, which formally compares the pooled estimator with the panel estimator.

As an alternative to the random-effects specification, you might want to fit an equal-correlation population-averaged cloglog model by typing

(Continued on next page)

```
. xtcloglog union age grade not_smsa south southXt, pa
Iteration 1: tolerance = .06580809
Iteration 2: tolerance = .00606963
Iteration 3: tolerance = .00032265
Iteration 4: tolerance = .00001658
Iteration 5: tolerance = 8.864e-07
```

```
GEE population-averaged model                   Number of obs      =      26200
Group variable:                    idcode       Number of groups   =       4434
Link:                              cloglog      Obs per group: min =          1
Family:                            binomial                    avg =        5.9
Correlation:                  exchangeable                    max =         12
                                                Wald chi2(5)       =     232.44
Scale parameter:                        1       Prob > chi2        =     0.0000
```

union	Coef.	Std. Err.	z	P>|z|	[95% Conf. Interval]	
age	.0045777	.0021754	2.10	0.035	.0003139	.0088415
grade	.0544267	.0095097	5.72	0.000	.035788	.0730654
not_smsa	-.1051731	.0430512	-2.44	0.015	-.189552	-.0207943
south	-.6578891	.061857	-10.64	0.000	-.7791266	-.5366515
southXt	.0142329	.004133	3.44	0.001	.0061325	.0223334
_cons	-2.074687	.1358008	-15.28	0.000	-2.340851	-1.808522

◁

▷ Example 2

In [R] **cloglog**, we showed these results and compared them with cloglog, vce(cluster id). xtcloglog with the pa option allows a vce(robust) option (the random-effects estimator does not allow the vce(robust) specification), so we can obtain the population-averaged cloglog estimator with the robust variance calculation by typing

```
. xtcloglog union age grade not_smsa south southXt, pa vce(robust)
```
(output omitted)

```
GEE population-averaged model                   Number of obs      =      26200
Group variable:                    idcode       Number of groups   =       4434
Link:                              cloglog      Obs per group: min =          1
Family:                            binomial                    avg =        5.9
Correlation:                  exchangeable                    max =         12
                                                Wald chi2(5)       =     153.64
Scale parameter:                        1       Prob > chi2        =     0.0000
                        (Std. Err. adjusted for clustering on idcode)
```

union	Coef.	Semi-robust Std. Err.	z	P>|z|	[95% Conf. Interval]	
age	.0045777	.003261	1.40	0.160	-.0018138	.0109692
grade	.0544267	.0117512	4.63	0.000	.0313948	.0774585
not_smsa	-.1051731	.0548342	-1.92	0.055	-.2126462	.0022999
south	-.6578891	.0793619	-8.29	0.000	-.8134355	-.5023427
southXt	.0142329	.005975	2.38	0.017	.0025221	.0259438
_cons	-2.074687	.1770236	-11.72	0.000	-2.421647	-1.727727

These standard errors are similar to those shown for cloglog, vce(cluster id) in [R] **cloglog**.

◁

Saved Results

xtcloglog, re saves the following in e():

Scalars

e(N)	# of observations	e(sigma_u)	panel-level standard deviation
e(N_g)	# of groups	e(n_quad)	# of quadrature points
e(N_cd)	# of completely determined obs.	e(k)	# of parameters
e(df_m)	model degrees of freedom	e(k_eq)	# of equations
e(ll)	log likelihood	e(k_eq_model)	# of equations in model Walt test
e(ll_0)	log likelihood, constant-only model	e(k_dv)	# of dependent variables
e(ll_c)	log likelihood, comparison model	e(p)	significance
e(g_max)	largest group size	e(rank)	rank of e(V)
e(g_min)	smallest group size	e(rank0)	rank of e(V) for constant-only model
e(g_avg)	average group size	e(ic)	# of iterations
e(chi2)	χ^2	e(rc)	return code
e(chi2_c)	χ^2 for comparison test	e(converged)	1 if converged, 0 otherwise
e(rho)	ρ		

Macros

e(cmd)	xtcloglog	e(distrib)	Gaussian; the distribution of the
e(cmdline)	command as typed		random effect
e(depvar)	name of dependent variable	e(vce)	*vcetype* specified in vce()
e(ivar)	variable denoting groups	e(vcetype)	title used to label Std. Err.
e(wtype)	weight type	e(opt)	type of optimization
e(wexp)	weight expression	e(ml_method)	type of ml method
e(title)	title in estimation output	e(user)	name of likelihood-evaluator program
e(offset)	offset	e(technique)	maximization technique
e(chi2type)	Wald or LR; type of model χ^2 test	e(crittype)	optimization criterion
e(chi2_ct)	Wald or LR; type of model χ^2 test corresponding to e(chi2_c)	e(properties)	b V
		e(predict)	program used to implement predict
e(intmethod)	integration method		

Matrices

e(b)	coefficient vector	e(ilog)	iteration log
e(V)	variance–covariance matrix of the estimators	e(gradient)	gradient vector

Functions

e(sample)	marks estimation sample

(Continued on next page)

xtcloglog, pa saves the following in e():

Scalars

e(N)	number of observations	e(chi2_dev)	χ^2 test of deviance
e(N_g)	number of groups	e(chi2_dis)	χ^2 test of deviance dispersion
e(df_m)	model degrees of freedom	e(deviance)	deviance
e(df_pear)	degrees of freedom for Pearson χ^2	e(dispers)	deviance dispersion
e(g_max)	largest group size	e(tol)	target tolerance
e(g_min)	smallest group size	e(dif)	achieved tolerance
e(g_avg)	average group size	e(phi)	scale parameter
e(chi2)	χ^2	e(rc)	return code

Macros

e(cmd)	xtgee	e(crittype)	optimization criterion
e(cmd2)	xtcloglog	e(scale)	x2, dev, phi, or #; scale parameter
e(cmdline)	command as typed	e(ivar)	variable denoting groups
e(depvar)	name of dependent variable	e(vce)	*vcetype* specified in vce()
e(wtype)	weight type	e(vcetype)	title used to label Std. Err.
e(wexp)	weight expression	e(chi2type)	Wald; type of model χ^2 test
e(family)	binomial	e(offset)	offset
e(link)	cloglog; link function	e(properties)	b V
e(corr)	correlation structure	e(predict)	program used to implement predict

Matrices

e(b)	coefficient vector	e(R)	estimated working correlation matrix
e(V)	variance–covariance matrix of the estimators		

Functions

e(sample)	marks estimation sample

Methods and Formulas

xtcloglog is implemented as an ado-file.

xtcloglog, pa reports the population-averaged results obtained by using xtgee, family(binomial) link(cloglog) to obtain estimates.

For the random-effects model, assume a normal distribution, $N(0, \sigma_\nu^2)$, for the random effects ν_i,

$$\Pr(y_{i1}, \ldots, y_{in_i} | \mathbf{x}_{i1}, \ldots, \mathbf{x}_{in_i}) = \int_{-\infty}^{\infty} \frac{e^{-\nu_i^2/2\sigma_\nu^2}}{\sqrt{2\pi}\sigma_\nu} \left\{ \prod_{t=1}^{n_i} F(y_{it}, \mathbf{x}_{it}\boldsymbol{\beta} + \nu_i) \right\} d\nu_i$$

where

$$F(y, z) = \begin{cases} 1 - \exp\left\{ -\exp(z) \right\} & \text{if } y \neq 0 \\ \exp\left\{ -\exp(z) \right\} & \text{otherwise} \end{cases}$$

The panel-level likelihood l_i is given by

$$l_i = \int_{-\infty}^{\infty} \frac{e^{-\nu_i^2/2\sigma_\nu^2}}{\sqrt{2\pi}\sigma_\nu} \left\{ \prod_{t=1}^{n_i} F(y_{it}, \mathbf{x}_{it}\boldsymbol{\beta} + \nu_i) \right\} d\nu_i$$

$$\equiv \int_{-\infty}^{\infty} g(y_{it}, x_{it}, \nu_i) d\nu_i$$

This integral can be approximated with M-point Gauss–Hermite quadrature

$$\int_{-\infty}^{\infty} e^{-x^2} h(x) dx \approx \sum_{m=1}^{M} w_m^* h(a_m^*)$$

This is equivalent to

$$\int_{-\infty}^{\infty} f(x) dx \approx \sum_{m=1}^{M} w_m^* \exp\left\{(a_m^*)^2\right\} f(a_m^*)$$

where the w_m^* denote the quadrature weights and the a_m^* denote the quadrature abscissas. The log likelihood, L, is the sum of the logs of the panel-level likelihoods l_i.

The default approximation of the log likelihood is by adaptive Gauss–Hermite quadrature, which approximates the panel-level likelihood with

$$l_i \approx \sqrt{2}\widehat{\sigma}_i \sum_{m=1}^{M} w_m^* \exp\left\{(a_m^*)^2\right\} g(y_{it}, x_{it}, \sqrt{2}\widehat{\sigma}_i a_m^* + \widehat{\mu}_i)$$

where $\widehat{\sigma}_i$ and $\widehat{\mu}_i$ are the adaptive parameters for panel i. Therefore, with the definition of $g(y_{it}, x_{it}, \nu_i)$, the total log likelihood is approximated by

$$L \approx \sum_{i=1}^{n} w_i \log\left[\sqrt{2}\widehat{\sigma}_i \sum_{m=1}^{M} w_m^* \exp\left\{(a_m^*)^2\right\} \frac{\exp\left\{-(\sqrt{2}\widehat{\sigma}_i a_m^* + \widehat{\mu}_i)^2 / 2\sigma_\nu^2\right\}}{\sqrt{2\pi}\sigma_\nu}\right.$$

$$\left.\prod_{t=1}^{n_i} F(y_{it}, x_{it}\beta + \sqrt{2}\widehat{\sigma}_i a_m^* + \widehat{\mu}_i)\right]$$

where w_i is the user-specified weight for panel i; if no weights are specified, $w_i = 1$.

The default method of adaptive Gauss–Hermite quadrature is to calculate the posterior mean and variance and use those parameters for $\widehat{\mu}_i$ and $\widehat{\sigma}_i$ by following the method of Naylor and Smith (1982), further discussed in Skrondal and Rabe-Hesketh (2004). We start with $\widehat{\sigma}_{i,0} = 1$ and $\widehat{\mu}_{i,0} = 0$, and the posterior means and variances are updated in the kth iteration. That is, at the kth iteration of the optimization for l_i, we use

$$l_{i,k} \approx \sum_{m=1}^{M} \sqrt{2}\widehat{\sigma}_{i,k-1} w_m^* \exp\left\{a_m^*\right\}^2\right\} g(y_{it}, x_{it}, \sqrt{2}\widehat{\sigma}_{i,k-1} a_m^* + \widehat{\mu}_{i,k-1})$$

Letting

$$\tau_{i,m,k-1} = \sqrt{2}\widehat{\sigma}_{i,k-1} a_m^* + \widehat{\mu}_{i,k-1}$$

$$\widehat{\mu}_{i,k} = \sum_{m=1}^{M} (\tau_{i,m,k-1}) \frac{\sqrt{2}\widehat{\sigma}_{i,k-1} w_m^* \exp\left\{(a_m^*)^2\right\} g(y_{it}, x_{it}, \tau_{i,m,k-1})}{l_{i,k}}$$

and

$$\widehat{\sigma}_{i,k} = \sum_{m=1}^{M} (\tau_{i,m,k-1})^2 \frac{\sqrt{2}\widehat{\sigma}_{i,k-1} w_m^* \exp\left\{(a_m^*)^2\right\} g(y_{it}, x_{it}, \tau_{i,m,k-1})}{l_{i,k}} - (\widehat{\mu}_{i,k})^2$$

and this is repeated until $\widehat{\mu}_{i,k}$ and $\widehat{\sigma}_{i,k}$ have converged for this iteration of the maximization algorithm. This adaptation is applied on every iteration until the log-likelihood change from the preceding iteration is less than a relative difference of 1e–6; after this, the quadrature parameters are fixed.

One can instead use the adaptive quadrature method of Liu and Pierce (1994), option `intmethod(aghermite)`, which uses the mode and curvature of the mode as approximations for the mean and variance. We take the integrand

$$g(y_{it}, x_{it}, \nu_i) = \frac{e^{-\nu_i^2/2\sigma_\nu^2}}{\sqrt{2\pi}\sigma_\nu} \left\{ \prod_{t=1}^{n_i} F(y_{it}, \mathbf{x}_{it}\boldsymbol{\beta} + \nu_i) \right\}$$

and find α_i the mode of $g(y_{it}, x_{it}, \nu_i)$. We calculate

$$\gamma_i = -\frac{\partial^2}{\partial \nu_i^2} \log\{g(y_{it}, x_{it}, \nu_i)\}\Big|_{\nu_i = \alpha_i}$$

Then

$$\int_{-\infty}^{\infty} g(y_{it}, x_{it}, \nu_i) d\nu_i \approx \left(\frac{2}{\gamma_i}\right)^{1/2} \sum_{m=1}^{M} w_m^* \exp\{(a_m^*)^2\} g\left\{ y_{it}, x_{it}, \left(\frac{2}{\gamma_i}\right)^{1/2} a_m^* + \alpha_i \right\}$$

This adaptation is performed on the first iteration only; that is, the α_i and γ_i are calculated once at the first iteration and then held constant throughout the subsequent iterations.

The log likelihood can also be calculated by nonadaptive Gauss–Hermite quadrature, option `intmethod(ghermite)`, where $\rho = \sigma_\nu^2/(\sigma_\nu^2 + 1)$:

$$L = \sum_{i=1}^{n} w_i \log\left\{ \Pr(y_{i1}, \ldots, y_{in_i} | \mathbf{x}_{i1}, \ldots, \mathbf{x}_{in_i}) \right\}$$

$$\approx \sum_{i=1}^{n} w_i \log\left[\frac{1}{\sqrt{\pi}} \sum_{m=1}^{M} w_m^* \prod_{t=1}^{n_i} F\left\{ y_{it}, \mathbf{x}_{it}\boldsymbol{\beta} + a_m^* \left(\frac{2\rho}{1-\rho}\right)^{1/2} \right\} \right]$$

All three quadrature formulas require that the integrated function be well approximated by a polynomial of degree equal to the number of quadrature points. The number of periods (panel size) can affect whether

$$\prod_{t=1}^{n_i} F(y_{it}, \mathbf{x}_{it}\boldsymbol{\beta} + \nu_i)$$

is well approximated by a polynomial. As panel size and ρ increase, the quadrature approximation can become less accurate. For large ρ, the random-effects model can also become unidentified. Adaptive quadrature gives better results for correlated data and large panels than nonadaptive quadrature; however, we recommend that you use the `quadchk` command to verify the quadrature approximation used in this command, whichever approximation you choose.

References

Liang, K.-Y., and S. L. Zeger. 1986. Longitudinal data analysis using generalized linear models. *Biometrika* 73: 13–22.

Liu, Q., and D. A. Pierce 1994. A note on Gauss–Hermite quadrature. *Biometrika* 81: 624–629.

Naylor, J. C., and A. F. M. Smith. 1982. Applications of a method for the efficient computation of posterior distributions. *Journal of the Royal Statistical Society, Series C* 31: 214–225.

Neuhaus, J. M. 1992. Statistical methods for longitudinal and clustered designs with binary responses. *Statistical Methods in Medical Research* 1: 249–273.

Neuhaus, J. M., J. D. Kalbfleisch, and W. W. Hauck. 1991. A comparison of cluster-specific and population-averaged approaches for analyzing correlated binary data. *International Statistical Review* 59: 25–35.

Pendergast, J. F., S. J. Gange, M. A. Newton, M. J. Lindstrom, M. Palta, and M. R. Fisher. 1996. A survey of methods for analyzing clustered binary response data. *International Statistical Review* 64: 89–118.

Skrondal, A., and S. Rabe-Hesketh. 2004. *Generalized Latent Variable Modeling: Multilevel, Longitudinal, and Structural Equation Models*. Boca Raton, FL: Chapman & Hall/CRC.

Also See

[XT] **xtcloglog postestimation** — Postestimation tools for xtcloglog

[XT] **quadchk** — Check sensitivity of quadrature approximation

[R] **constraint** — Define and list constraints

[XT] **xtgee** — Fit population-averaged panel-data models by using GEE

[XT] **xtlogit** — Fixed-effects, random-effects, and population-averaged logit models

[XT] **xtprobit** — Random-effects and population-averaged probit models

[R] **cloglog** — Complementary log-log regression

[U] **20 Estimation and postestimation commands**

Title

> **xtcloglog postestimation** — Postestimation tools for xtcloglog

Description

The following postestimation commands are available for `xtcloglog`:

command	description
adjust[1]	adjusted predictions of $\mathbf{x}\beta$, probabilities, or $\exp(\mathbf{x}\beta)$
*estat	AIC, BIC, VCE, and estimation sample summary
estimates	cataloging estimation results
lincom	point estimates, standard errors, testing, and inference for linear combinations of coefficients
lrtest	likelihood-ratio test
mfx	marginal effects or elasticities
nlcom	point estimates, standard errors, testing, and inference for nonlinear combinations of coefficients
predict	predictions, residuals, influence statistics, and other diagnostic measures
predictnl	point estimates, standard errors, testing, and inference for generalized predictions
test	Wald tests for simple and composite linear hypotheses
testnl	Wald tests of nonlinear hypotheses

[1] `adjust` is not appropriate with time-series operators.

* `estat ic` is not appropriate after `xtcloglog, pa`.

See the corresponding entries in the *Stata Base Reference Manual* for details.

Syntax for predict

Random-effects (RE) model

> predict [*type*] *newvar* [*if*] [*in*] [, *RE_statistics* <u>nooff</u>set]

Population-averaged (PA) model

> predict [*type*] *newvar* [*if*] [*in*] [, *PA_statistics* <u>nooff</u>set]

RE_statistics	description
Main	
xb	linear prediction; the default
pu0	probability of a positive outcome
stdp	standard error of the linear prediction

PA_statistics	description
Main	
mu	predicted probability of *depvar*; considers the offset(); the default
rate	predicted probability of *depvar*
xb	linear prediction
stdp	standard error of the linear prediction
score	first derivative of the log likelihood with respect to $x_j\beta$

These statistics are available both in and out of sample; type predict ... if e(sample) ... if wanted only for the estimation sample.

Options for predict

⌐ Main ⌐

xb calculates the linear prediction. This is the default for the random-effects model.

pu0 calculates the probability of a positive outcome, assuming that the random effect for that observation's panel is zero ($\nu = 0$). This may not be similar to the proportion of observed outcomes in the group.

stdp calculates the standard error of the linear prediction.

mu and rate both calculate the predicted probability of *depvar*. mu takes into account the offset(). rate ignores those adjustments. mu and rate are equivalent if you did not specify offset(). mu is the default for the population-averaged model.

score calculates the equation-level score, $u_j = \partial \ln L_j(x_j\beta)/\partial(x_j\beta)$.

nooffset is relevant only if you specified offset(*varname*) for xtcloglog. It modifies the calculations made by predict so that they ignore the offset variable; the linear prediction is treated as $x_{it}\beta$ rather than $x_{it}\beta + \text{offset}_{it}$.

Remarks

▷ Example 1

In example 1 of [XT] **xtcloglog**, we fitted the model

```
. use http://www.stata-press.com/data/r10/union
(NLS Women 14-24 in 1968)
. xtcloglog union age grade not_smsa south southXt
(output omitted )
```

Here we use mfx to determine how changes in the regressors affect the probability of a positive outcome, assuming that the random effect for each panel is zero:

(Continued on next page)

```
. mfx compute, predict(pu0)
Marginal effects after xtcloglog
      y  = Pr(union=1 assuming u_i=0) (predict, pu0)
         = .08678013
```

variable	dy/dx	Std. Err.	z	P>|z|	[95% C.I.]	X
age	.0010172	.00027	3.71	0.000	.00048 .001554	30.4322
grade	.0057883	.00116	5.01	0.000	.003523 .008054	12.7615
not_smsa*	−.0158421	.00501	−3.16	0.002	−.025658 −.006027	.283702
south*	−.0710282	.00704	−10.09	0.000	−.084819 −.057237	.413015
southXt	.0013577	.0005	2.73	0.006	.000382 .002333	3.96874

(*) dy/dx is for discrete change of dummy variable from 0 to 1

We see that an additional year of schooling increases the probability that a woman belongs to a union by about six-tenths of a percentage point.

◁

Also See

[XT] **xtcloglog** — Random-effects and population-averaged cloglog models

[U] **20 Estimation and postestimation commands**

Title

> **xtdata** — Faster specification searches with xt data

Syntax

$$\texttt{xtdata} \; [\textit{varlist}] \; [\textit{if}] \; [\textit{in}] \; [, \; \textit{options}]$$

options	description
Main	
re	convert data to a form suitable for random-effects estimation
ratio(#)	ratio of random effect to pure residual (standard deviations)
be	convert data to a form suitable for between estimation
fe	convert data to a form suitable for fixed-effects (within) estimation
nodouble	keep original variable type; default is to recast type as double
clear	overwrite current data in memory

A panel variable must be specified; use xtset; see [XT] **xtset**.

Description

xtdata produces a transformed dataset of the variables specified in *varlist* or of all the variables in the data. Once the data are transformed, Stata's regress command may be used to perform specification searches more quickly than xtreg; see [R] **regress** and [XT] **xtreg**. Using xtdata, re also creates a variable named constant. When using regress after xtdata, re, specify noconstant and include constant in the regression. After xtdata, be and xtdata, fe, you need not include constant or specify regress's noconstant option.

Options

> Main

re specifies that the data are to be converted into a form suitable for random-effects estimation. re is the default if be, fe, or re is not specified. ratio() must also be specified.

ratio(#) (use with xtdata, re only) specifies the ratio $\sigma_\nu / \sigma_\epsilon$, which is the ratio of the random effect to the pure residual. This is the ratio of the standard deviations, not the variances.

be specifies that the data are to be converted into a form suitable for between estimation.

fe specifies that the data are to be converted into a form suitable for fixed-effects (within) estimation.

nodouble specifies that transformed variables keep their original types, if possible. The default is to recast variables to double.

Remember that xtdata transforms variables to be differences from group means, pseudodifferences from group means, or group means. Specifying nodouble will decrease the size of the resulting dataset but may introduce roundoff errors in these calculations.

clear specifies that the data may be converted even though the dataset has changed since it was last saved on disk.

Remarks

If you have not read [XT] **xt** and [XT] **xtreg**, please do so.

The formal estimation commands of xtreg—see [XT] **xtreg**—do not produce results instanta-neously, especially with large datasets. Equations (2), (3), and (4) of [XT] **xtreg** describe the data necessary to fit each of the models with OLS. The idea here is to transform the data once to the appropriate form and then use regress to fit such models more quickly.

▷ Example 1

We will use the example in [XT] **xtreg** demonstrating between-effects regression. Another way to estimate the between equation is to convert the data in memory to the between data:

```
. use http://www.stata-press.com/data/r10/nlswork
(National Longitudinal Survey.  Young Women 14-26 years of age in 1968)

. generate age2=age^2
(24 missing values generated)

. generate ttl_exp2 = ttl_exp^2

. generate tenure2=tenure^2
(433 missing values generated)

. generate byte black = race==2

. xtdata ln_w grade age* ttl_exp* tenure* black not_smsa south, be clear

. regress ln_w grade age* ttl_exp* tenure* black not_smsa south
```

Source	SS	df	MS		
Model	415.021613	10	41.5021613		
Residual	431.954995	4686	.092179896		
Total	846.976608	4696	.180361288		

Number of obs = 4697
F(10, 4686) = 450.23
Prob > F   = 0.0000
R-squared   = 0.4900
Adj R-squared = 0.4889
Root MSE   = .30361

ln_wage	Coef.	Std. Err.	t	P>|t|	[95% Conf. Interval]	
grade	.0607602	.0020006	30.37	0.000	.0568382	.0646822
age	.0323158	.0087251	3.70	0.000	.0152105	.0494211
age2	-.0005997	.0001429	-4.20	0.000	-.0008799	-.0003194
(output omitted)						
south	-.0993378	.010136	-9.80	0.000	-.1192091	-.0794665
_cons	.3339113	.1210434	2.76	0.006	.0966093	.5712133

The output is the same as that produced by xtreg, be; the reported R^2 is the R^2 between. Using xtdata followed by just one regress does not save time. Using xtdata is justified when you intend to explore the specification of the model by running many alternative regressions.

◁

❑ Technical Note

When using xtdata, you must eliminate any variables that you do not intend to use and that have missing values. xtdata follows a casewise-deletion rule, which means that an observation is excluded from the conversion if it is missing on any of the variables. In the example above, we specified that the variables be converted on the command line. We could also drop the variables first, and it might even be useful to preserve our estimation sample:

```
. use http://www.stata-press.com/data/r10/nlswork, clear
(National Longitudinal Survey.  Young Women 14-26 years of age in 1968)
. generate age2 = age^2
(24 missing values generated)
. generate ttl_exp2 = ttl_exp^2
. generate tenure2 = tenure^2
(433 missing values generated)
. generate byte black = race==2
. keep id year ln_w grade age* ttl_exp* tenure* black not_smsa south
. save xtdatasmpl
file xtdatasmpl.dta saved
```

❏

▷ Example 2

`xtdata` with the `fe` option converts the data so that results are equivalent to those from estimating by using `xtreg` with the `fe` option.

```
. xtdata, fe
. regress ln_w grade age* ttl_exp* tenure* black not_smsa south
```

Source	SS	df	MS			Number of obs = 28091
						F(9, 28081) = 651.21
Model	412.443881	9	45.8270979			Prob > F = 0.0000
Residual	1976.12232	28081	.07037222			R-squared = 0.1727
						Adj R-squared = 0.1724
Total	2388.5662	28090	.085032617			Root MSE = .26528

ln_wage	Coef.	Std. Err.	t	P>|t|	[95% Conf. Interval]	
grade	-.0147051	4.97e+08	-0.00	1.000	-9.75e+08	9.75e+08
age	.0359987	.0030904	11.65	0.000	.0299414	.0420559
age2	-.000723	.0000486	-14.88	0.000	-.0008183	-.0006277
ttl_exp	.0334668	.0027061	12.37	0.000	.0281626	.0387709
ttl_exp2	.0002163	.0001166	1.86	0.064	-.0000122	.0004448
tenure	.0357539	.0016871	21.19	0.000	.0324471	.0390607
tenure2	-.0019701	.0001141	-17.27	0.000	-.0021937	-.0017465
black	(dropped)					
not_smsa	-.0890108	.0086984	-10.23	0.000	-.10606	-.0719616
south	-.0606309	.0099763	-6.08	0.000	-.0801849	-.0410769
_cons	1.221668	6.23e+09	0.00	1.000	-1.22e+10	1.22e+10

The coefficients reported by `regress` after `xtdata, fe` are the same as those reported by `xtreg, fe`, but the standard errors are slightly smaller. This is because no adjustment has been made to the estimated covariance matrix for the estimation of the person means. The difference is small, however, and results are adequate for a specification search.

◁

▷ Example 3

To use `xtdata, re`, you must specify the ratio $\sigma_\nu/\sigma_\epsilon$, which is the ratio of the standard deviations of the random effect and pure residual. Merely to show the relationship of `regress` after `xtdata, re` to `xtreg, re`, we will specify this ratio as $.25790313/.29069544 = .88719358$, which is the number `xtreg` reports when the model is fitted from the outset; see the random-effects example in [XT] **xtreg**. For specification searches, however, it is adequate to specify this number more crudely, and, when performing the specification search for this manual entry, we used `ratio(1)`.

```
. use http://www.stata-press.com/data/r10/xtdatasmpl, clear
(National Longitudinal Survey.  Young Women 14-26 years of age in 1968)
. xtdata, clear re ratio(.88719358)
```

───── theta ───────				
min	5%	median	95%	max
0.2520	0.2520	0.5499	0.7016	0.7206

xtdata reports the distribution of θ based on the specified ratio. If these were balanced data, θ would have been constant.

When running regressions with these data, you must specify the noconstant option and include the variable constant:

```
. regress ln_w grade age* ttl_exp* tenure* black not_smsa south constant,
> noconstant
```

Source	SS	df	MS		Number of obs =	28091
					F(11, 28080) =14303.11	
Model	13272.3241	11	1206.57492		Prob > F = 0.0000	
Residual	2368.75918	28080	.084357521		R-squared = 0.8486	
					Adj R-squared = 0.8485	
Total	15641.0833	28091	.556800517		Root MSE = .29044	

ln_wage	Coef.	Std. Err.	t	P>|t|	[95% Conf. Interval]	
grade	.0646499	.0017811	36.30	0.000	.0611588	.068141
age	.0368059	.0031195	11.80	0.000	.0306915	.0429204
age2	-.0007133	.00005	-14.27	0.000	-.0008113	-.0006153
(output omitted)						
south	-.0868927	.0073031	-11.90	0.000	-.1012072	-.0725781
constant	.238721	.0494688	4.83	0.000	.1417598	.3356822

Results are the same coefficients and standard errors that xtreg, re previously estimated. The summaries at the top, however, should be ignored, as they are expressed in terms of (4) of [XT] **xtreg**, and, moreover, for a model without a constant.

◁

❑ Technical Note

Using xtdata requires some caution. The following guidelines may help:

1. xtdata is intended for use only during the specification search phase of analysis. Results should be estimated with xtreg on unconverted data.

2. After converting the data, you may use regress to obtain estimates of the coefficients and their standard errors. For regress after xtdata, fe, the standard errors are too small, but only slightly.

3. You may loosely interpret the coefficient's significance tests and confidence intervals. However, for results after xtdata, fe and re, an incorrect (but close to correct) distribution is assumed.

4. You should ignore the summary statistics reported at the top of regress's output.

5. After converting the data, you may form linear, but not nonlinear, combinations of regressors; that is, if your data contained age, it would not be correct to convert the data and then form age squared. All nonlinear transformations should be done before conversion. (For xtdata, be, you can get away with forming nonlinear combinations ex post, but the results will not be exact.) ❑

☐ Technical Note

The `xtdata` command can be used to help you examine data, especially with `scatter`.

```
. use http://www.stata-press.com/data/r10/xtdatasmpl, clear
(National Longitudinal Survey.  Young Women 14-26 years of age in 1968)
. xtdata, be
. scatter ln_wage age, title(Between data) msymbol(o) msize(tiny)
```

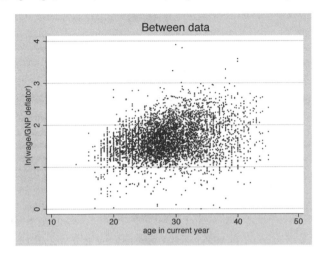

```
. use http://www.stata-press.com/data/r10/xtdatasmpl, clear
(National Longitudinal Survey.  Young Women 14-26 years of age in 1968)
. xtdata, fe
. scatter ln_wage age, title(Within data) msymbol(o) msize(tiny)
```

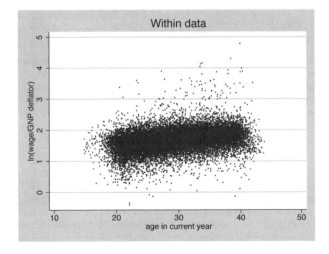

```
. use http://www.stata-press.com/data/r10/xtdatasmpl, clear
(National Longitudinal Survey.  Young Women 14-26 years of age in 1968)
. scatter ln_wage age, title(Overall data) msymbol(o) msize(tiny)
```

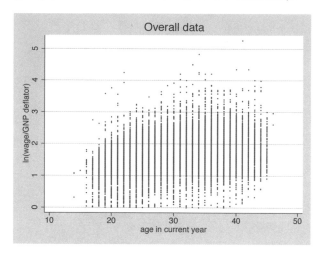

Methods and Formulas

xtdata is implemented as an ado-file.

(This section is a continuation of the *Methods and Formulas* of [XT] **xtreg**.)

xtdata, be, fe, and re transform the data according to (2), (3), and (4), respectively, of [XT] **xtreg**, except that xtdata, fe adds back in the overall mean, thus forming the transformation

$$\mathbf{x}_{it} - \overline{x}_i + \overline{\overline{x}}$$

xtdata, re requires the user to specify r as an estimate of $\sigma_\nu/\sigma_\epsilon$. θ_i is calculated from

$$\theta_i = 1 - \frac{1}{\sqrt{T_i r^2 + 1}}$$

Also See

[XT] **xtsum** — Summarize xt data

Title

> **xtdescribe** — Describe pattern of xt data

Syntax

xtdescribe [*if*] [*in*] [, *options*]

options	description
Main	
patterns(*#*)	maximum participation patterns; default is patterns(9)
width(*#*)	display *#* width of participation patterns; default is width(100)

A panel variable and a time variable must be specified; use xtset; see [XT] **xtset**.
by is allowed; see [D] **by**.

Description

xtdescribe describes the participation pattern of cross-sectional time-series (xt) data.

Options

> Main

patterns(*#*) specifies the maximum number of participation patterns to be reported; patterns(9) is the default. Specifying patterns(50) would list up to 50 patterns. Specifying patterns(1000) is taken to mean patterns(∞); all the patterns will be listed.

width(*#*) specifies the desired width of the participation patterns to be displayed; width(100) is the default. If the number of times is greater than width(), then each column in the participation pattern represents multiple periods as indicated in a footnote at the bottom of the table. The actual width may differ slightly from the requested width depending on the span of the time variable and the number of periods.

Remarks

If you have not read [XT] **xt**, please do so.

xtdescribe describes the cross-sectional and time-series aspects of the data in memory.

▷ Example 1

In [XT] **xt**, we introduced data based on a subsample of the NLSY data on young women aged 14–26 years in 1968. Here is a description of the data used in many of the [XT] **xt** examples:

```
. use http://www.stata-press.com/data/r10/nlswork
(National Longitudinal Survey.  Young Women 14-26 years of age in 1968)

. xtdescribe

   idcode:  1, 2, ..., 5159                               n =      4711
     year:  68, 69, ..., 88                               T =        15
            Delta(year) = 1 unit
            Span(year)  = 21 periods
            (idcode*year uniquely identifies each observation)

Distribution of T_i:    min     5%    25%      50%    75%    95%    max
                          1      1      3        5      9     13     15

     Freq.   Percent   Cum.  | Pattern
 ----------------------------+---------------------------------
       136      2.89   2.89  | 1..................
       114      2.42   5.31  | .................1
        89      1.89   7.20  | ................1.11
        87      1.85   9.04  | .................11
        86      1.83  10.87  | 111111.1.11.1.11.1.11
        61      1.29  12.16  | ............11.1.11
        56      1.19  13.35  | 11................
        54      1.15  14.50  | .............1.1.11
        54      1.15  15.64  | .......1.11.1.11.1.11
      3974     84.36 100.00  | (other patterns)
 ----------------------------+---------------------------------
      4711    100.00         | XXXXXX.X.XX.X.XX.X.XX
```

`xtdescribe` tells us that we have 4,711 women in our data and that the `idcode` that identifies each ranges from 1 to 5,159. We are also told that the maximum number of individual years over which we observe any woman is 15, though the `year` variable spans 21 years. The delta or periodicity of `year` is one unit, meaning that in principle we could observe each woman yearly. We are reassured that `idcode` and `year`, taken together, uniquely identify each observation in our data. We are also shown the distribution of T_i; 50% of our women are observed 5 years or less. Only 5% of our women are observed for 13 years or more.

Finally, we are shown the participation pattern. A 1 in the pattern means one observation that year; a dot means no observation. The largest fraction of our women (still only 2.89%) was observed in the single year 1968 and not thereafter; the next largest fraction was observed in 1988 but not before; and the next largest fraction was observed in 1985, 1987, and 1988.

At the bottom is the sum of the participation patterns, including the patterns that were not shown. We can see that none of the women were observed in six of the years (there are six dots). (The survey was not administered in those 6 years.)

We could see more of the patterns by specifying the `patterns()` option, or we could see all the patterns by specifying `patterns(1000)`.

◁

▷ Example 2

The strange participation patterns shown above have to do with our subsampling of the data, not with the administrators of the survey. Here are the data from which we drew the sample used in the [XT] **xt** examples:

```
. xtdescribe
```

```
  idcode:  1, 2, ..., 5159                                      n =      5159
    year:  68, 69, ..., 88                                      T =        15
           Delta(year) = 1; (88-68)+1 = 21
           (idcode*year does not uniquely identify observations)
```

```
Distribution of T_i:    min     5%    25%    50%    75%    95%    max
                          1      2     11     15     16     19     30
```

Freq.	Percent	Cum.	Pattern
1034	20.04	20.04	111111.1.11.1.11.1.11
153	2.97	23.01	1....................
147	2.85	25.86	112111.1.11.1.11.1.11
130	2.52	28.38	111112.1.11.1.11.1.11
122	2.36	30.74	111211.1.11.1.11.1.11
113	2.19	32.93	11...................
84	1.63	34.56	111111.1.11.1.11.1.12
79	1.53	36.09	111111.1.12.1.11.1.11
67	1.30	37.39	111111.1.11.1.11.1.1.
3230	62.61	100.00	(other patterns)
5159	100.00		XXXXXX.X.XX.X.XX.X.XX

We have multiple observations per year. In the pattern, 2 indicates that a woman appears twice in the year, 3 indicates 3 times, and so on—X indicates 10 or more, should that be necessary.

In fact, this is a dataset that was itself extracted from the NLSY, in which t is not time but job number. To simplify exposition, we made a simpler dataset by selecting the last job in each year.

◁

▷ Example 3

When the number of periods is greater than the width of the participation pattern, each column will represent more than one period.

```
. use http://www.stata-press.com/data/r10/xtdesxmpl
```

```
. xtdescribe
```

```
 patient:  1, 2, ..., 30                                        n =        30
    time:  09mar2007 16:00:00, 09mar2007 17:00:00, ...,         T =        32
           10mar2007 23:00:00
           Delta(time) = 1 hour
           Span(time)  = 32 periods
           (patient*time uniquely identifies each observation)
```

```
Distribution of T_i:    min     5%    25%    50%    75%    95%    max
                         30     30     31     32     32     32     32
```

Freq.	Percent	Cum.	Pattern
21	70.00	70.00	11111111111111111111111111111111
3	10.00	80.00	111111111111111111111111111111..
2	6.67	86.67	..111111111111111111111111111111
2	6.67	93.33	.1111111111111111111111111111111
2	6.67	100.00	1.111111111111111111111111111111
30	100.00		XXXXXXXXXXXXXXXXXXXXXXXXXXXXXXXX

We have data for 30 patients who were observed hourly between 4:00 PM on March 9, 2007, and 11:00 PM on March 10, a span of 32 hours. We have complete records for 21 of the patients. The footnote indicates that each column in the pattern represents two periods, so for four patients we have an observation taken at either 4:00 PM or 5:00 PM on March 9, but we do not have observations for both times. There are three patients for whom we are missing both the 10:00 PM and 11:00 PM observations on March 10, and there are two patients for whom we are missing the 4:00 PM and 5:00 PM observations for March 9.

◁

Methods and Formulas

xtdescribe is implemented as an ado-file.

Also See

[XT] **xtsum** — Summarize xt data

[XT] **xttab** — Tabulate xt data

Title

xtdpd — Linear dynamic panel-data estimation

Syntax

xtdpd *depvar* [*indepvars*] [*if*] [*in*], dgmmiv(*varlist* [...]) [*options*]

options	description
Model	
*dgmmiv(*varlist*[...])	GMM-type instruments for the difference equation; can be specified more than once
lgmmiv(*varlist*[...])	GMM-type instruments for the level equation; can be specified more than once
iv(*varlist*[...])	standard instruments for the difference and level equations; can be specified more than once
div(*varlist*[...])	standard instruments for the difference equation only; can be specified more than once
liv(*varlist*)	standard instruments for the level equation only; can be specified more than once
noconstant	suppress constant term
twostep	compute the two-step estimator instead of the one-step estimator
hascons	check for collinearity only among levels of independent variables; by default checks occur among levels and differences
fodeviation	specifies that forward-orthogonal deviations are to be used instead of first differences
SE/Robust	
vce(*vcetype*)	*vcetype* may be gmm or robust
Reporting	
level(*#*)	set confidence level; default is level(95)
artests(*#*)	use # as maximum order for AR tests; default is artests(2)

*dgmmiv() is required.

A panel variable and a time variable must be specified; use xtset; see [XT] **xtset**.

depvar, *indepvars*, and all *varlists* may contain time-series operators; see [U] **11.4.3 Time-series varlists**.

by and statsby are allowed; see [U] **11.1.10 Prefix commands**.

See [U] **20 Estimation and postestimation commands** for more capabilities of estimation commands.

Description

Linear dynamic panel-data models include p lags of the dependent variable as covariates and contain unobserved panel-level effects, fixed or random. By construction, the unobserved panel-level effects are correlated with the lagged dependent variables, making standard estimators inconsistent. xtdpd fits a dynamic panel-data model using the Arellano–Bond (1991) or the Arellano–Bover/Blundell–Bond (1995, 1998) estimator.

At the cost of a more complicated syntax, xtdpd can fit models with low-order moving-average correlation in the idiosyncratic errors or predetermined variables with a more complicated structure than allowed for xtabond or xtdpdsys; see [XT] **xtabond** and [XT] **xtdpdsys**.

Options

─────┐ Model └──

dgmmiv(*varlist* [, <u>la</u>grange(*flag* [*llag*])]) specifies GMM-type instruments for the differenced equation. Levels of the variables are used to form GMM-type instruments for the difference equation. All possible lags are used, unless lagrange(*flag llag*) restricts the lags to begin with *flag* and end with *llag*. You may specify as many sets of GMM-type instruments for the differenced equation as you need within the standard Stata limits on matrix size. Each set may have its own *flag* and *llag*. dgmmiv() is required.

lgmmiv(*varlist* [, <u>la</u>g(#)]) specifies GMM-type instruments for the level equation. Differences of the variables are used to form GMM-type instruments for the level equation. The first lag of the differences is used unless lag(#) is specified, indicating that #th lag of the differences be used. You may specify as many sets of GMM-type instruments for the level equation as you need within the standard Stata limits on matrix size. Each set may have its own *lag*.

iv(*varlist* [, <u>nodifference</u>]) specifies standard instruments for both the differenced and level equations. Differences of the variables are used as instruments for the differenced equations, unless nodifference is specified, which requests that levels be used. Levels of the variables are used as instruments for the level equations. You may specify as many sets of standard instruments for both the differenced and level equations as you need within the standard Stata limits on matrix size.

div(*varlist* [, <u>nodifference</u>]) specifies additional standard instruments for the differenced equation. Specified variables may not be included in iv() or in liv(). Differences of the variables are used, unless nodifference is specified, which requests that levels of the variables be used as instruments for the differenced equation. You may specify as many additional sets of standard instruments for the differenced equation as you need within the standard Stata limits on matrix size.

liv(*varlist*) specifies additional standard instruments for the level equation. Specified variables may not be included in iv() or in div(). Levels of the variables are used as instruments for the level equation. You may specify as many additional sets of standard instruments for the level equation as you need within the standard Stata limits on matrix size.

noconstant; see [XT] **estimation options**.

twostep specifies that the two-step estimator be calculated.

hascons specifies that xtdpd check for collinearity only among levels of independent variables; by default checks occur among levels and differences.

fodeviation specifies that forward-orthogonal deviations are to be used instead of first differences. fodeviation is not allowed when there are gaps in the data or when lgmmiv() is specified.

⌐ SE/Robust ⌐

vce(*vcetype*) specifies the type of standard error reported, which includes types that are derived from asymptotic theory and that are robust to some kinds of misspecification; see *Methods and Formulas*.

     vce(gmm), the default, uses the conventionally derived variance estimator for generalized method of moments estimation.

     vce(robust) uses the robust estimator. After one-step estimation, this is the Arellano–Bond robust VCE estimator. After two-step estimation, this is the Windmeijer (2005) WC-robust estimator.

⌐ Reporting ⌐

level(*#*); see [XT] **estimation options**.

artests(*#*) specifies the maximum order of the autocorrelation test to be calculated. The tests are reported by estat abond; see [XT] **xtdpd postestimation**. Specifying the order of the highest test at estimation time is more efficient than specifying it to estat abond, because estat abond must refit the model to obtain the test statistics. The maximum order must be less than or equal to the number of periods in the longest panel. The default is artests(2).

Remarks

If you have not read [XT] **xtabond** and [XT] **xtdpdsys**, you should do so before continuing.

Consider the dynamic panel-data model

$$y_{it} = \sum_{j=1}^{p} \alpha_j y_{i,t-j} + \mathbf{x}_{it}\boldsymbol{\beta}_1 + \mathbf{w}_{it}\boldsymbol{\beta}_2 + \nu_i + \epsilon_{it} \qquad i = \{1, \ldots, N\}; \ t = \{1, \ldots, T_i\} \qquad (1)$$

where

the $\alpha_1, \ldots, \alpha_p$ are p parameters to be estimated,

$\mathbf{x}_{it}$ is a $1 \times k_1$ vector of strictly exogenous covariates,

$\boldsymbol{\beta}_1$ is a $k_1 \times 1$ vector of parameters to be estimated,

$\mathbf{w}_{it}$ is a $1 \times k_2$ vector of predetermined covariates,

$\boldsymbol{\beta}_2$ is a $k_2 \times 1$ vector of parameters to be estimated,

ν_i are the panel-level effects (which may be correlated with x_{it} or w_{it}), and

and ϵ_{it} are i.i.d. or come from a low-order moving-average process, with variance σ_ϵ^2.

Building on the work of Anderson and Hsiao (1981, 1982) and Holtz-Eakin, Newey, and Rosen (1988), Arellano and Bond (1991) derived one-step and two-step GMM estimators using moment conditions in which lagged levels of the dependent and predetermined variables were instruments for the differenced equation. Blundell and Bond (1998) show that the lagged-level instruments in the Arellano–Bond estimator become weak as the autoregressive process becomes too persistent or the ratio of the variance of the panel-level effect ν_i to the variance of the idiosyncratic error ϵ_{it} becomes too large. Building on the work of Arellano and Bover (1995), Blundell and Bond (1998) proposed a system estimator that uses moment conditions in which lagged differences are used as instruments for the level equation in addition to the moment conditions of lagged levels as instruments for the differenced equation. The additional moment conditions are valid only if the initial condition $E[\nu_i \Delta y_{i2}] = 0$ holds for all i; see Blundell and Bond (1998) and Blundell, Bond, and Windmeijer (2000).

xtdpd fits dynamic panel-data models using the Arellano–Bond or the Arellano–Bover/Blundell–Bond system estimator. The parameters of many standard models can be more easily estimated using the Arellano–Bond estimator implemented in xtabond or using the Arellano–Bover/Blundell–Bond system estimator implemented in xtdpdsys; see [XT] **xtabond** and [XT] **xtdpdsys**. xtdpd can fit more complex models at the cost of a more complicated syntax. That the idiosyncratic errors follow a low-order MA process and that the predetermined variables have a more complicated structure than accommodated by xtabond and xtdpdsys are two common reasons for using xtdpd instead of xtabond or xtdpdsys.

The standard GMM robust two-step estimator of the VCE is known to be seriously biased. Windmeijer (2005) derived a bias-corrected robust estimator for two-step VCEs from GMM estimators known as the WC-robust estimator, which is implemented in xtdpd.

The Arellano–Bond test of autocorrelation of order m and the Sargan test of overidentifying restrictions derived by Arellano and Bond (1991) are computed by xtdpd but reported by estat abond and estat sargan, respectively; see [XT] **xtdpd postestimation**.

Because xtdpd extends xtabond and xtdpdsys, [XT] **xtabond** and [XT] **xtdpdsys** provide useful background.

▷ Example 1

Arellano and Bond (1991) apply their new estimators and test statistics to a model of dynamic labor demand that had previously been considered by Layard and Nickell (1986), using data from an unbalanced panel of firms from the United Kingdom. All variables are indexed over the firm i and time t. In this dataset, n_{it} is the log of employment in firm i inside the United Kingdom at time t, w_{it} is the natural log of the real product wage, k_{it} is the natural log of the gross capital stock, and ys_{it} is the natural log of industry output. The model also includes time dummies yr1980, yr1981, yr1982, yr1983, and yr1984. To gain some insight into the syntax for xtdpd, we reproduce the first example from [XT] **xtabond** using xtdpd:

```
. use http://www.stata-press.com/data/r10/abdata

. xtdpd L(0/2).n L(0/1).w L(0/2).(k ys) yr1980-yr1984 year, noconstant
> div(L(0/1).w L(0/2).(k ys) yr1980-yr1984 year) dgmmiv(n)
```

Dynamic panel-data estimation				Number of obs		=	611
Group variable: id				Number of groups		=	140
Time variable: year							
				Obs per group:	min =		4
					avg =		4.364286
					max =		6
Number of instruments =		41		Wald chi2(16)		=	1757.07
				Prob > chi2		=	0.0000

One-step results

n	Coef.	Std. Err.	z	P>|z|	[95% Conf. Interval]	
n						
L1.	.6862261	.1486163	4.62	0.000	.3949435	.9775088
L2.	-.0853582	.0444365	-1.92	0.055	-.1724523	.0017358
w						
--.	-.6078208	.0657694	-9.24	0.000	-.7367265	-.4789151
L1.	.3926237	.1092374	3.59	0.000	.1785222	.6067251
k						
--.	.3568456	.0370314	9.64	0.000	.2842653	.4294259
L1.	-.0580012	.0583051	-0.99	0.320	-.172277	.0562747
L2.	-.0199475	.0416274	-0.48	0.632	-.1015357	.0616408
ys						
--.	.6085073	.1345412	4.52	0.000	.3448115	.8722031
L1.	-.7111651	.1844599	-3.86	0.000	-1.0727	-.3496304
L2.	.1057969	.1428568	0.74	0.459	-.1741974	.3857912
yr1980	.0029062	.0212705	0.14	0.891	-.0387832	.0445957
yr1981	-.0404378	.0354707	-1.14	0.254	-.1099591	.0290836
yr1982	-.0652767	.048209	-1.35	0.176	-.1597646	.0292111
yr1983	-.0690928	.0627354	-1.10	0.271	-.1920521	.0538664
yr1984	-.0650302	.0781322	-0.83	0.405	-.2181665	.0881061
year	.0095545	.0142073	0.67	0.501	-.0182912	.0374002

```
Instruments for differenced equation
        GMM-type: L(2/.).n
        Standard: D.w LD.w D.k LD.k L2D.k D.ys LD.ys L2D.ys D.yr1980
                  D.yr1981 D.yr1982 D.yr1983 D.yr1984 D.year
```

Unlike most instrumental-variables estimation commands, the independent variables in the varlist are not automatically used as instruments. In this example, all the independent variables are strictly exogenous, so we include them in div(), a list of variables whose first differences will be instruments for the differenced equation. We include the dependent variable in dgmmiv(), a list of variables whose lagged levels will be used to create GMM-type instruments for the differenced equation. (GMM-type instruments are discussed in a technical note below.)

The footer in the output reports the instruments used. The first line indicates that xtdpd used lags from 2 on back to create the GMM-type instruments described in Arellano and Bond (1991) and Holtz-Eakin, Newey, and Rosen (1988). The second line says that the first difference of all the variables included in the div() varlist were used as standard instruments for the differenced equation.

◁

❏ Technical Note

GMM-type instruments are built from lags of one variable. Ignoring the strictly exogenous variables for simplicity, our model is

$$n_{it} = \alpha_1 n_{it-1} + \alpha_2 n_{it-2} + \nu_i + \epsilon_{it} \tag{2}$$

After differencing we have

$$\Delta n_{it} = \Delta \alpha_1 n_{it-1} + \Delta \alpha_2 n_{it-2} + \Delta \epsilon_{it} \tag{3}$$

Equation (3) implies that we need instruments that are not correlated with either ϵ_{it} or ϵ_{it-1}. Equation (2) shows that L2.n is the first lag of n that is not correlated with ϵ_{it} or ϵ_{it-1}, so it is the first lag of n that can be used to instrument the differenced equation.

Consider the following data from one of the complete panels in the previous example:

```
. list id year n L2.n dl2.n if id==140
```

	id	year	n	L2.n	L2D.n
1023.	140	1976	.4324315	.	.
1024.	140	1977	.3694925	.	.
1025.	140	1978	.3541718	.4324315	.
1026.	140	1979	.3632532	.3694925	-.0629391
1027.	140	1980	.3371863	.3541718	-.0153207
1028.	140	1981	.285179	.3632532	.0090815
1029.	140	1982	.1756326	.3371863	-.026067
1030.	140	1983	.1275133	.285179	-.0520073
1031.	140	1984	.0889263	.1756326	-.1095464

The missing values in L2D.n show that we lose 3 observations because of lags and the difference that removes the panel-level effects. The first nonmissing observation occurs in 1979 and observations on n from 1976 and 1977 are available to instrument the 1979 differenced equation. The table below gives the observations available to instrument the differenced equation for the data above.

Year of difference errors	Years of instruments	Number of instruments
1979	1976–1977	2
1980	1976–1978	3
1981	1976–1979	4
1982	1976–1980	5
1983	1976–1981	6
1984	1976–1982	7

The table shows that there are a total of 27 GMM-type instruments.

The output in the example above informs us that there were a total of 41 instruments applied to the differenced equation. Because there are 14 standard instruments, there must have been 27 GMM-type instruments, which matches our above calculation.

❏

▷ Example 2

Sometimes we cannot assume strict exogeneity. Recall that a variable x_{it} is said to be strictly exogenous if $E[x_{it}\epsilon_{is}] = 0$ for all t and s. If $E[x_{it}\epsilon_{is}] \neq 0$ for $s < t$ but $E[x_{it}\epsilon_{is}] = 0$ for all $s \geq t$, the variable is said to be predetermined. Intuitively, if the error term at time t has some feedback on the subsequent realizations of x_{it}, x_{it} is a predetermined variable. In the output below, we use xtdpd to reproduce an example in [XT] **xtabond**.

```
. xtdpd L(0/2).n L(0/1).(w ys) L(0/2).k yr1980-yr1984 year,
> div(L(0/1).(ys) yr1980-yr1984 year) dgmmiv(n) dgmmiv(L.w L2.k, lag(1 .))
> twostep noconstant vce(robust)
```

Dynamic panel-data estimation			Number of obs	=	611
Group variable: id			Number of groups	=	140
Time variable: year					

	Obs per group:	min =	4
		avg =	4.364286
		max =	6

Number of instruments =	83	Wald chi2(15)	=	958.30
		Prob > chi2	=	0.0000

Two-step results

n	Coef.	WC-Robust Std. Err.	z	P>|z|	[95% Conf. Interval]	
n						
L1.	.8580958	.1265515	6.78	0.000	.6100594	1.106132
L2.	-.081207	.0760703	-1.07	0.286	-.2303022	.0678881
w						
--.	-.6910855	.1387684	-4.98	0.000	-.9630666	-.4191044
L1.	.5961712	.1497338	3.98	0.000	.3026982	.8896441
ys						
--.	.6936392	.1728623	4.01	0.000	.3548354	1.032443
L1.	-.8773678	.2183085	-4.02	0.000	-1.305245	-.449491
k						
--.	.4140654	.1382788	2.99	0.003	.1430439	.6850868
L1.	-.1537048	.1220244	-1.26	0.208	-.3928681	.0854586
L2.	-.1025833	.0710886	-1.44	0.149	-.2419143	.0367477
yr1980	-.0072451	.017163	-0.42	0.673	-.0408839	.0263938
yr1981	-.0609608	.030207	-2.02	0.044	-.1201655	-.0017561
yr1982	-.1130369	.0454826	-2.49	0.013	-.2021812	-.0238926
yr1983	-.1335249	.0600213	-2.22	0.026	-.2511645	-.0158853
yr1984	-.1623177	.0725434	-2.24	0.025	-.3045001	-.0201352
year	.0264501	.0119329	2.22	0.027	.003062	.0498381

```
Instruments for differenced equation
        GMM-type: L(2/.).n L(1/.).L.w L(1/.).L2.k
        Standard: D.ys LD.ys D.yr1980 D.yr1981 D.yr1982 D.yr1983 D.yr1984
                  D.year
```

The footer informs us that we are now including GMM-type instruments from the first lag of L.w on back and from the first lag of L2.k on back.

◁

▷ Example 3

As discussed in [XT] **xtabond** and [XT] **xtdpdsys**, xtabond and xtdpdsys both use a strict definition of predetermined variables with lags. In the strict definition, the most recent lag of the variable in pre() is considered predetermined. (Here specifying pre(w, lag(1, .)) to xtabond means that

L.w is a predetermined variable and pre(k, lag(2, .)) means that L2.k is a predetermined variable.) In a weaker definition, the current observation is considered predetermined, but subsequent lags are included in the model. Here w and k would be predetermined instead of L.w and L2.w. The output below implements this weaker definition for the previous example.

```
. xtdpd L(0/2).n L(0/1).(w ys) L(0/2).k yr1980-yr1984 year,
> div(L(0/1).(ys) yr1980-yr1984 year) dgmmiv(n) dgmmiv(w k, lag(1 .))
> twostep noconstant vce(robust)
```

Dynamic panel-data estimation	Number of obs	=	611
Group variable: id	Number of groups	=	140
Time variable: year			

	Obs per group:	min =	4
		avg =	4.364286
		max =	6

Number of instruments = 101	Wald chi2(15)	=	879.53
	Prob > chi2	=	0.0000

Two-step results

n	Coef.	WC-Robust Std. Err.	z	P>|z|	[95% Conf. Interval]	
n						
L1.	.6343155	.1221058	5.19	0.000	.3949925	.8736384
L2.	-.0871247	.0704816	-1.24	0.216	-.2252661	.0510168
w						
--.	-.720063	.1133359	-6.35	0.000	-.9421973	-.4979287
L1.	.238069	.1223186	1.95	0.052	-.0016712	.4778091
ys						
--.	.5999718	.1653036	3.63	0.000	.2759827	.923961
L1.	-.5674808	.1656411	-3.43	0.001	-.8921314	-.2428303
k						
--.	.3931997	.0986673	3.99	0.000	.1998153	.5865842
L1.	-.0019641	.0772814	-0.03	0.980	-.1534329	.1495047
L2.	-.0231165	.0487317	-0.47	0.635	-.1186288	.0723958
yr1980	-.006209	.0162138	-0.38	0.702	-.0379875	.0255694
yr1981	-.0398491	.0313794	-1.27	0.204	-.1013516	.0216535
yr1982	-.0525715	.0397346	-1.32	0.186	-.1304498	.0253068
yr1983	-.0451175	.051418	-0.88	0.380	-.145895	.05566
yr1984	-.0437772	.0614391	-0.71	0.476	-.1641955	.0766412
year	.0173374	.0108665	1.60	0.111	-.0039605	.0386352

```
Instruments for differenced equation
        GMM-type: L(2/.).n L(1/.).w L(1/.).k
        Standard: D.ys LD.ys D.yr1980 D.yr1981 D.yr1982 D.yr1983 D.yr1984
                  D.year
```

As expected, the output shows that the additional 18 instruments available under the weaker definition can affect the magnitudes of the estimates. Applying the stricter definition when the true model was generated by the weaker definition yielded consistent but inefficient results; there were some additional moment conditions that could have been included but were not. In contrast, applying the weaker definition when the true model was generated by the stricter definition yields inconsistent estimates.

◁

▷ Example 4

Here we use xtdpd to reproduce an example from [XT] **xtdpdsys** in which we used the system estimator to fit a model with predetermined variables.

```
. xtdpd L(0/1).n L(0/2).(w k) yr1980-yr1984 year,
> div(yr1980-yr1984 year) dgmmiv(n) dgmmiv(L2.(w k), lag(1 .))
> lgmmiv(n L1.(w k)) vce(robust) hascons
```

```
Dynamic panel-data estimation               Number of obs      =        751
Group variable: id                          Number of groups   =        140
Time variable: year
                                            Obs per group:   min =          5
                                                             avg =   5.364286
                                                             max =          7

Number of instruments =       95           Wald chi2(13)      =    7562.80
                                            Prob > chi2        =     0.0000
```

One-step results

n	Coef.	Robust Std. Err.	z	P>|z|	[95% Conf. Interval]
n					
L1.	.913278	.0460602	19.83	0.000	.8230017	1.003554
w					
--.	-.728159	.1019044	-7.15	0.000	-.927888	-.5284301
L1.	.5602737	.1939617	2.89	0.004	.1801156	.9404317
L2.	-.0523028	.1487653	-0.35	0.725	-.3438775	.2392718
k					
--.	.4820097	.0760787	6.34	0.000	.3328983	.6311212
L1.	-.2846944	.0831902	-3.42	0.001	-.4477442	-.1216446
L2.	-.1394181	.0405709	-3.44	0.001	-.2189356	-.0599006
yr1980	-.0325146	.0216371	-1.50	0.133	-.0749226	.0098935
yr1981	-.0726116	.0346482	-2.10	0.036	-.1405207	-.0047024
yr1982	-.0477038	.0451914	-1.06	0.291	-.1362772	.0408696
yr1983	-.0396264	.0558734	-0.71	0.478	-.1491362	.0698835
yr1984	-.0810383	.0736648	-1.10	0.271	-.2254186	.063342
year	.0192741	.0145326	1.33	0.185	-.0092092	.0477574
_cons	-37.34972	28.77747	-1.30	0.194	-93.75253	19.05308

```
Instruments for differenced equation
        GMM-type: L(2/.).n L(1/.).L2.w L(1/.).L2.k
        Standard: D.yr1980 D.yr1981 D.yr1982 D.yr1983 D.yr1984 D.year
Instruments for level equation
        GMM-type: LD.n L2D.w L2D.k
        Standard: _cons
```

The first lags of the variables included in lgmmiv() are used to create GMM-type instruments for the level equation. Only the first lags of the variables in lgmmiv() are used because the moment conditions using higher lags are redundant; see Blundell and Bond (1998) and Blundell, Bond, and Windmeijer (2000).

◁

▷ Example 5

All the previous examples have used moment conditions that are valid only if the idiosyncratic errors are i.i.d. This example shows how to use xtdpd to estimate the parameters of a model with first-order moving-average [MA(1)] errors using either the Arellano–Bond estimator or the Arellano–Bover/Blundell–Bond system estimator. For simplicity, we assume that the independent variables are strictly exogenous.

We begin by noting that the Sargan test rejects the null hypothesis that the overidentifying restrictions are valid in the model with i.i.d. errors.

```
. xtdpd L(0/1).n L(0/2).(w k) yr1980-yr1984 year,
> div(L(0/1).(w k) yr1980-yr1984 year) dgmmiv(n) hascons
  (output omitted)

. estat sargan
Sargan test of overidentifying restrictions
        H0: overidentifying restrictions are valid

        chi2(24)      =   49.70094
        Prob > chi2   =    0.0015
```

Assuming that the idiosyncratic errors are MA(1) implies that only lags three or higher are valid instruments for the differenced equation. (See the technical note below.)

```
. xtdpd L(0/1).n L(0/2).(w k) yr1980-yr1984 year,
> div(L(0/1).(w k) yr1980-yr1984 year) dgmmiv(n, lag(3 .)) hascons
```

Dynamic panel-data estimation		Number of obs	=	751
Group variable: id		Number of groups	=	140
Time variable: year				
		Obs per group: min =		5
		avg =		5.364286
		max =		7
Number of instruments =	32	Wald chi2(13)	=	1195.04
		Prob > chi2	=	0.0000

One-step results

n	Coef.	Std. Err.	z	P>|z|	[95% Conf. Interval]	
n						
L1.	.8696303	.2014473	4.32	0.000	.4748008	1.26446
w						
--.	-.5802971	.0762659	-7.61	0.000	-.7297756	-.4308187
L1.	.2918658	.1543883	1.89	0.059	-.0107296	.5944613
L2.	-.5903459	.2995123	-1.97	0.049	-1.177379	-.0033126
k						
--.	.3428139	.0447916	7.65	0.000	.2550239	.4306039
L1.	-.1383918	.0825823	-1.68	0.094	-.3002502	.0234665
L2.	-.0260956	.1535855	-0.17	0.865	-.3271177	.2749265
yr1980	-.0036873	.0301587	-0.12	0.903	-.0627973	.0554226
yr1981	.00218	.0592014	0.04	0.971	-.1138526	.1182125
yr1982	.0782939	.0897622	0.87	0.383	-.0976367	.2542246
yr1983	.1734231	.1308914	1.32	0.185	-.0831193	.4299655
yr1984	.2400685	.1734456	1.38	0.166	-.0998787	.5800157
year	-.0354681	.0309963	-1.14	0.253	-.0962198	.0252836
_cons	73.13706	62.61443	1.17	0.243	-49.58496	195.8591

```
Instruments for differenced equation
        GMM-type: L(3/.).n
        Standard: D.w LD.w D.k LD.k D.yr1980 D.yr1981 D.yr1982 D.yr1983
                  D.yr1984 D.year
Instruments for level equation
        Standard: _cons
```

The results from `estat sargan` no longer reject the null hypothesis that the overidentifying restrictions are valid.

```
. estat sargan
Sargan test of overidentifying restrictions
        H0: overidentifying restrictions are valid
        chi2(18)     =   20.80081
        Prob > chi2  =    0.2896
```

Moving on to the system estimator, we note that the Sargan test rejects the null hypothesis after fitting the model with i.i.d. errors.

```
. xtdpd L(0/1).n L(0/2).(w k) yr1980-yr1984 year,
> div(L(0/1).(w k) yr1980-yr1984 year) dgmmiv(n) lgmmiv(n) hascons
  (output omitted )
. estat sargan
Sargan test of overidentifying restrictions
        H0: overidentifying restrictions are valid
        chi2(31)     =   59.22907
        Prob > chi2  =    0.0017
```

Now we fit the model using the additional moment conditions constructed from the second lag of n as an instrument for the level equation.

```
. xtdpd L(0/1).n L(0/2).(w k) yr1980-yr1984 year,
> div(L(0/1).(w k) yr1980-yr1984 year) dgmmiv(n, lag(3 .)) lgmmiv(n, lag(2))
> hascons
Dynamic panel-data estimation              Number of obs       =        751
Group variable: id                         Number of groups    =        140
Time variable: year
                                           Obs per group: min  =          5
                                                          avg  =   5.364286
                                                          max  =          7

Number of instruments =       38          Wald chi2(13)        =    3680.01
                                          Prob > chi2          =     0.0000
One-step results
```

n	Coef.	Std. Err.	z	P>|z|	[95% Conf. Interval]	
n						
L1.	.9603675	.095608	10.04	0.000	.7729794	1.147756
w						
--.	-.5433987	.068835	-7.89	0.000	-.6783128	-.4084845
L1.	.4356183	.0881727	4.94	0.000	.262803	.6084336
L2.	-.2785721	.1115061	-2.50	0.012	-.4971201	-.0600241
k						
--.	.3139331	.0419054	7.49	0.000	.2317999	.3960662
L1.	-.160103	.0546915	-2.93	0.003	-.2672963	-.0529096
L2.	-.1295766	.0507752	-2.55	0.011	-.2290943	-.030059
yr1980	-.0200704	.0248954	-0.81	0.420	-.0688644	.0287236
yr1981	-.0425838	.0422155	-1.01	0.313	-.1253246	.040157
yr1982	.0048723	.0600938	0.08	0.935	-.1129093	.122654
yr1983	.0458978	.0785687	0.58	0.559	-.1080941	.1998897
yr1984	.0633219	.1026188	0.62	0.537	-.1378074	.2644511
year	-.0075599	.019059	-0.40	0.692	-.0449148	.029795
_cons	16.20856	38.00619	0.43	0.670	-58.28221	90.69932

```
Instruments for differenced equation
        GMM-type: L(3/.).n
        Standard: D.w LD.w D.k LD.k D.yr1980 D.yr1981 D.yr1982 D.yr1983
                  D.yr1984 D.year
Instruments for level equation
        GMM-type: L2D.n
        Standard: _cons
```

The estimate of the coefficient on L.n is now .96. Blundell, Bond, and Windmeijer (2000, 63–65) show that the moment conditions in the system estimator remain informative as the true coefficient on L.n approaches unity. Holtz-Eakin, Newey, and Rosen (1988) show that because the large-sample distribution of the estimator is derived for fixed number of periods and a growing number of individuals there is no "unit-root" problem.

The results from estat sargan no longer reject the null hypothesis that the overidentifying restrictions are valid.

```
. estat sargan
Sargan test of overidentifying restrictions
        H0: overidentifying restrictions are valid
        chi2(24)    =   27.22585
        Prob > chi2 =    0.2940
```

◁

❑ Technical Note

To find the valid moment conditions for the model with MA(1) errors, we begin by writing the model

$$n_{it} = \alpha n_{it-1} + \beta x_{it} + \nu_i + \epsilon_{it} + \gamma \epsilon_{it-1}$$

where the ϵ_{it} are assumed to be i.i.d.

Because the composite error, $\epsilon_{it} + \gamma \epsilon_{it-1}$, is MA(1), only lags two or higher are valid instruments for the level equation, assuming the initial condition that $E[\nu_i \Delta n_{i2}] = 0$. The key to this point is that lagging the above equation two periods shows that ϵ_{it-2} and ϵ_{it-3} appear in the equation for n_{it-2}. Because the ϵ_{it} are i.i.d., n_{it-2} is a valid instrument for the level equation with errors $\nu_i + \epsilon_{it} + \gamma \epsilon_{it-1}$. ($n_{it-2}$ will be correlated with n_{it-1} but uncorrelated with the errors $\nu_i + \epsilon_{it} + \gamma \epsilon_{it-1}$.) An analogous argument works for higher lags.

First-differencing the above equation yields

$$\Delta n_{it} = \alpha \Delta n_{it-1} + \beta \Delta x_{it} + \Delta \epsilon_{it} + \gamma \Delta \epsilon_{it-1}$$

Because ϵ_{it-2} is the farthest lag of ϵ_{it} that appears in the differenced equation, lags three or higher are valid instruments for the differenced composite errors. (Lagging the level equation three periods shows that only ϵ_{it-3} and ϵ_{it-4} appear in the equation for n_{it-3}, which implies that n_{it-3} is a valid instrument for the current differenced equation. An analogous argument works for higher lags.)

❑

Saved Results

xtdpd saves the following in e():

Scalars

e(N)	number of observations
e(N_g)	number of groups
e(df_m)	model degrees of freedom
e(g_max)	largest group size
e(g_min)	smallest group size
e(g_avg)	average group size
e(t_max)	maximum time in sample
e(t_min)	minimum time in sample
e(chi2)	model χ^2 statistic
e(arm#)	test for autocorrelation of order #
e(artests)	number of AR tests computed
e(sig2)	estimate of σ_ϵ^2
e(rss)	sum squared differenced residuals
e(artests)	number of AR tests performed
e(sargan)	Sargan test statistic
e(zrank)	rank of instrument matrix

Macros

e(cmd)	xtdpd
e(cmdline)	command as typed
e(depvar)	name of dependent variable
e(twostep)	twostep, if specified
e(ivar)	variable denoting groups
e(tvar)	time variable
e(vce)	*vcetype* specified in vce()
e(vcetype)	title used to label Std. Err.
e(system)	system, if system estimator
e(hascons)	hascons, if specified
e(transform)	specified transform
e(datasignature)	checksum from datasignature
e(engine)	xtdpd
e(div_odvars)	differenced variables used as standard instruments for differenced equation and not for level equation
e(div_olvars)	level variables used as standard instruments for differenced equation and not for level equation
e(liv_olvars)	level variables used as standard instruments for level equation and not for differenced equation
e(div_dvars)	differenced variables used as standard instruments for differenced equation
e(div_lvars)	level variables used as standard instruments for differenced equation
e(liv_lvars)	level variables used as standard instruments for level equation
e(dgmmiv_vars)	variables used to create GMM-type instruments for differenced equation
e(dgmmiv_flag)	first lags of variables used to create GMM-type instruments for differenced equation
e(dgmmiv_llag)	last lags of variables used to create GMM-type instruments for differenced equation
e(lgmmiv_vars)	variables used to create GMM-type instruments for level equation
e(lgmmiv_flag)	first lags used to create GMM-type instruments for level equation
e(properties)	b V
e(estat_cmd)	program used to implement estat
e(predict)	program used to implement predict

Matrices

    e(b)   coefficient vector

    e(V)   variance–covariance matrix of the estimators

Functions

    e(sample) marks estimation sample

Methods and Formulas

xtdpd is implemented as an ado-file.

Consider dynamic panel-data models of the form

$$y_{it} = \sum_{j=1}^{p} \alpha_j y_{i,t-j} + \mathbf{x}_{it}\boldsymbol{\beta}_1 + \mathbf{w}_{it}\boldsymbol{\beta}_2 + \nu_i + \epsilon_{it}$$

where the variables are as defined as in (1).

$\mathbf{x}$ and $\mathbf{w}$ may contain lagged independent variables and time dummies.

Let $\mathbf{X}_{it}^{L} = (y_{i,t-1}, y_{i,t-2}, \ldots, y_{i,t-p}, \mathbf{x}_{it}, \mathbf{w}_{it})$ be the $1 \times K$ vector of covariates for i at time t, where $K = p + k_1 + k_2$, p is the number of included lags, k_1 is the number of strictly exogenous variables in x_{it}, and k_2 is the number of predetermined variables in w_{it}. (The superscript L stands for levels.)

Now rewrite this relationship as a set of T_i equations for each individual,

$$\mathbf{y}_i^{L} = \mathbf{X}_i^{L}\boldsymbol{\delta} + \nu_i\boldsymbol{\iota}_i + \boldsymbol{\epsilon}_i$$

where T_i is the number of observations available for individual i; $\mathbf{y}_i$, $\boldsymbol{\iota}_i$, and $\boldsymbol{\epsilon}_i$ are $T_i \times 1$, whereas $\mathbf{X}_i$ is $T_i \times K$.

The estimators use both the levels and a transform of the variables in the above equation. Denote the transformed variables by an $*$, so that $\mathbf{y}_i^{*}$ is the transformed $\mathbf{y}_i^{L}$ and $\mathbf{X}_i^{*}$ is the transformed $\mathbf{X}_i^{L}$. The transform may be either the first difference or the forward-orthogonal deviations (FOD) transform. The (i, t)th observation of the FOD transform of a variable $\mathbf{x}$ is given by

$$x_{it}^{*} = c_t \left\{ x_{it} - \frac{1}{T-t}(x_{it+1} + x_{it+2} + \cdots + x_{iT}) \right\}$$

where $c_t^2 = (T-t)/(T-t+1)$ and T is the number of observations on $\mathbf{x}$; see Arellano and Bover (1995) and Arellano (2003).

Here we present the formulas for the Arellano–Bover/Blundell–Bond system estimator. The formulas for the Arellano–Bond estimator are obtained by setting the additional level matrices in the system estimator to null matrices.

Stacking the transformed and untransformed vectors of the dependent variable for a given i yields

$$\mathbf{y}_i = \begin{pmatrix} \mathbf{y}_i^{*} \\ \mathbf{y}_i^{L} \end{pmatrix}$$

Similarly, stacking the transformed and untransformed matrices of the covariates for a given i yields

$$\mathbf{X}_i = \begin{pmatrix} \mathbf{X}_i^* \\ \mathbf{X}_i^L \end{pmatrix}$$

$\mathbf{Z}_i$ is a matrix of instruments,

$$\mathbf{Z}_i = \begin{pmatrix} \mathbf{Z}_{di} & \mathbf{0} & \mathbf{D}_i & \mathbf{0} & \mathbf{I}_i^d \\ \mathbf{0} & \mathbf{Z}_{Li} & \mathbf{0} & \mathbf{L}_i & \mathbf{I}_i^L \end{pmatrix}$$

where $\mathbf{Z}_{di}$ is the matrix of GMM-type instruments created from the dgmmiv() options, $\mathbf{Z}_{Li}$ is the matrix of GMM-type instruments created from the lgmmiv() options, $\mathbf{D}_i$ is the matrix of standard instruments created from the div() options, $\mathbf{L}_i$ is the matrix of standard instruments created from the liv() options, $\mathbf{I}_i^d$ is the matrix of standard instruments created from the iv() options for the differenced errors, and $\mathbf{I}_i^L$ is the matrix of standard instruments created from the iv() options for the level errors.

div(), liv(), and iv() simply add columns to instrument matrix. The GMM-type instruments are more involved. Begin by considering a simple balanced-panel example in which our model is

$$y_{it} = \alpha_1 y_{i,t-1} + \alpha_2 y_{i,t-2} + \nu_i + \epsilon_{it}$$

We do not need to consider covariates because strictly exogenous variables are handled using div(), iv(), or liv(), and predetermined or endogenous variables are handled analogous to the dependent variable.

Assume that the data come from a balanced panel in which there are no missing values. After first-differencing the equation, we have

$$\Delta y_{it} = \alpha_1 \Delta y_{i,t-1} + \alpha_2 \Delta y_{i,t-2} + \Delta \epsilon_{it}$$

The first 3 observations are lost to lags and differencing. If we assume that the ϵ_{it} are not autocorrelated, for each i at $t = 4$, y_{i1} and y_{i2} are valid instruments for the differenced equation. Similarly, at $t = 5$, y_{i1}, y_{i2}, and y_{i3} are valid instruments. We specify dgmmiv(y) to obtain an instrument matrix with one row for each period that we are instrumenting:

$$\mathbf{Z}_{di} = \begin{pmatrix} y_{i1} & y_{i2} & 0 & 0 & 0 & \cdots & 0 & 0 & 0 \\ 0 & 0 & y_{i1} & y_{i2} & y_{i3} & \cdots & 0 & 0 & 0 \\ \vdots & \vdots & \vdots & \vdots & \ddots & \vdots & \vdots & \vdots & \vdots \\ 0 & 0 & 0 & 0 & \cdots & 0 & y_{i1} & \cdots & y_{i,T-2} \end{pmatrix}$$

Since $p = 2$, $\mathbf{Z}_{di}$ has $T - p - 1$ rows and $\sum_{m=p}^{T-2} m$ columns.

Specifying lgmmiv(y) creates the instrument matrix

$$\mathbf{Z}_{Li} = \begin{pmatrix} \Delta.y_{i2} & 0 & 0 & \dots & 0 \\ 0 & \Delta.y_{i3} & 0 & \dots & 0 \\ \vdots & \vdots & \vdots & \ddots & \vdots \\ 0 & 0 & 0 & \dots & \Delta.y_{i(T_i-1)} \end{pmatrix}$$

This extends to other lag structures with complete data. Unbalanced data and missing observations are handled by dropping the rows for which there are no data and filling in zeros in columns where missing data are required. Suppose that, for some i, the $t = 1$ observation was missing but was not missing for some other panels. `dgmmiv(y)` would then create the instrument matrix

$$\mathbf{Z}_{di} = \begin{pmatrix} 0 & 0 & 0 & y_{i2} & y_{i3} & 0 & 0 & 0 & 0 & \dots & 0 & 0 & 0 \\ 0 & 0 & 0 & 0 & 0 & 0 & y_{i2} & y_{i3} & 0 & \dots & 0 & 0 & 0 \\ \vdots & \vdots & \vdots & \vdots & \vdots & \vdots & \vdots & \vdots & \ddots & \vdots & \vdots & \vdots & \vdots \\ 0 & 0 & 0 & 0 & 0 & 0 & 0 & 0 & \dots & 0 & y_{i2} & \dots & y_{iT-2} \end{pmatrix}$$

$\mathbf{Z}_{di}$ has $T_i - p - 1$ rows and $\sum_{m=p}^{\tau-2} m$ columns, where $\tau = \max_i \tau_i$ and τ_i is the number of nonmissing observations in panel i.

After defining

$$\mathbf{Q}_{xz} = \sum_i \mathbf{X}_i' \mathbf{Z}_i$$

$$\mathbf{Q}_{zy} = \sum_i \mathbf{Z}_i' \mathbf{y}_i$$

$$\mathbf{W}_1 = \mathbf{Q}_{xz} \mathbf{A}_1 \mathbf{Q}_{xz}'$$

$$\mathbf{A}_1 = \left(\sum_i \mathbf{Z}_i' \mathbf{H}_{1i} \mathbf{Z}_i \right)^{-1}$$

and

$$\mathbf{H}_{1i} = \begin{pmatrix} \mathbf{H}_{di} & \mathbf{0} \\ \mathbf{0} & \mathbf{H}_{Li} \end{pmatrix}$$

the one-step estimates are given by

$$\widehat{\beta}_1 = \mathbf{W}_1^{-1} \mathbf{Q}_{xz} \mathbf{A}_1 \mathbf{Q}_{zy}$$

When using the first-difference transform $\mathbf{H}_{di}$, is given by

$$\mathbf{H}_{di} = \begin{pmatrix} 1 & -.5 & 0 & \dots & 0 & 0 \\ -.5 & 1 & -.5 & \dots & 0 & 0 \\ \vdots & \vdots & \vdots & \ddots & \vdots & \vdots \\ 0 & 0 & 0 & \dots & 1 & -.5 \\ 0 & 0 & 0 & \dots & -.5 & 1 \end{pmatrix}$$

and $\mathbf{H}_{Li}$ is given by .5 times the identity matrix. When using the FOD transform, both $\mathbf{H}_{di}$ and $\mathbf{H}_{Li}$ are equal to the identity matrix.

The transformed one-step residuals are given by

$$\widehat{\epsilon}_{1i}^* = \mathbf{y}_i^* - \widehat{\beta}_1 \mathbf{X}_i^*$$

which are used to compute

$$\widehat{\sigma}_1^2 = (1/(N-K)) \sum_i^N \widehat{\epsilon}_{1i}^{*\prime} \widehat{\epsilon}_{1i}^*$$

The GMM one-step VCE is then given by

$$\widehat{V}_{\mathrm{GMM}}[\widehat{\beta}_1] = \widehat{\sigma}_1^2 \mathbf{W}_1^{-1}$$

The one-step level residuals are given by

$$\widehat{\epsilon}_{1i}^L = \mathbf{y}_i^L - \widehat{\beta}_1 \mathbf{X}_i^L$$

Stacking the residual vectors yields

$$\widehat{\epsilon}_{1i} - \begin{pmatrix} \widehat{\epsilon}_{1i}^* \\ \widehat{\epsilon}_{1i}^L \end{pmatrix}$$

which is used to compute $\mathbf{H}_{2i} = \widehat{\epsilon}_{1i}^{\prime} \widehat{\epsilon}_{1i}$ which is used in

$$\mathbf{A}_2 = \left(\sum_i \mathbf{Z}_i^{\prime} \mathbf{H}_{2i} \mathbf{Z}_i \right)^{-1}$$

and the robust one-step VCE is given by

$$\widehat{V}_{\mathrm{robust}}[\widehat{\beta}_1] = \mathbf{W}_1^{-1} \mathbf{Q}_{xz} \mathbf{A}_1 \mathbf{A}_2^{-1} \mathbf{A}_1 \mathbf{Q}_{xz}^{\prime} \mathbf{W}_1^{-1}$$

$\widehat{V}_{\mathrm{robust}}[\widehat{\beta}_1]$ is robust to heteroskedasticity in the errors.

After defining

$$\mathbf{W}_2 = \mathbf{Q}_{xz} \mathbf{A}_2 \mathbf{Q}_{xz}^{\prime}$$

the two-step estimates are given by

$$\widehat{\beta}_2 = \mathbf{W}_2^{-1} \mathbf{Q}_{xz} \mathbf{A}_2 \mathbf{Q}_{zy}$$

The GMM two-step VCE is then given by

$$\widehat{V}_{\mathrm{GMM}}[\widehat{\beta}_2] = \mathbf{W}_2^{-1}$$

The GMM two-step VCE is known to be severely biased. Windmeijer (2005) derived the Windmeijer bias-corrected (WC) estimator for the robust VCE of two-step GMM estimators. xtdpd implements this WC-robust estimator of the VCE. The formulas for this method are involved; see Windmeijer (2005). The WC-robust estimator of the VCE is robust to heteroskedasticity in the errors.

Acknowledgment

We thank David Roodman of the Center for Global Development, who wrote xtabond2.

References

Anderson, T. W., and C. Hsiao. 1981. Estimation of dynamic models with error components. *Journal of the American Statistical Association* 76: 598–606.

———. 1982. Formulation and estimation of dynamic models using panel data. *Journal of Econometrics* 18: 47–82.

Arellano, M. 2003. *Panel-data Econometrics.* Oxford: Oxford University Press.

Arellano, M., and S. Bond. 1991. Some tests of specification for panel data: Monte Carlo evidence and an application to employment equations. *Review of Economic Studies* 58: 277–297.

Arellano, M., and O. Bover. 1995. Another look at the instrumental variable estimation of error-components models. *Journal of Econometrics* 68: 29–51.

Baltagi, B. H. 2005. *Econometric Analysis of Panel Data.* 3rd ed. New York: Wiley.

Blundell, R., and S. Bond. 1998. Initial conditions and moment restrictions in dynamic panel-data models. *Journal of Econometrics* 87: 115–143.

Blundell, R., S. Bond, and F. Windmeijer. 2000. Estimation in dynamic panel-data models: Improving the performance of the standard GMM estimator. In *Nonstationary Panels, Cointegrating Panels and Dynamic Panels,* ed B. Baltagi, 53–92. New York: Elsevier.

Bruno, G. S. F. 2005. Estimation and inference in dynamic unbalanced panel-data models with a small number of individuals. *Stata Journal* 5: 473–500.

Hansen, L. P. 1982. Large sample properties of generalized method of moments estimators. *Econometrica* 50: 1029–1054.

Holtz-Eakin, D., W. Newey, and H. S. Rosen. 1988. Estimating vector autoregressions with panel data. *Econometrica* 56: 1371–1395.

Layard, R., and S. J. Nickell. 1986. Unemployment in Britain. *Economica* 53: S121–S169.

Windmeijer, F. 2005. A finite sample correction for the variance of linear efficient two-step GMM estimators. *Journal of Econometrics* 126: 25–52.

Also See

Title

> **xtdpd postestimation** — Postestimation tools for xtdpd

Description

The following postestimation commands are of special interest after `xtdpd`:

command	description
estat abond	test for autocorrelation
estat sargan	Sargan test of overidentifying restrictions

For information about these commands, see below.

The following standard postestimation commands are also available:

command	description
estat	VCE and estimation sample summary
estimates	cataloging estimation results
lincom	point estimates, standard errors, testing, and inference for linear combinations of coefficients
mfx	marginal effects or elasticities
nlcom	point estimates, standard errors, testing, and inference for nonlinear combinations of coefficients
predict	predictions, residuals, influence statistics, and other diagnostic measures
predictnl	point estimates, standard errors, testing, and inference for generalized predictions
test	Wald tests for simple and composite linear hypotheses
testnl	Wald tests of nonlinear hypotheses

See the corresponding entries in the *Stata Base Reference Manual* for details.

Special-interest postestimation commands

`estat abond` reports the Arellano–Bond test for serial correlation in the first-differenced residuals.

`estat sargan` reports the Sargan test of the overidentifying restrictions.

Syntax for predict

predict [*type*] *newvar* [*if*] [*in*] [, xb e stdp difference]

Options for predict

⌐ Main ⌐

xb, the default, calculates the linear prediction.

e calculates the residual error.

stdp calculates the standard error of the prediction, which can be thought of as the standard error of
the predicted expected value or mean for the observation's covariate pattern. The standard error
of the prediction is also referred to as the standard error of the fitted value. stdp may not be
combined with difference.

difference specifies that the statistic be calculated for the first differences instead of the levels, the
default.

Syntax for estat abond

estat abond [, artests(#)]

Option for estat abond

artests(#) specifies the highest order of serial correlation to be tested. By default, the tests computed
during estimation are reported. The model will be refitted when artests(#) specifies a higher
order than that computed during the original estimation. The model can be refitted only if the data
have not changed.

Syntax for estat sargan

estat sargan

Remarks

Remarks are presented under the following headings:

> estat abond
> estat sargan

estat abond

The moment conditions used by xtdpd are valid only if there is no serial correlation in the
idiosyncratic errors. Testing for serial correlation in dynamic panel-data models is tricky because one
needs to apply a transform to remove the panel-level effects, but the transformed errors have a more
complicated error structure than the idiosyncratic errors. The Arellano–Bond test for serial correlation
reported by estat abond tests for serial correlation in the first-differenced errors.

Because the first difference of independently and identically distributed idiosyncratic errors will be
autocorrelated, rejecting the null hypothesis of no serial correlation at order one in the first-differenced
errors does not imply that the model is misspecified. Rejecting the null hypothesis at higher orders
implies that the moment conditions are not valid. See [XT] **xtdpd** for an example that uses alternative
moment conditions.

After the one-step system estimator, the test can be computed only when vce(robust) has been
specified.

estat sargan

Like all GMM estimators, the estimator in `xtdpd` can produce consistent estimates only if the moment conditions used are valid. Although there is no method to test if the moment conditions from an exactly identified model are valid, one can test whether the overidentifying moment conditions are valid. `estat sargan` implements the Sargan test of overidentifying conditions discussed in Arellano and Bond (1991).

Only for a homoskedastic error term does the Sargan test have an asymptotic chi-squared distribution. In fact, Arellano and Bond (1991) show that the one-step Sargan test overrejects in the presence of heteroskedasticity. Since its asymptotic distribution is not known under the assumptions of the `vce(robust)` model, `xtdpd` does not compute it when `vce(robust)` is specified.

Methods and Formulas

All postestimation commands listed above are implemented as ado-files.

The notation for $\widehat{\epsilon}_{1i}^*$, $\widehat{\epsilon}_{1i}$, $\mathbf{H}_{1i}$, $\mathbf{H}_{2i}$, $\mathbf{X}_i$, $\mathbf{Z}_i$, $\mathbf{W}_1$, $\mathbf{W}_2$, $\widehat{\mathbf{V}}_*[\widehat{\beta}_*]$, $\mathbf{A}_1$, $\mathbf{A}_2$, $\mathbf{Q}_{xz}$, and $\widehat{\sigma}_1^2$ has been defined in *Methods and Formulas* of [XT] **xtdpd**.

The Arellano–Bond test for zero mth-order autocorrelation in the first-differenced errors is given by

$$A(m) = \frac{s_0}{\sqrt{s_1 + s_2 + s_3}}$$

where the definitions of s_0, s_1, s_2 and s_3 vary over the estimators and transforms.

We begin by defining $\widehat{\mathbf{u}}_{1i}^* = Lm.\widehat{\epsilon}_{1i}^*$, with the missing values filled in with zeros. Letting $j = 1$ for the one-step estimator, $j = 2$ for the two-step estimator, $c = $ GMM for the GMM VCE estimator, and $c = $ robust for the robust VCE estimator, we can now define s_0, s_1, s_2, and s_3:

$$s_0 = \sum_i \widehat{\mathbf{u}}_{ji}^{*\prime} \widehat{\epsilon}_{ji}^*$$

$$s_1 = \sum_i \widehat{\mathbf{u}}_{ji}^{*\prime} \mathbf{H}_{ji} \widehat{\mathbf{u}}_{ji}^*$$

$$s_2 = -2\mathbf{q}_{ji} \mathbf{W}_j^{-1} \mathbf{Q}_{xz} \mathbf{A}_j \mathbf{Q}_{zu}$$

$$s_3 = \mathbf{q}_{jx} \widehat{\mathbf{V}}_c \left[\widehat{\beta}_j\right] \mathbf{q}_{jx}'$$

where

$$\mathbf{q}_{jx} = \left(\sum_i \widehat{\mathbf{u}}_{ji}^{*\prime} \mathbf{X}_i \right)$$

and $\mathbf{Q}_{zu}$ varies over estimator and transform.

For the Arellano–Bond estimator with the first-differenced transform,

$$\mathbf{Q}_{zu} = \left(\sum_i \mathbf{Z}_i' \mathbf{H}_{ji} \widehat{\mathbf{u}}_{ji}^* \right)$$

For the Arellano–Bond estimator with the FOD transform,

$$\mathbf{Q}_{zu} = \left(\sum_i \mathbf{Z}_i' \mathbf{Q}_{\text{fod}} \right)$$

where

$$\mathbf{Q}_{\text{fod}} = \begin{pmatrix} -\sqrt{\frac{T_i+1}{T_i}} & 0 & \cdots & 0 \\ \sqrt{\frac{T_i-1}{T_i}} & \sqrt{\frac{T_i}{T_i-1}} & \cdots & 0 \\ 0 & \cdot & \cdot & \vdots \\ 0 & \cdots & \sqrt{\frac{1}{2}} & -\sqrt{\frac{2}{1}} \end{pmatrix} \widehat{\mathbf{u}}_{ji}^*$$

and * implies the first-differenced transform instead of the FOD transform.

For the Arellano–Bover/Blundell–Bond system estimator with the first-differenced transform,

$$\mathbf{Q}_{zu} = \left(\sum_i \mathbf{Z}_i' \widehat{\boldsymbol{\epsilon}}_{ji} \widehat{\boldsymbol{\epsilon}}_{ji}^{*\prime} \widehat{\mathbf{u}}_{ji}^* \right)$$

After a one-step estimator, the Sargan test is

$$S_1 = \frac{1}{\widehat{\sigma}_1^2} \left(\sum_i \widehat{\boldsymbol{\epsilon}}_{1i}' \mathbf{Z}_i \right) \mathbf{A}_1 \left(\sum_i \mathbf{Z}_i' \widehat{\boldsymbol{\epsilon}}_{1i} \right)$$

The transformed two-step residuals are given by

$$\widehat{\boldsymbol{\epsilon}}_{2i}^* = \mathbf{y}_i^* - \widehat{\boldsymbol{\beta}}_2 \mathbf{X}_i^*$$

and the level two-step residuals are given by

$$\widehat{\boldsymbol{\epsilon}}_{2i}^L = \mathbf{y}_i^L - \widehat{\boldsymbol{\beta}}_2 \mathbf{X}_i^L$$

Stacking the residual vectors yields

$$\widehat{\boldsymbol{\epsilon}}_{2i} = \begin{pmatrix} \widehat{\boldsymbol{\epsilon}}_{2i}^* \\ \widehat{\boldsymbol{\epsilon}}_{2i}^L \end{pmatrix}$$

After a two-step estimator, the Sargan test is

$$S_2 = \left(\sum_i \widehat{\epsilon}'_{2i} \mathbf{Z}_i \right) \mathbf{A}_2 \left(\sum_i \mathbf{Z}'_i \widehat{\epsilon}_{2i} \right)$$

Reference

Arellano, M., and S. Bond. 1991. Some tests of specification for panel data: Monte Carlo evidence and an application to employment equations. *Review of Economic Studies* 58: 277–297.

Also See

[XT] **xtdpd** — Linear dynamic panel-data estimation

Title

> **xtdpdsys** — Arellano–Bover/Blundell–Bond linear dynamic panel-data estimation

Syntax

> xtdpdsys *depvar* [*indepvars*] [*if*] [*in*] [, *options*]

options	description
Model	
noconstant	suppress constant term
lags(*#*)	use *#* lags of dependent variable as covariates; default is lags(1)
maxldep(*#*)	maximum lags of dependent variable for use as instruments
maxlags(*#*)	maximum lags of predetermined and endogenous variables for use as instruments
twostep	compute the two-step estimator instead of the one-step estimator
Predetermined	
pre(*varlist*[...])	predetermined variables; can be specified more than once
Endogenous	
endogenous(*varlist* [...])	endogenous variables; can be specified more than once
SE/Robust	
vce(*vcetype*)	*vcetype* may be gmm or robust
Reporting	
level(*#*)	set confidence level; default is level(95)
artests(*#*)	use *#* as maximum order for AR tests; default is artests(2)

A panel variable and a time variable must be specified; use [XT] **xtset**.

indepvars and all *varlists*, except pre(*varlist*[...]) and endogenous(*varlist*[...]), may contain time-series operators; see [U] **11.4.3 Time-series varlists**. The specification of *depvar* may not contain time-series operators.

by, statsby, and xi are allowed; see [U] **11.1.10 Prefix commands**.

See [U] **20 Estimation and postestimation commands** for more capabilities of estimation commands.

Description

Linear dynamic panel-data models include p lags of the dependent variable as covariates and contain unobserved panel-level effects, fixed or random. By construction, the unobserved panel-level effects are correlated with the lagged dependent variables, making standard estimators inconsistent. Arellano and Bond (1991) derived a consistent generalized method-of-moments (GMM) estimator for this model. The Arellano and Bond estimator can perform poorly if the autoregressive parameters are too large or the ratio of the variance of the panel-level effect to the variance of idiosyncratic error is too large. Building on the work of Arellano and Bover (1995), Blundell and Bond (1998) developed a system estimator that uses additional moment conditions; xtdpdsys implements this estimator.

This estimator is designed for datasets with many panels and few periods. This method assumes that there is no autocorrelation in the idiosyncratic errors and requires the initial condition that the panel-level effects be uncorrelated with the first difference of the first observation of the dependent variable.

Options

      Model

noconstant; see [XT] **estimation options**.

lags(#) sets p, the number of lags of the dependent variable to be included in the model. The default is $p = 1$.

maxldep(#) sets the maximum number of lags of the dependent variable that can be used as instruments. The default is to use all $T_i - p - 2$ lags.

maxlags(#) sets the maximum number of lags of the predetermined and endogenous variables that can be used as instruments. For predetermined variables, the default is to use all $T_i - p - 1$ lags. For endogenous variables, the default is to use all $T_i - p - 2$ lags.

twostep specifies that the two-step estimator be calculated.

      Predetermined

pre(*varlist* [, lagstruct(*prelags*, *premaxlags*)]) specifies that a set of predetermined variables be included in the model. Optionally, you may specify that *prelags* lags of the specified variables also be included. The default for *prelags* is 0. Specifying *premaxlags* sets the maximum number of further lags of the predetermined variables that can be used as instruments. The default is to include $T_i - p - 1$ lagged levels as instruments for predetermined variables. You may specify as many sets of predetermined variables as you need within the standard Stata limits on matrix size. Each set of predetermined variables may have its own number of *prelags* and *premaxlags*.

      Endogenous

endogenous(*varlist* [, lagstruct(*endlags*, *endmaxlags*)]) specifies that a set of endogenous variables be included in the model. Optionally, you may specify that *endlags* lags of the specified variables also be included. The default for *endlags* is 0. Specifying *endmaxlags* sets the maximum number of further lags of the endogenous variables that can be used as instruments. The default is to include $T_i - p - 2$ lagged levels as instruments for endogenous variables. You may specify as many sets of endogenous variables as you need within the standard Stata limits on matrix size. Each set of endogenous variables may have its own number of *endlags* and *endmaxlags*.

      SE/Robust

vce(*vcetype*) specifies the type of standard error reported, which includes types that are derived from asymptotic theory and that are robust to some kinds of misspecification.

vce(gmm), the default, uses the conventionally derived variance estimator for generalized method of moments estimation.

vce(robust) uses the robust estimator. After one-step estimation, this is the Arellano–Bond robust VCE estimator. After two-step estimation, this is the Windmeijer (2005) WC-robust estimator.

⌐ Reporting ⌐

`level(#)`; see [XT] **estimation options**.

`artests(#)` specifies the maximum order of the autocorrelation test to be calculated. The tests are reported by `estat abond`; see [XT] **xtdpdsys postestimation**. Specifying the order of the highest test at estimation time is more efficient than specifying it to `estat abond`, because `estat abond` must refit the model to obtain the test statistics. The maximum order must be less than or equal the number of periods in the longest panel. The default is `artests(2)`.

Remarks

If you have not read [XT] **xtabond**, you may want to do so before continuing.

Consider the dynamic panel-data model

$$y_{it} = \sum_{j=1}^{p} \alpha_j y_{i,t-j} + \mathbf{x}_{it}\boldsymbol{\beta}_1 + \mathbf{w}_{it}\boldsymbol{\beta}_2 + \nu_i + \epsilon_{it} \quad i = 1, \ldots, N \quad t = 1, \ldots, T_i \quad (1)$$

where

the α_j are p parameters to be estimated,
$\mathbf{x}_{it}$ is a $1 \times k_1$ vector of strictly exogenous covariates,
$\boldsymbol{\beta}_1$ is a $k_1 \times 1$ vector of parameters to be estimated,
$\mathbf{w}_{it}$ is a $1 \times k_2$ vector of predetermined or endogenous covariates,
$\boldsymbol{\beta}_2$ is a $k_2 \times 1$ vector of parameters to be estimated,
ν_i are the panel-level effects (which may be correlated with the covariates), and
ϵ_{it} are i.i.d. over the whole sample with variance σ_ϵ^2.

The ν_i and the ϵ_{it} are assumed to be independent for each i over all t.

By construction, the lagged dependent variables are correlated with the unobserved panel-level effects, making standard estimators inconsistent. With many panels and few periods, the Arellano–Bond estimator is constructed by first-differencing to remove the panel-level effects and using instruments to form moment conditions.

Blundell and Bond (1998) show that the lagged-level instruments in the Arellano–Bond estimator become weak as the autoregressive process becomes too persistent or the ratio of the variance of the panel-level effects ν_i to the variance of the idiosyncratic error ϵ_{it} becomes too large. Building on the work of Arellano and Bover (1995), Blundell and Bond (1998) proposed a system estimator that uses moment conditions in which lagged differences are used as instruments for the level equation in addition to the moment conditions of lagged levels as instruments for the differenced equation. The additional moment conditions are valid only if the initial condition $E[\nu_i \Delta y_{i2}] = 0$ holds for all i; see Blundell and Bond (1998) and Blundell, Bond, and Windmeijer (2000).

`xtdpdsys` fits dynamic panel-data estimators with the Arellano–Bover/Blundell–Bond system estimator. Because `xtdpdsys` extends `xtabond`, [XT] **xtabond** provides useful background.

▷ Example 1

In their article, Arellano and Bond (1991) apply their estimators and test statistics to a model of dynamic labor demand that had previously been considered by Layard and Nickell (1986), using data from an unbalanced panel of firms from the United Kingdom. All variables are indexed over the firm

i and time t. In this dataset, n_{it} is the log of employment in firm i at time t, w_{it} is the natural log of the real product wage, k_{it} is the natural log of the gross capital stock, and ys_{it} is the natural log of industry output. The model also includes time dummies yr1980, yr1981, yr1982, yr1983, and yr1984.

For comparison, we begin by using `xtabond` to fit a model to these data.

```
. use http://www.stata-press.com/data/r10/abdata

. xtabond n L(0/2).(w k) yr1980-yr1984 year, vce(robust)
```

```
Arellano-Bond dynamic panel-data estimation   Number of obs      =        611
Group variable: id                            Number of groups   =        140
Time variable: year
                                              Obs per group:   min =          4
                                                               avg =   4.364286
                                                               max =          6
Number of instruments =      40               Wald chi2(13)      =    1318.68
                                              Prob > chi2        =     0.0000
One-step results
```

	n	Coef.	Robust Std. Err.	z	P>|z|	[95% Conf. Interval]	
n	L1.	.6286618	.1161942	5.41	0.000	.4009254	.8563983
w	--.	-.5104249	.1904292	-2.68	0.007	-.8836592	-.1371906
	L1.	.2891446	.140946	2.05	0.040	.0128954	.5653937
	L2.	-.0443653	.0768135	-0.58	0.564	-.194917	.1061865
k	--.	.3556923	.0603274	5.90	0.000	.2374528	.4739318
	L1.	-.0457102	.0699732	-0.65	0.514	-.1828552	.0914348
	L2.	-.0619721	.0328589	-1.89	0.059	-.1263743	.0024301
yr1980		-.0282422	.0166363	-1.70	0.090	-.0608488	.0043643
yr1981		-.0694052	.028961	-2.40	0.017	-.1261677	-.0126426
yr1982		-.0523678	.0423433	-1.24	0.216	-.1353591	.0306235
yr1983		-.0256599	.0533747	-0.48	0.631	-.1302723	.0789525
yr1984		-.0093229	.0696241	-0.13	0.893	-.1457837	.1271379
year		.0019575	.0119481	0.16	0.870	-.0214604	.0253754
_cons		-2.543221	23.97919	-0.11	0.916	-49.54158	44.45514

```
Instruments for differenced equation
        GMM-type: L(2/.).n
        Standard: D.w LD.w L2D.w D.k LD.k L2D.k D.yr1980 D.yr1981 D.yr1982
                  D.yr1983 D.yr1984 D.year
Instruments for level equation
        Standard: _cons
```

Now we fit the same model by using `xtdpdsys`:

(Continued on next page)

```
. xtdpdsys n L(0/2).(w k) yr1980-yr1984 year, vce(robust)
```

```
System dynamic panel-data estimation          Number of obs      =        751
Group variable: id                             Number of groups   =        140
Time variable: year
                                               Obs per group:   min =          5
                                                                avg =   5.364286
                                                                max =          7

Number of instruments =      47                Wald chi2(13)      =    2579.96
                                               Prob > chi2        =     0.0000
One-step results
```

n	Coef.	Robust Std. Err.	z	P>|z|	[95% Conf. Interval]	
n						
L1.	.8221535	.093387	8.80	0.000	.6391184	1.005189
w						
--.	-.5427935	.1881721	-2.88	0.004	-.911604	-.1739831
L1.	.3703602	.1656364	2.24	0.025	.0457189	.6950015
L2.	-.0726314	.0907148	-0.80	0.423	-.2504292	.1051664
k						
--.	.3638069	.0657524	5.53	0.000	.2349346	.4926792
L1.	-.1222996	.0701521	-1.74	0.081	-.2597951	.015196
L2.	-.0901355	.0344142	-2.62	0.009	-.1575862	-.0226849
yr1980	-.0308622	.016946	-1.82	0.069	-.0640757	.0023512
yr1981	-.0718417	.0293223	-2.45	0.014	-.1293123	-.014371
yr1982	-.0384806	.0373631	-1.03	0.303	-.1117111	.0347498
yr1983	-.0121768	.0498519	-0.24	0.807	-.1098847	.0855311
yr1984	-.0050903	.0655011	-0.08	0.938	-.1334701	.1232895
year	.0058631	.0119867	0.49	0.625	-.0176304	.0293566
_cons	-10.59198	23.92087	-0.44	0.658	-57.47602	36.29207

```
Instruments for differenced equation
        GMM-type: L(2/.).n
        Standard: D.w LD.w L2D.w D.k LD.k L2D.k D.yr1980 D.yr1981 D.yr1982
                  D.yr1983 D.yr1984 D.year
Instruments for level equation
        GMM-type: LD.n
        Standard: _cons
```

If you are unfamiliar with the L().() notation, see [U] **13.8 Time-series operators**. That the system estimator produces a much higher estimate of the coefficient on lagged employment agrees with the results in Blundell and Bond (1998), who show that the system estimator does not have the downward bias that the Arellano–Bond estimator has when the true value is high.

Comparing the footers illustrates the difference between the two estimators; xtdpdsys includes lagged differences of n as instruments for the level equation, whereas xtabond does not. Comparing the headers shows that xtdpdsys has seven more instruments than xtabond. (As it should; there are 7 observations on LD.n available in the complete panels that run from 1976–1984, after accounting for the first 2 years that are lost because the model has two lags.) Only the first lags of the variables are used because the moment conditions using higher lags are redundant; see Blundell and Bond (1998) and Blundell, Bond, and Windmeijer (2000).

estat abond reports the Arellano–Bond test for serial correlation in the first-differenced errors. The moment conditions are valid only if there is no serial correlation in the idiosyncratic errors. Because the first difference of independently and identically distributed idiosyncratic errors will be autocorrelated, rejecting the null hypothesis of no serial correlation at order one in the first-differenced errors does not imply that the model is misspecified. Rejecting the null hypothesis at higher orders implies that the moment conditions are not valid. See [XT] **xtdpd** for an alternative estimator in this case.

```
. estat abond
Arellano-Bond test for zero autocorrelation in first-differenced errors
```

Order	z	Prob > z
1	-4.6414	0.0000
2	-1.0572	0.2904

```
H0: no autocorrelation
```

The above output does not present evidence that the model is misspecified.

◁

▷ Example 2

Sometimes we cannot assume strict exogeneity. Recall that a variable x_{it} is said to be strictly exogenous if $E[x_{it}\epsilon_{is}] = 0$ for all t and s. If $E[x_{it}\epsilon_{is}] \neq 0$ for $s < t$ but $E[x_{it}\epsilon_{is}] = 0$ for all $s \geq t$, the variable is said to be predetermined. Intuitively, if the error term at time t has some feedback on the subsequent realizations of x_{it}, x_{it} is a predetermined variable. Because unforecastable errors today might affect future changes in the real wage and in the capital stock, we might suspect that the log of the real product wage and the log of the gross capital stock are predetermined instead of strictly exogenous.

(*Continued on next page*)

```
. xtdpdsys n yr1980-yr1984 year, pre(w k, lag(2, .)) vce(robust)
```

System dynamic panel-data estimation   Number of obs   =   751
Group variable: id   Number of groups   =   140
Time variable: year

Obs per group: min =   5
    avg =   5.364286
    max =   7

Number of instruments =   95   Wald chi2(13)   =   7562.80
    Prob > chi2   =   0.0000

One-step results

n	Coef.	Robust Std. Err.	z	P>|z|	[95% Conf. Interval]	
n						
L1.	.913278	.0460602	19.83	0.000	.8230017	1.003554
w						
--.	-.728159	.1019044	-7.15	0.000	-.927888	-.5284301
L1.	.5602737	.1939617	2.89	0.004	.1801156	.9404317
L2.	-.0523028	.1487653	-0.35	0.725	-.3438775	.2392718
k						
--.	.4820097	.0760787	6.34	0.000	.3328983	.6311212
L1.	-.2846944	.0831902	-3.42	0.001	-.4477442	-.1216446
L2.	-.1394181	.0405709	-3.44	0.001	-.2189356	-.0599006
yr1980	-.0325146	.0216371	-1.50	0.133	-.0749226	.0098935
yr1981	-.0726116	.0346482	-2.10	0.036	-.1405207	-.0047024
yr1982	-.0477038	.0451914	-1.06	0.291	-.1362772	.0408696
yr1983	-.0396264	.0558734	-0.71	0.478	-.1491362	.0698835
yr1984	-.0810383	.0736648	-1.10	0.271	-.2254186	.063342
year	.0192741	.0145326	1.33	0.185	-.0092092	.0477574
_cons	-37.34972	28.77747	-1.30	0.194	-93.75253	19.05308

```
Instruments for differenced equation
        GMM-type: L(2/.).n L(1/.).L2.w L(1/.).L2.k
        Standard: D.yr1980 D.yr1981 D.yr1982 D.yr1983 D.yr1984 D.year
Instruments for level equation
        GMM-type: LD.n L2D.w L2D.k
        Standard: _cons
```

The footer informs us that we are now including GMM-type instruments from the first lag of L.w on back and from the first lag of L2.k on back for the differenced errors and the second lags of the differences of w and k as instruments for the level errors.

◁

❏ Technical Note

The above example illustrates that xtdpdsys understands pre(w k, lag(2, .)) to mean that L2.w and L2.k are predetermined variables. This is a stricter definition than the alternative that pre(w k, lag(2, .)) means only that w k are predetermined but to include two lags of w and two lags of k in the model. If you prefer the weaker definition, xtdpdsys still gives you consistent estimates, but it is not using all possible instruments; see [XT] **xtdpd** for an example of how to include all possible instruments.

❏

Saved Results

xtdpdsys saves the following in e():

Scalars

e(N)	number of observations
e(N_g)	number of groups
e(df_m)	model degrees of freedom
e(g_max)	largest group size
e(g_min)	smallest group size
e(g_avg)	average group size
e(t_max)	maximum time in sample
e(t_min)	minimum time in sample
e(chi2)	model χ^2 statistic
e(arm#)	test for autocorrelation of order #
e(artests)	number of AR tests computed
e(sig2)	estimate of σ_ϵ^2
e(rss)	sum squared differenced residuals
e(artests)	number of AR tests performed
e(sargan)	Sargan test statistic
e(zrank)	rank of instrument matrix

Macros

e(cmd)	xtdpdsys
e(cmdline)	command as typed
e(depvar)	name of dependent variable
e(twostep)	twostep, if specified
e(ivar)	variable denoting groups
e(tvar)	time variable
e(vce)	*vcetype* specified in vce()
e(vcetype)	title used to label Std. Err.
e(system)	system, if system estimator
e(hascons)	hascons, if specified
e(transform)	specified transform
e(datasignature)	checksum from datasignature
e(engine)	xtdpd
e(div_odvars)	differenced variables used as standard instruments for differenced equation and not for level equation
e(div_olvars)	level variables used as standard instruments for differenced equation and not for level equation
e(liv_olvars)	level variables used as standard instruments for level equation and not for differenced equation
e(div_dvars)	differenced variables used as standard instruments for differenced equation
e(div_lvars)	level variables used as standard instruments for differenced equation
e(liv_lvars)	level variables used as standard instruments for level equation
e(dgmmiv_vars)	variables used to create GMM-type instruments for differenced equation
e(dgmmiv_flag)	first lags of variables used to create GMM-type instruments for differenced equation
e(dgmmiv_llag)	last lags of variables used to create GMM-type instruments for differenced equation
e(lgmmiv_vars)	variables used to create GMM-type instruments for level equation
e(lgmmiv_flag)	first lags used to create GMM-type instruments for level equation
e(properties)	b V
e(estat_cmd)	program used to implement estat
e(predict)	program used to implement predict

Matrices
    e(b)   coefficient vector
    e(V)   variance–covariance matrix of the estimators

Functions
    e(sample) marks estimation sample

Results e(div_odvars), e(div_olvars), e(liv_olvars), e(div_dvars), e(div_lvars), e(liv_lvars), e(dgmmiv_vars), e(dgmmiv_flag), e(dgmmiv_llag), e(lgmmiv_vars), and e(lgmmiv_flag) describe the instruments used by xtdpdsys. These results are rarely of interest; see the options of xtdpd for more details.

Methods and Formulas

xtdpdsys is implemented as an ado-file.

xtdpdsys uses xtdpd to perform its computations, so the formulas are given in *Methods and Formulas* of [XT] **xtdpd**.

Acknowledgment

We thank David Roodman of the Center for Global Development, who wrote xtabond2.

References

Anderson, T. W., and C. Hsiao. 1981. Estimation of dynamic models with error components. *Journal of the American Statistical Association* 76: 598–606.

———. 1982. Formulation and estimation of dynamic models using panel data. *Journal of Econometrics* 18: 47–82.

Arellano, M., and S. Bond. 1991. Some tests of specification for panel data: Monte Carlo evidence and an application to employment equations. *Review of Economic Studies* 58: 277–297.

Arellano, M., and O. Bover. 1995. Another look at the instrumental variable estimation of error-components models. *Journal of Econometrics* 68: 29–51.

Baltagi, B. H. 2005. *Econometric Analysis of Panel Data*. 3rd ed. New York: Wiley.

Blundell, R., and S. Bond. 1998. Initial conditions and moment restrictions in dynamic panel-data models. *Journal of Econometrics* 87: 115–143.

Blundell, R., S. Bond, and Windmeijer, F. 2000. Estimation in dynamic panel-data models: Improving the performance of the standard GMM estimator. In *Nonstationary Panels, Cointegrating Panels and Dynamic Panels*, ed B. Baltagi, 53–92. New York: Elsevier.

Bruno, G. S. F. 2005. Estimation and inference in dynamic unbalanced panel-data models with a small number of individuals. *Stata Journal* 5: 473–500.

Hansen, L. P. 1982. Large sample properties of generalized method of moments estimators. *Econometrica* 50: 1029–1054.

Holtz-Eakin, D., W. Newey, and H. S. Rosen. 1988. Estimating vector autoregressions with panel data. *Econometrica* 56: 1371–1395.

Layard, R., and S. J. Nickell. 1986. Unemployment in Britain. *Economica* 53: S121–S169.

Windmeijer, F. 2005. A finite sample correction for the variance of linear efficient two-step GMM estimators. *Journal of Econometrics* 126: 25–52.

Also See

[XT] **xtdpdsys postestimation** — Postestimation tools for xtdpdsys

[XT] **xtset** — Declare data to be panel data

[XT] **xtabond** — Arellano–Bond linear dynamic panel-data estimation

[XT] **xtdpd** — Linear dynamic panel-data estimation

[XT] **xtivreg** — Instrumental variables and two-stage least squares for panel-data models

[XT] **xtreg** — Fixed-, between-, and random-effects, and population-averaged linear models

[XT] **xtregar** — Fixed- and random-effects linear models with an AR(1) disturbance

Title

xtdpdsys postestimation — Postestimation tools for xtdpdsys

Description

The following postestimation commands are of special interest after `xtdpdsys`:

command	description
estat abond	test for autocorrelation
estat sargan	Sargan test of overidentifying restrictions

For information about these commands, see below.

The following standard postestimation commands are also available:

command	description
estat	VCE and estimation sample summary
estimates	cataloging estimation results
lincom	point estimates, standard errors, testing, and inference for linear combinations of coefficients
mfx	marginal effects or elasticities
nlcom	point estimates, standard errors, testing, and inference for nonlinear combinations of coefficients
predict	predictions, residuals, influence statistics, and other diagnostic measures
predictnl	point estimates, standard errors, testing, and inference for generalized predictions
test	Wald tests for simple and composite linear hypotheses
testnl	Wald tests of nonlinear hypotheses

See the corresponding entries in the *Stata Base Reference Manual* for details.

Special-interest postestimation commands

estat abond reports the Arellano–Bond test for serial correlation in the first-differenced residuals.

estat sargan reports the Sargan test of the overidentifying restrictions.

Syntax for predict

predict [*type*] *newvar* [*if*] [*in*] [, xb e stdp difference]

Options for predict

▔▔▔ Main ▔▔▔

xb, the default, calculates the linear prediction.

102

e calculates the residual error.

stdp calculates the standard error of the prediction, which can be thought of as the standard error of the predicted expected value or mean for the observation's covariate pattern. The standard error of the prediction is also referred to as the standard error of the fitted value. stdp may not be combined with difference.

difference specifies that the statistic be calculated for the first differences instead of the levels, the default.

Syntax for estat abond

estat abond $\left[\,,\ \underline{art}ests(\#)\,\right]$

Option for estat abond

artests(#) specifies the highest order of serial correlation to be tested. By default, the tests computed during estimation are reported. The model will be refitted when artests(#) specifies a higher order than that computed during the original estimation. The model can be refitted only if the data have not changed.

Syntax for estat sargan

estat sargan

Remarks

Remarks are presented under the following headings:

> *estat abond*
> *estat sargan*

estat abond

The moment conditions used by xtdpdsys are valid only if there is no serial correlation in the idiosyncratic errors. Testing for serial correlation in dynamic panel-data models is tricky because a transform is required to remove the panel-level effects, but the transformed errors have a more complicated error structure than that of the idiosyncratic errors. The Arellano–Bond test for serial correlation reported by estat abond tests for serial correlation in the first-differenced errors.

Because the first difference of independently and identically distributed idiosyncratic errors will be serially correlated, rejecting the null hypothesis of no serial correlation in the first-differenced errors at order one does not imply that the model is misspecified. Rejecting the null hypothesis at higher orders implies that the moment conditions are not valid. See [XT] **xtdpd** for an example of how to fit the model by using an alternative set of moment conditions.

After the one-step system estimator, the test can be computed only when vce(robust) has been specified.

estat sargan

Like all GMM estimators, the estimator in `xtdpdsys` can produce consistent estimates only if the moment conditions used are valid. Although there is no method to test if the moment conditions from an exactly identified model are valid, one can test whether the overidentifying moment conditions are valid. `estat sargan` implements the Sargan test of overidentifying conditions discussed in Arellano and Bond (1991).

Only for a homoskedastic error term does the Sargan test have an asymptotic chi-squared distribution. In fact, Arellano and Bond (1991) show that the one-step Sargan test overrejects in the presence of heteroskedasticity. Since its asymptotic distribution is not known under the assumptions of the `vce(robust)` model, `xtdpdsys` does not compute it when `vce(robust)` is specified. See [XT] **xtdpd** for an example in which the null hypothesis of the Sargan test is not rejected.

```
. use http://www.stata-press.com/data/r10/abdata
. xtdpdsys n L(0/2).(w k) yr1980-yr1984 year,
  (output omitted)
. estat sargan
Sargan test of overidentifying restrictions
        H0: overidentifying restrictions are valid
        chi2(33)    =  63.63911
        Prob > chi2 =    0.0011
```

The output above presents strong evidence against the null hypothesis that the overidentifying restrictions are valid. Rejecting this null hypothesis implies that we need to reconsider our model or our instruments, unless we attribute the rejection to heteroskedasticity in the data-generating process. Although performing the Sargan test after the two-step estimator is an alternative, Arellano and Bond (1991) found a tendency for this test to underreject in the presence of heteroskedasticity

Methods and Formulas

The formulas are given in *Methods and Formulas* of [XT] **xtdpd postestimation**.

Reference

Arellano, M., and S. Bond. 1991. Some tests of specification for panel data: Monte Carlo evidence and an application to employment equations. *Review of Economic Studies* 58: 277–297.

Also See

[XT] **xtdpdsys** — Arellano–Bover/Blundell–Bond linear dynamic panel-data estimation

Title

xtfrontier — Stochastic frontier models for panel data

Syntax

Time-invariant model

> xtfrontier *depvar* [*indepvars*] [*if*] [*in*] [*weight*] , ti [*ti_options*]

Time-varying decay model

> xtfrontier *depvar* [*indepvars*] [*if*] [*in*] [*weight*] , tvd [*tvd_options*]

ti_options	description
Model	
noconstant	suppress constant term
ti	use time-invariant model
cost	fit cost frontier model
constraints(*constraints*)	apply specified linear constraints
collinear	keep collinear variables
SE	
vce(*vcetype*)	*vcetype* may be oim, bootstrap, or jackknife
Reporting	
level(*#*)	set confidence level; default is level(95)
Max options	
maximize_options	control the maximization process; seldom used

tvd_options	description
Model	
noconstant	suppress constant term
tvd	use time-varying decay model
cost	fit cost frontier model
constraints(*constraints*)	apply specified linear constraints
collinear	keep collinear variables
SE	
vce(*vcetype*)	*vcetype* may be oim, bootstrap, or jackknife
Reporting	
level(*#*)	set confidence level; default is level(95)
Max options	
maximize_options	control the maximization process; seldom used

A panel variable must be specified. For xtfrontier, tvd, a time variable must also be specified. Use xtset; see [XT] **xtset**.

depvar and *indepvars* may contain time-series operators; see [U] **11.4.3 Time-series varlists**.

by, statsby, and xi are allowed; see [U] **11.1.10 Prefix commands**.

fweights and iweights are allowed; see [U] **11.1.6 weight**. Weights must be constant within panel.

See [U] **20 Estimation and postestimation commands** for more capabilities of estimation commands.

Description

xtfrontier fits stochastic production or cost frontier models for panel data. More precisely, xtfrontier estimates the parameters of a linear model with a disturbance generated by specific mixture distributions.

The disturbance term in a stochastic frontier model is assumed to have two components. One component is assumed to have a strictly nonnegative distribution, and the other component is assumed to have a symmetric distribution. In the econometrics literature, the nonnegative component is often referred to as the *inefficiency term*, and the component with the symmetric distribution as the *idiosyncratic error*. xtfrontier permits two different parameterizations of the inefficiency term: a time-invariant model and the Battese–Coelli (1992) parameterization of time effects. In the time-invariant model, the inefficiency term is assumed to have a truncated-normal distribution. In the Battese–Coelli (1992) parameterization of time effects, the inefficiency term is modeled as a truncated-normal random variable multiplied by a specific function of time. In both models, the idiosyncratic error term is assumed to have a normal distribution. The only panel-specific effect is the random inefficiency term.

See Kumbhakar and Lovell (2000) for a detailed introduction to frontier analysis.

Options for time-invariant model

⌐‾‾| Model |‾‾

noconstant; see [XT] **estimation options**.

ti specifies that the parameters of the time-invariant technical inefficiency model be estimated.

cost specifies that the frontier model be fitted in terms of a cost function instead of a production function. By default, xtfrontier fits a production frontier model.

constraints(*constraints*), collinear; see [XT] **estimation options**.

⌐‾‾| SE |‾‾

vce(*vcetype*) specifies the type of standard error reported, which includes types that are derived from asymptotic theory and that use bootstrap or jackknife methods; see [XT] *vce_options*.

⌐‾‾| Reporting |‾‾

level(#); see [XT] **estimation options**.

⌐ Max options ⌐

maximize_options: di<u>ff</u>icult, <u>tech</u>nique(*algorithm_spec*), <u>iter</u>ate(*#*), [<u>no</u>]<u>log</u>, <u>tra</u>ce, gradient, showstep, <u>hess</u>ian, <u>shownr</u>tolerance, <u>tol</u>erance(*#*), <u>ltol</u>erance(*#*), <u>gtol</u>erance(*#*), <u>nrtol</u>erance(*#*), <u>nonrtol</u>erance, from(*init_specs*); see [R] **maximize**. These options are seldom used.

Options for time-varying decay model

⌐ Model ⌐

noconstant; see [XT] **estimation options**.

tvd specifies that the parameters of the time-varying decay model be estimated.

cost specifies that the frontier model be fitted in terms of a cost function instead of a production function. By default, xtfrontier fits a production frontier model.

constraints(*constraints*), collinear; see [XT] **estimation options**.

⌐ SE ⌐

vce(*vcetype*) specifies the type of standard error reported, which includes types that are derived from asymptotic theory and that use bootstrap or jackknife methods; see [XT] *vce_options*.

⌐ Reporting ⌐

level(*#*); see [XT] **estimation options**.

⌐ Max options ⌐

maximize_options: di<u>ff</u>icult, <u>tech</u>nique(*algorithm_spec*), <u>iter</u>ate(*#*), [<u>no</u>]<u>log</u>, <u>tra</u>ce, gradient, showstep, <u>hess</u>ian, <u>shownr</u>tolerance, <u>tol</u>erance(*#*), <u>ltol</u>erance(*#*), <u>gtol</u>erance(*#*), <u>nrtol</u>erance(*#*), <u>nonrtol</u>erance, from(*init_specs*); see [R] **maximize**. These options are seldom used.

Remarks

Remarks are presented under the following headings:

Introduction
Time-invariant model
Time-varying decay model

Introduction

Stochastic production frontier models were introduced by Aigner, Lovell, and Schmidt (1977) and Meeusen and van den Broeck (1977). Since then, stochastic frontier models have become a popular subfield in econometrics; see Kumbhakar and Lovell (2000) for an introduction. xtfrontier fits two stochastic frontier models with distinct specifications of the inefficiency term and can fit both production- and cost-frontier models.

Let's review the nature of the stochastic frontier problem. Suppose that a producer has a production function $f(\mathbf{z}_{it}, \beta)$. In a world without error or inefficiency, in time t, the ith firm would produce

$$q_{it} = f(\mathbf{z}_{it}, \beta)$$

A fundamental element of stochastic frontier analysis is that each firm potentially produces less than it might because of a degree of inefficiency. Specifically,

$$q_{it} = f(\mathbf{z}_{it}, \beta)\xi_{it}$$

where ξ_{it} is the level of efficiency for firm i at time t; ξ_i must be in the interval $(0, 1]$. If $\xi_{it} = 1$, the firm is achieving the optimal output with the technology embodied in the production function $f(\mathbf{z}_{it}, \beta)$. When $\xi_{it} < 1$, the firm is not making the most of the inputs $\mathbf{z}_{it}$ given the technology embodied in the production function $f(\mathbf{z}_{it}, \beta)$. Since the output is assumed to be strictly positive (i.e., $q_{it} > 0$), the degree of technical efficiency is assumed to be strictly positive (i.e., $\xi_{it} > 0$).

Output is also assumed to be subject to random shocks, implying that

$$q_{it} = f(\mathbf{z}_{it}, \beta)\xi_{it}\exp(v_{it})$$

Taking the natural log of both sides yields

$$\ln(q_{it}) = \ln\{f(\mathbf{z}_{it}, \beta)\} + \ln(\xi_{it}) + v_{it}$$

Assuming that there are k inputs and that the production function is linear in logs, defining $u_{it} = -\ln(\xi_{it})$ yields

$$\ln(q_{it}) = \beta_0 + \sum_{j=1}^{k} \beta_j \ln(z_{jit}) + v_{it} - u_{it} \tag{1}$$

Since u_{it} is subtracted from $\ln(q_{it})$, restricting $u_{it} \geq 0$ implies that $0 < \xi_{it} \leq 1$, as specified above.

Kumbhakar and Lovell (2000) provide a detailed version of this derivation, and they show that performing an analogous derivation in the dual cost function problem allows us to specify the problem as

$$\ln(c_{it}) = \beta_0 + \beta_q \ln(q_{it}) + \sum_{j=1}^{k} \beta_j \ln(p_{jit}) + v_{it} - su_{it} \tag{2}$$

where q_{it} is output, the z_{jit} are input quantities, c_{it} is cost, the p_{jit} are input prices, and

$$s = \begin{cases} 1, & \text{for production functions} \\ -1, & \text{for cost functions} \end{cases}$$

Intuitively, the inefficiency effect is required to lower output or raise expenditure, depending on the specification.

❑ Technical Note

The model that `xtfrontier` actually fits has the form

$$y_{it} = \beta_0 + \sum_{j=1}^{k} \beta_j x_{jit} + v_{it} - su_{it}$$

so in the context of the discussion above, $y_{it} = \ln(q_{it})$ and $x_{jit} = \ln(z_{jit})$ for a production function; for a cost function, $y_{it} = \ln(c_{it})$, the x_{jit} are the $\ln(p_{jit})$, and $\ln(q_{it})$. You must perform the natural logarithm transformation of the data before estimation to interpret the estimation results correctly for a stochastic frontier production or cost model. xtfrontier does not perform any transformations on the data.

❏

Equation (2) is a variant of a panel-data model in which v_{it} is the idiosyncratic error and u_{it} is a time-varying panel-level effect. Much of the literature on this model has focused on deriving estimators for different specifications of the u_{it} term. Kumbhakar and Lovell (2000) provide a survey of this literature.

xtfrontier provides estimators for two different specifications of u_{it}. To facilitate the discussion, let $N^+(\mu, \sigma^2)$ denote the truncated-normal distribution, which is truncated at zero with mean μ and variance σ^2, and let $\overset{\text{iid}}{\sim}$ stand for independently and identically distributed.

Consider the simplest specification in which u_{it} is a time-invariant truncated-normal random variable. In the time-invariant model, $u_{it} = u_i$, $u_i \overset{\text{iid}}{\sim} N^+(\mu, \sigma_\mu^2)$, $v_{it} \overset{\text{iid}}{\sim} N(0, \sigma_v^2)$, and u_i and v_{it} are distributed independently of each other and the covariates in the model. Specifying option ti causes xtfrontier to estimate the parameters of this model.

In the time-varying decay specification,

$$u_{it} = \exp\big\{-\eta(t - T_i)\big\}u_i$$

where T_i is the last period in the ith panel, η is the decay parameter, $u_i \overset{\text{iid}}{\sim} N^+(\mu, \sigma_\mu^2)$, $v_{it} \overset{\text{iid}}{\sim} N(0, \sigma_v^2)$, and u_i and v_{it} are distributed independently of each other and the covariates in the model. Specifying option tvd causes xtfrontier to estimate the parameters of this model.

Time-invariant model

▷ Example 1

xtfrontier, ti provides maximum likelihood estimates for the parameters of the time-invariant decay model. In this model, the inefficiency effects are modeled as $u_{it} = u_i$, $u_i \overset{\text{iid}}{\sim} N^+(\mu, \sigma_\mu^2)$, $v_{it} \overset{\text{iid}}{\sim} N(0, \sigma_v^2)$, and u_i and v_{it} are distributed independently of each other and the covariates in the model. In this example, firms produce a product called a widget, using a constant-returns-to-scale technology. We have 948 observations—91 firms, with 6–14 observations per firm. Our dataset contains variables representing the quantity of widgets produced, the number of machine hours used in production, the number of labor hours used in production, and three additional variables that are the natural logarithm transformations of the three aforementioned variables.

(Continued on next page)

We fit a time-invariant model using the transformed variables:

```
. use http://www.stata-press.com/data/r10/xtfrontier1

. xtfrontier lnwidgets lnmachines lnworkers, ti
Iteration 0:   log likelihood = -1473.8703
Iteration 1:   log likelihood = -1473.0565
Iteration 2:   log likelihood = -1472.6155
Iteration 3:   log likelihood =  -1472.607
Iteration 4:   log likelihood = -1472.6069
```

Time-invariant inefficiency model

Group variable: id

Number of obs	=	948
Number of groups	=	91

Obs per group:		
min =		6
avg =		10.4
max =		14

Log likelihood = -1472.6069

Wald chi2(2)	=	661.76
Prob > chi2	=	0.0000

lnwidgets	Coef.	Std. Err.	z	P>|z|	[95% Conf. Interval]	
lnmachines	.2904551	.0164219	17.69	0.000	.2582688	.3226415
lnworkers	.2943333	.0154352	19.07	0.000	.2640808	.3245858
_cons	3.030983	.1441022	21.03	0.000	2.748548	3.313418
/mu	1.125667	.6479217	1.74	0.082	-.144236	2.39557
/lnsigma2	1.421979	.2672745	5.32	0.000	.898131	1.945828
/ilgtgamma	1.138685	.3562642	3.20	0.001	.4404204	1.83695
sigma2	4.145318	1.107938			2.455011	6.999424
gamma	.7574382	.0654548			.6083592	.8625876
sigma_u2	3.139822	1.107235			.9696821	5.309962
sigma_v2	1.005496	.0484143			.9106055	1.100386

In addition to the coefficients, the output reports estimates for the parameters `sigma_v2`, `sigma_u2`, `gamma`, `sigma2`, `ilgtgamma`, `lnsigma2`, and `mu`. `sigma_v2` is the estimate of σ_v^2. `sigma_u2` is the estimate of σ_u^2. `gamma` is the estimate of $\gamma = \sigma_u^2/\sigma_S^2$. `sigma2` is the estimate of $\sigma_S^2 = \sigma_v^2 + \sigma_u^2$. Since γ must be between 0 and 1, the optimization is parameterized in terms of the inverse logit of γ, and this estimate is reported as `ilgtgamma`. Since σ_S^2 must be positive, the optimization is parameterized in terms of $\ln(\sigma_S^2)$, and this estimate is reported as `lnsigma2`. Finally, `mu` is the estimate of μ.

◁

❑ Technical Note

Our simulation results indicate that this estimator requires relatively large samples to achieve any reasonable degree of precision in the estimates of μ and $\sigma_\mu{}^2$.

❑

Time-varying decay model

`xtfrontier, tvd` provides maximum likelihood estimates for the parameters of the time-varying decay model. In this model, the inefficiency effects are modeled as

$$u_{it} = \exp\{-\eta(t - T_i)\}u_i$$

where $u_i \overset{\text{iid}}{\sim} N^+(\mu, \sigma_\mu^2)$.

When $\eta > 0$, the degree of inefficiency decreases over time; when $\eta < 0$, the degree of inefficiency increases over time. Since $t = T_i$ in the last period, the last period for firm i contains the base level of inefficiency for that firm. If $\eta > 0$, the level of inefficiency decays toward the base level. If $\eta < 0$, the level of inefficiency increases to the base level.

▷ Example 2

When $\eta = 0$, the time-varying decay model reduces to the time-invariant model. The following example illustrates this property and demonstrates how to specify constraints and starting values in these models.

Let's begin by fitting the time-varying decay model on the same data that were used in the previous example for the time-invariant model.

```
. xtfrontier lnwidgets lnmachines lnworkers, tvd
Iteration 0:   log likelihood = -1551.3798  (not concave)
Iteration 1:   log likelihood = -1502.2637
Iteration 2:   log likelihood = -1476.3093  (not concave)
Iteration 3:   log likelihood = -1472.9845
Iteration 4:   log likelihood = -1472.5365
Iteration 5:   log likelihood =  -1472.529
Iteration 6:   log likelihood = -1472.5289
```

Time-varying decay inefficiency model		Number of obs	=	948
Group variable: id		Number of groups	=	91
Time variable: t		Obs per group: min =		6
		avg =		10.4
		max =		14
		Wald chi2(2)	=	661.93
Log likelihood = -1472.5289		Prob > chi2	=	0.0000

lnwidgets	Coef.	Std. Err.	z	P>|z|	[95% Conf. Interval]	
lnmachines	.2907555	.0164376	17.69	0.000	.2585384	.3229725
lnworkers	.2942412	.0154373	19.06	0.000	.2639846	.3244978
_cons	3.028939	.1436046	21.09	0.000	2.74748	3.310399
/mu	1.110831	.6452809	1.72	0.085	-.1538967	2.375558
/eta	.0016764	.00425	0.39	0.693	-.0066535	.0100064
/lnsigma2	1.410723	.2679485	5.26	0.000	.885554	1.935893
/ilgtgamma	1.123982	.3584243	3.14	0.002	.4214828	1.82648
sigma2	4.098919	1.098299			2.424327	6.930228
gamma	.7547265	.0663495			.603838	.8613419
sigma_u2	3.093563	1.097606			.9422943	5.244832
sigma_v2	1.005356	.0484079			.9104785	1.100234

The estimate of η is close to zero, and the other estimates are not too far from those of the time-invariant model.

We can use `constraint` to constrain $\eta = 0$ and obtain the same results produced by the time-invariant model. Although there is only one statistical equation to be estimated in this model, the model fits five of Stata's [R] **ml** equations; see [R] **ml** or Gould, Pitblado, and Sribney (2003). The equation names can be seen by listing the matrix of estimated coefficients.

```
. matrix list e(b)

e(b)[1,7]
        lnwidgets:   lnwidgets:   lnwidgets:   lnsigma2:   ilgtgamma:        mu:
        lnmachines    lnworkers       _cons       _cons       _cons      _cons
y1     .29075546     .2942412   3.0289395   1.4107233   1.1239816   1.1108307

              eta:
             _cons
y1        .00167642
```

To constrain a parameter to a particular value in any equation, except the first equation, you must specify both the equation name and the parameter name by using the syntax

constraint # [*eqname*] _b[*varname*] = *value*   or

constraint # [*eqname*] *coefficient* = *value*

where *eqname* is the equation name, *varname* is the name of variable in a linear equation, and *coefficient* refers to any parameter that has been estimated. More elaborate specifications with expressions are possible; see the example with constant returns to scale below, and see [R] **constraint** for general reference.

Suppose that we impose the constraint $\eta = 0$; we get the same results as those reported above for the time-invariant model, except for some minute differences attributable to an alternate convergence path in the optimization.

```
. constraint 1 [eta]_cons = 0

. xtfrontier lnwidgets lnmachines lnworkers, tvd constraints(1)

Iteration 0:   log likelihood = -1540.7124   (not concave)
Iteration 1:   log likelihood = -1515.7726
Iteration 2:   log likelihood = -1473.0162
Iteration 3:   log likelihood = -1472.9223
Iteration 4:   log likelihood = -1472.6254
Iteration 5:   log likelihood =  -1472.607
Iteration 6:   log likelihood = -1472.6069

Time-varying decay inefficiency model          Number of obs     =        948
Group variable: id                             Number of groups  =         91
Time variable: t                               Obs per group: min =          6
                                                              avg =       10.4
                                                              max =         14

                                               Wald chi2(2)      =     661.76
Log likelihood  = -1472.6069                   Prob > chi2       =     0.0000
```

lnwidgets	Coef.	Std. Err.	z	P>|z|	[95% Conf. Interval]	
lnmachines	.2904551	.0164219	17.69	0.000	.2582688	.3226414
lnworkers	.2943332	.0154352	19.07	0.000	.2640807	.3245857
_cons	3.030963	.1440995	21.03	0.000	2.748534	3.313393
/mu	1.125507	.6480444	1.74	0.082	-.1446369	2.39565
/eta	0	.	.	.	.	.
/lnsigma2	1.422039	.2673128	5.32	0.000	.8981155	1.945962
/ilgtgamma	1.138764	.3563076	3.20	0.001	.4404135	1.837114
sigma2	4.145565	1.108162			2.454972	7.000366
gamma	.7574526	.0654602			.6083575	.862607
sigma_u2	3.140068	1.107459			.9694878	5.310649
sigma_v2	1.005496	.0484143			.9106057	1.100386

◁

Saved Results

xtfrontier saves the following in e():

Scalars

e(N)	number of observations	e(g_avg)	average number of observations
e(N_g)	number of groups		per group
e(k)	number of estimated parameters	e(g_max)	maximum number of observations
e(k_eq)	number of equations		per group
e(k_eq_model)	number of equations in model	e(sigma2)	sigma2
	Wald test	e(gamma)	gamma
e(k_dv)	number of dependent variables	e(Tcon)	1 if panels balanced; 0 otherwise
e(df_m)	model degrees of freedom	e(sigma_u)	standard deviation of
e(ll)	log likelihood		technical inefficiency
e(rc)	return code	e(chi2)	χ^2
e(converged)	1 if converged, 0 otherwise	e(sigma_v)	standard deviation of random error
e(g_min)	minimum number of observations	e(rank)	rank of e(V)
	per group	e(p)	model significance
		e(ic)	number of iterations

Macros

e(cmd)	xtfrontier	e(chi2type)	Wald; type of model χ^2 test
e(cmdline)	command as typed	e(vce)	*vcetype* specified in vce()
e(depvar)	name of dependent variable	e(vcetype)	title used to label Std. Err.
e(function)	production or cost	e(opt)	type of optimization
e(model)	ti, after time-invariant model; tvd,	e(ml_method)	type of ml method
	after time-varying decay model	e(user)	name of likelihood-evaluator program
e(ivar)	variable denoting groups	(e(technique)	maximization technique
e(tvar)	variable denoting time	e(crittype)	optimization criterion
e(wtype)	weight type	e(properties)	b V
e(wexp)	weight expression	e(predict)	program used to implement predict
e(title)	name of model		

Matrices

e(b)	coefficient vector	e(V)	variance–covariance matrix
e(ilog)	iteration log (up to 20 iterations)		of the estimators

Functions

e(sample)	marks estimation sample

Methods and Formulas

xtfrontier is implemented as an ado-file.

xtfrontier fits stochastic frontier models for panel data that can be expressed as

$$y_{it} = \beta_0 + \sum_{j=1}^{k} \beta_j x_{jit} + v_{it} - su_{it}$$

where y_{it} is the natural logarithm of output, the x_{jit} are the natural logarithm of the input quantities for the production efficiency problem, y_{it} is the natural logarithm of costs, the x_{it} are the natural logarithm of input prices for the cost efficiency problem, and

$$s = \begin{cases} 1, & \text{for production functions} \\ -1, & \text{for cost functions} \end{cases}$$

For the time-varying decay model, the log-likelihood function is derived as

$$\ln L = -\frac{1}{2}\left(\sum_{i=1}^{N} T_i\right)\left\{\ln(2\pi) + \ln(\sigma_S^2)\right\} - \frac{1}{2}\sum_{i=1}^{N}(T_i - 1)\ln(1 - \gamma)$$

$$-\frac{1}{2}\sum_{i=1}^{N}\ln\left\{1 + \left(\sum_{t=1}^{T_i}\eta_{it}^2 - 1\right)\gamma\right\} - N\ln\left\{1 - \Phi(-\widetilde{z})\right\} - \frac{1}{2}N\widetilde{z}^2$$

$$+\sum_{i=1}^{N}\ln\left\{1 - \Phi(-z_i^*)\right\} + \frac{1}{2}\sum_{i=1}^{N}z_i^{*2} - \frac{1}{2}\sum_{i=1}^{N}\sum_{t=1}^{T_i}\frac{\epsilon_{it}^2}{(1 - \gamma)\sigma_S^2}$$

where $\sigma_S = (\sigma_u^2 + \sigma_v^2)^{1/2}$, $\gamma = \sigma_u^2/\sigma_S^2$, $\epsilon_{it} = y_{it} - \mathbf{x}_{it}\boldsymbol{\beta}$, $\eta_{it} = \exp\{-\eta(t - T_i)\}$, $\widetilde{z} = \mu/\left(\gamma\sigma_S^2\right)^{1/2}$, $\Phi()$ is the cumulative distribution function of the standard normal distribution, and

$$z_i^* = \frac{\mu(1 - \gamma) - s\gamma\sum_{t=1}^{T_i}\eta_{it}\epsilon_{it}}{\left[\gamma(1 - \gamma)\sigma_S^2\left\{1 + \left(\sum_{t=1}^{T_i}\eta_{it}^2 - 1\right)\gamma\right\}\right]^{1/2}}$$

Maximizing the above log likelihood estimates the coefficients η, μ, σ_v, and σ_u.

References

Aigner, D. J., C. A. K. Lovell, and P. Schmidt. 1977. Formulation and estimation of stochastic frontier production function models. *Journal of Econometrics* 6: 21–37.

Battese, G. E., and T. J. Coelli. 1992. Frontier production functions, technical efficiency and panel data: With applications to paddy farmers in India. *Journal of Productivity Analysis* 3: 153–169.

——. 1995. A model for technical inefficiency effects in a stochastic frontier production for panel data. *Empirical Economics* 20: 325–332.

Caudill, S. B., J. M. Ford, and D. M. Gropper. 1995. Frontier estimation and firm-specific inefficiency measures in the presence of heteroskedasticity. *Journal of Business and Economic Statistics* 13: 105–111.

Coelli, T. J. 1995. Estimators and hypothesis tests for a stochastic frontier function: A Monte Carlo analysis. *Journal of Productivity Analysis* 6: 247–268.

Coelli, T. J., D. S. P. Rao, and G. E. Battese. 2005. *An Introduction to Efficiency and Productivity Analysis*. 2nd ed. New York: Springer.

Gould, W. W., J. S. Pitblado, and W. M. Sribney. 2006. *Maximum Likelihood Estimation with Stata*. 3rd ed. College Station, TX: Stata Press.

Kumbhakar, S. C., and C. A. K. Lovell. 2000. *Stochastic Frontier Analysis*. Cambridge: Cambridge University Press.

Meeusen, W., and J. van den Broeck. 1977. Efficiency estimation from Cobb–Douglas production functions with composed error. *International Economic Review* 18: 435–444.

Zellner, A., and N. Revankar. 1970. Generalized production functions. *Review of Economic Studies* 37: 241–250.

Also See

Title

xtfrontier postestimation — Postestimation tools for xtfrontier

Description

The following postestimation commands are available for xtfrontier:

command	description
adjust[1]	adjusted predictions of $\mathbf{x}\beta$
estat	AIC, BIC, VCE, and estimation sample summary
estimates	cataloging estimation results
lincom	point estimates, standard errors, testing, and inference for linear combinations of coefficients
lrtest	likelihood-ratio test
mfx	marginal effects or elasticities
nlcom	point estimates, standard errors, testing, and inference for nonlinear combinations of coefficients
predict	predictions, residuals, influence statistics, and other diagnostic measures
predictnl	point estimates, standard errors, testing, and inference for generalized predictions
test	Wald tests for simple and composite linear hypotheses
testnl	Wald tests of nonlinear hypotheses

[1] adjust is not appropriate with time-series operators.

See the corresponding entries in the *Stata Base Reference Manual* for details.

Syntax for predict

predict [*type*] *newvar* [*if*] [*in*] [, *statistic*]

statistic	description
Main	
xb	linear prediction; the default
stdp	standard error of the linear prediction
u	minus the natural log of the technical efficiency via $E\left(u_{it} \mid \epsilon_{it}\right)$
m	minus the natural log of the technical efficiency via $M\left(u_{it} \mid \epsilon_{it}\right)$
te	the technical efficiency via $E\left\{\exp(-su_{it}) \mid \epsilon_{it}\right\}$

where

$$s = \begin{cases} 1, & \text{for production functions} \\ -1, & \text{for cost functions} \end{cases}$$

Options for predict

xb, the default, calculates the linear prediction.

stdp calculates the standard error of the linear prediction.

u produces estimates of minus the natural log of the technical efficiency via $E\left(u_{it} \mid \epsilon_{it}\right)$.

m produces estimates of minus the natural log of the technical efficiency via the mode, $M\left(u_{it} \mid \epsilon_{it}\right)$.

te produces estimates of the technical efficiency via $E\left\{\exp(-su_{it}) \mid \epsilon_{it}\right\}$.

Remarks

▷ Example 1

A production function exhibits *constant returns to scale* if doubling the amount of each input results in a doubling in the quantity produced. When the production function is linear in logs, constant returns to scale implies that the sum of the coefficients on the inputs is one. In [XT] **xtfrontier**, we fitted a time-varying decay model. Here we test whether the estimated production function exhibits constant returns:

```
. use http://www.stata-press.com/data/r10/xtfrontier1
. xtfrontier lnwidgets lnmachines lnworkers, tvd
(output omitted )
. test lnmachines + lnworkers = 1
( 1)  [lnwidgets]lnmachines + [lnwidgets]lnworkers = 1
           chi2(  1) =   331.55
         Prob > chi2 =    0.0000
```

The test statistic is highly significant, so we reject the null hypothesis and conclude that this production function does not exhibit constant returns to scale.

The previous Wald χ^2 test indicated that the sum of the coefficients does not equal one. An alternative is to use lincom to compute the sum explicitly:

```
. lincom lnmachines + lnworkers
( 1)  [lnwidgets]lnmachines + [lnwidgets]lnworkers = 0
```

lnwidgets	Coef.	Std. Err.	z	P>|z|	[95% Conf. Interval]	
(1)	.5849967	.0227918	25.67	0.000	.5403256	.6296677

The sum of the coefficients is significantly less than one, so this production function exhibits *decreasing returns to scale*. If we doubled the number of machines and workers, we would obtain less than twice as much output.

◁

(*Continued on next page*)

Methods and Formulas

All postestimation commands listed above are implemented as ado-files.

Continuing from the *Methods and Formulas* section of [XT] **xtfrontier**, estimates for u_{it} can be obtained from the mean or the mode of the conditional distribution $f(u|\epsilon)$.

$$E\left(u_{it}\mid\epsilon_{it}\right)=\widetilde{\mu}_i+\widetilde{\sigma}_i\left\{\frac{\phi\left(-\widetilde{\mu}_i/\widetilde{\sigma}_i\right)}{1-\Phi\left(-\widetilde{\mu}_i/\widetilde{\sigma}_i\right)}\right\}$$

$$M\left(u_{it}\mid\epsilon_{it}\right)=\begin{cases}-\widetilde{\mu}_i,&\text{if }\widetilde{\mu}_i>=0\\0,&\text{otherwise}\end{cases}$$

where

$$\widetilde{\mu}_i=\frac{\mu\sigma_v^2-s\sum_{t=1}^{T_i}\eta_{it}\epsilon_{it}\sigma_u^2}{\sigma_v^2+\sum_{t=1}^{T_i}\eta_{it}^2\sigma_u^2}$$

$$\widetilde{\sigma}_i^2=\frac{\sigma_v^2\sigma_u^2}{\sigma_v^2+\sum_{t=1}^{T_i}\eta_{it}^2\sigma_u^2}$$

These estimates can be obtained from predict *newvar*, u and predict *newvar*, m, respectively, and are calculated by plugging in the estimated parameters.

predict *newvar*, te produces estimates of the technical-efficiency term. These estimates are obtained from

$$E\left\{\exp(-su_{it})\mid\epsilon_{it}\right\}=\left[\frac{1-\Phi\left\{s\eta_{it}\widetilde{\sigma}_i-(\widetilde{\mu}_i/\widetilde{\sigma}_i)\right\}}{1-\Phi\left(-\widetilde{\mu}_i/\widetilde{\sigma}_i\right)}\right]\exp\left(-s\eta_{it}\widetilde{\mu}_i+\frac{1}{2}\eta_{it}^2\widetilde{\sigma}_i^2\right)$$

Replacing $\eta_{it}=1$ and $\eta=0$ in these formulas produces the formulas for the time-invariant models.

Also See

[XT] **xtfrontier** — Stochastic frontier models for panel data

[U] **20 Estimation and postestimation commands**

Title

> **xtgee** — Fit population-averaged panel-data models by using GEE

Syntax

xtgee *depvar* [*indepvars*] [*if*] [*in*] [*weight*] [*, options*]

options	description
Model	
<u>f</u>amily(*family*)	distribution of *depvar*; see table below
<u>l</u>ink(*link*)	link function; see table below
Model 2	
<u>exp</u>osure(*varname*)	include ln(*varname*) in model with coefficient constrained to 1
<u>off</u>set(*varname*)	include *varname* in model with coefficient constrained to 1
<u>nocon</u>stant	suppress constant term
force	estimate even if observations unequally spaced in time
Correlation	
<u>c</u>orr(*correlation*)	within-group correlation structure; see table below
SE/Robust	
vce(*vcetype*)	*vcetype* may be conventional, <u>r</u>obust, <u>boot</u>strap, or <u>jack</u>knife
nmp	use divisor $N - P$ instead of the default N
rgf	multiply the robust variance estimate by $(N - 1)/(N - P)$
<u>s</u>cale(*parm*)	overrides the default scale parameter; *parm* may be x2, dev, phi, or #
Reporting	
<u>level</u>(#)	set confidence level; default is level(95)
<u>ef</u>orm	report exponentiated coefficients
Opt options	
optimize_options	control the optimization process; seldom used
† <u>nodis</u>play	suppress display of header and coefficients

---

† nodisplay is not shown in the dialog box.

A panel variable must be specified. For xtgee, pa, correlation structures other than exchangeable and independent require that a time variable also be specified. Use xtset; see [XT] **xtset**.

depvar and *indepvars* may contain time-series operators; see [U] **11.4 varlists**.

by, statsby, and xi are allowed; see [U] **11.1.10 Prefix commands**.

iweights, fweights, and pweights are allowed; see [U] **11.1.6 weight**. Weights must be constant within panel.

See [U] **20 Estimation and postestimation commands** for more capabilities of estimation commands.

family	description
<u>gau</u>ssian	Gaussian (normal); family(normal) is a synonym
<u>i</u>gaussian	inverse Gaussian
<u>b</u>inomial[# | *varname*]	Bernoulli/binomial
<u>poisson</u>	Poisson
<u>nb</u>inomial[#]	negative binomial
<u>gam</u>ma	gamma

link	link function/definition
<u>id</u>entity	identity; $y = y$
log	log; $\ln(y)$
<u>logit</u>	logit; $\ln\{y/(1-y)\}$, natural log of the odds
<u>pr</u>obit	probit; $\Phi^{-1}(y)$, where $\Phi(\ )$ is the normal cumulative distribution
<u>cl</u>oglog	cloglog; $\ln\{-\ln(1-y)\}$
<u>power</u>[#]	power; y^k with $k = \#$; $\# = 1$ if not specified
<u>op</u>ower[#]	odds power; $[\{y/(1-y)\}^k - 1]/k$ with $k = \#$; $\# = 1$ if not specified
<u>nb</u>inomial	negative binomial; $\ln\{y/(y+\alpha)\}$
<u>rec</u>iprocal	reciprocal; $1/y$

correlation	description
<u>exc</u>hangeable	exchangeable
<u>ind</u>ependent	independent
<u>uns</u>tructured	unstructured
<u>fix</u>ed *matname*	user-specified
ar #	autoregressive of order #
<u>sta</u>tionary #	stationary of order #
<u>non</u>stationary #	nonstationary of order #

For example,

```
. xtgee y x1 x2, family(gaussian) link(identity) corr(exchangeable)
```

would estimate a random-effects linear regression—corr(exchangeable) does not provide random effects. It actually fits an equal-correlation population-averaged model equivalent to the random-effects model for linear regression.

Description

xtgee fits population-averaged panel-data models. In particular, xtgee fits general linear models and allows you to specify the within-group correlation structure for the panels.

See [R] **logistic** and [R] **regress** for lists of related estimation commands.

Options

☐ Model ☐

family(*family*) specifies the distribution of *depvar*; family(gaussian) is the default.

link(*link*) specifies the link function; the default is the canonical link for the family() specified.

☐ Model 2 ☐

exposure(*varname*) and offset(*varname*) are different ways of specifying the same thing. exposure() specifies a variable that reflects the amount of exposure over which the *depvar* events were observed for each observation; ln(*varname*) with coefficient constrained to be 1 is entered into the regression equation. offset() specifies a variable that is to be entered directly into the log-link function with its coefficient constrained to be 1; thus, exposure is assumed to be $e^{varname}$. If you were fitting a Poisson regression model, family(poisson) link(log), for instance, you would account for exposure time by specifying offset() containing the log of exposure time.

noconstant specifies that the linear predictor has no intercept term, thus forcing it through the origin on the scale defined by the link function.

force; see [XT] **estimation options**.

☐ Correlation ☐

corr(*correlation*); see [XT] **estimation options**.

☐ SE/Robust ☐

vce(*vcetype*) specifies the type of standard error reported, which includes types that are derived from asymptotic theory, that are robust to some kinds of misspecification, and that use bootstrap or jackknife methods; see [XT] *vce_options*.

vce(conventional), the default, uses the conventionally derived variance estimator for generalized least-squares regression.

vce(robust) specifies that the Huber/White/sandwich estimator of variance is to be used in place of the default conventional variance estimator (see *Methods and Formulas* below). Use of this option causes xtgee to produce valid standard errors even if the correlations within group are not as hypothesized by the specified correlation structure. It does, however, require that the model correctly specifies the mean. The resulting standard errors are thus labeled "semirobust" instead of "robust". Although there is no vce(cluster *clustvar*) option, results are as if this option were included and you specified clustering on the panel variable.

nmp; see [XT] *vce_options*.

rgf specifies that the robust variance estimate is multiplied by $(N-1)/(N-P)$, where N is the total number of observations and P is the number of coefficients estimated. This option can be used only with family(gaussian) when vce(robust) is either specified or implied by the use of pweights. Using this option implies that the robust variance estimate is not invariant to the scale of any weights used.

scale(x2 | dev | phi | #); see [XT] *vce_options*.

☐ Reporting ☐

level(#); see [XT] **estimation options**.

`eform` displays the exponentiated coefficients and corresponding standard errors and confidence intervals as described in [R] **maximize**. For `family(binomial)` `link(logit)` (i.e., logistic regression), exponentiation results in odds ratios; for `family(poisson)` `link(log)` (i.e., Poisson regression), exponentiated coefficients are incidence-rate ratios.

⌐‾‾‾‾‾‾‾‾| Opt options |‾‾‾

optimize_options control the iterative optimization process. These options are seldom used.

  <u>iter</u>ate(#) specifies the maximum number of iterations. When the number of iterations equals #, the optimization stops and presents the current results, even if convergence has not been reached. The default is `iterate(100)`.

  <u>tol</u>erance(#) specifies the tolerance for the coefficient vector. When the relative change in the coefficient vector from one iteration to the next is less than or equal to #, the optimization process is stopped. `tolerance(1e-6)` is the default.

  `nolog` suppresses display of the iteration log.

  <u>tra</u>ce specifies that the current estimates be printed at each iteration.

The following option is available with `xtgee` but is not shown in the dialog box:

`nodisplay` is for programmers. It suppresses display of the header and coefficients.

Remarks

  For a thorough introduction to GEE in the estimation of GLM, see Hardin and Hilbe (2003). More information on linear models is presented in Nelder and Wedderburn (1972). Finally, there have been several illuminating articles on various applications of GEE in Zeger, Liang, and Albert (1988); Zeger and Liang (1986), and Liang (1987). Pendergast et al. (1996) surveys the current methods for analyzing clustered data in regard to binary response data. Our implementation follows that of Liang and Zeger (1986).

  `xtgee` fits generalized linear models of y_{it} with covariates $\mathbf{x}_{it}$

$$g\{E(y_{it})\} = \mathbf{x}_{it}\boldsymbol{\beta}, \qquad y \sim F \text{ with parameters } \theta_{it}$$

for $i = 1, \ldots, m$ and $t = 1, \ldots, n_i$, where there are n_i observations for each group identifier i. $g(\ )$ is called the link function, and F is the distributional family. Substituting various definitions for $g(\ )$ and F results in a wide array of models. For instance, if y_{it} is distributed Gaussian (normal) and $g(\ )$ is the identity function, we have

$$E(y_{it}) = \mathbf{x}_{it}\boldsymbol{\beta}, \qquad y \sim N(\ )$$

yielding linear regression, random-effects regression, or other regression-related models, depending on what we assume for the correlation structure.

  If $g(\ )$ is the logit function and y_{it} is distributed Bernoulli (binomial), we have

$$\text{logit}\{E(y_{it})\} = \mathbf{x}_{it}\boldsymbol{\beta}, \qquad y \sim \text{Bernoulli}$$

or logistic regression. If $g(\ )$ is the natural log function and y_{it} is distributed Poisson, we have

$$\ln\{E(y_{it})\} = \mathbf{x}_{it}\boldsymbol{\beta}, \qquad y \sim \text{Poisson}$$

or Poisson regression, also known as the log-linear model. Other combinations are possible.

You specify the link function with the `link()` option, the distributional family with `family()`, and the assumed within-group correlation structure with `corr()`.

The binomial distribution can be specified as (1) `family(binomial)`, (2) `family(binomial #)`, or (3) `family(binomial varname)`. In case 2, `#` is the value of the binomial denominator N, the number of trials. Specifying `family(binomial 1)` is the same as specifying `family(binomial)`; both mean that y has the Bernoulli distribution with values 0 and 1 only. In case 3, *varname* is the variable containing the binomial denominator, thus allowing the number of trials to vary across observations.

The negative binomial distribution must be specified as `family(nbinomial #)`, where `#` denotes the value of the parameter α in the negative binomial distribution. The results will be conditional on this value.

You do not have to specify both `family()` and `link()`; the default `link()` is the canonical link for the specified `family()`:

Family	Canonical link
`family(binomial)`	`link(logit)`
`family(gamma)`	`link(reciprocal)`
`family(gaussian)`	`link(identity)`
`family(igaussian)`	`link(power -2)`
`family(nbinomial)`	`link(log)`
`family(poisson)`	`link(log)`

If you specify both `family()` and `link()`, not all combinations make sense. You may choose among the following combinations:

	Gaussian	Inverse Gaussian	Binomial	Poisson	Negative Binomial	Gamma
Identity	X	X	X	X	X	X
Log	X	X	X	X	X	X
Logit			X			
Probit			X			
C. log-log			X			
Power	X	X	X	X	X	X
Odds Power			X			
Neg. binom.					X	
Reciprocal	X		X	X		X

You specify the assumed within-group correlation structure with the `corr()` option.

For example, call **R** the working correlation matrix for modeling the within-group correlation, a square $\max\{n_i\} \times \max\{n_i\}$ matrix. `corr()` specifies the structure of **R**. Let $\mathbf{R}_{t,s}$ denote the t, s element.

The `independent` structure is defined as

$$\mathbf{R}_{t,s} = \begin{cases} 1 & \text{if } t = s \\ 0 & \text{otherwise} \end{cases}$$

The `corr(exchangeable)` structure (corresponding to equal-correlation models) is defined as

$$\mathbf{R}_{t,s} = \begin{cases} 1 & \text{if } t = s \\ \rho & \text{otherwise} \end{cases}$$

The `corr(ar g)` structure is defined as the usual correlation matrix for an AR(g) model. This is sometimes called multiplicative correlation. For example, an AR(1) model is given by

$$\mathbf{R}_{t,s} = \begin{cases} 1 & \text{if } t = s \\ \rho^{|t-s|} & \text{otherwise} \end{cases}$$

The `corr(stationary g)` structure is a stationary(g) model. For example, a stationary(1) model is given by

$$\mathbf{R}_{t,s} = \begin{cases} 1 & \text{if } t = s \\ \rho & \text{if } |t - s| = 1 \\ 0 & \text{otherwise} \end{cases}$$

The `corr(nonstationary g)` structure is a nonstationary(g) model that imposes only the constraints that the elements of the working correlation matrix along the diagonal be 1 and the elements outside the gth band be zero,

$$\mathbf{R}_{t,s} = \begin{cases} 1 & \text{if } t = s \\ \rho_{ts} & \text{if } 0 < |t - s| \leq g, \ \rho_{ts} = \rho_{st} \\ 0 & \text{otherwise} \end{cases}$$

`corr(unstructured)` imposes only the constraint that the diagonal elements of the working correlation matrix be 1.

$$\mathbf{R}_{t,s} = \begin{cases} 1 & \text{if } t = s \\ \rho_{ts} & \text{otherwise}, \ \rho_{ts} = \rho_{st} \end{cases}$$

The `corr(fixed matname)` specification is taken from the user-supplied matrix, such that

$$\mathbf{R} = matname$$

Here the correlations are not estimated from the data. The user-supplied matrix must be a valid correlation matrix with 1s on the diagonal.

Full formulas for all the correlation structures are provided in the *Methods and Formulas* below.

❑ Technical Note

Some `family()`, `link()`, and `corr()` combinations result in models already fitted by Stata:

family()	link()	corr()	Other Stata estimation command
gaussian	identity	independent	regress
gaussian	identity	exchangeable	xtreg, re (see note 1)
gaussian	identity	exchangeable	xtreg, pa
binomial	cloglog	independent	cloglog (see note 2)
binomial	cloglog	exchangeable	xtcloglog, pa
binomial	logit	independent	logit or logistic
binomial	logit	exchangeable	xtlogit, pa
binomial	probit	independent	probit (see note 3)
binomial	probit	exchangeable	xtprobit, pa
nbinomial	nbinomial	independent	nbreg (see note 4)
poisson	log	independent	poisson
poisson	log	exchangeable	xtpoisson, pa
gamma	log	independent	streg, dist(exp) nohr (see note 5)
family	*link*	independent	glm, irls (see note 6)

Notes:

1. These methods produce the same results only for balanced panels; see [XT] **xt**.

2. For cloglog estimation, `xtgee` with `corr(independent)` and `cloglog` (see [R] **cloglog**) will produce the same coefficients, but the standard errors will be only asymptotically equivalent because cloglog is not the canonical link for the binomial family.

3. For probit estimation, `xtgee` with `corr(independent)` and `probit` will produce the same coefficients, but the standard errors will be only asymptotically equivalent because probit is not the canonical link for the binomial family. If the binomial denominator is not 1, the equivalent maximum-likelihood command is `bprobit`; see [R] **probit** and [R] **glogit**.

4. Fitting a negative binomial model using `xtgee` (or using `glm`) will yield results conditional on the specified value of α. The `nbreg` command, however, estimates that parameter and provides unconditional estimates; see [R] **nbreg**.

5. `xtgee` with `corr(independent)` can be used to fit exponential regressions, but this requires specifying `scale(1)`. As with probit, the `xtgee`-reported standard errors will be only asymptotically equivalent to those produced by `streg, dist(exp) nohr` (see [ST] **streg**) because log is not the canonical link for the gamma family. `xtgee` cannot be used to fit exponential regressions on censored data.

   Using the `independent` correlation structure, the `xtgee` command will fit the same model fitted with the `glm, irls` command if the family–link combination is the same.

6. If the `xtgee` command is equivalent to another command, using `corr(independent)` and the `vce(robust)` option with `xtgee` corresponds to using the `vce(cluster` *clustvar*`)` option in the equivalent command, where *clustvar* corresponds to the panel variable.

   ❑

`xtgee` is a generalization of the `glm, irls` command and gives the same output when the same family and link are specified together with an independent correlation structure. What makes `xtgee` useful is

1. the number of statistical models that it generalizes for use with panel data, many of which are not otherwise available in Stata;

2. the richer correlation structure `xtgee` allows, even when models are available through other `xt` commands; and

3. the availability of robust standard errors (see [U] **20.15 Obtaining robust variance estimates**), even when the model and correlation structure are available through other `xt` commands.

In the following examples, we illustrate the relationships of `xtgee` with other Stata estimation commands. Remember that, although `xtgee` generalizes many other commands, the computational algorithm is different; therefore, the answers you obtain will not be identical. The dataset we are using is a subset of the `nlswork` data (see [XT] **xt**); we are looking at observations before 1980.

▷ Example 1

We can use `xtgee` to perform ordinary least squares by `regress`:

```
. use http://www.stata-press.com/data/r10/nlswork2
(National Longitudinal Survey.  Young Women 14-26 years of age in 1968)

. generate age2 = age*age
(9 missing values generated)
```

```
. regress ln_w grade age age2
```

Source	SS	df	MS
Model	597.54468	3	199.18156
Residual	2265.74584	16081	.14089583
Total	2863.29052	16084	.178021047

Number of obs = 16085
F(3, 16081) = 1413.68
Prob > F = 0.0000
R-squared = 0.2087
Adj R-squared = 0.2085
Root MSE = .37536

ln_wage	Coef.	Std. Err.	t	P>|t|	[95% Conf. Interval]	
grade	.0724483	.0014229	50.91	0.000	.0696592	.0752374
age	.1064874	.0083644	12.73	0.000	.0900922	.1228825
age2	-.0016931	.0001655	-10.23	0.000	-.0020174	-.0013688
_cons	-.8681487	.1024896	-8.47	0.000	-1.06904	-.6672577

```
. xtgee ln_w grade age age2, corr(indep) nmp
Iteration 1: tolerance = 1.310e-12
```

GEE population-averaged model
Group variable: idcode
Link: identity
Family: Gaussian
Correlation: independent

Number of obs   =   16085
Number of groups   =   3913
Obs per group: min =   1
                  avg =   4.1
                  max =   9
Wald chi2(3)   =   4241.04
Prob > chi2   =   0.0000

Scale parameter: .1408958

Pearson chi2(16081):   2265.75
Dispersion (Pearson):   .1408958

Deviance   =   2265.75
Dispersion   =   .1408958

ln_wage	Coef.	Std. Err.	z	P>|z|	[95% Conf. Interval]	
grade	.0724483	.0014229	50.91	0.000	.0696594	.0752372
age	.1064874	.0083644	12.73	0.000	.0900935	.1228812
age2	-.0016931	.0001655	-10.23	0.000	-.0020174	-.0013688
_cons	-.8681487	.1024896	-8.47	0.000	-1.069025	-.6672728

When nmp is specified, the coefficients and the standard errors produced by the estimators are the same. Moreover, the scale parameter estimate from the xtgee command equals the MSE calculation from regress; both are estimates of the variance of the residuals.

◁

▷ Example 2

The identity link and Gaussian family produce regression-type models. With the independent correlation structure, we reproduce ordinary least squares. With the exchangeable correlation structure, we produce an equal-correlation linear regression estimator.

xtgee, fam(gauss) link(ident) corr(exch) is asymptotically equivalent to the weighted-GLS estimator provided by xtreg, re and to the full maximum-likelihood estimator provided by xtreg, mle. In balanced data, xtgee, fam(gauss) link(ident) corr(exch) and xtreg, mle produce the same results. With unbalanced data, the results are close but differ because the two estimators handle unbalanced data differently. For both balanced and unbalanced data, the results produced by xtgee, fam(gauss) link(ident) corr(exch) and xtreg, mle differ from those produced by xtreg, re. Below we demonstrate the use of the three estimators with unbalanced data. We begin with xtgee; show the maximum likelihood estimator xtreg, mle; show the GLS estimator xtreg, re; and finally show xtgee with the vce(robust) option.

```
. xtgee ln_w grade age age2, nolog
```

GEE population-averaged model		Number of obs	=	16085
Group variable:	idcode	Number of groups	=	3913
Link:	identity	Obs per group: min	=	1
Family:	Gaussian	avg	=	4.1
Correlation:	exchangeable	max	=	9
		Wald chi2(3)	=	2918.26
Scale parameter:	.1416586	Prob > chi2	=	0.0000

ln_wage	Coef.	Std. Err.	z	P>|z|	[95% Conf. Interval]	
grade	.0717731	.00211	34.02	0.000	.0676377	.0759086
age	.1077645	.006885	15.65	0.000	.0942701	.1212589
age2	-.0016381	.0001362	-12.03	0.000	-.001905	-.0013712
_cons	-.9480449	.0869277	-10.91	0.000	-1.11842	-.7776698

```
. xtreg ln_w grade age age2, mle

Fitting constant-only model:
Iteration 0:   log likelihood = -6035.2751
Iteration 1:   log likelihood = -5870.6718
Iteration 2:   log likelihood = -5858.9478
Iteration 3:   log likelihood = -5858.8244

Fitting full model:
Iteration 0:   log likelihood = -4591.9241
Iteration 1:   log likelihood = -4562.4406
Iteration 2:   log likelihood = -4562.3526
```

Random-effects ML regression		Number of obs	=	16085
Group variable: idcode		Number of groups	=	3913
Random effects u_i ~ Gaussian		Obs per group: min	=	1
		avg	=	4.1
		max	=	9
		LR chi2(3)	=	2592.94
Log likelihood = -4562.3526		Prob > chi2	=	0.0000

ln_wage	Coef.	Std. Err.	z	P>|z|	[95% Conf. Interval]	
grade	.0717747	.0021419	33.51	0.000	.0675766	.0759728
age	.1077899	.0068265	15.79	0.000	.0944102	.1211696
age2	-.0016364	.000135	-12.12	0.000	-.0019011	-.0013718
_cons	-.9500833	.0863831	-11.00	0.000	-1.119391	-.7807755
/sigma_u	.2689639	.004085			.2610754	.2770908
/sigma_e	.2669944	.0017113			.2636613	.2703695
rho	.5036748	.0086443			.486734	.5206089

Likelihood-ratio test of sigma_u=0: chibar2(01)= 4996.22 Prob>=chibar2 = 0.000

(Continued on next page)

```
. xtreg ln_w grade age age2, re
```

| Random-effects GLS regression | | | | Number of obs | = | 16085 |
| Group variable: idcode | | | | Number of groups | = | 3913 |

R-sq: within = 0.0983				Obs per group: min =		1
between = 0.2946				avg =		4.1
overall = 0.2076				max =		9

| Random effects u_i ~ Gaussian | | | | Wald chi2(3) | = | 2875.09 |
| corr(u_i, X)   = 0 (assumed) | | | | Prob > chi2 | = | 0.0000 |

ln_wage	Coef.	Std. Err.	z	P>|z|	[95% Conf. Interval]	
grade	.0717757	.0021665	33.13	0.000	.0675295	.076022
age	.1078042	.0068126	15.82	0.000	.0944518	.1211566
age2	-.0016355	.0001347	-12.14	0.000	-.0018996	-.0013714
_cons	-.9512088	.0863141	-11.02	0.000	-1.120381	-.7820363
sigma_u	.27383336					
sigma_e	.2662536					
rho	.51403157	(fraction of variance due to u_i)				

```
. xtgee ln_w grade age age2, vce(robust) nolog
```

GEE population-averaged model				Number of obs	=	16085
Group variable:			idcode	Number of groups	=	3913
Link:			identity	Obs per group: min =		1
Family:			Gaussian	avg =		4.1
Correlation:			exchangeable	max =		9
				Wald chi2(3)	=	2031.28
Scale parameter:			.1416586	Prob > chi2	=	0.0000

(Std. Err. adjusted for clustering on idcode)

ln_wage	Coef.	Semi-robust Std. Err.	z	P>|z|	[95% Conf. Interval]	
grade	.0717731	.0023341	30.75	0.000	.0671983	.0763479
age	.1077645	.0098097	10.99	0.000	.0885379	.1269911
age2	-.0016381	.0001964	-8.34	0.000	-.002023	-.0012532
_cons	-.9480449	.1195009	-7.93	0.000	-1.182262	-.7138274

In [R] **regress**, regress, vce(cluster *clustvar*) may produce inefficient coefficient estimates with valid standard errors for random-effects models. These standard errors are robust to model misspecification. The vce(robust) option of xtgee, on the other hand, requires that the model correctly specify the mean.

◁

Saved Results

xtgee saves the following in e():

Scalars

e(N)	number of observations	e(df_pear)	degrees of freedom for Pearson χ^2
e(N_g)	number of groups	e(deviance)	deviance
e(df_m)	model degrees of freedom	e(chi2_dev)	χ^2 test of deviance
e(g_max)	largest group size	e(dispers)	deviance dispersion
e(g_min)	smallest group size	e(chi2_dis)	χ^2 test of deviance dispersion
e(g_avg)	average group size	e(tol)	target tolerance
e(rc)	return code	e(dif)	achieved tolerance
e(chi2)	χ^2	e(phi)	scale parameter

Macros

e(cmd)	xtgee	e(tvar)	time variable
e(cmdline)	command as typed	e(vce)	*vcetype* specified in vce()
e(depvar)	name of dependent variable	e(vcetype)	title used to label Std. Err.
e(family)	distribution family	e(chi2type)	Wald; type of model χ^2 test
e(link)	link function	e(offset)	offset
e(wtype)	weight type	e(crittype)	optimization criterion
e(wexp)	weight expression	e(properties)	b V
e(corr)	correlation structure	e(estat_cmd)	program used to implement estat
e(scale)	x2, dev, phi, or #; scale parameter	e(predict)	program used to implement predict
e(ivar)	variable denoting groups		

Matrices

e(b)	coefficient vector	e(R)	estimated working correlation matrix
e(V)	variance–covariance matrix of the estimators		

Functions

e(sample)	marks estimation sample

Methods and Formulas

xtgee is implemented as an ado-file.

xtgee fits general linear models for panel data with the GEE approach described in Liang and Zeger (1986). A related method, referred to as GEE2, is described in Zhao and Prentice (1990) and Prentice and Zhao (1991). The GEE2 method attempts to gain efficiency in the estimation of β by specifying a parametric model for α and then assumes that the models for both the mean and dependency parameters are correct. Thus there is a tradeoff in robustness for efficiency. The preliminary work of Liang, Zeger, and Qaqish (1987), however, indicates that there is little efficiency gained with this alternative approach.

In the GLM approach (see McCullagh and Nelder 1989), we assume that

$$h(\boldsymbol{\mu}_{i,j}) = x_{i,j}^{\mathrm{T}}\boldsymbol{\beta}$$

$$\mathrm{Var}(y_{i,j}) = g(\mu_{i,j})\phi$$

$$\boldsymbol{\mu}_i = E(\mathbf{y}_i) = \{h^{-1}(x_{i,1}^{\mathrm{T}}\boldsymbol{\beta}), \ldots, h^{-1}(x_{i,n_i}^{\mathrm{T}}\boldsymbol{\beta})\}^{\mathrm{T}}$$

$$\mathbf{A}_i = \mathrm{diag}\{g(\mu_{i,1}), \ldots, g(\mu_{i,n_i})\}$$

$$\mathrm{Cov}(\mathbf{y}_i) = \phi\mathbf{A}_i \quad \text{for independent observations.}$$

In the absence of a convenient likelihood function with which to work, we can rely on a multivariate analog of the quasiscore function introduced by Wedderburn (1974):

$$\mathbf{S}_{\boldsymbol{\beta}}(\boldsymbol{\beta}, \boldsymbol{\alpha}) = \sum_{i=1}^{m} \left(\frac{\partial \boldsymbol{\mu}_i}{\partial \boldsymbol{\beta}} \right)^{\mathrm{T}} \mathrm{Var}(\mathbf{y}_i)^{-1}(\mathbf{y}_i - \boldsymbol{\mu}_i) = 0$$

We can solve for correlation parameters $\boldsymbol{\alpha}$ by simultaneously solving

$$\mathbf{S}_{\boldsymbol{\alpha}}(\boldsymbol{\beta}, \boldsymbol{\alpha}) = \sum_{i=1}^{m} \left(\frac{\partial \boldsymbol{\eta}_i}{\partial \boldsymbol{\alpha}} \right)^{\mathrm{T}} \mathbf{H}_i^{-1}(\mathbf{W}_i - \boldsymbol{\eta}_i) = 0$$

In the GEE approach to GLM, we let $\mathbf{R}_i(\boldsymbol{\alpha})$ be a "working" correlation matrix depending on the parameters in $\boldsymbol{\alpha}$ (see the *Correlation structures* section for the number of parameters), and we estimate $\boldsymbol{\beta}$ by solving the GEE,

$$\mathbf{U}(\boldsymbol{\beta}) = \sum_{i=1}^{m} \frac{\partial \boldsymbol{\mu}_i}{\partial \boldsymbol{\beta}} \mathbf{V}_i^{-1}(\boldsymbol{\alpha})(\mathbf{y}_i - \boldsymbol{\mu}_i) = 0$$
$$\text{where} \quad \mathbf{V}_i(\boldsymbol{\alpha}) = \mathbf{A}_i^{1/2} \mathbf{R}_i(\boldsymbol{\alpha}) \mathbf{A}_i^{1/2}$$

To solve this equation, we need only a crude approximation of the variance matrix, which we can obtain from a Taylor series expansion, where

$$\mathrm{Cov}(\mathbf{y}_i) = \mathbf{L}_i \mathbf{Z}_i \mathbf{D}_i \mathbf{Z}_i^{\mathrm{T}} \mathbf{L}_i + \phi \mathbf{A}_i = \widetilde{\mathbf{V}}_i$$
$$\mathbf{L}_i = \mathrm{diag}\{\partial h^{-1}(u)/\partial u, u = x_{i,j}^{\mathrm{T}} \boldsymbol{\beta}, j = 1, \ldots, n_i\}$$

which allows that

$$\widehat{\mathbf{D}}_i \approx (\mathbf{Z}_i^{\mathrm{T}} \mathbf{Z}_i)^{-1} \mathbf{Z}_i \widehat{\mathbf{L}}_i^{-1} \left\{ (\mathbf{y}_i - \widehat{\boldsymbol{\mu}}_i)(\mathbf{y}_i - \widehat{\boldsymbol{\mu}}_i)^{\mathrm{T}} - \widehat{\phi} \widehat{\mathbf{A}}_i \right\} \widehat{\mathbf{L}}_i^{-1} \mathbf{Z}_i^{\mathrm{T}} (\mathbf{Z}_i' \mathbf{Z}_i)^{-1}$$
$$\widehat{\phi} = \sum_{i=1}^{m} \sum_{j=1}^{n_i} \frac{(y_{i,j} - \widehat{\mu}_{i,j})^2 - (\widehat{\mathbf{L}}_{i,j})^2 \mathbf{Z}_{i,j}^{\mathrm{T}} \widehat{\mathbf{D}}_i \mathbf{Z}_{i,j}}{g(\widehat{\mu}_{i,j})}$$

Calculating GEE for GLM

Using the notation from Liang and Zeger (1986), let $\mathbf{y}_i = (y_{i,1}, \ldots, y_{i,n_i})^{\mathrm{T}}$ be the $n_i \times 1$ vector of outcome values, and let $\mathbf{X}_i = (x_{i,1}, \ldots, x_{i,n_i})^{\mathrm{T}}$ be the $n_i \times p$ matrix of covariate values for the ith subject $i = 1, \ldots, m$. We assume that the marginal density for $y_{i,j}$ may be written in exponential family notation as

$$f(y_{i,j}) = \exp\left[\{y_{i,j}\theta_{i,j} - a(\theta_{i,j}) + b(y_{i,j})\} \phi\right]$$

where $\theta_{i,j} = h(\eta_{i,j}), \eta_{i,j} = x_{i,j}\boldsymbol{\beta}$. Under this formulation, the first two moments are given by

$$E(y_{i,j}) = a'(\theta_{i,j}), \qquad \mathrm{Var}(y_{i,j}) = a''(\theta_{i,j})/\phi$$

We define the quantities, assuming that we have an $n \times n$ working correlation matrix $\mathbf{R}(\boldsymbol{\alpha})$,

$$\boldsymbol{\Delta}_i = \text{diag}(d\theta_{i,j}/d\eta_{i,j}) \qquad n \times n \text{ matrix}$$

$$\mathbf{A}_i = \text{diag}\{a''(\theta_{i,j})\} \qquad n \times n \text{ matrix}$$

$$\mathbf{S}_i = \mathbf{y}_i - a'(\boldsymbol{\theta}_i) \qquad n \times 1 \text{ matrix}$$

$$\mathbf{D}_i = \mathbf{A}_i \boldsymbol{\Delta}_i \mathbf{X}_i \qquad n \times p \text{ matrix}$$

$$\mathbf{V}_i = \mathbf{A}_i^{1/2}\mathbf{R}(\boldsymbol{\alpha})\mathbf{A}_i^{1/2} \qquad n \times n \text{ matrix}$$

such that the GEE becomes

$$\sum_{i=1}^{m} \mathbf{D}_i^{\mathrm{T}}\mathbf{V}_i^{-1}\mathbf{S}_i = 0$$

We then have that

$$\widehat{\boldsymbol{\beta}}_{j+1} = \widehat{\boldsymbol{\beta}}_j - \left\{\sum_{i=1}^{m}\mathbf{D}_i^{\mathrm{T}}(\widehat{\boldsymbol{\beta}}_j)\widetilde{\mathbf{V}}_i^{-1}(\widehat{\boldsymbol{\beta}}_j)\mathbf{D}_i(\widehat{\boldsymbol{\beta}}_j)\right\}^{-1} \left\{\sum_{i=1}^{m}\mathbf{D}_i^{\mathrm{T}}(\widehat{\boldsymbol{\beta}}_j)\widetilde{\mathbf{V}}_i^{-1}(\widehat{\boldsymbol{\beta}}_j)\mathbf{S}_i(\widehat{\boldsymbol{\beta}}_j)\right\}$$

where the term

$$\left\{\sum_{i=1}^{m}\mathbf{D}_i^{\mathrm{T}}(\widehat{\boldsymbol{\beta}}_j)\widetilde{\mathbf{V}}_i^{-1}(\widehat{\boldsymbol{\beta}}_j)\mathbf{D}_i(\widehat{\boldsymbol{\beta}}_j)\right\}^{-1}$$

is what we call the conventional variance estimate. It is used to calculate the standard errors if the `robust` option is not specified. See Liang and Zeger (1986) for the calculation of the robust variance estimator.

Define the following:

$$\mathbf{D} = (\mathbf{D}_1^{\mathrm{T}}, \dots, \mathbf{D}_m^{\mathrm{T}})$$

$$\mathbf{S} = (\mathbf{S}_1^{\mathrm{T}}, \dots, \mathbf{S}_m^{\mathrm{T}})^{\mathrm{T}}$$

$$\widetilde{\mathbf{V}} = nm \times nm \text{ block diagonal matrix with } \widetilde{\mathbf{V}}_i$$

$$\mathbf{Z} = \mathbf{D}\boldsymbol{\beta} - \mathbf{S}$$

At a given iteration, the correlation parameters $\boldsymbol{\alpha}$ and scale parameter ϕ can be estimated from the current Pearson residuals, defined by

$$\widehat{r}_{i,j} = \{y_{i,j} - a'(\widehat{\theta}_{i,j})\}/\{a''(\widehat{\theta}_{i,j})\}^{1/2}$$

where $\widehat{\theta}_{i,j}$ depends on the current value for $\widehat{\boldsymbol{\beta}}$. We can then estimate ϕ by

$$\widehat{\phi}^{-1} = \sum_{i=1}^{m}\sum_{j=1}^{n_i} \widehat{r}_{i,j}^2/(N-p)$$

As this general derivation is complicated, let's follow the derivation of the Gaussian family with the identity link (regression) to illustrate the generalization. After making appropriate substitutions, we will see a familiar updating equation. First, we rewrite the updating equation for β as

$$\widehat{\boldsymbol{\beta}}_{j+1} = \widehat{\boldsymbol{\beta}}_j - \mathbf{Z}_1^{-1}\mathbf{Z}_2$$

and then derive $\mathbf{Z}_1$ and $\mathbf{Z}_2$.

$$
\begin{aligned}
\mathbf{Z}_1 &= \sum_{i=1}^{m} \mathbf{D}_i^{\mathsf{T}}(\widehat{\beta}_j) \widetilde{\mathbf{V}}_i^{-1}(\widehat{\beta}_j) \mathbf{D}_i(\widehat{\beta}_j) = \sum_{i=1}^{m} \mathbf{X}_i^{\mathsf{T}} \boldsymbol{\Delta}_i^{\mathsf{T}} \mathbf{A}_i^{\mathsf{T}} \{\mathbf{A}_i^{1/2} \mathbf{R}(\boldsymbol{\alpha}) \mathbf{A}_i^{1/2}\}^{-1} \mathbf{A}_i \boldsymbol{\Delta}_i \mathbf{X}_i \\
&= \sum_{i=1}^{m} \mathbf{X}_i^{\mathsf{T}} \operatorname{diag}\left\{\frac{\partial \theta_{i,j}}{\partial (\mathbf{X}\boldsymbol{\beta})}\right\} \operatorname{diag}\{a''(\theta_{i,j})\} \left[\operatorname{diag}\{a''(\theta_{i,j})\}^{1/2} \mathbf{R}(\boldsymbol{\alpha}) \operatorname{diag}\{a''(\theta_{i,j})\}^{1/2}\right]^{-1} \\
&\qquad \operatorname{diag}\{a''(\theta_{i,j})\} \operatorname{diag}\left\{\frac{\partial \theta_{i,j}}{\partial (\mathbf{X}\boldsymbol{\beta})}\right\} \mathbf{X}_i \\
&= \sum_{i=1}^{m} \mathbf{X}_i^{\mathsf{T}} \mathbf{II}(\mathbf{III})^{-1} \mathbf{II} \mathbf{X}_i = \sum_{i=1}^{m} \mathbf{X}_i^{\mathsf{T}} \mathbf{X}_i = \mathbf{X}^{\mathsf{T}} \mathbf{X}
\end{aligned}
$$

$$
\begin{aligned}
\mathbf{Z}_2 &= \sum_{i=1}^{m} \mathbf{D}_i^{\mathsf{T}}(\widehat{\beta}_j) \widetilde{\mathbf{V}}_i^{-1}(\widehat{\beta}_j) \mathbf{S}_i(\widehat{\beta}_j) = \sum_{i=1}^{m} \mathbf{X}_i^{\mathsf{T}} \boldsymbol{\Delta}_i^{\mathsf{T}} \mathbf{A}_i^{\mathsf{T}} \{\mathbf{A}_i^{1/2} \mathbf{R}(\boldsymbol{\alpha}) \mathbf{A}_i^{1/2}\}^{-1} \left(\mathbf{y}_i - \mathbf{X}_i \widehat{\beta}_j\right) \\
&= \sum_{i=1}^{m} \mathbf{X}_i^{\mathsf{T}} \operatorname{diag}\left\{\frac{\partial \theta_{i,j}}{\partial (\mathbf{X}\boldsymbol{\beta})}\right\} \operatorname{diag}\{a''(\theta_{i,j})\} \left[\operatorname{diag}\{a''(\theta_{i,j})\}^{1/2} \mathbf{R}(\boldsymbol{\alpha}) \operatorname{diag}\{a''(\theta_{i,j})\}^{1/2}\right]^{-1} \\
&\qquad \left(\mathbf{y}_i - \mathbf{X}_i \widehat{\beta}_j\right) \\
&= \sum_{i=1}^{m} \mathbf{X}_i \mathbf{II}(\mathbf{III})^{-1} (\mathbf{y}_i - \mathbf{X}_i \widehat{\beta}_j) = \sum_{i=1}^{m} \mathbf{X}_i^{\mathsf{T}} (\mathbf{y}_i - \mathbf{X}_i \widehat{\beta}_j) = \mathbf{X}^{\mathsf{T}} \widehat{s}_j
\end{aligned}
$$

So, we may write the update formula as

$$
\widehat{\beta}_{j+1} = \widehat{\beta}_j - (\mathbf{X}^{\mathsf{T}} \mathbf{X})^{-1} \mathbf{X}^{\mathsf{T}} \widehat{s}_j
$$

which is the same formula for GLS in regression.

Correlation structures

The working correlation matrix $\mathbf{R}$ is a function of $\boldsymbol{\alpha}$ and is more accurately written as $\mathbf{R}(\boldsymbol{\alpha})$. Depending on the assumed correlation structure, $\boldsymbol{\alpha}$ might be

Independent	no parameters to estimate
Exchangeable	$\boldsymbol{\alpha}$ is a scalar
Autoregressive	$\boldsymbol{\alpha}$ is a vector
Stationary	$\boldsymbol{\alpha}$ is a vector
Nonstationary	$\boldsymbol{\alpha}$ is a matrix
Unstructured	$\boldsymbol{\alpha}$ is a matrix

Also, throughout the estimation of a general unbalanced panel, it is more proper to discuss $\mathbf{R}_i$, which is the upper left $n_i \times n_i$ submatrix of the ultimately saved matrix in e(R), $\max\{n_i\} \times \max\{n_i\}$.

The only panels that enter into the estimation for a lag-dependent correlation structure are those with $n_i > g$ (assuming a lag of g). xtgee drops panels with too few observations (and mentions when it does so).

Independent

The working correlation matrix $\mathbf{R}$ is an identity matrix.

Exchangeable

$$\alpha = \sum_{i=1}^{m} \left\{ \frac{\sum_{j=1}^{n_i} \sum_{k=1}^{n_i} \widehat{r}_{i,j}\widehat{r}_{i,k} - \sum_{j=1}^{n_i} \widehat{r}_{i,j}^2}{n_i(n_i-1)} \right\} \Bigg/ \left(\sum_{i=1}^{m} \frac{\sum_{j=1}^{n_i} \widehat{r}_{i,j}^2}{n_i} \right)$$

and the working correlation matrix is given by

$$\mathbf{R}_{s,t} = \begin{cases} 1 & s = t \\ \alpha & \text{otherwise} \end{cases}$$

Autoregressive and stationary

These two structures require g parameters to be estimated so that α is a vector of length $g+1$ (the first element of α is 1).

$$\alpha = \sum_{i=1}^{m} \left(\frac{\sum_{j=1}^{n_i} \widehat{r}_{i,j}^2}{n_i} , \frac{\sum_{j=1}^{n_i-1} \widehat{r}_{i,j}\widehat{r}_{i,j+1}}{n_i} , \dots , \frac{\sum_{j=1}^{n_i-g} \widehat{r}_{i,j}\widehat{r}_{i,j+g}}{n_i} \right) \Bigg/ \left(\sum_{i=1}^{m} \frac{\sum_{j=1}^{n_i} \widehat{r}_{i,j}^2}{n_i} \right)$$

The working correlation matrix for the AR model is calculated as a function of Toeplitz matrices formed from the α vector, see Newton (1988). The working correlation matrix for the stationary model is given by

$$\mathbf{R}_{s,t} = \begin{cases} \alpha_{1,|s-t|} & \text{if } |s-t| \leq g \\ 0 & \text{otherwise} \end{cases}$$

Nonstationary and unstructured

These two correlation structures require a matrix of parameters. α is estimated (where we replace $\widehat{r}_{i,j} = 0$ whenever $i > n_i$ or $j > n_i$) as

$$\alpha = \sum_{i=1}^{m} m \begin{pmatrix} N_{1,1}^{-1}\widehat{r}_{i,1}^2 & N_{1,2}^{-1}\widehat{r}_{i,1}\widehat{r}_{i,2} & \cdots & N_{1,n}^{-1}\widehat{r}_{i,1}\widehat{r}_{i,n} \\ N_{2,1}^{-1}\widehat{r}_{i,2}\widehat{r}_{i,1} & N_{2,2}^{-1}\widehat{r}_{i,2}^2 & \cdots & N_{2,n}^{-1}\widehat{r}_{i,2}\widehat{r}_{i,n} \\ \vdots & \vdots & \ddots & \vdots \\ N_{n,1}^{-1}\widehat{r}_{i,n_i}\widehat{r}_{i,1} & N_{n,2}^{-1}\widehat{r}_{i,n_i}\widehat{r}_{i,2} & \cdots & N_{n,n}^{-1}\widehat{r}_{i,n}^2 \end{pmatrix} \Bigg/ \left(\sum_{i=1}^{m} \frac{\sum_{j=1}^{n_i} \widehat{r}_{i,j}^2}{n_i} \right)$$

where $N_{p,q} = \sum_{i=1}^{m} I(i,p,q)$ and

$$I(i,p,q) = \begin{cases} 1 & \text{if panel } i \text{ has valid observations at times p and q} \\ 0 & \text{otherwise} \end{cases}$$

where $N_{i,j} = \min(N_i, N_j)$, N_i = number of panels observed at time i, and $n = \max(n_1, n_2, \dots, n_m)$.

The working correlation matrix for the nonstationary model is given by

$$\mathbf{R}_{s,t} = \begin{cases} 1 & \text{if } s = t \\ \alpha_{s,t} & \text{if } 0 < |s-t| \leq g \\ 0 & \text{otherwise} \end{cases}$$

The working correlation matrix for the unstructured model is given by

$$\mathbf{R}_{s,t} = \begin{cases} 1 & \text{if } s = t \\ \alpha_{s,t} & \text{otherwise} \end{cases}$$

such that the unstructured model is equal to the nonstationary model at lag $g = n - 1$, where the panels are balanced with $n_i = n$ for all i.

References

Hardin, J. W. 2002. The robust variance estimator for two-stage models. *Stata Journal* 2: 253–266.

Hardin, J. W., and J. M. Hilbe. 2003. *Generalized Estimating Equations.* Boca Raton, FL: Chapman & Hall/CRC.

Hosmer, D. W., Jr., and S. Lemeshow. 2002. *Applied Logistic Regression.* 2nd ed. New York: Wiley.

Kleinbaum, D. G., and M. Klein. 2002. *Logistic Regression: A Self-Learning Text.* 2nd ed. New York: Springer.

Liang, K.-Y. 1987. Estimating functions and approximate conditional likelihood. *Biometrika* 4: 695–702.

Liang, K.-Y., and S. L. Zeger. 1986. Longitudinal data analysis using generalized linear models. *Biometrika* 73: 13–22.

Liang, K.-Y., S. L. Zeger, and B. Qaqish. 1987. Multivariate regression analyses for categorical data. *Journal of the Royal Statistical Society, Series B* 54: 3–40.

McCullagh, P., and J. A. Nelder. 1989. *Generalized Linear Models.* 2nd ed. London: Chapman & Hall/CRC.

Nelder, J. A., and R. W. M. Wedderburn. 1972. Generalized linear models. *Journal of the Royal Statistical Society, Series A* 135: 370–384.

Newton, H. J. 1988. *TIMESLAB: A Time Series Analysis Laboratory.* Belmont, CA: Brooks/Cole.

Pendergast, J. F., S. J. Gange, M. A. Newton, M. J. Lindstrom, M. Palta, and M. R. Fisher. 1996. A survey of methods for analyzing clustered binary response data. *International Statistical Review* 64: 89–118.

Prentice, R. L., and L. P. Zhao. 1991. Estimating equations for parameters in means and covariances of multivariate discrete and continuous responses. *Biometrics* 47: 825–839.

Rabe-Hesketh, S., A. Pickles, and C. Taylor. 2000. sg129: Generalized linear latent and mixed models. *Stata Technical Bulletin* 53: 47–57. Reprinted in *Stata Technical Bulletin Reprints*, vol. 9, pp. 293–307.

Rabe-Hesketh, S., A. Skrondal, and A. Pickles. 2002. Reliable estimation of generalized linear mixed models using adaptive quadrature. *Stata Journal* 2: 1–21.

Twisk, J. W. R. 2003. *Applied Longitudinal Data Analysis for Epidemiology: A Practical Guide.* Cambridge: Cambridge University Press.

Wedderburn, R. W. M. 1974. Quasi-likelihood functions, generalized linear models, and the Gauss–Newton method. *Biometrika* 61: 439–447.

Zeger, S. L., and K.-Y. Liang. 1986. Longitudinal data analysis for discrete and continuous outcomes. *Biometrics* 42: 121–130.

Zeger, S. L., K.-Y. Liang, and P. S. Albert. 1988. Models for longitudinal data: A generalized estimating equation approach. *Biometrics* 44: 1049–1060.

Zhao, L. P., and R. L. Prentice. 1990. Correlated binary regression using a quadratic exponential model. *Biometrika* 77: 642–648.

Also See

Title

xtgee postestimation — Postestimation tools for xtgee

Description

The following postestimation command is of special interest after `xtgee`:

command	description
estat wcorrelation	estimated matrix of the within-group correlations

For information about `estat wcorrelation`, see below.

The following standard postestimation commands are also available:

command	description
adjust[1]	adjusted predictions of $\mathbf{x}\beta$, probabilities, or $\exp(\mathbf{x}\beta)$
estat	VCE and estimation sample summary
estimates	cataloging estimation results
hausman	Hausman's specification test
lincom	point estimates, standard errors, testing, and inference for linear combinations of coefficients
mfx	marginal effects or elasticities
nlcom	point estimates, standard errors, testing, and inference for nonlinear combinations of coefficients
predict	predictions, residuals, influence statistics, and other diagnostic measures
predictnl	point estimates, standard errors, testing, and inference for generalized predictions
test	Wald tests for simple and composite linear hypotheses
testnl	Wald tests of nonlinear hypotheses

[1] `adjust` is not appropriate with time-series operators.

See the corresponding entries in the *Stata Base Reference Manual* for details.

Special-interest postestimation commands

`estat wcorrelation` displays the estimated matrix of the within-group correlations.

Syntax for predict

predict [*type*] *newvar* [*if*] [*in*] [, *statistic* <u>nooff</u>set]

statistic	description
Main	
mu	predicted value of *depvar*; considers the offset() or exposure(); the default
rate	predicted value of *depvar*
xb	linear prediction
stdp	standard error of the linear prediction
score	first derivative of the log likelihood with respect to $\mathbf{x}_j\beta$

These statistics are available both in and out of sample; type predict ... if e(sample) ... if wanted only for the estimation sample.

Options for predict

⌐ Main ⌐

mu, the default, and rate calculate the predicted value of *depvar*. mu takes into account the offset() or exposure() together with the denominator if the family is binomial; rate ignores those adjustments. mu and rate are equivalent if (1) you did not specify offset() or exposure() when you fitted the xtgee model and (2) you did not specify family(binomial #) or family(binomial *varname*), meaning the binomial family and a denominator not equal to one.

Thus mu and rate are the same for link(identity) family(gaussian).

mu and rate are not equivalent for link(logit) family(binomial pop). Then mu would predict the number of positive outcomes and rate would predict the probability of a positive outcome.

mu and rate are not equivalent for link(log) family(poisson) exposure(time). Then mu would predict the number of events given exposure time and rate would calculate the incidence rate—the number of events given an exposure time of 1.

xb calculates the linear prediction.

stdp calculates the standard error of the linear prediction.

score calculates the equation-level score, $u_j = \partial \ln L_j(\mathbf{x}_j\beta)/\partial(\mathbf{x}_j\beta)$.

nooffset is relevant only if you specified offset(*varname*), exposure(*varname*), family(binomial #), or family(binomial *varname*) when you fitted the model. It modifies the calculations made by predict so that they ignore the offset or exposure variable and the binomial denominator. Thus predict ... , mu nooffset produces the same results as predict ... , rate.

Syntax for estat wcorrelation

    estat wcorrelation [, compact format(%*fmt*)]

Options for estat wcorrelation

compact specifies that only the parameters (alpha) of the estimated matrix of within-group correlations be displayed rather than the entire matrix.

format(%*fmt*) overrides the display format; see [D] **format**.

Remarks

▷ Example 1

xtgee can estimate rich correlation structures. In example 2 of [XT] **xtgee**, we fitted the model

```
. use http://www.stata-press.com/data/r10/nlswork2
(National Longitudinal Survey.  Young Women 14-26 years of age in 1968)

. generate age2 = age*age
(9 missing values generated)

. xtgee ln_w grade age age2
  (output omitted )
```

After estimation, `estat wcorrelation` reports the working correlation matrix **R**:

```
. estat wcorrelation

Estimated within-idcode correlation matrix R:

            c1         c2         c3         c4         c5         c6

   r1         1
   r2  .4851356          1
   r3  .4851356   .4851356          1
   r4  .4851356   .4851356   .4851356          1
   r5  .4851356   .4851356   .4851356   .4851356          1
   r6  .4851356   .4851356   .4851356   .4851356   .4851356          1
   r7  .4851356   .4851356   .4851356   .4851356   .4851356   .4851356
   r8  .4851356   .4851356   .4851356   .4851356   .4851356   .4851356
   r9  .4851356   .4851356   .4851356   .4851356   .4851356   .4851356

            c7         c8         c9

   r7         1
   r8  .4851356          1
   r9  .4851356   .4851356          1
```

The equal-correlation model corresponds to an exchangeable correlation structure, meaning that the correlation of observations within person is a constant. The working correlation estimated by **xtgee** is 0.4851. (**xtreg, re**, by comparison, reports .5140.) We constrained the model to have this simple correlation structure. What if we relaxed the constraint? To go to the other extreme, let's place no constraints on the matrix (other than its being symmetric). We do this by specifying `correlation(unstructured)`, although we can abbreviate the option.

```
. xtgee ln_w grade age age2, corr(unstr) nolog
GEE population-averaged model          Number of obs      =        16085
Group and time vars:        idcode year Number of groups   =         3913
Link:                          identity Obs per group: min =            1
Family:                        Gaussian                avg =          4.1
Correlation:               unstructured                max =            9
                                        Wald chi2(3)       =      2405.20
Scale parameter:                .1418513 Prob > chi2       =       0.0000

     ln_wage |      Coef.   Std. Err.      z    P>|z|     [95% Conf. Interval]
-------------+----------------------------------------------------------------
       grade |   .0720684    .002151    33.50   0.000     .0678525    .0762843
         age |   .1008095   .0081471    12.37   0.000     .0848416    .1167775
        age2 |  -.0015104   .0001617    -9.34   0.000    -.0018272   -.0011936
       _cons |  -.8645484   .1009488    -8.56   0.000    -1.062404   -.6666923
```

```
. estat wcorrelation
```

Estimated within-idcode correlation matrix R:

	c1	c2	c3	c4	c5	c6
r1	1					
r2	.4354838	1				
r3	.4280248	.5597329	1			
r4	.3772342	.5012129	.5475113	1		
r5	.4031433	.5301403	.502668	.6216227	1	
r6	.3663686	.4519138	.4783186	.5685009	.7306005	1
r7	.2819915	.3605743	.3918118	.4012104	.4642561	.50219
r8	.3162028	.3445668	.4285424	.4389241	.4696792	.5222537
r9	.2148737	.3078491	.3337292	.3584013	.4865802	.4613128

	c7	c8	c9
r7	1		
r8	.6475654	1	
r9	.5791417	.7386595	1

This correlation matrix looks different from the previously constrained one and shows, in particular, that the serial correlation of the residuals diminishes as the lag increases, although residuals separated by small lags are more correlated than, say, AR(1) would imply.

◁

▷ Example 2

In [XT] **xtprobit**, we showed a random-effects model of unionization using the union data described in [XT] **xt**. We performed the estimation using xtprobit but said that we could have used xtgee as well. Here we fit a population-averaged (equal correlation) model for comparison:

```
. use http://www.stata-press.com/data/r10/union, clear
(NLS Women 14-24 in 1968)

. xtgee union age grade not_smsa south southXt, family(binomial) link(probit)

Iteration 1: tolerance = .04796083
Iteration 2: tolerance = .00352657
Iteration 3: tolerance = .00017886
Iteration 4: tolerance = 8.654e-06
Iteration 5: tolerance = 4.150e-07
```

GEE population-averaged model				Number of obs	=	26200
Group variable:			idcode	Number of groups	=	4434
Link:			probit	Obs per group: min	=	1
Family:			binomial	avg	=	5.9
Correlation:			exchangeable	max	=	12
				Wald chi2(5)	=	241.66
Scale parameter:			1	Prob > chi2	=	0.0000

union	Coef.	Std. Err.	z	P>|z|	[95% Conf. Interval]	
age	.0031597	.0014678	2.15	0.031	.0002829	.0060366
grade	.0329992	.0062334	5.29	0.000	.020782	.0452163
not_smsa	-.0721799	.0275189	-2.62	0.009	-.1261159	-.0182439
south	-.409029	.0372213	-10.99	0.000	-.4819815	-.3360765
southXt	.0081828	.002545	3.22	0.001	.0031946	.0131709
_cons	-1.184799	.0890117	-13.31	0.000	-1.359259	-1.01034

Let us look at the correlation structure and then relax it:

```
. estat wcorrelation, format(%8.4f)
Estimated within-idcode correlation matrix R:
```

	c1	c2	c3	c4	c5	c6	c7
r1	1.0000						
r2	0.4630	1.0000					
r3	0.4630	0.4630	1.0000				
r4	0.4630	0.4630	0.4630	1.0000			
r5	0.4630	0.4630	0.4630	0.4630	1.0000		
r6	0.4630	0.4630	0.4630	0.4630	0.4630	1.0000	
r7	0.4630	0.4630	0.4630	0.4630	0.4630	0.4630	1.0000
r8	0.4630	0.4630	0.4630	0.4630	0.4630	0.4630	0.4630
r9	0.4630	0.4630	0.4630	0.4630	0.4630	0.4630	0.4630
r10	0.4630	0.4630	0.4630	0.4630	0.4630	0.4630	0.4630
r11	0.4630	0.4630	0.4630	0.4630	0.4630	0.4630	0.4630
r12	0.4630	0.4630	0.4630	0.4630	0.4630	0.4630	0.4630

	c8	c9	c10	c11	c12
r8	1.0000				
r9	0.4630	1.0000			
r10	0.4630	0.4630	1.0000		
r11	0.4630	0.4630	0.4630	1.0000	
r12	0.4630	0.4630	0.4630	0.4630	1.0000

We estimate the fixed correlation between observations within person to be 0.4630. We have many data (an average of 5.9 observations on 4,434 women), so estimating the full correlation matrix is feasible. Let's do that and then examine the results:

```
. xtgee union age grade not_smsa south southXt, family(binomial) link(probit)
> corr(unstr) nolog
```

```
GEE population-averaged model                    Number of obs      =      26200
Group and time vars:              idcode t0       Number of groups   =       4434
Link:                                 probit      Obs per group: min =          1
Family:                             binomial                     avg =        5.9
Correlation:                    unstructured                     max =         12
                                                  Wald chi2(5)       =     196.76
Scale parameter:                           1      Prob > chi2        =     0.0000
```

union	Coef.	Std. Err.	z	P>|z|	[95% Conf. Interval]	
age	.0020207	.0019768	1.02	0.307	-.0018539	.0058952
grade	.0349572	.0065627	5.33	0.000	.0220946	.0478198
not_smsa	-.0951058	.0291532	-3.26	0.001	-.152245	-.0379665
south	-.3891526	.0434868	-8.95	0.000	-.4743853	-.30392
southXt	.0078823	.0034032	2.32	0.021	.0012121	.0145524
_cons	-1.194276	.1000155	-11.94	0.000	-1.390303	-.9982495

```
. estat wcorrelation, format(%8.4f)
```

Estimated within-idcode correlation matrix R:

	c1	c2	c3	c4	c5	c6	c7
r1	1.0000						
r2	0.6796	1.0000					
r3	0.6272	0.6628	1.0000				
r4	0.5365	0.5800	0.6170	1.0000			
r5	0.3377	0.3716	0.4037	0.4810	1.0000		
r6	0.3079	0.3771	0.4283	0.4591	0.6435	1.0000	
r7	0.3053	0.3630	0.3887	0.4299	0.4949	0.6407	1.0000
r8	0.2807	0.3062	0.3251	0.3762	0.4691	0.5610	0.7000
r9	0.3045	0.3013	0.3042	0.3822	0.4620	0.5101	0.6093
r10	0.2324	0.2630	0.2779	0.3655	0.3987	0.4921	0.5878
r11	0.2369	0.2321	0.2716	0.3265	0.3555	0.4425	0.5094
r12	0.2400	0.2374	0.2561	0.3153	0.3478	0.3835	0.4782

	c8	c9	c10	c11	c12
r8	1.0000				
r9	0.6709	1.0000			
r10	0.5957	0.6308	1.0000		
r11	0.5607	0.5740	0.5706	1.0000	
r12	0.4985	0.5404	0.5302	0.6406	1.0000

As before, we find that the correlation of residuals decreases as the lag increases, but more slowly than an AR(1) process.

◁

▷ Example 3

In this example, we examine injury incidents among 20 airlines in each of 4 years. The data are fictional, and, as a matter of fact, are really from a random-effects model.

```
. use http://www.stata-press.com/data/r10/airacc
. generate lnpm = ln(pmiles)
. xtgee i_cnt inprog, family(poisson) eform offset(lnpm) nolog
```

GEE population-averaged model				Number of obs	=	80
Group variable:			airline	Number of groups	=	20
Link:			log	Obs per group: min =		4
Family:			Poisson	avg =		4.0
Correlation:			exchangeable	max =		4
				Wald chi2(1)	=	5.27
Scale parameter:			1	Prob > chi2	=	0.0217

i_cnt	IRR	Std. Err.	z	P>|z|	[95% Conf. Interval]	
inprog	.9059936	.0389528	-2.30	0.022	.8327758	.9856487
lnpm	(offset)					

```
. estat wcorrelation
```

Estimated within-airline correlation matrix R:

	c1	c2	c3	c4
r1	1			
r2	.4606406	1		
r3	.4606406	.4606406	1	
r4	.4606406	.4606406	.4606406	1

Now there are not really enough data here to reliably estimate the correlation without any constraints of structure, but here is what happens if we try:

```
. xtgee i_cnt inprog, family(poisson) eform offset(lnpm) corr(unstr) nolog
GEE population-averaged model              Number of obs      =        80
Group and time vars:          airline time  Number of groups   =        20
Link:                                  log  Obs per group: min =         4
Family:                             Poisson                avg =       4.0
Correlation:                  unstructured                max =         4
                                             Wald chi2(1)       =      0.36
Scale parameter:                        1    Prob > chi2        =    0.5496
```

i_cnt	IRR	Std. Err.	z	P>|z|	[95% Conf. Interval]
inprog	.9791082	.0345486	-0.60	0.550	.9136826 1.049219
lnpm	(offset)				

```
. estat wcorrelation
Estimated within-airline correlation matrix R:
```

	c1	c2	c3	c4
r1	1			
r2	.5700298	1		
r3	.716356	.4192126	1	
r4	.2383264	.3839863	.3521287	1

There is no sensible pattern to the correlations.

We created this dataset from a random-effects Poisson model. We reran our data-creation program and this time had it create 400 airlines rather than 20, still with 4 years of data each. Here are the equal-correlation model and estimated correlation structure

```
. use http://www.stata-press.com/data/r10/airacc2, clear

. xtgee i_cnt inprog, family(poisson) eform offset(lnpm) nolog
GEE population-averaged model              Number of obs      =      1600
Group variable:                    airline  Number of groups   =       400
Link:                                  log  Obs per group: min =         4
Family:                             Poisson                avg =       4.0
Correlation:                  exchangeable                max =         4
                                             Wald chi2(1)       =    111.80
Scale parameter:                        1    Prob > chi2        =    0.0000
```

i_cnt	IRR	Std. Err.	z	P>|z|	[95% Conf. Interval]
inprog	.8915304	.0096807	-10.57	0.000	.8727571 .9107076
lnpm	(offset)				

```
. estat wcorrelation
Estimated within-airline correlation matrix R:
```

	c1	c2	c3	c4
r1	1			
r2	.5291707	1		
r3	.5291707	.5291707	1	
r4	.5291707	.5291707	.5291707	1

The following estimation results assume unstructured correlation:

```
. xtgee i_cnt inprog, family(poisson) corr(unstr) eform offset(lnpm) nolog
GEE population-averaged model                Number of obs      =      1600
Group and time vars:            airline time Number of groups   =       400
Link:                                    log Obs per group: min =         4
Family:                              Poisson               avg =       4.0
Correlation:                    unstructured               max =         4
                                             Wald chi2(1)       =    113.43
Scale parameter:                         1   Prob > chi2        =    0.0000
```

i_cnt	IRR	Std. Err.	z	P>|z|	[95% Conf. Interval]	
inprog	.8914155	.0096208	-10.65	0.000	.8727572	.9104728
lnpm	(offset)					

```
. estat wcorrelation
Estimated within-airline correlation matrix R:
```

	c1	c2	c3	c4
r1	1			
r2	.4733189	1		
r3	.5240576	.5748868	1	
r4	.5139748	.5048895	.5840707	1

The equal-correlation model estimated a fixed correlation of .5292, and above we have correlations ranging between .4733 and .5841 with little pattern in their structure.

◁

Methods and Formulas

All postestimation commands listed above are implemented as ado-files.

Also See

[XT] **xtgee** — Fit population-averaged panel-data models by using GEE

[U] **20 Estimation and postestimation commands**

Title

---
xtgls — Fit panel-data models by using GLS

Syntax

xtgls *depvar* [*indepvars*] [*if*] [*in*] [*weight*] [, *options*]

options	description
Model	
<u>nocon</u>stant	suppress constant term
<u>p</u>anels(<u>i</u>id)	use i.i.d. error structure
<u>p</u>anels(<u>h</u>eteroskedastic)	use heteroskedastic but uncorrelated error structure
<u>p</u>anels(<u>c</u>orrelated)	use heteroskedastic and correlated error structure
<u>c</u>orr(independent)	use independent autocorrelation structure
<u>c</u>orr(<u>a</u>r1)	use AR1 autocorrelation structure
<u>c</u>orr(<u>p</u>sar1)	use panel-specific AR1 autocorrelation structure
<u>rho</u>type(*calc*)	specify method to compute autocorrelation parameter; see *Options* for details; seldom used
igls	use iterated GLS estimator instead of two-step GLS estimator
force	estimate even if observations unequally spaced in time
SE	
nmk	normalize standard error by $N - k$ instead of N
Reporting	
<u>l</u>evel(#)	set confidence level; default is level(95)
Opt options	
optimize_options	control the optimization process; seldom used

A panel variable must be specified. For correlation structures other than independent, a time variable must be specified. A time variable must also be specified if panels(correlated) is specified. Use xtset; see [XT] **xtset**.

depvar and *indepvars* may contain time-series operators; see [U] **11.4.3 Time-series varlists**.

by, statsby, and xi are allowed; see [U] **11.1.10 Prefix commands**.

aweights are allowed; see [U] **11.1.6 weight**. Weights must be constant within panel.

See [U] **20 Estimation and postestimation commands** for more capabilities of estimation commands.

Description

xtgls fits panel-data linear models by using feasible generalized least squares. This command allows estimation in the presence of AR(1) autocorrelation within panels and cross-sectional correlation and heteroskedasticity across panels.

Options

⌐ Model ⌐

noconstant; see [XT] **estimation options**.

panels(*pdist*) specifies the error structure across panels.

panels(iid) specifies a homoskedastic error structure with no cross-sectional correlation. This is the default.

panels(heteroskedastic) specifies a heteroskedastic error structure with no cross-sectional correlation.

panels(correlated) specifies a heteroskedastic error structure with cross-sectional correlation. If p(c) is specified, you must also specify a time variable (use xtset). The results will be based on a generalized inverse of a singular matrix unless $T \geq m$ (the number of periods is greater than or equal to the number of panels).

corr(*corr*) specifies the assumed autocorrelation within panels.

corr(independent) specifies that there is no autocorrelation. This is the default.

corr(ar1) specifies that, within panels, there is AR(1) autocorrelation and that the coefficient of the AR(1) process is common to all the panels. If c(ar1) is specified, you must also specify a time variable (use xtset).

corr(psar1) specifies that, within panels, there is AR(1) autocorrelation and that the coefficient of the AR(1) process is specific to each panel. psar1 stands for panel-specific AR(1). If c(psar1) is specified, a time variable must also be specified; use xtset.

rhotype(*calc*) specifies the method to be used to calculate the autocorrelation parameter:

regress	regression using lags; the default
dw	Durbin–Watson calculation
freg	regression using leads
nagar	Nagar calculation
theil	Theil calculation
tscorr	time-series autocorrelation calculation

All the calculations are asymptotically equivalent and consistent; this is a rarely used option.

igls requests an iterated GLS estimator instead of the two-step GLS estimator for a nonautocorrelated model or instead of the three-step GLS estimator for an autocorrelated model. The iterated GLS estimator converges to the MLE for the corr(independent) models but does not for the other corr() models.

force; see [XT] **estimation options**.

⌐ SE ⌐

nmk specifies that standard errors are to be normalized by $N - k$, where k is the number of parameters estimated, rather than N, the number of observations. Greene (2003, 322) recommends N and remarks that whether you use N or $N - k$ does not make the variance calculation unbiased in these models.

⌐ Reporting ⌐

level(#); see [XT] **estimation options**.

⌐ Opt options ⌐

optimize_options control the iterative optimization process. These options are seldom used.

iterate(*#*) specifies the maximum number of iterations. When the number of iterations equals *#*, the optimization stops and presents the current results, even if convergence has not been reached. The default is iterate(100).

tolerance(*#*) specifies the tolerance for the coefficient vector. When the relative change in the coefficient vector from one iteration to the next is less than or equal to *#*, the optimization process is stopped. tolerance(1e-7) is the default.

nolog suppresses display of the iteration log.

Remarks

Remarks are presented under the following headings:

Introduction
Heteroskedasticity across panels
Correlation across panels (cross-sectional correlation)
Autocorrelation within panels

Introduction

Information on GLS can be found in Greene (2003), Maddala (2001), Davidson and MacKinnon (1993), and Judge et al. (1985).

If you have many panels relative to periods, see [XT] **xtreg** and [XT] **xtgee**. xtgee, in particular, provides capabilities similar to those of xtgls but does not allow cross-sectional correlation. On the other hand, xtgee allows a richer description of the correlation within panels as long as the same correlations apply to all panels. xtgls provides two unique features:

1. Cross-sectional correlation may be modeled (panels(correlated)).

2. Within panels, the AR(1) correlation coefficient may be unique (corr(psar1)).

xtgls allows models with heteroskedasticity and no cross-sectional correlation, but, strictly speaking, xtgee does not. xtgee with the vce(robust) option relaxes the assumption of equal variances, at least as far as the standard error calculation is concerned.

Also, xtgls, panels(iid) corr(independent) nmk is equivalent to regress.

The nmk option uses $n - k$ rather than n to normalize the variance calculation.

To fit a model with autocorrelated errors (corr(ar1) or corr(psar1)), the data must be equally spaced in time. To fit a model with cross-sectional correlation (panels(correlated)), panels must have the same number of observations (be balanced).

The equation from which the models are developed is given by

$$y_{it} = \mathbf{x}_{it}\boldsymbol{\beta} + \epsilon_{it}$$

where $i = 1, \dots, m$ is the number of units (or panels) and $t = 1, \dots, T_i$ is the number of observations for panel i. This model can equally be written as

$$\begin{bmatrix} \mathbf{y}_1 \\ \mathbf{y}_2 \\ \vdots \\ \mathbf{y}_m \end{bmatrix} = \begin{bmatrix} \mathbf{X}_1 \\ \mathbf{X}_2 \\ \vdots \\ \mathbf{X}_m \end{bmatrix} \beta + \begin{bmatrix} \epsilon_1 \\ \epsilon_2 \\ \vdots \\ \epsilon_m \end{bmatrix}$$

The variance matrix of the disturbance terms can be written as

$$E[\epsilon\epsilon'] = \Omega = \begin{bmatrix} \sigma_{1,1}\Omega_{1,1} & \sigma_{1,2}\Omega_{1,2} & \cdots & \sigma_{1,m}\Omega_{1,m} \\ \sigma_{2,1}\Omega_{2,1} & \sigma_{2,2}\Omega_{2,2} & \cdots & \sigma_{2,m}\Omega_{2,m} \\ \vdots & \vdots & \ddots & \vdots \\ \sigma_{m,1}\Omega_{m,1} & \sigma_{m,2}\Omega_{m,2} & \cdots & \sigma_{m,m}\Omega_{m,m} \end{bmatrix}$$

For the $\Omega_{i,j}$ matrices to be parameterized to model cross-sectional correlation, they must be square (balanced panels).

In these models, we assume that the coefficient vector β is the same for all panels and consider a variety of models by changing the assumptions on the structure of Ω.

For the classic OLS regression model, we have

$$E[\epsilon_{i,t}] = 0$$
$$\mathrm{Var}[\epsilon_{i,t}] = \sigma^2$$
$$\mathrm{Cov}[\epsilon_{i,t}, \epsilon_{j,s}] = 0 \qquad \text{if } t \neq s \text{ or } i \neq j$$

This amounts to assuming that Ω has the structure given by

$$\Omega = \begin{bmatrix} \sigma^2\mathbf{I} & \mathbf{0} & \cdots & \mathbf{0} \\ \mathbf{0} & \sigma^2\mathbf{I} & \cdots & \mathbf{0} \\ \vdots & \vdots & \ddots & \vdots \\ \mathbf{0} & \mathbf{0} & \cdots & \sigma^2\mathbf{I} \end{bmatrix}$$

whether or not the panels are balanced (the $\mathbf{0}$ matrices may be rectangular). The classic OLS assumptions are the default panels(uncorrelated) and corr(independent) options for this command.

Heteroskedasticity across panels

In many cross-sectional datasets, the variance for each of the panels differs. It is common to have data on countries, states, or other units that have variation of scale. The heteroskedastic model is specified by including the panels(heteroskedastic) option, which assumes that

$$\Omega = \begin{bmatrix} \sigma_1^2\mathbf{I} & \mathbf{0} & \cdots & \mathbf{0} \\ \mathbf{0} & \sigma_2^2\mathbf{I} & \cdots & \mathbf{0} \\ \vdots & \vdots & \ddots & \vdots \\ \mathbf{0} & \mathbf{0} & \cdots & \sigma_m^2\mathbf{I} \end{bmatrix}$$

▷ Example 1

Greene (2003, 329) reprints data in a classic study of investment demand by Grunfeld and Griliches (1960). Below we allow the variances to differ for each of the five companies.

```
. use http://www.stata-press.com/data/r10/invest2

. xtgls invest market stock, panels(hetero)

Cross-sectional time-series FGLS regression

Coefficients:  generalized least squares
Panels:        heteroskedastic
Correlation:   no autocorrelation

Estimated covariances      =        5          Number of obs     =        100
Estimated autocorrelations =        0          Number of groups  =          5
Estimated coefficients     =        3          Time periods      =         20
                                               Wald chi2(2)      =     865.38
                                               Prob > chi2       =     0.0000
```

invest	Coef.	Std. Err.	z	P>|z|	[95% Conf. Interval]	
market	.0949905	.007409	12.82	0.000	.0804692	.1095118
stock	.3378129	.0302254	11.18	0.000	.2785722	.3970535
_cons	-36.2537	6.124363	-5.92	0.000	-48.25723	-24.25017

◁

Correlation across panels (cross-sectional correlation)

We may wish to assume that the error terms of panels are correlated, in addition to having different scale variances. The variance structure is specified by including the panels(correlated) option and is given by

$$\Omega = \begin{bmatrix} \sigma_1^2 \mathbf{I} & \sigma_{1,2} \mathbf{I} & \cdots & \sigma_{1,m} \mathbf{I} \\ \sigma_{2,1} \mathbf{I} & \sigma_2^2 \mathbf{I} & \cdots & \sigma_{2,m} \mathbf{I} \\ \vdots & \vdots & \ddots & \vdots \\ \sigma_{m,1} \mathbf{I} & \sigma_{m,2} \mathbf{I} & \cdots & \sigma_m^2 \mathbf{I} \end{bmatrix}$$

Since we must estimate cross-sectional correlation in this model, the panels must be balanced (and $T \geq m$ for valid results). A time variable must also be specified so that xtgls knows how the observations within panels are ordered. xtset shows us that this is true.

▷ Example 2

```
. xtset
       panel variable:  company (strongly balanced)
        time variable:  time, 1 to 20
                delta:  1 unit
```

```
. xtgls invest market stock, panels(correlated)

Cross-sectional time-series FGLS regression

Coefficients:   generalized least squares
Panels:         heteroskedastic with cross-sectional correlation
Correlation:    no autocorrelation

Estimated covariances      =         15      Number of obs      =        100
Estimated autocorrelations =          0      Number of groups   =          5
Estimated coefficients     =          3      Time periods       =         20
                                             Wald chi2(2)       =    1285.19
                                             Prob > chi2        =     0.0000
```

invest	Coef.	Std. Err.	z	P>|z|	[95% Conf. Interval]
market	.0961894	.0054752	17.57	0.000	.0854583 .1069206
stock	.3095321	.0179851	17.21	0.000	.2742819 .3447822
_cons	-38.36128	5.344871	-7.18	0.000	-48.83703 -27.88552

The estimated cross-sectional covariances are stored in e(Sigma).

```
. matrix list e(Sigma)

symmetric e(Sigma)[5,5]
            _ee        _ee2        _ee3        _ee4        _ee5
_ee    9410.9061
_ee2  -168.04631   755.85077
_ee3  -1915.9538  -4163.3434    34288.49
_ee4  -1129.2896  -80.381742   2259.3242   633.42367
_ee5   258.50132   4035.872   -27898.235  -1170.6801   33455.511
```

◁

> ## Example 3

We can obtain the MLE results by specifying the igls option, which iterates the GLS estimation technique to convergence:

```
. xtgls invest market stock, panels(correlated) igls

Iteration 1: tolerance = .2127384
Iteration 2: tolerance = .22817
  (output omitted)
Iteration 1046: tolerance = 1.000e-07

Cross-sectional time-series FGLS regression

Coefficients:   generalized least squares
Panels:         heteroskedastic with cross-sectional correlation
Correlation:    no autocorrelation

Estimated covariances      =         15      Number of obs      =        100
Estimated autocorrelations =          0      Number of groups   =          5
Estimated coefficients     =          3      Time periods       =         20
                                             Wald chi2(2)       =     558.51
Log likelihood             =  -515.4222      Prob > chi2        =     0.0000
```

invest	Coef.	Std. Err.	z	P>|z|	[95% Conf. Interval]
market	.023631	.004291	5.51	0.000	.0152207 .0320413
stock	.1709472	.0152526	11.21	0.000	.1410526 .2008417
_cons	-2.216508	1.958845	-1.13	0.258	-6.055774 1.622759

Here the log likelihood is reported in the header of the output.

◁

Autocorrelation within panels

The individual identity matrices along the diagonal of Ω may be replaced with more general structures to allow for serial correlation. xtgls allows three options so that you may assume a structure with corr(independent) (no autocorrelation); corr(ar1) (serial correlation where the correlation parameter is common for all panels); or corr(psar1) (serial correlation where the correlation parameter is unique for each panel).

The restriction of a common autocorrelation parameter is reasonable when the individual correlations are nearly equal and the time series are short.

If the restriction of a common autocorrelation parameter is reasonable, this allows us to use more information in estimating the autocorrelation parameter to produce a more reasonable estimate of the regression coefficients.

When you specify corr(ar1) or corr(psar1), the iterated GLS estimator does not converge to the MLE.

▷ Example 4

If corr(ar1) is specified, each group is assumed to have errors that follow the same AR(1) process; that is, the autocorrelation parameter is the same for all groups.

```
. xtgls invest market stock, panels(hetero) corr(ar1)

Cross-sectional time-series FGLS regression

Coefficients:   generalized least squares
Panels:         heteroskedastic
Correlation:    common AR(1) coefficient for all panels  (0.8651)

Estimated covariances      =        5          Number of obs      =        100
Estimated autocorrelations =        1          Number of groups   =          5
Estimated coefficients     =        3          Time periods       =         20
                                               Wald chi2(2)       =     119.69
                                               Prob > chi2        =     0.0000
```

invest	Coef.	Std. Err.	z	P>|z|	[95% Conf. Interval]
market	.0744315	.0097937	7.60	0.000	.0552362	.0936268
stock	.2874294	.0475391	6.05	0.000	.1942545	.3806043
_cons	-18.96238	17.64943	-1.07	0.283	-53.55464	15.62987

◁

▷ Example 5

If corr(psar1) is specified, each group is assumed to have errors that follow a different AR(1) process.

```
. xtgls invest market stock, panels(iid) corr(psar1)

Cross-sectional time-series FGLS regression

Coefficients:  generalized least squares
Panels:        homoskedastic
Correlation:   panel-specific AR(1)

Estimated covariances      =      1       Number of obs      =       100
Estimated autocorrelations =      5       Number of groups   =         5
Estimated coefficients     =      3       Time periods       =        20
                                          Wald chi2(2)       =    252.93
                                          Prob > chi2        =    0.0000
```

invest	Coef.	Std. Err.	z	P>|z|	[95% Conf. Interval]	
market	.0934343	.0097783	9.56	0.000	.0742693	.1125993
stock	.3838814	.0416775	9.21	0.000	.302195	.4655677
_cons	-10.1246	34.06675	-0.30	0.766	-76.8942	56.64499

◁

Saved Results

xtgls saves the following in e():

Scalars

e(N)	number of observations	e(ll)	log likelihood
e(N_g)	number of groups	e(g_max)	largest group size
e(N_t)	number of periods	e(g_min)	smallest group size
e(N_miss)	number of missing observations	e(g_avg)	average group size
e(n_cf)	number of estimated coefficients	e(rc)	return code
e(n_cv)	number of estimated covariances	e(chi2)	χ^2
e(n_cr)	number of estimated correlations	e(df_pear)	degrees of freedom for Pearson χ^2
e(df)	degrees of freedom		

Macros

e(cmd)	xtgls	e(chi2type)	Wald; type of model χ^2 test
e(cmdline)	command as typed	e(ivar)	variable denoting groups
e(depvar)	name of dependent variable	e(tvar)	variable denoting time
e(title)	title in estimation output	e(wtype)	weight type
e(coefftype)	estimation scheme	e(wexp)	weight expression
e(corr)	correlation structure	e(rho)	ρ
e(vt)	panel option	e(properties)	b V
e(rhotype)	type of estimated correlation	e(predict)	program used to implement predict

Matrices

e(b)	coefficient vector	e(Sigma)	$\widehat{\Sigma}$ matrix
e(V)	variance–covariance matrix of the estimators		

Functions

e(sample)	marks estimation sample

Methods and Formulas

`xtgls` is implemented as an ado-file.

The GLS results are given by

$$\widehat{\beta}_{\mathrm{GLS}} = (\mathbf{X}'\widehat{\Omega}^{-1}\mathbf{X})^{-1}\mathbf{X}'\widehat{\Omega}^{-1}\mathbf{y}$$
$$\widehat{\mathrm{Var}}(\widehat{\beta}_{\mathrm{GLS}}) = (\mathbf{X}'\widehat{\Omega}^{-1}\mathbf{X})^{-1}$$

For all our models, the Ω matrix may be written in terms of the Kronecker product:

$$\Omega = \boldsymbol{\Sigma}_{m \times m} \otimes \mathbf{I}_{T_i \times T_i}$$

The estimated variance matrix is obtained by substituting the estimator $\widehat{\boldsymbol{\Sigma}}$ for $\boldsymbol{\Sigma}$, where

$$\widehat{\boldsymbol{\Sigma}}_{i,j} = \frac{\widehat{\epsilon}_i{}'\widehat{\epsilon}_j}{T}$$

The residuals used in estimating $\boldsymbol{\Sigma}$ are first obtained from OLS regression. If the estimation is iterated, residuals are obtained from the last fitted model.

Maximum likelihood estimates may be obtained by iterating the FGLS estimates to convergence for models with no autocorrelation, `corr(independent)`.

The GLS estimates and their associated standard errors are calculated using $\widehat{\boldsymbol{\Sigma}}^{-1}$. As Beck and Katz (1995) point out, the $\boldsymbol{\Sigma}$ matrix is of rank at most $\min(T, m)$ when you use the `panels(correlated)` option. For the GLS results to be valid (not based on a generalized inverse), T must be at least as large as m, as you need at least as many period observations as there are panels.

Beck and Katz (1995) suggest using OLS parameter estimates with asymptotic standard errors that are corrected for correlation between the panels. This estimation can be performed with the `xtpcse` command; see [XT] **xtpcse**.

References

Baum, C. F. 2001. Residual diagnostics for cross-section time series regression models. *Stata Journal* 1: 101–104.

Beck, N., and J. N. Katz. 1995. What to do (and not to do) with time-series cross-section data. *American Political Science Review* 89: 634–647.

Blackwell, J. L., III. 2005. Estimation and testing of fixed-effect panel-data systems. *Stata Journal* 5: 202–207.

Davidson, R., and J. G. MacKinnon. 1993. *Estimation and Inference in Econometrics*. New York: Oxford University Press.

Greene, W. H. 2003. *Econometric Analysis*. 5th ed. Upper Saddle River, NJ: Prentice Hall.

Grunfeld, Y., and Z. Griliches. 1960. Is aggregation necessarily bad? *Review of Economics and Statistics* 42: 1–13.

Judge, G. G., W. E. Griffiths, R. C. Hill, H. Lütkepohl, and T.-C. Lee. 1985. *The Theory and Practice of Econometrics*. 2nd ed. New York: Wiley.

Maddala, G. S. 2001. *Introduction to Econometrics*. 3rd ed. New York: Wiley.

Also See

Title

> **xtgls postestimation** — Postestimation tools for xtgls

Description

The following postestimation commands are available for `xtgls`:

command	description
adjust[1]	adjusted predictions of $\mathbf{x}\beta$
estat[2]	AIC, BIC, VCE, and estimation sample summary
estimates	cataloging estimation results
lincom	point estimates, standard errors, testing, and inference for linear combinations of coefficients
lrtest[3]	likelihood-ratio test
mfx	marginal effects or elasticities
nlcom	point estimates, standard errors, testing, and inference for nonlinear combinations of coefficients
predict	predictions, residuals, influence statistics, and other diagnostic measures
predictnl	point estimates, standard errors, testing, and inference for generalized predictions
test	Wald tests for simple and composite linear hypotheses
testnl	Wald tests of nonlinear hypotheses

[1] adjust is not appropriate with time-series operators.

[2] AIC and BIC are available only if `igls` and `corr(independent)` were specified at estimation.

[3] Likelihood-ratio tests are available only if `igls` and `corr(independent)` were specified at estimation.

See the corresponding entries in the *Stata Base Reference Manual* for details.

Syntax for predict

> predict [*type*] *newvar* [*if*] [*in*] [, xb stdp]

These statistics are available both in and out of sample; type predict ... if e(sample) ... if wanted only for the estimation sample.

Options for predict

> Main

xb, the default, calculates the linear prediction.

stdp calculates the standard error of the linear prediction.

Also See

[XT] **xtgls** — Fit panel-data models by using GLS

[U] **20 Estimation and postestimation commands**

Title

> **xthtaylor** — Hausman–Taylor estimator for error-components models

Syntax

> xthtaylor *depvar* *indepvars* $[$ *if* $]$ $[$ *in* $]$ $[$ *weight* $]$, <u>en</u>dog(*varlist*) $[$ *options* $]$

options	description
Main	
<u>noc</u>onstant	suppress constant term
* <u>en</u>dog(*varlist*)	explanatory variables in *indepvars* to be treated as endogenous
<u>const</u>ant(*varlist*$_{ti}$)	independent variables that are constant within panel
<u>vary</u>ing(*varlist*$_{tv}$)	independent variables that are time varying within panel
<u>ama</u>curdy	fit model based on Amemiya and MaCurdy estimator
SE	
vce(*vcetype*)	*vcetype* may be <u>conv</u>entional, <u>boot</u>strap, or <u>jack</u>knife
Reporting	
<u>l</u>evel(#)	set confidence level; default is level(95)
<u>s</u>mall	report small-sample statistics

* endog(*varlist*) is required.

A panel variable must be specified. For xthtaylor, amacurdy, a time variable must also be specified. Use xtset; see [XT] **xtset**.

depvar, *indepvars*, and all *varlist*s may contain time-series operators; see [U] **11.4.3 Time-series varlists**.

by, statsby, and xi are allowed; see [U] **11.1.10 Prefix commands**.

iweights and fweights are allowed unless the amacurdy option is specified; fweights must be constant within panel; see [U] **11.1.6 weight**. Weights must be constant within panel.

See [U] **20 Estimation and postestimation commands** for more capabilities of estimation commands.

Description

xthtaylor fits panel-data random-effects models in which some of the covariates are correlated with the unobserved individual-level random effect. The estimators, originally proposed by Hausman and Taylor (1981) and by Amemiya and MaCurdy (1986), are based on instrumental variables. By default, xthtaylor uses the Hausman–Taylor estimator. When the amacurdy option is specified, xthtaylor uses the Amemiya–MaCurdy estimator.

Although the estimators implemented in xthtaylor and xtivreg (see [XT] **xtivreg**) use the method of instrumental variables, each command is designed for different problems. The estimators implemented in xtivreg assume that a subset of the explanatory variables in the model are correlated with the idiosyncratic error ϵ_{it}. In contrast, the Hausman–Taylor and Amemiya–MaCurdy estimators that are implemented in xthtaylor assume that some of the explanatory variables are correlated with the individual-level random effects, u_i, but that none of the explanatory variables are correlated with the idiosyncratic error, ϵ_{it}.

Options

noconstant; see [XT] **estimation options**.

endog(*varlist*) specifies that a subset of explanatory variables in *indepvars* be treated as endogenous variables, i.e., the explanatory variables that are assumed to be correlated with the unobserved random effect. endog() is required.

constant(*varlist*$_{ti}$) specifies the subset of variables in *indepvars* that are time invariant, that is, constant within panel. By using this option, you assert not only that the variables specified in *varlist*$_{ti}$ are time invariant but also that all other variables in *indepvars* are time varying. If this assertion is false, xthtaylor does not perform the estimation and will issue an error message. xthtaylor automatically detects which variables are time invariant and which are not. However, users may want to check their understanding of the data and specify which variables are time invariant and which are not.

varying(*varlist*$_{tv}$) specifies the subset of variables in *indepvars* that are time varying. By using this option, you assert not only that the variables specified in *varlist*$_{tv}$ are time varying but also that all other variables in *indepvars* are time invariant. If this assertion is false, xthtaylor does not perform the estimation and issues an error message. xthtaylor automatically detects which variables are time varying and which are not. However, users may want to check their understanding of the data and specify which variables are time varying and which are not.

amacurdy specifies that the Amemiya–MaCurdy estimator be used. This estimator uses extra instruments to gain efficiency at the cost of additional assumptions on the data-generating process. This option may be specified only for samples containing balanced panels, and weights may not be specified. The panels must also have a common initial period.

vce(*vcetype*) specifies the type of standard error reported, which includes types that are derived from asymptotic theory and that use bootstrap or jackknife methods; see [XT] *vce_options*.

vce(conventional), the default, uses the conventionally derived variance estimator for this Hausman–Taylor model.

level(*#*); see [XT] **estimation options**.

small specifies that the p-values from the Wald tests in the output and all subsequent Wald tests obtained via test use t and F distributions instead of the large-sample normal and χ^2 distributions. By default, the p-values are obtained using the normal and χ^2 distributions.

Remarks

If you have not read [XT] **xt**, please do so.

Consider a random-effects model of the form

$$y_{it} = \mathbf{X}_{1it}\boldsymbol{\beta}_1 + \mathbf{X}_{2it}\boldsymbol{\beta}_2 + \mathbf{Z}_{1i}\boldsymbol{\delta}_1 + \mathbf{Z}_{2i}\boldsymbol{\delta}_2 + \mu_i + \epsilon_{it}$$

where

$\mathbf{X}_{1it}$ is a $1 \times k_1$ vector of observations on exogenous, time-varying variables assumed to be uncorrelated with μ_i and ϵ_{it};

$\mathbf{X}_{2it}$ is a $1 \times k_2$ vector of observations on endogenous, time-varying variables assumed to be (possibly) correlated with μ_i but orthogonal to ϵ_{it};

$\mathbf{Z}_{1i}$ is a $1 \times g_1$ vector of observations on exogenous, time-invariant variables assumed to be uncorrelated with μ_i and ϵ_{it};

$\mathbf{Z}_{2i}$ is a $1 \times g_2$ vector of observations on endogenous, time-invariant variables assumed to be (possibly) correlated μ_i but orthogonal to ϵ_{it};

μ_i is the unobserved, panel-level random effect that is assumed to have zero mean and finite variance σ_μ^2 and to be independently and identically distributed (i.i.d.) over the panels;

ϵ_{it} is the idiosyncratic error that is assumed to have zero mean and finite variance σ_ϵ^2 and to be i.i.d. over all the observations in the data;

$\beta_1, \beta_2, \delta_1,$ and δ_2 are $k_1 \times 1$, $k_2 \times 1$, $g_1 \times 1$, and $g_2 \times 1$ coefficient vectors, respectively; and

$i = 1, \ldots, n$, where n is the number of panels in the sample and, for each i, $t = 1, \ldots, T_i$.

Since $\mathbf{X}_{2it}$ and $\mathbf{Z}_{2i}$ may be correlated with μ_i, the simple random-effects estimators—xtreg, re and xtreg, mle—are generally not consistent for the parameters in this model. Since the within estimator, xtreg, fe, removes the μ_i by mean-differencing the data before estimating β_1 and β_2, it is consistent for these parameters. However, in the process of removing the μ_i, the within estimator also eliminates the $\mathbf{Z}_{1i}$ and the $\mathbf{Z}_{2i}$. Thus it cannot estimate δ_1 nor δ_2. The Hausman–Taylor and Amemiya–MaCurdy estimators implemented in xthtaylor are designed to resolve this problem.

The within estimator consistently estimates β_1 and β_2. Using these estimates, we can obtain the within residuals, called $\widehat{d}_i$. Intermediate, albeit consistent, estimates of δ_1 and δ_2—called $\widehat{\delta}_{1\text{IV}}$ and $\widehat{\delta}_{2\text{IV}}$, respectively—are obtained by regressing the within residuals on $\mathbf{Z}_{1i}$ and $\mathbf{Z}_{2i}$, using $\mathbf{X}_{1it}$ and $\mathbf{Z}_{1i}$ as instruments. The order condition for identification requires that the number of variables in $\mathbf{X}_{1it}$, k_1, be at least as large as the number of elements in $\mathbf{Z}_{2i}$, g_2 and that there be sufficient correlation between the instruments and $\mathbf{Z}_{2i}$ to avoid a weak-instrument problem.

The within estimates of β_1 and β_2 and the intermediate estimates $\widehat{\delta}_{1\text{IV}}$ and $\widehat{\delta}_{2\text{IV}}$ can be used to obtain sets of within and overall residuals. These two sets of residuals can be used to estimate the variance components (see *Methods and Formulas* for details).

The estimated variance components can then be used to perform a GLS transform on each of the variables. For what follows, define the general notation $\breve{w}_{it}$ to represent the GLS transform of the variable w_{it}, $\overline{w}_i$ to represent the within-panel mean of w_{it}, and $\widetilde{w}_{it}$ to represent the within transform of w_{it}. With this notational convention, the Hausman–Taylor (1981) estimator of the coefficients of interest can be obtained by the instrumental-variables regression

$$\breve{y}_{it} = \breve{\mathbf{X}}_{1it}\beta_1 + \breve{\mathbf{X}}_{2it}\beta_2 + \breve{\mathbf{Z}}_{1i}\delta_1 + \breve{\mathbf{Z}}_{2i}\delta_2 + \breve{\mu}_i + \breve{\epsilon}_{it} \tag{1}$$

using $\widetilde{\mathbf{X}}_{1it}, \widetilde{\mathbf{X}}_{2it}, \overline{\mathbf{X}}_{1i}, \overline{\mathbf{X}}_{2i},$ and $\mathbf{Z}_{1i}$ as instruments.

For the instruments to be valid, this estimator requires that $\overline{\mathbf{X}}_{1i.}$ and $\mathbf{Z}_{1i}$ be uncorrelated with the random-effect μ_i. More precisely, the instruments are valid when

$$\text{plim}_{n \to \infty} \frac{1}{n} \sum_{i=1}^{n} \overline{\mathbf{X}}_{1i.} \mu_i = 0$$

and

$$\text{plim}_{n\to\infty} \frac{1}{n} \sum_{i=1}^{n} \mathbf{Z}_{1i}\mu_i = 0$$

Amemiya and MaCurdy (1986) place stricter requirements on the instruments that vary within panels to obtain a more efficient estimator. Specifically, Amemiya and MaCurdy (1986) assume that $\mathbf{X}_{1it}$ is orthogonal to μ_i in every period; i.e., $\text{plim}_{n\to\infty} \frac{1}{n} \sum_{i=1}^{n} \mathbf{X}_{1it}\mu_i = 0$ for $t = 1, \ldots, T$. With this restriction, they derive the Amemiya–MaCurdy estimator as the instrumental-variables regression of (1) using instruments $\widetilde{\mathbf{X}}_{1it}$, $\widetilde{\mathbf{X}}_{2it}$, $\mathbf{X}_{1it}^*$, and $\mathbf{Z}_{1i}$. The order condition for the Amemiya–MaCurdy estimator is now $Tk_1 > g_2$. xthtaylor uses the Amemiya–MaCurdy estimator when the amacurdy option is specified.

▷ Example 1

This example replicates the results of Baltagi and Khanti-Akom (1990, table II, column HT) using 595 observations on individuals over 1976–1982 that were extracted from the Panel Study of Income Dynamics (PSID). In the model, the log-transformed wage lwage is assumed to be a function of how long the person has worked for a firm, wks; binary variables indicating whether a person lives in a large metropolitan area or in the south, smsa and south; marital status is ms; years of education, ed; a quadratic of work experience, exp and exp2; occupation, occ; a binary variable indicating employment in a manufacture industry, ind; a binary variable indicating that wages are set by a union contract, union; a binary variable indicating gender, fem; and a binary variable indicating whether the individual is African American, blk.

We suspect that the time-varying variables exp, exp2, wks, ms, and union are all correlated with the unobserved individual random effect. We can inspect these variables to see if they exhibit sufficient within-panel variation to serve as their own instruments.

```
. use http://www.stata-press.com/data/r10/psidextract
. xtsum exp exp2 wks ms union
```

Variable		Mean	Std. Dev.	Min	Max	Observations	
exp	overall	19.85378	10.96637	1	51	N =	4165
	between		10.79018	4	48	n =	595
	within		2.00024	16.85378	22.85378	T =	7
exp2	overall	514.405	496.9962	1	2601	N =	4165
	between		489.0495	20	2308	n =	595
	within		90.44581	231.405	807.405	T =	7
wks	overall	46.81152	5.129098	5	52	N =	4165
	between		3.284016	31.57143	51.57143	n =	595
	within		3.941881	12.2401	63.66867	T =	7
ms	overall	.8144058	.3888256	0	1	N =	4165
	between		.3686109	0	1	n =	595
	within		.1245274	-.0427371	1.671549	T =	7
union	overall	.3639856	.4812023	0	1	N =	4165
	between		.4543848	0	1	n =	595
	within		.1593351	-.4931573	1.221128	T =	7

We are also going to assume that the exogenous variables occ, south, smsa, ind, fem, and blk are instruments for the endogenous, time-invariant variable ed. The output below indicates that although fem appears to be a weak instrument, the remaining instruments are probably sufficiently correlated to identify the coefficient on ed. (See Baltagi and Khanti-Akom [1990] for more discussion.)

```
. correlate fem blk occ south smsa ind ed
(obs=4165)
```

	fem	blk	occ	south	smsa	ind	ed
fem	1.0000						
blk	0.2086	1.0000					
occ	-0.0847	0.0837	1.0000				
south	0.0516	0.1218	0.0413	1.0000			
smsa	0.1044	0.1154	-0.2018	-0.1350	1.0000		
ind	-0.1778	-0.0475	0.2260	-0.0769	-0.0689	1.0000	
ed	-0.0012	-0.1196	-0.6194	-0.1216	0.1843	-0.2365	1.0000

We will assume that the correlations are strong enough and proceed with the estimation. The output below gives the Hausman–Taylor estimates for this model.

```
. xthtaylor lwage occ south smsa ind exp exp2 wks ms union fem blk ed,
> endog(exp exp2 wks ms union ed)
Hausman-Taylor estimation               Number of obs      =        4165
Group variable: id                      Number of groups   =         595

                                        Obs per group: min =           7
                                                       avg =           7
                                                       max =           7

Random effects u_i ~ i.i.d.             Wald chi2(12)      =     6891.87
                                        Prob > chi2        =      0.0000
```

lwage	Coef.	Std. Err.	z	P>|z|	[95% Conf.	Interval]
TVexogenous						
occ	-.0207047	.0137809	-1.50	0.133	-.0477149	.0063055
south	.0074398	.031955	0.23	0.816	-.0551908	.0700705
smsa	-.0418334	.0189581	-2.21	0.027	-.0789906	-.0046761
ind	.0136039	.0152374	0.89	0.372	-.0162608	.0434686
TVendogenous						
exp	.1131328	.002471	45.79	0.000	.1082898	.1179758
exp2	-.0004189	.0000546	-7.67	0.000	-.0005259	-.0003119
wks	.0008374	.0005997	1.40	0.163	-.0003381	.0020129
ms	-.0298508	.01898	-1.57	0.116	-.0670508	.0073493
union	.0327714	.0149084	2.20	0.028	.0035514	.0619914
TIexogenous						
fem	.1309236	.126659	-1.03	0.301	-.3791707	.1173234
blk	-.2857479	.1557019	-1.84	0.066	-.5909179	.0194221
TIendogenous						
ed	.137944	.0212485	6.49	0.000	.0962977	.1795902
_cons	2.912726	.2836522	10.27	0.000	2.356778	3.468674
sigma_u	.94180304					
sigma_e	.15180273					
rho	.97467788	(fraction of variance due to u_i)				

```
Note:  TV refers to time varying; TI refers to time invariant.
```

The estimated σ_μ and σ_ϵ are 0.9418 and 0.1518, respectively, indicating that a large fraction of the total error variance is attributed to μ_i. The z statistics indicate that several the coefficients may not be significantly different from zero. Whereas the coefficients on the time-invariant variables fem and blk have relatively large standard errors, the standard error for the coefficient on ed is relatively small.

Baltagi and Khanti-Akom (1990) also present evidence that the efficiency gains of the Amemiya–MaCurdy estimator over the Hausman–Taylor estimator are small for these data. This point is especially important given the additional restrictions that the estimator places on the data-generating process. The output below replicates the Baltagi and Khanti-Akom (1990) results from column AM of table II.

```
. xthtaylor lwage occ south smsa ind exp exp2 wks ms union fem blk ed,
> endog(exp exp2 wks ms union ed) amacurdy
```

Amemiya-MaCurdy estimation	Number of obs	=	4165
Group variable: id	Number of groups	=	595
Time variable: t	Obs per group: min =		7
	avg =		7
	max =		7
Random effects u_i ~ i.i.d.	Wald chi2(12)	=	6879.20
	Prob > chi2	=	0.0000

lwage	Coef.	Std. Err.	z	P>|z|	[95% Conf. Interval]	
TVexogenous						
occ	-.0208498	.0137653	-1.51	0.130	-.0478292	.0061297
south	.0072818	.0319365	0.23	0.820	-.0553126	.0698761
smsa	-.0419507	.0189471	-2.21	0.027	-.0790864	-.0048149
ind	.0136289	.015229	0.89	0.371	-.0162194	.0434771
TVendogenous						
exp	.1129704	.0024688	45.76	0.000	.1081316	.1178093
exp2	-.0004214	.0000546	-7.72	0.000	-.0005283	-.0003145
wks	.0008381	.0005995	1.40	0.162	-.0003368	.002013
ms	-.0300894	.0189674	-1.59	0.113	-.0672649	.0070861
union	.0324752	.0148939	2.18	0.029	.0032837	.0616667
TIexogenous						
fem	-.132008	.1266039	-1.04	0.297	-.380147	.1161311
blk	-.2859004	.1554857	-1.84	0.066	-.5906468	.0188459
TIendogenous						
ed	.1372049	.0205695	6.67	0.000	.0968894	.1775205
_cons	2.927338	.2751274	10.64	0.000	2.388098	3.466578
sigma_u	.94180304					
sigma_e	.15180273					
rho	.97467788	(fraction of variance due to u_i)				

Note: TV refers to time varying; TI refers to time invariant.

◁

❏ Technical Note

We mentioned earlier that insufficient correlation between an endogenous variable and the instruments can give rise to a weak-instrument problem. Suppose that we simulate data for a model of the form

$$y = 3 + 3x_{1a} + 3x_{1b} + 3x_2 + 3z_1 + 3z_2 + u_i + e_{it}$$

and purposely construct the instruments so that they exhibit little correlation with the endogenous variable z_2.

(Continued on next page)

```
. use http://www.stata-press.com/data/r10/xthtaylor1
. correlate ui z1 z2 x1a x1b x2 eit
(obs=10000)
```

	ui	z1	z2	x1a	x1b	x2	eit
ui	1.0000						
z1	0.0268	1.0000					
z2	0.8777	0.0286	1.0000				
x1a	-0.0145	0.0065	-0.0034	1.0000			
x1b	0.0026	0.0079	0.0038	-0.0030	1.0000		
x2	0.8765	0.0191	0.7671	-0.0192	0.0037	1.0000	
eit	0.0060	-0.0198	0.0123	-0.0100	-0.0138	0.0092	1.0000

In the output below, weak instruments have serious consequences on the estimates produced by xthtaylor. The estimate of the coefficient on z2 is three times larger than its true value, and its standard error is rather large. Without sufficient correlation between the endogenous variable and its instruments in a given sample, there is insufficient information for identifying the parameter. Also, given the results of Stock, Wright, and Yojo (2002), weak instruments will cause serious size distortions in any tests performed.

```
. xthtaylor yit x1a x1b x2 z1 z2, endog(x2 z2)
```

Hausman-Taylor estimation			Number of obs	=	10000
Group variable: id			Number of groups	=	1000
			Obs per group: min	=	10
			avg	=	10
			max	=	10
Random effects u_i ~ i.i.d.			Wald chi2(5)	=	24172.91
			Prob > chi2	=	0.0000

yit	Coef.	Std. Err.	z	P>|z|	[95% Conf. Interval]	
TVexogenous						
x1a	2.959736	.0330233	89.63	0.000	2.895011	3.02446
x1b	2.953891	.0333051	88.69	0.000	2.888614	3.019168
TVendogenous						
x2	3.022685	.033085	91.36	0.000	2.957839	3.08753
TIexogenous						
z1	2.709179	.587031	4.62	0.000	1.55862	3.859739
TIendogenous						
z2	9.525973	8.572966	1.11	0.266	-7.276732	26.32868
_cons	2.837072	.4276595	6.63	0.000	1.998875	3.675269
sigma_u	8.729479					
sigma_e	3.1657492					
rho	.88377062	(fraction of variance due to u_i)				

Note: TV refers to time varying; TI refers to time invariant.

▷ Example 2

Now let's consider why we might want to specify the constant(*varlist*ti) option. For this example, we will use simulated data. In the output below, we fit a model over the full sample. Note the placement in the output of the coefficient on the exogenous variable x1c.

```
. use http://www.stata-press.com/data/r10/xthtaylor2

. xthtaylor yit x1a x1b x1c x2 z1 z2, endog(x2 z2)
```

Hausman-Taylor estimation   Number of obs   =   10000
Group variable: id   Number of groups   =   1000

                                             Obs per group: min =   10
                                                            avg =   10
                                                            max =   10

Random effects u_i ~ i.i.d.   Wald chi2(6)   = 10341.63
                                             Prob > chi2   =   0.0000

yit	Coef.	Std. Err.	z	P>|z|	[95% Conf. Interval]	
TVexogenous						
x1a	3.023647	.0570274	53.02	0.000	2.911875	3.135418
x1b	2.966666	.0572659	51.81	0.000	2.854427	3.078905
x1c	.2355318	.123502	1.91	0.057	-.0065276	.4775912
TVendogenous						
x2	14.17476	3.128385	4.53	0.000	8.043234	20.30628
TIexogenous						
z1	1.741709	.4280022	4.07	0.000	.9028398	2.580578
TIendogenous						
z2	7.983849	.6970903	11.45	0.000	6.617577	9.350121
_cons	2.146038	.3794179	5.66	0.000	1.402393	2.889684
sigma_u	5.6787791					
sigma_e	3.1806188					
rho	.76120931	(fraction of variance due to u_i)				

Note: TV refers to time varying; TI refers to time invariant.

Now suppose that we want to fit the model using only the first eight periods. Below, x1c now appears under the TIexogenous heading rather than the TVexogenous heading because x1c is time invariant in the subsample defined by t<9.

(Continued on next page)

```
. xthtaylor yit x1a x1b x1c x2 z1 z2 if t<9, endog(x2 z2)
```

Hausman-Taylor estimation	Number of obs	=	8000
Group variable: id	Number of groups	=	1000
	Obs per group: min =		8
	avg =		8
	max =		8
Random effects u_i ~ i.i.d.	Wald chi2(6) =		15354.87
	Prob > chi2 =		0.0000

yit	Coef.	Std. Err.	z	P>|z|	[95% Conf. Interval]	
TVexogenous						
x1a	3.051966	.0367026	83.15	0.000	2.98003	3.123901
x1b	2.967822	.0368144	80.62	0.000	2.895667	3.039977
TVendogenous						
x2	.7361217	3.199764	0.23	0.818	-5.5353	7.007543
TIexogenous						
x1c	3.215907	.5657191	5.68	0.000	2.107118	4.324696
z1	3.347644	.5819756	5.75	0.000	2.206992	4.488295
TIendogenous						
z2	2.010578	1.143982	1.76	0.079	-.231586	4.252742
_cons	3.257004	.5295828	6.15	0.000	2.219041	4.294967
sigma_u	15.445594					
sigma_e	3.175083					
rho	.95945606	(fraction of variance due to u_i)				

```
Note:  TV refers to time varying; TI refers to time invariant.
```

To prevent a variable from becoming time invariant, you can use either constant($varlist_{ti}$) or varying($varlist_{tv}$). constant($varlist_{ti}$) specifies the subset of variables in *varlist* that are time invariant and requires the remaining variables in *varlist* to be time varying. If you specify constant($varlist_{ti}$) and any of the variables contained in $varlist_{ti}$ are time varying, or if any of the variables not contained in $varlist_{ti}$ are time invariant, xthtaylor will not perform the estimation and will issue an error message.

```
. xthtaylor yit x1a x1b x1c x2 z1 z2 if t<9, endog(x2 z2) constant(z1 z2)
x1c not included in -constant()-.
r(198);
```

The same thing happens when you use the varying($varlist_{tv}$) option.

◁

Saved Results

xthtaylor saves the following in e():

Scalars

e(N)	number of observations	e(chi2)	χ^2
e(N_g)	number of groups	e(rho)	ρ
e(df_m)	model degrees of freedom	e(Tcon)	1 if panels balanced; 0 otherwise
e(def_r)	residual degrees of freedom	e(sigma_u)	panel-level standard deviation
e(g_max)	largest group size	e(sigma_e)	standard deviation of ϵ_{it}
e(g_min)	smallest group size	e(F)	model F (small only)
e(g_avg)	average group size	e(Tbar)	harmonic mean of group sizes

Macros

e(cmd)	xthtaylor	e(TIexogenous)	exog. time-invariant variables
e(cmdline)	command as typed	e(TVendogenous)	endog. time-varying variables
e(depvar)	name of dependent variable	e(TIendogenous)	endog. time-invariant variables
e(wtype)	weight type	e(chi2type)	Wald; type of model χ^2 test
e(wexp)	weight expression	e(vce)	*vcetype* specified in vce()
e(title)	Hausman-Taylor or	e(vcetype)	title used to label Std. Err.
	Amemiya-MaCurdy	e(properties)	b V
e(ivar)	variable denoting groups	e(predict)	program used to implement
e(tvar)	time variable, amacurdy only		predict
e(TVexogenous)	exog. time-varying variables		

Matrices

e(b)	coefficient vector	e(V)	variance–covariance matrix of the estimators

Functions

e(sample)	marks estimation sample

Methods and Formulas

xthtaylor is implemented as an ado-file.

Consider an error-components model of the form

$$y_{it} = \mathbf{X}_{1it}\boldsymbol{\beta}_1 + \mathbf{X}_{2it}\boldsymbol{\beta}_2 + \mathbf{Z}_{1i}\delta_1 + \mathbf{Z}_{2i}\delta_2 + \mu_i + \epsilon_{it} \qquad (2)$$

for $i = 1, \ldots, n$ and, for each i, $t = 1, \ldots, T_i$, of which T_i periods are observed; n is the number of panels in the sample. The covariates in $\mathbf{X}$ are time varying, and the covariates in $\mathbf{Z}$ are time invariant. Both $\mathbf{X}$ and $\mathbf{Z}$ are decomposed into two parts. The covariates in $\mathbf{X}_1$ and $\mathbf{Z}_1$ are assumed to be uncorrelated with μ_i and e_{it}, whereas the covariates in $\mathbf{X}_2$ and $\mathbf{Z}_2$ are allowed to be correlated with μ_i but not with ϵ_{it}. Hausman and Taylor (1981) suggest an instrumental-variable estimator for this model.

For some variable w, the within transformation of w is defined as

$$\widetilde{w}_{it} = w_{it} - \overline{w}_{i.} \qquad \overline{w}_{i.} = \frac{1}{n} \sum_{t=1}^{T_i} w_{it}$$

Since the within estimator removes $\mathbf{Z}$, the within transformation reduces the model to

$$\widetilde{y}_{it} = \widetilde{\mathbf{X}}_{1it}\boldsymbol{\beta}_1 + \widetilde{\mathbf{X}}_{2it}\boldsymbol{\beta}_2 + \widetilde{\epsilon}_{it}$$

The within estimators $\widehat{\beta}_{1w}$ and $\widehat{\beta}_{2w}$ are consistent for $\boldsymbol{\beta}_1$ and $\boldsymbol{\beta}_2$, but they may not be efficient. Also, note that the within estimator cannot estimate $\boldsymbol{\delta}_1$ and $\boldsymbol{\delta}_2$.

The within estimator can be used to obtain the within residuals

$$\widetilde{d}_{it} = \widetilde{y}_{it} - \widetilde{\mathbf{X}}_{1it}\widehat{\beta}_{1w} - \widetilde{\mathbf{X}}_{2it}\widehat{\beta}_{2w}$$

allowing us to estimate the variance of the idiosyncratic error component, σ_ϵ^2, as

$$\widehat{\sigma}_\epsilon^2 = \frac{RSS}{N - n}$$

where RSS is the residual sum of squares from the within regression and N is the total number of observations in the sample.

Regressing $\widetilde{d}_{it}$ on $\mathbf{Z}_1$ and $\mathbf{Z}_2$, using $\mathbf{X}_1$ and $\mathbf{Z}_1$ as instruments, provides intermediate, consistent estimates of $\boldsymbol{\delta}_1$ and $\boldsymbol{\delta}_2$, which we will call $\widehat{\boldsymbol{\delta}}_{1IV}$ and $\widehat{\boldsymbol{\delta}}_{2IV}$.

Using the within estimates, $\widehat{\boldsymbol{\delta}}_{1IV}$, and $\widehat{\boldsymbol{\delta}}_{2IV}$, we can obtain an estimate of the variance of the random effect, σ_μ^2. First, let

$$\widehat{e}_{it} = \left(y_{it} - \mathbf{X}_{1it}\widehat{\beta}_{1w} - \mathbf{X}_{2it}\widehat{\beta}_{2w} - \mathbf{Z}_{1it}\widehat{\boldsymbol{\delta}}_{1IV} - \mathbf{Z}_{2it}\widehat{\boldsymbol{\delta}}_{2IV} \right)$$

Then define

$$s^2 = \frac{1}{N} \sum_{i=1}^{n} \sum_{t=1}^{T_i} \left(\frac{1}{T_i} \sum_{t=1}^{T_i} \widehat{e}_i \right)^2$$

Hausman and Taylor (1981) showed that, for balanced panels,

$$\text{plim}_{n \to \infty} s^2 = T\sigma_\mu^2 + \sigma_\epsilon^2$$

For unbalanced panels,

$$\text{plim}_{n \to \infty} s^2 = \overline{T}\sigma_\mu^2 + \sigma_\epsilon^2$$

where

$$\overline{T} = \frac{n}{\sum_{i=1}^{n} \frac{1}{T_i}}$$

After we plug in $\widehat{\sigma}_\epsilon^2$, our consistent estimate for σ_ϵ^2, a little algebra suggests the estimate

$$\widehat{\sigma}_\mu^2 = (s^2 - \widehat{\sigma}_\epsilon^2)(\overline{T})^{-1}$$

Define $\widehat{\theta}_i$ as

$$\widehat{\theta}_i = 1 - \left(\frac{\widehat{\sigma}_\epsilon^2}{\widehat{\sigma}_\epsilon^2 + T_i \widehat{\sigma}_\mu^2} \right)^{\frac{1}{2}}$$

With $\widehat{\theta}_i$ in hand, we can perform the standard random-effects GLS transform on each of the variables. The transform is given by

$$w_{it}^* = w_{it} - \widehat{\theta}_i \overline{w}_{i.}$$

where $\overline{w}_{i.}$ is the within-panel mean.

We can then obtain the Hausman–Taylor estimates of the coefficients in (2) and the conventional VCE by fitting an instrumental-variables regression of the GLS-transformed y_{it}^* on $\mathbf{X}_{it}^*$ and $\mathbf{Z}_{it}^*$, with instruments $\widetilde{\mathbf{X}}_{it}$, $\overline{\mathbf{X}}_{1i.}$, and $\mathbf{Z}_{1i}$.

We can obtain Amemiya–MaCurdy estimates of the coefficients in (2) and the conventional VCE by fitting an instrumental-variables regression of the GLS-transformed y_{it}^* on $\mathbf{X}_{it}^*$ and $\mathbf{Z}_{it}^*$, using $\widetilde{\mathbf{X}}_{it}$, $\breve{\mathbf{X}}_{1it}$, and $\mathbf{Z}_{1i}$ as instruments, where $\breve{\mathbf{X}}_{1it} = \mathbf{X}_{1i1}, \mathbf{X}_{1i2}, \ldots, \mathbf{X}_{1iT_i}$. The order condition for the Amemiya–MaCurdy estimator is $T k_1 > g_2$, and this estimator is available only for balanced panels.

References

Amemiya, T., and T. MaCurdy. 1986. Instrumental-variable estimation of an error-components model. *Econometrica* 54: 869–880.

Baltagi, B. H. 2005. *Econometric Analysis of Panel Data*. 3rd ed. New York: Wiley.

Baltagi, B. H., and S. Khanti-Akom. 1990. On efficient estimation with panel data: An empirical comparison of instrumental variables estimators. *Journal of Applied Econometrics* 5: 401–406.

Hausman, J. A., and W. E. Taylor. 1981. Panel data and unobservable individual effects. *Econometrica* 49: 1377–1398.

Stock, J. H., J. H. Wright, and M. Yogo. 2002. A survey of weak instruments and weak identification in generalized method of moments. *Journal of Business and Economic Statistics* 20: 518–529.

Also See

Title

xthtaylor postestimation — Postestimation tools for xthtaylor

Description

The following postestimation commands are available for xthtaylor:

command	description
adjust[1]	adjusted predictions of $\mathbf{x}\beta$
estat	VCE and estimation sample summary
estimates	cataloging estimation results
lincom	point estimates, standard errors, testing, and inference for linear combinations of coefficients
mfx	marginal effects or elasticities
nlcom	point estimates, standard errors, testing, and inference for nonlinear combinations of coefficients
predict	predictions, residuals, influence statistics, and other diagnostic measures
predictnl	point estimates, standard errors, testing, and inference for generalized predictions
test	Wald tests for simple and composite linear hypotheses
testnl	Wald tests of nonlinear hypotheses

[1] adjust is not appropriate with time-series operators.

See the corresponding entries in the *Stata Base Reference Manual* for details.

Syntax for predict

predict [*type*] *newvar* [*if*] [*in*] [, *statistic*]

statistic	description
Main	
xb	$\mathbf{X}_{it}\widehat{\beta} + \mathbf{Z}_i\widehat{\delta}$, fitted values; the default
stdp	standard error of the fitted values
ue	$\widehat{\mu}_i + \widehat{\epsilon}_{it}$, the combined residual
*xbu	$\mathbf{X}_{it}\widehat{\beta} + \mathbf{Z}_i\widehat{\delta} + \widehat{\mu}_i$, prediction including effect
*u	$\widehat{\mu}_i$, the random error component
*e	$\widehat{\epsilon}_{it}$, prediction of the idiosyncratic error component

Unstarred statistics are available both in and out of sample; type predict ... if e(sample) ... if wanted only for the estimation sample. Starred statistics are calculated only for the estimation sample, even when if e(sample) is not specified.

Options for predict

Main

xb, the default, calculates the linear prediction, that is, $\mathbf{X}_{it}\widehat{\beta} + \mathbf{Z}_{it}\widehat{\delta}$.

stdp calculates the standard error of the linear prediction.

ue calculates the prediction of $\widehat{\mu}_i + \widehat{\epsilon}_{it}$.

xbu calculates the prediction of $\mathbf{X}_{it}\widehat{\beta} + \mathbf{Z}_{it}\widehat{\delta} + \widehat{\nu}_i$, the prediction including the random effect.

u calculates the prediction of $\widehat{\mu}_i$, the estimated random effect.

e calculates the prediction of $\widehat{\epsilon}_{it}$.

Methods and Formulas

All postestimation commands listed above are implemented as ado-files.

Also See

[XT] **xthtaylor** — Hausman–Taylor estimator for error-components models

[U] **20 Estimation and postestimation commands**

Title

> **xtintreg** — Random-effects interval-data regression models

Syntax

$$\texttt{xtintreg } \textit{depvar}_{\text{lower}} \textit{ depvar}_{\text{upper}} \left[\textit{indepvars}\right] \left[\textit{if}\right] \left[\textit{in}\right] \left[\textit{weight}\right] \left[, \textit{ options}\right]$$

options	description
Model	
<u>nocon</u>stant	suppress constant term
<u>off</u>set(*varname*)	include *varname* in model with coefficient constrained to 1
<u>constra</u>ints(*constraints*)	apply specified linear constraints
<u>col</u>linear	keep collinear variables
SE	
vce(*vcetype*)	*vcetype* may be oim, <u>boot</u>strap, or <u>jack</u>knife
Reporting	
<u>level</u>(#)	set confidence level; default is level(95)
noskip	perform overall model test as a likelihood-ratio test
intreg	perform likelihood-ratio test against pooled model
Int opts (RE)	
<u>intm</u>ethod(*intmethod*)	integration method; *intmethod* may be <u>mvaghermite</u>, <u>agh</u>ermite, or <u>gh</u>ermite; default is intmethod(mvaghermite)
<u>intp</u>oints(#)	use # quadrature points; default is intpoints(12)
Max options	
maximize_options	control the maximization process; see [R] **maximize**

A panel variable must be specified; use xtset; see [XT] **xtset**.
*depvar*_{lower}, *depvar*_{upper}, and *indepvars* may contain time-series operators; see [U] **11.4.3 Time-series varlists**.
by, statsby, and xi are allowed; see [U] **11.1.10 Prefix commands**.
iweights are allowed; see [U] **11.1.6 weight**. Weights must be constant within panel.
See [U] **20 Estimation and postestimation commands** for more capabilities of estimation commands.

Description

xtintreg fits random-effects interval data regression models. There is no command for a conditional fixed-effects model, as there does not exist a sufficient statistic allowing the fixed effects to be conditioned out of the likelihood. Unconditional fixed-effects intreg models may be fitted with the intreg command, with indicator variables for the panels. The appropriate indicator variables can be generated using tabulate or xi. However, unconditional fixed-effects estimates are biased.

xtintreg is slow because the likelihood function is calculated by adaptive Gauss–Hermite quadrature; see *Methods and Formulas*. Computation time is roughly proportional to the number of points used for the quadrature. The default is intpoints(12). Increasing the number of quadrature points can improve the quadrature approximation. See [XT] **quadchk**.

Options

    ⌐ Model ⌐

noconstant, offset(*varname*), constraints(*constraints*), collinear; see [XT] **estimation options**.

    ⌐ SE ⌐

vce(*vcetype*) specifies the type of standard error reported, which includes types that are derived from asymptotic theory and that use bootstrap or jackknife methods; see [XT] ***vce_options***.

    ⌐ Reporting ⌐

level(*#*), noskip; see [XT] **estimation options**.

intreg specifies that a likelihood-ratio test comparing the random-effects model with the pooled (intreg) model be included in the output.

    ⌐ Int opts (RE) ⌐

intmethod(*intmethod*), intpoints(*#*); see [XT] **estimation options**.

    ⌐ Max options ⌐

maximize_options: <u>diff</u>icult, <u>tech</u>nique(*algorithm_spec*), <u>iter</u>ate(*#*), [<u>no</u>]<u>log</u>, <u>trace</u>, <u>grad</u>ient, showstep, <u>hess</u>ian, shownrtolerance, <u>tol</u>erance(*#*), <u>ltol</u>erance(*#*), <u>gtol</u>erance(*#*), <u>nrtol</u>erance(*#*), <u>nonrtol</u>erance, from(*init_specs*); see [R] **maximize**. Some of these options are not available if intmethod(ghermite) is specified. These options are seldom used.

Remarks

Consider the linear regression model with panel-level random effects

$$y_{it} = \mathbf{x}_{it}\boldsymbol{\beta} + \nu_i + \epsilon_{it}$$

for $i = 1, \ldots, n$ panels, where $t = 1, \ldots, n_i$. The random effects, ν_i, are i.i.d., $N(0, \sigma_\nu^2)$, and ϵ_{it} are i.i.d., $N(0, \sigma_\epsilon^2)$ independently of ν_i. The observed data consist of the couples, (y_{1it}, y_{2it}), such that all that is known is that $y_{1it} \le y_{it} \le y_{2it}$, where y_{1it} is possibly $-\infty$ and y_{2it} is possibly $+\infty$.

▷ Example 1

We begin with the dataset nlswork described in [XT] **xt** and create two fictional dependent variables, where the wages are instead reported sometimes as ranges. The wages have been adjusted to 1988 dollars and have further been recoded such that some of the observations are known exactly, some are left-censored, some are right-censored, and some are known only in an interval.

We wish to fit a random-effects interval regression model of adjusted (log) wages:

```
. use http://www.stata-press.com/data/r10/nlswork5
(National Longitudinal Survey.  Young Women 14-26 years of age in 1968)
. xtintreg ln_wage1 ln_wage2 union age grade south southXt occ_code, intreg
(output omitted)
```

Random-effects interval regression						Number of obs	=	19151
Group variable: idcode						Number of groups	=	4140

```
Random effects u_i ~ Gaussian                   Obs per group: min =          1
                                                               avg =        4.6
                                                               max =         12

                                                Wald chi2(6)       =    2523.84
Log likelihood  =  -23174.58                    Prob > chi2        =     0.0000
```

	Coef.	Std. Err.	z	P>|z|	[95% Conf. Interval]	
union	.1441626	.0094248	15.30	0.000	.1256903	.1626349
age	.0115741	.0007172	16.14	0.000	.0101685	.0129798
grade	.0795451	.0023455	33.91	0.000	.0749481	.0841421
south	-.1392074	.0162391	-8.57	0.000	-.1710355	-.1073794
southXt	.0036372	.0011738	3.10	0.002	.0013366	.0059378
occ_code	-.0198253	.0014084	-14.08	0.000	-.0225859	-.0170648
_cons	.4509353	.0379734	11.88	0.000	.3765088	.5253618
/sigma_u	.2986489	.00527	56.67	0.000	.2883199	.3089778
/sigma_e	.352846	.0030934	114.07	0.000	.3467831	.3589089
rho	.4173828	.0102538			.3974021	.4375792

```
Likelihood-ratio test of sigma_u=0: chibar2(01)= 2519.56 Prob>=chibar2 = 0.000

  Observation summary:      4757  left-censored observations
                            4792       uncensored observations
                            4830 right-censored observations
                            4772       interval observations
```

The output includes the overall and panel-level variance components (labeled `sigma_e` and `sigma_u`, respectively) together with ρ (labeled `rho`),

$$\rho = \frac{\sigma_\nu^2}{\sigma_\epsilon^2 + \sigma_\nu^2}$$

which is the proportion of the total variance contributed by the panel-level variance component.

When `rho` is zero, the panel-level variance component is unimportant, and the panel estimator is not different from the pooled estimator. A likelihood-ratio test of this is included at the bottom of the output. This test formally compares the pooled estimator (intreg) with the panel estimator.

◁

❏ Technical Note

The random-effects model is calculated using quadrature. As the panel sizes (or ρ) increase, the quadrature approximation can become less accurate. We can use the `quadchk` command to see if changing the number of quadrature points affects the results. If the results change, the quadrature approximation is not accurate, and the results of the model should not be interpreted. See [XT] **quadchk** for details and [XT] **xtprobit** for an example.

❏

Saved Results

xtintreg saves the following in e():

Scalars

e(N)	# of observations	e(rho)	ρ
e(N_g)	# of groups	e(sigma_u)	panel-level standard deviation
e(N_unc)	# of uncensored observations	e(sigma_e)	standard deviation of ϵ_{it}
e(N_lc)	# of left-censored observations	e(n_quad)	# of quadrature points
e(N_rc)	# of right-censored observations	e(rc)	return code
e(N_int)	# of interval observations	e(rank)	rank of e(V)
e(N_cd)	# of completely determined obs.	e(rank0)	rank of e(V) for constant-only model
e(df_m)	model degrees of freedom	e(k)	# of parameters
e(ll)	log likelihood	e(k_eq)	# of equations
e(ll_0)	log likelihood, constant-only model	e(k_eq_model)	# of equations in model Wald test
e(g_max)	largest group size	e(k_dv)	# of dependent variables
e(g_min)	smallest group size	e(ic)	# of iterations
e(g_avg)	average group size	e(p)	significance
e(chi2)	χ^2	e(converged)	1 if converged, 0 otherwise
e(chi2_c)	χ^2 for comparison test		

Macros

e(cmd)	xtintreg	e(distrib)	Gaussian; the distribution of the
e(cmdline)	command as typed		random effect
e(depvar)	names of dependent variables	e(vce)	*vcetype* specified in vce()
e(ivar)	variable denoting groups	e(vcetype)	title used to label Std. Err.
e(wtype)	weight type	e(opt)	type of optimization
e(wexp)	weight expression	e(ml_method)	type of ml method
e(title)	title in estimation output	e(user)	name of likelihood-evaluator program
e(offset1)	offset	e(technique)	maximization technique
e(chi2type)	Wald or LR; type of model χ^2 test	e(crittype)	optimization criterion
e(chi2_ct)	Wald or LR; type of model χ^2 test	e(properties)	b V
	corresponding to e(chi2_c)	e(predict)	program used to implement predict
e(intmethod)	integration method		

Matrices

e(b)	coefficient vector	e(ilog)	iteration log
e(V)	variance–covariance matrix of the estimators	e(gradient)	gradient vector

Functions

e(sample)	marks estimation sample

Methods and Formulas

xtintreg is implemented as an ado-file.

Assuming a normal distribution, $N(0, \sigma_\nu^2)$, for the random effects ν_i, we have the joint (unconditional of ν_i) density of the observed data for the ith panel

$$f\left\{(y_{1i1}, y_{2i1}), \ldots, (y_{1in_i}, y_{2in_i}) | \mathbf{x}_{1i}, \ldots, \mathbf{x}_{in_i}\right\} =$$
$$\int_{-\infty}^{\infty} \frac{e^{-\nu_i^2/2\sigma_\nu^2}}{\sqrt{2\pi}\sigma_\nu} \left\{\prod_{t=1}^{n_i} F(y_{1it}, y_{2it}, \mathbf{x}_{it}\boldsymbol{\beta} + \nu_i)\right\} d\nu_i$$

where

$$
F(y_{1it}, y_{2it}, \Delta_{it}) = \begin{cases} \left(\sqrt{2\pi}\sigma_\epsilon\right)^{-1} e^{-(y_{1it}-\Delta_{it})^2/(2\sigma_\epsilon^2)} & \text{if } (y_{1it}, y_{2it}) \in C \\[2ex] \Phi\left(\frac{y_{2it}-\Delta_{it}}{\sigma_\epsilon}\right) & \text{if } (y_{1it}, y_{2it}) \in L \\[2ex] 1 - \Phi\left(\frac{y_{1it}-\Delta_{it}}{\sigma_\epsilon}\right) & \text{if } (y_{1it}, y_{2it}) \in R \\[2ex] \Phi\left(\frac{y_{2it}-\Delta_{it}}{\sigma_\epsilon}\right) - \Phi\left(\frac{y_{1it}-\Delta_{it}}{\sigma_\epsilon}\right) & \text{if } (y_{1it}, y_{2it}) \in I \end{cases}
$$

where C is the set of noncensored observations ($y_{1it} = y_{2it}$ and both nonmissing), L is the set of left-censored observations (y_{1it} missing and y_{2it} nonmissing), R is the set of right-censored observations (y_{1it} nonmissing and y_{2it} missing), I is the set of interval observations ($y_{1it} < y_{2it}$ and both nonmissing), and $\Phi()$ is the cumulative normal distribution.

The panel-level likelihood l_i is given by

$$
l_i = \int_{-\infty}^{\infty} \frac{e^{-\nu_i^2/2\sigma_\nu^2}}{\sqrt{2\pi}\sigma_\nu} \left\{ \prod_{t=1}^{n_i} F(y_{1it}, y_{2it}, \mathbf{x}_{it}\boldsymbol{\beta} + \nu_i) \right\} d\nu_i
$$

$$
\equiv \int_{-\infty}^{\infty} g(y_{1it}, y_{2it}, x_{it}, \nu_i) d\nu_i
$$

This integral can be approximated with M-point Gauss–Hermite quadrature

$$
\int_{-\infty}^{\infty} e^{-x^2} h(x) dx \approx \sum_{m=1}^{M} w_m^* h(a_m^*)
$$

This is equivalent to

$$
\int_{-\infty}^{\infty} f(x) dx \approx \sum_{m=1}^{M} w_m^* \exp\left\{(a_m^*)^2\right\} f(a_m^*)
$$

where the w_m^* denote the quadrature weights and the a_m^* denote the quadrature abscissas. The log likelihood, L, is the sum of the logs of the panel-level likelihoods l_i.

The default approximation of the log likelihood is by adaptive Gauss–Hermite quadrature, which approximates the panel-level likelihood with

$$
l_i \approx \sqrt{2}\hat{\sigma}_i \sum_{m=1}^{M} w_m^* \exp\left\{(a_m^*)^2\right\} g(y_{1it}, y_{2it}, x_{it}, \sqrt{2}\hat{\sigma}_i a_m^* + \hat{\mu}_i)
$$

where $\hat{\sigma}_i$ and $\hat{\mu}_i$ are the adaptive parameters for panel i. Therefore, using the definition of $g(y_{1it}, y_{2it}, x_{it}, \nu_i)$, the total log likelihood is approximated by

$$
L \approx \sum_{i=1}^{n} w_i \log\Bigg[\sqrt{2}\hat{\sigma}_i \sum_{m=1}^{M} w_m^* \exp\{(a_m^*)^2\} \frac{\exp\{-(\sqrt{2}\hat{\sigma}_i a_m^* + \hat{\mu}_i)^2/2\sigma_\nu^2\}}{\sqrt{2\pi}\sigma_\nu}
$$

$$
\prod_{t=1}^{n_i} F(y_{1it}, y_{2it}, x_{it}\boldsymbol{\beta} + \sqrt{2}\hat{\sigma}_i a_m^* + \hat{\mu}_i) \Bigg]
$$

where w_i is the user-specified weight for panel i; if no weights are specified, $w_i = 1$.

The default method of adaptive Gauss–Hermite quadrature is to calculate the posterior mean and variance and use those parameters for $\widehat{\mu}_i$ and $\widehat{\sigma}_i$ by following the method of Naylor and Smith (1982), further discussed in Skrondal and Rabe-Hesketh (2004). We start with $\widehat{\sigma}_{i,0} = 1$ and $\widehat{\mu}_{i,0} = 0$, and the posterior means and variances are updated in the kth iteration. That is, at the kth iteration of the optimization for l_i we use

$$l_{i,k} \approx \sum_{m=1}^{M} \sqrt{2}\widehat{\sigma}_{i,k-1} w_m^* \exp\{a_m^*)^2\} g(y_{1it}, y_{2it}, x_{it}, \sqrt{2}\widehat{\sigma}_{i,k-1} a_m^* + \widehat{\mu}_{i,k-1})$$

Letting

$$\tau_{i,m,k-1} = \sqrt{2}\widehat{\sigma}_{i,k-1} a_m^* + \widehat{\mu}_{i,k-1}$$

$$\widehat{\mu}_{i,k} = \sum_{m=1}^{M} (\tau_{i,m,k-1}) \frac{\sqrt{2}\widehat{\sigma}_{i,k-1} w_m^* \exp\{(a_m^*)^2\} g(y_{1it}, y_{2it}, x_{it}, \tau_{i,m,k-1})}{l_{i,k}}$$

and

$$\widehat{\sigma}_{i,k} = \sum_{m=1}^{M} (\tau_{i,m,k-1})^2 \frac{\sqrt{2}\widehat{\sigma}_{i,k-1} w_m^* \exp\{(a_m^*)^2\} g(y_{1it}, y_{2it}, x_{it}, \tau_{i,m,k-1})}{l_{i,k}} - (\widehat{\mu}_{i,k})^2$$

and this is repeated until $\widehat{\mu}_{i,k}$ and $\widehat{\sigma}_{i,k}$ have converged for this iteration of the maximization algorithm. This adaptation is applied on every iteration until the log-likelihood change from the preceding iteration is less than a relative difference of 1e−6; after this, the quadrature parameters are fixed.

One can instead use the adaptive quadrature method of Liu and Pierce (1994), option int-method(aghermite), which uses the mode and curvature of the mode as approximations for the mean and variance. We take the integrand

$$g(y_{1it}, y_{2it}, x_{it}, \nu_i) = \frac{e^{-\nu_i^2/2\sigma_\nu^2}}{\sqrt{2\pi}\sigma_\nu} \left\{ \prod_{t=1}^{n_i} F(y_{1it}, y_{2it}, \mathbf{x}_{it}\boldsymbol{\beta} + \nu_i) \right\}$$

and find α_i the mode of $g(y_{1it}, y_{2it}, x_{it}, \nu_i)$. We calculate

$$\gamma_i = -\frac{\partial^2}{\partial \nu^2} \log\{g(y_{1it}, y_{2it}, x_{it}, \nu_i)\}\big|_{\nu_i = \alpha_i}$$

Then

$$\int_{-\infty}^{\infty} g(y_{1it}, y_{2it}, x_{it}, \nu_i) d\nu_i \approx \left(\frac{2}{\gamma_i}\right)^{1/2} \sum_{m=1}^{M} w_m^* \exp\{(a_m^*)^2\}$$

$$g\left\{ y_{1it}, y_{2it}, x_{it}, \left(\frac{2}{\gamma_i}\right)^{1/2} a_m^* + \alpha_i \right\}$$

This adaptation is performed on the first iteration only; that is, the α_i and γ_i are calculated once at the first iteration and then held constant throughout the subsequent iterations.

The log likelihood can also be calculated by nonadaptive Gauss–Hermite quadrature, option intmethod(ghermite):

$$
L = \sum_{i=1}^{n} w_i \log f\left\{ (y_{1i1}, y_{2i1}), \ldots, (y_{1in_i}, y_{2in_i}) | \mathbf{x}_{1i}, \ldots, \mathbf{x}_{in_i} \right\}
$$

$$
\approx \sum_{i=1}^{n} w_i \log\left\{ \frac{1}{\sqrt{\pi}} \sum_{m=1}^{M} w_m^* \prod_{t=1}^{n_i} F\left(y_{1it}, y_{2it}, \mathbf{x}_{it}\boldsymbol{\beta} + \sqrt{2}\sigma_\nu a_m^* \right) \right\}
$$

All three quadrature formulas require that the integrated function be well approximated by a polynomial of degree equal to the number of quadrature points. The number of periods (panel size) can affect whether

$$
\prod_{t=1}^{n_i} F(y_{1it}, y_{2it}, \mathbf{x}_{it}\boldsymbol{\beta} + \nu_i)
$$

is well approximated by a polynomial. As panel size and ρ increase, the quadrature approximation can become less accurate. For large ρ, the random-effects model can also become unidentified. Adaptive quadrature gives better results for correlated data and large panels than nonadaptive quadrature; however, we recommend that you use the quadchk command to verify the quadrature approximation used in this command, whichever approximation you choose.

References

Liu, Q., and D. A. Pierce 1994. A note on Gauss–Hermite quadrature. *Biometrika* 81: 624–629.

Naylor, J. C., and A. F. M. Smith. 1982. Applications of a method for the efficient computation of posterior distributions. *Journal of the Royal Statistical Society, Series C* 31: 214–225.

Neuhaus, J. M. 1992. Statistical methods for longitudinal and clustered designs with binary responses. *Statistical Methods in Medical Research* 1: 249–273.

Pendergast, J. F., S. J. Gange, M. A. Newton, M. J. Lindstrom, M. Palta, and M. R. Fisher. 1996. A survey of methods for analyzing clustered binary response data. *International Statistical Review* 64: 89–118.

Skrondal, A., and S. Rabe-Hesketh. 2004. *Generalized Latent Variable Modeling: Multilevel, Longitudinal, and Structural Equation Models*. Boca Raton, FL: Chapman & Hall/CRC.

Also See

[XT] **xtintreg postestimation** — Postestimation tools for xtintreg

[XT] **quadchk** — Check sensitivity of quadrature approximation

[XT] **xtreg** — Fixed-, between-, and random-effects, and population-averaged linear models

[XT] **xttobit** — Random-effects tobit models

[R] **intreg** — Interval regression

[R] **tobit** — Tobit regression

[U] **20 Estimation and postestimation commands**

Title

xtintreg postestimation — Postestimation tools for xtintreg	

Description

The following postestimation commands are available for `xtintreg`:

command	description
adjust[1]	adjusted predictions of $\mathbf{x}\beta$
estat	AIC, BIC, VCE, and estimation sample summary
estimates	cataloging estimation results
lincom	point estimates, standard errors, testing, and inference for linear combinations of coefficients
lrtest	likelihood-ratio test
mfx	marginal effects or elasticities
nlcom	point estimates, standard errors, testing, and inference for nonlinear combinations of coefficients
predict	predictions, residuals, influence statistics, and other diagnostic measures
predictnl	point estimates, standard errors, testing, and inference for generalized predictions
test	Wald tests for simple and composite linear hypotheses
testnl	Wald tests of nonlinear hypotheses

[1] `adjust` is not appropriate with time-series operators.

See the corresponding entries in the *Stata Base Reference Manual* for details.

Syntax for predict

> predict [*type*] *newvar* [*if*] [*in*] [, *statistic* <u>nooff</u>set]

statistic	description
Main	
xb	linear prediction assuming $\nu_i = 0$, the default
stdp	standard error of the linear prediction
stdf	standard error of the linear forecast
<u>pr</u>0(*a*,*b*)	$\Pr(a < y < b)$ assuming $\nu_i = 0$
<u>e</u>0(*a*,*b*)	$E(y \mid a < y < b)$ assuming $\nu_i = 0$
<u>ystar</u>0(*a*,*b*)	$E(y^*)$, $y^* = \max\{a, \min(y_j, b)\}$ assuming $\nu_i = 0$

These statistics are available both in and out of sample; type `predict ... if e(sample) ...` if wanted only for the estimation sample.

where *a* and *b* may be numbers or variables; *a* missing ($a \geq .$) means $-\infty$, and *b* missing ($b \geq .$) means $+\infty$; see [U] **12.2.1 Missing values**.

Options for predict

⌐ Main ⌐

xb, the default, calculates the linear prediction.

stdp calculates the standard error of the prediction. It can be thought of as the standard error of the predicted expected value or mean for the observation's covariate pattern. The standard error of the prediction is also referred to as the standard error of the fitted value.

stdf calculates the standard error of the forecast. This is the standard error of the point prediction for 1 observation. It is commonly referred to as the standard error of the future or forecast value. By construction, the standard errors produced by stdf are always larger than those produced by stdp; see [R] **regress** *Methods and Formulas*.

pr0(a,b) calculates estimates of $\Pr(a < y < b | \mathbf{x} = \mathbf{x}_{it}, \nu_i = 0)$, which is the probability that y would be observed in the interval (a, b), given the current values of the predictors, $\mathbf{x}_{it}$, and given a zero random effect. In the discussion that follows, these two conditions are implied.

> a and b may be specified as numbers or variable names; *lb* and *ub* are variable names;
> pr0(20,30) calculates $\Pr(20 < y < 30)$;
> pr0(*lb*,*ub*) calculates $\Pr(lb < y < ub)$; and
> pr0(20,*ub*) calculates $\Pr(20 < y < ub)$.

> a missing ($a \geq .$) means $-\infty$; pr0(.,30) calculates $\Pr(-\infty < y < 30)$;
> pr0(*lb*,30) calculates $\Pr(-\infty < y < 30)$ in observations for which *lb* $\geq .$
> (and calculates $\Pr(lb < y < 30)$ elsewhere).

> b missing ($b \geq .$) means $+\infty$; pr0(20,.) calculates $\Pr(+\infty > y > 20)$;
> pr0(20,*ub*) calculates $\Pr(+\infty > y > 20)$ in observations for which *ub* $\geq .$
> (and calculates $\Pr(20 < y < ub)$ elsewhere).

e0(a,b) calculates estimates of $E(y \mid a < y < b, \mathbf{x} = \mathbf{x}_{it}, \nu_i = 0)$, which is the expected value of y conditional on y being in the interval (a, b), meaning that y is censored. a and b are specified as they are for pr0().

ystar0(a,b) calculates estimates of $E(y^* | \mathbf{x} = \mathbf{x}_{it}, \nu_i = 0)$, where $y^* = a$ if $y \leq a$, $y^* = b$ if $y \geq b$, and $y^* = y$ otherwise, meaning that y^* is the truncated version of y. a and b are specified as they are for pr0().

nooffset is relevant only if you specified offset(*varname*) for xtintreg. It modifies the calculations made by predict so that they ignore the offset variable; the linear prediction is treated as $\mathbf{x}_{it}\beta$ rather than $\mathbf{x}_{it}\beta + \text{offset}_{it}$.

Remarks

▷ Example 1

In [XT] **xtintreg**, we fitted a random-effects model of wages. Say that we want to know how union membership status affects the probability that a worker's wage will be "low", where low means a log wage that is less than the 20th percentile of all observations in our dataset. First, we use centile to find the 20th percentile of ln_wage:

```
. use http://www.stata-press.com/data/r10/nlswork5
(National Longitudinal Survey.  Young Women 14-26 years of age in 1968)
. xtintreg ln_wage1 ln_wage2 union age grade south southXt occ_code, intreg
(output omitted )
```

```
. centile ln_wage, centile(20)
```

Variable	Obs	Percentile	Centile	— Binom. Interp. — [95% Conf. Interval]
ln_wage	28534	20	1.301507	1.297063 1.308635

Now we use **mfx** to obtain the effect of **union** on the probability that **ln_wage** is less than 1.30:

```
. mfx compute, predict(pr0(.,1.30))
```

```
Marginal effects after xtintreg
     y  = Pr(ln_wage1<1.30) (predict, pr0(.,1.30))
        =  .17686354
```

variable	dy/dx	Std. Err.	z	P>|z|	[95% C.I.]	X
union*	−.0746944	.00455	−16.43	0.000	−.083604 −.065785	.234348
age	−.0064975	.00041	−15.90	0.000	−.007299 −.005697	31.3587
grade	−.0446554	.00143	−31.18	0.000	−.047463 −.041848	12.7652
south*	.0799507	.00959	8.34	0.000	.061162 .098739	.414652
southXt	−.0020419	.00066	−3.10	0.002	−.003335 −.000749	4.35805
occ_code	.0111297	.0008	13.97	0.000	.009568 .012692	4.66623

(*) dy/dx is for discrete change of dummy variable from 0 to 1

Being in a union lowers the probability of being classified as a low-wage worker by nearly 7.5 percentage points. An additional year of schooling lowers the probability by nearly 4.5 percentage points.

◁

Methods and Formulas

All postestimation commands listed above are implemented as ado-files.

Also See

[XT] **xtintreg** — Random-effects interval-data regression models

[U] **20 Estimation and postestimation commands**

Title

> **xtivreg** — Instrumental variables and two-stage least squares for panel-data models

Syntax

GLS random-effects (RE) model

> xtivreg *depvar* [*varlist*₁] (*varlist*₂ = *varlist*ᵢᵥ) [*if*] [*in*] [, re *RE_options*]

Between-effects (BE) model

> xtivreg *depvar* [*varlist*₁] (*varlist*₂ = *varlist*ᵢᵥ) [*if*] [*in*], be [*BE_options*]

Fixed-effects (FE) model

> xtivreg *depvar* [*varlist*₁] (*varlist*₂ = *varlist*ᵢᵥ) [*if*] [*in*], fe [*FE_options*]

First-differenced (FD) estimator

> xtivreg *depvar* [*varlist*₁] (*varlist*₂ = *varlist*ᵢᵥ) [*if*] [*in*], fd [*FD_options*]

RE_options	description
Model	
re	use random-effects estimator; the default
ec2sls	use Baltagi's EC2SLS random-effects estimator
nosa	use the Baltagi–Chang estimators of the variance components
regress	treat covariates as exogenous and ignore instrument variables
SE	
vce(*vcetype*)	*vcetype* may be conventional, bootstrap, or jackknife
Reporting	
level(#)	set confidence level; default is level(95)
first	report first-stage estimates
small	report t and F statistics instead of Z and chi-squared statistics
theta	report θ

BE_options	description
Model	
be	use between-effects estimator
<u>reg</u>ress	treat covariates as exogenous and ignore instrument variables
SE	
vce(*vcetype*)	*vcetype* may be conventional, <u>boot</u>strap, or <u>jack</u>knife
Reporting	
<u>l</u>evel(*#*)	set confidence level; default is level(95)
first	report first-stage estimates
<u>sm</u>all	report t and F statistics instead of Z and chi-squared statistics

FE_options	description
Model	
fe	use fixed-effects estimator
<u>reg</u>ress	treat covariates as exogenous and ignore instrument variables
SE	
vce(*vcetype*)	*vcetype* may be conventional, <u>boot</u>strap, or <u>jack</u>knife
Reporting	
<u>l</u>evel(*#*)	set confidence level; default is level(95)
first	report first-stage estimates
<u>sm</u>all	report t and F statistics instead of Z and chi-squared statistics

FD_options	description
Model	
<u>nocon</u>stant	suppress constant term
fd	first-differenced estimator
<u>reg</u>ress	treat covariates as exogenous and ignore instrument variables
SE	
vce(*vcetype*)	*vcetype* may be conventional, <u>boot</u>strap, or <u>jack</u>knife
Reporting	
<u>l</u>evel(*#*)	set confidence level; default is level(95)
first	report first-stage estimates
<u>sm</u>all	report t and F statistics instead of Z and chi-squared statistics

A panel variable must be specified. For xtivreg, fd a time variable must also be specified. Use xtset; see [XT] **xtset**.

depvar, *varlist*$_1$, *varlist*$_2$, and *varlist*$_{iv}$ may contain time-series operators; see [U] **11.4.3 Time-series varlists**.

by, statsby, and xi are allowed; see [U] **11.1.10 Prefix commands**.

See [U] **20 Estimation and postestimation commands** for more capabilities of estimation commands.

Description

xtivreg offers five different estimators for fitting panel-data models in which some of the right-hand-side covariates are endogenous. These estimators are two-stage least-squares generalizations of simple panel-data estimators for exogenous variables. xtivreg with the be option uses the two-stage least-squares between estimator. xtivreg with the fe option uses the two-stage least-squares within estimator. xtivreg with the re option uses a two-stage least-squares random-effects estimator. There are two implementations: G2SLS from Balestra and Varadharajan-Krishnakumar (1987) and EC2SLS from Baltagi. The Balestra and Varadharajan-Krishnakumar G2SLS is the default because it is computationally less expensive. Baltagi's EC2SLS can be obtained by specifying the ec2sls option. xtivreg with the fd option requests the two-stage least-squares first-differenced estimator.

See Baltagi (2005) for an introduction to panel-data models with endogenous covariates. For the derivation and application of the first-differenced estimator, see Anderson and Hsiao (1981).

Options for RE model

> ___Model___

re requests the G2SLS random-effects estimator. re is the default.

ec2sls requests Baltagi's EC2SLS random-effects estimator instead of the default Balestra and Varadharajan-Krishnakumar estimator.

nosa specifies that the Baltagi–Chang estimators of the variance components be used instead of the default adapted Swamy–Arora estimators.

regress specifies that all the covariates be treated as exogenous and that the instrument list be ignored. Specifying regress causes xtivreg to fit the requested panel-data regression model of *depvar* on *varlist*$_1$ and *varlist*$_2$, ignoring *varlist*$_{iv}$.

> ___SE___

vce(*vcetype*) specifies the type of standard error reported, which includes types that are derived from asymptotic theory and that use bootstrap or jackknife methods; see [XT] *vce_options*.

vce(conventional), the default, uses the conventionally derived variance estimator for generalized least-squares regression.

> ___Reporting___

level(*#*); see [XT] **estimation options**.

first specifies that the first-stage regressions be displayed.

small specifies that t statistics be reported instead of Z statistics and that F statistics be reported instead of chi-squared statistics.

theta specifies that the output include the estimated value of θ used in combining the between and fixed estimators. For balanced data, this is a constant, and for unbalanced data, a summary of the values is presented in the header of the output.

Options for BE model

⌐ Model ⌐

be requests the between regression estimator.

regress specifies that all the covariates are to be treated as exogenous and that the instrument list is to be ignored. Specifying regress causes xtivreg to fit the requested panel-data regression model of *depvar* on *varlist*$_1$ and *varlist*$_2$, ignoring *varlist*$_{iv}$.

⌐ SE ⌐

vce(*vcetype*) specifies the type of standard error reported, which includes types that are derived from asymptotic theory and that use bootstrap or jackknife methods; see [XT] *vce_options*.

vce(conventional), the default, uses the conventionally derived variance estimator for generalized least-squares regression.

⌐ Reporting ⌐

level(*#*); see [XT] **estimation options**.

first specifies that the first-stage regressions be displayed.

small specifies that t statistics be reported instead of Z statistics and that F statistics be reported instead of chi-squared statistics.

Options for FE model

⌐ Model ⌐

fe requests the fixed-effects (within) regression estimator.

regress specifies that all the covariates are to be treated as exogenous and that the instrument list is to be ignored. Specifying regress causes xtivreg to fit the requested panel-data regression model of *depvar* on *varlist*$_1$ and *varlist*$_2$, ignoring *varlist*$_{iv}$.

⌐ SE ⌐

vce(*vcetype*) specifies the type of standard error reported, which includes types that are derived from asymptotic theory and that use bootstrap or jackknife methods; see [XT] *vce_options*.

vce(conventional), the default, uses the conventionally derived variance estimator for generalized least-squares regression.

⌐ Reporting ⌐

level(*#*); see [XT] **estimation options**.

first specifies that the first-stage regressions be displayed.

small specifies that t statistics be reported instead of Z statistics and that F statistics be reported instead of chi-squared statistics.

Options for FD model

⌐ Model ⌐

noconstant; see [XT] **estimation options**.

fd requests the first-differenced regression estimator.

regress specifies that all the covariates are to be treated as exogenous and that the instrument list is to be ignored. Specifying regress causes xtivreg to fit the requested panel-data regression model of *depvar* on *varlist*$_1$ and *varlist*$_2$, ignoring *varlist*$_{iv}$.

⌐ SE ⌐

vce(*vcetype*) specifies the type of standard error reported, which includes types that are derived from asymptotic theory and that use bootstrap or jackknife methods; see [XT] *vce_options*.

vce(conventional), the default, uses the conventionally derived variance estimator for generalized least-squares regression.

⌐ Reporting ⌐

level(#); see [XT] **estimation options**.

first specifies that the first-stage regressions be displayed.

small specifies that t statistics be reported instead of Z statistics and that F statistics be reported instead of chi-squared statistics.

Remarks

If you have not read [XT] **xt**, please do so.

Consider an equation of the form

$$y_{it} = \mathbf{Y}_{it}\boldsymbol{\gamma} + \mathbf{X}_{1it}\boldsymbol{\beta} + \mu_i + \nu_{it} = \mathbf{Z}_{it}\boldsymbol{\delta} + \mu_i + \nu_{it} \tag{1}$$

where

y_{it} is the dependent variable

$\mathbf{Y}_{it}$ is an $1 \times g_2$ vector of observations on g_2 endogenous variables included as covariates, and these variables are allowed to be correlated with the ν_{it}

$\mathbf{X}_{1it}$ is an $1 \times k_1$ vector of observations on the exogenous variables included as covariates

$\mathbf{Z}_{it} = [\mathbf{Y}_{it}\ \mathbf{X}_{it}]$

$\boldsymbol{\gamma}$ is a $g_2 \times 1$ vector of coefficients

$\boldsymbol{\beta}$ is a $k_1 \times 1$ vector of coefficients

$\boldsymbol{\delta}$ is a $K \times 1$ vector of coefficients, and $K = g_2 + k_1$

Assume that there is a $1 \times k_2$ vector of observations on the k_2 instruments in $\mathbf{X}_{2it}$. The order condition is satisfied if $k_2 \geq g_2$. Let $\mathbf{X}_{it} = [\mathbf{X}_{1it}\ \mathbf{X}_{2it}]$. xtivreg handles exogenously unbalanced panel data. Thus define T_i to be the number of observations on panel i, n to be the number of panels and N to be the total number of observations; i.e., $N = \sum_{i=1}^{n} T_i$.

xtivreg offers five different estimators, which may be applied to models having the form of (1). The first-differenced estimator (FD2SLS) removes the μ_i by fitting the model in first differences. The within estimator (FE2SLS) fits the model after sweeping out the μ_i by removing the panel-level means from each variable. The between estimator (BE2SLS) models the panel averages. The two random-effects estimators, G2SLS and EC2SLS, treat the μ_i as random variables that are independent and identically distributed (i.i.d.) over the panels. Except for (FD2SLS), all these estimators are generalizations of estimators in xtreg. See [XT] **xtreg** for a discussion of these estimators for exogenous covariates.

Although the estimators allow for different assumptions about the μ_i, all the estimators assume that the idiosyncratic error term ν_{it} has zero mean and is uncorrelated with the variables in $\mathbf{X}_{it}$. Just as when there are no endogenous covariates, as discussed in [XT] **xtreg**, there are various perspectives on what assumptions should be placed on the μ_i. If they are assumed to be fixed, the μ_i may be correlated with the variables in $\mathbf{X}_{it}$, and the within estimator is efficient within a class of limited information estimators. Alternatively, if the μ_i are assumed to be random, they are also assumed to be independent and identically distributed (i.i.d.) over the panels. If the μ_i are assumed to be uncorrelated with the variables in $\mathbf{X}_{it}$, the GLS random-effects estimators are more efficient than the within estimator. However, if the μ_i are correlated with the variables in $\mathbf{X}_{it}$, the random-effects estimators are inconsistent but the within estimator is consistent. The price of using the within estimator is that it is not possible to estimate coefficients on time-invariant variables, and all inference is conditional on the μ_i in the sample. See Mundlak (1978) and Hsiao (1986) for discussions of this interpretation of the within estimator.

▷ Example 1: First-differenced estimator

The two-stage least-squares first-differenced estimator (FD2SLS) has been used to fit both fixed-effect and random-effect models. If the μ_i are truly fixed-effects, the FD2SLS estimator is not as efficient as the two-stage least-squares within estimator for finite T_i. Similarly, if none of the endogenous variables are lagged dependent variables, the exogenous variables are all strictly exogenous, and the random effects are i.i.d. and independent of the $\mathbf{X}_{it}$, the two-stage GLS estimators are more efficient than the FD2SLS estimator. However, the FD2SLS estimator has been used to obtain consistent estimates when one of these conditions fails. Anderson and Hsiao (1981) used a version of the FD2SLS estimator to fit a panel-data model with a lagged dependent variable.

Arellano and Bond (1991) develop new one-step and two-step GMM estimators for dynamic panel data. See [XT] **xtabond** for a discussion of these estimators and Stata's implementation of them. In their article, Arellano and Bond (1991) apply their new estimators to a model of dynamic labor demand that had previously been considered by Layard and Nickell (1986). They also compare the results of their estimators with those from the Anderson–Hsiao estimator using data from an unbalanced panel of firms from the United Kingdom. As is conventional, all variables are indexed over the firm i and time t. In this dataset, $\mathbf{n}_{it}$ is the log of employment in firm i inside the United Kingdom at time t, $\mathbf{w}_{it}$ is the natural log of the real product wage, $\mathbf{k}_{it}$ is the natural log of the gross capital stock, and $\mathbf{ys}_{it}$ is the natural log of industry output. The model also includes time dummies yr1980, yr1981, yr1982, yr1983, and yr1984. In Arellano and Bond (1991, table 5, column e), the authors present the results from applying one version of the Anderson–Hsiao estimator to these data. This example reproduces their results for the coefficients, though standard errors are different because Arellano and Bond are using robust standard errors.

(Continued on next page)

```
. use http://www.stata-press.com/data/r10/abdata
. xtivreg n l2.n l(0/1).w l(0/2).(k ys) yr1981-yr1984 (l.n = l3.n), fd
```

First-differenced IV regression

Group variable: id		Number of obs =	471
Time variable: year		Number of groups =	140
R-sq: within = 0.0141		Obs per group: min =	3
between = 0.9165		avg =	3.4
overall = 0.9892		max =	5
		chi2(14) =	122.53
corr(u_i, Xb) = 0.9239		Prob > chi2 =	0.0000

d.n	Coef.	Std. Err.	z	P>|z|	[95% Conf. Interval]	
n						
LD.	1.422765	1.583053	0.90	0.369	-1.679962	4.525493
L2D.	-.1645517	.1647179	-1.00	0.318	-.4873928	.1582894
w						
D1.	-.7524675	.1765733	-4.26	0.000	-1.098545	-.4063902
LD.	.9627611	1.086506	0.89	0.376	-1.166752	3.092275
k						
D1.	.3221686	.1466086	2.20	0.028	.0348211	.6095161
LD.	-.3248778	.5800599	-0.56	0.575	-1.461774	.8120187
L2D.	-.0953947	.1960883	-0.49	0.627	-.4797207	.2889314
ys						
D1.	.7660906	.369694	2.07	0.038	.0415037	1.490678
LD.	-1.361881	1.156835	-1.18	0.239	-3.629237	.9054744
L2D.	.3212993	.5440403	0.59	0.555	-.745	1.387599
yr1981						
D1.	-.0574197	.0430158	-1.33	0.182	-.1417291	.0268896
yr1982						
D1.	-.0882952	.0706214	-1.25	0.211	-.2267106	.0501203
yr1983						
D1.	-.1063153	.10861	-0.98	0.328	-.319187	.1065563
yr1984						
D1.	-.1172108	.15196	-0.77	0.441	-.4150468	.1806253
_cons	.0161204	.0336264	0.48	0.632	-.0497861	.082027

sigma_u	.29069213	
sigma_e	.18855982	
rho	.70384993	(fraction of variance due to u_i)

Instrumented:	L.n
Instruments:	L2.n w L.w k L.k L2.k ys L.ys L2.ys yr1981 yr1982 yr1983 yr1984
	L3.n

◁

▷ Example 2: Fixed-effects model

For the within estimator, consider another version of the wage equation discussed in [XT] **xtreg**. The data for this example come from an extract of women from the National Longitudinal Survey of Youth that was described in detail in [XT] **xt**. Restricting ourselves to only time-varying covariates, we might suppose that the log of the real wage was a function of the individual's age, age^2, her tenure in the observed place of employment, whether she belonged to union, whether she lives in metropolitan area, and whether she lives in the south. The variables for these are, respectively, age, age2, tenure, union, not_smsa, and south. If we treat all the variables as exogenous, we can use the one-stage within estimator from xtreg, yielding

```
. use http://www.stata-press.com/data/r10/nlswork
(National Longitudinal Survey.  Young Women 14-26 years of age in 1968)
```

```
. generate age2 = age^2
(24 missing values generated)
. xtreg ln_w age* tenure not_smsa union south, fe
```

```
Fixed-effects (within) regression              Number of obs      =       19007
Group variable: idcode                         Number of groups   =        4134

R-sq:  within  = 0.1333                         Obs per group: min =           1
       between = 0.2375                                        avg =         4.6
       overall = 0.2031                                        max =          12

                                                F(6,14867)         =      381.19
corr(u_i, Xb)  = 0.2074                         Prob > F           =      0.0000
```

ln_wage	Coef.	Std. Err.	t	P>|t|	[95% Conf. Interval]	
age	.0311984	.0033902	9.20	0.000	.0245533	.0378436
age2	-.0003457	.0000543	-6.37	0.000	-.0004522	-.0002393
tenure	.0176205	.0008099	21.76	0.000	.0160331	.0192079
not_smsa	-.0972535	.0125377	-7.76	0.000	-.1218289	-.072678
union	.0975672	.0069844	13.97	0.000	.0838769	.1112576
south	-.0620932	.013327	-4.66	0.000	-.0882158	-.0359706
_cons	1.091612	.0523126	20.87	0.000	.9890729	1.194151
sigma_u	.3910683					
sigma_e	.25545969					
rho	.70091004	(fraction of variance due to u_i)				

```
F test that all u_i=0:     F(4133,14867) =       8.31        Prob > F = 0.0000
```

All the coefficients are statistically significant and have the expected signs.

Now suppose that we wish to model tenure as a function of union and south and that we believe that the errors in the two equations are correlated. Since we are still interested in the within estimates, we now need a two-stage least-squares estimator. The following output shows the command and the results from fitting this model:

```
. xtivreg ln_w age* not_smsa (tenure = union south), fe
```

```
Fixed-effects (within) IV regression           Number of obs      =       19007
Group variable: idcode                         Number of groups   =        4134

R-sq:  within  =      .                         Obs per group: min =           1
       between = 0.1304                                        avg =         4.6
       overall = 0.0897                                        max =          12

                                                Wald chi2(4)       =   147926.58
corr(u_i, Xb)  = -0.6843                         Prob > chi2        =      0.0000
```

ln_wage	Coef.	Std. Err.	z	P>|z|	[95% Conf. Interval]	
tenure	.2403531	.0373419	6.44	0.000	.1671643	.3135419
age	.0118437	.0090032	1.32	0.188	-.0058023	.0294897
age2	-.0012145	.0001968	-6.17	0.000	-.0016003	-.0008286
not_smsa	-.0167178	.0339236	-0.49	0.622	-.0832069	.0497713
_cons	1.678287	.1626657	10.32	0.000	1.359468	1.997106
sigma_u	.70661941					
sigma_e	.63029359					
rho	.55690561	(fraction of variance due to u_i)				

```
F  test that all u_i=0:     F(4133,14869) =       1.44        Prob > F   = 0.0000
```

```
Instrumented:   tenure
Instruments:    age age2 not_smsa union south
```

Although all the coefficients still have the expected signs, the coefficients on `age` and `not_smsa` are no longer statistically significant. Given that these variables have been found to be important in many other studies, we might want to rethink our specification.

◁

If we are willing to assume that the μ_i are uncorrelated with the other covariates, we can fit a random-effects model. The model is frequently known as the variance-components or error-components model. `xtivreg` has estimators for two-stage least-squares one-way error-components models. In the one-way framework, there are two variance components to estimate, the variance of the μ_i and the variance of the ν_{it}. Since the variance components are unknown, consistent estimates are required to implement feasible GLS. `xtivreg` offers two choices: a Swamy–Arora method and simple consistent estimators from Baltagi and Chang (2000).

Baltagi and Chang (1994) derived the Swamy–Arora estimators of the variance components for unbalanced panels. By default, `xtivreg` uses estimators that extend these unbalanced Swamy–Arora estimators to the case with instrumental variables. The default Swamy–Arora method contains a degree-of-freedom correction to improve its performance in small samples. Baltagi and Chang (2000) use variance-components estimators, which are based on the ideas of Amemiya (1971) and Swamy and Arora (1972), but they do not attempt to make small-sample adjustments. These consistent estimators of the variance components will be used if the `nosa` option is specified.

Using either estimator of the variance components, `xtivreg` offers two GLS estimators of the random-effects model. These two estimators differ only in how they construct the GLS instruments from the exogenous and instrumental variables contained in $\mathbf{X}_{it} = [\mathbf{X}_{1it}\ \mathbf{X}_{2it}]$. The default method, G2SLS, which is from Balestra and Varadharajan-Krishnakumar, uses the exogenous variables after they have been passed through the feasible GLS transform. In math, G2SLS uses $\mathbf{X}_{it}^*$ for the GLS instruments, where $\mathbf{X}_{it}^*$ is constructed by passing each variable in $\mathbf{X}_{it}$ through the GLS transform in (3) given in *Methods and Formulas*. If the `ec2sls` option is specified, `xtivreg` performs Baltagi's EC2SLS. In EC2SLS, the instruments are $\widetilde{\mathbf{X}}_{it}$ and $\overline{\mathbf{X}}_{it}$, where $\widetilde{\mathbf{X}}_{it}$ is constructed by passing each of the variables in $\mathbf{X}_{it}$ through the within transform, and $\overline{\mathbf{X}}_{it}$ is constructed by passing each variable through the between transform. The within and between transforms are given in the *Methods and Formulas* section. Baltagi and Li (1992) show that, although the G2SLS instruments are a subset of those contained in EC2SLS, the extra instruments in EC2SLS are redundant in the sense of White (2001). Given the extra computational cost, G2SLS is the default.

▷ Example 3: GLS random-effects model

Here is the output from applying the G2SLS estimator to this model:

```
. generate byte black = (race==2)
. xtivreg ln_w age* not_smsa black (tenure = union birth south), re
G2SLS random-effects IV regression              Number of obs      =      19007
Group variable: idcode                          Number of groups   =       4134

R-sq:  within  = 0.0664                          Obs per group: min =          1
       between = 0.2098                                         avg =        4.6
       overall = 0.1463                                         max =         12

                                                 Wald chi2(5)       =    1446.37
corr(u_i, X)        = 0 (assumed)                Prob > chi2        =     0.0000
```

ln_wage	Coef.	Std. Err.	z	P>|z|	[95% Conf. Interval]	
tenure	.1391798	.0078756	17.67	0.000	.123744	.1546157
age	.0279649	.0054182	5.16	0.000	.0173454	.0385843
age2	-.0008357	.0000871	-9.60	0.000	-.0010063	-.000665
not_smsa	-.2235103	.0111371	-20.07	0.000	-.2453386	-.2016821
black	-.2078613	.0125803	-16.52	0.000	-.2325183	-.1832044
_cons	1.337684	.0844988	15.83	0.000	1.172069	1.503299

sigma_u	.36582493					
sigma_e	.63031479					
rho	.25197078	(fraction of variance due to u_i)				

```
Instrumented:  tenure
Instruments:   age age2 not_smsa black union birth_yr south
```

We have included two time-invariant covariates, birth_yr and black. All the coefficients are statistically significant and are of the expected sign.

Applying the EC2SLS estimator yields similar results:

```
. xtivreg ln_w age* not_smsa black (tenure = union birth south), re ec2sls
EC2SLS random-effects IV regression             Number of obs      =      19007
Group variable: idcode                          Number of groups   =       4134

R-sq:  within  = 0.0898                          Obs per group: min =          1
       between = 0.2608                                         avg =        4.6
       overall = 0.1926                                         max =         12

                                                 Wald chi2(5)       =    2721.92
corr(u_i, X)        = 0 (assumed)                Prob > chi2        =     0.0000
```

ln_wage	Coef.	Std. Err.	z	P>|z|	[95% Conf. Interval]	
tenure	.064822	.0025647	25.27	0.000	.0597953	.0698486
age	.0380048	.0039549	9.61	0.000	.0302534	.0457562
age2	-.0006676	.0000632	-10.56	0.000	-.0007915	-.0005438
not_smsa	-.2298961	.0082993	-27.70	0.000	-.2461625	-.2136297
black	-.1823627	.0092005	-19.82	0.000	-.2003954	-.16433
_cons	1.110564	.0606538	18.31	0.000	.9916849	1.229443

sigma_u	.36582493					
sigma_e	.63031479					
rho	.25197078	(fraction of variance due to u_i)				

```
Instrumented:  tenure
Instruments:   age age2 not_smsa black union birth_yr south
```

Fitting the same model as above with the G2SLS estimator and the consistent variance components estimators yields

```
. xtivreg ln_w age* not_smsa black (tenure = union birth south), re nosa

G2SLS random-effects IV regression           Number of obs      =     19007
Group variable: idcode                        Number of groups   =      4134

R-sq:  within  = 0.0664                        Obs per group: min =         1
       between = 0.2098                                       avg =       4.6
       overall = 0.1463                                       max =        12

                                              Wald chi2(5)       =   1446.93
corr(u_i, X)        = 0 (assumed)              Prob > chi2        =    0.0000
```

ln_wage	Coef.	Std. Err.	z	P>|z|	[95% Conf. Interval]	
tenure	.1391859	.007873	17.68	0.000	.1237552	.1546166
age	.0279697	.005419	5.16	0.000	.0173486	.0385909
age2	−.0008357	.0000871	−9.60	0.000	−.0010064	−.000665
not_smsa	−.2235738	.0111344	−20.08	0.000	−.2453967	−.2017508
black	−.2078733	.0125751	−16.53	0.000	−.2325201	−.1832265
_cons	1.337522	.0845083	15.83	0.000	1.171889	1.503155

sigma_u	.36535633	
sigma_e	.63020883	
rho	.2515512	(fraction of variance due to u_i)

```
Instrumented:  tenure
Instruments:   age age2 not_smsa black union birth_yr south
```

◁

Acknowledgment

We thank Mead Over of the World Bank, who wrote an early implementation of `xtivreg`.

Saved Results

xtivreg, re saves the following in e():

Scalars

e(N)	number of observations	e(r2_o)	R-squared for overall model
e(N_g)	number of groups	e(r2_b)	R-squared for between model
e(df_m)	model degrees of freedom	e(Tcon)	1 if panels balanced; 0 otherwise
e(g_max)	largest group size	e(sigma)	ancillary parameter (gamma, lnormal)
e(g_min)	smallest group size	e(sigma_u)	panel-level standard deviation
e(g_avg)	average group size	e(sigma_e)	standard deviation of ϵ_{it}
e(chi2)	χ^2	e(thta_min)	minimum θ
e(rho)	ρ	e(thta_5)	θ, 5th percentile
e(Tbar)	harmonic mean of group sizes	e(thta_50)	θ, 50th percentile
e(F)	model F (small only)	e(thta_95)	θ, 95th percentile
e(df_rz)	residual degrees of freedom	e(thta_max)	maximum θ
e(r2_w)	R-squared for within model	e(m_p)	p-value from model test

Macros

e(cmd)	xtivreg	e(instd)	instrumented variables
e(cmdline)	command as typed	e(vce)	*vcetype* specified in vce()
e(depvar)	name of dependent variable	e(vcetype)	title used to label Std. Err.
e(model)	g2sls or ec2sls	e(chi2type)	Wald; type of model χ^2 test
e(ivar)	variable denoting groups	e(properties)	b V
e(tvar)	variable denoting time	e(predict)	program used to implement predict
e(insts)	instruments		

Matrices

e(b)	coefficient vector	e(V)	variance–covariance matrix of the estimators

Functions

e(sample)	marks estimation sample

(Continued on next page)

`xtivreg, be` saves the following in `e()`:

Scalars

e(N)	number of observations		e(F)	F statistic (small only)
e(N_g)	number of groups		e(rmse)	root mean squared error
e(mss)	model sum of squares		e(g_max)	largest group size
e(df_m)	model degrees of freedom		e(g_min)	smallest group size
e(rss)	residual sum of squares		e(g_avg)	average group size
e(rs_a)	adjusted R^2		e(Tcon)	1 if T is constant
e(df_r)	residual degrees of freedom		e(r2)	R-squared
e(df_rz)	residual degrees of freedom for first-differenced regression		e(r2_w)	R-squared for within model
			e(r2_o)	R-squared for overall model
e(chi2)	model Wald		e(r2_b)	R-squared for between model
e(chi2_p)	p-value for model χ^2 test			

Macros

e(cmd)	xtivreg		e(instd)	instrumented variables
e(cmdline)	command as typed		e(small)	small, if specified
e(depvar)	name of dependent variable		e(vce)	*vcetype* specified in vce()
e(model)	be		e(vcetype)	title used to label Std. Err.
e(ivar)	variable denoting groups		e(properties)	b V
e(tvar)	variable denoting time		e(predict)	program used to implement predict
e(insts)	instruments			

Matrices

e(b)	coefficient vector		e(V)	variance–covariance matrix of the estimators

Functions

e(sample)	marks estimation sample

xtivreg, fe saves the following in e():

Scalars

e(N)	number of observations	e(df_a)	degrees of freedom for
e(N_g)	number of groups		absorbed effect
e(mss)	model sum of squares	e(F_f)	F for H_0: $u_i=0$
e(tss)	total sum of squares	e(g_max)	largest group size
e(df_m)	model degrees of freedom	e(g_min)	smallest group size
e(rss)	residual sum of squares	e(g_avg)	average group size
e(df_r)	residual d.o.f. (small only)	e(rho)	ρ
e(df_rz)	residual d.o.f. for	e(Tbar)	harmonic mean of group sizes
	first-differenced regression	e(Tcon)	1 if T is constant
e(df_b)	d.o.f. for χ^2 statistic	e(r2_w)	R-squared for within model
e(r2)	R-squared	e(r2_o)	R-squared for overall model
e(r2_a)	adjusted R-squared	e(r2_b)	R-squared for between model
e(chi2)	model Wald (not small)	e(sigma)	ancillary parameter (gamma, lnormal)
e(chi2_p)	p-value for model χ^2 statistic	e(corr)	corr(u_i, Xb)
e(F)	F statistic (small only)	e(sigma_u)	panel-level standard deviation
e(F_fp)	p-value for F for H_0:$u_i=0$	e(sigma_e)	standard deviation of ϵ_{it}
e(rmse)	root mean squared error		

Macros

e(cmd)	xtivreg	e(insts)	instruments
e(cmdline)	command as typed	e(instd)	instrumented variables
e(depvar)	name of dependent variable	e(vce)	*vcetype* specified in vce()
e(model)	fe	e(vcetype)	title used to label Std. Err.
e(ivar)	variable denoting groups	e(properties)	b V
e(tvar)	variable denoting time	e(predict)	program used to implement predict

Matrices

e(b)	coefficient vector	e(V)	variance–covariance matrix of the estimators

Functions

e(sample)	marks estimation sample

(Continued on next page)

xtivreg, fd saves the following in e():

Scalars

e(N)	number of observations	e(df_a)	degrees of freedom for
e(N_g)	number of groups		absorbed effect
e(mss)	model sum of squares	e(F_f)	F for H_0: $u_i=0$
e(tss)	total sum of squares	e(g_max)	largest group size
e(df_m)	model degrees of freedom	e(g_min)	smallest group size
e(rss)	residual sum of squares	e(g_avg)	average group size
e(df_r)	residual d.o.f. (small only)	e(rho)	ρ
e(df_rz)	residual d.o.f. for	e(Tbar)	harmonic mean of group sizes
	first-differenced regression	e(Tcon)	1 if T is constant
e(df_b)	d.o.f. for the χ^2 statistic	e(r2_w)	R-squared for within model
e(r2)	R-squared	e(r2_o)	R-squared for overall model
e(r2_a)	adjusted R-squared	e(r2_b)	R-squared for between model
e(chi2)	model Wald (not small)	e(sigma)	ancillary parameter (gamma, lnormal)
e(chi2_p)	p-value for model χ^2 statistic	e(corr)	corr(u_i, Xb)
e(F)	F statistic (small only)	e(sigma_u)	panel-level standard deviation
e(rmse)	root mean squared error	e(sigma_e)	standard deviation of ϵ_{it}

Macros

e(cmd)	xtivreg	e(insts)	instruments
e(cmdline)	command as typed	e(instd)	instrumented variables
e(depvar)	name of dependent variable	e(vce)	*vcetype* specified in vce()
e(model)	fd	e(vcetype)	title used to label Std. Err.
e(ivar)	variable denoting groups	e(properties)	b V
e(tvar)	time variable	e(predict)	program used to implement predict

Matrices

e(b)	coefficient vector	e(V)	variance–covariance matrix of the estimators

Functions

e(sample)	marks estimation sample

Methods and Formulas

Consider an equation of the form

$$y_{it} = \mathbf{Y}_{it}\boldsymbol{\gamma} + \mathbf{X}_{1it}\boldsymbol{\beta} + \mu_i + \nu_{it} = \mathbf{Z}_{it}\boldsymbol{\delta} + \mu_i + \nu_{it} \tag{2}$$

where

y_{it} is the dependent variable;

$\mathbf{Y}_{it}$ is an $1 \times g_2$ vector of observations on g_2 endogenous variables included as covariates, and these variables are allowed to be correlated with the ν_{it};

$\mathbf{X}_{1it}$ is an $1 \times k_1$ vector of observations on the exogenous variables included as covariates;

$\mathbf{Z}_{it} = [\mathbf{Y}_{it} \ \mathbf{X}_{it}]$;

$\boldsymbol{\gamma}$ is a $g_2 \times 1$ vector of coefficients;

$\boldsymbol{\beta}$ is a $k_1 \times 1$ vector of coefficients;

$\boldsymbol{\delta}$ is a $K \times 1$ vector of coefficients, where $K = g_2 + k_1$.

Assume that there is a $1 \times k_2$ vector of observations on the k_2 instruments in $\mathbf{X}_{2it}$. The order condition is satisfied if $k_2 \geq g_2$. Let $\mathbf{X}_{it} = [\mathbf{X}_{1it} \ \mathbf{X}_{2it}]$. xtivreg handles exogenously unbalanced panel data. Thus define T_i to be the number of observations on panel i, n to be the number of panels and N to be the total number of observations; i.e., $N = \sum_{i=1}^{n} T_i$.

xtivreg, fd

As the name implies, this estimator obtains its estimates and conventional VCE from an instrumental-variables regression on the first-differenced data. Specifically, first differencing the data yields

$$y_{it} - y_{it-1} = (\mathbf{Z}_{it} - \mathbf{Z}_{i,t-1})\,\delta + \nu_{it} - \nu_{i,t-1}$$

With the μ_i removed by differencing, we can obtain the estimated coefficients and their estimated variance–covariance matrix from a standard two-stage least-squares regression of Δy_{it} on $\Delta \mathbf{Z}_{it}$ with instruments $\Delta \mathbf{X}_{it}$.

R^2 within is reported as $\left[\mathrm{corr}\{(\mathbf{Z}_{it} - \overline{\mathbf{Z}}_i)\widehat{\delta}, y_{it} - \overline{y}_i\}\right]^2$.

R^2 between is reported as $\left\{\mathrm{corr}(\overline{\mathbf{Z}}_i\widehat{\delta}, \overline{y}_i)\right\}^2$.

R^2 overall is reported as $\left\{\mathrm{corr}(\mathbf{Z}_{it}\widehat{\delta}, y_{it})\right\}^2$.

xtivreg, fe

At the heart of this model is the within transformation. The within transform of a variable w is

$$\widetilde{w}_{it} = w_{it} - \overline{w}_{i.} + \overline{w}$$

where

$$\overline{w}_{i.} = \frac{1}{n}\sum_{t=1}^{T_i} w_{it}$$

$$\overline{w} = \frac{1}{N}\sum_{i=1}^{n}\sum_{t=1}^{T_i} w_{it}$$

and n is the number of groups and N is the total number of observations on the variable.

The within transform of (2) is

$$\widetilde{y}_{it} = \widetilde{\mathbf{Z}}_{it} + \widetilde{\nu}_{it}$$

The within transform has removed the μ_i. With the μ_i gone, the within 2SLS estimator can be obtained from a two-stage least-squares regression of $\widetilde{y}_{it}$ on $\widetilde{\mathbf{Z}}_{it}$ with instruments $\widetilde{\mathbf{X}}_{it}$.

Suppose that there are K variables in $\mathbf{Z}_{it}$, including the mandatory constant. There are $K + n - 1$ parameters estimated in the model, and the conventional VCE for the within estimator is

$$\frac{N - K}{N - n - K + 1} V_{IV}$$

where V_{IV} is the VCE from the above two-stage least-squares regression.

From the estimate of $\widehat{\delta}$, estimates $\widehat{\mu}_i$ of μ_i are obtained as $\widehat{\mu}_i = \overline{y}_i - \overline{\mathbf{Z}}_i\widehat{\delta}$. Reported from the calculated $\widehat{\mu}_i$ is its standard deviation and its correlation with $\overline{\mathbf{Z}}_i\widehat{\delta}$. Reported as the standard deviation of ν_{it} is the regression's estimated root mean squared error, s^2, which is adjusted (as previously stated) for the $n - 1$ estimated means.

R^2 within is reported as the R^2 from the mean-deviated regression.

R^2 between is reported as $\left\{ \text{corr}(\overline{\mathbf{Z}}_i \widehat{\boldsymbol{\delta}}, \overline{y}_i) \right\}^2$.

R^2 overall is reported as $\left\{ \text{corr}(\mathbf{Z}_{it} \widehat{\boldsymbol{\delta}}, y_{it}) \right\}^2$.

At the bottom of the output, an F statistic against the null hypothesis that all the μ_i are zero is reported. This F statistic is an application of the results in Wooldridge (1990).

xtivreg, be

After passing (2) through the between transform, we are left with

$$\overline{y}_i = \alpha + \overline{\mathbf{Z}}_i \boldsymbol{\delta} + \mu_i + \overline{\nu}_i \tag{3}$$

where

$$\overline{w}_i = \frac{1}{T_i} \sum_{t=1}^{T_i} w_{it} \quad \text{for } w \in \{y, \mathbf{Z}, \nu\}$$

Similarly, define $\overline{\mathbf{X}}_i$ as the matrix of instruments $\mathbf{X}_{it}$ after they have been passed through the between transform.

The BE2SLS estimator of (3) obtains its coefficient estimates and its conventional VCE, a two-stage least-squares regression of $\overline{y}_i$ on $\overline{Z}_i$ with instruments $\overline{\mathbf{X}}_i$ in which each average appears T_i times.

R^2 between is reported as the R^2 from the fitted regression.

R^2 within is reported as $\left[\text{corr}\left\{ (\mathbf{Z}_{it} - \overline{\mathbf{Z}}_i)\widehat{\boldsymbol{\delta}}, y_{it} - \overline{y}_i \right\} \right]^2$.

R^2 overall is reported as $\left\{ \text{corr}(\mathbf{Z}_{it} \widehat{\boldsymbol{\delta}}, y_{it}) \right\}^2$.

xtivreg, re

Per Baltagi and Chang (2000), let

$$u = \mu_i + \nu_{it}$$

be the $N \times 1$ vector of combined errors. Then under the assumptions of the random-effects model,

$$E(uu') = \sigma_\nu^2 \text{diag}\left[I_{T_i} - \frac{1}{T_i} \iota_{T_i} \iota'_{T_i} \right] + \text{diag}\left[w_i \frac{1}{T_i} \iota_{T_i} \iota'_{T_i} \right]$$

where

$$\omega_i = T_i \sigma_\mu^2 + \sigma_\nu^2$$

and ι_{T_i} is a vector of ones of dimension T_i.

Since the variance components are unknown, consistent estimates are required to implement feasible GLS. xtivreg offers two choices. The default is a simple extension of the Swamy–Arora method for unbalanced panels.

Let

$$u_{it}^w = \widetilde{y}_{it} - \widetilde{\mathbf{Z}}_{it} \widehat{\boldsymbol{\delta}}_w$$

be the combined residuals from the within estimator. Let $\widetilde{u}_{it}$ be the within-transformed u_{it}. Then

$$\widehat{\sigma}_\nu = \frac{\sum_{i=1}^n \sum_{t=1}^{T_i} \widetilde{u}_{it}^2}{N - n - K + 1}$$

Let

$$u_{it}^b = y_{it} - \mathbf{Z}_{it}\boldsymbol{\delta}_b$$

be the combined residual from the between estimator. Let $\bar{u}_{i.}^b$ be the between residuals after they have been passed through the between transform. Then

$$\hat{\sigma}_\mu^2 = \frac{\sum_{i=1}^n \sum_{t=1}^{T_i} \bar{u}_{it}^2 - (n-K)\hat{\sigma}_\nu^2}{N-r}$$

where

$$r = \mathrm{trace}\left\{ \left(\bar{\mathbf{Z}}_i'\bar{\mathbf{Z}}_i\right)^{-1}\bar{\mathbf{Z}}_i'\mathbf{Z}_\mu\mathbf{Z}_\mu'\bar{\mathbf{Z}}_i \right\}$$

where

$$\mathbf{Z}_\mu = \mathrm{diag}\left(\iota_{T_i}\iota_{T_i}'\right)$$

If the `nosa` option is specified, the consistent estimators described in Baltagi and Chang (2000) are used. These are given by

$$\hat{\sigma}_\nu = \frac{\sum_{i=1}^n \sum_{t=1}^{T_i} \tilde{u}_{it}^2}{N-n}$$

and

$$\hat{\sigma}_\mu^2 = \frac{\sum_{i=1}^n \sum_{t=1}^{T_i} \bar{u}_{it}^2 - n\hat{\sigma}_\nu^2}{N}$$

The default Swamy–Arora method contains a degree-of-freedom correction to improve its performance in small samples.

Given estimates of the variance components, $\hat{\sigma}_\nu^2$ and $\hat{\sigma}_\mu^2$, the feasible GLS transform of a variable w is

$$w^* = w_{it} - \hat{\theta}_{it}\bar{w}_{i.} \tag{4}$$

where

$$\bar{w}_{i.} = \frac{1}{T_i}\sum_{t=1}^{T_i} w_{it}$$

$$\hat{\theta}_{it} = 1 - \left(\frac{\hat{\sigma}_\nu^2}{\hat{\omega}_i}\right)^{-\frac{1}{2}}$$

and

$$\hat{\omega}_i = T_i\hat{\sigma}_\mu^2 + \hat{\sigma}_\nu^2$$

Using either estimator of the variance components, `xtivreg` contains two GLS estimators of the random-effects model. These two estimators differ only in how they construct the GLS instruments from the exogenous and instrumental variables contained in $\mathbf{X}_{it} = [\mathbf{X}_{1it}\mathbf{X}_{2it}]$. The default method, G2SLS, which is from Balestra and Varadharajan-Krishnakumar, uses the exogenous variables after they have been passed through the feasible GLS transform. Mathematically, G2SLS uses $\mathbf{X}^*$ for the GLS instruments, where $\mathbf{X}^*$ is constructed by passing each variable in $\mathbf{X}$ though the GLS transform in (4). The G2SLS estimator obtains its coefficient estimates and conventional VCE from an instrumental variable regression of y_{it}^* on $\mathbf{Z}_{it}^*$ with instruments $\mathbf{X}_{it}^*$.

If the ec2sls option is specified, xtivreg performs Baltagi's EC2SLS. In EC2SLS, the instruments are $\widetilde{\mathbf{X}}_i t$ and $\overline{\mathbf{X}}_{it}$, where $\widetilde{X}_{it}$ is constructed by each of the variables in $\mathbf{X}_{it}$ throughout the GLS transform in (4), and $\overline{\mathbf{X}}_{it}$ is made of the group means of each variable in $\mathbf{X}_{it}$. The EC2SLS estimator obtains its coefficient estimates and its VCE from an instrumental variables regression of y_{it}^* on $\mathbf{Z}_{it}^*$ with instruments $\widetilde{\mathbf{X}}_{it}$ and $\overline{\mathbf{X}}_{it}$.

Baltagi and Li (1992) show that although the G2SLS instruments are a subset of those in EC2SLS, the extra instruments in EC2SLS are redundant in the sense of White (2001). Given the extra computational cost, G2SLS is the default.

The standard deviation of $\mu_i + \nu_{it}$ is calculated as $\sqrt{\widehat{\sigma}_\mu^2 + \widehat{\sigma}_\nu^2}$.

R^2 between is reported as $\left\{ \mathrm{corr}(\overline{\mathbf{Z}}_i\widehat{\boldsymbol{\delta}}, \overline{y}_i) \right\}^2$.

R^2 within is reported as $\left[\mathrm{corr}\left\{ (\mathbf{Z}_{it} - \overline{\mathbf{Z}}_i)\widehat{\boldsymbol{\delta}}, y_{it} - \overline{y}_i \right\} \right]^2$.

R^2 overall is reported as $\left\{ \mathrm{corr}(\mathbf{Z}_{it}\widehat{\boldsymbol{\delta}}, y_{it}) \right\}^2$.

References

Amemiya, T. 1971. The estimation of the variances is a variance-components model. *International Economic Review* 12: 1–13.

Anderson, T. W., and C. Hsiao. 1981. Estimation of dynamic models with error components. *Journal of the American Statistical Association* 76: 598–606.

Balestra, P., and J. Varadharajan-Krishnakumar. 1987. Full-information estimations of a system of simultaneous equations with error component structure. *Econometric Theory* 3: 223–246.

Baltagi, B. H. 2005. *Econometric Analysis of Panel Data*. 3rd ed. New York: Wiley.

Baltagi, B. H., and Y. Chang. 1994. Incomplete panels: A comparative study of alternative estimators for the unbalanced one-way error component regression model. *Journal of Econometrics* 62: 67–89.

——. 2000. Simultaneous equations with incomplete panels. *Econometric Theory* 16: 269–279.

Baltagi, B. H., and Q. Li. 1992. A note on the estimation of simultaneous equations with error components. *Econometric Theory* 8: 113–119.

Swamy, P. A. V. B., and S. S. Arora. 1972. The exact finite sample properties of the estimators of coefficients in the error components regression models. *Econometrica* 40: 261–275.

White, H. 2001. *Asymptotic Theory for Econometricians*. Rev. ed. New York: Academic Press.

Wooldridge, J. M. 1990. A note on the Lagrange multiple and F statistics for two-stage least squares regressions. *Economics Letters* 34: 151–155.

Also See

Title

> **xtivreg postestimation** — Postestimation tools for xtivreg

Description

The following postestimation commands are available for xtivreg:

command	description
adjust[1]	adjusted predictions of $\mathbf{x}\beta$
estat	VCE and estimation sample summary
estimates	cataloging estimation results
hausman	Hausman's specification test
lincom	point estimates, standard errors, testing, and inference for linear combinations of coefficients
mfx	marginal effects or elasticities
nlcom	point estimates, standard errors, testing, and inference for nonlinear combinations of coefficients
predict	predictions, residuals, influence statistics, and other diagnostic measures
predictnl	point estimates, standard errors, testing, and inference for generalized predictions
test	Wald tests for simple and composite linear hypotheses
testnl	Wald tests of nonlinear hypotheses

[1] adjust is not appropriate with time-series operators.

See the corresponding entries in the *Stata Base Reference Manual* for details.

Syntax for predict

For all but the first-differenced estimator

> predict [*type*] *newvar* [*if*] [*in*] [, *statistic*]

First-differenced estimator

> predict [*type*] *newvar* [*if*] [*in*] [, *FD_statistic*]

statistic	description
Main	
xb	$\mathbf{Z}_{it}\widehat{\delta}$, fitted values; the default
ue	$\widehat{\mu}_i + \widehat{\nu}_{it}$, the combined residual
*xbu	$\mathbf{Z}_{it}\widehat{\delta} + \widehat{\mu}_i$, prediction including effect
*u	$\widehat{\mu}_i$, the fixed or random error component
*e	$\widehat{\nu}_{it}$, the overall error component

Unstarred statistics are available both in and out of sample; type predict ... if e(sample) ... if wanted only for the estimation sample. Starred statistics are calculated only for the estimation sample, even when if e(sample) is not specified.

199

FD_statistic	description
Main	
xb	$\mathbf{x}_j\mathbf{b}$, fitted values for the first-differenced model; the default
e	$e_{it} - e_{it-1}$, the first-differenced overall error component

These statistics are available both in and out of sample; type `predict ... if e(sample) ...` if wanted only for the estimation sample.

Options for predict

⌐ Main ⌐

xb, the default, calculates the linear prediction, that is, $\mathbf{Z}_{it}\widehat{\boldsymbol{\delta}}$.

ue calculates the prediction of $\widehat{\mu}_i + \widehat{\nu}_{it}$. This is not available after the first-differenced model.

xbu calculates the prediction of $\mathbf{Z}_{it}\widehat{\boldsymbol{\delta}} + \widehat{\mu}_i$, the prediction including the fixed or random component. This is not available after the first-differenced model.

u calculates the prediction of $\widehat{\mu}_i$, the estimated fixed or random effect. This is not available after the first-differenced model.

e calculates the prediction of $\widehat{\nu}_{it}$.

Also See

[XT] **xtivreg** — Instrumental variables and two-stage least squares for panel-data models

[U] **20 Estimation and postestimation commands**

Title

xtline — Panel-data line plots

Syntax

Graph by panel

xtline *varlist* $\left[\,if\,\right]$ $\left[\,in\,\right]$ $\left[\,,\ panel\_options\,\right]$

Overlaid panels

xtline *varname* $\left[\,if\,\right]$ $\left[\,in\,\right]$, <u>ov</u>erlay $\left[\,overlaid\_options\,\right]$

panel_options	description
Main	
i(*varname$_i$*)	use *varname$_i$* as the panel ID variable
t(*varname$_t$*)	use *varname$_t$* as the time variable
Plot	
cline_options	affect rendition of the plotted points connected by lines
Add plots	
addplot(*plot*)	add other plots to the generated graph
Y axis, Time axis, Titles, Legend, Overall	
twoway_options	any options other than by() documented in [G] *twoway_options*
<u>by</u>opts(*by_suboptions*)	affect appearance of the combined graph

overlaid_options	description
Main	
<u>ov</u>erlay	overlay each panel on the same graph
i(*varname$_i$*)	use *varname$_i$* as the panel ID variable
t(*varname$_t$*)	use *varname$_t$* as the time variable
Plots	
<u>plot</u>#opts(*cline_options*)	affect rendition of the # panel line
Add plots	
addplot(*plot*)	add other plots to the generated graph
Y axis, Time axis, Titles, Legend, Overall	
twoway_options	any options other than by() documented in [G] *twoway_options*

A panel variable and a time variable must be specified. Use xtset (see [XT] **xtset**) or specify the i() and t() options. The t() option allows noninteger values for the time variable, whereas xtset does not.

Description

xtline draws line plots for panel data.

Options for graph by panel

___Main___

i(*varname_i*) and t(*varname_t*) override the panel settings from xtset. *varname_i* is allowed to be a string variable. *varname_t* can take on noninteger values and have repeated values within panel. That is to say, it can be any numeric variable that you would like to specify for the x-dimension of the graph. It is an error to specify i() without t() and vice versa.

___Plot___

cline_options affect the rendition of the plotted points connected by lines; see [G] *cline_options*.

___Add plots___

addplot(*plot*) provides a way to add other plots to the generated graph; see [G] *addplot_option*.

___Y axis, Time axis, Titles, Legend, Overall___

twoway_options are any of the options documented in [G] *twoway_options*, excluding by(). These include options for titling the graph (see [G] *title_options*) and for saving the graph to disk (see [G] *saving_option*).

byopts(*by_suboptions*) allows all the options documented in [G] *by_option*. These options affect the appearance of the by-graph. byopts() may not be combined with overlay.

Options for overlaid panels

___Main___

overlay causes the plot from each panel to be overlaid on the same graph. The default is to generate plots by panel. This option may not be combined with byopts() or be specified when there are multiple variables in *varlist*.

i(*varname_i*) and t(*varname_t*) override the panel settings from xtset. *varname_i* is allowed to be a string variable. *varname_t* can take on noninteger values and have repeated values within panel. That is to say, it can be any numeric variable that you would like to specify for the x-dimension of the graph. It is an error to specify i() without t() and vice versa.

___Plots___

plot#opts(*cline_options*) affect the rendition of the #th panel (in sorted order). The *cline_options* can affect whether and how the points are connected; see [G] *cline_options*.

___Add plots___

addplot(*plot*) provides a way to add other plots to the generated graph; see [G] *addplot_option*.

┌─── Y axis, Time axis, Titles, Legend, Overall └───────────────────────────────

twoway_options are any of the options documented in [G] *twoway_options*, excluding by(). These include options for titling the graph (see [G] *title_options*) and for saving the graph to disk (see [G] *saving_option*).

Remarks

▷ Example 1

Suppose that Tess, Sam, and Arnold kept a calorie log for an entire calendar year. At the end of the year, if they pooled their data together, they would have a dataset (e.g., xtline1.dta) that contains the number of calories each of them consumed for 365 days. They could then use xtset to identify the date variable and treat each person as a panel and use xtline to plot the calories versus time for each person separately.

```
. use http://www.stata-press.com/data/r10/xtline1
. xtset person day
        panel variable:  person (strongly balanced)
         time variable:  day, 01jan2002 to 31dec2002
                 delta:  1 day
. xtline calories, tlabel(#3)
```

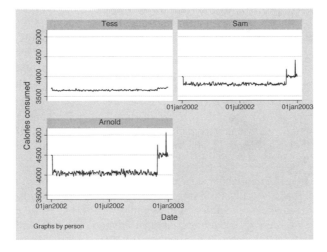

Specify the overlay option so that the values are plotted on the same graph to provide a better comparison among Tess, Sam, and Arnold.

(*Continued on next page*)

. xtline calories, overlay

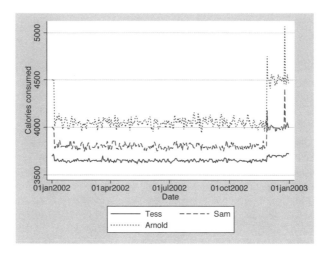

◁

Methods and Formulas

xtline is implemented as an ado-file.

Also See

[XT] **xtset** — Declare data to be panel data

[G] **graph twoway** — Twoway graphs

[TS] **tsline** — Plot time-series data

Title

> **xtlogit** — Fixed-effects, random-effects, and population-averaged logit models

Syntax

Random-effects (RE) model

> xtlogit *depvar* [*indepvars*] [*if*] [*in*] [*weight*] [, re *RE_options*]

Conditional fixed-effects (FE) model

> xtlogit *depvar* [*indepvars*] [*if*] [*in*] [*weight*] , fe [*FE_options*]

Population-averaged (PA) model

> xtlogit *depvar* [*indepvars*] [*if*] [*in*] [*weight*] , pa [*PA_options*]

RE_options	description
Model	
<u>nocon</u>stant	suppress constant term
re	use random-effects estimator; the default
<u>off</u>set(*varname*)	include *varname* in model with coefficient constrained to 1
<u>constra</u>ints(*constraints*)	apply specified linear constraints
<u>coll</u>inear	keep collinear variables
SE	
vce(*vcetype*)	*vcetype* may be oim, <u>boot</u>strap, or <u>jack</u>knife
Reporting	
<u>level</u>(#)	set confidence level; default is level(95)
or	report odds ratios
noskip	perform overall model test as a likelihood-ratio test
Int opts (RE)	
<u>intm</u>ethod(*intmethod*)	integration method; *intmethod* may be <u>mvag</u>hermite, <u>ag</u>hermite, or <u>g</u>hermite; default is intmethod(mvaghermite)
<u>intp</u>oints(#)	use # quadrature points; default is intpoints(12)
Max options	
maximize_options	control the maximization process; seldom used
† <u>nodis</u>play	suppress display of header and coefficients

FE_options	description
Model	
<u>fe</u>	use fixed-effects estimator
<u>off</u>set(*varname*)	include *varname* in model with coefficient constrained to 1
<u>cons</u>traints(*constraints*)	apply specified linear constraints
<u>coll</u>inear	keep collinear variables
SE	
vce(*vcetype*)	*vcetype* may be oim, <u>boot</u>strap, or <u>jack</u>knife
Reporting	
<u>level</u>(#)	set confidence level; default is level(95)
or	report odds ratios
<u>nos</u>kip	perform overall model test as a likelihood-ratio test
Max options	
maximize_options	control the maximization process; seldom used
† <u>nodi</u>splay	suppress display of header and coefficients

PA_options	description
Model	
<u>nocon</u>stant	suppress constant term
pa	use population-averaged estimator
<u>off</u>set(*varname*)	include *varname* in model with coefficient constrained to 1
PA options	
<u>corr</u>(*correlation*)	within-group correlation structure
force	estimate even if observations unequally spaced in time
SE/Robust	
vce(*vcetype*)	*vcetype* may be conventional, <u>r</u>obust, <u>boot</u>strap, or jackknife
nmp	use divisor $N - P$ instead of the default N
<u>s</u>cale(*parm*)	overrides the default scale parameter; *parm* may be x2, dev, phi, or #
Reporting	
<u>level</u>(#)	set confidence level; default is level(95)
or	report odds ratios
Opt options	
optimize_options	control the optimization process; seldom used
† <u>nodi</u>splay	do not display the header and coefficients

† <u>nodi</u>splay is not shown in the dialog box.

correlation	description
exchangeable	exchangeable
independent	independent
unstructured	unstructured
fixed *matname*	user-specified
ar #	autoregressive of order #
stationary #	stationary of order #
nonstationary #	nonstationary of order #

A panel variable must be specified. For xtlogit, pa, correlation structures other than exchangeable and
independent require that a time variable also be specified. Use xtset; see [XT] **xtset**.

depvar and *indepvars* may contain time-series operators; see [U] **11.4.3 Time-series varlists**.

by, statsby, and xi are allowed; see [U] **11.1.10 Prefix commands**.

iweights, fweights, and pweights are allowed for the population-averaged model, and iweights are
allowed for the fixed-effects and random-effects models; see [U] **11.1.6 weight**. Weights must be constant
within panel.

See [U] **20 Estimation and postestimation commands** for more capabilities of estimation commands.

Description

xtlogit fits random-effects, conditional fixed-effects, and population-averaged logit models.
Whenever we refer to a fixed-effects model, we mean the conditional fixed-effects model.

xtlogit, re is slow because the likelihood function is calculated by adaptive Gauss–Hermite
quadrature; see *Methods and Formulas*. Computation time is roughly proportional to the number of
points used for the quadrature. The default is intpoints(12). Increasing the number of quadrature
points can improve the quadrature approximation. See [XT] **quadchk**.

By default, the population-averaged model is an equal-correlation model; xtlogit, pa assumes
corr(exchangeable). See [XT] **xtgee** for details on how to fit other population-averaged models.

See [R] **logistic** for a list of related estimation commands.

Options for RE model

⌐ Model ⌐

noconstant; see [XT] **estimation options**.

re requests the random-effects estimator, which is the default.

offset(*varname*) constraints(*constraints*), collinear; see [XT] **estimation options**.

⌐ SE ⌐

vce(*vcetype*) specifies the type of standard error reported, which includes types that are derived from
asymptotic theory and that use bootstrap or jackknife methods; see [XT] *vce_options*.

⌐ Reporting ⌐

level(#); see [XT] **estimation options**.

or reports the estimated coefficients transformed to odds ratios, i.e., e^b rather than b. Standard errors and confidence intervals are similarly transformed. This option affects how results are displayed, not how they are estimated. or may be specified at estimation or when replaying previously estimated results.

noskip; see [XT] **estimation options**.

⌐──────⌐ Int opts (RE) ⌐───

intmethod(*intmethod*), intpoints(*#*); see [XT] **estimation options**.

⌐──────⌐ Max options ⌐──

maximize_options: <u>diff</u>icult, <u>tech</u>nique(*algorithm_spec*), <u>iter</u>ate(*#*), [<u>no</u>]<u>log</u>, <u>tra</u>ce, gradient, showstep, <u>hess</u>ian, <u>shownr</u>tolerance, <u>tol</u>erance(*#*), <u>ltol</u>erance(*#*), <u>gtol</u>erance(*#*), <u>nrtol</u>erance(*#*), <u>nonrtol</u>erance, from(*init_specs*); see [R] **maximize**. These options are seldom used.

The following option is available with xtlogit but is not shown in the dialog box:

nodisplay is for programmers. It suppresses the display of the header and the coefficients.

Options for FE model

⌐──────⌐ Model ⌐──

fe requests the fixed-effects estimator.

offset(*varname*), constraints(*constraints*), collinear; see [XT] **estimation options**.

⌐──────⌐ SE ⌐───

vce(*vcetype*) specifies the type of standard error reported, which includes types that are derived from asymptotic theory and that use bootstrap or jackknife methods; see [XT] *vce_options*.

⌐──────⌐ Reporting ⌐──

level(*#*); see [XT] **estimation options**.

or reports the estimated coefficients transformed to odds ratios, i.e., e^b rather than b. Standard errors and confidence intervals are similarly transformed. This option affects how results are displayed, not how they are estimated. or may be specified at estimation or when replaying previously estimated results.

noskip; see [XT] **estimation options**.

⌐──────⌐ Max options ⌐──

maximize_options: <u>diff</u>icult, <u>tech</u>nique(*algorithm_spec*), <u>iter</u>ate(*#*), [<u>no</u>]<u>log</u>, <u>tra</u>ce, gradient, showstep, <u>hess</u>ian, <u>shownr</u>tolerance, <u>tol</u>erance(*#*), <u>ltol</u>erance(*#*), <u>gtol</u>erance(*#*), <u>nrtol</u>erance(*#*), <u>nonrtol</u>erance, from(*init_specs*); see [R] **maximize**. These options are seldom used.

The following option is available with xtlogit but is not shown in the dialog box:

nodisplay is for programmers. It suppresses the display of the header and the coefficients.

Options for PA model

⌐‾‾‾‾‾⌐ Model ⌐‾‾

noconstant; see [XT] **estimation options**.

pa requests the population-averaged estimator.

offset(*varname*); see [XT] **estimation options**.

⌐‾‾‾‾‾⌐ Correlation ⌐‾‾‾

corr(*correlation*), force; see [XT] **estimation options**.

⌐‾‾‾‾‾⌐ SE/Robust ⌐‾‾‾

vce(*vcetype*) specifies the type of standard error reported, which includes types that are derived from asymptotic theory, that are robust to some kinds of misspecification, and that use bootstrap or jackknife methods; see [XT] *vce_options*.

vce(conventional), the default, uses the conventionally derived variance estimator for generalized least-squares regression.

nmp, scale(x2 | dev | phi | #); see [XT] *vce_options*.

⌐‾‾‾‾‾⌐ Reporting ⌐‾‾‾

level(*#*); see [XT] **estimation options**.

or reports the estimated coefficients transformed to odds ratios, i.e., e^b rather than b. Standard errors and confidence intervals are similarly transformed. This option affects how results are displayed, not how they are estimated. or may be specified at estimation or when replaying previously estimated results.

⌐‾‾‾‾‾⌐ Opt options ⌐‾‾‾

optimize_options control the iterative optimization process. These options are seldom used.

iterate(*#*) specifies the maximum number of iterations. When the number of iterations equals *#*, the optimization stops and presents the current results, even if convergence has not been reached. The default is iterate(100).

tolerance(*#*) specifies the tolerance for the coefficient vector. When the relative change in the coefficient vector from one iteration to the next is less than or equal to *#*, the optimization process is stopped. tolerance(1e-6) is the default.

nolog suppresses display of the iteration log.

trace specifies that the current estimates be printed at each iteration.

The following option is available with xtlogit but is not shown in the dialog box:

nodisplay is for programmers. It suppresses the display of the header and the coefficients.

Remarks

xtlogit is a convenience command if you want the population-averaged model. Typing

    . xtlogit ..., pa ...

is equivalent to typing

```
. xtgee ..., ... family(binomial) link(logit) corr(exchangeable)
```

It is also a convenience command if you want the fixed-effects model. Typing

```
. xtlogit ..., fe ...
```

is equivalent to typing

```
. clogit ..., group(varname_i) ...
```

See also [XT] **xtgee** and [R] **clogit** for information about `xtlogit`.

By default or when `re` is specified, `xtlogit` fits via maximum likelihood the random-effects model

$$\Pr(y_{it} \neq 0 | \mathbf{x}_{it}) = P(\mathbf{x}_{it}\boldsymbol{\beta} + \nu_i)$$

for $i = 1, \ldots, n$ panels, where $t = 1, \ldots, n_i$, ν_i are i.i.d., $N(0, \sigma_\nu^2)$, and $P(z) = \{1 + \exp(-z)\}^{-1}$.

Underlying this model is the variance components model

$$y_{it} \neq 0 \iff \mathbf{x}_{it}\boldsymbol{\beta} + \nu_i + \epsilon_{it} > 0$$

where ϵ_{it} are i.i.d. logistic distributed with mean zero and variance $\sigma_\epsilon^2 = \pi^2/3$, independently of ν_i.

▷ Example 1

We are studying unionization of women in the United States and are using the `union` dataset; see [XT] **xt**. We wish to fit a random-effects model of union membership:

```
. use http://www.stata-press.com/data/r10/union
(NLS Women 14-24 in 1968)

. xtlogit union age grade not_smsa south southXt

(output omitted)
```

Random-effects logistic regression   Number of obs   =   26200
Group variable: idcode   Number of groups   =   4434

Random effects u_i ~ Gaussian   Obs per group: min =   1
                                                             avg =   5.9
                                                             max =   12

                                              Wald chi2(5)   =   227.30
Log likelihood = -10540.366   Prob > chi2   =   0.0000

union	Coef.	Std. Err.	z	P>|z|	[95% Conf. Interval]	
age	.0093936	.004454	2.11	0.035	.000664	.0181232
grade	.0867878	.0176345	4.92	0.000	.0522247	.1213508
not_smsa	-.2519379	.082334	-3.06	0.002	-.4133095	-.0905663
south	-1.163769	.1114164	-10.45	0.000	-1.382141	-.945397
southXt	.023245	.0078497	2.96	0.003	.0078599	.0386302
_cons	-3.360131	.2586306	-12.99	0.000	-3.867038	-2.853225
/lnsig2u	1.749534	.0469964			1.657423	1.841645
sigma_u	2.398317	.0563561			2.290366	2.511356
rho	.6361486	.0108779			.6145729	.6571902

Likelihood-ratio test of rho=0: chibar2(01) = 6010.74 Prob >= chibar2 = 0.000

The output includes the additional panel-level variance component. This is parameterized as the log of the variance $\ln(\sigma_\nu^2)$ (labeled lnsig2u in the output). The standard deviation σ_ν is also included in the output and labeled sigma_u together with ρ (labeled rho),

$$\rho = \frac{\sigma_\nu^2}{\sigma_\nu^2 + \sigma_\epsilon^2}$$

which is the proportion of the total variance contributed by the panel-level variance component.

When rho is zero, the panel-level variance component is unimportant, and the panel estimator is no different from the pooled estimator. A likelihood-ratio test of this is included at the bottom of the output. This test formally compares the pooled estimator (logit) with the panel estimator.

As an alternative to the random-effects specification, we might want to fit an equal-correlation logit model:

```
. xtlogit union age grade not_smsa south southXt, pa

Iteration 1: tolerance = .07495101
Iteration 2: tolerance = .00626455
Iteration 3: tolerance = .00030986
Iteration 4: tolerance = .00001432
Iteration 5: tolerance = 6.699e-07

GEE population-averaged model              Number of obs      =      26200
Group variable:                   idcode   Number of groups   =       4434
Link:                              logit   Obs per group: min =          1
Family:                         binomial                  avg =        5.9
Correlation:                exchangeable                  max =         12
                                           Wald chi2(5)       =     233.60
Scale parameter:                       1   Prob > chi2        =     0.0000
```

union	Coef.	Std. Err.	z	P>|z|	[95% Conf. Interval]	
age	.0053241	.0024988	2.13	0.033	.0004265	.0102216
grade	.0595076	.0108311	5.49	0.000	.0382791	.0807361
not_smsa	-.1224955	.0483137	-2.54	0.011	-.2171887	-.0278024
south	-.7270863	.0675522	-10.76	0.000	-.8594861	-.5946865
southXt	.0151984	.0045586	3.33	0.001	.0062638	.024133
_cons	-2.01111	.15439	-13.03	0.000	-2.313709	-1.708512

◁

▷ Example 2

xtlogit with the pa option allows a vce(robust) option, so we can obtain the population-averaged logit estimator with the robust variance calculation by typing

(Continued on next page)

```
. xtlogit union age grade not_smsa south southXt, pa vce(robust) nolog
```

| GEE population-averaged model | | | | | Number of obs | = | 26200 |

Group variable: idcode   Number of groups =   4434
Link: logit   Obs per group: min =   1
Family: binomial   avg =   5.9
Correlation: exchangeable   max =   12
                                                        Wald chi2(5)   =   152.01
Scale parameter: 1   Prob > chi2   =   0.0000

(Std. Err. adjusted for clustering on idcode)

union	Coef.	Semi-robust Std. Err.	z	P>|z|	[95% Conf. Interval]	
age	.0053241	.0037494	1.42	0.156	-.0020246	.0126727
grade	.0595076	.0133482	4.46	0.000	.0333455	.0856697
not_smsa	-.1224955	.0613646	-2.00	0.046	-.2427678	-.0022232
south	-.7270863	.0870278	-8.35	0.000	-.8976577	-.5565149
southXt	.0151984	.006613	2.30	0.022	.0022371	.0281596
_cons	-2.01111	.2016405	-9.97	0.000	-2.406319	-1.615902

These standard errors are somewhat larger than those obtained without the vce(robust) option.

Finally, we can also fit a fixed-effects model to these data (see also [R] **clogit** for details):

```
. xtlogit union age grade not_smsa south southXt, fe
note: multiple positive outcomes within groups encountered.
note: 2744 groups (14165 obs) dropped because of all positive or
      all negative outcomes.
Iteration 0:   log likelihood = -4516.5769
Iteration 1:   log likelihood = -4511.1069
Iteration 2:   log likelihood = -4511.1042
Iteration 3:   log likelihood = -4511.1042
```

Conditional fixed-effects logistic regression   Number of obs   =   12035
Group variable: idcode   Number of groups =   1690

                                                 Obs per group: min =   2
                                                                avg =   7.1
                                                                max =   12

                                                 LR chi2(5)   =   78.16
Log likelihood = -4511.1042   Prob > chi2   =   0.0000

union	Coef.	Std. Err.	z	P>|z|	[95% Conf. Interval]	
age	.0079706	.0050283	1.59	0.113	-.0018848	.0178259
grade	.0811808	.0419138	1.94	0.053	-.0009687	.1633303
not_smsa	.0210368	.1131542	0.19	0.853	-.2007414	.242815
south	-1.007318	.1500498	-6.71	0.000	-1.30141	-.7132256
southXt	.0263495	.0083244	3.17	0.002	.010034	.042665

◁

Saved Results

xtlogit, re saves the following in e():

Scalars

e(N)	# of observations	e(sigma_u)	panel-level standard deviation
e(N_g)	# of groups	e(n_quad)	# of quadrature points
e(N_cd)	# of completely determined obs.	e(k)	# of parameters
e(df_m)	model degrees of freedom	e(k_eq)	# of equations
e(ll)	log likelihood	e(k_eq_model)	# of equations in model Wald test
e(ll_0)	log likelihood, constant-only model	e(k_dv)	# of dependent variables
e(ll_c)	log likelihood, comparison model	e(p)	significance
e(g_max)	largest group size	e(rank)	rank of e(V)
e(g_min)	smallest group size	e(rank0)	rank of e(V) for constant-only model
e(g_avg)	average group size	e(ic)	# of iterations
e(chi2)	χ^2	e(rc)	return code
e(chi2_c)	χ^2 for comparison test	e(converged)	1 if converged, 0 otherwise
e(rho)	ρ		

Macros

e(cmd)	xtlogit	e(distrib)	Gaussian; the distribution of the random effect
e(cmdline)	command as typed		
e(depvar)	name of dependent variable	e(vce)	*vcetype* specified in vce()
e(ivar)	variable denoting groups	e(vcetype)	title used to label Std. Err.
e(wtype)	weight type	e(opt)	type of optimization
e(wexp)	weight expression	e(ml_method)	type of ml method
e(title)	title in estimation output	e(user)	name of likelihood-evaluator program
e(offset)	offset	e(technique)	maximization technique
e(chi2type)	Wald or LR; type of model χ^2 test	e(crittype)	optimization criterion
e(chi2_ct)	Wald or LR; type of model χ^2 test corresponding to e(chi2_c)	e(properties)	b V
		e(predict)	program used to implement predict
e(intmethod)	integration method		

Matrices

e(b)	coefficient vector	e(ilog)	iteration log
e(V)	variance–covariance matrix of the estimators	e(gradient)	gradient vector

Functions

e(sample)	marks estimation sample

(Continued on next page)

xtlogit, fe saves the following in e():

Scalars

e(N)	number of observations	e(k)	# of parameters
e(N_g)	number of groups	e(k_eq)	# of equations
e(df_m)	model degrees of freedom	e(k_eq_model)	# of equations in model Wald test
e(ll)	log likelihood	e(k_dv)	# of dependent variables
e(ll_0)	log likelihood, constant-only model	e(p)	significance
e(g_max)	largest group size	e(rank)	rank of e(V)
e(g_min)	smallest group size	e(ic)	# of iterations
e(g_avg)	average group size	e(rc)	return code
e(r2_p)	pseudo R-squared	e(converged)	1 if converged, 0 otherwise
e(chi2)	χ^2		

Macros

e(cmd)	clogit	e(group)	name of group() variable
e(cmd2)	xtlogit	e(vce)	*vcetype* specified in vce()
e(cmdline)	command as typed	e(vcetype)	title used to label Std. Err.
e(depvar)	name of dependent variable	e(opt)	type of optimization
e(ivar)	variable denoting groups	e(ml_method)	type of ml method
e(offset)	offset	e(user)	name of likelihood-evaluator program
e(wtype)	weight type	e(technique)	maximization technique
e(wexp)	weight expression	e(crittype)	optimization criterion
e(title)	title in estimation output	e(properties)	b V
e(chi2type)	LR; type of model χ^2 test	e(predict)	program used to implement predict

Matrices

e(b)	coefficient vector	e(ilog)	iteration log
e(V)	variance–covariance matrix of the estimators	e(gradient)	gradient vector

Functions

e(sample)	marks estimation sample

`xtlogit, pa` saves the following in `e()`:

Scalars

`e(N)`	number of observations	`e(deviance)`	deviance
`e(N_g)`	number of groups	`e(chi2_dev)`	χ^2 test of deviance
`e(df_m)`	model degrees of freedom	`e(dispers)`	deviance dispersion
`e(g_max)`	largest group size	`e(chi2_dis)`	χ^2 test of deviance dispersion
`e(g_min)`	smallest group size	`e(tol)`	target tolerance
`e(g_avg)`	average group size	`e(dif)`	achieved tolerance
`e(chi2)`	χ^2	`e(phi)`	scale parameter
`e(df_pear)`	degrees of freedom for Pearson χ^2	`e(rc)`	return code

Macros

`e(cmd)`	xtgee	`e(crittype)`	optimization criterion
`e(cmd2)`	xtlogit	`e(scale)`	x2, dev, phi, or #; scale parameter
`e(cmdline)`	command as typed	`e(ivar)`	variable denoting groups
`e(depvar)`	name of dependent variable	`e(vce)`	*vcetype* specified in vce()
`e(wtype)`	weight type	`e(vcetype)`	title used to label Std. Err.
`e(wexp)`	weight expression	`e(chi2type)`	Wald; type of model χ^2 test
`e(family)`	binomial	`e(offset)`	offset
`e(link)`	logit; link function	`e(properties)`	b V
`e(corr)`	correlation structure	`e(predict)`	program used to implement predict

Matrices

`e(b)`	coefficient vector	`e(R)`	estimated working correlation matrix
`e(V)`	variance–covariance matrix of the estimators		

Functions

`e(sample)`	marks estimation sample

Methods and Formulas

`xtlogit` is implemented as an ado-file.

`xtlogit` reports the population-averaged results obtained by using `xtgee`, `family(binomial)` `link(logit)` to obtain estimates. The fixed-effects results are obtained using `clogit`. See [XT] **xtgee** and [R] **clogit** for details on the methods and formulas.

If we assume a normal distribution, $N(0, \sigma_\nu^2)$, for the random effects ν_i,

$$\Pr(y_{i1}, \ldots, y_{in_i} | \mathbf{x}_{i1}, \ldots, \mathbf{x}_{in_i}) = \int_{-\infty}^{\infty} \frac{e^{-\nu_i^2/2\sigma_\nu^2}}{\sqrt{2\pi}\sigma_\nu} \left\{ \prod_{t=1}^{n_i} F(y_{it}, \mathbf{x}_{it}\boldsymbol{\beta} + \nu_i) \right\} d\nu_i$$

where

$$F(y, z) = \begin{cases} \dfrac{1}{1 + \exp(-z)} & \text{if } y \neq 0 \\[2mm] \dfrac{1}{1 + \exp(z)} & \text{otherwise} \end{cases}$$

The panel-level likelihood l_i is given by

$$l_i = \int_{-\infty}^{\infty} \frac{e^{-\nu_i^2/2\sigma_\nu^2}}{\sqrt{2\pi}\sigma_\nu} \left\{ \prod_{t=1}^{n_i} F(y_{it}, \mathbf{x}_{it}\boldsymbol{\beta} + \nu_i) \right\} d\nu_i$$

$$\equiv \int_{-\infty}^{\infty} g(y_{it}, x_{it}, \nu_i) d\nu_i$$

This integral can be approximated with M-point Gauss–Hermite quadrature

$$\int_{-\infty}^{\infty} e^{-x^2} h(x) dx \approx \sum_{m=1}^{M} w_m^* h(a_m^*)$$

This is equivalent to

$$\int_{-\infty}^{\infty} f(x) dx \approx \sum_{m=1}^{M} w_m^* \exp\left\{ (a_m^*)^2 \right\} f(a_m^*)$$

where the w_m^* denote the quadrature weights and the a_m^* denote the quadrature abscissas. The log likelihood, L, is the sum of the logs of the panel-level likelihoods l_i.

The default approximation of the log likelihood is by adaptive Gauss–Hermite quadrature, which approximates the panel-level likelihood with

$$l_i \approx \sqrt{2}\widehat{\sigma}_i \sum_{m=1}^{M} w_m^* \exp\left\{ (a_m^*)^2 \right\} g(y_{it}, x_{it}, \sqrt{2}\widehat{\sigma}_i a_m^* + \widehat{\mu}_i)$$

where $\widehat{\sigma}_i$ and $\widehat{\mu}_i$ are the adaptive parameters for panel i. Therefore, with the definition of $g(y_{it}, x_{it}, \nu_i)$, the total log likelihood is approximated by

$$L \approx \sum_{i=1}^{n} w_i \log\left[\sqrt{2}\widehat{\sigma}_i \sum_{m=1}^{M} w_m^* \exp\left\{ (a_m^*)^2 \right\} \frac{\exp\left\{ -(\sqrt{2}\widehat{\sigma}_i a_m^* + \widehat{\mu}_i)^2/2\sigma_\nu^2 \right\}}{\sqrt{2\pi}\sigma_\nu} \right.$$

$$\left. \prod_{t=1}^{n_i} F(y_{it}, x_{it}\boldsymbol{\beta} + \sqrt{2}\widehat{\sigma}_i a_m^* + \widehat{\mu}_i) \right]$$

where w_i is the user-specified weight for panel i; if no weights are specified, $w_i = 1$.

The default method of adaptive Gauss–Hermite quadrature is to calculate the posterior mean and variance and use those parameters for $\widehat{\mu}_i$ and $\widehat{\sigma}_i$ by following the method of Naylor and Smith (1982), further discussed in Skrondal and Rabe-Hesketh (2004). We start with $\widehat{\sigma}_{i,0} = 1$ and $\widehat{\mu}_{i,0} = 0$, and the posterior means and variances are updated in the kth iteration. That is, at the kth iteration of the optimization for l_i, we use

$$l_{i,k} \approx \sum_{m=1}^{M} \sqrt{2}\widehat{\sigma}_{i,k-1} w_m^* \exp\left\{ a_m^* \right\}^2 \} g(y_{it}, x_{it}, \sqrt{2}\widehat{\sigma}_{i,k-1} a_m^* + \widehat{\mu}_{i,k-1})$$

Letting

$$\tau_{i,m,k-1} = \sqrt{2}\widehat{\sigma}_{i,k-1} a_m^* + \widehat{\mu}_{i,k-1}$$

$$\widehat{\mu}_{i,k} = \sum_{m=1}^{M} (\tau_{i,m,k-1}) \frac{\sqrt{2}\widehat{\sigma}_{i,k-1} w_m^* \exp\{(a_m^*)^2\} g(y_{it}, x_{it}, \tau_{i,m,k-1})}{l_{i,k}}$$

and

$$\widehat{\sigma}_{i,k} = \sum_{m=1}^{M} (\tau_{i,m,k-1})^2 \frac{\sqrt{2}\widehat{\sigma}_{i,k-1} w_m^* \exp\{(a_m^*)^2\} g(y_{it}, x_{it}, \tau_{i,m,k-1})}{l_{i,k}} - (\widehat{\mu}_{i,k})^2$$

and this is repeated until $\widehat{\mu}_{i,k}$ and $\widehat{\sigma}_{i,k}$ have converged for this iteration of the maximization algorithm. This adaptation is applied on every iteration until the log-likelihood change from the preceding iteration is less than a relative difference of 1e–6; after this, the quadrature parameters are fixed.

One can instead use the adaptive quadrature method of Liu and Pierce (1994), option `int-method(aghermite)`, which uses the mode and curvature of the mode as approximations for the mean and variance. We take the integrand

$$g(y_{it}, x_{it}, \nu_i) = \frac{e^{-\nu_i^2/2\sigma_\nu^2}}{\sqrt{2\pi}\sigma_\nu} \left\{ \prod_{t=1}^{n_i} F(y_{it}, \mathbf{x}_{it}\boldsymbol{\beta} + \nu_i) \right\}$$

and find α_i the mode of $g(y_{it}, x_{it}, \nu_i)$. We calculate

$$\gamma_i = -\frac{\partial^2}{\partial \nu_i^2} \log\{g(y_{it}, x_{it}, \nu_i)\}\Big|_{\nu_i=\alpha_i}$$

Then

$$\int_{-\infty}^{\infty} g(y_{it}, x_{it}, \nu_i) d\nu_i \approx \left(\frac{2}{\gamma_i}\right)^{1/2} \sum_{m=1}^{M} w_m^* \exp\{(a_m^*)^2\} g\left\{y_{it}, x_{it}, \left(\frac{2}{\gamma_i}\right)^{1/2} a_m^* + \alpha_i\right\}$$

This adaptation is performed on the first iteration only; that is, the α_i and γ_i are calculated once at the first iteration and then held constant throughout the subsequent iterations.

The log likelihood can also be calculated by nonadaptive Gauss–Hermite quadrature, option `intmethod(ghermite)`, where $\rho = \sigma_\nu^2/(\sigma_\nu^2 + 1)$:

$$L = \sum_{i=1}^{n} w_i \log\left\{\Pr(y_{i1}, \ldots, y_{in_i} | \mathbf{x}_{i1}, \ldots, \mathbf{x}_{in_i})\right\}$$

$$\approx \sum_{i=1}^{n} w_i \log\left[\frac{1}{\sqrt{\pi}} \sum_{m=1}^{M} w_m^* \prod_{t=1}^{n_i} F\left\{y_{it}, \mathbf{x}_{it}\boldsymbol{\beta} + a_m^* \left(\frac{2\rho}{1-\rho}\right)^{1/2}\right\}\right]$$

All three quadrature formulas require that the integrated function be well approximated by a polynomial of degree equal to the number of quadrature points. The number of periods (panel size) can affect whether

$$\prod_{t=1}^{n_i} F(y_{it}, \mathbf{x}_{it}\boldsymbol{\beta} + \nu_i)$$

is well approximated by a polynomial. As panel size and ρ increase, the quadrature approximation can become less accurate. For large ρ, the random-effects model can also become unidentified. Adaptive quadrature gives better results for correlated data and large panels than nonadaptive quadrature; however, we recommend that you use the `quadchk` command to verify the quadrature approximation used in this command, whichever approximation you choose.

References

Conway, M. R. 1990. A random effects model for binary data. *Biometrics* 46: 317–328.

Liang, K.-Y., and S. L. Zeger. 1986. Longitudinal data analysis using generalized linear models. *Biometrika* 73: 13–22.

Liu, Q., and D. A. Pierce 1994. A note on Gauss–Hermite quadrature. *Biometrika* 81: 624–629.

Naylor, J. C., and A. F. M. Smith. 1982. Applications of a method for the efficient computation of posterior distributions. *Journal of the Royal Statistical Society, Series C* 31: 214–225.

Neuhaus, J. M. 1992. Statistical methods for longitudinal and clustered designs with binary responses. *Statistical Methods in Medical Research* 1: 249–273.

Neuhaus, J. M., J. D. Kalbfleisch, and W. W. Hauck. 1991. A comparison of cluster-specific and population-averaged approaches for analyzing correlated binary data. *International Statistical Review* 59: 25–35.

Pendergast, J. F., S. J. Gange, M. A. Newton, M. J. Lindstrom, M. Palta, and M. R. Fisher. 1996. A survey of methods for analyzing clustered binary response data. *International Statistical Review* 64: 89–118.

Skrondal, A., and S. Rabe-Hesketh. 2004. *Generalized Latent Variable Modeling: Multilevel, Longitudinal, and Structural Equation Models*. Boca Raton, FL: Chapman & Hall/CRC.

Twisk, J. W. R. 2003. *Applied Longitudinal Data Analysis for Epidemiology: A Practical Guide*. Cambridge: Cambridge University Press.

Also See

[XT] **xtlogit postestimation** — Postestimation tools for xtlogit

[XT] **quadchk** — Check sensitivity of quadrature approximation

[R] **constraint** — Define and list constraints

[XT] **xtcloglog** — Random-effects and population-averaged cloglog models

[XT] **xtgee** — Fit population-averaged panel-data models by using GEE

[XT] **xtprobit** — Random-effects and population-averaged probit models

[R] **clogit** — Conditional (fixed-effects) logistic regression

[R] **logit** — Logistic regression, reporting coefficients

[R] **logistic** — Logistic regression, reporting odds ratios

[U] **20 Estimation and postestimation commands**

Title

---

xtlogit postestimation — Postestimation tools for xtlogit

Description

The following postestimation commands are available for `xtlogit`:

command	description
adjust[1]	adjusted predictions of $\mathbf{x}\beta$, probabilities, or $\exp(\mathbf{x}\beta)$ predictions
*estat	AIC, BIC, VCE, and estimation sample summary
estimates	cataloging estimation results
lincom	point estimates, standard errors, testing, and inference for linear combinations of coefficients
lrtest	likelihood-ratio test
mfx	marginal effects or elasticities
nlcom	point estimates, standard errors, testing, and inference for nonlinear combinations of coefficients
predict	predictions, residuals, influence statistics, and other diagnostic measures
predictnl	point estimates, standard errors, testing, and inference for generalized predictions
test	Wald tests for simple and composite linear hypotheses
testnl	Wald tests of nonlinear hypotheses

[1] `adjust` is not appropriate with time-series operators.

* `estat ic` is not appropriate after `xtlogit, pa`.

See the corresponding entries in the *Stata Base Reference Manual* for details.

Syntax for predict

Random-effects model

> predict [*type*] *newvar* [*if*] [*in*] [, *RE_statistic* <u>nooff</u>set]

Fixed-effects model

> predict [*type*] *newvar* [*if*] [*in*] [, *FE_statistic* <u>nooff</u>set]

Population-averaged model

> predict [*type*] *newvar* [*if*] [*in*] [, *PA_statistic* <u>nooff</u>set]

RE_statistic	description
Main	
xb	linear prediction; the default
pu0	probability of a positive outcome assuming that the random effect is zero
stdp	standard error of the linear prediction

FE_statistic	description
Main	
pc1	predicted probability of a positive outcome conditional on one positive outcome within group; the default
pu0	probability of a positive outcome assuming that the fixed effect is zero
xb	linear prediction
stdp	standard error of the linear prediction

PA_statistic	description
Main	
mu	predicted probability of *depvar*; considers the offset()
rate	predicted probability of *depvar*
xb	linear prediction
stdp	standard error of the linear prediction
score	first derivative of the log likelihood with respect to $\mathbf{x}_j\beta$

These statistics are available both in and out of sample; type predict ... if e(sample) ... if wanted only for the estimation sample.

The predicted probability for the fixed-effects model is conditional on there being only one outcome per group. See [R] **clogit** for details.

Options for predict

⌐ Main ⌐

xb calculates the linear prediction. This is the default for the random-effects model.

pc1 calculates the predicted probability of a positive outcome conditional on one positive outcome within group. This is the default for the fixed-effects model.

mu and rate both calculate the predicted probability of *depvar*. mu takes into account the offset(), and rate ignores those adjustments. mu and rate are equivalent if you did not specify offset(). mu is the default for the population-averaged model.

pu0 calculates the probability of a positive outcome, assuming that the fixed or random effect for that observation's panel is zero ($\nu = 0$). This may not be similar to the proportion of observed outcomes in the group.

stdp calculates the standard error of the linear prediction.

score calculates the equation-level score, $u_j = \partial \ln L_j(\mathbf{x}_j\beta)/\partial(\mathbf{x}_j\beta)$.

nooffset is relevant only if you specified offset(*varname*) for xtlogit. This option modifies the calculations made by predict so that they ignore the offset variable; the linear prediction is treated as $\mathbf{x}_{it}\beta$ rather than $\mathbf{x}_{it}\beta + \text{offset}_{it}$.

Remarks

▷ Example 1

In [XT] **xtlogit**, we fitted a random-effects model of union status on the person's age and level of schooling, whether she lived in an urban area, and whether she lived in the south. In fact, we included both the dummy variable south and a term called southXt to capture the interaction between south and time of observation. To test whether residing in the south affects union status, we must determine whether south and southXt are jointly significant. First, we refit our model, save the estimation results for later use, and use test to conduct a Wald test of the joint significance of those two variables' parameters:

```
. use http://www.stata-press.com/data/r10/union
(NLS Women 14-24 in 1968)
. xtlogit union age grade not_smsa south southXt
 (output omitted )
. estimates store fullmodel
. test south southXt
 ( 1)  [union]south = 0
 ( 2)  [union]southXt = 0
          chi2(  2) =  143.72
        Prob > chi2 =    0.0000
```

The test statistic is clearly significant, so we reject the null hypothesis that the coefficients are jointly zero and conclude that living in the south does significantly affect union status.

We can also test our hypothesis with a likelihood-ratio test. Here we fit the model without south and southXt and then call lrtest to compare this restricted model to the full model:

```
. xtlogit union age grade not_smsa
 (output omitted )
. lrtest fullmodel .
Likelihood-ratio test                           LR chi2(2)  =     146.36
(Assumption: . nested in fullmodel)             Prob > chi2 =     0.0000
```

These results confirm our finding that living in the south affects union status.

◁

Methods and Formulas

All postestimation commands listed above are implemented as ado-files.

Also See

[XT] **xtlogit** — Fixed-effects, random-effects, and population-averaged logit models

[U] **20 Estimation and postestimation commands**

Title

xtmelogit — Multilevel mixed-effects logistic regression

Syntax

xtmelogit *depvar fe_equation* || *re_equation* [|| *re_equation* ...] [, *options*]

where the syntax of *fe_equation* is

[*indepvars*] [*if*] [*in*] [, *fe_options*]

and the syntax of *re_equation* is one of the following:

for random coefficients and intercepts

levelvar: [*varlist*] [, *re_options*]

for random effects among the values of a factor variable

levelvar: R.*varname* [, *re_options*]

levelvar is a variable identifying the group structure for the random effects at that level, or _all representing one group comprising all observations.

fe_options	description
Model	
noconstant	suppress the constant term from the fixed-effects equation
offset(*varname*)	include *varname* in model with coefficient constrained to 1

re_options	description
Model	
covariance(*vartype*)	variance–covariance structure of the random effects
noconstant	suppress the constant term from the random-effects equation
collinear	keep collinear variables

options	description
Model	
binomial(*varname* | #)	set binomial trials if data are in binomial form
Integration	
laplace	use Laplacian approximation; equivalent to intpoints(1)
intpoints(# [# ...])	set the number of integration (quadrature) points; default is 7

Reporting

level(#)	set confidence level; default is level(95)
or	report fixed-effects coefficients as odds ratios
variance	show random-effects parameter estimates as variances and covariances
noretable	suppress random-effects table
nofetable	suppress fixed-effects table
estmetric	show parameter estimates in the estimation metric
noheader	suppress output header
nogroup	suppress table summarizing groups
nolrtest	do not perform LR test comparing to logistic regression

Max options

maximize_options	control the maximization process during gradient-based optimization
retolerance(#)	tolerance for random-effects estimates; default is retolerance(1e-8); seldom used
reiterate(#)	maximum number of iterations for random-effects estimation; default is reiterate(50); seldom used
matlog	parameterize variance components using matrix logarithms
refineopts(maximize_options)	control the maximization process during refinement of starting values

vartype	description
independent	one unique variance parameter per random effect, all covariances zero; the default unless a factor variable is specified
exchangeable	equal variances for random effects, and one common pairwise covariance
identity	equal variances for random effects, all covariances zero
unstructured	all variances–covariances distinctly estimated

indepvars may contain time-series operators; see [U] **11.4.3 Time-series varlists**.

by, rolling, statsby, and xi are allowed; see [U] **11.1.10 Prefix commands**.

See [U] **20 Estimation and postestimation commands** for more capabilities of estimation commands.

Description

xtmelogit fits mixed-effects models for binary/binomial responses. Mixed models contain both *fixed effects* and *random effects*. The fixed effects are analogous to standard regression coefficients and are estimated directly. The random effects are not directly estimated (although they may be obtained postestimation) but are summarized according to their estimated variances and covariances. Random effects may take the form of either random intercepts or random coefficients, and the grouping structure of the data may consist of multiple levels of nested groups. The distribution of the random effects is assumed to be Gaussian. The conditional distribution of the response given the random effects is assumed to be Bernoulli, with success probability determined by the logistic cumulative distribution function (c.d.f.). Since the log likelihood for this model has no closed form, it is approximated by adaptive Gaussian quadrature.

Options

noconstant suppresses the constant (intercept) term and may be specified for the fixed-effects equation and for any or all of the random-effects equations.

offset(*varname*) specifies that *varname* be included in the fixed-effects portion of the model with the coefficient constrained to be 1.

covariance(*vartype*), where *vartype* is

independent | exchangeable | identity | unstructured

specifies the structure of the covariance matrix for the random effects and may be specified for each random-effects equation. An independent covariance structure allows for a distinct variance for each random effect within a random-effects equation and assumes that all covariances are zero. exchangeable structure specifies one common variance for all random effects and one common pairwise covariance. identity is short for "multiple of the identity"; that is, all variances are equal and all covariances are zero. unstructured allows all variances and covariances to be distinct. If an equation consists of p random-effects terms, the unstructured covariance matrix will have $p(p+1)/2$ unique parameters.

covariance(independent) is the default, except when the random-effects equation is a factor-variable specification R.*varname*, in which case covariance(identity) is the default.

Only covariance(identity) and covariance(exchangeable) are allowed with the factor-variable specification.

collinear specifies that xtmelogit not remove the collinear variables from a random-effects equation. Usually there is no reason to leave collinear variables in place, and in fact doing so usually causes the estimation to fail because of the matrix singularity caused by the collinearity. However, with certain models (for example, a random-effects model with a full set of contrasts), the variables may be collinear, yet the model is fully identified because of restrictions on the random-effects covariance structure. In such cases, using option collinear allows the estimation to take place with the random-effects equation intact.

binomial(*varname* | #) specifies that the data are in binomial form; that is, *depvar* records the number of successes from a series of binomial trials. This number of trials is given either as *varname*, which allows this number to vary over the observations, or as the constant #. If binomial() is not specified (the default), *depvar* is treated as Bernoulli, with any nonzero, nonmissing values indicating positive responses.

laplace specifies that log likelihoods be calculated using the Laplacian approximation, equivalent to adaptive Gaussian quadrature with one integration point for each level in the model; laplace is equivalent to intpoints(1). Computation time increases as a function of the number of quadrature points raised to a power equaling the dimension of the random-effects specification. The computational time saved by using laplace can thus be substantial, especially when you have many levels and/or random coefficients.

The Laplacian approximation has been known to produce biased parameter estimates, but the bias tends to be more prominent in the estimates of the variance components rather than in estimates of the fixed effects. If your interest lies primarily with the fixed-effects estimates, the Laplace approximation may be a viable faster alternative to adaptive quadrature with multiple integration points.

Specifying a factor variable, R. *varname*, increases the dimension of the random effects by the number of distinct values of *varname*, i.e., the number of factor levels. Even when this number is small to moderate, it increases the total random-effects dimension to the point where estimation with more than one quadrature point is prohibitively intensive.

For this reason, when you have factor variables in your random-effects equations, option laplace is assumed. You can override this behavior by using option intpoints().

intpoints(#[# ...]) sets the number of integration points for adaptive Gaussian quadrature. The more points, the more accurate the approximation to the log likelihood. However, computation time increases with the number of quadrature points, and in models with many levels and/or many random coefficients, this increase can be substantial.

You may specify one number of integration points applying to all levels of random effects in the model, or you may specify distinct numbers of points for each level. intpoints(7) is the default; that is, by default seven quadrature points are used for each level.

_____⌐ Reporting ⌐_____

level(#); see [XT] **estimation options**.

or reports the fixed-effects coefficients transformed to odds ratios, i.e., $\exp(b)$ rather than b. Standard errors and confidence intervals are similarly transformed. This option affects how results are displayed, not how they are estimated. or may be specified at estimation or when replaying previously estimated results.

variance displays the random-effects parameter estimates as variances and covariances. The default is to display them as standard deviations and correlations.

noretable suppresses the table of random effects.

nofetable suppresses the table of fixed effects.

estmetric displays all parameter estimates in the estimation metric. Fixed-effects estimates are unchanged from those normally displayed, but random-effects parameter estimates are displayed as log-standard deviations and hyperbolic arctangents of correlations, with equation names that organize them by model level.

noheader suppresses the output header, either at estimation or upon replay.

nogroup suppresses the display of group summary information (number of groups, average group size, minimum, and maximum) from the output header.

nolrtest prevents xtmelogit from performing a likelihood-ratio test that compares the mixed-effects logistic model to standard (marginal) logistic regression. This option may also be specified upon replay to suppress this test from the output.

_____⌐ Max options ⌐_____

maximize_options: difficult, technique(*algorithm_spec*), iterate(#), [no]log, trace, gradient, showstep, hessian, shownrtolerance, tolerance(#), ltolerance(#), gtolerance(#), nrtolerance(#), nonrtolerance; see [R] **maximize**.

For option technique(), the default is technique(nr), and algorithm bhhh is not allowed.

retolerance(#) specifies the convergence tolerance for the estimated random effects used by adaptive Gaussian quadrature. Although not estimated as model parameters, random-effects estimators are used to adapt the quadrature points. Estimating these random effects is an iterative procedure, with convergence declared when the maximum relative change in the random effects is less than retolerance(). The default is retolerance(1e-8). You should seldom have to use this option.

reiterate(*#*) specifies the maximum number of iterations used when estimating the random effects to be used in adapting the Gaussian quadrature points; see above. The default is reiterate(50). You should seldom have to use this option.

matlog, during optimization, parameterizes variance components by using the matrix logarithms of the variance–covariance matrices formed by these components at each model level. By default, a parameterization using the matrix square root is used. Both methods ensure variance–covariance matrices that are positive semidefinite. For most problems the matrix square root is more stable near the boundary of the parameter space. However, if convergence is problematic, one option may be to try the alternate matlog parameterization. When convergence is not an issue, both parameterizations yield equivalent results.

refineopts(*maximize_options*) controls the maximization process during the refinement of starting values. Estimation in xtmelogit takes place in two stages. In the first stage, starting values are refined by holding the quadrature points fixed between iterations. During the second stage, quadrature points are adapted with each evaluation of the log likelihood. Maximization options specified within refineopts() control the first stage of optimization; i.e., they control the refining of starting values.

maximize_options specified outside refineopts() control the second stage.

The one exception to the above rule is option nolog, which when specified outside refineopts() applies globally.

Refining starting values helps make the iterations of the second stage (those that lead toward the solution) more numerically stable. In this regard, of particular interest is refineopts(iterate(*#*)), with two iterations being the default. Should the maximization fail because of instability in the Hessian calculations, one possible solution may be to increase the number of iterations here.

Remarks

Remarks are presented under the following headings:

     Introduction
     One-level models
     Other covariance structures
     Distribution theory for likelihood-ratio tests
     Multilevel models
     Computation time and the Laplacian approximation
     Crossed-effects models

Introduction

Mixed-effects logistic regression is logistic regression containing both fixed effects and random effects. In longitudinal/panel data, random effects are useful for modeling intrapanel correlation; that is, observations in the same panel are correlated because they share common panel-level random effects.

xtmelogit allows for not just one, but many levels of nested panels. For example, in a two-level model you can specify random effects for schools and then random effects for classes nested within schools.

However, for simplicity, for now we consider the one-level model where, for a series of M independent panels, and conditional on a set of *random effects* $\mathbf{u}_i$,

$$P(y_{ij} = 1|\mathbf{u}_i) = H\left(\mathbf{x}_{ij}\boldsymbol{\beta} + \mathbf{z}_{ij}\mathbf{u}_i\right) \tag{1}$$

for $i = 1, \ldots, M$ panels, with panel i consisting of $j = 1, \ldots, n_i$ observations. The responses are the binary-valued y_{ij}, and we follow the standard Stata convention of treating $y_{ij} = 1$ if $depvar_{ij} \neq 0$, and $y_{ij} = 0$ otherwise. The $1 \times p$ row vector $\mathbf{x}_{ij}$ are the covariates for the fixed effects, analogous to the covariates you would find in a standard logistic regression model, with regression coefficients (fixed effects) $\boldsymbol{\beta}$.

The $1 \times q$ vector $\mathbf{z}_{ij}$ are the covariates corresponding to the random effects and can be used to represent both random intercepts and random coefficients. For example, in a random intercept model, $\mathbf{z}_{ij}$ is simply the scalar 1. The random effects $\mathbf{u}_i$ are M realizations from a multivariate normal distribution with mean $\mathbf{0}$ and $q \times q$ variance matrix $\boldsymbol{\Sigma}$. The random effects are not directly estimated as model parameters but are instead summarized according to the unique elements of $\boldsymbol{\Sigma}$, known as *variance components*. One special case of (1) places $\mathbf{z}_{ij} = \mathbf{x}_{ij}$, so that all covariate effects are essentially random and distributed as multivariate normal with mean $\boldsymbol{\beta}$ and variance $\boldsymbol{\Sigma}$.

Finally, since this is logistic regression, $H(\cdot)$ is the logistic cumulative distribution function (c.d.f.). The logistic c.d.f. maps the linear predictor to the probability of a success ($y_{ij} = 1$), with $H(v) = \exp(v)/\{1 + \exp(v)\}$.

Model (1) may also be stated in terms of a latent linear response, where only $y_{ij} = I(y_{ij}^* > 0)$ is observed for the latent

$$y_{ij}^* = \mathbf{x}_{ij}\boldsymbol{\beta} + \mathbf{z}_{ij}\mathbf{u}_i + \epsilon_{ij}$$

The errors ϵ_{ij} are distributed as logistic with mean zero and variance $\pi^2/3$ and are independent of $\mathbf{u}_i$.

Model (1) is an example of a generalized linear mixed model (GLMM), which generalizes the linear mixed-effects (LME) model to non-Gaussian responses. You can fit LMEs in Stata by using `xtmixed`. Because of the relationship between LMEs and GLMMs, there is insight to be gained through examination of the linear mixed model. This is especially true for Stata users since the terminology, syntax, options, and output for fitting these types of models are nearly identical. See [XT] **xtmixed** and the references therein, particularly in the *Introduction*, for more information.

Multilevel models with binary responses have been used extensively in the health and social sciences. As just one example, Leyland and Goldstein (2001, sec. 3.6) describe a study of equity of health care in Great Britain. Multilevel models with binary and other limited dependent responses also have a long history in econometrics; Rabe-Hesketh, Skrondal, and Pickles (2005) provide an excellent survey.

Log-likelihood calculations for fitting any mixed-effects model (LME, logistic, or otherwise) require integrating out the random effects. For LME, this integral has a closed-form solution, but this is not so with the logistic or any other GLMM. In dealing with this difficulty, early estimation methods avoided the integration altogether. Two such popular methods are the closely related penalized quasilikelihood (PQL) and marginal quasilikelihood (MQL) (Breslow and Clayton 1993). Both PQL and MQL use a combination of iterative reweighted least squares (see [R] **glm**) and standard estimation techniques for fitting LMEs. Efficient computational methods for fitting LMEs have existed for some time (Bates and Pinheiro 1998; Littell et al. 1996), and PQL and MQL inherit this computational efficiency. However, both these methods suffer from two key disadvantages. First, they have been shown to be biased, and this bias can be severe when panels are small and/or intrapanel correlation is high (Rodríguez and Goldman 1995; Lin and Breslow 1996). Second, because they are "quasilikelihood" methods and not true likelihood methods, their use prohibits comparing nested models via likelihood-ratio tests, blocking the main avenue of inference involving variance components.

The advent of modern computers has brought with it the development of more computationally intensive methods, such as bias-corrected PQL (Lin and Breslow 1996), Bayesian Markov-Chain Monte Carlo, and simulated maximum likelihood, just to name a few; see Ng et al. (2006) for a discussion of these alternate strategies (and more) for mixed-effects models for binary outcomes.

One widely used modern method is to directly estimate the integral required to calculate the log likelihood by Gauss–Hermite quadrature, or some variation thereof. Since the log likelihood itself is estimated, this method has the advantage of permitting LR tests for comparing nested models. Also, if done correctly, quadrature approximations can be quite accurate, thus minimizing bias.

In discussing quadrature, it is easiest to relate to the simplest form of (1)—the simplest model you can fit using xtmelogit—the single-level model with a random intercept,

$$P(y_{ij} = 1) = H\left(\mathbf{x}_{ij}\boldsymbol{\beta} + u_i\right)$$

This model can also be fit using xtlogit with option re. xtlogit supports three types of Gauss–Hermite quadrature; see [XT] **xtlogit**. The estimation method used by xtmelogit is a multicoefficient and multilevel extension of one of these quadrature types, namely, adaptive Gaussian quadrature (AGQ) based on conditional modes, with the multicoefficient extension from Pinheiro and Bates (1995) and the multilevel extension from Pinheiro and Chao (2006); see *Methods and Formulas*.

Finally, using formulation (1) and its multilevel extensions requires one important convention of terminology. Model (1) is what we call a *one-level* model, with extensions to two, three, or any number of levels. In our hypothetical two-level model with classes nested within schools, the schools are considered the first level and classes, the second level of the model. This is generally accepted terminology but differs from that of the literature on hierarchical models, e.g., Skrondal and Rabe-Hesketh (2004); Raudenbush and Bryk (2002). In that literature, our schools and classes model would be considered a three-level model, with the pupils (presumably) forming the first level, classes the second, and schools the third. Not only is there one more level, pupils, but the order is reversed.

One-level models

We begin with a simple application of (1).

▷ Example 1

Ng et al. (2006) analyze a subsample of data from the 1989 Bangladesh fertility survey (Huq and Cleland 1990), which polled 1,934 Bangladeshi women on their use of contraception.

```
. use http://www.stata-press.com/data/r10/bangladesh
(Bangladesh Fertility Survey, 1989)

. describe

Contains data from http://www.stata-press.com/data/r10/bangladesh.dta
  obs:         1,934                          Bangladesh Fertility Survey,
                                                1989
 vars:             7                          24 May 2007 13:22
 size:        34,812 (99.7% of memory free)   (_dta has notes)
```

variable name	storage type	display format	value label	variable label
district	byte	%9.0g		District
c_use	byte	%9.0g	yesno	Use contraception
urban	byte	%9.0g	urban	Urban or rural
age	float	%9.0g		Age, mean centered
child1	byte	%9.0g		1 child
child2	byte	%9.0g		2 children
child3	byte	%9.0g		3 or more children

```
Sorted by:  district
```

The women sampled were from 60 districts, identified by variable `district`. Each district contained either urban or rural areas (variable `urban`) or both. Variable `c_use` is the binary response, with a value of one indicating contraceptive use. Other covariates include mean-centered `age` and three indicator variables recording number of children.

Consider a standard logistic regression model, amended to have random effects for each district. Defining $\pi_{ij} = \Pr(c\_use_{ij} = 1)$, we have

$$\text{logit}(\pi_{ij}) = \beta_0 + \beta_1 \text{urban}_{ij} + \beta_2 \text{age}_{ij} + \beta_3 \text{child1}_{ij} + \beta_4 \text{child2}_{ij} + \beta_5 \text{child3}_{ij} + u_i \quad (2)$$

for $i = 1, \dots, 60$ districts, with $j = 1, \dots, n_i$ women in district i.

```
. xtmelogit c_use urban age child* || district:

Refining starting values:

Iteration 0:    log likelihood = -1219.2682
Iteration 1:    log likelihood = -1209.3544
Iteration 2:    log likelihood = -1207.1908

Performing gradient-based optimization:

Iteration 0:    log likelihood = -1207.1908
Iteration 1:    log likelihood = -1206.8323
Iteration 2:    log likelihood = -1206.8322
Iteration 3:    log likelihood = -1206.8322
```

```
Mixed-effects logistic regression            Number of obs      =        1934
Group variable: district                      Number of groups   =          60

                                              Obs per group: min =           2
                                                             avg =        32.2
                                                             max =         118

Integration points =    7                     Wald chi2(5)       =      109.60
Log likelihood = -1206.8322                   Prob > chi2        =      0.0000
```

c_use	Coef.	Std. Err.	z	P>|z|	[95% Conf. Interval]	
urban	.7322764	.1194857	6.13	0.000	.4980887	.9664641
age	-.0264982	.0078916	-3.36	0.001	-.0419654	-.0110309
child1	1.116002	.1580921	7.06	0.000	.8061466	1.425856
child2	1.365895	.174669	7.82	0.000	1.02355	1.70824
child3	1.344031	.1796549	7.48	0.000	.9919141	1.696148
_cons	-1.68929	.1477592	-11.43	0.000	-1.978892	-1.399687

Random-effects Parameters	Estimate	Std. Err.	[95% Conf. Interval]	
district: Identity				
sd(_cons)	.4643477	.0789531	.3327464	.6479975

```
LR test vs. logistic regression: chibar2(01) =     43.39 Prob>=chibar2 = 0.0000
```

Those of you familiar with `xtmixed`, Stata's command for fitting linear mixed models, will recognize the syntax and output. Whether you are familiar with `xtmixed`, however, there are enough nuances in `xtmelogit` to warrant the guided tour:

1. By typing "`c_use urban age child*`", we specified the binary response, `c_use`, and the fixed portion of the model in the same way we would if we were using `logit` or any other estimation command. Our fixed effects are a constant term (intercept) and coefficients on `urban`, `age`, and the indicator variables `child1`, `child2` and `child3`.

2. When we added "`|| district:`", we specified random effects at the level identified by group variable `district`. Since we wanted only a random intercept, that is all we had to type.

3. The estimation log consists of two parts:

   (a) A set of iterations aimed at refining starting values. These are designed to be relatively quick iterations aimed at getting the parameter estimates within a neighborhood of the eventual solution, making the iterations in (b) more numerically stable.

   (b) A set of "gradient-based" iterations. By default, these are Newton–Raphson iterations, but other methods are available by specifying the appropriate *maximize_options*; see [R] **maximize**.

4. Within the output header you'll find a series of group (district) statistics. District sizes vary greatly, ranging the all way from $n_i = 2$ to $n_i = 118$.

5. Just above the reported log likelihood, the number of "Integration Points" is displayed as 7, the default. As stated previously in *Introduction*, log likelihoods are approximated using adaptive Gaussian quadrature, and the more integration points you use, the better the approximation; see *Methods and Formulas*. You can specify an alternate number of integration points by using option intpoints().

   In any case, refitting this model with more integration points would demonstrate that seven integration points is sufficient.

6. The first estimation table reports the fixed effects, and these can be interpreted just as you would the output from logit. You can also specify option or at estimation or on replay to display the fixed effects as odds ratios instead.

   If you did display results as odds ratios, you would find urban women to have roughly double the odds of using contraception as that of their rural counterparts. Having any number of children will increase the odds from three- to fourfold, when compared with the base category of no children. Contraceptive use also decreases with age.

7. The second estimation table shows the estimated variance components. The first section of the table is labeled "district: Identity", meaning that these are random effects at the district level and that their variance–covariance matrix is a multiple of the identity matrix; that is, $\Sigma = \sigma_u^2 \mathbf{I}$. Since we have only one random effect at this level, xtmelogit knew that Identity is the only possible covariance structure. In any case, σ_u was estimated as 0.464 with standard error 0.079.

   If you prefer variance estimates, $\widehat{\sigma}_u^2$, to standard deviation estimates, $\widehat{\sigma}_u$, specify option variance either at estimation or on replay.

8. A likelihood-ratio test comparing the model to ordinary logistic regression, model (2) without u_i, is provided and is highly significant for these data.

9. Finally, since (2) is a simple random-intercept model, you can also fit it with xtlogit, specifying option re.

   We now store our estimates for later use.

   ```
   . estimates store r_int
   ```

   ◁

In what follows we will be extending (2), focusing on variable urban. Before we begin, to keep things short we restate (2) as

$$\text{logit}(\pi_{ij}) = \beta_0 + \beta_1 \text{urban}_{ij} + \mathcal{F}_{ij} + u_i$$

where $\mathcal{F}_{ij}$ is merely shorthand for the portion of the fixed-effects specification having to do with age and children.

▷ Example 2

Extending (2) to allow for a random slope on the indicator variable urban yields the model

$$\text{logit}(\pi_{ij}) = \beta_0 + \beta_1 \text{urban}_{ij} + \mathcal{F}_{ij} + u_i + v_i \text{urban}_{ij} \tag{3}$$

which we can fit by typing

```
. xtmelogit c_use urban age child* || district: urban
(output omitted)
. estimates store r_urban
```

Extending the model was as simple as adding urban to the random effects specification, so that the model now includes a random intercept *and* a random coefficient on urban. We dispense with the output because, although this is an improvement over the random-intercept model (2),

```
. lrtest r_int r_urban
Likelihood-ratio test                          LR chibar2(01)   =      3.66
(Assumption: r_int nested in r_urban)          Prob > chibar2   =    0.0279
```

we find the default covariance structure for (u_i, v_i), covariance(Independent),

$$\Sigma = \text{Var}\begin{bmatrix} u_i \\ v_i \end{bmatrix} = \begin{bmatrix} \sigma_u^2 & 0 \\ 0 & \sigma_v^2 \end{bmatrix}$$

to be inadequate. We see below that we can reject this model in favor of one that allows correlation between u_i and v_i.

```
. xtmelogit c_use urban age child* || district: urban, covariance(unstructured)
> variance
(output omitted)
```

| Mixed-effects logistic regression | | Number of obs | = | 1934 |
| Group variable: district | | Number of groups | = | 60 |

		Obs per group: min =	2
		avg =	32.2
		max =	118

| Integration points = 7 | Wald chi2(5) | = | 97.50 |
| Log likelihood = -1199.315 | Prob > chi2 | = | 0.0000 |

c_use	Coef.	Std. Err.	z	P>|z|	[95% Conf. Interval]	
urban	.8157872	.1715519	4.76	0.000	.4795516	1.152023
age	-.026415	.008023	-3.29	0.001	-.0421398	-.0106902
child1	1.13252	.1603285	7.06	0.000	.818282	1.446758
child2	1.357739	.1770522	7.67	0.000	1.010724	1.704755
child3	1.353827	.1828801	7.40	0.000	.9953881	1.712265
_cons	-1.71165	.1605617	-10.66	0.000	-2.026345	-1.396954

Random-effects Parameters	Estimate	Std. Err.	[95% Conf. Interval]	
district: Unstructured				
var(urban)	.6663221	.3224714	.2580709	1.7204
var(_cons)	.3897435	.1292459	.2034723	.7465388
cov(urban,_cons)	-.4058846	.1755418	-.7499403	-.0618289

LR test vs. logistic regression: chi2(3) =   58.42   Prob > chi2 = 0.0000

Note: LR test is conservative and provided only for reference.

```
. estimates store r_urban_corr
. lrtest r_urban r_urban_corr
Likelihood-ratio test                               LR chi2(1)  =      11.38
(Assumption: r_urban nested in r_urban_corr)        Prob > chi2 =     0.0007
```

By specifying `covariance(unstructured)` above, we told `xtmelogit` to allow correlation between random effects at the "`district level`"; i.e.,

$$\Sigma = \text{Var}\begin{bmatrix} u_i \\ v_i \end{bmatrix} = \begin{bmatrix} \sigma_u^2 & \sigma_{uv} \\ \sigma_{uv} & \sigma_v^2 \end{bmatrix}$$

Option `variance` is a display option that does not affect estimation but merely displays the variance components as variances and covariances instead of standard deviations and correlations. This feature will prove convenient in the discussion that follows.

◁

▷ Example 3

The purpose of introducing a random coefficient on the binary variable `urban` in (3) was to allow for separate random effects, within each district, for the urban and rural areas of that district. Hence, if we had the binary variable `rural` in our data such that $\text{rural}_{ij} = 1 - \text{urban}_{ij}$, then we can reformulate (3) as

$$\text{logit}(\pi_{ij}) = \beta_0\text{rural}_{ij} + (\beta_0 + \beta_1)\text{urban}_{ij} + \mathcal{F}_{ij} + u_i\text{rural}_{ij} + (u_i + v_i)\text{urban}_{ij} \qquad (3a)$$

where we have translated both the fixed portion and random portion to be in terms of `rural` rather than a random intercept. Translating the fixed portion is not necessary to make the point we make below, but we do so anyway for uniformity.

Translating the estimated random-effects parameters from the previous output to ones appropriate for (3a), we get $\text{Var}(u_i) = \widehat{\sigma}_u^2 = 0.390$,

$$\text{Var}(u_i + v_i) = \widehat{\sigma}_u^2 + \widehat{\sigma}_v^2 + 2\widehat{\sigma}_{uv}$$
$$= 0.390 + 0.666 - 2(0.406) = 0.244$$

and $\text{Cov}(u_i, u_i + v_i) = \widehat{\sigma}_u^2 + \widehat{\sigma}_{uv} = 0.390 - 0.406 = -0.016$.

An alternative that does not require remembering how to calculate variances and covariances involving sums—and one that also gives you standard errors—is to let Stata do the work for you:

```
. gen byte rural = 1 - urban

. xtmelogit c_use rural urban age child*, nocons || district: rural urban,
> nocons cov(unstr) var

(output omitted )
```

```
Mixed-effects logistic regression              Number of obs      =        1934
Group variable: district                       Number of groups   =          60

                                               Obs per group: min =           2
                                                              avg =        32.2
                                                              max =         118

Integration points =   7                       Wald chi2(6)       =      120.24
Log likelihood =  -1199.315                    Prob > chi2        =      0.0000
```

c_use	Coef.	Std. Err.	z	P>|z|	[95% Conf. Interval]	
rural	-1.71165	.1605618	-10.66	0.000	-2.026345	-1.396954
urban	-.8958623	.1704961	-5.25	0.000	-1.230028	-.5616961
age	-.026415	.008023	-3.29	0.001	-.0421398	-.0106902
child1	1.13252	.1603285	7.06	0.000	.818282	1.446758
child2	1.357739	.1770522	7.67	0.000	1.010724	1.704755
child3	1.353827	.1828801	7.40	0.000	.9953882	1.712265

Random-effects Parameters	Estimate	Std. Err.	[95% Conf. Interval]	
district: Unstructured				
var(rural)	.3897438	.1292459	.2034726	.7465393
var(urban)	.2442966	.1450674	.0762886	.7823031
cov(rural,urban)	-.0161411	.1057469	-.2234012	.1911189

```
LR test vs. logistic regression:      chi2(3) =    58.42    Prob > chi2 = 0.0000
Note: LR test is conservative and provided only for reference.
```

The above output demonstrates an equivalent fit to that we displayed for model (3) in example 2, with the added benefit of a more direct comparison of the parameters for rural and urban areas.

◁

❏ Technical Note

Our model fits for (3) and (3a) are equivalent only because we allowed for correlation in the random effects for both. Had we used the default "Independent" covariance structure, we would be fitting different models; in (3) we would be making the restriction that $Cov(u_i, v_i) = 0$, whereas in (3a) we would be assuming that $Cov(u_i, u_i + v_i) = 0$.

The moral here is that, although xtmelogit will do this by default, one should be cautious when imposing an independent covariance structure, since the correlation between random effects is not invariant to model translations that would otherwise yield equivalent results in standard regression models. In our example we remapped an intercept and binary coefficient to two complementary binary coefficients, something we could do in standard logistic regression without consequence, but that here required more consideration.

Rabe-Hesketh and Skrondal (2005, 66–67) provide a nice discussion of this phenomenon in the related case of recentering a continuous covariate.

❏

Other covariance structures

In the above examples, we demonstrated the Independent and Unstructured covariance structures. Also available are Identity (seen previously in output but not directly specified), which restricts random effects to be uncorrelated and share a common variance, and Exchangeable, which assumes a common variance and a common pairwise covariance.

You can also specify multiple random-effects equations at the same level, in which case the above four covariance types can be combined to form more complex blocked-diagonal covariance structures. This could be used, for example, to impose an equality constraint on a subset of variance components or to otherwise group together a set of related random effects.

Continuing the previous example: typing

```
. xtmelogit c_use urban age child* || district: child*, cov(exchangeable) || district:
```

would fit a model with the same fixed effects as (3) but with random-effects structure

$$\text{logit}(\pi_{ij}) = \beta_0 + \cdots + u_{1i}\texttt{child1}_{ij} + u_{2i}\texttt{child2}_{ij} + u_{3i}\texttt{child3}_{ij} + v_i$$

That is, we have random coefficients on each indicator variable for children (the first district: specification) and an overall district random intercept (the second district: specification). The above syntax fits a model with overall covariance structure

$$\Sigma = \text{Var}\begin{bmatrix} u_{1i} \\ u_{2i} \\ u_{3i} \\ v_i \end{bmatrix} = \begin{bmatrix} \sigma_u^2 & \sigma_c & \sigma_c & 0 \\ \sigma_c & \sigma_u^2 & \sigma_c & 0 \\ \sigma_c & \sigma_c & \sigma_u^2 & 0 \\ 0 & 0 & 0 & \sigma_v^2 \end{bmatrix}$$

reflecting the relationship among the random coefficients for children. We did not have to specify noconstant on the first district: specification. xtmelogit automatically avoids collinearity by including an intercept on only the final specification among repeated level equations.

Of course, if we fitted the above model we would heed our own advice from the previous technical note and make sure that not only our data but also our specification characterization of the random effects permitted the above structure. That is, we would check the above against a model that had an Unstructured covariance for all four random effects and then perhaps against a model that assumed an Unstructured covariance among the three random coefficients on children, coupled with independence with the random intercept. All comparisons can be made by storing estimates (command estimates store) and then using lrtest, as demonstrated previously.

Distribution theory for likelihood-ratio tests

A keen observer of the output for fitting the equivalent models (3) and (3a) may have noticed that, in the output for (3a), the covariance parameter does not appear at all significant. In fact, an LR test would confirm this. In the results for (3), however, all three variance components appear to be significant, and you would be hard pressed to prove otherwise. We thus have two entirely equivalent model fits, yet the first fit relies on all three variance components, whereas with the second you could presumably drop the covariance between the random coefficients. Whether generalizing from model (2) to model (3)/(3a) requires one or two additional parameters is unclear. Asked another way: do the models differ by 1 or 2 degrees of freedom?

Such paradoxical cases are at the core of the central issue concerning distribution theory for LR tests, where oftentimes significance levels cannot be exactly computed when models differ by (or appear to differ by) more than one variance component. We won't go into the details here but instead direct you to the section in [XT] **xtmixed** with the same name as this one. What is stated there applies equally to xtmelogit.

When significance levels cannot be computed exactly, both `xtmelogit` and `lrtest` will caution you, and you may have noticed the following message at the bottom of some of the output we have produced:

```
Note: LR test is conservative and provided only for reference.
```

In Stata, part of that message is blue, meaning that you can click on it for more details. If you aren't interested in all the details, it suffices to know that by "conservative" we mean that the p-value displayed is an upper bound on the actual p-value. If you choose to reject the null hypothesis of a reduced model on the basis of the displayed p-value, you would also reject based on the actual p-value, since it would be even smaller.

Multilevel models

The methods we have discussed so far extend from one-level models to two or more nested levels of random effects. By *nested* we mean that the random effects shared within lower-level subgroups are unique to the upper-level groups. For example, assuming that classroom effects would be nested within schools would be natural, since classrooms are unique to schools.

▷ Example 4

Rabe-Hesketh, Touloupoulou, and Murray (2001) analyzed data from a study measuring the cognitive ability of patients with schizophrenia, compared with their relatives and control subjects. Cognitive ability was measured as the successful completion of the "Tower of London", a computerized task, measured at three levels of difficulty. For all but one of the 226 subjects, there were three measurements (one for each difficulty level), and since patients' relatives were also tested, a family identifier, `family`, was also recorded.

```
. use http://www.stata-press.com/data/r10/towerlondon
(Tower of London data)
. describe
Contains data from http://www.stata-press.com/data/r10/towerlondon.dta
  obs:           677                          Tower of London data
  vars:            5                          31 May 2007 10:41
  size:        7,447 (99.9% of memory free)   (_dta has notes)
```

variable name	storage type	display format	value label	variable label
family	int	%8.0g		Family id
subject	int	%9.0g		Subject id
dtlm	byte	%9.0g		1 = task completed
difficulty	byte	%9.0g		Level of difficulty: -1, 0, or 1
group	byte	%8.0g		1: controls; 2: relatives; 3: schizophrenics

```
Sorted by:  family  subject
```

We fit a logistic model with response `dtlm`, the indicator of cognitive function, and with covariates `difficulty` and a set of indicator variables for `group`, with the controls (`group==1`) being the base category. We also allow for random effects due to families and due to subjects within families.

```
. xi: xtmelogit dtlm difficulty i.group || family: || subject:
i.group          _Igroup_1-3       (naturally coded; _Igroup_1 omitted)
```
  (*output omitted*)

```
Mixed-effects logistic regression              Number of obs      =      677
```

Group Variable	No. of Groups	Observations per Group			Integration Points
		Minimum	Average	Maximum	
family	118	2	5.7	27	7
subject	226	2	3.0	3	7

```
                                            Wald chi2(3)       =     74.89
Log likelihood = -305.12043                 Prob > chi2        =    0.0000
```

dtlm	Coef.	Std. Err.	z	P>|z|	[95% Conf. Interval]	
difficulty	-1.648506	.1932139	-8.53	0.000	-2.027198	-1.269814
_Igroup_2	-.24868	.3544065	-0.70	0.483	-.943304	.445944
_Igroup_3	-1.0523	.3999896	-2.63	0.009	-1.836265	-.2683349
_cons	-1.485861	.2848469	-5.22	0.000	-2.04415	-.927571

Random-effects Parameters	Estimate	Std. Err.	[95% Conf. Interval]	
family: Identity				
sd(_cons)	.7544415	.345725	.3072982	1.852214
subject: Identity				
sd(_cons)	1.066739	.3214235	.5909884	1.925472

```
LR test vs. logistic regression:    chi2(2) =    17.54   Prob > chi2 = 0.0002
Note: LR test is conservative and provided only for reference.
```

But we would prefer to see odds ratios and variances for the random-effects parameters:

```
. xtmelogit, or variance
Mixed-effects logistic regression              Number of obs      =      677
```

Group Variable	No. of Groups	Observations per Group			Integration Points
		Minimum	Average	Maximum	
family	118	2	5.7	27	7
subject	226	2	3.0	3	7

```
                                            Wald chi2(3)       =     74.89
Log likelihood = -305.12043                 Prob > chi2        =    0.0000
```

dtlm	Odds Ratio	Std. Err.	z	P>|z|	[95% Conf. Interval]	
difficulty	.192337	.0371622	-8.53	0.000	.131704	.2808839
_Igroup_2	.7798295	.2763766	-0.70	0.483	.3893393	1.561964
_Igroup_3	.3491338	.1396499	-2.63	0.009	.1594117	.7646517

Random-effects Parameters	Estimate	Std. Err.	[95% Conf. Interval]	
family: Identity				
var(_cons)	.5691819	.5216585	.0944322	3.430696
subject: Identity				
var(_cons)	1.137931	.6857498	.3492672	3.707441

LR test vs. logistic regression: chi2(2) =   17.54   Prob > chi2 = 0.0002
Note: LR test is conservative and provided only for reference.

Notes:

1. This model has two random-effects equations, separated by ||. The first is a random intercept (constant only) at the `family` level, and the second is a random intercept at the `subject` level. The order in which these are specified (from left to right) is important—xtmelogit assumes that `subject` is nested within `family`.

2. The information on groups is now displayed as a table, with one row for each model level. Among other things, we see that we have 226 subjects from 118 families. Also, the number of integration points for adaptive Gaussian quadrature is displayed within this table, since you can choose to have it vary by model level. As with one-level models, the default is seven points.

   You can suppress this table with option `nogroup` or with `noheader`, which will suppress the rest of the header as well.

3. The variance-component estimates are now organized and labeled according to level.

   After adjusting for the random-effects structure, the odds of successful completion of the Tower of London decrease dramatically as the level of difficulty increases. Also, schizophrenics (`group==3`) tended not to perform as well as the control subjects. Of course we would make similar conclusions from a standard logistic model fitted to the same data, but the odds ratios would differ somewhat.

   ◁

❏ Technical Note

In the previous example, the subjects are coded with unique values between 1 and 251 (with some gaps), but such coding is not necessary to produce nesting within families. Once we specified the nesting structure to xtmelogit, all that was important was the relative coding of `subject` within each unique value of `family`. We could have coded `subjects` as the numbers 1, 2, 3, and so on, restarting at 1 with each new family, and xtmelogit would have produced the same results.

Group identifiers may also be coded using string variables.

❏

The above extends to models with more than two levels of nesting in the obvious manner, by adding more random-effects equations, each separated by ||. The order of nesting goes from left to right as the groups go from biggest (highest level) to smallest (lowest level).

Computation time and the Laplacian approximation

Like many programs that fit generalized linear mixed models, xtmelogit can be computationally intensive. This is particularly true for large datasets with many lowest-level panels, models with many random coefficients, models with many estimable parameters (both fixed effects and variance components), or any combination thereof.

Computation time will also depend on hardware and other external factors but in general is (roughly) a function of $p^2\{M + M(N_Q)^{q_t}\}$, where p is the number of estimable parameters, M is the number of lowest-level (smallest) panels, N_Q is the number of quadrature points, and q_t is the total dimension of the random effects, that is, the total number of random intercepts and coefficients at all levels.

For a given model and a given dataset, the only prevailing factor influencing computation time is $(N_Q)^{q_t}$. However, since this is a power function, this factor can get prohibitively large. Consider a model with one random intercept and three random coefficients, such as that discussed in *Other covariance structures*. For such a model, $(N_Q)^{q_t} = 7^4 = 2,401$ using the default number of quadrature points. Even a modest reduction to five quadrature points would reduce this factor by almost fourfold ($5^4 = 625$) which, depending on M and p, could drastically speed up estimation.

Ideally, you want to use enough quadrature points such that your estimates are stable and that adding more quadrature points would not change the estimates much. If you want accurate estimates, we recommend that you perform this check. We have tacitly followed this advice in all the models we have fitted thus far. In each example, increasing the number of quadrature points from the default of seven did not make much of a difference.

However, we don't deny a tradeoff between speed and accuracy, and in that spirit we give you the option to choose a (possibly) less accurate solution in the interest of getting quicker results. Toward this end is the limiting case of $N_Q = 1$, otherwise known as the Laplacian approximation; see *Methods and Formulas*. You can obtain this estimate either by using option `laplace` or by directly setting `intpoints(1)`. The computational benefit is evident—one raised to any power equals one—and the Laplacian approximation has been shown to perform well in certain situations (Liu and Pierce 1994; Tierney and Kadane 1986).

In the previous section, we fitted a two-level model to the Tower of London data using seven quadrature points. We refit the same model, this time via the Laplacian approximation:

```
. xi: xtmelogit dtlm difficulty i.group || family: || subject:, laplace or variance
(output omitted)
Mixed-effects logistic regression              Number of obs      =        677
```

Group Variable	No. of Groups	Observations per Group			Integration Points
		Minimum	Average	Maximum	
family	118	2	5.7	27	1
subject	226	2	3.0	3	1

```
                                               Wald chi2(3)       =      76.09
Log likelihood = -306.51035                    Prob > chi2        =     0.0000
```

dtlm	Odds Ratio	Std. Err.	z	P>|z|	[95% Conf. Interval]	
difficulty	.2044132	.0377578	-8.60	0.000	.1423248	.2935872
_Igroup_2	.7860452	.2625197	-0.72	0.471	.4084766	1.512613
_Igroup_3	.3575718	.1354592	-2.71	0.007	.1701774	.7513195

Random-effects Parameters	Estimate	Std. Err.	[95% Conf. Interval]	
family: Identity				
var(_cons)	.5229424	.4704256	.0896881	3.049109
subject: Identity				
var(_cons)	.790933	.5699271	.1926569	3.247094

LR test vs. logistic regression: chi2(2) =   14.76   Prob > chi2 = 0.0006
Note: LR test is conservative and provided only for reference.
Note: Log likelihood calculations are based on the Laplacian approximation.

Comparing these results to those previously obtained, we observe the following:

1. Odds ratios and their standard errors are well approximated by the Laplacian method. Therefore, if your interest lies primarily here, then `laplace` may be a viable alternative.

2. Estimates of variance components exhibit bias, particularly at the lower (`subject`) level.

3. The model log-likelihood and comparison LR test are in fair agreement.

Although this is by no means the rule, we find the above observations to be fairly typical based on our own experience. Pinheiro and Chao (2006) also make observations similar to points 1 and 2 on the basis of their simulation studies: bias due to Laplace (when present) tends to exhibit itself more in the estimated variance components than in the estimates of the fixed effects.

Item 3 is of particular interest, because it demonstrates that `laplace` can produce a decent estimate of the model log likelihood. Consequently, you can use `laplace` during the model building phase of your analysis, during which you are comparing competing models by using LR tests. Once you settle on a parsimonious model that fits well, you can then increase the number of quadrature points and obtain more accurate parameter estimates for further study.

We discuss such a scenario in *Other covariance structures*, where we posit a blocked-diagonal exchangeable/identity covariance structure and recommend comparing against more complex structures to verify our assumptions. The comparisons ruling out the more complex structures can be performed more quickly using `laplace`.

Of course, sometimes the Laplacian approximation will perform either better or worse than observed here. This behavior depends primarily on panel size and intrapanel correlation, but the relative influence of these factors is unclear. The idea behind Laplace is to approximate the posterior density of the random effects given the response with a normal distribution; see *Methods and Formulas*. Asymptotic theory dictates that this approximation improves with larger panels. Of course, the key question, as always, is "How large is large enough?" Also, there are data situations where Laplace performs well even with small panels. Therefore, it is difficult to make a definitive call as to when you can expect `laplace` to yield accurate results across all aspects of the model.

In conclusion, consider our above advice as a rule of thumb based on empirical evidence.

Crossed-effects models

Not all mixed-effects models contain nested random effects.

▷ Example 5

Rabe-Hesketh and Skrondal (2005, 257ff.) perform an analysis on school data from Fife, Scotland. The data, originally from Paterson (1991), are from a study measuring students' attainment as an integer score from 1 to 10, based on the Scottish school exit examination taken at age 16. The study comprises 3,435 students who first attended any one of 148 primary schools and then any one of 19 secondary schools.

```
. use http://www.stata-press.com/data/r10/fifeschool
(School data from Fife, Scotland)

. describe

Contains data from http://www.stata-press.com/data/r10/fifeschool.dta
  obs:         3,435                          School data from Fife, Scotland
 vars:             5                          28 May 2007 10:08
 size:        37,785 (99.6% of memory free)   (_dta has notes)
```

variable name	storage type	display format	value label	variable label
pid	int	%9.0g		Primary school id
sid	byte	%9.0g		Secondary school id
attain	byte	%9.0g		Attainment score at age 16
vrq	int	%9.0g		Verbal-reasoning score from final year of primary school
sex	byte	%9.0g		1: female; 0: male

```
Sorted by:
. gen byte attain_gt_6 = attain > 6
```

To make the analysis relevant to our present discussion, we focus not on the attainment score itself but instead on whether the score is greater than 6. We wish to model this indicator as a function of the fixed effect `sex` and of random effects due to primary and secondary schools.

For this analysis, it would make sense to assume that the random effects are not nested, but instead *crossed*, meaning that the effect due to primary school is the same regardless of the secondary school attended. Our model is thus

$$\text{logit}\{\Pr(\texttt{attain}_{ijk} > 6)\} = \beta_0 + \beta_1 \texttt{sex}_{ijk} + u_i + v_j \tag{4}$$

for student k, $k = 1, \ldots, n_{ij}$, who attended primary school i, $i = 1, \ldots, 148$, and then secondary school j, $j = 1, \ldots, 19$.

Since there is no evident nesting, one solution would be to consider the data as a whole and fit a one-level, one-panel model with random-effects structure

$$\mathbf{u} = \begin{bmatrix} u_1 \\ \vdots \\ u_{148} \\ v_1 \\ \vdots \\ v_{19} \end{bmatrix} \sim N(\mathbf{0}, \mathbf{\Sigma}); \quad \mathbf{\Sigma} = \begin{bmatrix} \sigma_u^2 \mathbf{I}_{148} & \mathbf{0} \\ \mathbf{0} & \sigma_v^2 \mathbf{I}_{19} \end{bmatrix}$$

We can fit such a model by using the group designation `_all:`, which tells `xtmelogit` to treat the whole dataset as one panel, and the factor notation R.*varname*, which mimics the creation of indicator variables identifying schools:

```
. xtmelogit attain_gt_6 sex || _all:R.pid || _all:R.sid, or variance
```

But we do not recommend fitting this model this way, because of high total dimension $(148+19 = 167)$ of the random effects. This would require working with matrices of column dimension 167, which is probably not a problem for most current hardware, but would be if this number got much larger.

An equivalent way to fit (4) that has smaller dimension is to treat the panels identified by primary schools as nested within the entire data, i.e., as nested within the "_all" group.

```
. xtmelogit attain_gt_6 sex || _all:R.sid || pid:, or variance
Note: factor variables specified; option laplace assumed
(output omitted )
Mixed-effects logistic regression              Number of obs    =      3435
```

Group Variable	No. of Groups	Observations per Group Minimum	Average	Maximum	Integration Points
_all	1	3435	3435.0	3435	1
pid	148	1	23.2	72	1

```
                                               Wald chi2(1)     =     14.28
Log likelihood = -2220.0035                    Prob > chi2      =    0.0002
```

attain_gt_6	Odds Ratio	Std. Err.	z	P>|z|	[95% Conf. Interval]	
sex	1.32512	.0986967	3.78	0.000	1.145135	1.533395

Random-effects Parameters	Estimate	Std. Err.	[95% Conf. Interval]	
_all: Identity				
var(R.sid)	.1239741	.0694743	.0413354	.3718255
pid: Identity				
var(_cons)	.4520491	.0953864	.2989334	.6835916

```
LR test vs. logistic regression:     chi2(2) =    195.80   Prob > chi2 = 0.0000
Note: LR test is conservative and provided only for reference.
Note: log-likelihood calculations are based on the Laplacian approximation.
```

Choosing the primary schools as those to nest was no accident; since there are far fewer secondary schools than primary schools, the above required only 19 random coefficients for the secondary schools, and one random intercept at the primary school level, for a total dimension of 20. Our data also include a measurement of verbal reasoning, variable vrq. Adding a fixed effect due to vrq in (4) would negate the effect due to secondary school, a fact we leave to you to verify as an exercise.

◁

See [XT] **xtmixed** for a similar discussion of crossed effects in the context of linear mixed models. Also see Rabe-Hesketh and Skrondal (2005, chap. 8) for more examples of crossed-effects models, including models with random interactions, and for more techniques on how to avoid high-dimensional estimation.

❑ Technical Note

The estimation in the previous example was performed using a Laplacian approximation, even though we did not specify this. Whenever factor variables are used (the R. *varname* notation), estimation reverts to the Laplacian method because of the high dimension induced by having factor variables.

In the above example, through some creative nesting we reduced the dimension of the random effects to 20, but this is still too large to permit estimation via adaptive Gaussian quadrature; see *Computation time and the Laplacian approximation*. Even with two quadrature points, our rough formula for computation time would contain within it a factor of $2^{20} = 1,048,576$.

Option `laplace` is therefore assumed when you use factor variables. If the number of distinct levels of your factors is small enough (say, five or fewer) to permit estimation via AGQ, you can override the imposition of `laplace` by specifying option `intpoints()`.

❏

Saved Results

`xtmelogit` saves the following in `e()`:

Scalars

e(N)	number of observations	e(p)	p-value for χ^2
e(k)	number of parameters	e(ll_c)	log-likelihood, comparison model
e(k_f)	number of FE parameters	e(chi2_c)	χ^2, comparison model
e(k_r)	number of RE parameters	e(df_c)	d.f., comparison model
e(k_rs)	number of std. deviations	e(p_c)	p-value, comparison model
e(k_rc)	number of correlations	e(converged)	1 if converged, 0 otherwise
e(df_m)	model degrees of freedom	e(reparm_rc)	return code, final
e(ll)	log-likelihood		reparameterization
e(chi2)	χ^2	e(rc)	return code

Macros

e(cmd)	xtmelogit	e(laplace)	laplace, if Laplace approx.
e(cmdline)	command as typed	e(chi2type)	Wald, type of model χ^2
e(title)	title in estimation output	e(opt)	type of optimization
e(model)	logistic	e(ml_method)	type of ml method
e(depvar)	name of dependent variable	e(technique)	maximization technique
e(offset)	offset	e(crittype)	optimization criterion
e(binomial)	binomial number of trials	e(datasignature)	the checksum
e(method)	ML	e(datasignaturevars)	variables used in checksum
e(ivars)	grouping variables	e(properties)	b V
e(redim)	random-effects dimensions	e(estat_cmd)	program used to implement
e(vartypes)	variance-structure types		estat
e(revars)	random-effects covariates	e(predict)	program used to implement
e(n_quad)	number of integration pts.		predict

Matrices

e(b)	coefficient vector	e(V)	variance–covariance matrix of
e(N_g)	group counts		the estimator
e(g_min)	group size minimums	e(g_avg)	group size averages
e(g_max)	group size maximums		

Functions

e(sample)	marks estimation sample

Methods and Formulas

`xtmelogit` is implemented as an ado-file.

Model (1) assumes Bernoulli data, a special case of the binomial. Since binomial data are also supported by `xtmelogit` (option `binomial()`), the methods presented below are in terms of the more general binomial mixed-effects model.

For a one-level binomial model, consider the response y_{ij} as the number of successes from a series of r_{ij} Bernoulli trials (replications). For panel i, $i = 1, \ldots, M$, the conditional distribution of $\mathbf{y}_i = (y_{i1}, \ldots, y_{in_i})'$, given a set of panel-level random effects $\mathbf{u}_i$, is

$$f(\mathbf{y}_i | \mathbf{u}_i) = \prod_{j=1}^{n_i} \left[\binom{r_{ij}}{y_{ij}} \left\{ H\left(\mathbf{x}_{ij}\boldsymbol{\beta} + \mathbf{z}_{ij}\mathbf{u}_i\right) \right\}^{y_{ij}} \left\{ 1 - H\left(\mathbf{x}_{ij}\boldsymbol{\beta} + \mathbf{z}_{ij}\mathbf{u}_i\right) \right\}^{r_{ij} - y_{ij}} \right]$$

$$= \exp\left(\sum_{j=1}^{n_i} \left[y_{ij}\left(\mathbf{x}_{ij}\boldsymbol{\beta} + \mathbf{z}_{ij}\mathbf{u}_i\right) - r_{ij}\log\left\{1 + \exp\left(\mathbf{x}_{ij}\boldsymbol{\beta} + \mathbf{z}_{ij}\mathbf{u}_i\right)\right\} + \log\binom{r_{ij}}{y_{ij}} \right] \right)$$

for $H(v) = \exp(v)/\{1 + \exp(v)\}$.

Defining $\mathbf{r}_i = (r_{i1}, \ldots, r_{in_i})'$ and

$$c(\mathbf{y}_i, \mathbf{r}_i) = \sum_{j=1}^{n_i} \log\binom{r_{ij}}{y_{ij}}$$

where $c(\mathbf{y}_i, \mathbf{r}_i)$ does not depend on the model parameters, we can express the above compactly in matrix notation,

$$f(\mathbf{y}_i | \mathbf{u}_i) = \exp\left[\mathbf{y}_i'\left(\mathbf{X}_i\boldsymbol{\beta} + \mathbf{Z}_i\mathbf{u}_i\right) - \mathbf{r}_i'\log\left\{1 + \exp\left(\mathbf{X}_i\boldsymbol{\beta} + \mathbf{Z}_i\mathbf{u}_i\right)\right\} + c(\mathbf{y}_i, \mathbf{r}_i)\right]$$

where $\mathbf{X}_i$ is formed by stacking the row vectors $\mathbf{x}_{ij}$, $\mathbf{Z}_i$ is formed by stacking the row vectors $\mathbf{z}_{ij}$, and we extend the definitions of the functions $\log()$ and $\exp()$ to be vector functions where necessary.

Since the prior distribution of $\mathbf{u}_i$ is multivariate normal with mean $\mathbf{0}$ and $q \times q$ variance matrix $\boldsymbol{\Sigma}$, the likelihood contribution for the i panel is obtained by integrating $\mathbf{u}_i$ out the joint density $f(\mathbf{y}_i, \mathbf{u}_i)$,

$$\mathcal{L}_i(\boldsymbol{\beta}, \boldsymbol{\Sigma}) = (2\pi)^{-q/2} |\boldsymbol{\Sigma}|^{-1/2} \int f(\mathbf{y}_i | \mathbf{u}_i) \exp\left(-\mathbf{u}_i'\boldsymbol{\Sigma}^{-1}\mathbf{u}_i/2\right) d\mathbf{u}_i$$

$$= \exp\{c(\mathbf{y}_i, \mathbf{r}_i)\} (2\pi)^{-q/2} |\boldsymbol{\Sigma}|^{-1/2} \int \exp\{g(\boldsymbol{\beta}, \boldsymbol{\Sigma}, \mathbf{u}_i)\} d\mathbf{u}_i \tag{5}$$

where

$$g(\boldsymbol{\beta}, \boldsymbol{\Sigma}, \mathbf{u}_i) = \mathbf{y}_i'\left(\mathbf{X}_i\boldsymbol{\beta} + \mathbf{Z}_i\mathbf{u}_i\right) - \mathbf{r}_i'\log\left\{1 + \exp\left(\mathbf{X}_i\boldsymbol{\beta} + \mathbf{Z}_i\mathbf{u}_i\right)\right\} - \mathbf{u}_i'\boldsymbol{\Sigma}^{-1}\mathbf{u}_i/2$$

and for convenience, in the arguments of $g()$ we suppress the dependence on the observable data $(\mathbf{y}_i, \mathbf{r}_i, \mathbf{X}_i, \mathbf{Z}_i)$.

The integration in (5) has no closed form and thus must be approximated. The Laplacian approximation (Tierney and Kadane 1986; Pinheiro and Bates 1995) is based on a second-order Taylor expansion of $g(\boldsymbol{\beta}, \boldsymbol{\Sigma}, \mathbf{u}_i)$ about the value of $\mathbf{u}_i$ that maximizes it. Taking first and second derivatives, we obtain

$$g'(\boldsymbol{\beta}, \boldsymbol{\Sigma}, \mathbf{u}_i) = \frac{\partial g(\boldsymbol{\beta}, \boldsymbol{\Sigma}, \mathbf{u}_i)}{\partial \mathbf{u}_i} = \mathbf{Z}_i'\{\mathbf{y}_i - \mathbf{m}(\boldsymbol{\beta}, \mathbf{u}_i)\} - \boldsymbol{\Sigma}^{-1}\mathbf{u}_i$$

$$g''(\boldsymbol{\beta}, \boldsymbol{\Sigma}, \mathbf{u}_i) = \frac{\partial^2 g(\boldsymbol{\beta}, \boldsymbol{\Sigma}, \mathbf{u}_i)}{\partial \mathbf{u}_i \partial \mathbf{u}_i'} = -\left\{\mathbf{Z}_i'\mathbf{V}(\boldsymbol{\beta}, \mathbf{u}_i)\mathbf{Z}_i + \boldsymbol{\Sigma}^{-1}\right\}$$

where $\mathbf{m}(\boldsymbol{\beta}, \mathbf{u}_i)$ is the vector function with jth element equal to the conditional mean of y_{ij} given $\mathbf{u}_i$, i.e., $r_{ij}H(\mathbf{x}_{ij}\boldsymbol{\beta} + \mathbf{z}_{ij}\mathbf{u}_i)$. $\mathbf{V}(\boldsymbol{\beta}, \mathbf{u}_i)$ is the diagonal matrix whose diagonal entries v_{ij} are the conditional variances of y_{ij} given $\mathbf{u}_i$, namely,

$$v_{ij} = r_{ij}H\left(\mathbf{x}_{ij}\boldsymbol{\beta} + \mathbf{z}_{ij}\mathbf{u}_i\right)\left\{1 - H\left(\mathbf{x}_{ij}\boldsymbol{\beta} + \mathbf{z}_{ij}\mathbf{u}_i\right)\right\}$$

The maximizer of $g\left(\boldsymbol{\beta}, \boldsymbol{\Sigma}, \mathbf{u}_i\right)$ is $\widehat{\mathbf{u}}_i$ such that $g'\left(\boldsymbol{\beta}, \boldsymbol{\Sigma}, \widehat{\mathbf{u}}_i\right) = \mathbf{0}$. The integrand in (5) is proportional to the posterior density $f(\mathbf{u}_i|\mathbf{y}_i)$, so $\widehat{\mathbf{u}}_i$ also represents the posterior mode, a plausible estimator of $\mathbf{u}_i$ in its own right.

Given the above derivatives, the second-order Taylor approximation then takes the form

$$g\left(\boldsymbol{\beta}, \boldsymbol{\Sigma}, \mathbf{u}_i\right) \approx g\left(\boldsymbol{\beta}, \boldsymbol{\Sigma}, \widehat{\mathbf{u}}_i\right) + \frac{1}{2}\left(\mathbf{u}_i - \widehat{\mathbf{u}}_i\right)' g''\left(\boldsymbol{\beta}, \boldsymbol{\Sigma}, \widehat{\mathbf{u}}_i\right)\left(\mathbf{u}_i - \widehat{\mathbf{u}}_i\right) \tag{6}$$

The first-derivative term vanishes because $g'\left(\boldsymbol{\beta}, \boldsymbol{\Sigma}, \widehat{\mathbf{u}}_i\right) = \mathbf{0}$. Therefore,

$$\int \exp\left\{g\left(\boldsymbol{\beta}, \boldsymbol{\Sigma}, \mathbf{u}_i\right)\right\} d\mathbf{u}_i \approx \exp\left\{g\left(\boldsymbol{\beta}, \boldsymbol{\Sigma}, \widehat{\mathbf{u}}_i\right)\right\}$$
$$\times \int \exp\left[-\frac{1}{2}\left(\mathbf{u}_i - \widehat{\mathbf{u}}_i\right)'\left\{-g''\left(\boldsymbol{\beta}, \boldsymbol{\Sigma}, \widehat{\mathbf{u}}_i\right)\right\}\left(\mathbf{u}_i - \widehat{\mathbf{u}}_i\right)\right] d\mathbf{u}_i \tag{7}$$
$$= \exp\left\{g\left(\boldsymbol{\beta}, \boldsymbol{\Sigma}, \widehat{\mathbf{u}}_i\right)\right\}\left(2\pi\right)^{q/2}\left|-g''\left(\boldsymbol{\beta}, \boldsymbol{\Sigma}, \widehat{\mathbf{u}}_i\right)\right|^{-1/2}$$

since the latter integrand can be recognized as the "kernel" of a multivariate normal density.

Combining the above with (5) (and taking logs) gives the Laplacian log-likelihood contribution of the ith panel,

$$L_i^{\text{Lap}}(\boldsymbol{\beta}, \boldsymbol{\Sigma}) = -\frac{1}{2}\log|\boldsymbol{\Sigma}| - \log|\mathbf{R}_i| + g\left(\boldsymbol{\beta}, \boldsymbol{\Sigma}, \widehat{\mathbf{u}}_i\right) + c(\mathbf{y}_i, \mathbf{r}_i)$$

where $\mathbf{R}_i$ is an upper-triangular matrix such that $-g''\left(\boldsymbol{\beta}, \boldsymbol{\Sigma}, \widehat{\mathbf{u}}_i\right) = \mathbf{R}_i\mathbf{R}_i'$. Pinheiro and Chao (2006) show that $\widehat{\mathbf{u}}_i$ and $\mathbf{R}_i$ can be efficiently computed as the iterative solution to a least-squares problem using matrix decomposition methods similar to those used in fitting LME models (Bates and Pinheiro 1998; Pinheiro and Bates 2000; [XT] **xtmixed**).

The fidelity of the Laplacian approximation is determined wholly by the accuracy of the approximation in (6). An alternative that does not depend so heavily on this approximation is integration via adaptive Gaussian quadrature (AGQ; Naylor and Smith 1982; Liu and Pierce 1994).

The application of AGQ to this particular problem is from Pinheiro and Bates (1995). When we reexamine the integral in question, a transformation of integration variables yields

$$\int \exp\left\{g\left(\boldsymbol{\beta}, \boldsymbol{\Sigma}, \mathbf{u}_i\right)\right\} d\mathbf{u}_i = \left|\mathbf{R}_i\right|^{-1}\int \exp\left\{g\left(\boldsymbol{\beta}, \boldsymbol{\Sigma}, \widehat{\mathbf{u}}_i + \mathbf{R}_i^{-1}\mathbf{t}\right)\right\} d\mathbf{t}$$
$$= (2\pi)^{q/2}\left|\mathbf{R}_i\right|^{-1}\int \exp\left\{g\left(\boldsymbol{\beta}, \boldsymbol{\Sigma}, \widehat{\mathbf{u}}_i + \mathbf{R}_i^{-1}\mathbf{t}\right) + \mathbf{t}'\mathbf{t}/2\right\}\phi(\mathbf{t})d\mathbf{t} \tag{8}$$

where $\phi()$ is the standard multivariate normal density. Since the integrand is now expressed as some function multiplied by a normal density, it can be estimated by applying the rules of standard Gauss–Hermite quadrature. For a predetermined number of quadrature points N_Q, define $a_k = \sqrt{2}a_k^*$ and $w_k = w_k^*/\sqrt{\pi}$, for $k = 1, \dots, N_Q$, where (a_k^*, w_k^*) are a set of abscissas and weights for Gauss–Hermite quadrature approximations of $\int \exp(-x^2)f(x)dx$, as obtained from Abramowitz and Stegun (1972, 924).

Define $\mathbf{a_k} = (a_{k_1}, a_{k_2}, \ldots, a_{k_q})'$; that is, $\mathbf{a_k}$ is a vector that spans the N_Q abscissas over the dimension q of the random effects. Applying quadrature rules to (8) yields the AGQ approximation,

$$\int \exp\{g(\boldsymbol{\beta}, \boldsymbol{\Sigma}, \mathbf{u}_i)\}\, d\mathbf{u}_i$$

$$\approx (2\pi)^{q/2} |\mathbf{R}_i|^{-1} \sum_{k_1=1}^{N_Q} \cdots \sum_{k_q=1}^{N_Q} \left[\exp\left\{g\left(\boldsymbol{\beta}, \boldsymbol{\Sigma}, \widehat{\mathbf{u}}_i + \mathbf{R}_i^{-1}\mathbf{a_k}\right) + \mathbf{a_k'}\mathbf{a_k}/2\right\} \prod_{p=1}^{q} w_{k_p} \right]$$

$$\equiv (2\pi)^{q/2} \widehat{G}_i(\boldsymbol{\beta}, \boldsymbol{\Sigma})$$

resulting in the AGQ log-likelihood contribution of the ith panel,

$$L_i^{\mathrm{AGQ}}(\boldsymbol{\beta}, \boldsymbol{\Sigma}) = -\frac{1}{2}\log|\boldsymbol{\Sigma}| + \log\left\{\widehat{G}_i(\boldsymbol{\beta}, \boldsymbol{\Sigma})\right\} + c(\mathbf{y}_i, \mathbf{r}_i)$$

The "adaptive" part of adaptive Gaussian quadrature lies in the translation and rescaling of the integration variables in (8) by using $\widehat{\mathbf{u}}_i$ and $\mathbf{R}_i^{-1}$ respectively. This transformation of quadrature abscissas (centered at zero in standard form) is chosen to better capture the features of the integrand, which through (7) can be seen to resemble a multivariate normal distribution with mean $\widehat{\mathbf{u}}_i$ and variance $\mathbf{R}_i^{-1}\mathbf{R}_i^{-T}$. AGQ is therefore not as dependent as the Laplace method upon the approximation in (6). In AGQ, (6) serves merely to redirect the quadrature abscissas, with the AGQ approximation improving as the number of quadrature points, N_Q, increases. In fact, Pinheiro and Bates (1995) point out that AGQ with only one quadrature point ($a = 0$ and $w = 1$) reduces to the Laplacian approximation.

The log likelihood for the entire dataset is then simply the sum of the contributions of the M individual panels, namely, $L(\boldsymbol{\beta}, \boldsymbol{\Sigma}) = \sum_{i=1}^{M} L_i^{\mathrm{Lap}}(\boldsymbol{\beta}, \boldsymbol{\Sigma})$ for Laplace and $L(\boldsymbol{\beta}, \boldsymbol{\Sigma}) = \sum_{i=1}^{M} L_i^{\mathrm{AGQ}}(\boldsymbol{\beta}, \boldsymbol{\Sigma})$ for adaptive Gaussian quadrature.

Maximization of $L(\boldsymbol{\beta}, \boldsymbol{\Sigma})$ is performed with respect to $(\boldsymbol{\beta}, \boldsymbol{\theta})$, where $\boldsymbol{\theta}$ is a vector comprising the unique elements of the matrix square root of $\boldsymbol{\Sigma}$. This is done to ensure that $\boldsymbol{\Sigma}$ is always positive semidefinite. If option `matlog` is specified, then $\boldsymbol{\theta}$ instead consists of the unique elements of the matrix logarithm of $\boldsymbol{\Sigma}$. For well-conditioned problems both methods produce equivalent results, yet our experience deems the former as more numerically stable near the boundary of the parameter space.

Once maximization is achieved, parameter estimates are mapped from $(\widehat{\boldsymbol{\beta}}, \widehat{\boldsymbol{\theta}})$ to $(\widehat{\boldsymbol{\beta}}, \widehat{\boldsymbol{\gamma}})$, where $\widehat{\boldsymbol{\gamma}}$ is a vector containing the unique (estimated) elements of $\boldsymbol{\Sigma}$, expressed as logarithms of standard deviations for the diagonal elements and hyperbolic arctangents of the correlations for off-diagonal elements. This last step is necessary to (a) obtain a parameterization under which parameter estimates can be displayed and interpreted individually, rather than as elements of a matrix square root (or logarithm), and (b) parameterize these elements such that their ranges each encompass the entire real line.

Parameter estimates are stored in `e(b)` as $(\widehat{\boldsymbol{\beta}}, \widehat{\boldsymbol{\gamma}})$, with the corresponding variance–covariance matrix stored in `e(V)`. Parameter estimates can be displayed in this metric by specifying option `estmetric`. However, in `xtmelogit` output, variance components are most often displayed either as variances and covariances (option `variance`) or as standard deviations and correlations (the default).

The approach outlined above can be extended from one-level models to models with two or more nested levels of random effects; see Pinheiro and Chao (2006) for details.

Acknowledgments

We are indebted to Sophia Rabe-Hesketh, University of California, Berkeley; Anders Skrondal, London School of Economics and Norweigian Institute of Public Health; and Andrew Pickles, University of Manchester, for their extensive body of work in Stata, both previous and ongoing, in this area.

References

Abramowitz, M., and I. Stegun (eds.) 1972. *Handbook of Mathematical Functions*. New York: Dover.

Andrews, M., T. Schank, and R. Upward. 2006. Practical fixed-effects estimation methods for the three-way error-components model. *Stata Journal* 6: 461–481.

Bates, D. M., and J. C. Pinheiro. 1998. Computational methods for multilevel models. *Technical Memorandum BL0112140-980226-01TM*. Murray Hill, NJ: Bell Labs, Lucent Technologies.

Breslow, N. E., and D. G. Clayton. 1993. Approximate inference in generalized linear mixed models. *Journal of the American Statistical Association* 88: 9–25.

Gutierrez, R. G., S. L. Carter, and D. M. Drukker. 2001. sg160: On boundary-value likelihood-ratio tests. *Stata Technical Bulletin* 60: 15–18. Reprinted in *Stata Technical Bulletin Reprints*, vol. 10, pp. 269–273.

Huq, N. M., and J. Cleland. 1990. *Bangladesh Fertility Survey 1989 (Main Report)*. National Institute of Population Research and Training.

Laird, N. M., and J. H. Ware. 1982. Random-effects models for longitudinal data. *Biometrics* 38: 963–974.

Lin, X., and N. E. Breslow. 1996. Bias correction in generalised linear mixed models with multiple components of dispersion. *Journal of the American Statistical Association* 91: 1007–1016.

Liu, Q., and D. A. Pierce. 1994. A note on Gauss–Hermite quadrature. *Biometrika* 81: 624–629.

Leyland, A. H., and H. Goldstein (eds.) 2001. *Multilevel Modelling of Health Statistics*. New York: Wiley.

Littell, R. C., G. A. Milliken, W. W. Stroup, and R. D. Wolfinger. 1996. *SAS System for Mixed Models*. Cary, NC: SAS Institute.

Marchenko, Y. 2006. Estimating variance components in Stata. *Stata Journal* 6: 1–21.

McCulloch, C. E., and S. R. Searle. 2001. *Generalized, Linear, and Mixed Models*. New York: Wiley.

McLachlan, G. J., and K. E. Basford. 1988. *Mixture Models*. New York: Dekker.

Naylor, J. C., and A. F. M. Smith. 1982 Applications of a method for the efficient computation of posterior distributions. *Applied Statistics* 31: 214–225.

Ng, E. S. W., J. R. Carpenter, H. Goldstein, and J. Rasbash. 2006. Estimation in generalised linear mixed models with binary outcomes by simulated maximum likelihood. *Statistical Modelling* 6: 23–42.

Paterson, L. 1991. Socio-economic status and educational attainment: A multidimensional and multilevel study. *Evaluation and Research in Education* 5: 97–121.

Pinheiro, J. C., and D. M. Bates. 1995. Approximations to the log likelihood function in the nonlinear mixed-effects model. *Journal of Computational and Graphical Statistics* 4: 12–35.

———. 2000. *Mixed-Effects Models in S and S-PLUS*. New York: Springer.

Pinheiro, J. C., and E. C. Chao. 2006. Efficient Laplacian and adaptive Gaussian quadrature algorithms for multilevel generalized linear mixed models. *Journal of Computational and Graphical Statistics* 15: 58–81.

Rabe-Hesketh, S., and A. Skrondal. 2005. *Multilevel and Longitudinal Modeling Using Stata*. College Station, TX: Stata Press.

Rabe-Hesketh, S., A. Skrondal, and A. Pickles. 2005. Maximum likelihood estimation of limited and discrete dependent variable models with nested random effects. *Journal of Econometrics* 128: 301–323.

Rabe-Hesketh, S., R. Touloupoulou, and R. M. Murray. 2001. Multilevel modeling of cognitive function in schizophrenics and their first degree relatives. *Multivariate Behavioral Research* 36: 279–298.

Raudenbush, S. W., and A. S. Bryk. 2002. *Hierarchical Linear Models: Applications and Data Analysis Methods*. 2nd ed. Thousand Oaks, CA: Sage.

Rodríguez, G., and N. Goldman. 1995. An assessment of estimation procedures for multilevel models with binary responses. *Journal of the Royal Statistical Society, Series A* 158: 73–89.

Self, S. G., and K.-Y. Liang. 1987. Asymptotic properties of maximum likelihood estimators and likelihood ratio tests under nonstandard conditions. *Journal of the American Statistical Association* 82: 605–610.

Skrondal, A., and S. Rabe-Hesketh. 2004. *Generalized Latent Variable Modeling: Multilevel, Longitudinal and Structural Equation Models.* Boca Raton, FL: Chapman & Hall/CRC Press.

Tierney, L., and J. B. Kadane. Accurate approximations for posterior moments and marginal densities. 1986. *Journal of the American Statistical Association* 81: 82–86.

Also See

[XT] **xtmelogit postestimation** — Postestimation tools for xtmelogit

[XT] **xtmepoisson** — Multilevel mixed-effects Poisson regression

[XT] **xtmixed** — Multilevel mixed-effects linear regression

[XT] **xtlogit** — Fixed-effects, random-effects, and population-averaged logit models

[XT] **xtreg** — Fixed-, between-, and random-effects, and population-averaged linear models

[XT] **xtrc** — Random-coefficients model

[XT] **xtgee** — Fit population-averaged panel-data models by using GEE

[U] **20 Estimation and postestimation commands**

Title

Description

The following postestimation commands are of special interest after `xtmelogit`:

command	description
estat group	summarizes the composition of the nested groups
estat recovariance	displays the estimated random-effects covariance matrix (or matrices)

For information about these commands, see below.

The following standard postestimation commands are also available:

command	description
adjust	adjusted predictions of $x\beta$
estat	AIC, BIC, VCE, and estimation sample summary
estimates	cataloging estimation results
lincom	point estimates, standard errors, testing, and inference for linear combinations of coefficients
lrtest	likelihood-ratio test
mfx	marginal effects or elasticities
nlcom	point estimates, standard errors, testing, and inference for nonlinear combinations of coefficients
predict	predicted probabilities, estimated linear predictor and its standard error
predictnl	point estimates, standard errors, testing, and inference for generalized predictions
test	Wald tests for simple and composite linear hypotheses
testnl	Wald tests of nonlinear hypotheses

See the corresponding entries in the *Stata Base Reference Manual* for details.

Special-interest postestimation commands

`estat group` reports number of groups and minimum, average, and maximum group sizes for each level of the model. Model levels are identified by the corresponding group variable in the data. Since groups are treated as nested, the information in this summary may differ from what you would get if you `tabulated` each group variable individually.

`estat recovariance` displays the estimated variance–covariance matrix of the random effects for each level in the model. Random effects can be either random intercepts, in which case the corresponding rows and columns of the matrix are labeled as _cons, or random coefficients, in which case the label is the name of the associated variable in the data.

Syntax for predict

Syntax for obtaining estimated random effects or their standard errors

> predict [*type*] { *stub** | *newvarlist* } [*if*] [*in*], { <u>ref</u>fects | <u>res</u>es }
>
>   [<u>l</u>evel(*levelvar*)]

Syntax for obtaining other predictions

> predict [*type*] *newvar* [*if*] [*in*] [, *statistic* <u>fixed</u>only <u>nooff</u>set]

statistic	description
Main	
<u>mu</u>	the predicted mean, i.e., the predicted success probability; the default
xb	linear prediction for the *fixed* portion of the model only
stdp	standard error of the fixed-portion linear prediction
<u>pearson</u>	Pearson residuals
<u>deviance</u>	Deviance residuals
<u>ans</u>combe	Anscombe residuals

Statistics are available both in and out of sample; type predict ... if e(sample) ... if wanted only for the estimation sample.

Options for predict

> Main

reffects calculates posterior modal estimates of the random effects. By default, estimates for all random effects in the model are calculated. However, if option level(*levelvar*) is specified, then estimates for only level *levelvar* in the model are calculated. For example, if classes are nested within schools, then typing

>   . predict b*, reffects level(school)

would yield random-effects estimates at the school level. You must specify q new variables, where q is the number of random-effects terms in the model (or level). However, it is much easier to just specify *stub** and let Stata name the variables *stub*1, *stub*2, ..., *stub*q for you.

reses calculates standard errors for the random-effects estimates obtained by using option reffects. By default, standard errors for all random effects in the model are calculated. However, if option level(*levelvar*) is specified, then standard errors for only level *levelvar* in the model are calculated. For example, if classes are nested within schools, then typing

>   . predict se*, reses level(school)

would yield standard errors at the school level. You must specify q new variables, where q is the number of random-effects terms in the model (or level). However, it is much easier to just specify *stub** and let Stata name the variables *stub*1, *stub*2, ..., *stub*q for you.

Options `reffects` and `reses` often generate multiple new variables at once. When this occurs, the random effects (or standard errors) contained in the generated variables correspond to the order in which the variance components are listed in the output of `xtmelogit`. Still, examining the variable labels of the generated variables (using [D] **describe**, for instance) can be useful in deciphering which variables correspond to which terms in the model.

`level(levelvar)` specifies the level in the model at which predictions for random effects and their standard errors are to be obtained. *levelvar* is the name of the model level and is either the name of the variable describing the grouping at that level or _all, a special designation for a group comprising all the estimation data.

`mu`, the default, calculates the predicted mean, i.e., the predicted success probability. By default, this is based on a linear predictor that includes *both* the fixed effects and the random effects, and the predicted mean is conditional on the values of the random effects. Use option `fixedonly` (see below) if you want predictions that include only the fixed portion of the model, i.e., if you want random effects set to zero.

`xb` calculates the linear prediction $x\beta$ based on the estimated fixed effects (coefficients) in the model. This is equivalent to fixing all random effects in the model to their theoretical (prior) mean value of zero.

`stdp` calculates the standard error of the fixed-effects linear predictor $x\beta$.

`pearson` calculates Pearson residuals. Pearson residuals large in absolute value may indicate a lack of fit. By default, residuals include both the fixed portion and the random portion of the model. Option `fixedonly` modifies the calculation to include the fixed portion only.

`deviance` calculates deviance residuals. Deviance residuals are recommended by McCullagh and Nelder (1989) as having the best properties for examining the goodness of fit of a GLM. They are approximately normally distributed if the model is correctly specified. They may be plotted against the fitted values or against a covariate to inspect the model's fit. By default, residuals include both the fixed portion and the random portion of the model. Option `fixedonly` modifies the calculation to include the fixed portion only.

`anscombe` calculates Anscombe residuals, residuals that are designed to closely follow a normal distribution. By default, residuals include both the fixed portion and the random portion of the model. Option `fixedonly` modifies the calculation to include the fixed portion only.

`fixedonly` modifies predictions to include only the fixed portion of the model, equivalent to setting all random effects equal to zero; see above.

`nooffset` is relevant only if you specified `offset(varname)` for `xtmelogit`. It modifies the calculations made by `predict` so that they ignore the offset variable; the linear prediction is treated as $\mathbf{X}\beta + \mathbf{Z}\mathbf{u}$ rather than $\mathbf{X}\beta + \mathbf{Z}\mathbf{u} +$ offset.

Syntax for estat group

        estat g̲roup

Syntax for estat recovariance

estat <u>recov</u>ariance [, <u>level</u>(*levelvar*) <u>corr</u>elation *matlist_options*]

Options for estat recovariance

level(*levelvar*) specifies the level in the model for which the random-effects covariance matrix is to be displayed and returned in r(cov). By default, the covariance matrices for all levels in the model are displayed. *levelvar* is the name of the model level and is either the name of variable describing the grouping at that level or _all, a special designation for a group comprising all the estimation data.

correlation displays the covariance matrix as a correlation matrix and returns the correlation matrix in r(corr).

matlist_options are style and formatting options that control how the matrix (or matrices) are displayed; see [P] **matlist** for a list of what is available.

Remarks

Various predictions, statistics, and diagnostic measures are available after fitting a logistic mixed-effects model with xtmelogit. For the most part, calculation centers around obtaining estimates of the subject/group-specific random effects. Random effects are not provided as estimates when the model is fitted but instead need to be predicted after estimation.

▷ Example 1

In example 3 of [XT] **xtmelogit**, we represented the probability of contraceptive use among Bangladeshi women by using the model (stated with slightly different notation here)

$$\text{logit}(\pi_{ij}) = \beta_0 \text{rural}_{ij} + \beta_1 \text{urban}_{ij} + \beta_2 \text{age}_{ij} +$$
$$\beta_3 \text{child1}_{ij} + \beta_4 \text{child2}_{ij} + \beta_5 \text{child3}_{ij} + a_i \text{rural}_{ij} + b_i \text{urban}_{ij}$$

where π_{ij} is the probability of contraceptive use, $i = 1, \ldots, 60$ districts, $j = 1, \ldots, n_i$ women within each district, and a_i and b_i are normally distributed with mean zero and variance–covariance matrix

$$\Sigma = \text{Var} \begin{bmatrix} a_i \\ b_i \end{bmatrix} = \begin{bmatrix} \sigma_a^2 & \sigma_{ab} \\ \sigma_{ab} & \sigma_b^2 \end{bmatrix}$$

(Continued on next page)

```
. use http://www.stata-press.com/data/r10/bangladesh
(Bangladesh Fertility Survey, 1989)
. gen byte rural = 1 - urban
. xtmelogit c_use rural urban age child*, nocons || district: rural urban,
> nocons cov(un)
 (output omitted )
```

```
Mixed-effects logistic regression        Number of obs      =      1934
Group variable: district                 Number of groups   =        60

                                         Obs per group: min =         2
                                                        avg =      32.2
                                                        max =       118

Integration points =   7                 Wald chi2(6)       =    120.24
Log likelihood = -1199.315               Prob > chi2        =    0.0000
```

c_use	Coef.	Std. Err.	z	P>|z|	[95% Conf. Interval]	
rural	-1.71165	.1605618	-10.66	0.000	-2.026345	-1.396954
urban	-.8958623	.1704961	-5.25	0.000	-1.230028	-.5616961
age	-.026415	.008023	-3.29	0.001	-.0421398	-.0106902
child1	1.13252	.1603285	7.06	0.000	.818282	1.446758
child2	1.357739	.1770522	7.67	0.000	1.010724	1.704755
child3	1.353827	.1828801	7.40	0.000	.9953882	1.712265

Random-effects Parameters	Estimate	Std. Err.	[95% Conf. Interval]	
district: Unstructured				
sd(rural)	.6242947	.1035136	.4510793	.8640251
sd(urban)	.4942637	.146751	.2762039	.884479
corr(rural,urban)	-.0523101	.3384598	-.6153877	.5461171

```
LR test vs. logistic regression:       chi2(3) =      58.42   Prob > chi2 = 0.0000
Note: LR test is conservative and provided only for reference.
```

Rather than see the estimated variance components listed as standard deviations and correlations as above, we can instead see them as variance–covariances in matrix form; i.e., we can see $\widehat{\Sigma}$

```
. estat recovariance
Random-effects covariance matrix for level district
```

	rural	urban
rural	.3897438	
urban	-.0161411	.2442966

or we can see $\widehat{\Sigma}$ as a correlation matrix

```
. estat recovariance, correlation
Random-effects correlation matrix for level district
```

	rural	urban
rural	1	
urban	-.0523101	1

The purpose of using this particular model was to allow for district random effects that were specific to the rural and urban areas of that district and that could be interpreted as such. We can obtain predictions of these random effects

```
. predict re_rural re_urban, reffects
```

and their corresponding standard errors

      . predict se_rural se_urban, reses

The order in which we specified the variables to be generated corresponds to the order in which the variance components are listed in xtmelogit output. If in doubt, a simple describe will show how these newly generated variables are labeled just to be sure.

Having generated estimated random effects and standard errors, we can now list them for the first 10 districts:

      . by district, sort: generate tolist = (_n==1)
      . list district re_rural se_rural re_urban se_urban if district <= 10 & tolist,
      > sep(0)

	district	re_rural	se_rural	re_urban	se_urban
1.	1	-.9206641	.3129662	-.5551252	.2321872
118.	2	-.0307772	.3784629	.0012746	.4938357
138.	3	-.0149148	.6242094	.2257356	.4689535
140.	4	-.2684802	.3951617	.5760576	.3970433
170.	5	.0787537	.3078451	.004534	.4675104
209.	6	-.3842217	.2741989	.2727723	.4184852
274.	7	-.1742786	.4008164	.0072177	.493866
292.	8	.0447142	.315396	.2256406	.4679901
329.	9	-.3561363	.3885605	.0733451	.4555068
352.	10	-.5368572	.4743089	.0222338	.4939777

◁

❑ Technical Note

When these data were first introduced in [XT] **xtmelogit**, we noted that not all districts contained both urban and rural areas. This fact is somewhat demonstrated by the random effects that are nearly zero in the above. A closer examination of the data would reveal that disrict 3 has no rural areas, and districts 2, 7, and 10 have no urban areas.

The estimated random effects are not exactly zero in these cases is because of the correlation between urban and rural effects. For instance, if a district has no urban areas, it can still yield a nonzero (albeit small) random-effect estimate for a nonexistent urban area because of the correlation with its rural counterpart.

Had we imposed an independent covariance structure in our model, the estimated random effects in the cases in question would be exactly zero.

❑

❑ Technical Note

The estimated standard errors produced above using option reses are conditional on the values of the estimated model parameters: β and the components of Σ. Their interpretation is therefore not one of standard sample-to-sample variability but instead one that does not incorporate uncertainty in the estimated model parameters; see *Methods and Formulas*.

That stated, conditional standard errors can still be used as a measure of relative precision, provided that you keep this caveat in mind.

❑

▷ Example 2

Continuing with example 1, we can obtain predicted probabilities, the default prediction:

```
. predict p
(option mu assumed; predicted means)
```

These predictions are based on a linear predictor that includes *both* the fixed effects and random effects due to district. Specifying option `fixedonly` gives predictions that set the random effects to their prior mean of zero. Below, we compare both over the first 20 observations:

```
. predict p_fixed, fixedonly
(option mu assumed; predicted means)

. list c_use p p_fixed age child* in 1/20
```

	c_use	p	p_fixed	age	child1	child2	child3
1.	no	.3579543	.4927183	18.44	0	0	1
2.	no	.2134724	.3210403	-5.56	0	0	0
3.	no	.4672256	.6044016	1.44	0	1	0
4.	no	.4206505	.5584864	8.44	0	0	1
5.	no	.2510909	.3687281	-13.56	0	0	0
6.	no	.2412878	.3565185	-11.56	0	0	0
7.	no	.3579543	.4927183	18.44	0	0	1
8.	no	.4992191	.6345999	-3.56	0	0	1
9.	no	.4572049	.594723	-5.56	1	0	0
10.	no	.4662518	.6034657	1.44	0	0	1
11.	yes	.2412878	.3565185	-11.56	0	0	0
12.	no	.2004691	.3040173	-2.56	0	0	0
13.	no	.4506573	.5883407	-4.56	1	0	0
14.	no	.4400747	.5779263	5.44	0	0	1
15.	no	.4794194	.616036	-0.56	0	0	1
16.	yes	.4465936	.5843561	4.44	0	0	1
17.	no	.2134724	.3210403	-5.56	0	0	0
18.	yes	.4794194	.616036	-0.56	0	0	1
19.	yes	.4637673	.6010735	-6.56	1	0	0
20.	no	.5001973	.6355067	-3.56	0	1	0

◁

❏ Technical Note

Out-of-sample predictions are permitted after `xtmelogit`, but if these predictions involve estimated random effects, the integrity of the estimation data must be preserved. If the estimation data have changed since the model was fitted, `predict` will be unable to obtain predicted random effects that are appropriate for the fitted model and will give an error. Thus, to obtain out-of-sample predictions that contain random-effects terms, be sure that the data for these predictions are in observations that augment the estimation data.

❏

Saved Results

estat recovariance saves the last-displayed random-effects covariance matrix in r(cov) or in r(corr) if it is displayed as a correlation matrix.

Methods and Formulas

Continuing the discussion in *Methods and Formulas* of [XT] **xtmelogit**, and using the definitions and formulas defined there, we begin by considering the "prediction" of the random effects $\mathbf{u}_i$ for the ith panel in a one-level model.

Given a set of estimated xtmelogit parameters, $(\widehat{\boldsymbol{\beta}}, \widehat{\boldsymbol{\Sigma}})$, a profile likelihood in $\mathbf{u}_i$ is derived from the joint distribution $f(\mathbf{y}_i, \mathbf{u}_i)$ as

$$\mathcal{L}_i(\mathbf{u}_i) = \exp\left\{c\left(\mathbf{y}_i, \mathbf{r}_i\right)\right\} (2\pi)^{-q/2} |\widehat{\boldsymbol{\Sigma}}|^{-1/2} \exp\left\{g\left(\widehat{\boldsymbol{\beta}}, \widehat{\boldsymbol{\Sigma}}, \mathbf{u}_i\right)\right\} \tag{1}$$

The conditional MLE of $\mathbf{u}_i$—conditional on fixed $(\widehat{\boldsymbol{\beta}}, \widehat{\boldsymbol{\Sigma}})$—is the maximizer of $\mathcal{L}_i(\mathbf{u}_i)$, or equivalently, the value of $\widehat{\mathbf{u}}_i$ that solves

$$\mathbf{0} = g'\left(\widehat{\boldsymbol{\beta}}, \widehat{\boldsymbol{\Sigma}}, \widehat{\mathbf{u}}_i\right) = \mathbf{Z}_i'\left\{\mathbf{y}_i - \mathbf{m}(\widehat{\boldsymbol{\beta}}, \widehat{\mathbf{u}}_i)\right\} - \widehat{\boldsymbol{\Sigma}}^{-1}\widehat{\mathbf{u}}_i$$

Since (1) is proportional to the conditional density $f(\mathbf{u}_i|\mathbf{y}_i)$, you can also refer to $\widehat{\mathbf{u}}_i$ as the *conditional mode* (or *posterior mode* if you lean toward Bayesian terminology). Regardless, you are referring to the same estimator.

Conditional standard errors for the estimated random effects are derived from standard theory of maximum likelihood, which dictates that the asymptotic variance matrix of $\widehat{\mathbf{u}}_i$ is the negative inverse of the Hessian, which is estimated as

$$g''\left(\widehat{\boldsymbol{\beta}}, \widehat{\boldsymbol{\Sigma}}, \widehat{\mathbf{u}}_i\right) = -\left\{\mathbf{Z}_i'\mathbf{V}(\widehat{\boldsymbol{\beta}}, \widehat{\mathbf{u}}_i)\mathbf{Z}_i + \widehat{\boldsymbol{\Sigma}}^{-1}\right\}$$

Similar calculations extend to models with more than one level of random effects; see Pinheiro and Chao (2006).

For any j observation in the i panel in a one-level model, define the linear predictor as

$$\widehat{\eta}_{ij} = \mathbf{x}_{ij}\widehat{\boldsymbol{\beta}} + \mathbf{z}_{ij}\widehat{\mathbf{u}}_i$$

In a two-level model, for the kth observation within the jth level-two panel within the ith level-one panel,

$$\widehat{\eta}_{ijk} = \mathbf{x}_{ijk}\widehat{\boldsymbol{\beta}} + \mathbf{z}_{ijk}^{(1)}\widehat{\mathbf{u}}_i^{(1)} + \mathbf{z}_{ijk}^{(2)}\widehat{\mathbf{u}}_{ij}^{(2)}$$

where the $\mathbf{z}^{(k)}$ and $\mathbf{u}^{(k)}$ refer to the level k design variables and random effects, respectively. For models with more than two levels, the definition of $\widehat{\eta}$ extends in the natural way, with only the notation become more complicated.

If option fixedonly is specified, $\widehat{\eta}$ contains the linear predictor for only the fixed portion of the model, e.g., in a one-level model $\widehat{\eta}_{ij} = \mathbf{x}_{ij}\widehat{\boldsymbol{\beta}}$. In what follows, we assume a one-level model, with the only necessary modification for multilevel models being the indexing.

The predicted mean, conditional on the random effects $\widehat{\mathbf{u}}_i$, is

$$\widehat{\mu}_{ij} = r_{ij}H(\widehat{\eta}_{ij})$$

Pearson residuals are calculated as

$$\nu_{ij}^P = \frac{y_{ij} - \widehat{\mu}_{ij}}{\{V(\widehat{\mu}_{ij})\}^{1/2}}$$

for $V(\widehat{\mu}_{ij}) = \widehat{\mu}_{ij}(1 - \widehat{\mu}_{ij}/r_{ij})$.

Deviance residuals are calculated as

$$\nu_{ij}^D = \text{sign}(y_{ij} - \widehat{\mu}_{ij})\sqrt{\widehat{d_{ij}^2}}$$

where

$$\widehat{d_{ij}^2} = \begin{cases} 2r_{ij}\log\left(\dfrac{r_{ij}}{r_{ij} - \widehat{\mu}_{ij}}\right) & \text{if } y_{ij} = 0 \\[2ex] 2y_{ij}\log\left(\dfrac{y_{ij}}{\widehat{\mu}_{ij}}\right) + 2(r_{ij} - y_{ij})\log\left(\dfrac{r_{ij} - y_{ij}}{r_{ij} - \widehat{\mu}_{ij}}\right) & \text{if } 0 < y_{ij} < r_{ij} \\[2ex] 2r_{ij}\log\left(\dfrac{r_{ij}}{\widehat{\mu}_{ij}}\right) & \text{if } y_{ij} = r_{ij} \end{cases}$$

Anscombe residuals are calculated as

$$\nu_{ij}^A = \frac{3\left\{y_{ij}^{2/3}\mathcal{H}(y_{ij}/r_{ij}) - \widehat{\mu}^{2/3}\mathcal{H}(\widehat{\mu}_{ij}/r_{ij})\right\}}{2\left(\widehat{\mu}_{ij} - \widehat{\mu}_{ij}^2/r_{ij}\right)^{1/6}}$$

where $\mathcal{H}(t)$ is a specific univariate case of the Hypergeometric2F1 function (Wolfram 1999, 771–772). For Anscombe residuals for binomial regression, the specific form of the Hypergeometric2F1 function that we require is $\mathcal{H}(t) = {}_2F_1(2/3, 1/3, 5/3, t)$.

For a discussion of the general properties of the above residuals, see Hardin and Hilbe (2007, chap. 4).

References

Hardin, J. W., and J. M. Hilbe. 2007. *Generalized Linear Models and Extensions*. 2nd ed. College Station, TX: Stata Press.

McCullagh, P., and J. A. Nelder. 1989. *Generalized Linear Models*. 2nd ed. London: Chapman & Hall/CRC.

Pinheiro, J. C., and E. C. Chao. 2006. Efficient Laplacian and adaptive Gaussian quadrature algorithms for multilevel generalized linear mixed models. *Journal of Computational and Graphical Statistics* 15: 58–81.

Rabe-Hesketh, S., and A. Skrondal. 2005. *Multilevel and Longitudinal Modeling Using Stata*. College Station, TX: Stata Press.

Wolfram, S. 1999. *The Mathematica Book*. 4th ed. Cambridge: Cambridge University Press.

Also See

[XT] **xtmelogit** — Multilevel mixed-effects logistic regression

[U] **20 Estimation and postestimation commands**

Title

> **xtmepoisson** — Multilevel mixed-effects Poisson regression

Syntax

xtmepoisson *depvar fe_equation* || *re_equation* [|| *re_equation* ...] [, *options*]

where the syntax of *fe_equation* is

[*indepvars*] [*if*] [*in*] [, *fe_options*]

and the syntax of *re_equation* is one of the following:

for random coefficients and intercepts

levelvar: [*varlist*] [, *re_options*]

for random effects among the values of a factor variable

levelvar: R.*varname* [, *re_options*]

levelvar is a variable identifying the group structure for the random effects at that level, or _all representing one group comprising all observations.

fe_options	description
Model	
<u>noc</u>onstant	suppress the constant term from the fixed-effects equation
<u>exp</u>osure(*varname$_e$*)	include ln(*varname$_e$*) in model with coefficient constrained to 1
<u>off</u>set(*varname$_o$*)	include *varname$_o$* in model with coefficient constrained to 1

re_options	description
Model	
<u>cov</u>ariance(*vartype*)	variance–covariance structure of the random effects
<u>noc</u>onstant	suppress the constant term from the random-effects equation
<u>col</u>linear	keep collinear variables

options	description
Integration	
<u>lap</u>lace	use Laplacian approximation; equivalent to intpoints(1)
<u>intp</u>oints(*# [# ...]*)	set the number of integration (quadrature) points; default is 7

Reporting

level(#)	set confidence level; default is level(95)
irr	report fixed-effects coefficients as incidence-rate ratios
variance	show random-effects parameter estimates as variances and covariances
noretable	suppress random-effects table
nofetable	suppress fixed-effects table
estmetric	show parameter estimates in the estimation metric
noheader	suppress output header
nogroup	suppress table summarizing groups
nolrtest	do not perform LR test comparing to Poisson regression

Max options

maximize_options	control the maximization process during gradient-based optimization
retolerance(#)	tolerance for random-effects estimates; default is retolerance(1e-8); seldom used
reiterate(#)	maximum number of iterations for random-effects estimation; default is reiterate(50); seldom used
matlog	parameterize variance components using matrix logarithms
refineopts(maximize_options)	control the maximization process during refinement of starting values

vartype	description
independent	one unique variance parameter per random effect, all covariances zero; the default unless a factor variable is specified
exchangeable	equal variances for random effects, and one common pairwise covariance
identity	equal variances for random effects, all covariances zero
unstructured	all variances–covariances distinctly estimated

indepvars may contain time-series operators; see [U] **11.4.3 Time-series varlists**.
by, rolling, statsby, and xi are allowed; see [U] **11.1.10 Prefix commands**.
See [U] **20 Estimation and postestimation commands** for more capabilities of estimation commands.

Description

xtmepoisson fits mixed-effects models for count responses. Mixed models contain both *fixed effects* and *random effects*. The fixed effects are analogous to standard regression coefficients and are estimated directly. The random effects are not directly estimated (although they may be obtained postestimation) but are summarized according to their estimated variances and covariances. Random effects may take the form of either random intercepts or random coefficients, and the grouping structure of the data may consist of multiple levels of nested groups. The distribution of the random effects is assumed to be Gaussian. The conditional distribution of the response given the random effects is assumed to be Poisson. Since the log likelihood for this model has no closed form, it is approximated by adaptive Gaussian quadrature.

Options

Model

noconstant suppresses the constant (intercept) term and may be specified for the fixed-effects equation and for any or all of the random-effects equations.

exposure($varname_e$) specifies a variable that reflects the amount of exposure over which the *depvar* events were observed for each observation; ln($varname_e$) is included in the fixed-effects portion of the model with the coefficient constrained to be 1.

offset($varname_o$) specifies that $varname_o$ be included in the fixed-effects portion of the model with the coefficient constrained to be 1.

covariance(*vartype*), where *vartype* is

independent | exchangeable | identity | unstructured

specifies the structure of the covariance matrix for the random effects and may be specified for each random-effects equation. An independent covariance structure allows for a distinct variance for each random effect within a random-effects equation and assumes that all covariances are zero. exchangeable structure specifies one common variance for all random effects and one common pairwise covariance. identity is short for "multiple of the identity"; that is, all variances are equal and all covariances are zero. unstructured allows all variances and covariances to be distinct. If an equation consists of p random-effects terms, the unstructured covariance matrix will have $p(p+1)/2$ unique parameters.

covariance(independent) is the default, except when the random-effects equation is a factor-variable specification R.*varname*, in which case covariance(identity) is the default.

Only covariance(identity) and covariance(exchangeable) are allowed with the factor-variable specification.

collinear specifies that xtmepoisson not remove the collinear variables from a random-effects equation. Usually there is no reason to leave collinear variables in place, and in fact doing so usually causes the estimation to fail because of the matrix singularity caused by the collinearity. However, with certain models (for example, a random-effects model with a full set of contrasts), the variables may be collinear, yet the model is fully identified because of restrictions on the random-effects covariance structure. In such cases, using option collinear allows the estimation to take place with the random-effects equation intact.

Integration

laplace specifies that log likelihoods be calculated using the Laplacian approximation, equivalent to adaptive Gaussian quadrature with one integration point for each level in the model; laplace is equivalent to intpoints(1). Computation time increases as a function of the number of quadrature points raised to a power equaling the dimension of the random-effects specification. The computational time saved by using laplace can thus be substantial, especially when you have many levels and/or random coefficients.

The Laplacian approximation has been known to produce biased parameter estimates, but the bias tends to be more prominent in the estimates of the variance components rather than in estimates of the fixed effects. If your interest lies primarily with the fixed-effects estimates, the Laplace approximation may be a viable faster alternative to adaptive quadrature with multiple integration points.

Specifying a factor variable, R.*varname*, increases the dimension of the random effects by the number of distinct values of *varname*, i.e., the number of factor levels. Even when this number is small to moderate, it increases the total random-effects dimension to the point where estimation with more than one quadrature point is prohibitively intensive.

For this reason, when you have factor variables in your random-effects equations, option `laplace` is assumed. You can override this behavior by using option `intpoints()`, but doing so is not recommended.

`intpoints(#[#...])` sets the number of integration points for adaptive Gaussian quadrature. The more points, the more accurate the approximation to the log likelihood. However, computation time increases with the number of quadrature points, and in models with many levels and/or many random coefficients, this increase can be substantial.

You may specify one number of integration points applying to all levels of random effects in the model, or you may specify distinct numbers of points for each level. `intpoints(7)` is the default; that is, by default seven quadrature points are used for each level.

    Reporting

`level(#)`; see [XT] **estimation options**.

`irr` reports the fixed-effects coefficients transformed to incidence-rate ratios, i.e., $\exp(b)$ rather than b. Standard errors and confidence intervals are similarly transformed. This option affects how results are displayed, not how they are estimated. `irr` may be specified at estimation or when replaying previously estimated results.

`variance` displays the random-effects parameter estimates as variances and covariances. The default is to display them as standard deviations and correlations.

`noretable` suppresses the table of random effects.

`nofetable` suppresses the table of fixed effects.

`estmetric` displays all parameter estimates in the estimation metric. Fixed-effects estimates are unchanged from those normally displayed, but random-effects parameter estimates are displayed as log-standard deviations and hyperbolic arctangents of correlations, with equation names that organize them by model level.

`noheader` suppresses the output header, either at estimation or upon replay.

`nogroup` suppresses the display of group summary information (number of groups, average group size, minimum, and maximum) from the output header.

`nolrtest` prevents `xtmepoisson` from performing a likelihood-ratio test that compares the mixed-effects Poisson model to standard (marginal) Poisson regression. This option may also be specified upon replay to suppress this test from the output.

    Max options

maximize_options: <u>difficult</u>, <u>tech</u>nique(*algorithm_spec*), <u>iter</u>ate(*#*), [<u>no</u>] log, <u>trace</u>, gradient, showstep, <u>hess</u>ian, <u>shownrtol</u>erance, <u>tol</u>erance(*#*), <u>ltol</u>erance(*#*), <u>gtol</u>erance(*#*), <u>nrtol</u>erance(*#*), <u>nonrtol</u>erance; see [R] **maximize**.

For option `technique()`, the default is `technique(nr)`, and algorithm `bhhh` is not allowed.

`retolerance(#)` specifies the convergence tolerance for the estimated random effects used by adaptive Gaussian quadrature. Although not estimated as model parameters, random-effects estimators are used to adapt the quadrature points. Estimating these random effects is an iterative procedure, with convergence declared when the maximum relative change in the random effects is less than `retolerance()`. The default is `retolerance(1e-8)`. You should seldom have to use this option.

reiterate(*#*) specifies the maximum number of iterations used when estimating the random effects to be used in adapting the Gaussian quadrature points; see above. The default is reiterate(50). You should seldom have to use this option.

matlog, during optimization, parameterizes variance components by using the matrix logarithms of the variance–covariance matrices formed by these components at each model level. By default, a parameterization using the matrix square root is used. Both methods ensure variance–covariance matrices that are positive semidefinite. For most problems the matrix square root is more stable near the boundary of the parameter space. However, if convergence is problematic, one option may be to try the alternate matlog parameterization. When convergence is not an issue, both parameterizations yield equivalent results.

refineopts(*maximize_options*) controls the maximization process during the refinement of starting values. Estimation in xtmepoisson takes place in two stages. In the first stage starting values are refined by holding the quadrature points fixed between iterations. During the second stage, quadrature points are adapted with each evaluation of the log likelihood. Maximization options specified within refineopts() control the first stage of optimization; i.e., they control the refining of starting values.

maximize_options specified outside refineopts() control the second stage.

The one exception to the above rule is option nolog, which when specified outside refineopts() applies globally.

Refining starting values helps make the iterations of the second stage (those that lead toward the solution) more numerically stable. In this regard, of particular interest is refineopts(iterate(*#*)), with two iterations being the default. Should the maximization fail because of instability in the Hessian calculations, one possible solution may be to increase the number of iterations here.

Remarks

Remarks are presented under the following headings:

> *Introduction*
> *A one-level model*
> *A multilevel model*

Introduction

Mixed-effects Poisson regression is Poisson regression containing both fixed effects and random effects. In longitudinal/panel data, random effects are useful for modeling intrapanel correlation; that is, observations in the same panel are correlated because they share common panel-level random effects.

xtmepoisson allows for not just one, but many levels of nested panels. For example, in a two-level model you can specify random effects for schools and then random effects for classes nested within schools.

However, for simplicity, for now we consider the one-level model where, for a series of M independent panels and, conditional on a set of *random effects* $\mathbf{u}_i$,

$$P(y_{ij} = y | \mathbf{u}_i) = \exp\left(-\mu_{ij}\right) \mu_{ij}^y / y! \tag{1}$$

for $\mu_{ij} = \exp(\mathbf{x}_{ij}\boldsymbol{\beta} + \mathbf{z}_{ij}\mathbf{u}_i)$, $i = 1, \ldots, M$ panels, and with panel i consisting of $j = 1, \ldots, n_i$ observations. The responses are counts y_{ij}. The $1 \times p$ row vector $\mathbf{x}_{ij}$ are the covariates for the fixed effects, analogous to the covariates you would find in a standard Poisson regression model, with regression coefficients (fixed effects) $\boldsymbol{\beta}$.

The $1 \times q$ vector $\mathbf{z}_{ij}$ are the covariates corresponding to the random effects and can be used to represent both random intercepts and random coefficients. For example, in a random intercept model, $\mathbf{z}_{ij}$ is simply the scalar 1. The random effects $\mathbf{u}_i$ are M realizations from a multivariate normal distribution with mean $\mathbf{0}$ and $q \times q$ variance matrix $\mathbf{\Sigma}$. The random effects are not directly estimated as model parameters but are instead summarized according to the unique elements of $\mathbf{\Sigma}$, known as *variance components*. One special case of (1) places $\mathbf{z}_{ij} = \mathbf{x}_{ij}$, so that all covariate effects are essentially random and distributed as multivariate normal with mean $\boldsymbol{\beta}$ and variance $\mathbf{\Sigma}$.

Model (1) is a member of the class of generalized linear mixed models (GLMMs), which generalize the linear mixed-effects (LME) model to non-Gaussian responses. In particular, model (1) deals with count responses. Stata also has the command xtmelogit for fitting another type of GLMM, the logistic model for binary and binomial responses.

From a general prospective, there is not much to distinguish xtmepoisson from xtmelogit, and most everything said about xtmelogit in [XT] **xtmelogit** applies to xtmepoisson. If you are anxious to get started applying xtmepoisson to your count data, continue reading this entry. Examples are provided below.

We encourarge you to read [XT] **xtmelogit**, however. In addition to some history and guided tours of syntax and output, substantive issues are discussed, and these apply equally to Poisson data. These include Stata conventions for multilevel terminology, specifying covariance structures for random effects, constructing complex blocked-diagonal covariance structures, distribution theory for likelihood-ratio tests, factors that affect computation time, the Laplacian approximation, advice on model building, and fitting crossed-effects models.

A one-level model

We begin with a simple application of (1).

▷ Example 1

Breslow and Clayton (1993) fitted a mixed-effects Poisson model to data from a randomized trial of the drug progabide for the treatment of epilepsy.

```
. use http://www.stata-press.com/data/r10/epilepsy
(Epilepsy data; progabide drug treatment)
. describe
Contains data from epilepsy.dta
  obs:           236                          Epilepsy data; progabide drug
                                                treatment
  vars:            8                          31 May 2007 14:09
  size:        6,844 (99.9% of memory free)   (_dta has notes)
```

variable name	storage type	display format	value label	variable label
subject	byte	%9.0g		Subject id: 1-59
seizures	int	%9.0g		No. of seizures
treat	byte	%9.0g		1: progabide; 0: placebo
visit	float	%9.0g		Dr. visit; coded as (-.3, -.1, .1, .3)
lage	float	%9.0g		log(age), mean-centered
lbas	float	%9.0g		log(0.25*baseline seizures), mean-centered
lbas_trt	float	%9.0g		lbas/treat interaction
v4	byte	%8.0g		Fourth visit indicator

```
Sorted by:  subject
```

Originally from Thall and Vail (1990), data were collected on 59 subjects (31 on progabide, 28 placebo). The number of epileptic seizures (seizures) was recorded during the 2 weeks prior to each of four doctor visits (visit). The treatment group is identified by the indicator variable treat. Data were also collected on the logarithm of age (lage) and the logarithm of one-quarter the number of seizures during the 8 weeks prior to the study (lbas). Variable lbas_trt represents the interaction between lbas and treatment. lage, lbas, and lbas_trt are mean centered. Since the study originally noted a substantial decrease in seizures prior to the fourth doctor visit, an indicator, v4, for the fourth visit was also recorded.

Breslow and Clayton (1993) fitted a random-effects Poisson model for the number of observed seizures

$$\log(\mu_{ij}) = \beta_0 + \beta_1 \text{treat}_{ij} + \beta_2 \text{lbas}_{ij} + \beta_3 \text{lbas\_trt}_{ij} + \beta_4 \text{lage}_{ij} + \beta_5 \text{v4}_{ij} + u_i$$

for $i = 1, \ldots, 59$ subjects and $j = 1, \ldots, 4$ visits. The random effects u_i are assumed to be normally distributed with mean zero and variance σ_u^2.

```
. xtmepoisson seizures treat lbas lbas_trt lage v4 || subject:

Refining starting values:

Iteration 0:   log likelihood = -680.40577  (not concave)
Iteration 1:   log likelihood = -668.60112
Iteration 2:   log likelihood = -666.36624

Performing gradient-based optimization:

Iteration 0:   log likelihood = -666.36624
Iteration 1:   log likelihood = -665.45274
Iteration 2:   log likelihood = -665.29075
Iteration 3:   log likelihood = -665.29068

Mixed-effects Poisson regression            Number of obs      =        236
Group variable: subject                     Number of groups   =         59

                                            Obs per group: min =          4
                                                           avg =        4.0
                                                           max =          4

Integration points =    7                   Wald chi2(5)       =     121.67
Log likelihood = -665.29068                 Prob > chi2        =     0.0000
```

seizures	Coef.	Std. Err.	z	P>|z|	[95% Conf. Interval]	
treat	-.9330388	.4008344	-2.33	0.020	-1.71866	-.1474177
lbas	.8844329	.1312313	6.74	0.000	.6272243	1.141641
lbas_trt	.3382609	.2033384	1.66	0.096	-.0602751	.7367968
lage	.4842386	.3472775	1.39	0.163	-.1964129	1.16489
v4	-.1610871	.0545758	-2.95	0.003	-.2680537	-.0541206
_cons	2.154574	.2200425	9.79	0.000	1.723299	2.58585

Random-effects Parameters	Estimate	Std. Err.	[95% Conf. Interval]	
subject: Identity				
sd(_cons)	.5028186	.0586255	.4000981	.6319113

```
LR test vs. Poisson regression:  chibar2(01) =    304.74 Prob>=chibar2 = 0.0000
```

The number of seizures before the fourth visit does exhibit a significant drop, and the patients on progabide demonstrate a decrease in frequency of seizures compared with the placebo group. The subject-specific random effects also appear significant, $\hat{\sigma}_u = 0.503$ with standard error 0.059. The above results are also in good agreement with those of Breslow and Clayton (1993, table 4), who fitted this model by the method of penalized quasilikelihood (PQL).

Since this is a simple random-intercept model, you can obtain equivalent results by using `xtmepoisson` with options `re` and `normal`.

See *One-level models* in [XT] **xtmelogit** for a detailed description of syntax and of reading the resulting output.

◁

▷ Example 2

In their study of PQL, Breslow and Clayton (1993) also fitted a model where they dropped the fixed effect on v4 and replaced it with a random subject-specific linear trend over the four doctor visits. The model they fitted is

$$\log(\mu_{ij}) = \beta_0 + \beta_1 \texttt{treat}_{ij} + \beta_2 \texttt{lbas}_{ij} + \beta_3 \texttt{lbas\_trt}_{ij} +$$
$$\beta_4 \texttt{lage}_{ij} + \beta_5 \texttt{visit}_{ij} + u_i + v_i \texttt{visit}_{ij}$$

where (u_i, v_i) are bivariate normal with zero mean and variance–covariance matrix:

$$\Sigma = \text{Var}\begin{bmatrix} u_i \\ v_i \end{bmatrix} = \begin{bmatrix} \sigma_u^2 & \sigma_{uv} \\ \sigma_{uv} & \sigma_v^2 \end{bmatrix}$$

```
. xtmepoisson seizures treat lbas lbas_trt lage visit || subject: visit,
> cov(unstructured) intpoints(9)
  (output omitted )
Mixed-effects Poisson regression               Number of obs      =        236
Group variable: subject                        Number of groups   =         59

                                               Obs per group: min =          4
                                                              avg =        4.0
                                                              max =          4

Integration points =    9                      Wald chi2(5)       =     115.56
Log likelihood = -655.68103                    Prob > chi2        =     0.0000
```

seizures	Coef.	Std. Err.	z	P>|z|	[95% Conf. Interval]	
treat	-.9286588	.4021642	-2.31	0.021	-1.716886	-.1404314
lbas	.8849767	.1312519	6.74	0.000	.6277276	1.142226
lbas_trt	.3379757	.2044444	1.65	0.098	-.062728	.7386794
lage	.4767192	.353622	1.35	0.178	-.2163673	1.169806
visit	-.2664098	.1647096	-1.62	0.106	-.5892347	.0564151
_cons	2.099555	.2203711	9.53	0.000	1.667635	2.531474

Random-effects Parameters	Estimate	Std. Err.	[95% Conf. Interval]	
subject: Unstructured				
sd(visit)	.7290273	.1573227	.4775909	1.112837
sd(_cons)	.5014906	.0586145	.3988172	.6305967
corr(visit,_cons)	.0078542	.2426514	-.43639	.4490197

LR test vs. Poisson regression: chi2(3) =   324.54   Prob > chi2 = 0.0000

Note: LR test is conservative and provided only for reference.

In the above, we specified option `cov(unstructured)` to allow correlation between u_i and v_i, although on the basis of the above output it probably was not necessary—the default `Independent` structure would have sufficed. In the interest of getting more accurate estimates, we also increased the number of quadrature points to nine, although the estimates do not change much when compared to estimates based on the default seven quadrature points.

The essence of the above-fitted model is that, after adjusting for other covariates, the log trend in seizures is modeled as a random subject-specific line, with intercept distributed as $N(\beta_0, \sigma_u^2)$ and slope distributed as $N(\beta_5, \sigma_v^2)$. From the above output, $\widehat{\beta}_0 = 2.100$, $\widehat{\sigma}_u = 0.501$, $\widehat{\beta}_5 = -0.266$, and $\widehat{\sigma}_v = 0.729$.

You can predict the random effects u_i and v_i by using predict after xtmepoisson; see [XT] **xtmepoisson postestimation**. Better still, you can obtain a predicted number of seizures that takes these random effects into account.

xtmepoisson also offers a myriad of display options. Among the most useful are variance for displaying estimated variance components as variance and covariances, and irr for displaying fixed effects as incidence-rate ratios.

```
. xtmepoisson, variance irr
Mixed-effects Poisson regression                Number of obs      =        236
Group variable: subject                         Number of groups   =         59

                                                Obs per group: min =          4
                                                               avg =        4.0
                                                               max =          4

Integration points =    9                       Wald chi2(5)       =     115.56
Log likelihood = -655.68103                     Prob > chi2        =     0.0000
```

seizures	IRR	Std. Err.	z	P>|z|	[95% Conf. Interval]	
treat	.3950833	.1588883	-2.31	0.021	.1796246	.8689833
lbas	2.422928	.318014	6.74	0.000	1.873349	3.133735
lbas_trt	1.402106	.2866528	1.65	0.098	.9391989	2.093169
lage	1.610781	.5696077	1.35	0.178	.8054394	3.221366
visit	.7661251	.1261882	-1.62	0.106	.5547517	1.058037

Random-effects Parameters	Estimate	Std. Err.	[95% Conf. Interval]	
subject: Unstructured				
var(visit)	.5314808	.2293851	.2280931	1.238406
var(_cons)	.2514928	.0587892	.1590552	.3976522
cov(visit,_cons)	.0028715	.0887018	-.1709808	.1767238

```
LR test vs. Poisson regression:       chi2(3) =    324.54   Prob > chi2 = 0.0000
Note: LR test is conservative and provided only for reference.
```

◁

A multilevel model

xtmepoisson can also fit models with more than one level of nested random effects.

▷ Example 3

Rabe-Hesketh and Skrondal (2005, exercise 6.4) describe data from the *Atlas of Cancer Mortality in the European Economic Community* (EEC) (Smans, Muir, and Boyle 1992). The data were analyzed in Langford, Bentham, and McDonald (1998) and record the number of deaths among males because of malignant melanoma during 1971–1980.

```
. use http://www.stata-press.com/data/r10/melanoma
(Skin cancer (melanoma) data)
```

```
. describe
Contains data from melanoma.dta
  obs:          354                          Skin cancer (melanoma) data
  vars:           6                          30 May 2007 17:10
  size:       7,788 (99.9% of memory free)   (_dta has notes)
```

variable name	storage type	display format	value label	variable label
nation	byte	%11.0g	n	Nation id
region	byte	%9.0g		Region id: EEC level-I areas
county	int	%9.0g		County id: EEC level-II/level-III areas
deaths	int	%9.0g		No. deaths during 1971-1980
expected	float	%9.0g		No. expected deaths
uv	float	%9.0g		UV dose, mean-centered

```
Sorted by:
```

Nine European nations (variable `nation`) are represented, and data were collected over geographical regions defined by EEC statistical services as level I areas (variable `region`), with deaths being recorded for each of 354 counties, which are level II or level III EEC-defined areas (variable `county`, which identifies the observations). Counties are nested within regions, and regions are nested within nations.

Variable `deaths` records the number of deaths for each county, and `expected` records the expected number of deaths (the exposure) on the basis of crude rates for the combined countries. Finally, variable uv is a measure of exposure to ultraviolet (UV) radiation.

In modeling the number of deaths, one possibility is to include dummy variables for the nine nations as fixed effects. Another is to treat these as random effects and fit the two-level random-intercept Poisson model,

$$\log(\mu_{ijk}) = \log(\text{expected}_{ijk}) + \beta_0 + \beta_1 \text{uv}_{ijk} + \beta_2 \text{uv}^2_{ijk} + u_i + v_{ij}$$

for nation i, region j, and county k. The model includes an exposure term for expected deaths and a quadratic term for UV radiation.

```
. gen uv2 = uv^2
. xtmepoisson deaths uv uv2, exposure(expected) || nation: || region:
  (output omitted )
Mixed-effects Poisson regression                Number of obs      =       354
```

Group Variable	No. of Groups	Observations per Group Minimum	Average	Maximum	Integration Points
nation	9	3	39.3	95	7
region	78	1	4.5	13	7

```
                                      Wald chi2(2)       =      25.69
Log likelihood = -1089.411            Prob > chi2        =     0.0000
```

deaths	Coef.	Std. Err.	z	P>|z|	[95% Conf. Interval]	
uv	.0056975	.0137931	0.41	0.680	-.0213364	.0327314
uv2	-.0058374	.001388	-4.21	0.000	-.0085579	-.0031169
_cons	.1289976	.1581122	0.82	0.415	-.1808966	.4388918
expected	(exposure)					

Random-effects Parameters	Estimate	Std. Err.	[95% Conf. Interval]	
nation: Identity				
sd(_cons)	.4290364	.1101666	.2593733	.7096807
region: Identity				
sd(_cons)	.1956382	.0224569	.1562233	.2449974

LR test vs. Poisson regression: chi2(2) = 1267.13 Prob > chi2 = 0.0000

Note: LR test is conservative and provided only for reference.

By including an exposure variable that is an expected rate, we are in effect specifying a linear model for the log of the standardized mortality ratio (SMR), the ratio of observed deaths to expected deaths that is based on a reference population. Here the reference population is all nine nations.

We now add a random-intercept for counties nested within regions, making this a three-level model. Since counties also identify the observations, the corresponding variance component can be interpreted as a measure of overdispersion, variability above and beyond that allowed by standard Poisson; see [R] **nbreg**.

```
. xtmepoisson deaths uv uv2, exposure(expected) || nation: || region: || county:,
> laplace
```

(output omitted)

Mixed-effects Poisson regression   Number of obs   =   354

Group Variable	No. of Groups	Observations per Group			Integration Points
		Minimum	Average	Maximum	
nation	9	3	39.3	95	1
region	78	1	4.5	13	1
county	354	1	1.0	1	1

Log likelihood = -1078.8598   Wald chi2(2)   =   28.12
                                                Prob > chi2   =   0.0000

deaths	Coef.	Std. Err.	z	P>|z|	[95% Conf. Interval]	
uv	.0043977	.0142978	0.31	0.758	-.0236254	.0324208
uv2	-.0058104	.0014047	-4.14	0.000	-.0085635	-.0030572
_cons	.1127634	.1555188	0.73	0.468	-.1920479	.4175747
expected	(exposure)					

Random-effects Parameters	Estimate	Std. Err.	[95% Conf. Interval]	
nation: Identity				
sd(_cons)	.4192799	.1077695	.253347	.6938927
region: Identity				
sd(_cons)	.1704024	.0254158	.1272089	.2282621
county: Identity				
sd(_cons)	.1220659	.0218334	.0859693	.1733186

LR test vs. Poisson regression: chi2(3) = 1288.23 Prob > chi2 = 0.0000

Note: LR test is conservative and provided only for reference.
Note: log-likelihood calculations are based on the Laplacian approximation.

In the above, we used a Laplacian approximation, which is not only faster but also produces estimates that closely agree with those obtained with the default seven quadrature points.

See *Computation time and the Laplacian approximation* in [XT] **xtmelogit** for a discussion comparing Laplacian approximation with adaptive quadrature.

◁

Saved Results

xtmepoisson saves the following in e():

Scalars

e(N)	number of observations	e(p)	p-value for χ^2
e(k)	number of parameters	e(ll_c)	log-likelihood, comparison model
e(k_f)	number of FE parameters	e(chi2_c)	χ^2, comparison model
e(k_r)	number of RE parameters	e(df_c)	d.f., comparison model
e(k_rs)	number of std. deviations	e(p_c)	p-value, comparison model
e(k_rc)	number of correlations	e(converged)	1 if converged, 0 otherwise
e(df_m)	model degrees of freedom	e(reparm_rc)	return code, final
e(ll)	log likelihood		reparameterization
e(chi2)	χ^2	e(rc)	return code

Macros

e(cmd)	xtmepoisson	e(laplace)	laplace, if Laplace approx.
e(cmdline)	command as typed	e(chi2type)	Wald, type of model χ^2
e(title)	title in estimation output	e(opt)	type of optimization
e(model)	Poisson	e(ml_method)	type of ml method
e(depvar)	name of dependent variable	e(technique)	maximization technique
e(offset)	offset	e(crittype)	optimization criterion
e(exposurevar)	exposure variable	e(datasignature)	the checksum
e(method)	ML	e(datasignaturevars)	variables used in checksum
e(ivars)	grouping variables	e(properties)	b V
e(redim)	random-effects dimensions	e(estat_cmd)	program used to implement
e(vartypes)	variance-structure types		estat
e(revars)	random-effects covariates	e(predict)	program used to implement
e(n_quad)	number of integration pts.		predict

Matrices

e(b)	coefficient vector	e(V)	variance–covariance matrix of
e(N_g)	group counts		the estimator
e(g_min)	group size minimums	e(g_avg)	group size averages
e(g_max)	group size maximums		

Functions

e(sample)	marks estimation sample

Methods and Formulas

xtmepoisson is implemented as an ado-file.

In a one-level Poisson model, for panel i, $i = 1, \ldots, M$, the conditional distribution of $\mathbf{y}_i = (y_{i1}, \ldots, y_{in_i})'$, given a set of panel-level random effects $\mathbf{u}_i$, is

$$f(\mathbf{y}_i | \mathbf{u}_i) = \prod_{j=1}^{n_i} \left[\{\exp(\mathbf{x}_{ij}\boldsymbol{\beta} + \mathbf{z}_{ij}\mathbf{u}_i)\}^{y_{ij}} \exp\{-\exp(\mathbf{x}_{ij}\boldsymbol{\beta} + \mathbf{z}_{ij}\mathbf{u}_i)\} / y_{ij}! \right]$$

$$= \exp\left[\sum_{j=1}^{n_i} \{y_{ij}(\mathbf{x}_{ij}\boldsymbol{\beta} + \mathbf{z}_{ij}\mathbf{u}_i) - \exp(\mathbf{x}_{ij}\boldsymbol{\beta} + \mathbf{z}_{ij}\mathbf{u}_i) - \log(y_{ij}!)\} \right]$$

Defining $c(\mathbf{y}_i) = \sum_{j=1}^{n_i} \log(y_{ij}!)$, where $c(\mathbf{y}_i)$ does not depend on the model parameters, we can express the above compactly in matrix notation,

$$f(\mathbf{y}_i | \mathbf{u}_i) = \exp\{\mathbf{y}_i'(\mathbf{X}_i\boldsymbol{\beta} + \mathbf{Z}_i\mathbf{u}_i) - \mathbf{1}'\exp(\mathbf{X}_i\boldsymbol{\beta} + \mathbf{Z}_i\mathbf{u}_i) - c(\mathbf{y}_i)\}$$

where $\mathbf{X}_i$ is formed by stacking the row vectors $\mathbf{x}_{ij}$, $\mathbf{Z}_i$ is formed by stacking the row vectors $\mathbf{z}_{ij}$, and we extend the definition of $\exp()$ to be a vector function where necessary.

Since the prior distribution of $\mathbf{u}_i$ is multivariate normal with mean $\mathbf{0}$ and $q \times q$ variance matrix $\boldsymbol{\Sigma}$, the likelihood contribution for the i panel is obtained by integrating $\mathbf{u}_i$ out the joint density $f(\mathbf{y}_i, \mathbf{u}_i)$,

$$\mathcal{L}_i(\boldsymbol{\beta}, \boldsymbol{\Sigma}) = (2\pi)^{-q/2} |\boldsymbol{\Sigma}|^{-1/2} \int f(\mathbf{y}_i | \mathbf{u}_i) \exp\left(-\mathbf{u}_i'\boldsymbol{\Sigma}^{-1}\mathbf{u}_i/2\right) d\mathbf{u}_i$$

$$= \exp\{-c(\mathbf{y}_i)\} (2\pi)^{-q/2} |\boldsymbol{\Sigma}|^{-1/2} \int \exp\{g(\boldsymbol{\beta}, \boldsymbol{\Sigma}, \mathbf{u}_i)\} d\mathbf{u}_i \tag{2}$$

where

$$g(\boldsymbol{\beta}, \boldsymbol{\Sigma}, \mathbf{u}_i) = \mathbf{y}_i'(\mathbf{X}_i\boldsymbol{\beta} + \mathbf{Z}_i\mathbf{u}_i) - \mathbf{1}'\exp(\mathbf{X}_i\boldsymbol{\beta} + \mathbf{Z}_i\mathbf{u}_i) - \mathbf{u}_i'\boldsymbol{\Sigma}^{-1}\mathbf{u}_i/2$$

and for convenience, in the arguments of $g()$ we suppress the dependence on the observable data $(\mathbf{y}_i, \mathbf{X}_i, \mathbf{Z}_i)$.

The integration in (2) has no closed form and thus must be approximated. The Laplacian approximation (Tierney and Kadane 1986; Pinheiro and Bates 1995) is based on a second-order Taylor expansion of $g(\boldsymbol{\beta}, \boldsymbol{\Sigma}, \mathbf{u}_i)$ about the value of $\mathbf{u}_i$ that maximizes it. Taking first and second derivatives, we obtain

$$g'(\boldsymbol{\beta}, \boldsymbol{\Sigma}, \mathbf{u}_i) = \frac{\partial g(\boldsymbol{\beta}, \boldsymbol{\Sigma}, \mathbf{u}_i)}{\partial \mathbf{u}_i} = \mathbf{Z}_i'\{\mathbf{y}_i - \mathbf{m}(\boldsymbol{\beta}, \mathbf{u}_i)\} - \boldsymbol{\Sigma}^{-1}\mathbf{u}_i$$

$$g''(\boldsymbol{\beta}, \boldsymbol{\Sigma}, \mathbf{u}_i) = \frac{\partial^2 g(\boldsymbol{\beta}, \boldsymbol{\Sigma}, \mathbf{u}_i)}{\partial \mathbf{u}_i \partial \mathbf{u}_i'} = -\{\mathbf{Z}_i'\mathbf{V}(\boldsymbol{\beta}, \mathbf{u}_i)\mathbf{Z}_i + \boldsymbol{\Sigma}^{-1}\}$$

where $\mathbf{m}(\boldsymbol{\beta}, \mathbf{u}_i)$ is the vector function with jth element equal to the conditional mean of y_{ij} given $\mathbf{u}_i$, i.e., $\exp(\mathbf{x}_{ij}\boldsymbol{\beta} + \mathbf{z}_{ij}\mathbf{u}_i)$. $\mathbf{V}(\boldsymbol{\beta}, \mathbf{u}_i)$ is the diagonal matrix whose diagonal entries v_{ij} are the conditional variances of y_{ij} given $\mathbf{u}_i$, namely,

$$v_{ij} = \exp(\mathbf{x}_{ij}\boldsymbol{\beta} + \mathbf{z}_{ij}\mathbf{u}_i)$$

since equality of mean and variance is a characteristic of the Poisson distribution.

The maximizer of $g(\boldsymbol{\beta}, \boldsymbol{\Sigma}, \mathbf{u}_i)$ is $\widehat{\mathbf{u}}_i$ such that $g'(\boldsymbol{\beta}, \boldsymbol{\Sigma}, \widehat{\mathbf{u}}_i) = \mathbf{0}$. The integrand in (2) is proportional to the posterior density $f(\mathbf{u}_i | \mathbf{y}_i)$, so $\widehat{\mathbf{u}}_i$ also represents the posterior mode, a plausible estimator of $\mathbf{u}_i$ in its own right.

Given the above derivatives, the second-order Taylor approximation then takes the form

$$g(\boldsymbol{\beta}, \boldsymbol{\Sigma}, \mathbf{u}_i) \approx g(\boldsymbol{\beta}, \boldsymbol{\Sigma}, \widehat{\mathbf{u}}_i) + \frac{1}{2}(\mathbf{u}_i - \widehat{\mathbf{u}}_i)' g''(\boldsymbol{\beta}, \boldsymbol{\Sigma}, \widehat{\mathbf{u}}_i)(\mathbf{u}_i - \widehat{\mathbf{u}}_i) \tag{3}$$

The first-derivative term vanishes because $g'(\boldsymbol{\beta}, \boldsymbol{\Sigma}, \widehat{\mathbf{u}}_i) = \mathbf{0}$. Therefore,

$$
\int \exp\{g(\boldsymbol{\beta}, \boldsymbol{\Sigma}, \mathbf{u}_i)\} d\mathbf{u}_i \approx \exp\{g(\boldsymbol{\beta}, \boldsymbol{\Sigma}, \widehat{\mathbf{u}}_i)\}
$$
$$
\times \int \exp\left[-\frac{1}{2}(\mathbf{u}_i - \widehat{\mathbf{u}}_i)'\{-g''(\boldsymbol{\beta}, \boldsymbol{\Sigma}, \widehat{\mathbf{u}}_i)\}(\mathbf{u}_i - \widehat{\mathbf{u}}_i)\right] d\mathbf{u}_i \quad (4)
$$
$$
= \exp\{g(\boldsymbol{\beta}, \boldsymbol{\Sigma}, \widehat{\mathbf{u}}_i)\}(2\pi)^{q/2} \left|-g''(\boldsymbol{\beta}, \boldsymbol{\Sigma}, \widehat{\mathbf{u}}_i)\right|^{-1/2}
$$

since the latter integrand can be recognized as the "kernel" of a multivariate normal density.

Combining the above with (2) (and taking logs) gives the Laplacian log-likelihood contribution of the ith panel,

$$
L_i^{\text{Lap}}(\boldsymbol{\beta}, \boldsymbol{\Sigma}) = -\frac{1}{2}\log|\boldsymbol{\Sigma}| - \log|\mathbf{R}_i| + g(\boldsymbol{\beta}, \boldsymbol{\Sigma}, \widehat{\mathbf{u}}_i) - c(\mathbf{y}_i)
$$

where $\mathbf{R}_i$ is an upper-triangular matrix such that $-g''(\boldsymbol{\beta}, \boldsymbol{\Sigma}, \widehat{\mathbf{u}}_i) = \mathbf{R}_i \mathbf{R}_i'$. Pinheiro and Chao (2006) show that $\widehat{\mathbf{u}}_i$ and $\mathbf{R}_i$ can be efficiently computed as the iterative solution to a least-squares problem using matrix decomposition methods similar to those used in fitting LME models (Bates and Pinheiro 1998; Pinheiro and Bates 2000; [XT] **xtmixed**).

The fidelity of the Laplacian approximation is determined wholly by the accuracy of the approximation in (3). An alternative that does not depend so heavily on this approximation is integration via adaptive Gaussian quadrature (AGQ; Naylor and Smith 1982; Liu and Pierce 1994).

The application of AGQ to this particular problem is from Pinheiro and Bates (1995). When we reexamine the integral in question, a transformation of integration variables yields

$$
\int \exp\{g(\boldsymbol{\beta}, \boldsymbol{\Sigma}, \mathbf{u}_i)\} d\mathbf{u}_i = |\mathbf{R}_i|^{-1} \int \exp\{g(\boldsymbol{\beta}, \boldsymbol{\Sigma}, \widehat{\mathbf{u}}_i + \mathbf{R}_i^{-1}\mathbf{t})\} d\mathbf{t}
$$
$$
= (2\pi)^{q/2} |\mathbf{R}_i|^{-1} \int \exp\{g(\boldsymbol{\beta}, \boldsymbol{\Sigma}, \widehat{\mathbf{u}}_i + \mathbf{R}_i^{-1}\mathbf{t}) + \mathbf{t}'\mathbf{t}/2\} \phi(\mathbf{t}) d\mathbf{t}
$$
$$(5)$$

where $\phi()$ is the standard multivariate normal density. Since the integrand is now expressed as some function multiplied by a normal density, it can be estimated by applying the rules of standard Gauss–Hermite quadrature. For a predetermined number of quadrature points N_Q, define $a_k = \sqrt{2}a_k^*$ and $w_k = w_k^*/\sqrt{\pi}$, for $k = 1, \ldots, N_Q$, where (a_k^*, w_k^*) are a set of abscissas and weights for Gauss–Hermite quadrature approximations of $\int \exp(-x^2)f(x)dx$, as obtained from Abramowitz and Stegun (1972, 924).

Define $\mathbf{a_k} = (a_{k_1}, a_{k_2}, \ldots, a_{k_q})'$; that is, $\mathbf{a_k}$ is a vector that spans the N_Q abscissas over the dimension q of the random effects. Applying quadrature rules to (5) yields the AGQ approximation,

$$
\int \exp\{g(\boldsymbol{\beta}, \boldsymbol{\Sigma}, \mathbf{u}_i)\} d\mathbf{u}_i
$$
$$
\approx (2\pi)^{q/2} |\mathbf{R}_i|^{-1} \sum_{k_1=1}^{N_Q} \cdots \sum_{k_q=1}^{N_Q} \left[\exp\{g(\boldsymbol{\beta}, \boldsymbol{\Sigma}, \widehat{\mathbf{u}}_i + \mathbf{R}_i^{-1}\mathbf{a_k}) + \mathbf{a_k}'\mathbf{a_k}/2\} \prod_{p=1}^{q} w_{k_p}\right]
$$
$$
\equiv (2\pi)^{q/2} \widehat{G}_i(\boldsymbol{\beta}, \boldsymbol{\Sigma})
$$

resulting in the AGQ log-likelihood contribution of the ith panel,

$$
L_i^{\text{AGQ}}(\boldsymbol{\beta}, \boldsymbol{\Sigma}) = -\frac{1}{2}\log|\boldsymbol{\Sigma}| + \log\left\{\widehat{G}_i(\boldsymbol{\beta}, \boldsymbol{\Sigma})\right\} - c(\mathbf{y}_i)
$$

The "adaptive" part of adaptive Gaussian quadrature lies in the translation and rescaling of the integration variables in (5) by using $\widehat{\mathbf{u}}_i$ and $\mathbf{R}_i^{-1}$ respectively. This transformation of quadrature abscissas (centered at zero in standard form) is chosen to better capture the features of the integrand, which through (4) can be seen to resemble a multivariate normal distribution with mean $\widehat{\mathbf{u}}_i$ and variance $\mathbf{R}_i^{-1}\mathbf{R}_i^{-T}$. AGQ is therefore not as dependent as the Laplace method upon the approximation in (3). In AGQ, (3) serves merely to redirect the quadrature abscissas, with the AGQ approximation improving as the number of quadrature points, N_Q, increases. In fact, Pinheiro and Bates (1995) point out that AGQ with only one quadrature point ($a = 0$ and $w = 1$) reduces to the Laplacian approximation.

The log likelihood for the entire dataset is then simply the sum of the contributions of the M individual panels, namely, $L(\boldsymbol{\beta}, \boldsymbol{\Sigma}) = \sum_{i=1}^{M} L_i^{\text{Lap}}(\boldsymbol{\beta}, \boldsymbol{\Sigma})$ for Laplace and $L(\boldsymbol{\beta}, \boldsymbol{\Sigma}) = \sum_{i=1}^{M} L_i^{\text{AGQ}}(\boldsymbol{\beta}, \boldsymbol{\Sigma})$ for adaptive Gaussian quadrature.

Maximization of $L(\boldsymbol{\beta}, \boldsymbol{\Sigma})$ is performed with respect to $(\boldsymbol{\beta}, \boldsymbol{\theta})$, where $\boldsymbol{\theta}$ is a vector comprising the unique elements of the matrix square root of $\boldsymbol{\Sigma}$. This is done to ensure that $\boldsymbol{\Sigma}$ is always positive semidefinite. If option `matlog` is specified, then $\boldsymbol{\theta}$ instead consists of the unique elements of the matrix logarithm of $\boldsymbol{\Sigma}$. For well-conditioned problems both methods produce equivalent results, yet our experience deems the former as more numerically stable near the boundary of the parameter space.

Once maximization is achieved, parameter estimates are mapped from $(\widehat{\boldsymbol{\beta}}, \widehat{\boldsymbol{\theta}})$ to $(\widehat{\boldsymbol{\beta}}, \widehat{\boldsymbol{\gamma}})$, where $\widehat{\boldsymbol{\gamma}}$ is a vector containing the unique (estimated) elements of $\boldsymbol{\Sigma}$, expressed as logarithms of standard deviations for the diagonal elements and hyperbolic arctangents of the correlations for off-diagonal elements. This last step is necessary to (a) obtain a parameterization under which parameter estimates can be displayed and interpreted individually, rather than as elements of a matrix square root (or logarithm), and (b) parameterize these elements such that their ranges each encompass the entire real line.

Parameter estimates are stored in `e(b)` as $(\widehat{\boldsymbol{\beta}}, \widehat{\boldsymbol{\gamma}})$, with the corresponding variance–covariance matrix stored in `e(V)`. Parameter estimates can be displayed in this metric by specifying option `estmetric`. However, in `xtmepoisson` output, variance components are most often displayed either as variances and covariances (option `variance`) or as standard deviations and correlations (the default).

The approach outlined above can be extended from one-level models to models with two or more nested levels of random effects; see Pinheiro and Chao (2006) for details.

Acknowledgments

We are indebted to Sophia Rabe-Hesketh, University of California, Berkeley; Anders Skrondal, London School of Economics and Norweigian Institute of Public Health; and Andrew Pickles, University of Manchester, for their extensive body of work in Stata, both previous and ongoing, in this area.

References

Abramowitz, M., and I. Stegun (eds.) 1972. *Handbook of Mathematical Functions.* New York: Dover.

Andrews, M., T. Schank, and R. Upward. 2006. Practical fixed-effects estimation methods for the three-way error-components model. *Stata Journal* 6: 461–481.

Bates, D. M., and J. C. Pinheiro. 1998. Computational methods for multilevel models. *Technical Memorandum BL0112140-980226-01TM.* Murray Hill, NJ: Bell Labs, Lucent Technologies.

Breslow, N. E., and D. G. Clayton. 1993. Approximate inference in generalized linear mixed models. *Journal of the American Statistical Association* 88: 9–25.

Gutierrez, R. G., S. L. Carter, and D. M. Drukker. 2001. sg160: On boundary-value likelihood-ratio tests. *Stata Technical Bulletin* 60: 15–18. Reprinted in *Stata Technical Bulletin Reprints*, vol. 10, pp. 269–273.

Laird, N. M., and J. H. Ware. 1982. Random-effects models for longitudinal data. *Biometrics* 38: 963–974.

Langford, I. H., G. Bentham, and A. McDonald. 1998. Multilevel modelling of geographically aggregated health data: a case study on malignant melanoma mortality and UV exposure in the European community. *Statistics in Medicine* 17: 41–58.

Lin, X., and N. E. Breslow. 1996. Bias correction in generalised linear mixed models with multiple components of dispersion. *Journal of the American Statistical Association* 91: 1007–1016.

Liu, Q., and D. A. Pierce. 1994. A note on Gauss–Hermite quadrature. *Biometrika* 81: 624–629.

Leyland, A. H., and H. Goldstein (eds.) 2001. *Multilevel Modelling of Health Statistics*. New York: Wiley.

Marchenko, Y. 2006. Estimating variance components in Stata. *Stata Journal* 6: 1–21.

McCulloch, C. E., and S. R. Searle. 2001. *Generalized, Linear, and Mixed Models*. New York: Wiley.

McLachlan, G. J., and K. E. Basford. 1988. *Mixture Models*. New York: Dekker.

Naylor, J. C., and A. F. M. Smith. 1982 Applications of a method for the efficient computation of posterior distributions. *Applied Statistics* 31: 214–225.

Pinheiro, J. C., and D. M. Bates. 1995. Approximations to the log-likelihood function in the nonlinear mixed-effects model. *Journal of Computational and Graphical Statistics* 4: 12–35.

——. 2000. *Mixed-Effects Models in S and S-PLUS*. New York: Springer.

Pinheiro, J. C., and E. C. Chao. 2006. Efficient Laplacian and adaptive Gaussian quadrature algorithms for multilevel generalized linear mixed models. *Journal of Computational and Graphical Statistics* 15: 58–81.

Rabe-Hesketh, S., and A. Skrondal. 2005. *Multilevel and Longitudinal Modeling Using Stata*. College Station, TX: Stata Press.

Rabe-Hesketh, S., A. Skrondal, and A. Pickles. 2005. Maximum likelihood estimation of limited and discrete dependent variable models with nested random effects. *Journal of Econometrics* 128: 301–323.

Raudenbush, S. W., and A. S. Bryk. 2002. *Hierarchical Linear Models: Applications and Data Analysis Methods*. 2nd ed. Thousand Oaks, CA: Sage.

Self, S. G., and K.-Y. Liang. 1987. Asymptotic properties of maximum likelihood estimators and likelihood ratio tests under nonstandard conditions. *Journal of the American Statistical Association* 82: 605–610.

Skrondal, A., and S. Rabe-Hesketh. 2004. *Generalized Latent Variable Modeling: Multilevel, Longitudinal and Structural Equation Models*. Boca Raton, FL: Chapman & Hall/CRC Press.

Smans, M., C. S. Muir, and P. Boyle. 1992. *Atlas of Cancer Mortality in the European Economic Community*. Lyon, France: IARC Scientific Publications.

Thall, P. F., and S. C. Vail. 1990. Some covariance models for longitudinal count data with overdisperson. *Biometrics* 46: 657–671.

Tierney, L., and J. B. Kadane. Accurate approximations for posterior moments and marginal densities. 1986. *Journal of the American Statistical Association* 81: 82–86.

Also See

Title

xtmepoisson postestimation — Postestimation tools for xtmepoisson

Description

The following postestimation commands are of special interest after `xtmepoisson`:

command	description
estat group	summarizes the composition of the nested groups
estat recovariance	displays the estimated random-effects covariance matrix (or matrices)

For information about these commands, see below.

The following standard postestimation commands are also available:

command	description
adjust	adjusted predictions of $x\beta$
estat	AIC, BIC, VCE, and estimation sample summary
estimates	cataloging estimation results
lincom	point estimates, standard errors, testing, and inference for linear combinations of coefficients
lrtest	likelihood-ratio test
mfx	marginal effects or elasticities
nlcom	point estimates, standard errors, testing, and inference for nonlinear combinations of coefficients
predict	predicted probabilities, estimated linear predictor and its standard error
predictnl	point estimates, standard errors, testing, and inference for generalized predictions
test	Wald tests for simple and composite linear hypotheses
testnl	Wald tests of nonlinear hypotheses

See the corresponding entries in the *Stata Base Reference Manual* for details.

Special-interest postestimation commands

`estat group` reports number of groups and minimum, average, and maximum group sizes for each level of the model. Model levels are identified by the corresponding group variable in the data. Since groups are treated as nested, the information in this summary may differ from what you would get if you `tabulated` each group variable individually.

`estat recovariance` displays the estimated variance–covariance matrix of the random effects for each level in the model. Random effects can be either random intercepts, in which case the corresponding rows and columns of the matrix are labeled as _cons, or random coefficients, in which case the label is the name of the associated variable in the data.

Syntax for predict

Syntax for obtaining estimated random effects or their standard errors

> predict $[type]$ $\{ stub* \, | \, newvarlist \}$ $[if]$ $[in]$, $\{ \underline{ref}fects \, | \, \underline{res}es \}$
>
> $[\underline{l}evel(levelvar)]$

Syntax for obtaining other predictions

> predict $[type]$ *newvar* $[if]$ $[in]$ $[$, *statistic* $\underline{fixed}only \ \underline{nooff}set]$

statistic	description
Main	
$\underline{mu}$	the predicted mean count; the default
xb	linear prediction for the *fixed* portion of the model only
stdp	standard error of the fixed-portion linear prediction
$\underline{pearson}$	Pearson residuals
$\underline{deviance}$	Deviance residuals
$\underline{anscombe}$	Anscombe residuals

Statistics are available both in and out of sample; type predict ... if e(sample) ... if wanted only for the estimation sample.

Options for predict

    ┐ Main └

reffects calculates posterior modal estimates of the random effects. By default, estimates for all random effects in the model are calculated. However, if option level(*levelvar*) is specified, then estimates for only level *levelvar* in the model are calculated. For example, if classes are nested within schools, then typing

> . predict b*, reffects level(school)

would yield random-effects estimates at the school level. You must specify q new variables, where q is the number of random-effects terms in the model (or level). However, it is much easier to just specify *stub** and let Stata name the variables *stub*1, *stub*2, ..., *stubq* for you.

reses calculates standard errors for the random-effects estimates obtained by using option reffects. By default, standard errors for all random effects in the model are calculated. However, if option level(*levelvar*) is specified, then standard errors for only level *levelvar* in the model are calculated. For example, if classes are nested within schools, then typing

> . predict se*, reses level(school)

would yield standard errors at the school level. You must specify q new variables, where q is the number of random-effects terms in the model (or level). However, it is much easier to just specify *stub** and let Stata name the variables *stub*1, *stub*2, ..., *stubq* for you.

Options `reffects` and `reses` often generate multiple new variables at once. When this occurs, the random effects (or standard errors) contained in the generated variables correspond to the order in which the variance components are listed in the output of `xtmepoisson`. Still, examining the variable labels of the generated variables (using [D] **describe**, for instance) can be useful in deciphering which variables correspond to which terms in the model.

`level`(*levelvar*) specifies the level in the model at which predictions for random effects and their standard errors are to be obtained. *levelvar* is the name of the model level and is either the name of the variable describing the grouping at that level or _all, a special designation for a group comprising all the estimation data.

`mu`, the default, calculates the predicted mean, i.e., the predicted count. By default, this is based on a linear predictor that includes *both* the fixed effects and the random effects, and the predicted mean is conditional on the values of the random effects. Use option `fixedonly` (see below) if you want predictions that include only the fixed portion of the model, i.e., if you want random effects set to zero.

`xb` calculates the linear prediction $\mathbf{x}\beta$ based on the estimated fixed effects (coefficients) in the model. This is equivalent to fixing all random effects in the model to their theoretical (prior) mean value of zero.

`stdp` calculates the standard error of the fixed-effects linear predictor $\mathbf{x}\beta$.

`pearson` calculates Pearson residuals. Pearson residuals large in absolute value may indicate a lack of fit. By default, residuals include both the fixed portion and the random portion of the model. Option `fixedonly` modifies the calculation to include the fixed portion only.

`deviance` calculates deviance residuals. Deviance residuals are recommended by McCullagh and Nelder (1989) as having the best properties for examining the goodness of fit of a GLM. They are approximately normally distributed if the model is correctly specified. They may be plotted against the fitted values or against a covariate to inspect the model's fit. By default, residuals include both the fixed portion and the random portion of the model. Option `fixedonly` modifies the calculation to include the fixed portion only.

`anscombe` calculates Anscombe residuals, residuals that are designed to closely follow a normal distribution. By default, residuals include both the fixed portion and the random portion of the model. Option `fixedonly` modifies the calculation to include the fixed portion only.

`fixedonly` modifies predictions to include only the fixed portion of the model, equivalent to setting all random effects equal to zero; see above.

`nooffset` is relevant only if you specified `offset`(*varname_o*) or `exposure`(*varname_e*) for `xtmepoisson`. It modifies the calculations made by `predict` so that they ignore the off-set variable; the linear prediction is treated as $\mathbf{X}\beta + \mathbf{Z}\mathbf{u}$ rather than $\mathbf{X}\beta + \mathbf{Z}\mathbf{u}$ + offset, or $\mathbf{X}\beta + \mathbf{Z}\mathbf{u}$ + ln(exposure), whichever is relevant.

Syntax for estat group

```
estat group
```

Syntax for estat recovariance

```
estat recovariance [ , level(levelvar) correlation matlist_options ]
```

Options for estat recovariance

level(*levelvar*) specifies the level in the model for which the random-effects covariance matrix is to be displayed and returned in r(cov). By default, the covariance matrices for all levels in the model are displayed. *levelvar* is the name of the model level and is either the name of variable describing the grouping at that level or _all, a special designation for a group comprising all the estimation data.

correlation displays the covariance matrix as a correlation matrix and returns the correlation matrix in r(corr).

matlist_options are style and formatting options that control how the matrix (or matrices) are displayed; see [P] **matlist** for a list of what is available.

Remarks

Various predictions, statistics, and diagnostic measures are available after fitting a Poisson mixed-effects model with xtmepoisson. For the most part, calculation centers around obtaining estimates of the subject/group-specific random effects. Random effects are not estimated when the model is fitted but instead need to be predicted after estimation.

▷ Example 1

In example 2 of [XT] **xtmepoisson**, we modeled the number of observed epileptic seizures as a function of treatment with the drug progabide and other covariates

$$\log(\mu_{ij}) = \beta_0 + \beta_1 \text{treat}_{ij} + \beta_2 \text{lbas}_{ij} + \beta_3 \text{lbas\_trt}_{ij} +$$
$$\beta_4 \text{lage}_{ij} + \beta_5 \text{visit}_{ij} + u_i + v_i \text{visit}_{ij}$$

where (u_i, v_i) are bivariate normal with zero mean and variance–covariance matrix

$$\Sigma = \text{Var} \begin{bmatrix} u_i \\ v_i \end{bmatrix} = \begin{bmatrix} \sigma_u^2 & \sigma_{uv} \\ \sigma_{uv} & \sigma_v^2 \end{bmatrix}$$

```
. use http://www.stata-press.com/data/r10/epilepsy
(Epilepsy data; Progabide drug treatment)
. xtmepoisson seizures treat lbas lbas_trt lage visit || subject: visit,
> cov(unstructured) intpoints(9)
 (output omitted )
```

| Mixed-effects Poisson regression | | | | Number of obs | = | 236 |
| Group variable: subject | | | | Number of groups | = | 59 |

				Obs per group: min =		4
				avg =		4.0
				max =		4

| Integration points = 9 | | | | Wald chi2(5) | = | 115.56 |
| Log likelihood = -655.68103 | | | | Prob > chi2 | = | 0.0000 |

seizures	Coef.	Std. Err.	z	P>|z|	[95% Conf. Interval]	
treat	-.9286589	.4021644	-2.31	0.021	-1.716887	-.1404311
lbas	.8849766	.131252	6.74	0.000	.6277275	1.142226
lbas_trt	.3379757	.2044445	1.65	0.098	-.0627281	.7386796
lage	.4767192	.353622	1.35	0.178	-.2163673	1.169806
visit	-.2664098	.1647096	-1.62	0.106	-.5892347	.0564151
_cons	2.099555	.2203712	9.53	0.000	1.667635	2.531474

Random-effects Parameters	Estimate	Std. Err.	[95% Conf. Interval]	
subject: Unstructured				
sd(visit)	.7290273	.1573227	.4775909	1.112837
sd(_cons)	.5014906	.0586145	.3988172	.6305967
corr(visit,_cons)	.0078542	.2426514	-.4363901	.4490197

LR test vs. Poisson regression: chi2(3) =   324.54   Prob > chi2 = 0.0000

Note: LR test is conservative and provided only for reference.

The purpose of this model was to allow subject-specific linear log trends over each subject's four doctor visits, after adjusting for the other covariates. The intercepts of these lines are distributed $N(\beta_0, \sigma_u^2)$, and the slopes $N(\beta_5, \sigma_v^2)$, based on the fixed effects and assumed distribution of the random effects.

We can use predict to obtain estimates of the random effects u_i and v_i and combine these with our estimates of β_0 and β_5 to obtain the intercepts and slopes of the linear log trends.

```
. predict re_visit re_cons, reffects
. gen b1 = _b[visit] + re_visit
. gen b0 = _b[_cons] + re_cons
. by subject, sort: gen tolist = _n==1
. list subject treat b1 b0 if tolist & (subject <=5 | subject >-55)
```

	subject	treat	b1	b0
1.	1	0	-.4284563	2.164691
5.	2	0	-.2727145	2.179111
9.	3	0	.0026486	2.450811
13.	4	0	-.3194157	2.268827
17.	5	0	.6063656	2.123723
217.	55	1	-.2304782	2.311494
221.	56	1	.2904741	3.211369
225.	57	1	-.4831492	1.457486
229.	58	1	-.252236	1.168154
233.	59	1	-.1266651	2.204869

We list these slopes (b1) and intercepts (b0) for five control subjects and five subjects on the treatment.

```
. count if tolist & treat
    31
. count if tolist & treat   & b1 < 0
    25
. count if tolist & !treat
    28
. count if tolist & !treat & b1 < 0
    20
```

We also find that 25 of the 31 subjects taking progabide were estimated to have a downward trend in seizures over their four doctor visits, compared with 20 of the 28 control subjects.

We also obtain predictions for number of seizures, and unless we specify option fixedonly, these predictions will incorporate the estimated subject-specific random effects.

```
. predict n
(option mu assumed; predicted means)
. list subject treat visit seizures n if subject <= 2 | subject >= 58, sep(0)
```

	subject	treat	visit	seizures	n
1.	1	0	-.3	5	3.887582
2.	1	0	-.1	3	3.568324
3.	1	0	.1	3	3.275285
4.	1	0	.3	3	3.00631
5.	2	0	-.3	3	3.705628
6.	2	0	-.1	5	3.508926
7.	2	0	.1	3	3.322664
8.	2	0	.3	3	3.14629
229.	58	1	-.3	0	.9972093
230.	58	1	-.1	0	.9481507
231.	58	1	.1	0	.9015056
232.	58	1	.3	0	.8571552
233.	59	1	-.3	1	2.487858
234.	59	1	-.1	4	2.425625
235.	59	1	.1	3	2.364948
236.	59	1	.3	2	2.305789

◁

❑ Technical Note

Out-of-sample predictions are permitted after xtmepoisson, but if these predictions involve estimated random effects, the integrity of the estimation data must be preserved. If the estimation data have changed since the model was fitted, predict will be unable to obtain predicted random effects that are appropriate for the fitted model and will give an error. Thus, to obtain out-of-sample predictions that contain random-effects terms, be sure that the data for these predictions are in observations that augment the estimation data.

❑

Saved Results

estat recovariance saves the last-displayed random-effects covariance matrix in r(cov) or in r(corr) if it is displayed as a correlation matrix.

Methods and Formulas

Continuing the discussion in *Methods and Formulas* of [XT] **xtmepoisson**, and using the definitions and formulas defined there, we begin by considering the "prediction" of the random effects $\mathbf{u}_i$ for the ith panel in a one-level model.

Given a set of estimated xtmepoisson parameters, $(\widehat{\beta}, \widehat{\Sigma})$, a profile likelihood in $\mathbf{u}_i$ is derived from the joint distribution $f(\mathbf{y}_i, \mathbf{u}_i)$ as

$$\mathcal{L}_i(\mathbf{u}_i) = \exp\left\{-c\left(\mathbf{y}_{ij}\right)\right\} (2\pi)^{-q/2} |\widehat{\Sigma}|^{-1/2} \exp\left\{g\left(\widehat{\beta}, \widehat{\Sigma}, \mathbf{u}_i\right)\right\} \tag{1}$$

The conditional MLE of $\mathbf{u}_i$—conditional on fixed $(\widehat{\boldsymbol{\beta}}, \widehat{\boldsymbol{\Sigma}})$—is the maximizer of $\mathcal{L}_i(\mathbf{u}_i)$, or equivalently, the value of $\widehat{\mathbf{u}}_i$ that solves

$$\mathbf{0} = g'\left(\widehat{\boldsymbol{\beta}}, \widehat{\boldsymbol{\Sigma}}, \widehat{\mathbf{u}}_i\right) = \mathbf{Z}_i'\left\{\mathbf{y}_i - \mathbf{m}(\widehat{\boldsymbol{\beta}}, \widehat{\mathbf{u}}_i)\right\} - \widehat{\boldsymbol{\Sigma}}^{-1}\widehat{\mathbf{u}}_i$$

Since (1) is proportional to the conditional density $f(\mathbf{u}_i|\mathbf{y}_i)$, you can also refer to $\widehat{\mathbf{u}}_i$ as the *conditional mode* (or *posterior mode* if you lean toward Bayesian terminology). Regardless, you are referring to the same estimator.

Conditional standard errors for the estimated random effects are derived from standard theory of maximum likelihood, which dictates that the asymptotic variance matrix of $\widehat{\mathbf{u}}_i$ is the negative inverse of the Hessian, which is estimated as

$$g''\left(\widehat{\boldsymbol{\beta}}, \widehat{\boldsymbol{\Sigma}}, \widehat{\mathbf{u}}_i\right) = -\left\{\mathbf{Z}_i'\mathbf{V}(\widehat{\boldsymbol{\beta}}, \widehat{\mathbf{u}}_i)\mathbf{Z}_i + \widehat{\boldsymbol{\Sigma}}^{-1}\right\}$$

Similar calculations extend to models with more than one level of random effects; see Pinheiro and Chao (2006).

For any j observation in the i panel in a one-level model, define the linear predictor as

$$\widehat{\eta}_{ij} = \mathbf{x}_{ij}\widehat{\boldsymbol{\beta}} + \mathbf{z}_{ij}\widehat{\mathbf{u}}_i$$

In a two-level model, for the kth observation within the jth level-two panel within the ith level-one panel,

$$\widehat{\eta}_{ijk} = \mathbf{x}_{ijk}\widehat{\boldsymbol{\beta}} + \mathbf{z}_{ijk}^{(1)}\widehat{\mathbf{u}}_i^{(1)} + \mathbf{z}_{ijk}^{(2)}\widehat{\mathbf{u}}_{ij}^{(2)}$$

where the $\mathbf{z}^{(k)}$ and $\mathbf{u}^{(k)}$ refer to the level k design variables and random effects, respectively. For models with more than two levels, the definition of $\widehat{\eta}$ extends in the natural way, with only the notation become more complicated.

If option `fixedonly` is specified, $\widehat{\eta}$ contains the linear predictor for only the fixed portion of the model, e.g., in a one-level model $\widehat{\eta}_{ij} = \mathbf{x}_{ij}\widehat{\boldsymbol{\beta}}$. In what follows, we assume a one-level model, with the only necessary modification for multilevel models being the indexing.

The predicted mean, conditional on the random effects $\widehat{\mathbf{u}}_i$, is

$$\widehat{\mu}_{ij} = \exp(\widehat{\eta}_{ij})$$

Pearson residuals are calculated as

$$\nu_{ij}^P = \frac{y_{ij} - \widehat{\mu}_{ij}}{\{V(\widehat{\mu}_{ij})\}^{1/2}}$$

for $V(\widehat{\mu}_{ij}) = \widehat{\mu}_{ij}$.

Deviance residuals are calculated as

$$\nu_{ij}^D = \text{sign}(y_{ij} - \widehat{\mu}_{ij})\sqrt{\widehat{d}_{ij}^2}$$

where

$$
\widehat{d}_{ij}^2 = \begin{cases} 2\widehat{\mu}_{ij} & \text{if } y_{ij} = 0 \\ 2 \left\{ y_{ij} \log\left(\dfrac{y_{ij}}{\widehat{\mu}_{ij}} \right) - (y_{ij} - \widehat{\mu}_{ij}) \right\} & \text{otherwise} \end{cases}
$$

Anscombe residuals are calculated as

$$
\nu_{ij}^A = \frac{3 \left(y_{ij}^{2/3} - \widehat{\mu}_{ij}^{2/3} \right)}{2\widehat{\mu}_{ij}^{1/6}}
$$

For a discussion of the general properties of the above residuals, see Hardin and Hilbe (2007, chap. 4).

References

Hardin, J. W., and J. M. Hilbe. 2007. *Generalized Linear Models and Extensions.* 2nd ed. College Station, TX: Stata Press.

McCullagh, P., and J. A. Nelder. 1989. *Generalized Linear Models.* 2nd ed. London: Chapman & Hall/CRC.

Pinheiro, J. C., and E. C. Chao. 2006. Efficient Laplacian and adaptive Gaussian quadrature algorithms for multilevel generalized linear mixed models. *Journal of Computational and Graphical Statistics* 15: 58–81.

Rabe-Hesketh, S., and A. Skrondal. 2005. *Multilevel and Longitudinal Modeling Using Stata.* College Station, TX: Stata Press.

Also See

[XT] **xtmepoisson** — Multilevel mixed-effects Poisson regression

[U] **20 Estimation and postestimation commands**

Title

xtmixed — Multilevel mixed-effects linear regression

Syntax

xtmixed *depvar fe_equation* $\begin{bmatrix} || & re\_equation \end{bmatrix}$ $\begin{bmatrix} || & re\_equation \dots \end{bmatrix}$ $\begin{bmatrix} , & options \end{bmatrix}$

where the syntax of *fe_equation* is

$\begin{bmatrix} indepvars \end{bmatrix}$ $\begin{bmatrix} if \end{bmatrix}$ $\begin{bmatrix} in \end{bmatrix}$ $\begin{bmatrix} , & fe\_options \end{bmatrix}$

and the syntax of *re_equation* is one of the following:

for random coefficients and intercepts

levelvar: $\begin{bmatrix} varlist \end{bmatrix}$ $\begin{bmatrix} , & re\_options \end{bmatrix}$

for random effects among the values of a factor variable

levelvar: R.*varname* $\begin{bmatrix} , & re\_options \end{bmatrix}$

levelvar is a variable identifying the group structure for the random effects at that level, or _all representing one group comprising all observations.

fe_options	description
Model	
<u>no</u>constant	suppress the constant term from the fixed-effects equation

re_options	description
Model	
<u>cov</u>ariance(*vartype*)	variance–covariance structure of the random effects
<u>no</u>constant	suppress the constant term from the random-effects equation
<u>col</u>linear	keep collinear variables

options	description
Estimation	
reml	fit model via maximum restricted likelihood; the default
<u>ml</u>e	fit model via maximum likelihood

Reporting

level(#)	set confidence level; default is level(95)
variance	show random-effects parameter estimates as variances and covariances
noretable	suppress random-effects table
nofetable	suppress fixed-effects table
estmetric	show parameter estimates in the estimation metric
noheader	suppress output header
nogroup	suppress table summarizing groups
nostderr	do not estimate standard errors of random-effects parameters
nolrtest	do not perform LR test comparing to linear regression

EM options

emiterate(#)	number of EM iterations; default is 20
emtolerance(#)	EM convergence tolerance; default is 1e-10
emonly	fit model exclusively using EM
emlog	show EM iteration log
emdots	show EM iterations as dots

Max options

maximize_options	control the maximization process

vartype	description
independent	one unique variance parameter per random effect, all covariances zero; the default unless a factor variable is specified
exchangeable	equal variances for random effects, and one common pairwise covariance
identity	equal variances for random effects, all covariances zero
unstructured	all variances–covariances distinctly estimated

depvar and indepvars may contain time-series operators; see [U] **11.4.3 Time-series varlists**.

by, rolling, statsby, and xi are allowed; see [U] **11.1.10 Prefix commands**.

See [U] **20 Estimation and postestimation commands** for more capabilities of estimation commands.

Description

xtmixed fits linear mixed models. Mixed models are characterized as containing both *fixed effects* and *random effects*. The fixed effects are analogous to standard regression coefficients and are estimated directly. The random effects are not directly estimated but are summarized according to their estimated variances and covariances. Although random effects are not directly estimated, you can form best linear unbiased predictions (BLUPs) of them by using predict after xtmixed; see [XT] **xtmixed postestimation**. Random effects may take the form of either random intercepts or random coefficients, and the grouping structure of the data may consist of multiple levels of nested groups. The error distribution of the linear mixed model is assumed to be Gaussian.

Options

Model

noconstant suppresses the constant (intercept) term and may be specified for the fixed-effects equation and for any or all of the random-effects equations.

covariance(*vartype*), where *vartype* is

independent | exchangeable | identity | unstructured

specifies the structure of the covariance matrix for the random effects and may be specified for each random-effects equation. An independent covariance structure allows for a distinct variance for each random effect within a random-effects equation and assumes that all covariances are zero. exchangeable structure specifies one common variance for all random effects and one common pairwise covariance. identity is short for "multiple of the identity"; that is, all variances are equal, and all covariances are zero. unstructured allows for all variances and covariances to be distinct. If an equation consists of p random-effects terms, the unstructured covariance matrix will have $p(p+1)/2$ unique parameters.

covariance(independent) is the default, except when the random-effects equation is a factor-variable specification R.*varname*, in which case covariance(identity) is the default.

Only covariance(identity) and covariance(exchangeable) are allowed with the factor-variable specification.

collinear specifies that xtmixed not remove the collinear variables from the random-effects equation. Usually there is no reason to leave collinear variables in place, and in fact doing so usually causes the estimation to fail because of the matrix singularity caused by the collinearity. However, with certain models (for example, a random-effects model with a full set of contrasts), the variables may be collinear, yet the model is fully identified because of restrictions on the random-effects covariance structure. In such cases, using option collinear allows the estimation to take place with the random-effects equation intact.

Estimation

reml and mle specify the statistical method for fitting the model.

reml, the default, specifies that the model be fitted using maximum restricted likelihood (REML), also known as maximum residual likelihood.

mle specifies that the model be fitted using maximum likelihood (ML).

Reporting

level(#); see [XT] **estimation options**.

variance displays the random-effects parameter estimates as variances and covariances. The default is to display them as standard deviations and correlations.

noretable suppresses the table of random effects.

nofetable suppresses the table of fixed effects.

estmetric displays all parameter estimates in the estimation metric. Fixed-effects estimates are unchanged from those normally displayed, but random-effects parameter estimates are displayed as log-standard deviations and hyperbolic arctangents of correlations, with equation names that organize them by model level.

noheader suppresses the output header, either at estimation or upon replay.

nogroup suppresses the display of group summary information (number of groups, average group size, minimum, and maximum) from the output header.

nostderr prevents xtmixed from calculating standard errors for the estimated random-effects parameters, although standard errors are still provided for the fixed-effects parameters. Specifying this option will speed up computation times.

nolrtest prevents xtmixed from fitting a reference linear regression model and using this model to calculate a likelihood-ratio test comparing the mixed model to ordinary regression. This option may also be specified on replay to suppress this test from the output.

⌐ EM options ⌐

emiter(#) specifies the number of EM (expectation-maximization) iterations to perform. The default is 20.

emtolerance(#) specifies the convergence tolerance for the EM algorithm. The default is 1e-10. EM iterations stop once the log (restricted) likelihood changes by a relative amount less than #. At that point, maximization switches to a gradient-based method, unless emonly is specified, in which case maximization stops.

emonly specifies that the likelihood be maximized exclusively using EM. The advantage of specifying emonly is that EM iterations are typically much faster than those for gradient-based methods. The disadvantages are that EM iterations can be slow to converge (if at all) and that EM provides no facility for estimating standard errors for the random-effects parameters.

emlog specifies that the EM iteration log be shown. The EM iteration log is, by default, not displayed unless option emonly is specified.

emdots specifies that the EM iterations be shown as dots. This option can be convenient since the EM algorithm may require many iterations to converge.

⌐ Max options ⌐

maximize_options: <u>diff</u>icult, <u>technique</u>(*algorithm_spec*), <u>iterate</u>(#), [<u>no</u>]<u>log</u>, <u>trace</u>, gradient, showstep, <u>hess</u>ian, <u>shownrtolerance</u>, <u>tol</u>erance(#), <u>ltol</u>erance(#), <u>gtol</u>erance(#), <u>nrtol</u>erance(#), <u>nonrtol</u>erance; see [R] **maximize**.

For option technique(), the default is technique(nr), and algorithm bhhh is not allowed.

Remarks

Remarks are presented under the following headings:

> *Introduction*
> *One-level models*
> *Covariance structures*
> *Likelihood versus restricted likelihood*
> *Two-level models*
> *Blocked-diagonal covariance structures*
> *Factor notation and crossed-effects models*
> *Diagnosing convergence problems*
> *Distribution theory for likelihood-ratio tests*

Introduction

Linear mixed models are models containing both fixed effects and random effects. They are a generalization of linear regression allowing for the inclusion of random deviations (effects) other than those associated with the overall error term. In matrix notation,

$$\mathbf{y} = \mathbf{X}\boldsymbol{\beta} + \mathbf{Z}\mathbf{u} + \boldsymbol{\epsilon} \tag{1}$$

where $\mathbf{y}$ is the $n \times 1$ vector of responses, $\mathbf{X}$ is a $n \times p$ design/covariate matrix for the fixed effects $\boldsymbol{\beta}$, and $\mathbf{Z}$ is the $n \times q$ design/covariate matrix for the random effects $\mathbf{u}$. The $n \times 1$ vector of errors, $\boldsymbol{\epsilon}$, is assumed to be multivariate normal with mean zero and variance matrix $\sigma_\epsilon^2 \mathbf{I}_n$.

The fixed portion of (1), $\mathbf{X}\boldsymbol{\beta}$, is analogous to the linear predictor from a standard OLS regression model with $\boldsymbol{\beta}$ the regression coefficients to be estimated. For the random portion of (1), $\mathbf{Z}\mathbf{u} + \boldsymbol{\epsilon}$, we assume that $\mathbf{u}$ has variance–covariance matrix $\mathbf{G}$ and that $\mathbf{u}$ is orthogonal to $\boldsymbol{\epsilon}$ so that

$$\text{Var}\begin{bmatrix} \mathbf{u} \\ \boldsymbol{\epsilon} \end{bmatrix} = \begin{bmatrix} \mathbf{G} & \mathbf{0} \\ \mathbf{0} & \sigma_\epsilon^2 \mathbf{I}_n \end{bmatrix}$$

The random effects $\mathbf{u}$ are not directly estimated (although they may be predicted), but instead are characterized by the elements of $\mathbf{G}$, known as *variance components*, that are estimated along with the residual variance σ_ϵ^2.

The general forms of the design matrices $\mathbf{X}$ and $\mathbf{Z}$ allow estimation for a broad class of linear models: blocked designs, split-plot designs, growth curves, multilevel or hierarchical designs, etc. They also allow a flexible method of modeling within-panel correlation. Subjects within the same panel can be correlated as a result of a shared random intercept, or through a shared random slope on (say) age, or both. The general specification of $\mathbf{G}$ also provides additional flexibility—the random intercept and random slope could themselves be modeled as independent, or correlated, or independent with equal variances, and so forth.

Overviews of mixed models are provided by, among others, Searle, Casella, and McCulloch (1992); McCulloch and Searle (2001); Verbeke and Molenberghs (2000); Raudenbush and Bryk (2002); and Pinheiro and Bates (2000). In particular, chapter 2 of Searle, Casella, and McCulloch (1992) provides an excellent history.

The key to fitting mixed models lies in estimating the variance components, and for that, there exist many methods. Most of the early literature in mixed models dealt with estimating variance components in ANOVA models. For simple models with balanced data, estimating variance components amounts to solving a system of equations obtained by setting expected mean-squares expressions equal to their observed counterparts. Much of the work in extending the "ANOVA method" to unbalanced data for general ANOVA designs is due to Henderson (1953).

The ANOVA method, however, has its shortcomings. Among these is a lack of uniqueness in that alternative, unbiased estimates of variance components could be derived using other quadratic forms of the data in place of observed mean squares (Searle, Casella, and McCulloch 1992, 38–39). As a result, ANOVA methods gave way to more modern methods, such as minimum norm quadratic unbiased estimation (MINQUE) and minimum variance quadratic unbiased estimation (MIVQUE); see Rao (1973) for MINQUE and Lamotte (1973) for MIVQUE. Both methods involve finding optimal quadratic forms of the data that are unbiased for the variance components.

The most popular methods, however, are maximum likelihood (ML) and restricted maximum-likelihood (REML), and these are the two methods that are supported by `xtmixed`. The ML estimates are based on the usual application of likelihood theory, given the distributional assumptions of the model. The basic idea behind REML (Thompson 1962) is that you can form a set of linear contrasts of the response that do not depend on the fixed effects, $\boldsymbol{\beta}$, but instead depend only on the variance components to be estimated. You then apply ML methods using the distribution of the linear contrasts to form the likelihood.

Returning to (1): in panel-data situations it is convenient not to consider all n observations at once but instead to organize the mixed model as a series of M independent panels

$$\mathbf{y}_i = \mathbf{X}_i\boldsymbol{\beta} + \mathbf{Z}_i\mathbf{u}_i + \boldsymbol{\epsilon}_i \tag{2}$$

for $i = 1, \ldots, M$, with panel i consisting of n_i observations. The response, $\mathbf{y}_i$, comprises the rows of $\mathbf{y}$ corresponding to the ith panel, with $\mathbf{X}_i$ and $\boldsymbol{\epsilon}_i$ defined analogously. The random effects, $\mathbf{u}_i$, can now be thought of as M realizations of a $q \times 1$ vector that is normally distributed with mean $\mathbf{0}$ and $q \times q$ variance matrix $\boldsymbol{\Sigma}$. The matrix $\mathbf{Z}_i$ is the $n_i \times q$ design matrix for the ith panel random effects. Relating this to (1), note that

$$\mathbf{Z} = \begin{bmatrix} \mathbf{Z}_1 & \mathbf{0} & \cdots & \mathbf{0} \\ \mathbf{0} & \mathbf{Z}_2 & \cdots & \mathbf{0} \\ \vdots & \vdots & \ddots & \vdots \\ \mathbf{0} & \mathbf{0} & \mathbf{0} & \mathbf{Z}_M \end{bmatrix}; \quad \mathbf{u} = \begin{bmatrix} \mathbf{u}_1 \\ \vdots \\ \mathbf{u}_M \end{bmatrix}; \quad \mathbf{G} = \mathbf{I}_M \otimes \boldsymbol{\Sigma}$$

The mixed-model formulation (2) is from Laird and Ware (1982) and offers two key advantages. First, it makes specifications of random-effects terms easier. If the panels are schools, you can simply specify a random effect "at the school level", as opposed to thinking of what a school-level random effect would mean when all the data are considered as a whole (if it helps, think Kronecker products). Second, representing a mixed-model with (2) generalizes easily to more than one level of random variation. For example, if classes are nested within schools, then (2) can be generalized to allow random effects at both the school and at the class-within-school levels. This we demonstrate later.

Finally, using formulation (2) and its multilevel extensions requires one important convention of terminology. Model (2) is what we call a *one-level* model, with extensions to two, three, or any number of levels. In our hypothetical two-level model with classes nested within schools, the schools are considered the first level and classes, the second level of the model. This is generally accepted terminology but differs from that of the literature on hierarchical models, e.g., Skrondal and Rabe-Hesketh (2004). In that literature, our schools and classes model would be considered a three-level model, with the students forming the first level, classes the second, and schools the third. Not only is there one more level, students, but the order is reversed.

One-level models

We begin with a simple application of (2).

▷ Example 1

Consider a longitudinal dataset used by both Ruppert, Wand, and Carroll (2003) and Diggle et al. (2002), consisting of **weight** measurements of 48 pigs on 9 successive **weeks**. Pigs are identified by variable **id**. Below is a plot of the growth curves for the first 10 pigs.

```
. use http://www.stata-press.com/data/r10/pig
(Longitudinal analysis of pig weights)
```

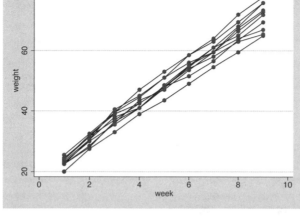

It seems clear that each pig experiences a linear trend in growth and that overall weight measurements vary from pig to pig. Because we are not really interested in these particular 48 pigs per se, we instead treat them as a random sample from a larger population and model the between-pig variability as a random effect or, in the terminology of (2), as a random intercept term at the pig level. We thus wish to fit the following model

$$\texttt{weight}_{ij} = \beta_0 + \beta_1 \texttt{week}_{ij} + u_i + \epsilon_{ij} \tag{3}$$

for $i = 1, \ldots, 48$ pigs and $j = 1, \ldots, 9$ weeks. The fixed portion of the model, $\beta_0 + \beta_1 \texttt{week}_{ij}$, simply states that we want one overall regression line representing the population average. The random effect u_i serves to shift this regression line up or down according to each pig. Since the random effects occur at the pig level (id), we fit the model by typing

Charles Roy Henderson (1911–1989) was born in Iowa and grew up on the family farm. His education in animal husbandry, animal nutrition, and statistics at Iowa State was interspersed with jobs in the Iowa Extension Service, Ohio University, and the U.S. Army. After completing his Ph.D., Henderson joined the Animal Science faculty at Cornell. He developed and applied statistical methods in the improvement of farm livestock productivity through genetic selection, with particular focus on dairy cattle. His methods are general and have been used worldwide in livestock breeding and beyond agriculture. Henderson's work on variance components and best linear unbiased prediction has proved to be one of the main roots of current mixed-model methods.

```
. xtmixed weight week || id:

Performing EM optimization:

Performing gradient-based optimization:

Iteration 0:    log restricted-likelihood = -1016.8984
Iteration 1:    log restricted-likelihood = -1016.8984

Computing standard errors:
```

Mixed-effects REML regression	Number of obs	=	432
Group variable: id	Number of groups	=	48

	Obs per group: min	=	9
	avg	=	9.0
	max	=	9

	Wald chi2(1)	=	25271.50
Log restricted-likelihood = -1016.8984	Prob > chi2	=	0.0000

weight	Coef.	Std. Err.	z	P>|z|	[95% Conf. Interval]	
week	6.209896	.0390633	158.97	0.000	6.133333	6.286458
_cons	19.35561	.603139	32.09	0.000	18.17348	20.53774

Random-effects Parameters	Estimate	Std. Err.	[95% Conf. Interval]	
id: Identity				
sd(_cons)	3.891253	.4143198	3.158334	4.794252
sd(Residual)	2.096356	.0757444	1.953034	2.250195

LR test vs. linear regression: chibar2(01) =   473.15 Prob >= chibar2 = 0.0000

At this point, a guided tour of the model specification and output is in order:

1. By typing "`weight week`", we specified the response, `weight`, and the fixed portion of the model in the same way we would if we were using `regress` or any other estimation command. Our fixed effects are a coefficient on `week` and a constant term.

2. When we added "`|| id:`", we specified random effects at the level identified by group variable id, i.e., the pig level. Since we wanted only a random intercept, that is all we had to type.

3. The estimation log consists of three parts:

    (a) A set of expectation-maximization (EM) iterations used to refine starting values. By default, the iterations themselves are not displayed, but you can display them with option `emlog`.

    (b) A set of "gradient-based" iterations. By default, these are Newton–Raphson iterations, but other methods are available by specifying the appropriate `maximize` options; see [R] **maximize**.

    (c) The message "Computing standard errors:". This is just to inform you that `xtmixed` has finished its iterative maximization and is now reparameterizing from a matrix-based parameterization (see *Methods and Formulas*) to the natural metric of variance components and their estimated standard errors.

4. The output title, "Mixed-effects REML regression", informs us that our model was fitted using REML, the default. For ML estimates, use option `mle`.

    Since this model is a simple random-intercept model, specifying option `mle` would be equivalent to using `xtreg`, also with option `mle`.

5. The first estimation table reports the fixed effects. We estimate $\beta_0 = 19.36$ and $\beta_1 = 6.21$.

6. The second estimation table shows the estimated variance components. The first section of the table is labeled "`id: Identity`", meaning that these are random effects at the `id` (pig) level and that their variance–covariance matrix is a multiple of the identity matrix; that is, $\Sigma = \sigma_u^2 I$. Since we have only one random effect at this level, `xtmixed` knew that `Identity` is the only possible covariance structure. In any case, σ_u is estimated as 3.89 with standard error 0.414.

   If you prefer variance estimates, $\widehat{\sigma}_u^2$, to standard deviation estimates, $\widehat{\sigma}_u$, specify option `variance` either at estimation or on replay.

7. The row labeled "`sd(Residual)`" displays the estimated standard deviation of the overall error term; i.e., $\widehat{\sigma}_\epsilon = 2.10$.

8. Finally, a likelihood-ratio test comparing the model to ordinary linear regression, model (3) without u_i, is provided and is highly significant for these data.

   We now store our estimates for later use.

   ```
   . estimates store randint
   ```
   ◁

▷ Example 2

Extending (3) to allow for a random slope on `week` yields the model

$$\texttt{weight}_{ij} = \beta_0 + \beta_1 \texttt{week}_{ij} + u_{0i} + u_{1i}\texttt{week}_{ij} + \epsilon_{ij} \tag{4}$$

fitted using `xtmixed`:

```
. xtmixed weight week || id: week
Performing EM optimization:
Performing gradient-based optimization:
Iteration 0:   log restricted-likelihood = -870.51473
Iteration 1:   log restricted-likelihood = -870.51473
Computing standard errors:
```

Mixed-effects REML regression			Number of obs	=	432
Group variable: id			Number of groups	=	48
			Obs per group: min =		9
			avg =		9.0
			max =		9
			Wald chi2(1)	=	4592.10
Log restricted-likelihood = -870.51473			Prob > chi2	=	0.0000

weight	Coef.	Std. Err.	z	P>|z|	[95% Conf. Interval]	
week	6.209896	.0916386	67.77	0.000	6.030287	6.389504
_cons	19.35561	.4021142	48.13	0.000	18.56748	20.14374

Random-effects Parameters	Estimate	Std. Err.	[95% Conf. Interval]	
id: Independent				
sd(week)	.6135471	.0673971	.4947035	.7609409
sd(_cons)	2.630132	.302883	2.098719	3.296105
sd(Residual)	1.26443	.0487971	1.172317	1.363781

```
LR test vs. linear regression:      chi2(2) = 765.92   Prob > chi2 = 0.0000
Note: LR test is conservative and provided only for reference.
. estimates store randslope
```

Since we didn't specify a covariance structure for the random effects $(u_{0i}, u_{1i})'$, xtmixed used the default Independent structure; that is,

$$\Sigma = \text{Var} \begin{bmatrix} u_{0i} \\ u_{1i} \end{bmatrix} = \begin{bmatrix} \sigma_{u0}^2 & 0 \\ 0 & \sigma_{u1}^2 \end{bmatrix} \tag{5}$$

with $\widehat{\sigma}_{u0} = 2.63$ and $\widehat{\sigma}_{u1} = 0.61$. Our point estimates of the fixed affects are essentially identical to those from model (3), but note that this does not hold generally. Given the 95% confidence interval for $\widehat{\sigma}_{u1}$, it would seem that the random slope is significant, and we can use lrtest and our two saved estimation results to verify this fact

```
. lrtest randslope randint
Likelihood-ratio test                        LR chibar2(01)   =    292.77
(Assumption: randint nested in randslope)    Prob > chibar2   =    0.0000
Note: LR tests based on REML are valid only when the fixed-effects
      specification is identical for both models.
```

❏ Technical Note

LR tests with REML require identical fixed-effects specifications for both models. As stated in Ruppert, Wand, and Carroll (2003), "The reason for this is that restricted likelihood is the likelihood of the residuals after fitting the fixed effects and so is not appropriate when there is more than one fixed effects model under consideration." To compare models with different fixed-effects specifications, use a Wald test, or fit the models by ML (option mle).

In our example, the fixed-effects specifications for both models are identical ($\beta_0 + \beta_1$week), so our REML-based test is valid.

❏

The results thus favor the model that allows for a random pig-specific regression line over the model that allows only for a pig-specific shift.

Finally, we also note the message at the bottom of our xtmixed output informing us that our overall LR test comparing to linear regression is conservative. For an explanation, see *Distribution theory for likelihood-ratio tests* later in this entry.

◁

Covariance structures

In example 2, we fitted a model with the default Independent covariance given in (5). Within any random-effects level specification, we can override this default by specifying an alternative covariance structure via option covariance().

▷ Example 3

We generalize (5) to allow u_{0i} and u_{1i} to be correlated; that is,

$$\Sigma = \text{Var} \begin{bmatrix} u_{0i} \\ u_{1i} \end{bmatrix} = \begin{bmatrix} \sigma_{u0}^2 & \sigma_{01} \\ \sigma_{01} & \sigma_{u1}^2 \end{bmatrix}$$

```
. xtmixed weight week || id: week, covariance(unstructured) variance
```

(*output omitted*)

```
Mixed-effects REML regression              Number of obs     =         432
Group variable: id                         Number of groups  =          48

                                           Obs per group: min =          9
                                                          avg =        9.0
                                                          max =          9

                                           Wald chi2(1)      =     4552.31
Log restricted-likelihood = -870.43562     Prob > chi2       =      0.0000
```

weight	Coef.	Std. Err.	z	P>|z|	[95% Conf. Interval]	
week	6.209896	.0920382	67.47	0.000	6.029504	6.390287
_cons	19.35561	.4038677	47.93	0.000	18.56405	20.14718

Random-effects Parameters	Estimate	Std. Err.	[95% Conf. Interval]	
id: Unstructured				
var(week)	.3799957	.0839023	.2465103	.5857635
var(_cons)	6.986465	1.616357	4.439432	10.99481
cov(week,_cons)	-.1033632	.2627309	-.6183063	.41158
var(Residual)	1.596829	.1231981	1.372736	1.857506

```
LR test vs. linear regression:       chi2(3) =    766.07   Prob > chi2 = 0.0000
```
Note: LR test is conservative and provided only for reference.

But we don't find the correlation to be at all significant.

```
. lrtest . randslope
Likelihood-ratio test                      LR chi2(1)   =       0.16
(Assumption: randslope nested in .)        Prob > chi2  =     0.6908
```
Note: LR tests based on REML are valid only when the fixed-effects
      specification is identical for both models.

In addition to specifying an alternate covariance structure, we specified option variance to display variance components in the variance–covariance metric, rather than the default, which displays them as standard deviations and correlations.

◁

We could instead have also specified covariance(identity), restricting u_{0i} and u_{1i} to not only be independent but also to have common variance, or we could have specified covariance(exchangeable), which imposes a common variance but allows for a nonzero correlation.

Likelihood versus restricted likelihood

Thus far, all our examples have used restricted maximum likelihood (REML) to estimate variance components. We could have just as easily asked for ML estimates. Refitting the model in example 2 by ML, we get

```
. xtmixed weight week || id: week, ml
```

  (*output omitted*)

Mixed-effects ML regression   Number of obs   =   432
Group variable: id   Number of groups   =   48

                                            Obs per group: min =   9
                                                           avg =   9.0
                                                           max =   9

                                            Wald chi2(1)   =   4689.52
Log likelihood = -869.03825   Prob > chi2   =   0.0000

weight	Coef.	Std. Err.	z	P>|z|	[95% Conf. Interval]	
week	6.209896	.0906818	68.48	0.000	6.032163	6.387629
_cons	19.35561	.3979158	48.64	0.000	18.57571	20.13551

Random-effects Parameters	Estimate	Std. Err.	[95% Conf. Interval]	
id: Independent				
sd(week)	.6066848	.0660293	.4901415	.7509392
sd(_cons)	2.599299	.2969071	2.077912	3.251513
sd(Residual)	1.264441	.0487958	1.172331	1.363789

LR test vs. linear regression: chi2(2) =   764.42   Prob > chi2 = 0.0000

Note: LR test is conservative and provided only for reference.

Although ML estimators are based on the usual likelihood theory, the idea behind REML is to transform the response into a set of linear contrasts whose distribution is free of the fixed effects β. The restricted likelihood is then formed by considering the distribution of the linear contrasts. Not only does this make the maximization problem free of β, it also incorporates the degrees of freedom used to estimate β into the estimation of the variance components. This follows since, by necessity, the rank of the linear contrasts must be less than the number of observations.

As a simple example, consider a constant-only regression where $y_i \sim N(\mu, \sigma^2)$ for $i = 1, \ldots, n$. The ML estimate of σ^2 can be derived theoretically as the n-divided sample variance. The REML estimate can be derived by considering the first $n - 1$ error contrasts, $y_i - \bar{y}$, whose joint distribution is free of μ. Applying maximum likelihood to this distribution results in an estimate of σ^2, that is, the $(n - 1)$ divided sample variance, which is unbiased for σ^2.

The unbiasedness property of REML extends to all mixed models when the data are balanced, and thus REML would seem the clear choice in balanced-data problems, although in large samples the difference between ML and REML is negligible. One disadvantage of REML is that LR tests based on REML are inappropriate for comparing models with different fixed-effects specifications. ML is appropriate for such LR tests and has the advantage of being easy to explain and being the method of choice for other estimators. The question of which method to use thus remains a matter of personal taste.

Examining the ML output, we find that the estimates of the variance components are slightly smaller than the REML estimates. This is typical, since ML estimates, which do not incorporate the degrees of freedom used to estimate the fixed effects, tend to be biased downward.

Two-level models

The panel-data representation of the mixed model given in (2) can be extended to two nested levels. Formally

$$\mathbf{y}_{ij} = \mathbf{X}_{ij}\boldsymbol{\beta} + \mathbf{Z}_{ij}^{(1)}\mathbf{u}_i^{(1)} + \mathbf{Z}_{ij}^{(2)}\mathbf{u}_{ij}^{(2)} + \boldsymbol{\epsilon}_{ij} \tag{6}$$

for $i = 1, \ldots, M$ first-level groups and $j = 1, \ldots, M_i$ second-level groups that are nested within group i. Group i, j consists of n_{ij} observations, so $\mathbf{y}_{ij}$, $\mathbf{X}_{ij}$, and $\boldsymbol{\epsilon}_{ij}$ each have row dimension n_{ij}. $\mathbf{Z}_{ij}^{(1)}$ is the $n_{ij} \times q_1$ design matrix for the first-level random effects $\mathbf{u}_i^{(1)}$, and $\mathbf{Z}_{ij}^{(2)}$ is the $n_{ij} \times q_2$ design matrix for the second-level random effects $\mathbf{u}_{ij}^{(2)}$. Furthermore, assume that

$$\mathbf{u}_i^{(1)} \sim N(\mathbf{0}, \boldsymbol{\Sigma}_1); \quad \mathbf{u}_{ij}^{(2)} \sim N(\mathbf{0}, \boldsymbol{\Sigma}_2); \quad \boldsymbol{\epsilon}_{ij} \sim N(\mathbf{0}, \sigma_\epsilon^2 \mathbf{I})$$

and that $\mathbf{u}_i^{(1)}$, $\mathbf{u}_{ij}^{(2)}$, and $\boldsymbol{\epsilon}_{ij}$ are independent.

Fitting a two-level model requires you to specify two random-effects "equations", one for each level. The variable list for the first equation represents $\mathbf{Z}_{ij}^{(1)}$, and the second equation, $\mathbf{Z}_{ij}^{(2)}$.

▷ Example 4

Baltagi, Song, and Jung (2001) estimate a Cobb–Douglas production function examining the productivity of public capital in each state's private output. Originally provided by Munnell (1990), the data were recorded over 1970–1986 for 48 states grouped into nine regions.

```
. use http://www.stata-press.com/data/r10/productivity, clear
(Public Capital Productivity)

. describe

Contains data from productivity.dta
  obs:            816                      Public Capital Productivity
  vars:            11                      29 Mar 2007 10:57
  size:        32,640 (99.7% of memory free)  (_dta has notes)
```

variable name	storage type	display format	value label	variable label
state	byte	%9.0g		states 1-48
region	byte	%9.0g		regions 1-9
year	int	%9.0g		years 1970-1986
public	float	%9.0g		public capital stock
hwy	float	%9.0g		log(highway component of public)
water	float	%9.0g		log(water component of public)
other	float	%9.0g		log(bldg/other component of public)
private	float	%9.0g		log(private capital stock)
gsp	float	%9.0g		log(gross state product)
emp	float	%9.0g		log(nonagriculture payrolls)
unemp	float	%9.0g		state unemployment rate

```
Sorted by:
```

Since the states are nested within regions, we fit a two-level mixed model with random intercepts at both the region and at the state-within-region levels. That is, we use (6) with both $\mathbf{Z}_{ij}^{(1)}$ and $\mathbf{Z}_{ij}^{(2)}$ set to the $n_{ij} \times 1$ column of ones, and $\boldsymbol{\Sigma}_1 = \sigma_1^2$ and $\boldsymbol{\Sigma}_2 = \sigma_2^2$ are both scalars.

```
. xtmixed gsp private emp hwy water other unemp || region: || state:
```
 (*output omitted*)

```
Mixed-effects REML regression                    Number of obs      =        816
```

Group Variable	No. of Groups	Observations per Group		
		Minimum	Average	Maximum
region	9	51	90.7	136
state	48	17	17.0	17

```
                                             Wald chi2(6)      =   18382.39
Log restricted-likelihood = 1404.7101        Prob > chi2       =     0.0000
```

gsp	Coef.	Std. Err.	z	P>|z|	[95% Conf. Interval]	
private	.2660308	.0215471	12.35	0.000	.2237993	.3082624
emp	.7555059	.0264556	28.56	0.000	.7036539	.8073579
hwy	.0718857	.0233478	3.08	0.002	.0261249	.1176464
water	.0761552	.0139952	5.44	0.000	.0487251	.1035853
other	-.1005396	.0170173	-5.91	0.000	-.1338929	-.0671862
unemp	-.0058815	.0009093	-6.47	0.000	-.0076636	-.0040994
_cons	2.126995	.1574864	13.51	0.000	1.818327	2.435663

Random-effects Parameters	Estimate	Std. Err.	[95% Conf. Interval]	
region: Identity				
sd(_cons)	.0435471	.0186292	.0188287	.1007161
state: Identity				
sd(_cons)	.0802737	.0095512	.0635762	.1013567
sd(Residual)	.0368008	.0009442	.034996	.0386987

```
LR test vs. linear regression:      chi2(2) =  1162.40    Prob > chi2 = 0.0000
```
Note: LR test is conservative and provided only for reference.

Some items of note:

1. Our model now has two random-effects equations, separated by ||. The first is a random intercept (constant only) at the `region` level, and the second is a random intercept at the `state` level. The order in which these are specified (from left to right) is significant—xtmixed assumes that `state` is nested within `region`.

2. The information on groups is now displayed as a table, with one row for each model level. You can suppress this table with option `nogroup` or with `noheader`, which will suppress the rest of the header, as well.

3. The variance-component estimates are now organized and labeled according to level.

After adjusting for the nested-level error structure, we find that the highway and water components of public capital had significant positive effects on private output, whereas the other public buildings component had a negative effect.

◁

❏ Technical Note

In the previous example, the states are coded 1–48 and are nested within nine regions. xtmixed treated the states as nested within regions, regardless of whether the codes for each state are unique between regions. That is, even if codes for states were duplicated between regions, xtmixed would have enforced the nesting and produced the same results.

The group information at the top of xtmixed output and that produced by the postestimation command estat group (see [XT] **xtmixed postestimation**) take the nesting into account. The statistics are thus not necessarily what you would get if you instead tabulated each group variable individually.

❏

Model (6) extends in a straightforward manner to more than two nested levels of random effects, as does the specification of such models in xtmixed.

Blocked-diagonal covariance structures

Covariance matrices of random effects within an equation can be modeled either as a multiple of the identity matrix, diagonal (i.e., Independent), exchangeable, or as general symmetric (Unstructured). These may also be combined to produce more complex blocked-diagonal covariance structures, effectively placing constraints on the variance components.

▷ Example 5

Returning to our productivity data, we now add random coefficients on hwy and unemp at the region level. This only slightly changes the estimates of the fixed effects, so we focus our attention on the variance components

```
. xtmixed gsp private emp hwy water other unemp || region: hwy unemp || state:,
> nolog nogroup nofetable
Mixed-effects REML regression              Number of obs     =       816
                                           Wald chi2(6)      =  16803.51
Log restricted-likelihood =  1423.3455     Prob > chi2       =    0.0000
```

Random-effects Parameters	Estimate	Std. Err.	[95% Conf. Interval]	
region: Independent				
sd(hwy)	.0052752	.0108846	.0000925	.3009897
sd(unemp)	.0052895	.001545	.002984	.0093764
sd(_cons)	.0596008	.0758296	.0049235	.721487
state: Identity				
sd(_cons)	.0807543	.009887	.0635259	.1026551
sd(Residual)	.0353932	.000914	.0336464	.0372307

```
LR test vs. linear regression:       chi2(4) =  1199.67    Prob > chi2 = 0.0000
Note: LR test is conservative and provided only for reference.
. estimates store prodrc
```

This model is the same as that fitted in example 4, except that $\mathbf{Z}_{ij}^{(1)}$ is now the $n_{ij} \times 3$ matrix with columns determined by the values of hwy, unemp, and an intercept term (one), in that order, and (since we used the default Independent structure) $\mathbf{\Sigma}_1$ is

$$
\mathbf{\Sigma}_1 = \begin{array}{c} \begin{array}{ccc} \text{hwy} & \text{unemp} & \text{\_cons} \end{array} \\ \begin{pmatrix} \sigma_a^2 & 0 & 0 \\ 0 & \sigma_b^2 & 0 \\ 0 & 0 & \sigma_c^2 \end{pmatrix} \end{array}
$$

The random-effects specification at the state level remains unchanged; i.e., $\mathbf{\Sigma}_2$ is still treated as the scalar variance of the random intercepts at the state level.

An LR test comparing this model with that from example 4 favors the inclusion of the two random coefficients, a fact we leave to the interested reader to verify.

Examining the estimated variance components reveals that the variances of the random coefficients on hwy and unemp could be treated as equal. That is

$$
\mathbf{\Sigma}_1 = \begin{array}{c} \begin{array}{ccc} \text{hwy} & \text{unemp} & \text{\_cons} \end{array} \\ \begin{pmatrix} \sigma_a^2 & 0 & 0 \\ 0 & \sigma_a^2 & 0 \\ 0 & 0 & \sigma_c^2 \end{pmatrix} \end{array}
$$

looks plausible. We can impose this equality constraint by treating $\mathbf{\Sigma}_1$ as blocked diagonal: the first block is a 2×2 multiple of the identity matrix, i.e., $\sigma_a^2 \mathbf{I}_2$; the second is a scalar, equivalently a 1×1 multiple of the identity.

We construct blocked-diagonal covariances by repeating level specifications

```
. xtmixed gsp private emp hwy water other unemp || region: hwy unemp,
> cov(identity) || region: || state:, nolog nogroup nofetable
Mixed-effects REML regression                  Number of obs     =       816
                                               Wald chi2(6)      =  16803.41
Log restricted-likelihood =  1423.3455         Prob > chi2       =    0.0000
```

Random-effects Parameters	Estimate	Std. Err.	[95% Conf. Interval]	
region: Identity				
sd(hwy unemp)	.0052896	.0015446	.0029844	.0093752
region: Identity				
sd(_cons)	.0595029	.0318238	.0208589	.1697401
state: Identity				
sd(_cons)	.080752	.0097453	.0637425	.1023006
sd(Residual)	.0353932	.0009139	.0336465	.0372306

```
LR test vs. linear regression:       chi2(3) =   1199.67    Prob > chi2 = 0.0000
```
Note: LR test is conservative and provided only for reference.

We specified two equations for the region level: the first for the random coefficients on hwy and unemp with covariance set to Identity and the second for the random intercept _cons, whose covariance defaults to Identity because it is of dimension one. xtmixed labeled the estimate of σ_a as "sd(hwy unemp)" to designate that it is common to the random coefficients on both hwy and unemp.

An LR test shows that the constrained model fits equally well.

```
. lrtest . prodrc
Likelihood-ratio test                           LR chibar2(01)  =      0.00
(Assumption: . nested in prodrc)                Prob > chibar2  =    1.0000
Note: LR tests based on REML are valid only when the fixed-effects
       specification is identical for both models.
```

◁

You can repeat level specifications as often as you like, defining successive blocks of a blocked-diagonal covariance matrix. However, repeated level equations must be listed consecutively; otherwise, xtmixed will give an error.

❏ Technical Note

In the previous estimation output, there was no constant term included in the first region equation, even though we did not use option noconstant. When you specify repeated level equations, xtmixed knows not to put constant terms in each equation since such a model would be unidentified. By default, it places the constant in the last repeated level equation, but you can use noconstant creatively to override this.

❏

Factor notation and crossed-effects models

Not all mixed models contain nested levels of random effects.

▷ Example 6

Returning to our longitudinal analysis of pig weights, suppose that instead of (4) we wish to fit

$$\texttt{weight}_{ij} = \beta_0 + \beta_1 \texttt{week}_{ij} + u_i + v_j + \epsilon_{ij} \tag{7}$$

for the $i = 1, \ldots, 48$ pigs and $j = 1, \ldots, 9$ weeks and

$$u_i \sim N(0, \sigma_u^2); \quad v_j \sim N(0, \sigma_v^2); \quad \epsilon_{ij} \sim N(0, \sigma_\epsilon^2)$$

all independently. Both (4) and (7) assume an overall population-average growth curve $\beta_0 + \beta_1 \texttt{week}$ and a random pig-specific shift.

The models differ in how week enters into the random part of the model. In (4), we assume that the effect due to week is linear and pig specific (a random slope); in (7), we assume that the effect due to week, v_j, is systematic to that week and common to all pigs. The rationale behind (7) could be that, assuming that the pigs were measured contemporaneously, we might be concerned that week-specific random factors such as weather and feeding patterns had significant systematic effects on all pigs.

Model (7) is a an example of a two-way *crossed-effects* model, with the pig effects u_i being crossed with the week effects v_j. One way to fit such models is to consider all the data as one big panel and treat the u_i and v_j as a series of $48 + 9 = 57$ random coefficients on indicator variables for pig and week. In the notation of (1),

$$
\mathbf{u} = \begin{bmatrix} u_1 \\ \vdots \\ u_{48} \\ v_1 \\ \vdots \\ v_9 \end{bmatrix} \sim N(\mathbf{0}, \mathbf{G}); \quad \mathbf{G} = \begin{bmatrix} \sigma_u^2 \mathbf{I}_{48} & \mathbf{0} \\ \mathbf{0} & \sigma_v^2 \mathbf{I}_9 \end{bmatrix}
$$

Since $\mathbf{G}$ is blocked diagonal, it can be represented in xtmixed as repeated level equations. All we need is an ID variable to identify all the observations as one big group and a way to tell xtmixed to treat pig and week as factor variables (or equivalently, as two sets of overparameterized indicator variables identifying pigs and weeks, respectively). xtmixed supports the special group designation _all for the former and the factor notation R.*varname* for the latter.

```
. use http://www.stata-press.com/data/r10/pig, clear
(Longitudinal analysis of pig weights)

. xtmixed weight week || _all: R.id || _all: R.week

Performing EM optimization:

Performing gradient-based optimization:

Iteration 0:   log restricted-likelihood = -1015.4214
Iteration 1:   log restricted-likelihood = -1015.4214

Computing standard errors:
```

```
Mixed-effects REML regression              Number of obs      =       432
Group variable: _all                       Number of groups   =         1

                                           Obs per group: min =       432
                                                          avg =     432.0
                                                          max =       432

                                           Wald chi2(1)       =  11516.16
Log restricted-likelihood = -1015.4214     Prob > chi2        =    0.0000
```

weight	Coef.	Std. Err.	z	P>|z|	[95% Conf. Interval]	
week	6.209896	.0578669	107.31	0.000	6.096479	6.323313
_cons	19.35561	.6493996	29.81	0.000	18.08281	20.62841

Random-effects Parameters	Estimate	Std. Err.	[95% Conf. Interval]	
_all: Identity				
sd(R.id)	3.892648	.4141707	3.15994	4.795252
_all: Identity				
sd(R.week)	.3337581	.1611824	.1295268	.8600111
sd(Residual)	2.072917	.0755915	1.929931	2.226496

```
LR test vs. linear regression:       chi2(2) =    476.10   Prob > chi2 = 0.0000
```
Note: LR test is conservative and provided only for reference.

```
. estimates store crossed
```

and thus we estimate $\widehat{\sigma}_u = 3.89$ and $\widehat{\sigma}_v = 0.33$. Both (4) and (7) estimate a total of five parameters, two fixed effects and three variance components. The models, however, are not nested within each other, which precludes the use of an LR test to compare both models. Refitting model (4) and looking at the AIC values using estimates stats

```
. quietly xtmixed weight week || id:week

. estimates stats crossed .
```

Model	Obs	ll(null)	ll(model)	df	AIC	BIC
crossed	432	.	-1015.421	5	2040.843	2061.185
.	432	.	-870.5147	5	1751.029	1771.372

definitely favors model (4). This finding is not surprising, given that our rationale behind (7) was somewhat fictitious. In our estimates stats output, the values of ll(null) are missing. xtmixed does not fit a constant-only model as part of its usual estimation of the full model, but we can use xtmixed to fit a constant-only model directly.

◁

The R. *varname* notation is equivalent to giving a list of overparameterized (none dropped) indicator variables for use in a random-effects specification. When you use R. *varname*, xtmixed handles the calculations internally rather than creating the indicators in the data. Since the set of indicators is overparameterized, R. *varname* implies noconstant. To include indicator variables in the fixed-effects specification, use xi; see [R] **xi**.

❏ Technical Note

Although we were able to fit the crossed-effects model (7), it came at the expense of increasing the column dimension of our random-effects design from two in model (4) to 57 in model (7). Computation time and memory requirements grow (roughly) quadratically with the dimension of the random effects. As a result, fitting such crossed-effects models is feasible only when the total column dimension is small to moderate.

Reexamining model (7), we note that if we drop v_j, we end up with a model equivalent to (3), meaning that we could have fitted (3) by typing

```
. xtmixed weight week || _all: R.id
```

instead of

```
. xtmixed weight week || id:
```

as we did when we originally fitted the model. The results of both estimations are identical, but the latter specification, organized at the panel (pig) level with random-effects dimension one (a random intercept) is much more computationally efficient. Whereas with the first form we are limited in how many pigs we can analyze, there is no such limitation with the second form.

Furthermore, we fit model (7) by using

```
. xtmixed weight week || _all: R.id || _all: R.week
```

as a direct way to demonstrate factor notation. However, we can technically treat pigs as nested within the "_all" group, yielding the equivalent and more efficient (total column dimension 10) way to fit (7)

```
. xtmixed weight week || _all: R.week || id:
```

We leave it to you to verify that both produce identical results.

❏

▷ Example 7

As another example of how the same model may be fitted different ways by using `xtmixed` (and as a way to demonstrate `covariance(exchangeable)`), consider the model used in example 4

$$y_{ij} = X_{ij}\beta + u_i^{(1)} + u_{ij}^{(2)} + \epsilon_{ij}$$

where y_{ij} represents the logarithms of gross state products for the $n_{ij} = 17$ observations from state j in region i, X_{ij} is a set of regressors, $u_i^{(1)}$ is a random intercept at the region level, and $u_{ij}^{(2)}$ is a random intercept at the state (nested within region) level. We assume that $u_i^{(1)} \sim N(0, \sigma_1^2)$ and $u_{ij}^{(2)} \sim N(0, \sigma_2^2)$ independently. Define

$$\mathbf{v}_i = \begin{bmatrix} u_i^{(1)} + u_{i1}^{(2)} \\ u_i^{(1)} + u_{i2}^{(2)} \\ \vdots \\ u_i^{(1)} + u_{iM_i}^{(2)} \end{bmatrix}$$

where M_i is the number of states in region i. Making this substitution, we can stack the observations for all the states within region i to get

$$y_i = X_i\beta + Z_i\mathbf{v}_i + \epsilon_i$$

where Z_i is a set of indicators identifying the states within each region; that is,

$$Z_i = I_{M_i} \otimes J_{17}$$

for a k-column vector of ones J_k, and

$$\Sigma = \text{Var}(\mathbf{v}_i) = \begin{bmatrix} \sigma_1^2 + \sigma_2^2 & \sigma_1^2 & \cdots & \sigma_1^2 \\ \sigma_1^2 & \sigma_1^2 + \sigma_2^2 & \cdots & \sigma_1^2 \\ \vdots & \vdots & \ddots & \vdots \\ \sigma_1^2 & \sigma_1^2 & \sigma_1^2 & \sigma_1^2 + \sigma_2^2 \end{bmatrix}_{M_i \times M_i}$$

Since Σ is an exchangeable matrix, we can fit this alternative form of the model by specifying the `exchangeable` covariance structure.

```
. use http://www.stata-press.com/data/r10/productivity, clear
(Public Capital Productivity)
```

```
. xtmixed gsp private emp hwy water other unemp || region: R.state,
> cov(exchangeable) variance
```
  (*output omitted*)

```
Mixed-effects REML regression                 Number of obs      =        816
Group variable: region                        Number of groups   =          9

                                              Obs per group: min =         51
                                                             avg =       90.7
                                                             max =        136

                                              Wald chi2(6)       =   18382.39
Log restricted-likelihood =  1404.7101        Prob > chi2        =     0.0000
```

gsp	Coef.	Std. Err.	z	P>|z|	[95% Conf. Interval]	
private	.2660308	.0215471	12.35	0.000	.2237993	.3082623
emp	.7555059	.0264556	28.56	0.000	.7036539	.8073579
hwy	.0718857	.0233478	3.08	0.002	.0261249	.1176464
water	.0761552	.0139952	5.44	0.000	.0487251	.1035853
other	-.1005396	.0170173	-5.91	0.000	-.1338929	-.0671862
unemp	-.0058815	.0009093	-6.47	0.000	-.0076636	-.0040994
_cons	2.126995	.1574864	13.51	0.000	1.818327	2.435663

Random-effects Parameters	Estimate	Std. Err.	[95% Conf. Interval]	
region: Exchangeable				
var(R.state)	.0083402	.0020718	.0051254	.0135715
cov(R.state)	.0018963	.0016225	-.0012836	.0050763
var(Residual)	.0013543	.0000695	.0012247	.0014976

```
LR test vs. linear regression:      chi2(2) =   1162.40   Prob > chi2 = 0.0000
```
Note: LR test is conservative and provided only for reference.

The estimates of the fixed effects and their standard errors are equivalent to those from example 4, and remapping the variance components from $(\sigma_1^2 + \sigma_2^2, \sigma_1^2, \sigma_e^2)$, as displayed here, to (τ_1, τ_2, τ_e), as displayed in example 4, will show that they are equivalent as well.

Of course, given the discussion in the previous technical note, it is more efficient to fit this model as we did originally, as a two-level model.

◁

Diagnosing convergence problems

Given the flexibility of the class of linear mixed models, you will find that some models "fail to converge" when used with your data. The default gradient-based method used by xtmixed is the Newton–Raphson algorithm, requiring the calculation of a gradient vector and Hessian (second derivative) matrix; see [R] **ml**.

A failure to converge can take any one of three forms:

1. repeated "nonconcave" or "backed-up" iterations without convergence;

2. a Hessian (second derivative) calculation that has become asymmetric, unstable, or has missing values;

3. the message "standard error calculation has failed" when computing standard errors.

All three situations essentially amount to the same thing: the Hessian calculation has become unstable, most likely because of a ridge in the likelihood function, a subsurface of the likelihood in which all points give the same value of the likelihood and for which there is no unique solution.

Such behavior is usually the result of either

A. a model that is not identified given the data. For example, fitting the two-level nested random intercept model

$$y_{ij} = \mathbf{x}_{ij}\boldsymbol{\beta} + u_i^{(1)} + u_{ij}^{(2)} + \epsilon_{ij}$$

without any replicated measurements at the (i, j) level. This model is unidentified for such data since the random intercepts $u_{ij}^{(2)}$ are confounded with the overall errors ϵ_{ij}; or

B. a model that contains a variance component whose estimate is really close to zero. When this occurs, a ridge is formed by an interval of values near zero, which produce the same likelihood and look equally good to the optimizer.

One useful way to diagnose problems of nonconvergence is to rely on the expectation-maximization (EM) algorithm (Dempster, Laird, and Rubin 1977), normally used by xtmixed only as a means of refining starting values. The advantages of EM are that it does not require a Hessian calculation, each successive EM iteration will result in a larger likelihood, iterations can be calculated quickly, and iterations will quickly bring parameter estimates into a neighborhood of the solution. The disadvantages of EM are that, once in a neighborhood of the solution, it can be slow to converge, if at all, and EM provides no facility for estimating standard errors of the estimated variance components.

One useful property of EM is that it is always willing to provide a solution if you allow it to iterate enough times, if you are satisfied with being in a neighborhood of the optimum rather than right on the optimum, and if standard errors of variance components are not crucial to your analysis. If you encounter a nonconvergent model, try using option emonly to bypass gradient-based optimization. Use emiterate(#) to specify the maximum number of EM iterations, which you will usually want to set much higher than the default of 20. If your EM solution shows an estimated variance component that is near zero, this provides evidence that B is the cause of the nonconvergence of the gradient-based method, in which case the solution would be to drop the offending variance component from the model. If no estimated variance components are near zero, reason A could be the culprit.

If your data and model are nearly unidentified, as opposed to fully unidentified, you may be able to obtain convergence with standard errors by changing some of the settings of the gradient-based optimization. Adding option difficult can be particularly helpful if you are seeing many "nonconcave" messages; you may also consider changing the technique() or using option nonrtolerance; see [R] maximize.

Distribution theory for likelihood-ratio tests

When determining the asymptotic distribution of a likelihood-ratio (LR) test comparing two nested models fitted by xtmixed, issues concerning boundary problems imposed by estimating strictly positive quantities (i.e., variances) can complicate the situation. When performing LR tests involving mixed models (whether comparing with linear regression within xtmixed or comparing two separate mixed models with lrtest), you may thus sometimes see a test labeled as "chibar" rather than the usual "chi2" or see a chi2 test with a note attached stating that the test is conservative.

At the heart of the issue is the number of variances being restricted to zero in the reduced model. If there are none, the usual asymptotic theory holds and the distribution of the test statistic is χ^2 with degrees of freedom equal to the difference in the number of estimated parameters between both models.

When there is only one variance being set to zero in the reduced model, the asymptotic distribution of the likelihood-ratio test statistic is a 50:50 mixture of a χ^2_k and a χ^2_{k+1} distribution, where k is the number of other restricted parameters in the reduced model that are unaffected by boundary conditions. Stata labels such test statistics as `chibar` and adjusts the significance levels accordingly. See Self and Liang (1987) for the appropriate theory or Gutierrez, Carter, and Drukker (2001) for a Stata-specific discussion.

When more than one variance parameter is being set to zero in the reduced model, however, the situation becomes more complicated. For example, consider a comparison test versus linear regression for a mixed model with two random coefficients and unstructured covariance matrix

$$\Sigma = \begin{bmatrix} \sigma_0^2 & \sigma_{01} \\ \sigma_{01} & \sigma_1^2 \end{bmatrix}$$

Since the random component of the mixed model comprises three parameters $(\sigma_0^2, \sigma_{01}, \sigma_1^2)$, on the surface it would seem that the LR comparison test would be distributed as χ^2_3. However, two complications need to be considered. First, the variances σ_0^2 and σ_1^2 are restricted to be positive, and second, constraints such as $\sigma_1^2 = 0$ implicitly restrict the covariance σ_{01} to be zero as well. From a technical standpoint, it is unclear how many parameters must be restricted to reduce the model to linear regression.

Because of these complications, appropriate and sufficiently general distribution theory for the more-than-one-variance case has yet to be developed. Theory (e.g., Stram and Lee 1994) and empirical studies (e.g., McLachlan and Basford 1988) have demonstrated that, whatever the distribution of the LR test statistic, its tail probabilities are bounded above by those of the χ^2 distribution with degrees of freedom equal to the full number of restricted parameters (three in the above example).

`xtmixed` uses this reference distribution, the χ^2 with full degrees of freedom, to produce a conservative test and places a note in the output labeling the test as such. Since the displayed significance level is an upper bound, rejection of the null hypothesis based on the reported level would imply rejection on the basis of the actual level.

❑ Technical Note

It may seem that `xtmixed` does not follow Stata's standard syntax for multipleequation models, but it does. In example 2, we typed

```
. xtmixed weight week || id:
```

but we could have used the standard multi-equation syntax:

```
. xtmixed (weight week) (id:)
```

`xtmixed` will understand either and produce the same results. We prefer the syntax using || because it better emphasizes the nested structure of the levels.

❑

Saved Results

xtmixed saves the following in e():

Scalars

e(N)	number of observations	e(chi2)	χ^2
e(k)	number of parameters	e(p)	p-value for χ^2
e(k_f)	number of FE parameters	e(ll_c)	log-likelihood, comparison model
e(k_r)	number of RE parameters	e(chi2_c)	χ^2, comparison model
e(k_rs)	number of std. deviations	e(df_c)	degrees of freedom, comparison model
e(k_rc)	number of correlations	e(p_c)	p-value, comparison model
e(df_m)	model degrees of freedom	e(converged)	1 if converged, 0 otherwise
e(ll)	log (restricted)-likelihood	e(rc)	return code

Macros

e(cmd)	xtmixed	e(chi2type)	Wald, type of model χ^2
e(cmdline)	command as typed	e(opt)	type of optimization
e(title)	title in estimation output	e(ml_method)	type of ml method
e(depvar)	name of dependent variable	e(technique)	maximization technique
e(method)	ML or REML	e(crittype)	optimization criterion
e(ivars)	grouping variables	e(properties)	b V
e(redim)	random-effects dimensions	e(estat_cmd)	program used to implement estat
e(vartypes)	variance-structure types	e(predict)	program used to implement predict
e(revars)	random-effects covariates		

Matrices

e(b)	coefficient vector	e(V)	variance–covariance matrix of the estimator
e(N_g)	group counts		
e(g_min)	group size minimums	e(g_avg)	group size averages
e(g_max)	group size maximums		

Functions

e(sample)	marks estimation sample

Methods and Formulas

xtmixed is implemented as an ado-file.

As given by (1), we have the linear mixed model

$$\mathbf{y} = \mathbf{X}\boldsymbol{\beta} + \mathbf{Z}\mathbf{u} + \boldsymbol{\epsilon}$$

where $\mathbf{y}$ is the $n \times 1$ vector of responses, $\mathbf{X}$ is a $n \times p$ design/covariate matrix for the fixed effects $\boldsymbol{\beta}$, and $\mathbf{Z}$ is the $n \times q$ design/covariate matrix for the random effects $\mathbf{u}$. The $n \times 1$ vector of errors, $\boldsymbol{\epsilon}$, is assumed to be multivariate normal with mean zero and variance matrix $\sigma_{\epsilon}^2 \mathbf{I}_n$. We also assume that $\mathbf{u}$ has variance–covariance matrix $\mathbf{G}$ and that $\mathbf{u}$ is orthogonal to $\boldsymbol{\epsilon}$ so that

$$\mathrm{Var}\begin{bmatrix} \mathbf{u} \\ \boldsymbol{\epsilon} \end{bmatrix} = \begin{bmatrix} \mathbf{G} & \mathbf{0} \\ \mathbf{0} & \sigma_{\epsilon}^2 \mathbf{I}_n \end{bmatrix}$$

Considering the combined error term $\mathbf{Z}\mathbf{u} + \boldsymbol{\epsilon}$, we see that $\mathbf{y}$ is multivariate normal with mean $\mathbf{X}\boldsymbol{\beta}$ and $n \times n$ variance–covariance matrix

$$\mathbf{V} = \mathbf{Z}\mathbf{G}\mathbf{Z}' + \sigma_{\epsilon}^2 \mathbf{I}_n$$

Defining θ as the vector of unique elements of $\mathbf{G}$ results in the log likelihood

$$L(\boldsymbol{\beta}, \boldsymbol{\theta}, \sigma_\epsilon^2) = -\frac{1}{2} \left\{ n \log(2\pi) + \log |\mathbf{V}| + (\mathbf{y} - \mathbf{X}\boldsymbol{\beta})' \mathbf{V}^{-1} (\mathbf{y} - \mathbf{X}\boldsymbol{\beta}) \right\} \tag{8}$$

which is maximized as a function of $\boldsymbol{\beta}$, $\boldsymbol{\theta}$, and σ_ϵ^2. As explained in chapter 6 of Searle, Casella, and McCulloch (1992), considering instead the likelihood of a set of linear contrasts, $\mathbf{Ky}$, that do not depend on $\boldsymbol{\beta}$ results in the restricted log likelihood

$$L_R(\boldsymbol{\beta}, \boldsymbol{\theta}, \sigma_\epsilon^2) = L(\boldsymbol{\beta}, \boldsymbol{\theta}, \sigma_\epsilon^2) - \frac{1}{2} \log \left| \mathbf{X}' \mathbf{V}^{-1} \mathbf{X} \right| \tag{9}$$

Given the high dimension of $\mathbf{V}$, however, the log-likelihood and restricted log-likelihood criteria are not usually computed by brute-force application of the above expressions. Instead, you can simplify the problem by subdividing the data into independent panels (and subpanels if possible) and using matrix decomposition methods on the smaller matrices that result from treating each panel one at time.

Consider the one-level model described previously in (2)

$$\mathbf{y}_i = \mathbf{X}_i \boldsymbol{\beta} + \mathbf{Z}_i \mathbf{u}_i + \boldsymbol{\epsilon}_i$$

for $i = 1, \dots, M$ panels with panel i containing n_i observations, with $\mathrm{Var}(\mathbf{u}_i) = \boldsymbol{\Sigma}$, a $q \times q$ matrix.

Efficient methods for computing (8) and (9) are given in chapter 2 of Pinheiro and Bates (2000). Namely, for the one-level model, define $\boldsymbol{\Delta}$ to be the Cholesky factor of $\sigma_\epsilon^2 \boldsymbol{\Sigma}^{-1}$, such that $\sigma_\epsilon^2 \boldsymbol{\Sigma}^{-1} = \boldsymbol{\Delta}' \boldsymbol{\Delta}$. For $i = 1, \dots, M$, decompose

$$\begin{bmatrix} \mathbf{Z}_i \\ \boldsymbol{\Delta} \end{bmatrix} = \mathbf{Q}_i \begin{bmatrix} \mathbf{R}_{11i} \\ \mathbf{0} \end{bmatrix}$$

using an orthogonal-triangular (QR) decomposition, with $\mathbf{Q}_i$ a $(n_i + q)$-square matrix and $\mathbf{R}_{11i}$ a q-square matrix. We then apply $\mathbf{Q}_i$ as follows

$$\begin{bmatrix} \mathbf{R}_{10i} \\ \mathbf{R}_{00i} \end{bmatrix} = \mathbf{Q}_i' \begin{bmatrix} \mathbf{X}_i \\ \mathbf{0} \end{bmatrix}; \qquad \begin{bmatrix} \mathbf{c}_{1i} \\ \mathbf{c}_{0i} \end{bmatrix} = \mathbf{Q}_i' \begin{bmatrix} \mathbf{y}_i \\ \mathbf{0} \end{bmatrix}$$

stack the $\mathbf{R}_{00i}$ and $\mathbf{c}_{0i}$ matrices, and perform the additional QR decomposition

$$\begin{bmatrix} \mathbf{R}_{001} & \mathbf{c}_{01} \\ \vdots & \vdots \\ \mathbf{R}_{00M} & \mathbf{c}_{0M} \end{bmatrix} = \mathbf{Q}_0 \begin{bmatrix} \mathbf{R}_{00} & \mathbf{c}_0 \\ \mathbf{0} & \mathbf{c}_1 \end{bmatrix}$$

Pinheiro and Bates (2000) show that ML estimates of $\boldsymbol{\beta}$, σ_ϵ^2, and $\boldsymbol{\Delta}$ (the unique elements of $\boldsymbol{\Delta}$, that is) are obtained by maximizing the profile log-likelihood (profiled in $\boldsymbol{\Delta}$)

$$L(\boldsymbol{\Delta}) = \frac{n}{2} \left\{ \log n - \log(2\pi) - 1 \right\} - n \log \|\mathbf{c}_1\| + \sum_{i=1}^{M} \log \left| \frac{\det(\boldsymbol{\Delta})}{\det(\mathbf{R}_{11i})} \right| \tag{10}$$

where $\| \cdot \|$ denotes the 2-norm, and following this maximization with

$$\widehat{\boldsymbol{\beta}} = \mathbf{R}_{00}^{-1} \mathbf{c}_0; \qquad \widehat{\sigma}_\epsilon^2 = n^{-1} \|\mathbf{c}_1\|^2 \tag{11}$$

REML estimates are obtained by maximizing

$$L_R(\boldsymbol{\Delta}) = \frac{n-p}{2} \left\{ \log(n-p) - \log(2\pi) - 1 \right\} - (n-p)\log\|\mathbf{c}_1\|$$
$$- \log|\det(\mathbf{R}_{00})| + \sum_{i=1}^{M} \log\left| \frac{\det(\boldsymbol{\Delta})}{\det(\mathbf{R}_{11i})} \right| \tag{12}$$

followed by

$$\widehat{\boldsymbol{\beta}} = \mathbf{R}_{00}^{-1}\mathbf{c}_0; \quad \widehat{\sigma}_\epsilon^2 = (n-p)^{-1}\|\mathbf{c}_1\|^2$$

For numerical stability, maximization of (10) and (12) is not performed with respect to the unique elements of $\boldsymbol{\Delta}$ but instead with respect to the unique elements of the matrix logarithm of $\boldsymbol{\Sigma}/\sigma_\epsilon^2$; define $\boldsymbol{\gamma}$ to be the vector containing these elements.

Once maximization with respect to $\boldsymbol{\gamma}$ is completed, $(\boldsymbol{\gamma}, \sigma_\epsilon^2)$ is reparameterized to $\{\boldsymbol{\alpha}, \log(\sigma_\epsilon)\}$, where $\boldsymbol{\alpha}$ is a vector containing the unique elements of $\boldsymbol{\Sigma}$, expressed as logarithms of standard deviations for the diagonal elements and hyperbolic arctangents of the correlations for off-diagonal elements. This last step is necessary to (a) obtain a joint variance–covariance estimate of the elements of $\boldsymbol{\Sigma}$ and σ_ϵ^2; (b) obtain a parameterization under which parameter estimates can be interpreted individually, rather than as elements of a matrix logarithm; and (c) parameterize these elements such that their ranges each encompass the entire real line.

Obtaining a joint variance–covariance matrix for the estimated $\{\boldsymbol{\alpha}, \log(\sigma_\epsilon)\}$ requires the evaluation of the log likelihood (or log-restricted likelihood) with only $\boldsymbol{\beta}$ profiled out. For ML, we have

$$L^*\{\boldsymbol{\alpha}, \log(\sigma_\epsilon)\} = L\{\boldsymbol{\Delta}(\boldsymbol{\alpha}, \sigma_\epsilon^2), \sigma_\epsilon^2\}$$
$$= -\frac{n}{2}\log(2\pi\sigma_\epsilon^2) - \frac{\|\mathbf{c}_1\|^2}{2\sigma_\epsilon^2} + \sum_{i=1}^{M} \log\left| \frac{\det(\boldsymbol{\Delta})}{\det(\mathbf{R}_{11i})} \right|$$

with the analogous expression for REML.

The variance–covariance matrix of $\widehat{\boldsymbol{\beta}}$ is estimated as

$$\widehat{\mathrm{Var}}(\widehat{\boldsymbol{\beta}}) = \widehat{\sigma}_\epsilon^2 \mathbf{R}_{00}^{-1} \left(\mathbf{R}_{00}^{-1}\right)'$$

but this does not mean that $\widehat{\mathrm{Var}}(\widehat{\boldsymbol{\beta}})$ is identical under both ML and REML since $\mathbf{R}_{00}$ depends on $\boldsymbol{\Delta}$. Since $\widehat{\boldsymbol{\beta}}$ is asymptotically uncorrelated with $\{\widehat{\boldsymbol{\alpha}}, \log(\widehat{\sigma}_\epsilon)\}$, the covariance of $\widehat{\boldsymbol{\beta}}$ with the other estimated parameters is treated as zero.

Parameter estimates are stored in e(b) as $\{\widehat{\boldsymbol{\beta}}, \widehat{\boldsymbol{\alpha}}, \log(\widehat{\sigma}_\epsilon)\}$, with the corresponding (blocked diagonal) variance–covariance matrix stored in e(V). Parameter estimates can be displayed in this metric by specifying option estmetric. However, in xtmixed output, variance components are most often displayed either as variances and covariances or as standard deviations and correlations.

EM iterations are derived by considering the $\mathbf{u}_i$ in (2) as missing data. Here we describe the procedure for maximizing the log likelihood via EM; the procedure for maximizing the restricted log likelihood is similar. The log likelihood for the full data $(\mathbf{y}, \mathbf{u})$ is

$$L_F(\boldsymbol{\beta}, \boldsymbol{\Sigma}, \sigma_\epsilon^2) = \sum_{i=1}^{M} \left\{ \log f_1(\mathbf{y}_i|\mathbf{u}_i, \boldsymbol{\beta}, \sigma_\epsilon^2) + \log f_2(\mathbf{u}_i|\boldsymbol{\Sigma}) \right\}$$

where $f_1()$ is the density function for multivariate normal with mean $\mathbf{X}_i\boldsymbol{\beta} + \mathbf{Z}_i\mathbf{u}_i$ and variance $\sigma_\epsilon^2\mathbf{I}_{n_i}$, and $f_2()$ is the density for multivariate normal with mean $\mathbf{0}$ and $q \times q$ covariance matrix $\boldsymbol{\Sigma}$. As before, we can profile $\boldsymbol{\beta}$ and σ_ϵ^2 out of the optimization, yielding the following EM iterative procedure:

1. For the current iterated value of $\boldsymbol{\Sigma}^{(t)}$, fix $\widehat{\boldsymbol{\beta}} = \widehat{\boldsymbol{\beta}}(\boldsymbol{\Sigma}^{(t)})$ and $\widehat{\sigma}_\epsilon^2 = \widehat{\sigma}_\epsilon^2(\boldsymbol{\Sigma}^{(t)})$ according to (11).

2. E-step: calculate

$$D(\boldsymbol{\Sigma}) \equiv E\left\{L_F(\widehat{\boldsymbol{\beta}}, \boldsymbol{\Sigma}, \widehat{\sigma}_\epsilon^2)|\mathbf{y}\right\}$$

$$= C - \frac{M}{2}\log\det(\boldsymbol{\Sigma}) - \frac{1}{2}\sum_{i=1}^{M}E\left(\mathbf{u}_i'\boldsymbol{\Sigma}^{-1}\mathbf{u}_i|\mathbf{y}\right)$$

where C is a constant that does not depend on $\boldsymbol{\Sigma}$, and the expected value of the quadratic form $\mathbf{u}_i'\boldsymbol{\Sigma}^{-1}\mathbf{u}_i$ is taken with respect to the conditional density $f(\mathbf{u}_i|\mathbf{y}, \widehat{\boldsymbol{\beta}}, \boldsymbol{\Sigma}^{(t)}, \widehat{\sigma}_\epsilon^2)$.

3. M-step: Maximize $D(\boldsymbol{\Sigma})$ to produce $\boldsymbol{\Sigma}^{(t+1)}$.

For general, symmetric $\boldsymbol{\Sigma}$, the maximizer of $D(\boldsymbol{\Sigma})$ can be derived explicitly, making EM iterations quite fast.

For extensions to two or more nested levels of random effects, see Bates and Pinheiro (1998).

Acknowledgments

We thank Badi Baltagi, Department of Economics, Syracuse University, and Ray Carroll, Department of Statistics, Texas A&M University, for providing us with the datasets used in this entry.

References

Andrews, M., T. Schank, and R. Upward. 2006. Practical fixed-effects estimation methods for the three-way error-components model. *Stata Journal* 6: 461–481.

Baltagi, B. H., S. H. Song, and B. C. Jung. 2001. The unbalanced nested error component regression model. *Journal of Econometrics* 101: 357–381.

Bates, D. M., and J. C. Pinheiro. 1998. Computational methods for multilevel models. *Technical Memorandum BL0112140-980226-01TM*. Murray Hill, NJ: Bell Labs, Lucent Technologies.

Dempster, A. P., N. M. Laird, and D. B. Rubin. 1977. Maximum likelihood from incomplete data via the EM algorithm. *Journal of the Royal Statistical Society, Series B* 39: 1–22.

Diggle, P. J., P. Heagerty, K.-Y. Liang, and S. L. Zeger. 2002. *Analysis of Longitudinal Data*. 2nd ed. Oxford: Oxford University Press.

Gutierrez, R. G., S. L. Carter, and D. M. Drukker. 2001. sg160: On boundary-value likelihood-ratio tests. *Stata Technical Bulletin* 60: 15–18. Reprinted in *Stata Technical Bulletin Reprints*, vol. 10, pp. 269–273.

Harville, D. A. 1977. Maximum likelihood approaches to variance component estimation and to related problems. *Journal of the American Statistical Association* 72: 320–340.

Henderson, C. R. 1953. Estimation of variance and covariance components. *Biometrics* 9: 226–252.

Hocking, R. R. 1985. *The Analysis of Linear Models*. Monterey, CA: Brooks/Cole.

Laird, N. M., and J. H. Ware. 1982. Random-effects models for longitudinal data. *Biometrics* 38: 963–974.

LaMotte, L. R. 1973. Quadratic estimation of variance components. *Biometrics* 29: 311–330.

Marchenko, Y. 2006. Estimating variance components in Stata. *Stata Journal* 6: 1–21.

McCulloch, C. E., and S. R. Searle. 2001. *Generalized, Linear, and Mixed Models.* New York: Wiley.

McLachlan, G. J., and K. E. Basford. 1988. *Mixture Models.* New York: Dekker.

Munnell, A. 1990. Why has productivity growth declined? Productivity and public investment. *New England Economic Review* Jan./Feb.: 3–22.

Pinheiro, J. C., and D. M. Bates. 2000. *Mixed-Effects Models in S and S-PLUS.* New York: Springer.

Rabe-Hesketh, S., and A. Skrondal. 2006. *Multilevel and Longitudinal Modeling Using Stata.* College Station, TX: Stata Press.

Rao, C. R. 1973. *Linear Statistical Inference and Its Applications.* 2nd ed. New York: Wiley.

Raudenbush, S. W., and A. S. Bryk. 2002. *Hierarchical Linear Models: Applications and Data Analysis Methods.* 2nd ed. Thousand Oaks, CA: Sage.

Ruppert, D., M. P. Wand, and R. J. Carroll. 2003. *Semiparametric Regression.* Cambridge: Cambridge University Press.

Searle, S. R. 1989. Charles Roy Henderson 1911–1989. *Biometrics* 45: 1333–1335.

Searle, S. R., G. Casella, and C. E. McCulloch. 1992. *Variance Components.* New York: Wiley.

Self, S. G., and K.-Y. Liang. 1987. Asymptotic properties of maximum likelihood estimators and likelihood ratio tests under nonstandard conditions. *Journal of the American Statistical Association* 82: 605–610.

Skrondal, A., and S. Rabe-Hesketh. 2004. *Generalized Latent Variable Modeling: Multilevel, Longitudinal and Structural Equation Models.* Boca Raton, FL: Chapman & Hall/CRC Press.

Stram, D. O., and J. W. Lee. 1994. Variance components testing in the longitudinal mixed effects model. *Biometrics* 50: 1171–1177.

Thompson, W. A. 1962. The problem of negative estimates of variance components. *Annals of Mathematical Statistics* 33: 273–289.

Verbeke, G., and G. Molenberghs. 2000. *Linear Mixed Models for Longitudinal Data.* New York: Springer.

Also See

[XT] **xtmixed postestimation** — Postestimation tools for xtmixed

[XT] **xtmelogit** — Multilevel mixed-effects logistic regression

[XT] **xtmepoisson** — Multilevel mixed-effects Poisson regression

[XT] **xtreg** — Fixed-, between-, and random-effects, and population-averaged linear models

[XT] **xtrc** — Random-coefficients model

[XT] **xtgee** — Fit population-averaged panel-data models by using GEE

[U] **20 Estimation and postestimation commands**

Title

> **xtmixed postestimation** — Postestimation tools for xtmixed

Description

The following postestimation commands are of special interest after `xtmixed`:

command	description
estat group	summarize the composition of the nested groups
estat recovariance	display the estimated random-effects covariance matrix (or matrices)

For information about these commands, see below.

The following standard postestimation commands are also available:

command	description
adjust	adjusted predictions of $x\beta$
estat	AIC, BIC, VCE, and estimation sample summary
estimates	cataloging estimation results
lincom	point estimates, standard errors, testing, and inference for linear combinations of coefficients
lrtest	likelihood-ratio test
mfx	marginal effects or elasticities
nlcom	point estimates, standard errors, testing, and inference for nonlinear combinations of coefficients
predict	predicted probabilities, estimated linear predictor and its standard error
predictnl	point estimates, standard errors, testing, and inference for generalized predictions
test	Wald tests for simple and composite linear hypotheses
testnl	Wald tests of nonlinear hypotheses

See the corresponding entries in the *Stata Base Reference Manual* for details.

Special-interest postestimation commands

`estat group` reports number of groups, and minimum, average, and maximum group sizes for each level of the model. Model levels are identified by the corresponding group variable in the data. Since groups are treated as nested, the information in this summary may differ from what you would get if you `tabulate` each group variable individually.

`estat recovariance` displays the estimated variance–covariance matrix of the random effects for each level in the model. Random effects can be either random intercepts, in which case the corresponding rows and columns of the matrix are labeled as _cons, or random coefficients, in which case the label is the name of the associated variable in the data.

Syntax for predict

Syntax for obtaining best linear unbiased predictions (BLUPs) *of random effects*

> predict $\big[$ *type* $\big]$ $\big\{$ *stub** | *newvarlist* $\big\}$ $\big[$ *if* $\big]$ $\big[$ *in* $\big]$, <u>ref</u>fects $\big[$ <u>l</u>evel(*levelvar*)$\big]$

Syntax for obtaining other predictions

> predict $\big[$ *type* $\big]$ *newvar* $\big[$ *if* $\big]$ $\big[$ *in* $\big]$ $\big[$, *statistic* <u>l</u>evel(*levelvar*) $\big]$

statistic	description
Main	
xb	linear prediction for the *fixed* portion of the model only; the default
stdp	standard error of the fixed-portion linear prediction
<u>fit</u>ted	fitted values, fixed-portion linear prediction plus contributions based on predicted random effects
<u>res</u>iduals	residuals, response minus fitted values
<u>rstan</u>dard	standardized residuals

Statistics are available both in and out of sample; type predict ... if e(sample) ... if wanted only for the estimation sample.

Options for predict

 ⌐ Main └──

xb, the default, calculates the linear prediction $\mathbf{x}\beta$ based on the estimated fixed effects (coefficients) in the model. This is equivalent to fixing all random effects in the model to their theoretical mean value of zero.

stdp calculates the standard error of the linear predictor $\mathbf{x}\beta$.

level(*levelvar*) specifies the level in the model at which predictions involving random effects are to be obtained; see the options below for the specifics. *levelvar* is the name of the model level and is either the name of the variable describing the grouping at that level or _all, a special designation for a group comprising all the estimation data.

reffects calculates best linear unbiased predictions (BLUPs) of the random effects. By default, BLUPs for all random effects in the model are calculated. However, if option level(*levelvar*) is specified, then BLUPs for only level *levelvar* in the model are calculated. For example, if classes are nested within schools, then typing

> . predict b*, reffects level(school)

would produce BLUPs at the school level. You must specify q new variables, where q is the number of random-effects terms in the model (or level). However, it is much easier to just specify *stub** and let Stata name the variables *stub*1 ... *stub*q for you.

fitted calculates fitted values, which are equal to the fixed-portion linear predictor *plus* contributions based on predicted random effects, or in mixed-model notation, $\mathbf{x}\beta + \mathbf{Zu}$. By default, the fitted values take into account random effects from all levels in the model; however, if option level(*levelvar*) is specified, the fitted values are fitted beginning with the topmost level down to and including level *levelvar*. For example, if classes are nested within schools, then typing

> . predict yhat_school, fitted level(school)

would produce school-level predictions. That is, the predictions would incorporate school-specific random effects but not those for each class nested within each school.

residuals calculates residuals, equal to the responses minus fitted values. By default, the fitted values take into account random effects from all levels in the model; however, if option level(*levelvar*) is specified, the fitted values are fitted beginning at the topmost level down to and including level *levelvar*.

rstandard calculates standardized residuals, equal to the residuals described above, divided by the estimated residual standard deviation (listed as "sd(Residual)" in xtmixed output).

Syntax for estat group

    estat group

Syntax for estat recovariance

    estat recovariance [, level(*levelvar*) correlation *matlist_options*]

Options for estat recovariance

level(*levelvar*) specifies the level in the model for which the random-effects covariance matrix is to be displayed and returned in r(cov). By default, the covariance matrices for all levels in the model are displayed. *levelvar* is the name of the model level and is either the name of variable describing the grouping at that level or _all, a special designation for a group comprising all the estimation data.

correlation displays the covariance matrix as a correlation matrix and returns the correlation matrix in r(corr).

matlist_options are style and formatting options that control how the matrix (or matrices) are displayed; see [P] **matlist** for a list of what is available.

Remarks

Various predictions, statistics, and diagnostic measures are available after fitting a mixed model using xtmixed. For the most part, calculation centers around obtaining best linear unbiased predictors (BLUPs) of the random effects. Random effects are not estimated when the model is fitted but instead need to be predicted after estimation.

▷ Example 1

In example 3 of [XT] **xtmixed**, we modeled the weights of 48 pigs measured on nine successive weeks as

$$\text{weight}_{ij} = \beta_0 + \beta_1 \text{week}_{ij} + u_{0i} + u_{1i}\text{week}_{ij} + \epsilon_{ij} \tag{1}$$

for $i = 1, \ldots, 48$, $j = 1, \ldots, 9$, $\epsilon_{ij} \sim N(0, \sigma_\epsilon^2)$, and u_{0i} and u_{1i} normally distributed with mean zero and variance–covariance matrix

$$\Sigma = \text{Var}\begin{bmatrix} u_{0i} \\ u_{1i} \end{bmatrix} = \begin{bmatrix} \sigma_{u0}^2 & \sigma_{01} \\ \sigma_{01} & \sigma_{u1}^2 \end{bmatrix}$$

```
. use http://www.statapress.com/data/r10/pig
(Longitudinal analysis of pig weights)

. xtmixed weight week || id: week, covariance(unstructured) variance
  (output omitted )
```

```
Mixed-effects REML regression                 Number of obs      =        432
Group variable: id                            Number of groups   =         48

                                              Obs per group: min =          9
                                                             avg =        9.0
                                                             max =          9

                                              Wald chi2(1)       =    4552.31
Log restricted-likelihood = -870.43562        Prob > chi2        =     0.0000
```

weight	Coef.	Std. Err.	z	P>|z|	[95% Conf. Interval]	
week	6.209896	.0920382	67.47	0.000	6.029504	6.390287
_cons	19.35561	.4038677	47.93	0.000	18.56405	20.14718

Random-effects Parameters	Estimate	Std. Err.	[95% Conf. Interval]	
id: Unstructured				
var(week)	.3799957	.0839023	.2465103	.5857635
var(_cons)	6.986465	1.616357	4.439432	10.99481
cov(week,_cons)	-.1033632	.2627309	-.6183063	.41158
var(Residual)	1.596829	.1231981	1.372736	1.857506

```
LR test vs. linear regression:       chi2(3) =   766.07   Prob > chi2 = 0.0000
Note: LR test is conservative and provided only for reference.
```

Rather than see the estimated variance components listed as above, we can instead see them in matrix form; i.e., we can see $\widehat{\Sigma}$

```
. estat recovariance
Random-effects covariance matrix for level id
```

	week	_cons
week	.3799957	
_cons	-.1033632	6.986465

or we can see $\widehat{\Sigma}$ as a correlation matrix

```
. estat recovariance, correlation
Random-effects correlation matrix for level id
```

	week	_cons
week	1	
_cons	-.0634377	1

We can also obtain BLUPs of the pig-level random effects (u_{0i} and u_{1i}). We need to specify the variables to be created in the order u1 u0 since that is the order in which the corresponding variance components are listed in the output (week _cons). We obtain the predictions and list them for the first 10 pigs.

```
. predict u1 u0, reffects
. by id, sort: generate tolist = (_n==1)
```

```
. list id u0 u1 if id <=10 & tolist
```

	id	u0	u1
1.	1	.2402243	-.3964052
10.	2	-1.591519	.5113588
19.	3	-3.537457	.321844
28.	4	1.974493	-.7738019
37.	5	1.308741	-.9259342
46.	6	-1.146433	-.5451292
55.	7	-2.597208	.0405007
64.	8	-1.138727	-.1694532
73.	9	-3.192426	-.7363427
82.	10	1.163175	.0026334

If you forget how to order your variables in predict, or if you use predict *stub**, remember that predict labels the generated variables for you to avoid confusion.

```
. describe u0 u1
```

variable name	storage type	display format	value label	variable label
u0	float	%9.0g		BLUP r.e. for id: _cons
u1	float	%9.0g		BLUP r.e. for id: week

Examining (1), we see that, within each pig, the successive weight measurements are modeled as simple linear regression with intercept $\beta_0 + u_{i0}$ and slope $\beta_1 + u_{i1}$. We can generate estimates of the pig-level intercepts and slopes with

```
. gen intercept = _b[_cons] + u0
. gen slope = _b[week] + u1
. list id intercept slope if id<=10 & tolist
```

	id	intercept	slope
1.	1	19.59584	5.81349
10.	2	17.7641	6.721255
19.	3	15.81816	6.53174
28.	4	21.33011	5.436094
37.	5	20.66435	5.283962
46.	6	18.20918	5.664767
55.	7	16.75841	6.250397
64.	8	18.21689	6.040442
73.	9	16.16319	5.473553
82.	10	20.51879	6.212529

Thus we can plot estimated regression lines for each of the pigs. Equivalently, we can just plot the fitted values since they are based on both the fixed and random effects:

```
. predict fitweight, fitted
. twoway connected fitweight week if id<=10, connect(L)
```

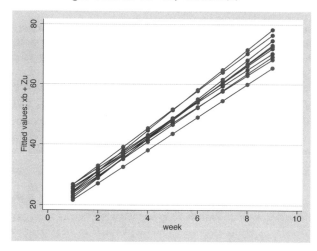

We can also generate standardized residuals and see if they follow a standard normal distribution, as they should in any good-fitting model:

```
. predict rs, rstandard
. sum rs
```

Variable	Obs	Mean	Std. Dev.	Min	Max
rs	432	-4.42e-10	.8925255	-3.620188	2.993914

```
. qnorm rs
```

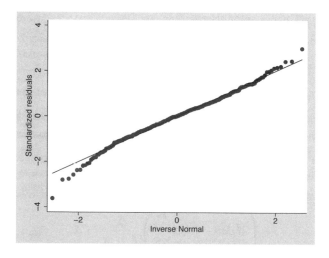

▷ Example 2

In example 4 of [XT] **xtmixed**, we estimated a Cobb–Douglas production function with random intercepts at the region level and at the state-within-region level:

$$\mathbf{y}_{ij} = \mathbf{X}_{ij}\boldsymbol{\beta} + u_i^{(1)} + u_{ij}^{(2)} + \epsilon_{ij}$$

```
. use http://www.statapress.com/data/r10/productivity, clear
(Public Capital Productivity)
. xtmixed gsp private emp hwy water other unemp || region: || state:
(output omitted )
```

We can use `estat group` to see how the data are broken down by state and region

```
. estat group
```

	No. of	Observations per Group		
Group Variable	Groups	Minimum	Average	Maximum
region	9	51	90.7	136
state	48	17	17.0	17

and we are reminded that we have balanced productivity data for 17 years for each state.

We can use `predict, fitted` to get the fitted values

$$\widehat{\mathbf{y}}_{ij} = \mathbf{X}_{ij}\widehat{\boldsymbol{\beta}} + \widehat{u}_i^{(1)} + \widehat{u}_{ij}^{(2)}$$

but if we instead want fitted values at the region level, i.e.,

$$\widehat{\mathbf{y}}_{ij} = \mathbf{X}_{ij}\widehat{\boldsymbol{\beta}} + \widehat{u}_i^{(1)}$$

we need to use option `level()`;

```
. predict gsp_region, fitted level(region)
. list gsp gsp_region in 1/10
```

	gsp	gsp_re~n
1.	10.25478	10.40034
2.	10.2879	10.4184
3.	10.35147	10.46851
4.	10.41721	10.52158
5.	10.42671	10.54457
6.	10.4224	10.53043
7.	10.4847	10.60275
8.	10.53111	10.64228
9.	10.59573	10.70008
10.	10.62082	10.72299

◁

❑ Technical Note

Out-of-sample predictions are permitted after `xtmixed`, but if these predictions involve BLUPs of random effects, the integrity of the estimation data must be preserved. If the estimation data have changed since the mixed model was fitted, `predict` will be unable to obtain predicted random effects that are appropriate for the fitted model and will give an error. Thus, to obtain out-of-sample predictions that contain random-effects terms, be sure that the data for these predictions are in observations that augment the estimation data.

❑

Saved Results

`estat recovariance` saves the last-displayed random-effects covariance matrix in `r(cov)` or in `r(corr)` if it is displayed as a correlation matrix.

Methods and Formulas

Following the notation defined in the *Methods and Formulas* section of [XT] **xtmixed**, best linear unbiased predictions (BLUPs) of random effects **u** are obtained as

$$\widetilde{\mathbf{u}} = \widetilde{\mathbf{G}} \mathbf{Z}' \widetilde{\mathbf{V}}^{-1} \left(\mathbf{y} - \mathbf{X}\widehat{\beta} \right)$$

where $\widetilde{\mathbf{G}}$ and $\widetilde{\mathbf{V}}$ are $\mathbf{G}$ and $\mathbf{V}$ with ML or REML estimates of the variance components plugged in. Fitted values are given by $\mathbf{X}\widehat{\beta} + \mathbf{Z}\widetilde{\mathbf{u}}$, residuals as $\mathbf{y} - \mathbf{X}\widehat{\beta} - \mathbf{Z}\widetilde{\mathbf{u}}$, and standardized residuals as residuals divided by $\widehat{\sigma}_\epsilon$.

If option `level(levelvar)` is specified, fitted values, residuals, and standardized residuals consider only those random-effects terms up to and including level *levelvar* in the model.

Also See

[XT] **xtmixed** — Multilevel mixed-effects linear regression

[U] **20 Estimation and postestimation commands**

Title

> **xtnbreg** — Fixed-effects, random-effects, & population-averaged negative binomial models

Syntax

Random-effects (RE) and conditional fixed-effects (FE) overdispersion models

> xtnbreg *depvar* [*indepvars*] [*if*] [*in*] [*weight*] [, [re | fe] *RE/FE_options*]

Population-averaged (PA) model

> xtnbreg *depvar* [*indepvars*] [*if*] [*in*] [*weight*] , pa [*PA_options*]

RE/FE_options	description
Model	
<u>nocon</u>stant	suppress constant term; not available with fe
re	use random-effects estimator; the default
fe	use fixed-effects estimator
<u>exp</u>osure(*varname*)	include ln(*varname*) in model with coefficient constrained to 1
<u>off</u>set(*varname*)	include *varname* in model with coefficient constrained to 1
<u>constra</u>ints(*constraints*)	apply specified linear constraints
<u>col</u>linear	keep collinear variables
SE	
vce(*vcetype*)	*vcetype* may be oim, <u>boot</u>strap, or <u>jack</u>knife
Reporting	
<u>level</u>(#)	set confidence level; default is level(95)
<u>irr</u>	report incidence-rate ratios
noskip	perform overall model test as a likelihood-ratio test
Max options	
maximize_options	control the maximization process; seldom used

PA_options	description
Model	
<u>nocon</u>stant	suppress constant term
pa	use population-averaged estimator
<u>exp</u>osure(*varname*)	include ln(*varname*) in model with coefficient constrained to 1
<u>off</u>set(*varname*)	include *varname* in model with coefficient constrained to 1
PA options	
<u>corr</u>(*correlation*)	within-group correlation structure
force	estimate even if observations unequally spaced in time

SE/Robust

vce(*vcetype*)	*vcetype* may be conventional, <u>r</u>obust, <u>boot</u>strap, or <u>jack</u>knife
nmp	use divisor $N - P$ instead of the default N
<u>sc</u>ale(*parm*)	overrides the default scale parameter; *parm* may be x2, dev, phi, or #

Reporting

<u>l</u>evel(#)	set confidence level; default is level(95)
<u>ir</u>r	report incidence-rate ratios

Opt options

optimize_options	control the optimization process; seldom used

correlation	description
<u>exch</u>angeable	exchangeable
<u>ind</u>ependent	independent
<u>uns</u>tructured	unstructured
<u>fix</u>ed *matname*	user-specified
ar #	autoregressive of order #
<u>stat</u>ionary #	stationary of order #
<u>non</u>stationary #	nonstationary of order #

A panel variable must be specified. For xtnbreg, pa, correlation structures other than exchangeable and independent require that a time variable also be specified. Use xtset; see [XT] **xtset**.

depvar and *indepvars* may contain time-series operators; see [U] **11.4.3 Time-series varlists**.

by, statsby, and xi are allowed; see [U] **11.1.10 Prefix commands**.

iweights, fweights, and pweights are allowed for the population-averaged model, and iweights are allowed in the random-effects and fixed-effects models; see [U] **11.1.6 weight**. Weights must be constant within panel.

See [U] **20 Estimation and postestimation commands** for more capabilities of estimation commands.

Description

xtnbreg fits random-effects overdispersion models, conditional fixed-effects overdispersion models, and population-averaged negative binomial models. Here "random effects" and "fixed effects" apply to the distribution of the dispersion parameter, not to the $x\beta$ term in the model. In the random-effects and fixed-effects overdispersion models, the dispersion is the same for all elements in the same group (i.e., elements with the same value of the panel variable). In the random-effects model, the dispersion varies randomly from group to group, such that the inverse of one plus the dispersion follows a $\text{Beta}(r, s)$ distribution. In the fixed-effects model, the dispersion parameter in a group can take on any value, since a conditional likelihood is used in which the dispersion parameter drops out of the estimation.

By default, the population-averaged model is an equal-correlation model; xtnbreg, pa assumes corr(exchangeable). See [XT] **xtgee** for details on this option to fit other population-averaged models.

Options for RE/FE models

Model

noconstant; see [XT] **estimation options**.

re requests the random-effects estimator, which is the default.

fe requests the conditional fixed-effects estimator.

exposure(*varname*), offset(*varname*), constraints(*constraints*), collinear; see [XT] **estimation options**.

SE

vce(*vcetype*) specifies the type of standard error reported, which includes types that are derived from asymptotic theory and that use bootstrap or jackknife methods; see [XT] *vce_options*.

Reporting

level(*#*); see [XT] **estimation options**.

irr reports exponentiated coefficients e^b rather than coefficients b. For the negative binomial model, exponentiated coefficients have the interpretation of incidence-rate ratios.

noskip; see [XT] **estimation options**.

Max options

maximize_options: difficult, technique(*algorithm_spec*), iterate(*#*), [no]log, trace, gradient, showstep, hessian, shownrtolerance, tolerance(*#*), ltolerance(*#*), gtolerance(*#*), nrtolerance(*#*), nonrtolerance, from(*init_specs*); see [R] **ml** and [R] **maximize**. These options are seldom used.

Options for PA model

Model

noconstant; see [XT] **estimation options**.

pa requests the population-averaged estimator.

exposure(*varname*), offset(*varname*); see [XT] **estimation options**.

PA options

corr(*correlation*), force; see [XT] **estimation options**.

SE/Robust

vce(*vcetype*) specifies the type of standard error reported, which includes types that are derived from asymptotic theory, that are robust to some kinds of misspecification, and that use bootstrap or jackknife methods; see [XT] *vce_options*.

vce(conventional), the default, uses the conventionally derived variance estimator for generalized least-squares regression.

nmp, scale(x2 | dev | phi | *#*); see [XT] *vce_options*.

level(#); see [XT] **estimation options**.

irr reports exponentiated coefficients e^b rather than coefficients b. For the negative binomial model, exponentiated coefficients have the interpretation of incidence-rate ratios.

optimize_options control the iterative optimization process. These options are seldom used.

iterate(#) specifies the maximum number of iterations. When the number of iterations equals #, the optimization stops and presents the current results, even if convergence has not been reached. The default is iterate(100).

tolerance(#) specifies the tolerance for the coefficient vector. When the relative change in the coefficient vector from one iteration to the next is less than or equal to #, the optimization process is stopped. tolerance(1e-6) is the default.

nolog suppresses display of the iteration log.

trace specifies that the current estimates be printed at each iteration.

Remarks

xtnbreg is a convenience command if you want the population-averaged model. Typing

        . xtnbreg ..., ... pa exposure(time)

is equivalent to typing

        . xtgee ..., ... family(nbinomial) link(log) corr(exchangeable) exposure(time)

See also [XT] **xtgee** for information about xtnbreg.

By default, or when re is specified, xtnbreg fits a maximum-likelihood random-effects overdispersion model.

▷ Example 1

You have (fictional) data on injury "incidents" incurred among 20 airlines in each of 4 years. (Incidents range from major injuries to exceedingly minor ones.) The government agency in charge of regulating airlines has run an experimental safety training program, and, in each of the years, some airlines have participated and some have not. You now wish to analyze whether the "incident" rate is affected by the program. You choose to estimate using random-effects negative binomial regression, as the dispersion might vary across the airlines for unidentified airline-specific reasons. Your measure of exposure is passenger miles for each airline in each year.

```
. use http://www.stata-press.com/data/r10/airacc

. xtnbreg i_cnt inprog, exposure(pmiles) irr
Fitting negative binomial (constant dispersion) model:
Iteration 0:   log likelihood = -293.57997
Iteration 1:   log likelihood = -293.57997
  (output omitted )
Fitting full model:
Iteration 0:   log likelihood = -295.72633
Iteration 1:   log likelihood = -270.49929  (not concave)
  (output omitted )
```

Random-effects negative binomial regression	Number of obs	=	80
Group variable: airline	Number of groups	=	20
Random effects u_i ~ Beta	Obs per group: min =		4
	avg =		4.0
	max =		4
	Wald chi2(1)	=	2.04
Log likelihood = -265.38202	Prob > chi2	=	0.1532

i_cnt	IRR	Std. Err.	z	P>|z|	[95% Conf. Interval]
inprog	.911673	.0590277	-1.43	0.153	.8030206 1.035027
pmiles	(exposure)				
/ln_r	4.794991	.951781			2.929535 6.660448
/ln_s	3.268052	.4709033			2.345098 4.191005
r	120.9033	115.0735			18.71892 780.9007
s	26.26013	12.36598			10.4343 66.08918

```
Likelihood-ratio test vs. pooled: chibar2(01) =    19.03 Prob>=chibar2 = 0.000
```

In the output above, the /ln_r and /ln_s lines refer to $\ln(r)$ and $\ln(s)$, where the inverse of one plus the dispersion is assumed to follow a Beta(r, s) distribution. The output also includes a likelihood-ratio test, which compares the panel estimator with the pooled estimator (i.e., a negative binomial estimator with constant dispersion).

You find that the incidence rate for accidents is not significantly different for participation in the program and that the panel estimator is significantly different from the pooled estimator.

We may alternatively fit a fixed-effects overdispersion model:

```
. xtnbreg i_cnt inprog, exposure(pmiles) irr fe nolog
```

Conditional FE negative binomial regression	Number of obs	=	80
Group variable: airline	Number of groups	=	20
	Obs per group: min =		4
	avg =		4.0
	max =		4
	Wald chi2(1)	=	2.11
Log likelihood = -174.25143	Prob > chi2	=	0.1463

i_cnt	IRR	Std. Err.	z	P>|z|	[95% Conf. Interval]
inprog	.9062669	.0613917	-1.45	0.146	.793587 1.034946
pmiles	(exposure)				

◁

▷ Example 2

We rerun our previous example, but this time we fit a robust equal-correlation population-averaged model:

```
. xtnbreg i_cnt inprog, exposure(pmiles) irr vce(robust) pa
Iteration 1: tolerance = .02499392
Iteration 2: tolerance = .0000482
Iteration 3: tolerance = 2.929e-07
```

```
GEE population-averaged model              Number of obs      =        80
Group variable:                  airline   Number of groups   =        20
Link:                               log    Obs per group: min =         4
Family:            negative binomial(k=1)                 avg =       4.0
Correlation:                 exchangeable                 max =         4
                                           Wald chi2(1)       =      1.28
Scale parameter:                      1    Prob > chi2        =    0.2571
```
                    (Std. Err. adjusted for clustering on airline)

i_cnt	IRR	Semi-robust Std. Err.	z	P>|z|	[95% Conf. Interval]	
inprog	.927275	.0617857	-1.13	0.257	.8137513	1.056636
pmiles	(exposure)					

We compare this with a pooled estimator with clustered robust-variance estimates:

```
. nbreg i_cnt inprog, exposure(pmiles) vce(cluster airline) irr
Fitting Poisson model:
Iteration 0:   log pseudolikelihood = -293.57997
Iteration 1:   log pseudolikelihood = -293.57997
Fitting constant-only model:
Iteration 0:   log pseudolikelihood = -335.13615
Iteration 1:   log pseudolikelihood = -279.43327
Iteration 2:   log pseudolikelihood = -276.09296
Iteration 3:   log pseudolikelihood = -274.84036
Iteration 4:   log pseudolikelihood = -274.81076
Iteration 5:   log pseudolikelihood = -274.81075
Fitting full model:
Iteration 0:   log pseudolikelihood = -274.56985
Iteration 1:   log pseudolikelihood = -274.55077
Iteration 2:   log pseudolikelihood = -274.55077
```

```
Negative binomial regression               Number of obs      =        80
Dispersion          = mean                 Wald chi2(1)       =      0.60
Log pseudolikelihood = -274.55077          Prob > chi2        =    0.4369
```
                    (Std. Err. adjusted for 20 clusters in airline)

i_cnt	IRR	Robust Std. Err.	z	P>|z|	[95% Conf. Interval]	
inprog	.9429015	.0713091	-0.78	0.437	.8130032	1.093555
pmiles	(exposure)					
/lnalpha	-2.835089	.3351784			-3.492027	-2.178151
alpha	.0587133	.0196794			.0304391	.1132507

Likelihood-ratio test of alpha=0:   chibar2(01) =   38.06 Prob>=chibar2 = 0.000

◁

Saved Results

xtnbreg, re saves the following in e():

Scalars

e(N)	# of observations	e(s)	value of s in Beta(r, s)
e(N_g)	number of groups	e(k)	# of parameters
e(df_m)	model degrees of freedom	e(k_eq)	# of equations
e(ll)	log likelihood	e(k_eq_model)	# of equations in model Wald test
e(ll_0)	log likelihood, constant-only model	e(k_dv)	# of dependent variables
e(ll_c)	log likelihood, comparison model	e(p)	significance
e(g_max)	largest group size	e(rank)	rank of e(V)
e(g_min)	smallest group size	e(rank0)	rank of e(V) for constant-only model
e(g_avg)	average group size	e(ic)	# of iterations
e(chi2)	χ^2	e(rc)	return code
e(chi2_c)	χ^2 for comparison test	e(converged)	1 if converged, 0 otherwise
e(r)	value of r in Beta(r, s)		

Macros

e(cmd)	xtnbreg	e(method)	estimation method
e(cmd2)	xtn_re	e(distrib)	Beta; the distribution of the random effect
e(cmdline)	command as typed		
e(depvar)	name of dependent variable	e(vce)	*vcetype* specified in vce()
e(ivar)	variable denoting groups	e(vcetype)	title used to label Std. Err.
e(wtype)	weight type	e(opt)	type of optimization
e(wexp)	weight expression	e(ml_method)	type of ml method
e(title)	title in estimation output	e(user)	name of likelihood-evaluator program
e(offset)	offset	e(technique)	maximization technique
e(chi2type)	Wald or LR; type of model χ^2 test	e(crittype)	optimization criterion
e(chi2_ct)	Wald or LR; type of model χ^2 test corresponding to e(chi2_c)	e(properties)	b V
		e(predict)	program used to implement predict

Matrices

e(b)	coefficient vector	e(ilog)	iteration log
e(V)	variance–covariance matrix of the estimators	e(gradient)	gradient vector

Functions

e(sample)	marks estimation sample

(Continued on next page)

xtnbreg, fe saves the following in e():

Scalars

e(N)	number of observations	e(k)	# of parameters
e(N_g)	number of groups	e(k_eq)	# of equations
e(df_m)	model degrees of freedom	e(k_eq_model)	# of equations in model Wald test
e(ll)	log likelihood	e(k_dv)	# of dependent variables
e(ll_0)	log likelihood, constant-only model	e(p)	significance
e(g_max)	largest group size	e(rank)	rank of e(V)
e(g_min)	smallest group size	e(ic)	# of iterations
e(g_avg)	average group size	e(rc)	return code
e(r2_p)	pseudo R-squared	e(converged)	1 if converged, 0 otherwise
e(chi2)	χ^2		

Macros

e(cmd)	xtnbreg	e(method)	requested estimation method
e(cmd2)	xtn_re	e(vce)	*vcetype* specified in vce()
e(cmdline)	command as typed	e(vcetype)	title used to label Std. Err.
e(depvar)	name of dependent variable	e(opt)	type of optimization
e(ivar)	variable denoting groups	e(ml_method)	type of ml method
e(offset)	offset	e(user)	name of likelihood-evaluator program
e(wtype)	weight type	e(technique)	maximization technique
e(wexp)	weight expression	e(crittype)	optimization criterion
e(title)	title in estimation output	e(properties)	b V
e(chi2type)	LR; type of model χ^2 test	e(predict)	program used to implement predict

Matrices

e(b)	coefficient vector	e(ilog)	iteration log
e(V)	variance–covariance matrix of the estimators	e(gradient)	gradient vector

Functions

e(sample)	marks estimation sample

`xtnbreg, pa` saves the following in `e()`:

Scalars

`e(N)`	number of observations	`e(deviance)`	deviance
`e(N_g)`	number of groups	`e(chi2_dev)`	χ^2 test of deviance
`e(df_m)`	model degrees of freedom	`e(dispers)`	deviance dispersion
`e(g_max)`	largest group size	`e(chi2_dis)`	χ^2 test of deviance dispersion
`e(g_min)`	smallest group size	`e(tol)`	target tolerance
`e(g_avg)`	average group size	`e(dif)`	achieved tolerance
`e(chi2)`	χ^2	`e(phi)`	scale parameter
`e(df_pear)`	degrees of freedom for Pearson χ^2	`e(rc)`	return code

Macros

`e(cmd)`	xtgee	`e(scale)`	x2, dev, phi, or #; scale parameter
`e(cmd2)`	xtnbreg	`e(nbalpha)`	α
`e(cmdline)`	command as typed	`e(ivar)`	variable denoting groups
`e(depvar)`	name of dependent variable	`e(vce)`	*vcetype* specified in vce()
`e(family)`	negative binomial(k=1)	`e(vcetype)`	title used to label Std. Err.
`e(wtype)`	weight type	`e(chi2type)`	Wald; type of model χ^2 test
`e(wexp)`	weight expression	`e(offset)`	offset
`e(link)`	log; link function	`e(properties)`	b V
`e(corr)`	correlation structure	`e(predict)`	program used to implement predict
`e(crittype)`	optimization criterion		

Matrices

`e(b)`	coefficient vector	`e(V)`	variance–covariance matrix of the
`e(R)`	estimated working correlation matrix		estimators

Functions

`e(sample)`	marks estimation sample

Methods and Formulas

`xtnbreg` is implemented as an ado-file.

`xtnbreg, pa` reports the population-averaged results obtained by using `xtgee, family(nbreg)` `link(log)` to obtain estimates. See [XT] **xtgee** for details on the methods and formulas.

For the random-effects and fixed-effects overdispersion models, let y_{it} be the count for the tth observation in the ith group. We begin with the model $y_{it} \mid \gamma_{it} \sim \text{Poisson}(\gamma_{it})$, where $\gamma_{it} \mid \delta_i \sim \text{gamma}(\lambda_{it}, \delta_i)$ with $\lambda_{it} = \exp(\mathbf{x}_{it}\boldsymbol{\beta} + \text{offset}_{it})$ and δ_i is the dispersion parameter. This yields the model

$$\Pr(Y_{it} = y_{it} \mid \mathbf{x}_{it}, \delta_i) = \frac{\Gamma(\lambda_{it} + y_{it})}{\Gamma(\lambda_{it})\Gamma(y_{it} + 1)} \left(\frac{1}{1 + \delta_i}\right)^{\lambda_{it}} \left(\frac{\delta_i}{1 + \delta_i}\right)^{y_{it}}$$

(See Hausman, Hall, and Griliches [1984, equation 3.1, 922]; our δ is the inverse of their δ.) Looking at within-group effects only, we find that this specification yields a negative binomial model for the ith group with dispersion (variance divided by the mean) equal to $1 + \delta_i$, i.e., constant dispersion within group. This parameterization of the negative binomial model differs from the default parameterization of `nbreg`, which has dispersion equal to $1 + \alpha \exp(\mathbf{x}\boldsymbol{\beta} + \text{offset})$; see [R] **nbreg**.

For a random-effects overdispersion model, we allow δ_i to vary randomly across groups; namely, we assume that $1/(1 + \delta_i) \sim \text{Beta}(r, s)$. The joint probability of the counts for the ith group is

$$\Pr(Y_{i1} = y_{i1}, \ldots, Y_{in_i} = y_{in_i} | \mathbf{X}_i) = \int_0^\infty \prod_{t=1}^{n_i} \Pr(Y_{it} = y_{it} \mid \mathbf{x}_{it}, \delta_i) \, f(\delta_i) \, d\delta_i$$

$$= \frac{\Gamma(r+s)\Gamma(r+\sum_{t=1}^{n_i}\lambda_{it})\Gamma(s+\sum_{t=1}^{n_i}y_{it})}{\Gamma(r)\Gamma(s)\Gamma(r+s+\sum_{t=1}^{n_i}\lambda_{it}+\sum_{t=1}^{n_i}y_{it})} \prod_{t=1}^{n_i} \frac{\Gamma(\lambda_{it}+y_{it})}{\Gamma(\lambda_{it})\Gamma(y_{it}+1)}$$

for $\mathbf{X}_i = (\mathbf{x}_{i1}, \ldots, \mathbf{x}_{in_i})$ and where f is the probability density function for δ_i. The resulting log likelihood is

$$\ln L = \sum_{i=1}^n w_i \left[\ln\Gamma(r+s) + \ln\Gamma\left(r+\sum_{k=1}^{n_i}\lambda_{ik}\right) + \ln\Gamma\left(s+\sum_{k=1}^{n_i}y_{ik}\right) - \ln\Gamma(r) - \ln\Gamma(s) \right.$$

$$\left. - \ln\Gamma\left(r+s+\sum_{k=1}^{n_i}\lambda_{ik}+\sum_{k=1}^{n_i}y_{ik}\right) + \sum_{t=1}^{n_i}\left\{ \ln\Gamma(\lambda_{it}+y_{it}) - \ln\Gamma(\lambda_{it}) - \ln\Gamma(y_{it}+1) \right\} \right]$$

where $\lambda_{it} = \exp(\mathbf{x}_{it}\boldsymbol{\beta} + \text{offset}_{it})$ and w_i is the weight for the ith group (Hausman, Hall, and Griliches 1984, equation 3.5, 927).

For the fixed-effects overdispersion model, we condition the joint probability of the counts for each group on the sum of the counts for the group (i.e., the observed $\sum_{t=1}^{n_i} y_{it}$). This yields

$$\Pr(Y_{i1} = y_{i1}, \ldots, Y_{in_i} = y_{in_i} \mid \mathbf{X}_i, \sum_{t=1}^{n_i}Y_{it} = \sum_{t=1}^{n_i}y_{it})$$

$$= \frac{\Gamma(\sum_{t=1}^{n_i}\lambda_{it})\Gamma(\sum_{t=1}^{n_i}y_{it}+1)}{\Gamma(\sum_{t=1}^{n_i}\lambda_{it}+\sum_{t=1}^{n_i}y_{it})} \prod_{t=1}^{n_i} \frac{\Gamma(\lambda_{it}+y_{it})}{\Gamma(\lambda_{it})\Gamma(y_{it}+1)}$$

The conditional log likelihood is

$$\ln L = \sum_{i=1}^n w_i \left[\ln\Gamma\left(\sum_{t=1}^{n_i}\lambda_{it}\right) + \ln\Gamma\left(\sum_{t=1}^{n_i}y_{it}+1\right) - \ln\Gamma\left(\sum_{t=1}^{n_i}\lambda_{it}+\sum_{t=1}^{n_i}y_{it}\right) \right.$$

$$\left. + \sum_{t=1}^{n_i}\left\{ \ln\Gamma(\lambda_{it}+y_{it}) - \ln\Gamma(\lambda_{it}) - \ln\Gamma(y_{it}+1) \right\} \right]$$

See Hausman, Hall, and Griliches (1984) for a more thorough development of the random-effects and fixed-effects models. Also, see Cameron and Trivedi (1998) for a good textbook treatment of this model.

References

Cameron, A. C., and P. K. Trivedi. 1998. *Regression Analysis of Count Data*. New York: Cambridge University Press.

Guimarães, P. 2005. A simple approach to fit the beta-binomial model. *Stata Journal* 5: 385–394.

Hausman, J., B. H. Hall, and Z. Griliches. 1984. Econometric models for count data with an application to the patents–R & D relationship. *Econometrica* 52: 909–938.

Liang, K.-Y., and S. L. Zeger. 1986. Longitudinal data analysis using generalized linear models. *Biometrika* 73: 13–22.

Also See

[XT] **xtnbreg postestimation** — Postestimation tools for xtnbreg

[R] **constraint** — Define and list constraints

[XT] **xtgee** — Fit population-averaged panel-data models by using GEE

[XT] **xtpoisson** — Fixed-effects, random-effects, and population-averaged Poisson models

[R] **nbreg** — Negative binomial regression

[U] **20 Estimation and postestimation commands**

Title

> **xtnbreg postestimation** — Postestimation tools for xtnbreg

Description

The following postestimation commands are available for `xtnbreg`:

command	description
adjust[1]	adjusted predictions of $\mathbf{x}\beta$ or $\exp(\mathbf{x}\beta)$
*estat	AIC, BIC, VCE, and estimation sample summary
estimates	cataloging estimation results
hausman	Hausman's specification test
lincom	point estimates, standard errors, testing, and inference for linear combinations of coefficients
lrtest	likelihood-ratio test
mfx	marginal effects or elasticities
nlcom	point estimates, standard errors, testing, and inference for nonlinear combinations of coefficients
predict	predictions, residuals, influence statistics, and other diagnostic measures
predictnl	point estimates, standard errors, testing, and inference for generalized predictions
test	Wald tests for simple and composite linear hypotheses
testnl	Wald tests of nonlinear hypotheses

[1] `adjust` is not appropriate with time-series operators.

* `estat ic` is not appropriate after `xtnbreg, pa`.

See the corresponding entries in the *Stata Base Reference Manual* for details.

Syntax for predict

Random-effects (RE) and conditional fixed-effects (FE) overdispersion models

> predict [*type*] *newvar* [*if*] [*in*] [, *RE/FE_statistic* <u>nooff</u>set]

Population-averaged (PA) model

> predict [*type*] *newvar* [*if*] [*in*] [, *PA_statistic* <u>nooff</u>set]

RE/FE_statistic description

Main	
xb	linear prediction; the default
stdp	standard error of the linear prediction
nu0	predicted number of events; assuming fixed or random effect is zero
iru0	predicted incidence rate; assuming fixed or random effect is zero

328

PA_statistic	description
Main	
mu	predicted value of *depvar*; considers the offset(); the default
rate	predicted value of *depvar*
xb	linear prediction
stdp	standard error of the linear prediction
<u>sco</u>re	first derivative of the log likelihood with respect to $\mathbf{x}_j\beta$

These statistics are available both in and out of sample; type predict ... if e(sample) ... if wanted only for the estimation sample.

Options for predict

⌐ Main ⌐

xb calculates the linear prediction. This is the default for the random-effects and fixed-effects models.

stdp calculates the standard error of the linear prediction.

nu0 calculates the predicted number of events, assuming a zero fixed or random effect.

iru0 calculates the predicted incidence rate, assuming a zero fixed or random effect.

mu and rate both calculate the predicted value of *depvar* (i.e., the predicted count). mu takes into account the offset(), and rate ignores those adjustments. mu and rate are equivalent if you did not specify offset(). mu is the default for the population-averaged model.

score calculates the equation-level score, $u_j = \partial\ln L_j(\mathbf{x}_j\beta)/\partial(\mathbf{x}_j\beta)$.

nooffset is relevant only if you specified offset(*varname*) for xtnbreg. It modifies the calculations made by predict so that they ignore the offset variable; the linear prediction is treated as $\mathbf{x}_{it}\beta$ rather than $\mathbf{x}_{it}\beta + \text{offset}_{it}$.

Methods and Formulas

All postestimation commands listed above are implemented as ado-files.

Also See

[XT] **xtnbreg** — Fixed-effects, random-effects, & population-averaged negative binomial models

[U] **20 Estimation and postestimation commands**

Title

> **xtpcse** — Linear regression with panel-corrected standard errors

Syntax

> xtpcse *depvar* [*indepvars*] [*if*] [*in*] [*weight*] [, *options*]

options	description
Model	
<u>no</u>constant	suppress constant term
<u>c</u>orrelation(<u>i</u>ndependent)	use independent autocorrelation structure
<u>c</u>orrelation(<u>a</u>r1)	use AR1 autocorrelation structure
<u>c</u>orrelation(psar1)	use panel-specific AR1 autocorrelation structure
<u>rho</u>type(*calc*)	specify method to compute autocorrelation parameter; seldom used
np1	weight panel-specific autocorrelations by panel sizes
<u>het</u>only	assume panel-level heteroskedastic errors
<u>i</u>ndependent	assume independent errors across panels
by/if/in	
<u>c</u>asewise	include only observations with complete cases
<u>p</u>airwise	include all available observations with nonmissing pairs
SE	
nmk	normalize standard errors by $N - k$ instead of N
Reporting	
<u>l</u>evel(#)	set confidence level; default is level(95)
<u>d</u>etail	report list of gaps in time series

A panel variable and a time variable must be specified; use xtset; see [XT] **xtset**.

depvar and *indepvars* may contain time-series operators; see [U] **11.4.3 Time-series varlists**.

by, statsby, and xi are allowed; see [U] **11.1.10 Prefix commands**.

iweights and aweights are allowed; see [U] **11.1.6 weight**.

See [U] **20 Estimation and postestimation commands** for more capabilities of estimation commands.

Description

xtpcse calculates panel-corrected standard error (PCSE) estimates for linear cross-sectional time-series models where the parameters are estimated by either OLS or Prais–Winsten regression. When computing the standard errors and the variance–covariance estimates, xtpcse assumes that the disturbances are, by default, heteroskedastic and contemporaneously correlated across panels.

See [XT] **xtgls** for the generalized least-squares estimator for these models.

Options

Model

noconstant; see [XT] **estimation options**.

correlation(*corr*) specifies the form of assumed autocorrelation within panels.

> correlation(independent), the default, specifies that there is no autocorrelation.

> correlation(ar1) specifies that, within panels, there is first-order autocorrelation AR(1) and that the coefficient of the AR(1) process is common to all the panels.

> correlation(psar1) specifies that, within panels, there is first-order autocorrelation and that the coefficient of the AR(1) process is specific to each panel. psar1 stands for panel-specific AR(1).

rhotype(*calc*) specifies the method to be used to calculate the autocorrelation parameter. Allowed for *calc* are

> | | |
> |---|---|
> | regress | regression using lags; the default |
> | freg | regression using leads |
> | tscorr | time-series autocorrelation calculation |
> | dw | Durbin–Watson calculation |

> All above methods are consistent and asymptotically equivalent; this is a rarely used option.

np1 specifies that the panel-specific autocorrelations be weighted by T_i rather than by the default $T_i - 1$ when estimating a common ρ for all panels, where T_i is the number of observations in panel i. This option has an effect only when panels are unbalanced and option correlation(ar1) is specified.

hetonly and independent specify alternative forms for the assumed covariance of the disturbances across the panels. If neither is specified, the disturbances are assumed to be heteroskedastic (each panel has its own variance) and contemporaneously correlated across the panels (each pair of panels has its own covariance). This is the standard PCSE model.

> hetonly specifies that the disturbances are assumed to be panel-level heteroskedastic only with no contemporaneous correlation across panels.

> independent specifies that the disturbances are assumed to be independent across panels; that is, there is one disturbance variance common to all observations.

by/if/in

casewise and pairwise specify how missing observations in unbalanced panels are to be treated when estimating the interpanel covariance matrix of the disturbances. The default is casewise selection.

> casewise specifies that the entire covariance matrix be computed only on the observations (periods) that are available for all panels. If an observation has missing data, all observations of that period are excluded when estimating the covariance matrix of disturbances. Specifying casewise ensures that the estimated covariance matrix will be of full rank and will be positive definite.

> pairwise specifies that, for each element in the covariance matrix, all available observations (periods) that are common to the two panels contributing to the covariance be used to compute the covariance.

> Options casewise and pairwise have an effect only when the panels are unbalanced and neither hetonly nor independent is specified.

nmk specifies that standard errors be normalized by $N - k$, where k is the number of parameters estimated, rather than N, the number of observations. Different authors have used one or the other normalization. Greene (2003, 322) recommends N and notes that using N or $N - k$ does not make the variance calculation unbiased in these models.

Reporting

level(#); see [XT] **estimation options**.

detail specifies that a detailed list of any gaps in the series be reported.

Remarks

xtpcse is an alternative to feasible generalized least squares (FGLS)—see [XT] **xtgls**—for fitting linear cross-sectional time-series models when the disturbances are not assumed to be independent and identically distributed (i.i.d.). Instead, the disturbances are assumed to be either heteroskedastic across panels or heteroskedastic and contemporaneously correlated across panels. The disturbances may also be assumed to be autocorrelated within panel, and the autocorrelation parameter may be constant across panels or different for each panel.

We can write such models as

$$y_{it} = \mathbf{x}_{it}\beta + \epsilon_{it}$$

where $i = 1, \ldots, m$ is the number of units (or panels); $t = 1, \ldots, T_i$; T_i is the number of periods in panel i; and ϵ_{it} is a disturbance that may be autocorrelated along t or contemporaneously correlated across i.

This model can also be written panel by panel as

$$\begin{bmatrix} \mathbf{y}_1 \\ \mathbf{y}_2 \\ \vdots \\ \mathbf{y}_m \end{bmatrix} = \begin{bmatrix} \mathbf{X}_1 \\ \mathbf{X}_2 \\ \vdots \\ \mathbf{X}_m \end{bmatrix} \beta + \begin{bmatrix} \epsilon_1 \\ \epsilon_2 \\ \vdots \\ \epsilon_m \end{bmatrix}$$

For a model with heteroskedastic disturbances and contemporaneous correlation but with no autocorrelation, the disturbance covariance matrix is assumed to be

$$E[\epsilon\epsilon'] = \Omega = \begin{bmatrix} \sigma_{11}\mathbf{I}_{11} & \sigma_{12}\mathbf{I}_{12} & \cdots & \sigma_{1m}\mathbf{I}_{1m} \\ \sigma_{21}\mathbf{I}_{21} & \sigma_{22}\mathbf{I}_{22} & \cdots & \sigma_{2m}\mathbf{I}_{2m} \\ \vdots & \vdots & \ddots & \vdots \\ \sigma_{m1}\mathbf{I}_{m1} & \sigma_{m2}\mathbf{I}_{m2} & \cdots & \sigma_{mm}\mathbf{I}_{mm} \end{bmatrix}$$

where σ_{ii} is the variance of the disturbances for panel i, σ_{ij} is the covariance of the disturbances between panel i and panel j when the panels' periods are matched, and $\mathbf{I}$ is a T_i by T_i identity matrix with balanced panels. The panels need not be balanced for xtpcse, but the expression for the covariance of the disturbances will be more general if they are unbalanced.

This could also be written as

$$E(\epsilon'\epsilon) = \Sigma_{m \times m} \otimes \mathbf{I}_{T_i \times T_i}$$

where Σ is the panel-by-panel covariance matrix and $\mathbf{I}$ is an identity matrix.

See [XT] **xtgls** for a full taxonomy and description of possible disturbance covariance structures.

xtpcse and xtgls follow two different estimation schemes for this family of models. xtpcse produces OLS estimates of the parameters when no autocorrelation is specified, or Prais–Winsten (see [TS] **prais**) estimates when autocorrelation is specified. If autocorrelation is specified, the estimates of the parameters are conditional on the estimates of the autocorrelation parameter(s). The estimate of the variance–covariance matrix of the parameters is asymptotically efficient under the assumed covariance structure of the disturbances and uses the FGLS estimate of the disturbance covariance matrix; see Kmenta (1997, 121).

xtgls produces full FGLS parameter and variance–covariance estimates. These estimates are conditional on the estimates of the disturbance covariance matrix and are conditional on any autocorrelation parameters that are estimated; see Kmenta (1997), Greene (2003), Davidson and MacKinnon (1993), or Judge et al. (1985).

Both estimators are consistent, as long as the conditional mean ($\mathbf{x}_{it}\beta$) is correctly specified. If the assumed covariance structure is correct, FGLS estimates produced by xtgls are more efficient. Beck and Katz (1995) have shown, however, that the full FGLS variance–covariance estimates are typically unacceptably optimistic (anticonservative) when used with the type of data analyzed by most social scientists—10–20 panels with 10–40 periods per panel. They show that the OLS or Prais–Winsten estimates with PCSEs have coverage probabilities that are closer to nominal.

Since the covariance matrix elements, σ_{ij}, are estimated from panels i and j, using those observations that have common time periods, estimators for this model achieve their asymptotic behavior as the T_is approach infinity. In contrast, the random- and fixed-effects estimators assume a different model and are asymptotic in the number of panels m; see [XT] **xtreg** for details of the random- and fixed-effects estimators.

Although xtpcse allows other disturbance covariance structures, the term PCSE, as used in the literature, refers specifically to models that are both heteroskedastic and contemporaneously correlated across panels, with or without autocorrelation.

▷ Example 1

Grunfeld and Griliches (1960) analyzed a company's current-year gross investment (invest) as determined by the company's prior year market value (mvalue) and the prior year's value of the company's plant and equipment (kstock). The dataset includes ten companies over 20 years, from 1935 through 1954, and is a classic dataset for demonstrating cross-sectional time-series analysis. Greene (2003, 329) reproduces the dataset.

To use xtpcse, the data must be organized in "long form"; that is, each observation must represent a record for a specific company at a specific time; see [D] **reshape**. In the Grunfeld data, company is a categorical variable identifying the company, and year is a variable recording the year. Here are the first few records:

```
. use http://www.stata-press.com/data/r10/grunfeld
. list in 1/5
```

	company	year	invest	mvalue	kstock	time
1.	1	1935	317.6	3078.5	2.8	1
2.	1	1936	391.8	4661.7	52.6	2
3.	1	1937	410.6	5387.1	156.9	3
4.	1	1938	257.7	2792.2	209.2	4
5.	1	1939	330.8	4313.2	203.4	5

To compute PCSEs, Stata must be able to identify the panel to which each observation belongs and be able to match the periods across the panels. We tell Stata how to do this matching by specifying the panel and time variables with xtset; see [XT] **xtset**. Since the data are annual, we specify the yearly option.

```
. xtset company year, yearly
       panel variable:  company (strongly balanced)
        time variable:  year, 1935 to 1954
               delta:  1 year
```

We can obtain OLS parameter estimates for a linear model of invest on mvalue and kstock while allowing the standard errors (and variance–covariance matrix of the estimates) to be consistent when the disturbances from each observation are not independent. Specifically, we want the standard errors to be robust to each company having a different variance of the disturbances and to each company's observations being correlated with those of the other companies through time.

This model is fitted in Stata by typing

```
. xtpcse invest mvalue kstock

Linear regression, correlated panels corrected standard errors (PCSEs)

Group variable:    company                Number of obs      =       200
Time variable:     year                   Number of groups   =        10
Panels:            correlated (balanced)  Obs per group: min =        20
Autocorrelation:   no autocorrelation                    avg =        20
                                                          max =        20
Estimated covariances      =        55    R-squared          =    0.8124
Estimated autocorrelations =         0    Wald chi2(2)       =    637.41
Estimated coefficients     =         3    Prob > chi2        =    0.0000
```

	Coef.	Panel-corrected Std. Err.	z	P>|z|	[95% Conf. Interval]
mvalue	.1155622	.0072124	16.02	0.000	.101426	.1296983
kstock	.2306785	.0278862	8.27	0.000	.1760225	.2853345
_cons	-42.71437	6.780965	-6.30	0.000	-56.00482	-29.42392

◁

▷ Example 2

xtgls will produce more efficient FGLS estimates of the models' parameters, but with the disadvantage that the standard error estimates are conditional on the estimated disturbance covariance. Beck and Katz (1995) argue that the improvement in power using FGLS with such data is small and that the standard error estimates from FGLS are unacceptably optimistic (anticonservative).

The FGLS model is fitted by typing

```
. xtgls invest mvalue kstock, panels(correlated)

Cross-sectional time-series FGLS regression

Coefficients:  generalized least squares
Panels:        heteroskedastic with cross-sectional correlation
Correlation:   no autocorrelation

Estimated covariances      =         55     Number of obs      =        200
Estimated autocorrelations =          0     Number of groups   =         10
Estimated coefficients     =          3     Time periods       =         20
                                            Wald chi2(2)       =    3738.07
Log likelihood             = -879.4274      Prob > chi2        =     0.0000
```

invest	Coef.	Std. Err.	z	P>|z|	[95% Conf. Interval]	
mvalue	.1127515	.0022364	50.42	0.000	.1083683	.1171347
kstock	.2231176	.0057363	38.90	0.000	.2118746	.2343605
_cons	-39.84382	1.717563	-23.20	0.000	-43.21018	-36.47746

The coefficients between the two models are close; the constants differ substantially, but we are generally not interested in the constant. As Beck and Katz observed, the standard errors for the FGLS model are 50%–100% smaller than those for the OLS model with PCSE.

If we were also concerned about autocorrelation of the disturbances, we could obtain a model with a common AR(1) parameter by specifying correlation(ar1).

```
. xtpcse invest mvalue kstock, correlation(ar1)
(note: estimates of rho outside [-1,1] bounded to be in the range [-1,1])

Prais-Winsten regression, correlated panels corrected standard errors (PCSEs)

Group variable:  company          Number of obs      =        200
Time variable:   year             Number of groups   =         10
Panels:          correlated (balanced)  Obs per group: min =     20
Autocorrelation: common AR(1)                      avg =         20
                                                   max =         20
Estimated covariances      =         55     R-squared          =     0.5468
Estimated autocorrelations =          1     Wald chi2(2)       =      93.71
Estimated coefficients     =          3     Prob > chi2        =     0.0000
```

invest	Panel-corrected Coef.	Std. Err.	z	P>|z|	[95% Conf. Interval]	
mvalue	.0950157	.0129934	7.31	0.000	.0695492	.1204822
kstock	.306005	.0603718	5.07	0.000	.1876784	.4243317
_cons	-39.12569	30.50355	-1.28	0.200	-98.91154	20.66016
rho	.9059774					

The estimate of the autocorrelation parameter is high (.926), and the standard errors are larger than for the model without autocorrelation, which is to be expected if there is autocorrelation.

◁

▷ Example 3

Let's estimate panel-specific autocorrelation parameters and change the method of estimating the autocorrelation parameter to the one typically used to estimate autocorrelation in time-series analysis.

```
. xtpcse invest mvalue kstock, correlation(psar1) rhotype(tscorr)

Prais-Winsten regression, correlated panels corrected standard errors (PCSEs)

Group variable:    company              Number of obs      =        200
Time variable:     year                 Number of groups   =         10
Panels:            correlated (balanced)   Obs per group: min =       20
Autocorrelation:   panel-specific AR(1)                 avg =         20
                                                        max =         20
Estimated covariances      =        55   R-squared          =     0.8670
Estimated autocorrelations =        10   Wald chi2(2)       =     444.53
Estimated coefficients     =         3   Prob > chi2        =     0.0000
```

		Panel-corrected				
	Coef.	Std. Err.	z	P>|z|	[95% Conf.	Interval]
mvalue	.1052613	.0086018	12.24	0.000	.0884021	.1221205
kstock	.3386743	.0367568	9.21	0.000	.2666322	.4107163
_cons	-58.18714	12.63687	-4.60	0.000	-82.95496	-33.41933
rhos =	.5135627	.87017	.9023497	.63368	.8571502 ...	.8752707

Beck and Katz (1995, 121) make a case against estimating panel-specific AR parameters, as opposed to one AR parameter for all panels.

◁

▷ Example 4

We can also diverge from PCSEs to estimate standard errors that are panel corrected, but only for panel-level heteroskedasticity; that is, each company has a different variance of the disturbances. Allowing also for autocorrelation, we would type

```
. xtpcse invest mvalue kstock, correlation(ar1) hetonly
(note: estimates of rho outside [-1,1] bounded to be in the range [-1,1])

Prais-Winsten regression, heteroskedastic panels corrected standard errors

Group variable:    company              Number of obs      =        200
Time variable:     year                 Number of groups   =         10
Panels:            heteroskedastic (balanced)   Obs per group: min =    20
Autocorrelation:   common AR(1)                         avg =         20
                                                        max =         20
Estimated covariances      =        10   R-squared          =     0.5468
Estimated autocorrelations =         1   Wald chi2(2)       =      91.72
Estimated coefficients     =         3   Prob > chi2        =     0.0000
```

		Het-corrected				
	Coef.	Std. Err.	z	P>|z|	[95% Conf.	Interval]
mvalue	.0950157	.0130872	7.26	0.000	.0693653	.1206661
kstock	.306005	.061432	4.98	0.000	.1856006	.4264095
_cons	-39.12569	26.16935	-1.50	0.135	-90.41666	12.16529
rho	.9059774					

With this specification, we do not obtain what are referred to in the literature as PCSEs. These standard errors are in the same spirit as PCSEs but are from the asymptotic covariance estimates of OLS without allowing for contemporaneous correlation.

◁

Saved Results

xtpcse saves the following in e():

Scalars

e(N)	number of observations	e(rmse)	root mean squared error
e(N_g)	number of groups	e(g_max)	largest group size
e(n_cf)	number of estimated coefficients	e(g_min)	smallest group size
e(n_cv)	number of estimated covariances	e(g_avg)	average group size
e(n_cr)	number of estimated correlations	e(rc)	return code
e(mss)	model sum of squares	e(chi2)	χ^2
e(df)	degrees of freedom	e(p)	significance
e(df_m)	model degrees of freedom	e(N_gaps)	number of gaps
e(rss)	residual sum of squares	e(n_sigma)	obs used to estimate elements
e(r2)	R-squared		of Sigma

Macros

e(cmd)	xtpcse	e(tvar)	variable denoting time
e(cmdline)	command as typed	e(vcetype)	title used to label Std. Err.
e(depvar)	name of dependent variable	e(chi2type)	Wald; type of model χ^2 test
e(wtype)	weight type	e(rho)	ρ
e(wexp)	weight expression	e(cons)	noconstant or ""
e(title)	title in estimation output	e(missmeth)	casewise or pairwise
e(panels)	contemporaneous covariance structure	e(balance)	balanced or unbalanced
e(corr)	correlation structure	e(properties)	b V
e(rhotype)	type of estimated correlation	e(predict)	program used to implement predict
e(ivar)	variable denoting groups		

Matrices

e(b)	coefficient vector	e(Sigma)	$\widehat{\Sigma}$ matrix
e(V)	variance–covariance matrix	e(rhomat)	vector of autocorrelation
	of the estimators		parameter estimates

Functions

e(sample)	marks estimation sample

Methods and Formulas

xtpcse is implemented as an ado-file.

If no autocorrelation is specified, the parameters β are estimated by OLS; see [R] **regress**. If autocorrelation is specified, the parameters β are estimated by Prais–Winsten; see [TS] **prais**.

When autocorrelation with panel-specific coefficients of correlation is specified (by using option correlation(psar1)), each panel-level ρ_i is computed from the residuals of an OLS regression across all panels; see [TS] **prais**. When autocorrelation with a common coefficient of correlation is specified (by using option correlation(ar1)), the common correlation coefficient is computed as

$$\rho = \frac{\rho_1 + \rho_2 + \cdots + \rho_m}{m}$$

where ρ_i is the estimated autocorrelation coefficient for panel i and m is the number of panels.

The covariance of the OLS or Prais–Winsten coefficients is

$$\text{Var}(\beta) = (\mathbf{X}'\mathbf{X})^{-1}\mathbf{X}'\mathit{\Omega}\mathbf{X}(\mathbf{X}'\mathbf{X})^{-1}$$

where $\mathit{\Omega}$ is the full covariance matrix of the disturbances.

When the panels are balanced, we can write $\mathit{\Omega}$ as

$$\mathit{\Omega} = \mathbf{\Sigma}_{m \times m} \otimes \mathbf{I}_{T_i \times T_i}$$

where $\mathbf{\Sigma}$ is the m by m panel-by-panel covariance matrix of the disturbances; see *Remarks*.

xtpcse estimates the elements of $\mathbf{\Sigma}$ as

$$\widehat{\mathbf{\Sigma}}_{ij} = \frac{\epsilon_i{}'\epsilon_j}{T_{ij}}$$

where ϵ_i and ϵ_j are the residuals for panels i and j, respectively, that can be matched by period, and where T_{ij} is the number of residuals between the panels i and j that can be matched by time period.

When the panels are balanced (each panel has the same number of observations and all periods are common to all panels), $T_{ij} = T$, where T is the number of observations per panel.

When panels are unbalanced, xtpcse by default uses casewise selection, in which only those residuals from periods that are common to all panels are used to compute $\widehat{S}_{ij}$. Here $T_{ij} = T^*$, where T^* is the number of periods common to all panels. When pairwise is specified, each $\widehat{S}_{ij}$ is computed using all observations that can be matched by period between the panels i and j.

Acknowledgments

We thank the following people for helpful comments: Nathaniel Beck, Department of Politics, New York University; Jonathan Katz, Division of the Humanities and Social Science, California Institute of Technology; and Robert John Franzese Jr., Center for Political Studies, Institute for Social Research, University of Michigan.

References

Beck, N., and J. N. Katz. 1995. What to do (and not to do) with time-series cross-section data. *American Political Science Review* 89: 634–647.

Blackwell, J. L., III. 2005. Estimation and testing of fixed-effect panel-data systems. *Stata Journal* 5: 202–207.

Davidson, R., and J. G. MacKinnon. 1993. *Estimation and Inference in Econometrics.* New York: Oxford University Press.

Greene, W. H. 2003. *Econometric Analysis.* 5th ed. Upper Saddle River, NJ: Prentice Hall.

Grunfeld, Y., and Z. Griliches. 1960. Is aggregation necessarily bad? *Review of Economics and Statistics* 42: 1–13.

Judge, G. G., W. E. Griffiths, R. C. Hill, H. Lütkepohl, and T.-C. Lee. 1985. *The Theory and Practice of Econometrics.* 2nd ed. New York: Wiley.

Kmenta, J. 1997. *Elements of Econometrics.* 2nd ed. Ann Arbor: University of Michigan Press.

Also See

[XT] **xtpcse postestimation** — Postestimation tools for xtpcse

[XT] **xtset** — Declare data to be panel data

[XT] **xtgls** — Fit panel-data models by using GLS

[XT] **xtreg** — Fixed-, between-, and random-effects, and population-averaged linear models

[XT] **xtregar** — Fixed- and random-effects linear models with an AR(1) disturbance

[R] **regress** — Linear regression

[TS] **newey** — Regression with Newey–West standard errors

[TS] **prais** — Prais–Winsten and Cochrane–Orcutt regression

[U] **20 Estimation and postestimation commands**

Title

> **xtpcse postestimation** — Postestimation tools for xtpcse

Description

The following postestimation commands are available for `xtpcse`:

command	description
adjust[1]	adjusted predictions of $\mathbf{x}\beta$ or $\exp(\mathbf{x}\beta)$
estat	VCE and estimation sample summary
estimates	cataloging estimation results
lincom	point estimates, standard errors, testing, and inference for linear combinations of coefficients
mfx	marginal effects or elasticities
nlcom	point estimates, standard errors, testing, and inference for nonlinear combinations of coefficients
predict	predictions, residuals, influence statistics, and other diagnostic measures
predictnl	point estimates, standard errors, testing, and inference for generalized predictions
test	Wald tests for simple and composite linear hypotheses
testnl	Wald tests of nonlinear hypotheses

[1] `adjust` is not appropriate with time-series operators.

See the corresponding entries in the *Stata Base Reference Manual* for details.

Syntax for predict

> predict [*type*] *newvar* [*if*] [*in*] [, xb stdp]

These statistics are available both in and out of sample; type `predict ... if e(sample) ...` if wanted only for the estimation sample.

Options for predict

⌐ Main ⌐

`xb`, the default, calculates the linear prediction.

`stdp` calculates the standard error of the linear prediction.

Methods and Formulas

All postestimation commands listed above are implemented as ado-files.

Also See

[XT] **xtpcse** — Linear regression with panel-corrected standard errors

[U] **20 Estimation and postestimation commands**

Title

> **xtpoisson** — Fixed-effects, random-effects, and population-averaged Poisson models

Syntax

Random-effects (RE) model

> xtpoisson *depvar* [*indepvars*] [*if*] [*in*] [*weight*] [, re *RE_options*]

Conditional fixed-effects (FE) model

> xtpoisson *depvar* [*indepvars*] [*if*] [*in*] [*weight*] , fe [*FE_options*]

Population-averaged (PA) model

> xtpoisson *depvar* [*indepvars*] [*if*] [*in*] [*weight*] , pa [*PA_options*]

RE_options	description
Model	
<u>noco</u>nstant	suppress constant term
re	use random-effects estimator; the default
<u>e</u>xposure(*varname*)	include ln(*varname*) in model with coefficient constrained to 1
<u>off</u>set(*varname*)	include *varname* in model with coefficient constrained to 1
normal	use a normal distribution for random effects instead of gamma
<u>constr</u>aints(*constraints*)	apply specified linear constraints
<u>col</u>linear	keep collinear variables
SE	
vce(*vcetype*)	*vcetype* may be oim, <u>boot</u>strap, or <u>jack</u>knife
Reporting	
<u>l</u>evel(*#*)	set confidence level; default is level(95)
<u>irr</u>	report incidence-rate ratios
noskip	fit constant-only model and perform likelihood-ratio test
Int opts (RE)	
<u>intm</u>ethod(*intmethod*)	integration method; *intmethod* may be <u>mvag</u>hermite, <u>agh</u>ermite, or <u>gh</u>ermite; default is intmethod(mvaghermite)
<u>intp</u>oints(*#*)	use *#* quadrature points; default is intpoints(12)
Max options	
maximize_options	control the maximization process; seldom used

FE_options	description
Model	
fe	use fixed-effects estimator
<u>exp</u>osure(*varname*)	include ln(*varname*) in model with coefficient constrained to 1
<u>off</u>set(*varname*)	include *varname* in model with coefficient constrained to 1
<u>cons</u>traints(*constraints*)	apply specified linear constraints
<u>coll</u>inear	keep collinear variables
SE	
vce(*vcetype*)	*vcetype* may be oim, <u>boot</u>strap, or <u>jack</u>knife
Reporting	
<u>l</u>evel(*#*)	set confidence level; default is level(95)
<u>irr</u>	report incidence-rate ratios
noskip	fit constant-only model and perform likelihood-ratio test
Max options	
maximize_options	control the maximization process; seldom used

PA_options	description
Model	
<u>nocons</u>tant	suppress constant term
pa	use population-averaged estimator
<u>exp</u>osure(*varname*)	include ln(*varname*) in model with coefficient constrained to 1
<u>off</u>set(*varname*)	include *varname* in model with coefficient constrained to 1
Correlation	
<u>corr</u>(*correlation*)	within-group correlation structure
force	estimate if observations unequally spaced in time
SE/Robust	
vce(*vcetype*)	*vcetype* may be conventional, <u>r</u>obust, <u>boot</u>strap, or <u>jack</u>knife
nmp	use divisor $N - P$ instead of the default N
<u>sc</u>ale(*parm*)	overrides the default scale parameter; *parm* may be x2, dev, phi, or *#*
Reporting	
<u>l</u>evel(*#*)	set confidence level; default is level(95)
<u>irr</u>	report incidence-rate ratios
Opt options	
optimize_options	control the optimization process; seldom used

correlation	description
<u>exc</u>hangeable	exchangeable
<u>ind</u>ependent	independent
<u>uns</u>tructured	unstructured
<u>fix</u>ed *matname*	user-specified
ar *#*	autoregressive
<u>stat</u>ionary *#*	stationary
<u>non</u>stationary *#*	nonstationary

A panel variable must be specified. For xtpoisson, pa, correlation structures other than exchangeable and
   independent require that a time variable also be specified. Use xtset; see [XT] **xtset**.

depvar and *indepvars* may contain time-series operators; see [U] **11.4.3 Time-series varlists**.

by, statsby, and xi are allowed; see [U] **11.1.10 Prefix commands**.

iweights, fweights, and pweights are allowed for the population-averaged model and iweights are allowed
   in the random-effects and fixed-effects models; see [U] **11.1.6 weight**. Weights must be constant within panel.

See [U] **20 Estimation and postestimation commands** for more capabilities of estimation commands.

Description

xtpoisson fits random-effects, conditional fixed-effects, and population-averaged Poisson models.
Whenever we refer to a fixed-effects model, we mean the conditional fixed-effects model.

xtpoisson, re normal is slow because the likelihood function is calculated by adaptive Gauss–
Hermite quadrature; see *Methods and Formulas*. Computation time is roughly proportional to the
number of points used for the quadrature. The default is intpoints(12). Increasing the number of
quadrature points can improve the quadrature approximation. See [XT] **quadchk**.

By default, the population-averaged model is an equal-correlation model; xtpoisson, pa assumes
corr(exchangeable). See [XT] **xtgee** for information on how to fit other population-averaged
models.

Options for RE model

⎡ Model ⎤

noconstant; see [XT] **estimation options**.

re, the default, requests the random-effects estimator.

exposure(*varname*), offset(*varname*),

normal specifies that the random effects follow a normal distribution instead of a gamma distribution.

constraints(*constraints*), collinear; see [XT] **estimation options**.

⎡ SE ⎤

vce(*vcetype*) specifies the type of standard error reported, which includes types that are derived from
   asymptotic theory and that use bootstrap or jackknife methods; see [XT] *vce_options*.

⎡ Reporting ⎤

level(*#*); see [XT] **estimation options**.

irr reports exponentiated coefficients e^b rather than coefficients b. For the Poisson model, exponentiated coefficients are interpreted as incidence-rate ratios.

noskip; see [XT] **estimation options**.

_____| Int opts (RE) |_____

intmethod(*intmethod*), intpoints(*#*); see [XT] **estimation options**.

_____| Max options |_____

maximize_options: <u>diffi</u>cult, <u>techn</u>ique(*algorithm_spec*), <u>iter</u>ate(*#*), [<u>no</u>]log, <u>tra</u>ce, gradient, showstep, <u>hess</u>ian, <u>shownr</u>tolerance, <u>tol</u>erance(*#*), <u>ltol</u>erance(*#*), <u>gtol</u>erance(*#*), <u>nrtol</u>erance(*#*), <u>nonrtol</u>erance, from(*init_specs*); see [R] **maximize**. Some of these options are not available if intmethod(ghermite) is specified. These options are seldom used.

Options for FE model

_____| Model |_____

fe requests the fixed-effects estimator.

exposure(*varname*), offset(*varname*), constraints(*constraints*), collinear; see [XT] **estimation options**.

_____| SE |_____

vce(*vcetype*) specifies the type of standard error reported, which includes types that are derived from asymptotic theory and that use bootstrap or jackknife methods; see [XT] *vce_options*.

_____| Reporting |_____

level(*#*); see [XT] **estimation options**.

irr reports exponentiated coefficients e^b rather than coefficients b. For the Poisson model, exponentiated coefficients are interpreted as incidence-rate ratios.

noskip; see [XT] **estimation options**.

_____| Max options |_____

maximize_options: <u>diffi</u>cult, <u>techn</u>ique(*algorithm_spec*), <u>iter</u>ate(*#*), [<u>no</u>]log, <u>tra</u>ce, gradient, showstep, <u>hess</u>ian, <u>shownr</u>tolerance, <u>tol</u>erance(*#*), <u>ltol</u>erance(*#*), <u>gtol</u>erance(*#*), <u>nrtol</u>erance(*#*), <u>nonrtol</u>erance, from(*init_specs*); see [R] **maximize**. These options are seldom used.

Options for PA model

_____| Model |_____

noconstant; see [XT] **estimation options**.

pa requests the population-averaged estimator.

exposure(*varname*), offset(*varname*); see [XT] **estimation options**.

___ Correlation ___

corr(*correlation*), force; see [XT] **estimation options**.

___ SE/Robust ___

vce(*vcetype*) specifies the type of standard error reported, which includes types that are derived from asymptotic theory, that are robust to some kinds of misspecification, and that use bootstrap or jackknife methods; see [XT] **vce_options**.

vce(conventional), the default, uses the conventionally derived variance estimator for generalized least-squares regression.

nmp, scale(x2 | dev | phi | #); see [XT] **vce_options**.

___ Reporting ___

level(#); see [XT] **estimation options**.

irr reports exponentiated coefficients e^b rather than coefficients b. For the Poisson model, exponentiated coefficients are interpreted as incidence-rate ratios.

___ Opt options ___

optimize_options control the iterative optimization process. These options are seldom used.

iterate(#) specifies the maximum number of iterations. When the number of iterations equals #, the optimization stops and presents the current results, even if convergence has not been reached. The default is iterate(100).

tolerance(#) specifies the tolerance for the coefficient vector. When the relative change in the coefficient vector from one iteration to the next is less than or equal to #, the optimization process is stopped. tolerance(1e-6) is the default.

nolog suppresses display of the iteration log.

trace specifies that the current estimates be printed at each iteration.

Remarks

xtpoisson is a convenience command if you want the population-averaged model. Typing

```
. xtpoisson ..., ... pa exposure(time)
```

is equivalent to typing

```
. xtgee ..., ... family(poisson) link(log) corr(exchangeable) exposure(time)
```

Also see [XT] **xtgee** for information about xtpoisson.

By default or when re is specified, xtpoisson fits via maximum likelihood the random-effects model

$$\Pr(Y_{it} = y_{it}|\mathbf{x}_{it}) = F(y_{it}, \mathbf{x}_{it}\boldsymbol{\beta} + \nu_i)$$

for $i = 1, \ldots, n$ panels, where $t = 1, \ldots, n_i$, and $F(x, z) = \Pr(X = x)$, where X is Poisson distributed with mean $\exp(z)$. In the standard random-effects model, ν_i is assumed to be i.i.d. such that $\exp(\nu_i)$ is gamma with mean one and variance α, which is estimated from the data. If normal is specified, ν_i is assumed to be i.i.d. $N(0, \sigma_\nu^2)$.

▷ Example 1

We have data on the number of ship accidents for five different types of ships (McCullagh and Nelder 1989, 205). We wish to analyze whether the "incident" rate is affected by the period in which the ship was constructed and operated. Our measure of exposure is months of service for the ship, and in this model, we assume that the exponentiated random effects are distributed as gamma with mean one and variance α.

```
. use http://www.stata-press.com/data/r10/ships

. xtpoisson accident op_75_79 co_65_69 co_70_74 co_75_79, exposure(service) irr

Fitting Poisson model:

Iteration 0:   log likelihood = -147.37993
Iteration 1:   log likelihood = -80.372714
Iteration 2:   log likelihood = -80.116093
Iteration 3:   log likelihood = -80.115916
Iteration 4:   log likelihood = -80.115916

Fitting full model:

Iteration 0:   log likelihood = -79.653186
Iteration 1:   log likelihood = -76.990836  (not concave)
Iteration 2:   log likelihood = -74.824942
Iteration 3:   log likelihood = -74.811243
Iteration 4:   log likelihood = -74.811217
Iteration 5:   log likelihood = -74.811217
```

```
Random-effects Poisson regression              Number of obs      =        34
Group variable: ship                           Number of groups   =         5

Random effects u_i ~ Gamma                     Obs per group: min =         6
                                                              avg =       6.8
                                                              max =         7

                                               Wald chi2(4)       =     50.90
Log likelihood   = -74.811217                  Prob > chi2        =    0.0000
```

accident	IRR	Std. Err.	z	P>|z|	[95% Conf. Interval]	
op_75_79	1.466305	.1734005	3.24	0.001	1.162957	1.848777
co_65_69	2.032543	.304083	4.74	0.000	1.515982	2.72512
co_70_74	2.356853	.3999259	5.05	0.000	1.690033	3.286774
co_75_79	1.641913	.3811398	2.14	0.033	1.04174	2.58786
service	(exposure)					
/lnalpha	-2.368406	.8474597			-4.029397	-.7074155
alpha	.0936298	.0793475			.0177851	.4929165

```
Likelihood-ratio test of alpha=0: chibar2(01) =    10.61 Prob>=chibar2 = 0.001
```

The output also includes a likelihood-ratio test of $\alpha = 0$, which compares the panel estimator with the pooled (Poisson) estimator.

We find that the incidence rate for accidents is significantly different for the periods of construction and operation of the ships and that the random-effects model is significantly different from the pooled model.

We may alternatively fit a fixed-effects specification instead of a random-effects specification:

```
. xtpoisson accident op_75_79 co_65_69 co_70_74 co_75_79, exp(service) irr fe
Iteration 0:    log likelihood = -80.738973
Iteration 1:    log likelihood = -54.857546
Iteration 2:    log likelihood = -54.641897
Iteration 3:    log likelihood = -54.641859
Iteration 4:    log likelihood = -54.641859
```

Conditional fixed-effects Poisson regression   Number of obs   =   34
Group variable: ship   Number of groups   =   5

Obs per group: min =   6
avg =   6.8
max =   7

Wald chi2(4)   =   48.44
Log likelihood = -54.641859   Prob > chi2   =   0.0000

accident	IRR	Std. Err.	z	P>|z|	[95% Conf. Interval]	
op_75_79	1.468831	.1737218	3.25	0.001	1.164926	1.852019
co_65_69	2.008003	.3004803	4.66	0.000	1.497577	2.692398
co_70_74	2.26693	.384865	4.82	0.000	1.625274	3.161912
co_75_79	1.573695	.3669393	1.94	0.052	.9964273	2.485397
service	(exposure)					

Both of these models fit the same thing but will differ in efficiency, depending on whether the assumptions of the random-effects model are true.

We could have assumed that the random effects followed a normal distribution, $N(0, \sigma_\nu^2)$, instead of a "log-gamma" distribution, and obtained

```
. xtpoisson accident op_75_79 co_65_69 co_70_74 co_75_79, exp(service) irr
> normal nolog
```

Random-effects Poisson regression   Number of obs   =   34
Group variable: ship   Number of groups   =   5
Random effects u_i ~ Gaussian   Obs per group: min =   6
avg =   6.8
max =   7

Wald chi2(4)   =   50.95
Log likelihood = -74.780982   Prob > chi2   =   0.0000

accident	IRR	Std. Err.	z	P>|z|	[95% Conf. Interval]	
op_75_79	1.466677	.1734403	3.24	0.001	1.163259	1.849236
co_65_69	2.032604	.3040933	4.74	0.000	1.516025	2.725205
co_70_74	2.357045	.3998397	5.05	0.000	1.690338	3.286717
co_75_79	1.646935	.3820235	2.15	0.031	1.045278	2.594905
service	(exposure)					
/lnsig2u	-2.351868	.8586262	-2.74	0.006	-4.034745	-.6689918
sigma_u	.3085306	.1324562			.1330045	.7156988

Likelihood-ratio test of sigma_u=0: chibar2(01) =   10.67 Pr>=chibar2 = 0.001

The output includes the additional panel-level variance component. This is parameterized as the log of the variance $\ln(\sigma_\nu^2)$ (labeled lnsig2u in the output). The standard deviation σ_ν is also included in the output labeled sigma_u.

When sigma_u is zero, the panel-level variance component is unimportant and the panel estimator is no different from the pooled estimator. A likelihood-ratio test of this is included at the bottom of the output. This test formally compares the pooled estimator (poisson) with the panel estimator. Here σ_ν is significantly greater than zero, so a panel estimator is indicated. ◁

▷ Example 2

This time we fit a robust equal-correlation population-averaged model:

```
. xtpoisson accident op_75_79 co_65_69 co_70_74 co_75_79, exp(service) pa
> vce(robust) eform

Iteration 1: tolerance = .04083192
Iteration 2: tolerance = .00270188
Iteration 3: tolerance = .00030663
Iteration 4: tolerance = .00003466
Iteration 5: tolerance = 3.891e-06
Iteration 6: tolerance = 4.359e-07
```

GEE population-averaged model				Number of obs	=	34
Group variable:			ship	Number of groups	=	5
Link:			log	Obs per group: min =		6
Family:			Poisson	avg =		6.8
Correlation:			exchangeable	max =		7
				Wald chi2(3)	=	181.55
Scale parameter:			1	Prob > chi2	=	0.0000

(Std. Err. adjusted for clustering on ship)

accident	IRR	Semi-robust Std. Err.	z	P>|z|	[95% Conf. Interval]	
op_75_79	1.483299	.1197901	4.88	0.000	1.266153	1.737685
co_65_69	2.038477	.1809524	8.02	0.000	1.712955	2.425859
co_70_74	2.643467	.4093947	6.28	0.000	1.951407	3.580962
co_75_79	1.876656	.33075	3.57	0.000	1.328511	2.650966
service	(exposure)					

We may compare this with a pooled estimator with clustered robust-variance estimates:

```
. poisson accident op_75_79 co_65_69 co_70_74 co_75_79, exp(service)
> vce(cluster ship) irr

Iteration 0:   log pseudolikelihood = -147.37993
Iteration 1:   log pseudolikelihood = -80.372714
Iteration 2:   log pseudolikelihood = -80.116093
Iteration 3:   log pseudolikelihood = -80.115916
Iteration 4:   log pseudolikelihood = -80.115916
```

Poisson regression		Number of obs	=	34
		Wald chi2(3)	=	.
		Prob > chi2	=	.
Log pseudolikelihood = -80.115916		Pseudo R2	=	0.3438

(Std. Err. adjusted for 5 clusters in ship)

accident	IRR	Robust Std. Err.	z	P>|z|	[95% Conf. Interval]	
op_75_79	1.47324	.1287036	4.44	0.000	1.2414	1.748377
co_65_69	2.125914	.2850531	5.62	0.000	1.634603	2.764897
co_70_74	2.860138	.6213563	4.84	0.000	1.868384	4.378325
co_75_79	2.021926	.4265285	3.34	0.001	1.337221	3.057227
service	(exposure)					

◁

Saved Results

xtpoisson, re saves the following in e():

Scalars

e(N)	# of observations	e(sigma_u)	panel-level standard deviation
e(N_g)	# of groups	e(alpha)	the value of alpha
e(N_cd)	# of completely determined obs.	e(k)	# of parameters
e(df_m)	model degrees of freedom	e(k_eq)	# of equations
e(ll)	log likelihood	e(k_eq_model)	# of equations in model Wald test
e(ll_0)	log likelihood, constant-only model	e(k_dv)	# of dependent variables
e(ll_c)	log likelihood, comparison model	e(p)	significance
e(g_max)	largest group size	e(rank)	rank of e(V)
e(g_min)	smallest group size	e(rank0)	rank of e(V) for constant-only model
e(g_avg)	average group size	e(ic)	# of iterations
e(chi2)	χ^2	e(rc)	return code
e(chi2_c)	χ^2 for comparison test	e(converged)	1 if converged, 0 otherwise

Macros

e(cmd)	xtpoisson	e(distrib)	Gamma; the distribution of the random effect
e(cmdline)	command as typed		
e(depvar)	name of dependent variable	e(vce)	*vcetype* specified in vce()
e(ivar)	variable denoting groups	e(vcetype)	title used to label Std. Err.
e(wtype)	weight type	e(opt)	type of optimization
e(wexp)	weight expression	e(ml_method)	type of ml method
e(title)	title in estimation output	e(user)	name of likelihood-evaluator program
e(offset)	offset	e(technique)	maximization technique
e(chi2type)	Wald or LR; type of model χ^2 test	e(crittype)	optimization criterion
e(chi2_ct)	Wald or LR; type of model χ^2 test corresponding to e(chi2_c)	e(properties)	b V
		e(predict)	program used to implement predict
e(method)	requested estimation method		

Matrices

e(b)	coefficient vector	e(ilog)	iteration log
e(V)	variance–covariance matrix of the estimators	e(gradient)	gradient vector

Functions

e(sample)	marks estimation sample

xtpoisson, re normal saves the following in e():

Scalars

e(N)	# of observations	e(sigma_u)	panel-level standard deviation
e(N_g)	# of groups	e(n_quad)	# of quadrature points
e(N_cd)	# of completely determined obs.	e(k)	# of parameters
e(df_m)	model degrees of freedom	e(k_eq)	# of equations
e(ll)	log likelihood	e(k_eq_model)	# of equations in model Wald test
e(ll_0)	log likelihood, constant-only model	e(k_dv)	# of dependent variables
e(ll_c)	log likelihood, comparison model	e(p)	significance
e(g_max)	largest group size	e(rank)	rank of e(V)
e(g_min)	smallest group size	e(rank0)	rank of e(V) for constant-only model
e(g_avg)	average group size	e(ic)	# of iterations
e(chi2)	χ^2	e(rc)	return code
e(chi2_c)	χ^2 for comparison test	e(converged)	1 if converged, 0 otherwise

Macros

e(cmd)	xtpoisson	e(intmethod)	integration method
e(cmdline)	command as typed	e(distrib)	Gaussian; the distribution of the
e(depvar)	name of dependent variable		random effect
e(ivar)	variable denoting groups	e(vce)	*vcetype* specified in vce()
e(wtype)	weight type	e(vcetype)	title used to label Std. Err.
e(wexp)	weight expression	e(opt)	type of optimization
e(title)	title in estimation output	e(ml_method)	type of ml method
e(offset)	offset	e(user)	name of likelihood-evaluator program
e(offset1)	ln(*varname*), where *varname* is	e(technique)	maximization technique
	variable from exposure()	e(crittype)	optimization criterion
e(chi2type)	Wald or LR; type of model χ^2 test	e(properties)	b V
e(chi2_ct)	Wald or LR; type of model χ^2 test	e(predict)	program used to implement predict
	corresponding to e(chi2_c)		

Matrices

e(b)	coefficient vector	e(ilog)	iteration log
e(V)	variance–covariance matrix of the	e(gradient)	gradient vector
	estimators		

Functions

e(sample)	marks estimation sample

(*Continued on next page*)

`xtpoisson, fe` saves the following in `e()`:

Scalars

`e(N)`	number of observations	`e(k)`	# of parameters
`e(N_g)`	number of groups	`e(k_eq)`	# of equations
`e(df_m)`	model degrees of freedom	`e(k_eq_model)`	# of equations in model Wald test
`e(ll)`	log likelihood	`e(k_dv)`	# of dependent variables
`e(ll_0)`	log likelihood, constant-only model	`e(p)`	significance
`e(ll_c)`	log likelihood, comparison model	`e(rank)`	rank of `e(V)`
`e(g_max)`	largest group size	`e(ic)`	# of iterations
`e(g_min)`	smallest group size	`e(rc)`	return code
`e(g_avg)`	average group size	`e(converged)`	1 if converged, 0 otherwise
`e(chi2)`	χ^2		

Macros

`e(cmd)`	xtpoisson	`e(vce)`	*vcetype* specified in vce()
`e(cmdline)`	command as typed	`e(vcetype)`	title used to label Std. Err.
`e(depvar)`	name of dependent variable	`e(opt)`	type of optimization
`e(ivar)`	variable denoting groups	`e(ml_method)`	type of ml method
`e(offset)`	offset	`e(user)`	name of likelihood-evaluator program
`e(wtype)`	weight type	`e(technique)`	maximization technique
`e(wexp)`	weight expression	`e(crittype)`	optimization criterion
`e(title)`	title in estimation output	`e(properties)`	b V
`e(chi2type)`	LR; type of model χ^2 test	`e(predict)`	program used to implement predict
`e(method)`	requested estimation method		

Matrices

`e(b)`	coefficient vector	`e(ilog)`	iteration log
`e(V)`	variance–covariance matrix of the estimators	`e(gradient)`	gradient vector

Functions

`e(sample)`	marks estimation sample

xtpoisson, pa saves the following in e():

Scalars

e(N)	number of observations	e(chi2_dev)	χ^2 test of deviance
e(N_g)	number of groups	e(chi2_dis)	χ^2 test of deviance dispersion
e(df_m)	model degrees of freedom	e(deviance)	deviance
e(df_pear)	degrees of freedom for Pearson χ^2	e(dispers)	deviance dispersion
e(g_max)	largest group size	e(tol)	target tolerance
e(g_min)	smallest group size	e(dif)	achieved tolerance
e(g_avg)	average group size	e(phi)	scale parameter
e(chi2)	χ^2	e(rc)	return code

Macros

e(cmd)	xtgee	e(crittype)	optimization criterion
e(cmd2)	xtpoisson	e(scale)	x2, dev, phi, or #; scale parameter
e(cmdline)	command as typed	e(ivar)	variable denoting groups
e(depvar)	name of dependent variable	e(vce)	*vcetype* specified in vce()
e(wtype)	weight type	e(vcetype)	covariance estimation method
e(wexp)	weight expression	e(chi2type)	Wald; type of model χ^2 test
e(family)	Poisson	e(offset)	offset
e(link)	log; link function	e(predict)	program used to implement predict
e(corr)	correlation structure	e(properties)	b V

Matrices

e(b)	coefficient vector	e(R)	estimated working correlation matrix
e(V)	variance–covariance matrix of the estimators		

Functions

e(sample)	marks estimation sample

Methods and Formulas

xtpoisson is implemented as an ado-file.

xtpoisson, pa reports the population-averaged results obtained by using xtgee, family(poisson) link(log) to obtain estimates. See [XT] **xtgee** for details about the methods and formulas.

Although Hausman, Hall, and Griliches (1984) wrote the seminal article on the random-effects and fixed-effects models, Cameron and Trivedi (1998) provide a good textbook treatment.

For a random-effects specification, we know that

$$\Pr(y_{i1}, \ldots, y_{in_i} | \alpha_i, \mathbf{x}_{i1}, \ldots, \mathbf{x}_{in_i}) = \left(\prod_{t=1}^{n_i} \frac{\lambda_{it}^{y_{it}}}{y_{it}!} \right) \exp \left\{ - \exp(\alpha_i) \sum_{t=1}^{n_i} \lambda_{it} \right\} \exp \left(\alpha_i \sum_{t=1}^{n_i} y_{it} \right)$$

where $\lambda_{it} = \exp(\mathbf{x}_{it}\boldsymbol{\beta})$. We may rewrite the above as (defining $\epsilon_i = \exp(\alpha_i)$)

$$\Pr(y_{i1}, \ldots, y_{in_i} | \epsilon_i, \mathbf{x}_{i1}, \ldots, \mathbf{x}_{in_i}) = \left\{ \prod_{t=1}^{n_i} \frac{(\lambda_{it} \epsilon_i)^{y_{it}}}{y_{it}!} \right\} \exp\left(-\sum_{t=1}^{n_i} \lambda_{it} \epsilon_i \right)$$

$$= \left(\prod_{t=1}^{n_i} \frac{\lambda_{it}^{y_{it}}}{y_{it}!} \right) \exp\left(-\epsilon_i \sum_{t=1}^{n_i} \lambda_{it} \right) \epsilon_i^{\sum_{t=1}^{n_i} y_{it}}$$

We now assume that ϵ_i follows a gamma distribution with mean one and variance θ so that unconditional on ϵ_i

$$\Pr(y_{i1}, \ldots, y_{in_i} | \mathbf{X}_i) = \frac{\theta^{\theta}}{\Gamma(\theta)} \left(\prod_{t=1}^{n_i} \frac{\lambda_{it}^{y_{it}}}{y_{it}!} \right) \int_0^\infty \exp\left(-\epsilon_i \sum_{t=1}^{n_i} \lambda_{it} \right) \epsilon_i^{\sum_{t=1}^{n_i} y_{it}} \epsilon_i^{\theta-1} \exp(-\theta \epsilon_i) d\epsilon_i$$

$$= \frac{\theta^{\theta}}{\Gamma(\theta)} \left(\prod_{t=1}^{n_i} \frac{\lambda_{it}^{y_{it}}}{y_{it}!} \right) \int_0^\infty \exp\left\{ -\epsilon_i \left(\theta + \sum_{t=1}^{n_i} \lambda_{it} \right) \right\} \epsilon_i^{\theta + \sum_{t=1}^{n_i} y_{it} - 1} d\epsilon_i$$

$$= \left(\prod_{t=1}^{n_i} \frac{\lambda_{it}^{y_{it}}}{y_{it}!} \right) \frac{\Gamma\left(\theta + \sum_{t=1}^{n_i} y_{it} \right)}{\Gamma(\theta)} \left(\frac{\theta}{\theta + \sum_{t=1}^{n_i} \lambda_{it}} \right)^{\theta} \left(\frac{1}{\theta + \sum_{t=1}^{n_i} \lambda_{it}} \right)^{\sum_{t=1}^{n_i} y_{it}}$$

for $\mathbf{X}_i = (\mathbf{x}_{i1}, \ldots, \mathbf{x}_{in_i})$.

The log likelihood (assuming gamma heterogeneity) is then derived using

$$u_i = \frac{\theta}{\theta + \sum_{t=1}^{n_i} \lambda_{it}} \qquad \lambda_{it} = \exp(\mathbf{x}_{it}\boldsymbol{\beta})$$

$$\Pr(Y_{i1} = y_{i1}, \ldots, Y_{in_i} = y_{in_i} | \mathbf{X}_i) = \frac{\prod_{t=1}^{n_i} \lambda_{it}^{y_{it}} \Gamma\left(\theta + \sum_{t=1}^{n_i} y_{it} \right)}{\prod_{t=1}^{n_i} y_{it}! \Gamma(\theta) \left(\sum_{t=1}^{n_i} \lambda_{it} \right)^{\sum_{t=1}^{n_i} y_{it}}} u_i^{\theta} (1 - u_i)^{\sum_{t=1}^{n_i} y_{it}}$$

such that the log likelihood may be written as

$$L = \sum_{i=1}^{n} w_i \left\{ \log \Gamma\left(\theta + \sum_{t=1}^{n_i} y_{it} \right) - \sum_{t=1}^{n_i} \log \Gamma(1 + y_{it}) - \log \Gamma(\theta) + \theta \log u_i \right.$$

$$\left. + \log(1 - u_i) \sum_{t=1}^{n_i} y_{it} + \sum_{t=1}^{n_i} y_{it}(\mathbf{x}_{it}\boldsymbol{\beta}) - \left(\sum_{t=1}^{n_i} y_{it} \right) \log\left(\sum_{t=1}^{n_i} \lambda_{it} \right) \right\}$$

where w_i is the user-specified weight for panel i; if no weights are specified, $w_i = 1$.

Alternatively, if we assume a normal distribution, $N(0, \sigma_\nu^2)$, for the random effects ν_i

$$\Pr(y_{i1}, \ldots, y_{in_i} | \mathbf{X}_i) = \int_{-\infty}^{\infty} \frac{e^{-\nu_i^2/2\sigma_\nu^2}}{\sqrt{2\pi}\sigma_\nu} \left\{ \prod_{t=1}^{n_i} F(y_{it}, \mathbf{x}_{it}\boldsymbol{\beta} + \nu_i) \right\} d\nu_i$$

where

$$F(y, z) = \exp\left\{ -\exp(z) + yz - \log(y!) \right\}.$$

The panel-level likelihood l_i is given by

$$l_i = \int_{-\infty}^{\infty} \frac{e^{-\nu_i^2/2\sigma_\nu^2}}{\sqrt{2\pi}\sigma_\nu} \left\{ \prod_{t=1}^{n_i} F(y_{it}, \mathbf{x}_{it}\boldsymbol{\beta} + \nu_i) \right\} d\nu_i$$

$$\equiv \int_{-\infty}^{\infty} g(y_{it}, x_{it}, \nu_i) d\nu_i$$

This integral can be approximated with M-point Gauss–Hermite quadrature

$$\int_{-\infty}^{\infty} e^{-x^2} h(x) dx \approx \sum_{m=1}^{M} w_m^* h(a_m^*)$$

This is equivalent to

$$\int_{-\infty}^{\infty} f(x) dx \approx \sum_{m=1}^{M} w_m^* \exp\left\{ (a_m^*)^2 \right\} f(a_m^*)$$

where the w_m^* denote the quadrature weights and the a_m^* denote the quadrature abscissas. The log likelihood, L, is the sum of the logs of the panel-level likelihoods l_i.

The default approximation of the log likelihood is by adaptive Gauss–Hermite quadrature, which approximates the panel-level likelihood with

$$l_i \approx \sqrt{2}\widehat{\sigma}_i \sum_{m=1}^{M} w_m^* \exp\left\{ (a_m^*)^2 \right\} g(y_{it}, x_{it}, \sqrt{2}\widehat{\sigma}_i a_m^* + \widehat{\mu}_i)$$

where $\widehat{\sigma}_i$ and $\widehat{\mu}_i$ are the adaptive parameters for panel i. Therefore, with the definition of $g(y_{it}, x_{it}, \nu_i)$, the total log likelihood is approximated by

$$L \approx \sum_{i=1}^{n} w_i \log\left[\sqrt{2}\widehat{\sigma}_i \sum_{m=1}^{M} w_m^* \exp\{(a_m^*)^2\} \frac{\exp\{-(\sqrt{2}\widehat{\sigma}_i a_m^* + \widehat{\mu}_i)^2/2\sigma_\nu^2\}}{\sqrt{2\pi}\sigma_\nu} \right.$$

$$\left. \prod_{t=1}^{n_i} F(y_{it}, x_{it}\boldsymbol{\beta} + \sqrt{2}\widehat{\sigma}_i a_m^* + \widehat{\mu}_i) \right]$$

where w_i is the user-specified weight for panel i; if no weights are specified, $w_i = 1$.

The default method of adaptive Gauss–Hermite quadrature is to calculate the posterior mean and variance and use those parameters for $\widehat{\mu}_i$ and $\widehat{\sigma}_i$ by following the method of Naylor and Smith (1982), further discussed in Skrondal and Rabe-Hesketh (2004). We start with $\widehat{\sigma}_{i,0} = 1$ and $\widehat{\mu}_{i,0} = 0$, and the posterior means and variances are updated in the kth iteration. That is, at the kth iteration of the optimization for l_i, we use

$$l_{i,k} \approx \sum_{m=1}^{M} \sqrt{2}\widehat{\sigma}_{i,k-1} w_m^* \exp\{a_m^*)^2\} g(y_{it}, x_{it}, \sqrt{2}\widehat{\sigma}_{i,k-1} a_m^* + \widehat{\mu}_{i,k-1})$$

Letting

$$\tau_{i,m,k-1} = \sqrt{2}\widehat{\sigma}_{i,k-1} a_m^* + \widehat{\mu}_{i,k-1}$$

$$\widehat{\mu}_{i,k} = \sum_{m=1}^{M} (\tau_{i,m,k-1}) \frac{\sqrt{2}\widehat{\sigma}_{i,k-1} w_m^* \exp\{(a_m^*)^2\} g(y_{it}, x_{it}, \tau_{i,m,k-1})}{l_{i,k}}$$

and

$$\widehat{\sigma}_{i,k} = \sum_{m=1}^{M} (\tau_{i,m,k-1})^2 \frac{\sqrt{2}\widehat{\sigma}_{i,k-1} w_m^* \exp\{(a_m^*)^2\} g(y_{it}, x_{it}, \tau_{i,m,k-1})}{l_{i,k}} - (\widehat{\mu}_{i,k})^2$$

and this is repeated until $\widehat{\mu}_{i,k}$ and $\widehat{\sigma}_{i,k}$ have converged for this iteration of the maximization algorithm. This adaptation is applied on every iteration until the log-likelihood change from the preceding iteration is less than a relative difference of 1e–6; after this, the quadrature parameters are fixed.

One can instead use the adaptive quadrature method of Liu and Pierce (1994), option `int-method(aghermite)`, which uses the mode and curvature of the mode as approximations for the mean and variance. We take the integrand

$$g(y_{it}, x_{it}, \nu_i) = \frac{e^{-\nu_i^2/2\sigma_\nu^2}}{\sqrt{2\pi}\sigma_\nu} \left\{ \prod_{t=1}^{n_i} F(y_{it}, \mathbf{x}_{it}\boldsymbol{\beta} + \nu_i) \right\}$$

and find α_i the mode of $g(y_{it}, x_{it}, \nu_i)$. We calculate

$$\gamma_i = -\frac{\partial^2}{\partial \nu_i^2} \log\{g(y_{it}, x_{it}, \nu_i)\}\big|_{\nu_i = \alpha_i}$$

Then

$$\int_{-\infty}^{\infty} g(y_{it}, x_{it}, \nu_i) d\nu_i \approx \left(\frac{2}{\gamma_i}\right)^{1/2} \sum_{m=1}^{M} w_m^* \exp\{(a_m^*)^2\} g\left\{y_{it}, x_{it}, \left(\frac{2}{\gamma_i}\right)^{1/2} a_m^* + \alpha_i\right\}$$

This adaptation is performed on the first iteration only; that is, the α_i and γ_i are calculated once at the first iteration and then held constant throughout the subsequent iterations.

The log likelihood can also be calculated by nonadaptive Gauss–Hermite quadrature, option `intmethod(ghermite)`, where $\rho = \sigma_\nu^2/(\sigma_\nu^2 + 1)$:

$$L = \sum_{i=1}^{n} w_i \log\left\{\Pr(y_{i1}, \ldots, y_{in_i} | \mathbf{x}_{i1}, \ldots, \mathbf{x}_{in_i})\right\}$$

$$\approx \sum_{i=1}^{n} w_i \log\left[\frac{1}{\sqrt{\pi}} \sum_{m=1}^{M} w_m^* \prod_{t=1}^{n_i} F\left\{y_{it}, \mathbf{x}_{it}\boldsymbol{\beta} + a_m^* \left(\frac{2\rho}{1-\rho}\right)^{1/2}\right\}\right]$$

All three quadrature formulas require that the integrated function be well approximated by a polynomial of degree equal to the number of quadrature points. The number of periods (panel size) can affect whether

$$\prod_{t=1}^{n_i} F(y_{it}, \mathbf{x}_{it}\boldsymbol{\beta} + \nu_i)$$

is well approximated by a polynomial. As panel size and ρ increase, the quadrature approximation can become less accurate. For large ρ, the random-effects model can also become unidentified. Adaptive quadrature gives better results for correlated data and large panels than nonadaptive quadrature; however, we recommend that you use the quadchk command to verify the quadrature approximation used in this command, whichever approximation you choose.

For a fixed-effects specification, we know that

$$\Pr(Y_{it} = y_{it}|\mathbf{x}_{it}) = \exp\{-\exp(\alpha_i + \mathbf{x}_{it}\boldsymbol{\beta})\}\exp(\alpha_i + \mathbf{x}_{it}\boldsymbol{\beta})^{y_{it}}/y_{it}!$$

$$= \frac{1}{y_{it}!}\exp\{-\exp(\alpha_i)\exp(\mathbf{x}_{it}\boldsymbol{\beta}) + \alpha_i y_{it}\}\exp(\mathbf{x}_{it}\boldsymbol{\beta})^{y_{it}}$$

$$\equiv F_{it}$$

Since we know that the observations are independent, we may write the joint probability for the observations within a panel as

$$\Pr\left(Y_{i1} = y_{i1}, \ldots, Y_{in_i} = y_{in_i}|\mathbf{X}_i\right)$$

$$= \prod_{t=1}^{n_i} \frac{1}{y_{it}!}\exp\{-\exp(\alpha_i)\exp(\mathbf{x}_{it}\boldsymbol{\beta}) + \alpha_i y_{it}\}\exp(\mathbf{x}_{it}\boldsymbol{\beta})^{y_{it}}$$

$$= \left(\prod_{t=1}^{n_i} \frac{\exp(\mathbf{x}_{it}\boldsymbol{\beta})^{y_{it}}}{y_{it}!}\right)\exp\left\{-\exp(\alpha_i)\sum_t \exp(\mathbf{x}_{it}\boldsymbol{\beta}) + \alpha_i \sum_t y_{it}\right\}$$

and we also know that the sum of n_i Poisson independent random variables, each with parameter λ_{it} for $t = 1, \ldots, n_i$, is distributed as Poisson with parameter $\sum_t \lambda_{it}$. Thus

$$\Pr\left(\sum_t Y_{it} = \sum_t y_{it}\bigg|\mathbf{X}_i\right) =$$

$$\frac{1}{(\sum_t y_{it})!}\exp\left\{-\exp(\alpha_i)\sum_t \exp(\mathbf{x}_{it}\boldsymbol{\beta}) + \alpha_i \sum_t y_{it}\right\}\left\{\sum_t \exp(\mathbf{x}_{it}\boldsymbol{\beta})\right\}^{\sum_t y_{it}}$$

So, the conditional likelihood is conditioned on the sum of the outcomes in the set (panel). The appropriate function is given by

$$\Pr\left(Y_{i1} = y_{i1}, \ldots, Y_{in_i} = y_{in_i} \middle| \mathbf{X}_i, \sum_t Y_{it} = \sum_t y_{it}\right) =$$

$$\left[\left(\prod_{t=1}^{n_i} \frac{\exp(\mathbf{x}_{it}\boldsymbol{\beta})^{y_{it}}}{y_{it}!}\right) \exp\left\{-\exp(\alpha_i)\sum_t \exp(\mathbf{x}_{it}\boldsymbol{\beta}) + \alpha_i \sum_t y_{it}\right\}\right] \Big/$$

$$\left[\frac{1}{(\sum_t y_{it})!}\exp\left\{-\exp(\alpha_i)\sum_t \exp(\mathbf{x}_{it}\boldsymbol{\beta}) + \alpha_i \sum_t y_{it}\right\}\left\{\sum_t \exp(\mathbf{x}_{it}\boldsymbol{\beta})\right\}^{\sum_t y_{it}}\right]$$

$$= \left(\sum_t y_{it}\right)!\prod_{t=1}^{n_i} \frac{\exp(\mathbf{x}_{it}\boldsymbol{\beta})^{y_{it}}}{y_{it}!\left\{\sum_k \exp(\mathbf{x}_{ik}\boldsymbol{\beta})\right\}^{y_{it}}}$$

which is free of α_i.

The conditional log likelihood is given by

$$L = \log \prod_{i=1}^{n}\left[\left(\sum_{t=1}^{n_i} y_{it}\right)!\prod_{t=1}^{n_i} \frac{\exp(\mathbf{x}_{it}\boldsymbol{\beta})^{y_{it}}}{y_{it}!\left\{\sum_{\ell=1}^{n_\ell} \exp(\mathbf{x}_{i\ell}\boldsymbol{\beta})\right\}^{y_{it}}}\right]^{w_i}$$

$$= \log \prod_{i=1}^{n}\left\{\frac{(\sum_t y_{it})!}{\prod_{t=1}^{n_i} y_{it}!}\prod_{t=1}^{n_i} p_{it}^{y_{it}}\right\}^{w_i}$$

$$= \sum_{i=1}^{n} w_i \left\{\log \Gamma\left(\sum_{t=1}^{n_i} y_{it} + 1\right) - \sum_{t=1}^{n_i} \log \Gamma(y_{it} + 1) + \sum_{t=1}^{n_i} y_{it} \log p_{it}\right\}$$

where

$$p_{it} = e^{\mathbf{x}_{it}\boldsymbol{\beta}} \Big/ \sum_\ell e^{\mathbf{x}_{i\ell}\boldsymbol{\beta}}$$

References

Cameron, A. C., and P. K. Trivedi. 1998. *Regression Analysis of Count Data*. New York: Cambridge University Press.

Greene, W. H. 2003. *Econometric Analysis*. 5th ed. Upper Saddle River, NJ: Prentice Hall.

Hardin, J., and J. Hilbe. 2007. *Generalized Linear Models and Extensions*. 2nd ed. College Station, TX: Stata Press.

Hausman, J., B. H. Hall, and Z. Griliches. 1984. Econometric models for count data with an application to the patents–R & D relationship. *Econometrica* 52: 909–938.

Liang, K.-Y., and S. L. Zeger. 1986. Longitudinal data analysis using generalized linear models. *Biometrika* 73: 13–22.

Liu, Q., and D. A. Pierce. 1994. A note on Gauss–Hermite quadrature. *Biometrika* 81: 624–629.

Naylor, J. C., and A. F. M. Smith. 1982. Applications of a method for the efficient computation of posterior distributions. *Journal of the Royal Statistical Society, Series C* 31: 214–225.

McCullagh, P., and J. A. Nelder. 1989. *Generalized Linear Models*. 2nd ed. London: Chapman & Hall/CRC.

Skrondal, A., and S. Rabe-Hesketh. 2004. *Generalized Latent Variable Modeling: Multilevel, Longitudinal, and Structural Equation Models*. Boca Raton, FL: Chapman & Hall/CRC.

Also See

Title

> **xtpoisson postestimation** — Postestimation tools for xtpoisson

Description

The following postestimation commands are available for xtpoisson:

command	description
adjust[1]	adjusted predictions of $\mathbf{x}\beta$ or $\exp(\mathbf{x}\beta)$
*estat	AIC, BIC, VCE, and estimation sample summary
estimates	cataloging estimation results
hausman	Hausman's specification test
lincom	point estimates, standard errors, testing, and inference for linear combinations of coefficients
lrtest	likelihood-ratio test
mfx	marginal effects or elasticities
nlcom	point estimates, standard errors, testing, and inference for nonlinear combinations of coefficients
predict	predictions, residuals, influence statistics, and other diagnostic measures
predictnl	point estimates, standard errors, testing, and inference for generalized predictions
test	Wald tests for simple and composite linear hypotheses
testnl	Wald tests of nonlinear hypotheses

[1] adjust is not appropriate with time-series operators.

* estat ic is not appropriate after xtpoisson, pa.

See the corresponding entries in the *Stata Base Reference Manual* for details.

Syntax for predict

Random-effects (RE) and fixed-effects (FE) models

> predict [*type*] *newvar* [*if*] [*in*] [, *RE/FE_statistic* <u>nooff</u>set]

Population-averaged (PA) model

> predict [*type*] *newvar* [*if*] [*in*] [, *PA_statistic* <u>nooff</u>set]

RE/FE_statistic	description
Main	
xb	linear prediction; the default
stdp	standard error of the linear prediction
nu0	predicted number of events; assumes zero
iru0	predicted incidence rate; assumes zero

360

PA_statistic	description
Main	
mu	predicted value of *depvar*; considers the offset(); the default
rate	predicted value of *depvar*
xb	linear prediction
stdp	standard error of the linear prediction
score	first derivative of the log likelihood with respect to $x_j\beta$

These statistics are available both in and out of sample; type predict ... if e(sample) ... if wanted only for the estimation sample.

Options for predict

⌐ Main ⌐

xb calculates the linear prediction. This is the default for the random-effects and fixed-effects models.

mu and rate both calculate the predicted value of *depvar*, i.e., the predicted count. mu takes into account the offset(), and rate ignores those adjustments. mu and rate are equivalent if you did not specify offset(). mu is the default for the population-averaged model.

stdp calculates the standard error of the linear prediction.

nu0 calculates the predicted number of events, assuming a zero random or fixed effect.

iru0 calculates the predicted incidence rate, assuming a zero random or fixed effect.

score calculates the equation-level score, $u_j = \partial \ln L_j(x_j\beta)/\partial(x_j\beta)$.

nooffset is relevant only if you specified offset(*varname*) for xtpoisson. It modifies the calculations made by predict so that they ignore the offset variable; the linear prediction is treated as $x_{it}\beta$ rather than $x_{it}\beta + \text{offset}_{it}$.

Remarks

▷ Example 1

In [XT] **xtpoisson**, we fitted a random-effects model of the number of accidents experienced by five different types of ships on the basis of when the ships were constructed and operated. Here we obtain the predicted number of accidents for each observation, assuming that the random effect for each panel is zero:

```
. use http://www.stata-press.com/data/r10/ships
. xtpoisson accident op_75_79 co_65_69 co_70_74 co_75_79, exposure(service) irr
 (output omitted )
. predict n_acc, nu0
(6 missing values generated)
. summarize n_acc
```

Variable	Obs	Mean	Std. Dev.	Min	Max
n_acc	34	13.52307	23.15885	.0617592	83.31905

From these results, you may be tempted to conclude that some types of ships are safe, with a predicted number of accidents close to zero, whereas others are dangerous, since 1 observation is predicted to have more than 83 accidents.

However, when we fitted the model, we specified the option `exposure(service)`. The variable `service` records the total number of months of operation for each type of ship constructed in and operated during particular years. Because ships experienced different utilization rates and thus were exposed to different levels of accident risk, we included `service` as our exposure variable. When comparing different types of ships, we must therefore predict the number of accidents, assuming that all ships faced the same exposure to risk. To do that, we use the `iru0` option with `predict`:

```
. predict acc_rate, iru0

. summarize acc_rate
```

Variable	Obs	Mean	Std. Dev.	Min	Max
acc_rate	40	.002975	.0010497	.0013724	.0047429

These results show that if each ship were used for 1 month, the expected number of accidents is 0.002975. Depending on the type of ship and years of construction and operation, the *incidence rate* of accidents ranges from 0.00137 to 0.00474.

◁

Methods and Formulas

All postestimation commands listed above are implemented as ado-files.

Also See

[XT] **xtpoisson** — Fixed-effects, random-effects, and population-averaged Poisson models

[U] **20 Estimation and postestimation commands**

Title

> **xtprobit** — Random-effects and population-averaged probit models

Syntax

Random-effects (RE) model

> xtprobit *depvar* [*indepvars*] [*if*] [*in*] [*weight*] [, re *RE_options*]

Population-averaged (PA) model

> xtprobit *depvar* [*indepvars*] [*if*] [*in*] [*weight*] , pa [*PA_options*]

RE_options	description
Model	
noconstant	suppress constant term
re	use random-effects estimator; the default
offset(*varname*)	include *varname* in model with coefficient constrained to 1
constraints(*constraints*)	apply specified linear constraints
collinear	keep collinear variables
SE	
vce(*vcetype*)	*vcetype* may be oim, bootstrap, or jackknife
Reporting	
level(#)	set confidence level; default is level(95)
noskip	perform overall model test as a likelihood-ratio test
Int opts (RE)	
intmethod(*intmethod*)	integration method; *intmethod* may be mvaghermite, aghermite, or ghermite; default is intmethod(mvaghermite)
intpoints(#)	use # quadrature points; default is intpoints(12)
Max options	
maximize_options	control the maximization process; seldom used

(Continued on next page)

PA_options	description
Model	
<u>nocon</u>stant	suppress constant term
pa	use population-averaged estimator
<u>off</u>set(*varname*)	include *varname* in model with coefficient constrained to 1
Correlation	
<u>corr</u>(*correlation*)	within-group correlation structure
force	estimate even if observations unequally spaced in time
SE/Robust	
vce(*vcetype*)	*vcetype* may be conventional, <u>r</u>obust, <u>boot</u>strap, or <u>jack</u>knife
nmp	use divisor $N - P$ instead of the default N
<u>sc</u>ale(*parm*)	overrides the default scale parameter; *parm* may be x2, dev, phi, or #
Reporting	
<u>level</u>(#)	set confidence level; default is level(95)
Opt options	
optimize_options	control the optimization process; seldom used

correlation	description
<u>exc</u>hangeable	exchangeable
<u>ind</u>ependent	independent
<u>uns</u>tructured	unstructured
<u>fix</u>ed *matname*	user-specified
ar #	autoregressive of order #
<u>stat</u>ionary #	stationary of order #
<u>nons</u>tationary #	nonstationary of order #

A panel variable must be specified. For xtprobit, pa, correlation structures other than exchangeable and independent require that a time variable also be specified. Use xtset; see [XT] **xtset**.

depvar and *indepvars* may contain time-series operators; see [U] **11.4.3 Time-series varlists**.

by, statsby, and xi are allowed; see [U] **11.1.10 Prefix commands**.

iweights, fweights, and pweights are allowed for the population-averaged model, and iweights are allowed in the random-effects model; see [U] **11.1.6 weight**. Weights must be constant within panel.

See [U] **20 Estimation and postestimation commands** for more capabilities of estimation commands.

Description

xtprobit fits random-effects and population-averaged probit models. There is no command for a conditional fixed-effects model, as there does not exist a sufficient statistic allowing the fixed effects to be conditioned out of the likelihood. Unconditional fixed-effects probit models may be fitted with the probit command with indicator variables for the panels. The appropriate indicator variables can be generated using tabulate or xi. However, unconditional fixed-effects estimates are biased.

xtprobit, re, the default, is slow because the likelihood function is calculated by adaptive Gauss–Hermite quadrature; see *Methods and Formulas*. Computation time is roughly proportional to the number of points used for the quadrature. The default is intpoints(12). Increasing the number of quadrature points can improve the quadrature approximation. See [XT] **quadchk**.

By default, the population-averaged model is an equal-correlation model; xtprobit assumes the within-group correlation structure corr(exchangeable). See [XT] **xtgee** for information about how to fit other population-averaged models.

See [R] **logistic** for a list of related estimation commands.

Options for RE model

⌐ Model ⌐

noconstant; see [XT] **estimation options**.

re requests the random-effects estimator. re is the default if neither re nor pa is specified.

offset(*varname*), constraints(*constraints*), collinear; see [XT] **estimation options**.

⌐ SE ⌐

vce(*vcetype*) specifies the type of standard error reported, which includes types that are derived from asymptotic theory and that use bootstrap or jackknife methods; see [XT] *vce_options*.

⌐ Reporting ⌐

level(*#*), noskip; see [XT] **estimation options**.

⌐ Int opts (RE) ⌐

intmethod(*intmethod*), intpoints(*#*); see [XT] **estimation options**.

⌐ Max options ⌐

maximize_options: <u>dif</u>ficult, <u>tech</u>nique(*algorithm_spec*), <u>iter</u>ate(*#*), [<u>no</u>]<u>log</u>, <u>tra</u>ce, gradient, showstep, <u>hess</u>ian, <u>shownr</u>tolerance, <u>tol</u>erance(*#*), <u>ltol</u>erance(*#*), <u>gtol</u>erance(*#*), <u>nrtol</u>erance(*#*), nonrtolerance, from(*init_specs*); see [R] **maximize**. These options are seldom used.

Options for PA model

⌐ Model ⌐

noconstant; see [XT] **estimation options**.

pa requests the population-averaged estimator.

offset(*varname*); see [XT] **estimation options**.

⌐ Correlation ⌐

corr(*correlation*), force; see [XT] **estimation options**.

vce(*vcetype*) specifies the type of standard error reported, which includes types that are derived from asymptotic theory, that are robust to some kinds of misspecification, and that use bootstrap or jackknife methods; see [XT] *vce_options*.

vce(conventional), the default, uses the conventionally derived variance estimator for generalized least-squares regression.

nmp, scale(x2 | dev | phi | #); see [XT] *vce_options*.

Reporting

level(#); see [XT] **estimation options**.

Opt options

optimize_options control the iterative optimization process. These options are seldom used.

iterate(#) specifies the maximum number of iterations. When the number of iterations equals #, the optimization stops and presents the current results, even if convergence has not been reached. The default is iterate(100).

tolerance(#) specifies the tolerance for the coefficient vector. When the relative change in the coefficient vector from one iteration to the next is less than or equal to #, the optimization process is stopped. tolerance(1e-6) is the default.

nolog suppresses display of the iteration log.

trace specifies that the current estimates be printed at each iteration.

Remarks

xtprobit is a convenience command for obtaining the population-averaged model. Typing

    . xtprobit ..., pa ...

is equivalent to typing

    . xtgee ..., ... family(binomial) link(probit) corr(exchangeable)

See also [XT] **xtgee** for information about xtprobit.

By default or when re is specified, xtprobit fits via maximum likelihood the random-effects model

$$\Pr(y_{it} \neq 0 | \mathbf{x}_{it}) = \Phi(\mathbf{x}_{it}\boldsymbol{\beta} + \nu_i)$$

for $i = 1, \ldots, n$ panels, where $t = 1, \ldots, n_i$, ν_i are i.i.d., $N(0, \sigma_\nu^2)$, and Φ is the standard normal cumulative distribution function.

Underlying this model is the variance components model

$$y_{it} \neq 0 \iff \mathbf{x}_{it}\boldsymbol{\beta} + \nu_i + \epsilon_{it} > 0$$

where ϵ_{it} are i.i.d. Gaussian distributed with mean zero and variance $\sigma_\epsilon^2 = 1$, independently of ν_i.

▷ Example 1

We are studying unionization of women in the United States and are using the union dataset; see [XT] **xt**. We wish to fit a random-effects model of union membership:

```
. use http://www.stata-press.com/data/r10/union
(NLS Women 14-24 in 1968)
. xtprobit union age grade not_smsa south southXt
Fitting comparison model:
Iteration 0:   log likelihood =  -13864.23
Iteration 1:   log likelihood = -13548.436
Iteration 2:   log likelihood = -13547.308
Iteration 3:   log likelihood = -13547.308
Fitting full model:
rho =  0.0      log likelihood = -13547.308
rho =  0.1      log likelihood = -12239.207
rho =  0.2      log likelihood = -11591.449
rho =  0.3      log likelihood = -11212.156
rho =  0.4      log likelihood = -10982.153
rho =  0.5      log likelihood = -10853.488
rho =  0.6      log likelihood = -10809.372
rho =  0.7      log likelihood =  -10866.13
Iteration 0:    log likelihood = -10808.301
Iteration 1:    log likelihood = -10599.612
Iteration 2:    log likelihood = -10552.389
Iteration 3:    log likelihood = -10552.327
Iteration 4:    log likelihood = -10552.327
```

| Random-effects probit regression | | | | Number of obs | = | 26200 |
| Group variable: idcode | | | | Number of groups | = | 4434 |

Random effects u_i ~ Gaussian

			Obs per group: min =	1
			avg =	5.9
			max =	12

| | Wald chi2(5) | = | 220.73 |
| Log likelihood = -10552.327 | Prob > chi2 | = | 0.0000 |

union	Coef.	Std. Err.	z	P>|z|	[95% Conf. Interval]	
age	.0046532	.0025134	1.85	0.064	-.000273	.0095795
grade	.0481056	.0099402	4.84	0.000	.0286232	.0675881
not_smsa	-.1401136	.0460446	-3.04	0.002	-.2303594	-.0498679
south	-.6428989	.0619944	-10.37	0.000	-.7644058	-.521392
southXt	.0130454	.0043914	2.97	0.003	.0044384	.0216525
_cons	-1.872166	.1455716	-12.86	0.000	-2.157481	-1.586851
/lnsig2u	.6105518	.0458732			.5206419	.7004617
sigma_u	1.356999	.031125			1.297346	1.419395
rho	.6480667	.0104626			.6272979	.6682901

Likelihood-ratio test of rho=0: chibar2(01) = 5989.96 Prob >= chibar2 = 0.000

The output includes the additional panel-level variance component, which is parameterized as the log of the variance $\ln(\sigma_\nu^2)$ (labeled lnsig2u in the output). The standard deviation σ_ν is also included in the output (labeled sigma_u) together with ρ (labeled rho), where

$$\rho = \frac{\sigma_\nu^2}{\sigma_\nu^2 + 1}$$

which is the proportion of the total variance contributed by the panel-level variance component.

When `rho` is zero, the panel-level variance component is unimportant, and the panel estimator is not different from the pooled estimator. A likelihood-ratio test of this is included at the bottom of the output. This test formally compares the pooled estimator (probit) with the panel estimator.

◁

❏ Technical Note

The random-effects model is calculated using quadrature. Large panel sizes and ρ can cause the quadrature approximation and the random effects model to become less accurate. We can use the `quadchk` command to see if changing the number of quadrature points affects the results. If the results change, the quadrature approximation is not accurate. The number of quadrature points should be increased until the results are stable. If this cannot be achieved, the results of the model should not be interpreted.

```
. quadchk, nooutput
Refitting model intpoints() =  8
Refitting model intpoints() = 16
```

	Fitted quadrature 12 points	Comparison quadrature 8 points	Comparison quadrature 16 points	
Log likelihood	-10552.327	-10554.6 -2.2730052 .0002154	-10552.501 -.17421606 .00001651	Difference Relative difference
union: age	.00465324	.00464778 -5.451e-06 -.00117145	.00465651 3.276e-06 .00070403	Difference Relative difference
union: grade	.04810562	.04843597 .00033035 .00686714	.04809464 -.00001099 -.00022837	Difference Relative difference
union: not_smsa	-.14011361	-.1410318 -.00091819 .00655319	-.13999397 .00011964 -.00085389	Difference Relative difference
union: south	-.6428989	-.64653423 -.00363533 .00565459	-.64267246 .00022644 -.00035222	Difference Relative difference
union: southXt	.01304544	.01309238 .00004694 .00359797	.01304601 5.681e-07 .00004355	Difference Relative difference
union: _cons	-1.8721664	-1.8792684 -.00710208 .00379351	-1.8713416 .00082478 -.00044055	Difference Relative difference
lnsig2u: _cons	.61055183	.61800191 .00745008 .0122022	.60993729 -.00061454 -.00100654	Difference Relative difference

Quadrature check

The results obtained for 12 quadrature points were closer to the results for 16 points than to the results for eight points. Although the relative and absolute differences are a bit larger than we'd like, they are not large. We can increase the number of quadrature points with the `intpoints()` option; if we choose `intpoints(20)` and do another `quadchk` we will get acceptable results, with relative differences around .01%.

This is not the case if we use nonadaptive quadrature. Then the results we obtain are

```
. xtprobit union age grade not_smsa south southXt, intmethod(ghermite)
Fitting comparison model:
Iteration 0:   log likelihood = -13864.23
Iteration 1:   log likelihood = -13548.436
Iteration 2:   log likelihood = -13547.308
Iteration 3:   log likelihood = -13547.308

Fitting full model:
rho =  0.0     log likelihood = -13547.308
rho =  0.1     log likelihood = -12239.207
rho =  0.2     log likelihood = -11591.449
rho =  0.3     log likelihood = -11212.156
rho =  0.4     log likelihood = -10982.153
rho =  0.5     log likelihood = -10853.488
rho =  0.6     log likelihood = -10809.372
rho =  0.7     log likelihood =  -10866.13

Iteration 0:   log likelihood = -10809.372
Iteration 1:   log likelihood = -10595.191
Iteration 2:   log likelihood = -10561.107
Iteration 3:   log likelihood = -10561.065
Iteration 4:   log likelihood = -10561.065
```

Random-effects probit regression | Number of obs = 26200
Group variable: idcode | Number of groups = 4434

Random effects u_i ~ Gaussian | Obs per group: min = 1
avg = 5.9
max = 12

Wald chi2(5) = 218.90
Log likelihood = -10561.065 | Prob > chi2 = 0.0000

union	Coef.	Std. Err.	z	P>|z|	[95% Conf. Interval]
age	.0044483	.0025027	1.78	0.076	-.000457	.0093535
grade	.0482482	.0100413	4.80	0.000	.0285677	.0679287
not_smsa	-.1370699	.0462961	-2.96	0.003	-.2278087	-.0463312
south	-.6305824	.0614827	-10.26	0.000	-.7510863	-.5100785
southXt	.0131853	.0043819	3.01	0.003	.004597	.0217737
_cons	-1.846838	.1458222	-12.67	0.000	-2.132644	-1.561032
/lnsig2u	.5612193	.0431875			.4765733	.6458653
sigma_u	1.323937	.0285888			1.269073	1.381172
rho	.6367346	.0099894			.6169384	.6560781

Likelihood-ratio test of rho=0: chibar2(01) = 5972.49 Prob >= chibar2 = 0.000

We now check the stability of the quadrature technique for this nonadaptive quadrature model. We expect it to be less stable.

```
. quadchk, nooutput
```

Refitting model intpoints() = 8
Refitting model intpoints() = 16

Quadrature check

	Fitted quadrature 12 points	Comparison quadrature 8 points	Comparison quadrature 16 points	
Log likelihood	-10561.065	-10574.78 -13.714764 .00129862	-10555.853 5.2126898 -.00049358	Difference Relative difference
union: age	.00444829	.00478943 .00034115 .07669143	.00451117 .00006288 .01413655	Difference Relative difference
union: grade	.04824822	.05629525 .00804704 .16678412	.04411083 -.00413739 -.0857522	Difference Relative difference
union: not_smsa	-.13706993	-.1314541 .00561584 -.0409706	-.14109796 -.00402802 .02938663	Difference Relative difference
union: south	-.63058241	-.62309654 .00748587 -.01187136	-.64546964 -.01488724 .02360871	Difference Relative difference
union: southXt	.01318534	.01194434 -.001241 -.09411977	.01341722 .00023188 .01758651	Difference Relative difference
union: _cons	-1.8468379	-1.9306422 -.08380427 .04537716	-1.8066854 .04015255 -.02174124	Difference Relative difference
lnsig2u: _cons	.56121927	.49078989 -.07042938 -.12549352	.58080948 .01959021 .03490652	Difference Relative difference

Once again, the results obtained for 12 quadrature points were closer to the results for 16 points than to the results for eight points. However, here the convergence point seems to be sensitive to the number of quadrature points, so we should not trust these results. We should increase the number of quadrature points with the intpoints() option and then use quadchk again. We should not use the results of a random-effects specification when there is evidence that the numeric technique for calculating the model is not stable (as shown by quadchk).

Generally, the relative differences in the coefficients should not change by more than 1% if the quadrature technique is stable. See [XT] **quadchk** for details. Increasing the number of quadrature points can often improve the stability, and for models with high rho we may need many. We can also switch between adaptive and nonadaptive quadrature. As a rule, adaptive quadrature, which is the default integration method, is much more flexible and robust.

❑

▷ Example 2

As an alternative to the random-effects specification, we can fit an equal-correlation probit model:

```
. xtprobit union age grade not_smsa south southXt, pa
Iteration 1: tolerance = .04796083
Iteration 2: tolerance = .00352657
Iteration 3: tolerance = .00017886
Iteration 4: tolerance = 8.654e-06
Iteration 5: tolerance = 4.150e-07
```

GEE population-averaged model				Number of obs	=	26200
Group variable:		idcode		Number of groups	=	4434
Link:		probit		Obs per group: min	=	1
Family:		binomial		avg	=	5.9
Correlation:		exchangeable		max	=	12
				Wald chi2(5)	=	241.66
Scale parameter:		1		Prob > chi2	=	0.0000

union	Coef.	Std. Err.	z	P>|z|	[95% Conf. Interval]	
age	.0031597	.0014678	2.15	0.031	.0002829	.0060366
grade	.0329992	.0062334	5.29	0.000	.020782	.0452163
not_smsa	-.0721799	.0275189	-2.62	0.009	-.1261159	-.0182439
south	-.409029	.0372213	-10.99	0.000	-.4819815	-.3360765
southXt	.0081828	.002545	3.22	0.001	.0031946	.0131709
_cons	-1.184799	.0890117	-13.31	0.000	-1.359259	-1.01034

◁

▷ Example 3

In [R] **probit**, we showed the above results and compared them with probit, vce(cluster id). xtprobit with the pa option allows a vce(robust) option (the random-effects estimator does not allow the vce(robust) specification), so we can obtain the population-averaged probit estimator with the robust variance calculation by typing

```
. xtprobit union age grade not_smsa south southXt, pa vce(robust) nolog
```

GEE population-averaged model				Number of obs	=	26200
Group variable:		idcode		Number of groups	=	4434
Link:		probit		Obs per group: min	=	1
Family:		binomial		avg	=	5.9
Correlation:		exchangeable		max	=	12
				Wald chi2(5)	=	154.00
Scale parameter:		1		Prob > chi2	=	0.0000

(Std. Err. adjusted for clustering on idcode)

union	Coef.	Semi-robust Std. Err.	z	P>|z|	[95% Conf. Interval]	
age	.0031597	.0022027	1.43	0.151	-.0011575	.007477
grade	.0329992	.0076631	4.31	0.000	.0179797	.0480186
not_smsa	-.0721799	.0348772	-2.07	0.038	-.140538	-.0038218
south	-.409029	.0482545	-8.48	0.000	-.5036061	-.3144519
southXt	.0081828	.0037108	2.21	0.027	.0009097	.0154558
_cons	-1.184799	.116457	-10.17	0.000	-1.413051	-.9565479

These standard errors are similar to those shown for probit, vce(cluster id) in [R] **probit**.

◁

▷ Example 4

In a previous example, we showed how quadchk indicated that the quadrature technique was numerically unstable. Here we present an example in which the quadrature is stable.

In this example, we have (synthetic) data on whether workers complain to managers at fast-food restaurants. The covariates are age (in years of the worker), grade (years of schooling completed by the worker), south (equal to 1 if the restaurant is located in the South), tenure (the number of years spent on the job by the worker), gender (of the worker), race (of the worker), income (in thousands of dollars by the restaurant), genderm (gender of the manager), burger (equal to 1 if the restaurant specializes in hamburgers), and chicken (equal to 1 if the restaurant specializes in chicken). The model is given by

```
. use http://www.stata-press.com/data/r10/chicken
. xtprobit complain age grade south tenure gender race income genderm burger
> chicken, nolog
```

Random-effects probit regression   Number of obs   =   2763
Group variable: restaurant   Number of groups   =   500

Random effects u_i ~ Gaussian   Obs per group: min =   3
                                                          avg =   5.5
                                                          max =   8

                                           Wald chi2(10)   =   126.59
Log likelihood = -1318.2088   Prob > chi2   =   0.0000

complain	Coef.	Std. Err.	z	P>|z|	[95% Conf. Interval]	
age	-.0430409	.0130211	-3.31	0.001	-.0685617	-.01752
grade	.0330934	.0264572	1.25	0.211	-.0187618	.0849486
south	.1012	.0707196	1.43	0.152	-.037408	.2398079
tenure	-.0440079	.0987099	-0.45	0.656	-.2374758	.14946
gender	.3318499	.0601382	5.52	0.000	.2139812	.4497185
race	.3417901	.0382251	8.94	0.000	.2668703	.4167098
income	-.0022702	.0008885	-2.56	0.011	-.0040117	-.0005288
genderm	.0524577	.0706587	0.74	0.458	-.0860305	.1909459
burger	.0448931	.0956151	0.47	0.639	-.1425091	.2322953
chicken	.1904714	.0953067	2.00	0.046	.0036737	.3772691
_cons	-.2145311	.6240549	-0.34	0.731	-1.437656	1.008594
/lnsig2u	-1.704494	.2502057			-2.194888	-1.214099
sigma_u	.4264557	.0533508			.333723	.5449563
rho	.1538793	.0325769			.1002105	.2289765

Likelihood-ratio test of rho=0: chibar2(01) =   29.91 Prob >= chibar2 = 0.000

Again we would like to check the stability of the quadrature technique of the model before interpreting the results. Given the estimate of ρ and the small size of the panels (between 3 and 8), we should find that the quadrature technique is numerically stable.

```
. quadchk, nooutput
Refitting model intpoints() =  8
Refitting model intpoints() = 16
```

Quadrature check

	Fitted quadrature 12 points	Comparison quadrature 8 points	Comparison quadrature 16 points	
Log likelihood	-1318.2088	-1318.2088 -2.002e-06 1.519e-09	-1318.2088 -1.195e-09 9.064e-13	Difference Relative difference
complain: age	-.04304086	-.04304086 -3.896e-10 9.051e-09	-.04304086 -2.625e-12 6.100e-11	Difference Relative difference
complain: grade	.0330934	.0330934 2.208e-11 6.673e-10	.0330934 1.867e-12 5.643e-11	Difference Relative difference
complain: south	.10119998	.10119999 2.369e-09 2.341e-08	.10119998 3.957e-11 3.910e-10	Difference Relative difference
complain: tenure	-.04400789	-.0440079 -3.362e-09 7.640e-08	-.04400789 -2.250e-11 5.114e-10	Difference Relative difference
complain: gender	.33184986	.33184986 3.190e-09 9.612e-09	.33184986 2.546e-11 7.673e-11	Difference Relative difference
complain: race	.34179006	.34179007 3.801e-09 1.112e-08	.34179006 2.990e-11 8.749e-11	Difference Relative difference
complain: income	-.00227021	-.00227021 -4.468e-11 1.968e-08	-.00227021 -9.252e-13 4.075e-10	Difference Relative difference
complain: genderm	.05245769	.05245769 1.963e-09 3.742e-08	.05245769 4.481e-11 8.542e-10	Difference Relative difference
complain: burger	.04489311	.04489311 4.173e-10 9.296e-09	.04489311 6.628e-12 1.476e-10	Difference Relative difference
complain: chicken	.19047138	.19047139 3.096e-09 1.625e-08	.19047138 4.917e-11 2.581e-10	Difference Relative difference
complain: _cons	-.21453112	-.21453111 1.281e-08 -5.972e-08	-.21453112 2.682e-10 -1.250e-09	Difference Relative difference
lnsig2u: _cons	-1.7044935	-1.7044934 1.255e-07 -7.365e-08	-1.7044935 -4.135e-10 2.426e-10	Difference Relative difference

The relative and absolute differences are all small between the default 12 quadrature points and the result with 16 points. We don't have any coefficients that have a large difference between the default 12 quadrature points and eight quadrature points.

We conclude that the quadrature technique is stable. Since the differences here are so small, we would plan on using and interpreting these results rather than trying to rerun with more quadrature points.

◁

Saved Results

xtprobit, re saves the following in e():

Scalars

e(N)	# of observations	e(sigma_u)	panel-level standard deviation
e(N_g)	# of groups	e(n_quad)	# of quadrature points
e(N_cd)	# of completely determined obs.	e(k)	# of parameters
e(df_m)	model degrees of freedom	e(k_eq)	# of equations
e(ll)	log likelihood	e(k_eq_model)	# of equations in model Wald test
e(ll_0)	log likelihood, constant-only model	e(k_dv)	# of dependent variables
e(ll_c)	log likelihood, comparison model	e(p)	significance
e(g_max)	largest group size	e(rank)	rank of e(V)
e(g_min)	smallest group size	e(rank0)	rank of e(V) for constant-only model
e(g_avg)	average group size	e(ic)	# of iterations
e(chi2)	χ^2	e(rc)	return code
e(chi2_c)	χ^2 for comparison test	e(converged)	1 if converged, 0 otherwise
e(rho)	ρ		

Macros

e(cmd)	xtprobit	e(distrib)	Gaussian; the distribution of the random effect
e(cmdline)	command as typed		
e(depvar)	name of dependent variable	e(vce)	*vcetype* specified in vce()
e(ivar)	variable denoting groups	e(vcetype)	title used to label Std. Err.
e(wtype)	weight type	e(opt)	type of optimization
e(wexp)	weight expression	e(ml_method)	type of ml method
e(title)	title in estimation output	e(user)	name of likelihood-evaluator program
e(offset)	offset	e(technique)	maximization technique
e(chi2type)	Wald or LR; type of model χ^2 test	e(crittype)	optimization criterion
e(chi2_ct)	Wald or LR; type of model χ^2 test corresponding to e(chi2_c)	e(properties)	b V
		e(predict)	program used to implement predict
e(intmethod)	integration method		

Matrices

e(b)	coefficient vector	e(ilog)	iteration log
e(V)	variance–covariance matrix of the estimators	e(gradient)	gradient vector

Functions

e(sample)	marks estimation sample

`xtprobit, pa` saves the following in `e()`:

Scalars

`e(N)`	# of observations	`e(chi2_dev)`	χ^2 test of deviance
`e(N_g)`	# of groups	`e(chi2_dis)`	χ^2 test of deviance dispersion
`e(df_m)`	model degrees of freedom	`e(deviance)`	deviance
`e(df_pear)`	degrees of freedom for Pearson χ^2	`e(dispers)`	deviance dispersion
`e(g_max)`	largest group size	`e(tol)`	target tolerance
`e(g_min)`	smallest group size	`e(dif)`	achieved tolerance
`e(g_avg)`	average group size	`e(phi)`	scale parameter
`e(chi2)`	χ^2	`e(rc)`	return code

Macros

`e(cmd)`	xtgee	`e(crittype)`	optimization criterion
`e(cmd2)`	xtprobit	`e(scale)`	x2, dev, phi, or #; scale parameter
`e(cmdline)`	command as typed	`e(ivar)`	variable denoting groups
`e(wtype)`	weight type	`e(vce)`	*vcetype* specified in vce()
`e(wexp)`	weight expression	`e(vcetype)`	title used to label Std. Err.
`e(title)`	title in estimation output	`e(chi2type)`	Wald; type of model χ^2 test
`e(depvar)`	name of dependent variable	`e(offset)`	offset
`e(family)`	binomial	`e(properties)`	b V
`e(link)`	probit; link function	`e(predict)`	program used to implement predict
`e(corr)`	correlation structure		

Matrices

`e(b)`	coefficient vector	`e(R)`	estimated working correlation matrix
`e(V)`	variance–covariance matrix of the estimators		

Functions

`e(sample)`	marks estimation sample

Methods and Formulas

`xtprobit` is implemented as an ado-file.

`xtprobit` reports the population-averaged results obtained by using `xtgee, family(binomial)` `link(probit)` to obtain estimates.

Assuming a normal distribution, $N(0, \sigma_\nu^2)$, for the random effects ν_i

$$\Pr(y_{i1}, \ldots, y_{in_i} | \mathbf{x}_{i1}, \ldots, \mathbf{x}_{in_i}) = \int_{-\infty}^{\infty} \frac{e^{-\nu_i^2/2\sigma_\nu^2}}{\sqrt{2\pi}\sigma_\nu} \left\{ \prod_{t=1}^{n_i} F(y_{it}, \mathbf{x}_{it}\boldsymbol{\beta} + \nu_i) \right\} d\nu_i$$

where

$$F(y, z) = \begin{cases} \Phi(z) & \text{if } y \neq 0 \\ 1 - \Phi(z) & \text{otherwise} \end{cases}$$

where Φ is the cumulative normal distribution.

The panel-level likelihood l_i is given by

$$l_i = \int_{-\infty}^{\infty} \frac{e^{-\nu_i^2/2\sigma_\nu^2}}{\sqrt{2\pi}\sigma_\nu} \left\{ \prod_{t=1}^{n_i} F(y_{it}, \mathbf{x}_{it}\boldsymbol{\beta} + \nu_i) \right\} d\nu_i$$

$$\equiv \int_{-\infty}^{\infty} g(y_{it}, x_{it}, \nu_i) d\nu_i$$

This integral can be approximated with M-point Gauss–Hermite quadrature

$$\int_{-\infty}^{\infty} e^{-x^2} h(x) dx \approx \sum_{m=1}^{M} w_m^* h(a_m^*)$$

This is equivalent to

$$\int_{-\infty}^{\infty} f(x) dx \approx \sum_{m=1}^{M} w_m^* \exp\left\{(a_m^*)^2\right\} f(a_m^*)$$

where the w_m^* denote the quadrature weights and the a_m^* denote the quadrature abscissas. The log likelihood, L, is the sum of the logs of the panel-level likelihoods l_i.

The default approximation of the log likelihood is by adaptive Gauss–Hermite quadrature, which approximates the panel-level likelihood with

$$l_i \approx \sqrt{2}\widehat{\sigma}_i \sum_{m=1}^{M} w_m^* \exp\left\{(a_m^*)^2\right\} g(y_{it}, x_{it}, \sqrt{2}\widehat{\sigma}_i a_m^* + \widehat{\mu}_i)$$

where $\widehat{\sigma}_i$ and $\widehat{\mu}_i$ are the adaptive parameters for panel i. Therefore, with the definition of $g(y_{it}, x_{it}, \nu_i)$, the total log likelihood is approximated by

$$L \approx \sum_{i=1}^{n} w_i \log\left[\sqrt{2}\widehat{\sigma}_i \sum_{m=1}^{M} w_m^* \exp\left\{(a_m^*)^2\right\} \frac{\exp\left\{-(\sqrt{2}\widehat{\sigma}_i a_m^* + \widehat{\mu}_i)^2 / 2\sigma_\nu^2\right\}}{\sqrt{2\pi}\sigma_\nu} \right.$$

$$\left. \prod_{t=1}^{n_i} F(y_{it}, x_{it}\boldsymbol{\beta} + \sqrt{2}\widehat{\sigma}_i a_m^* + \widehat{\mu}_i) \right]$$

where w_i is the user-specified weight for panel i; if no weights are specified, $w_i = 1$.

The default method of adaptive Gauss–Hermite quadrature is to calculate the posterior mean and variance and use those parameters for $\widehat{\mu}_i$ and $\widehat{\sigma}_i$ by following the method of Naylor and Smith (1982), further discussed in Skrondal and Rabe-Hesketh (2004). We start with $\widehat{\sigma}_{i,0} = 1$ and $\widehat{\mu}_{i,0} = 0$, and the posterior means and variances are updated in the kth iteration. That is, at the kth iteration of the optimization for l_i, we use

$$l_{i,k} \approx \sum_{m-1}^{M} \sqrt{2}\widehat{\sigma}_{i,k-1} w_m^* \exp\left\{a_m^*)^2\right\} g(y_{it}, x_{it}, \sqrt{2}\widehat{\sigma}_{i,k-1} a_m^* + \widehat{\mu}_{i,k-1})$$

Letting

$$\tau_{i,m,k-1} = \sqrt{2}\widehat{\sigma}_{i,k-1} a_m^* + \widehat{\mu}_{i,k-1}$$

$$\widehat{\mu}_{i,k} = \sum_{m=1}^{M} (\tau_{i,m,k-1}) \frac{\sqrt{2}\widehat{\sigma}_{i,k-1} w_m^* \exp\left\{(a_m^*)^2\right\} g(y_{it}, x_{it}, \tau_{i,m,k-1})}{l_{i,k}}$$

and

$$\widehat{\sigma}_{i,k} = \sum_{m=1}^{M} (\tau_{i,m,k-1})^2 \frac{\sqrt{2}\widehat{\sigma}_{i,k-1} w_m^* \exp\left\{(a_m^*)^2\right\} g(y_{it}, x_{it}, \tau_{i,m,k-1})}{l_{i,k}} - (\widehat{\mu}_{i,k})^2$$

and this is repeated until $\widehat{\mu}_{i,k}$ and $\widehat{\sigma}_{i,k}$ have converged for this iteration of the maximization algorithm. This adaptation is applied on every iteration until the log-likelihood change from the preceding iteration is less than a relative difference of 1e–6; after this, the quadrature parameters are fixed.

One can instead use the adaptive quadrature method of Liu and Pierce (1994), option `intmethod(aghermite)`, which uses the mode and curvature of the mode as approximations for the mean and variance. We take the integrand

$$g(y_{it}, x_{it}, \nu_i) = \frac{e^{-\nu_i^2/2\sigma_\nu^2}}{\sqrt{2\pi}\sigma_\nu} \left\{ \prod_{t=1}^{n_i} F(y_{it}, \mathbf{x}_{it}\boldsymbol{\beta} + \nu_i) \right\}$$

and find α_i the mode of $g(y_{it}, x_{it}, \nu_i)$. We calculate

$$\gamma_i = -\frac{\partial^2}{\partial \nu_i^2} \log\{g(y_{it}, x_{it}, \nu_i)\}\Big|_{\nu_i = \alpha_i}$$

Then

$$\int_{-\infty}^{\infty} g(y_{it}, x_{it}, \nu_i) d\nu_i \approx \left(\frac{2}{\gamma_i}\right)^{1/2} \sum_{m=1}^{M} w_m^* \exp\{(a_m^*)^2\} g\left\{ y_{it}, x_{it}, \left(\frac{2}{\gamma_i}\right)^{1/2} a_m^* + \alpha_i \right\}$$

This adaptation is performed on the first iteration only; that is, the α_i and γ_i are calculated once at the first iteration and then held constant throughout the subsequent iterations.

The log likelihood can also be calculated by nonadaptive Gauss–Hermite quadrature, option `intmethod(ghermite)`, where $\rho = \sigma_\nu^2/(\sigma_\nu^2 + 1)$:

$$L = \sum_{i=1}^{n} w_i \log\left\{ \Pr(y_{i1}, \ldots, y_{in_i} | \mathbf{x}_{i1}, \ldots, \mathbf{x}_{in_i}) \right\}$$

$$\approx \sum_{i=1}^{n} w_i \log\left[\frac{1}{\sqrt{\pi}} \sum_{m=1}^{M} w_m^* \prod_{t=1}^{n_i} F\left\{ y_{it}, \mathbf{x}_{it}\boldsymbol{\beta} + a_m^* \left(\frac{2\rho}{1-\rho}\right)^{1/2} \right\} \right]$$

All three quadrature formulas require that the integrated function be well approximated by a polynomial of degree equal to the number of quadrature points. The number of periods (panel size) can affect whether

$$\prod_{t=1}^{n_i} F(y_{it}, \mathbf{x}_{it}\boldsymbol{\beta} + \nu_i)$$

is well approximated by a polynomial. As panel size and ρ increase, the quadrature approximation can become less accurate. For large ρ, the random-effects model can also become unidentified. Adaptive quadrature gives better results for correlated data and large panels than nonadaptive quadrature; however, we recommend that you use the `quadchk` command to verify the quadrature approximation used in this command, whichever approximation you choose.

References

Conway, M. R. 1990. A random effects model for binary data. *Biometrics* 46: 317–328.

Frechette, G. R. 2001a. sg158: Random-effects ordered probit. *Stata Technical Bulletin* 59: 23–27. Reprinted in *Stata Technical Bulletin Reprints*, vol. 10, pp. 261–266.

———. 2001b. sg158.1: Update to random-effects probit. *Stata Technical Bulletin* 61: 12. Reprinted in *Stata Technical Bulletin Reprints*, vol. 10, pp. 266–267.

Guilkey, D. K., and J. L. Murphy. 1993. Estimation and testing in the random effects probit model. *Journal of Econometrics* 59: 301–317.

Liang, K.-Y., and S. L. Zeger. 1986. Longitudinal data analysis using generalized linear models. *Biometrika* 73: 13–22.

Liu, Q., and D. A. Pierce. 1994. A note on Gauss–Hermite quadrature. *Biometrika* 81: 624–629.

Naylor, J. C., and A. F. M. Smith. 1982. Applications of a method for the efficient computation of posterior distributions. *Journal of the Royal Statistical Society, Series C* 31: 214–225.

Neuhaus, J. M. 1992. Statistical methods for longitudinal and clustered designs with binary responses. *Statistical Methods in Medical Research* 1: 249–273.

Neuhaus, J. M., J. D. Kalbfleisch, and W. W. Hauck. 1991. A comparison of cluster-specific and population-averaged approaches for analyzing correlated binary data. *International Statistical Review* 59: 25–35.

Pendergast, J. F., S. J. Gange, M. A. Newton, M. J. Lindstrom, M. Palta, and M. R. Fisher. 1996. A survey of methods for analyzing clustered binary response data. *International Statistical Review* 64: 89–118.

Skrondal, A., and S. Rabe-Hesketh. 2004. *Generalized Latent Variable Modeling: Multilevel, Longitudinal, and Structural Equation Models*. Boca Raton, FL: Chapman & Hall/CRC.

Stewart, M. 2006. Maximum simulated likelihood estimation of random-effects dynamic probit models with autocorrelated errors. *Stata Journal* 6: 256–272.

Also See

[XT] **xtprobit postestimation** — Postestimation tools for xtprobit

[XT] **quadchk** — Check sensitivity of quadrature approximation

[R] **constraint** — Define and list constraints

[XT] **xtcloglog** — Random-effects and population-averaged cloglog models

[XT] **xtgee** — Fit population-averaged panel-data models by using GEE

[XT] **xtlogit** — Fixed-effects, random-effects, and population-averaged logit models

[R] **probit** — Probit regression

[U] **20 Estimation and postestimation commands**

Title

> **xtprobit postestimation** — Postestimation tools for xtprobit

Description

The following postestimation commands are available for xtprobit:

command	description
adjust[1]	adjusted predictions of $\mathbf{x}\beta$ or probabilities
*estat	AIC, BIC, VCE, and estimation sample summary
estimates	cataloging estimation results
hausman	Hausman's specification test
lincom	point estimates, standard errors, testing, and inference for linear combinations of coefficients
lrtest	likelihood-ratio test
mfx	marginal effects or elasticities
nlcom	point estimates, standard errors, testing, and inference for nonlinear combinations of coefficients
predict	predictions, residuals, influence statistics, and other diagnostic measures
predictnl	point estimates, standard errors, testing, and inference for generalized predictions
test	Wald tests for simple and composite linear hypotheses
testnl	Wald tests of nonlinear hypotheses

[1] adjust is not appropriate with time-series operators.

* estat ic is not appropriate after xtprobit, pa.

See the corresponding entries in the *Stata Base Reference Manual* for details.

Syntax for predict

Random-effects model

> predict [*type*] *newvar* [*if*] [*in*] [, *RE_statistic* <u>nooff</u>set]

Population-averaged model

> predict [*type*] *newvar* [*if*] [*in*] [, *PA_statistic* <u>nooff</u>set]

RE_statistic	description
Main	
xb	linear prediction; the default
pu0	probability of a positive outcome
stdp	standard error of the linear prediction

PA_statistic	description
Main	
mu	probability of *depvar*; considers the offset(); the default
rate	probability of *depvar*
xb	linear prediction
stdp	standard error of the linear prediction
<u>sco</u>re	first derivative of the log likelihood with respect to $\mathbf{x}_j\beta$

These statistics are available both in and out of sample; type predict ... if e(sample) ... if wanted only for the estimation sample.

Options for predict

⌐ Main ⌐

xb calculates the linear prediction. This is the default for the random-effects model.

pu0 calculates the probability of a positive outcome, assuming that the random effect for that observation's panel is zero ($\nu = 0$). This probability may not be similar to the proportion of observed outcomes in the group.

stdp calculates the standard error of the linear prediction.

mu and rate both calculate the predicted probability of *depvar*. mu takes into account the offset(), and rate ignores those adjustments. mu and rate are equivalent if you did not specify offset(). mu is the default for the population-averaged model.

score calculates the equation-level score, $u_j = \partial \ln L_j(\mathbf{x}_j\beta)/\partial(\mathbf{x}_j\beta)$.

nooffset is relevant only if you specified offset(*varname*) for xtprobit. It modifies the calculations made by predict so that they ignore the offset variable; the linear prediction is treated as $\mathbf{x}_{it}\beta$ rather than $\mathbf{x}_{it}\beta + \text{offset}_{it}$.

Remarks

▷ Example 1

In [XT] **xtprobit**, we fitted a random-effects model of union status on the person's age and level of schooling, whether she lived in an urban area, and whether she lived in the south. Here we compute the marginal effects on the probability of being in a union, assuming that the random effect for each panel is zero:

```
. use http://www.stata-press.com/data/r10/union
(NLS Women 14-24 in 1968)
. xtprobit union age grade not_smsa south southXt
  (output omitted )
```

```
. mfx compute, predict(pu0)
```

```
Marginal effects after xtprobit
      y  = Pr(union=1 assuming u_i=0) (predict, pu0)
         =  .08531782
```

variable	dy/dx	Std. Err.	z	P>|z|	[95% C.I.]		X
age	.0007261	.00039	1.84	0.065	-.000046	.001498	30.4322
grade	.0075066	.00157	4.78	0.000	.004431	.010582	12.7615
not_smsa*	-.0209815	.00666	-3.15	0.002	-.03403	-.007933	.283702
south*	-.0943862	.00919	-10.27	0.000	-.112397	-.076375	.413015
southXt	.0020357	.00069	2.96	0.003	.000689	.003383	3.96874

(*) dy/dx is for discrete change of dummy variable from 0 to 1

Not living in a metropolitan area (not_smsa = 0) lowers the probability of being in a union by about 2.1 percentage points.

◁

Methods and Formulas

All postestimation commands listed above are implemented as ado-files.

Also See

[XT] **xtprobit** — Random-effects and population-averaged probit models

[U] **20 Estimation and postestimation commands**

Title

> **xtrc** — Random-coefficients model

Syntax

> xtrc *depvar* *indepvars* [*if*] [*in*] [, *options*]

options	description
Main	
<u>nocon</u>stant	suppress constant term
<u>off</u>set(*varname*)	include *varname* in model with coefficient constrained to 1
<u>beta</u>s	display group-specific best linear predictors
SE	
vce(*vcetype*)	*vcetype* may be conventional, <u>boot</u>strap, or <u>jack</u>knife
Reporting	
<u>level</u>(#)	set confidence level; default is level(95)

A panel variable must be specified; use xtset; see [XT] **xtset**.

by, statsby, and xi are allowed; see [U] **11.1.10 Prefix commands**.

See [U] **20 Estimation and postestimation commands** for more capabilities of estimation commands.

Description

xtrc fits the Swamy (1970) random-coefficients linear regression model.

Options

> Main

noconstant, offset(*varname*); see [XT] **estimation options**

betas requests that the group-specific best linear predictors also be displayed.

> SE

vce(*vcetype*) specifies the type of standard error reported, which includes types that are derived from asymptotic theory and that use bootstrap or jackknife methods; see [XT] *vce_options*.

vce(conventional), the default, uses the conventionally derived variance estimator for generalized least-squares regression.

> Reporting

level(#); see [XT] **estimation options**.

Remarks

In random-coefficients models, we wish to treat the parameter vector as a realization (in each panel) of a stochastic process. xtrc fits the Swamy (1970) random-coefficients model, which is suitable for linear regression of panel data. See Greene (2003) and Poi (2003) for more information about this and other panel-data models.

▷ Example 1

Greene (2003, 329) reprints data from a classic study of investment demand by Grunfeld and Griliches (1960). In [XT] **xtgls**, we use this dataset to illustrate many of the possible models that may be fitted with the xtgls command. Although the models included in the xtgls command offer considerable flexibility, they all assume that there is no parameter variation across firms (the cross-sectional units).

To take a first look at the assumption of parameter constancy, we should reshape our data so that we may fit a simultaneous-equation model with sureg; see [R] **sureg**. Since there are only five panels here, this is not too difficult.

```
. use http://www.stata-press.com/data/r10/invest2
. reshape wide invest market stock, i(time) j(company)
(note: j = 1 2 3 4 5)
```

Data	long	->	wide
Number of obs.	100	->	20
Number of variables	5	->	16
j variable (5 values)	company	->	(dropped)
xij variables:			
	invest	->	invest1 invest2 ... invest5
	market	->	market1 market2 ... market5
	stock	->	stock1 stock2 ... stock5

```
. sureg (invest1 market1 stock1) (invest2 market2 stock2) (invest3 market3 stock3)
> (invest4 market4 stock4) (invest5 market5 stock5)
Seemingly unrelated regression
```

Equation	Obs	Parms	RMSE	"R-sq"	chi2	P
invest1	20	2	84.94729	0.9207	261.32	0.0000
invest2	20	2	12.36322	0.9119	207.21	0.0000
invest3	20	2	26.46612	0.6876	46.88	0.0000
invest4	20	2	9.742303	0.7264	59.15	0.0000
invest5	20	2	95.85484	0.4220	14.97	0.0006

(*Continued on next page*)

	Coef.	Std. Err.	z	P>|z|	[95% Conf. Interval]	
invest1						
market1	.120493	.0216291	5.57	0.000	.0781007	.1628853
stock1	.3827462	.032768	11.68	0.000	.318522	.4469703
_cons	-162.3641	89.45922	-1.81	0.070	-337.7009	12.97279
invest2						
market2	.0695456	.0168975	4.12	0.000	.0364271	.1026641
stock2	.3085445	.0258635	11.93	0.000	.2578529	.3592362
_cons	.5043112	11.51283	0.04	0.965	-22.06042	23.06904
invest3						
market3	.0372914	.0122631	3.04	0.002	.0132561	.0613268
stock3	.130783	.0220497	5.93	0.000	.0875663	.1739997
_cons	-22.43892	25.51859	-0.88	0.379	-72.45443	27.57659
invest4						
market4	.0570091	.0113623	5.02	0.000	.0347395	.0792788
stock4	.0415065	.0412016	1.01	0.314	-.0392472	.1222602
_cons	1.088878	6.258805	0.17	0.862	-11.17815	13.35591
invest5						
market5	.1014782	.0547837	1.85	0.064	-.0058958	.2088523
stock5	.3999914	.1277946	3.13	0.002	.1495186	.6504642
_cons	85.42324	111.8774	0.76	0.445	-133.8525	304.6989

Here we instead fit a random-coefficients model:

```
. use http://www.stata-press.com/data/r10/invest2

. xtrc invest market stock
```

Random-coefficients regression		Number of obs	=	100
Group variable: company		Number of groups	=	5
		Obs per group: min =		20
		avg =		20.0
		max =		20
		Wald chi2(2)	=	17.55
		Prob > chi2	=	0.0002

invest	Coef.	Std. Err.	z	P>|z|	[95% Conf. Interval]	
market	.0807646	.0250829	3.22	0.001	.0316031	.1299261
stock	.2839885	.0677899	4.19	0.000	.1511229	.4168542
_cons	-23.58361	34.55547	-0.68	0.495	-91.31108	44.14386

Test of parameter constancy: chi2(12) =   603.99   Prob > chi2 = 0.0000

Just as the results of our simultaneous-equation model do not support the assumption of parameter constancy, the test included with the random-coefficients model also indicates that the assumption is not valid for these data. With large panel datasets, we would not want to take the time to look at a simultaneous-equations model (aside from the fact that our doing so was subjective).

◁

Saved Results

xtrc saves the following in e():

Scalars

e(N)	number of observations	e(g_avg)	average group size
e(N_g)	number of groups	e(chi2)	χ^2
e(df_m)	model degrees of freedom	e(chi2_c)	χ^2 for comparison test
e(g_max)	largest group size	e(df_chi2c)	degrees of freedom for comparison χ^2 test
e(g_min)	smallest group size		

Macros

e(cmd)	xtrc	e(chi2type)	Wald; type of model χ^2 test
e(cmdline)	command as typed	e(vce)	*vcetype* specified in vce()
e(depvar)	name of dependent variable	e(vcetype)	title used to label Std. Err.
e(title)	title in estimation output	e(properties)	b V
e(ivar)	variable denoting groups	e(predict)	program used to implement predict
e(offset)	offset		

Matrices

e(b)	coefficient vector	e(V)	variance–covariance matrix of the estimators
e(Sigma)	$\widehat{\Sigma}$ matrix		
e(beta_ps)	matrix of best linear predictors	e(V_ps)	matrix of variances for the best linear predictors; row i contains vec of variance matrix for group i predictor

Functions

e(sample)	marks estimation sample

Methods and Formulas

xtrc is implemented as an ado-file.

In a random-coefficients model, the parameter heterogeneity is treated as stochastic variation. Assume that we write

$$\mathbf{y}_i = \mathbf{X}_i \boldsymbol{\beta}_i + \boldsymbol{\epsilon}_i$$

where $i = 1, \ldots, m$, and $\boldsymbol{\beta}_i$ is the coefficient vector ($k \times 1$) for the ith cross-sectional unit, such that

$$\boldsymbol{\beta}_i = \boldsymbol{\beta} + \boldsymbol{\nu}_i \qquad E(\boldsymbol{\nu}_i) = \mathbf{0} \qquad E(\boldsymbol{\nu}_i \boldsymbol{\nu}_i') = \boldsymbol{\Sigma}$$

Our goal is to find $\widehat{\boldsymbol{\beta}}$ and $\widehat{\boldsymbol{\Sigma}}$.

The derivation of the estimator assumes that the cross-sectional specific coefficient vector $\boldsymbol{\beta}_i$ is the outcome of a random process with mean vector $\boldsymbol{\beta}$ and covariance matrix $\boldsymbol{\Sigma}$,

$$\mathbf{y}_i = \mathbf{X}_i \boldsymbol{\beta}_i + \boldsymbol{\epsilon}_i = \mathbf{X}_i (\boldsymbol{\beta} + \boldsymbol{\nu}_i) + \boldsymbol{\epsilon}_i = \mathbf{X}_i \boldsymbol{\beta} + (\mathbf{X}_i \boldsymbol{\nu}_i + \boldsymbol{\epsilon}_i) = \mathbf{X}_i \boldsymbol{\beta} + \boldsymbol{\omega}_i$$

where $E(\boldsymbol{\omega}_i) = \mathbf{0}$ and

$$E(\boldsymbol{\omega}_i \boldsymbol{\omega}_i') = E\left\{ (\mathbf{X}_i \boldsymbol{\nu}_i + \boldsymbol{\epsilon}_i)(\mathbf{X}_i \boldsymbol{\nu}_i + \boldsymbol{\epsilon}_i)' \right\} = E(\boldsymbol{\epsilon}_i \boldsymbol{\epsilon}_i') + \mathbf{X}_i E(\boldsymbol{\nu}_i \boldsymbol{\nu}_i') \mathbf{X}_i' = \sigma_i^2 \mathbf{I} + \mathbf{X}_i \boldsymbol{\Sigma} \mathbf{X}_i' = \boldsymbol{\Pi}_i$$

Stacking the m equations, we have

$$\mathbf{y} = \mathbf{X} \boldsymbol{\beta} + \boldsymbol{\omega}$$

where $\boldsymbol{\varPi} \equiv E(\boldsymbol{\omega}\boldsymbol{\omega}')$ is a block diagonal matrix with $\boldsymbol{\varPi}_i$, $i = 1...m$, along the main diagonal and zeros elsewhere. The GLS estimator of $\widehat{\beta}$ is then

$$\widehat{\beta} = \left(\sum_i \mathbf{X}_i' \boldsymbol{\varPi}_i^{-1} \mathbf{X}_i \right)^{-1} \sum_i \mathbf{X}_i' \boldsymbol{\varPi}_i^{-1} \mathbf{y}_i = \sum_{i=1}^m \mathbf{W}_i \mathbf{b}_i$$

where

$$\mathbf{W}_i = \left\{ \sum_{i=1}^m (\boldsymbol{\varSigma} + \mathbf{V}_i)^{-1} \right\}^{-1} (\boldsymbol{\varSigma} + \mathbf{V}_i)^{-1}$$

$\mathbf{b}_i = (\mathbf{X}_i' \mathbf{X}_i)^{-1} \mathbf{X}_i' \mathbf{y}_i$ and $\mathbf{V}_i = \sigma_i^2 (\mathbf{X}_i' \mathbf{X}_i)^{-1}$, showing that the resulting GLS estimator is a matrix-weighted average of the panel-specific OLS estimators. The variance of $\widehat{\beta}$ is

$$\mathrm{Var}(\widehat{\beta}) = \sum_{i=1}^m (\boldsymbol{\varSigma} + \mathbf{V}_i)^{-1}$$

To calculate the above estimator $\widehat{\beta}$ for the unknown $\boldsymbol{\varSigma}$ and $\mathbf{V}_i$ parameters, we use the two-step approach suggested by Swamy (1970):

$$\mathbf{b}_i = \text{OLS panel-specific estimator}$$

$$\widehat{\sigma}_i^2 = \frac{\widehat{\boldsymbol{\epsilon}}_i' \widehat{\boldsymbol{\epsilon}}_i}{n_i - k}$$

$$\widehat{\mathbf{V}}_i = \widehat{\sigma}_i^2 (\mathbf{X}_i' \mathbf{X}_i)^{-1}$$

$$\overline{\mathbf{b}} = \frac{1}{m} \sum_{i=1}^m \mathbf{b}_i$$

$$\widehat{\boldsymbol{\varSigma}} = \frac{1}{m-1} \left(\sum_{i=1}^m \mathbf{b}_i \mathbf{b}_i' - m \overline{\mathbf{b}}\, \overline{\mathbf{b}}' \right) - \frac{1}{m} \sum_{i=1}^m \widehat{\mathbf{V}}_i$$

The two-step procedure begins with the usual OLS estimates of β_i. With those estimates, we may proceed by obtaining estimates of $\widehat{\mathbf{V}}_i$ and $\widehat{\boldsymbol{\varSigma}}$ (and thus $\widehat{\mathbf{W}}_i$) and then obtain an estimate of β.

Swamy (1970) further points out that the matrix $\widehat{\boldsymbol{\varSigma}}$ may not be positive definite and that since the second term is of order $1/(mT)$, it is negligible in large samples. A simple and asymptotically expedient solution is simply to drop this second term and instead use

$$\widehat{\boldsymbol{\varSigma}} = \frac{1}{m-1} \left(\sum_{i=1}^m \mathbf{b}_i \mathbf{b}_i' - m \overline{\mathbf{b}}\, \overline{\mathbf{b}}' \right)$$

As discussed by Judge et al. (1985, 541), the feasible best linear predictor of β_i is given by

$$\widehat{\beta}_i = \widehat{\beta} + \widehat{\boldsymbol{\Sigma}}\mathbf{X}'_i \left(\mathbf{X}_i\widehat{\boldsymbol{\Sigma}}\mathbf{X}'_i + \widehat{\sigma}_i^2\mathbf{I} \right)^{-1} \left(\mathbf{y}_i - \mathbf{X}_i\widehat{\beta} \right)$$

$$= \left(\widehat{\boldsymbol{\Sigma}}^{-1} + \widehat{\mathbf{V}}_i^{-1} \right)^{-1} \left(\widehat{\boldsymbol{\Sigma}}^{-1}\widehat{\beta} + \widehat{\mathbf{V}}_i^{-1}\mathbf{b}_i \right)$$

The conventional variance of $\widehat{\beta}_i$ is given by

$$\mathrm{Var}(\widehat{\beta}_i) = \mathrm{Var}(\widehat{\beta}) + (\mathbf{I} - \mathbf{A}_i)\left\{\widehat{\mathbf{V}}_i - \mathrm{Var}(\widehat{\beta})\right\}(\mathbf{I} - \mathbf{A}_i)'$$

where

$$\mathbf{A}_i = \left(\widehat{\boldsymbol{\Sigma}}^{-1} + \widehat{\mathbf{V}}_i^{-1} \right)^{-1} \widehat{\boldsymbol{\Sigma}}^{-1}$$

To test the model, we may look at the difference between the OLS estimate of β, ignoring the panel structure of the data and the matrix-weighted average of the panel-specific OLS estimators. The test statistic suggested by Swamy (1970) is given by

$$\chi^2_{k(m-1)} = \sum_{i=1}^{m}(\mathbf{b}_i - \overline{\beta}^*)'\widehat{\mathbf{V}}_i^{-1}(\mathbf{b}_i - \overline{\beta}^*) \qquad \text{where} \qquad \overline{\beta}^* = \left(\sum_{i=1}^{m} \widehat{\mathbf{V}}_i^{-1} \right)^{-1} \sum_{i=1}^{m} \widehat{\mathbf{V}}_i^{-1}\mathbf{b}_i$$

Johnston and DiNardo (1997) has shown that the test is algebraically equivalent to testing

$$H_0 : \beta_1 = \beta_2 = \cdots = \beta_m$$

in the generalized (groupwise heteroskedastic) xtgls model, where $\mathbf{V}$ is block diagonal with ith diagonal element $\boldsymbol{\Pi}_i$.

References

Greene, W. H. 2003. *Econometric Analysis*. 5th ed. Upper Saddle River, NJ: Prentice Hall.

Grunfeld, Y., and Z. Griliches. 1960. Is aggregation necessarily bad? *Review of Economics and Statistics* 42: 1–13.

Johnston, J., and J. DiNardo. 1997. *Econometric Methods*. 4th ed. New York: McGraw–Hill.

Judge, G. G., W. E. Griffiths, R. C. Hill, H. Lütkepohl, and T.-C. Lee. 1985. *The Theory and Practice of Econometrics*. 2nd ed. New York: Wiley.

Poi, B. 2003. From the help desk: Swamy's random-coefficients model. *Stata Journal* 3: 302–308.

Swamy, P. 1970. Efficient inference in a random coefficient regression model. *Econometrica* 38: 311–323.

———. 1971. *Statistical Inference in Random Coefficient Regression Models*. New York: Springer.

Also See

[XT] **xtrc postestimation** — Postestimation tools for xtrc

[XT] **xtmixed** — Multilevel mixed-effects linear regression

[XT] **xtreg** — Fixed-, between-, and random-effects, and population-averaged linear models

[U] **20 Estimation and postestimation commands**

Title

---

xtrc postestimation — Postestimation tools for xtrc

Description

The following postestimation commands are available for xtrc:

command	description
adjust	adjusted predictions of $\mathbf{x}\beta$
estat	VCE and estimation sample summary
estimates	cataloging estimation results
lincom	point estimates, standard errors, testing, and inference for linear combination of coefficients
mfx	marginal effects or elasticities
nlcom	point estimates, standard errors, testing, and inference for nonlinear combinations of coefficients
predict	predictions, residuals, influence statistics, and other diagnostic measures
predictnl	point estimates, standard errors, testing, and inference for generalized predictions
test	Wald tests for simple and composite linear hypotheses
testnl	Wald tests of nonlinear hypotheses

See the corresponding entries in the *Stata Base Reference Manual* for details.

Syntax for predict

predict [*type*] *newvar* [*if*] [*in*] [, *statistic* <u>nooff</u>set]

statistic	description
Main	
xb	linear prediction; the default
stdp	standard error of the linear prediction
group(*group*)	linear prediction based on group *group*.

These statistics are available both in and out of sample; type predict ... if e(sample) ... if wanted only for the estimation sample.

Options for predict

⌐ Main ⌐

xb, the default, calculates the linear prediction using the mean parameter vector.

stdp calculates the standard error of the linear prediction.

group(*group*) calculates the linear prediction using the best linear predictors for group *group*.

388

`nooffset` is relevant only if you specified `offset(`*varname*`)` for `xtrc`. It modifies the calculations made by `predict` so that they ignore the offset variable; the linear prediction is treated as $\mathbf{x}_{it}\mathbf{b}$ rather than $\mathbf{x}_{it}\mathbf{b} + \text{offset}_{it}$.

Methods and Formulas

All postestimation commands listed above are implemented as ado-files.

Also See

[XT] **xtrc** — Random-coefficients model

[U] **20 Estimation and postestimation commands**

Title

> **xtreg** — Fixed-, between-, and random-effects, and population-averaged linear models

Syntax

GLS random-effects (RE) model

> xtreg *depvar* [*indepvars*] [*if*] [, re *RE_options*]

Between-effects (BE) model

> xtreg *depvar* [*indepvars*] [*if*] , be [*BE_options*]

Fixed-effects (FE) model

> xtreg *depvar* [*indepvars*] [*if*] [*weight*] , fe [*FE_options*]

ML random-effects (MLE) model

> xtreg *depvar* [*indepvars*] [*if*] [*weight*] , mle [*MLE_options*]

Population-averaged (PA) model

> xtreg *depvar* [*indepvars*] [*if*] [*weight*] , pa [*PA_options*]

RE_options	description
Model	
re	use random-effects estimator; the default
sa	use Swamy–Arora estimator of the variance components
SE/Robust	
vce(*vcetype*)	*vcetype* may be conventional, <u>r</u>obust, <u>cl</u>uster *clustvar*, <u>boot</u>strap, or jackknife
nonest	do not check that panels are nested within clusters
Reporting	
<u>level</u>(#)	set confidence level; default is level(95)
<u>theta</u>	report θ

BE_options	description
Model	
<u>be</u>	use between-effects estimator
<u>w</u>ls	use weighted least squares
SE	
vce(*vcetype*)	*vcetype* may be conventional, <u>boot</u>strap, or <u>jack</u>knife
Reporting	
<u>level</u>(*#*)	set confidence level; default is level(95)

FE_options	description
Model	
fe	use fixed-effects estimator
SE/Robust	
vce(*vcetype*)	*vcetype* may be conventional, <u>r</u>obust, <u>cl</u>uster *clustvar*, <u>boot</u>strap, or <u>jack</u>knife
nonest	do not check that panels are nested within clusters
dfadj	adjust the cluster–robust–VCE estimator for the within transform; seldom used
Reporting	
<u>level</u>(*#*)	set confidence level; default is level(95)

MLE_options	description
Model	
<u>nocons</u>tant	suppress constant term
mle	use ML random-effects estimator
SE	
vce(*vcetype*)	*vcetype* may be oim, <u>boot</u>strap, or <u>jack</u>knife
Reporting	
<u>level</u>(*#*)	set confidence level; default is level(95)
Max options	
maximize_options	control the maximization process; seldom used

PA_options	description
Model	
noconstant	suppress constant term
pa	use population-averaged estimator
offset(*varname*)	include *varname* in model with coefficient constrained to 1
Correlation	
corr(*correlation*)	within-group correlation structure
force	estimate even if observations unequally spaced in time
SE/Robust	
vce(*vcetype*)	*vcetype* may be conventional, robust, bootstrap, or jackknife
nmp	use divisor $N - P$ instead of the default N
rgf	multiply the robust variance estimate by $(N - 1)/(N - P)$
scale(*parm*)	overrides the default scale parameter; *parm* may be x2, dev, phi, or #
Reporting	
level(#)	set confidence level; default is level(95)
Opt options	
optimize_options	control the optimization process; seldom used

correlation	description
exchangeable	exchangeable
independent	independent
unstructured	unstructured
fixed *matname*	user-specified
ar #	autoregressive of order #
stationary #	stationary of order #
nonstationary #	nonstationary of order #

A panel variable must be specified. For xtreg, pa, correlation structures other than exchangeable and independent require that a time variable also be specified. Use xtset; see [XT] **xtset**.

depvar and *indepvars* may contain time-series operators; see [U] **11.4.3 Time-series varlists**.

by, statsby, xi are allowed; see [U] **11.1.10 Prefix commands**.

aweights, fweights, and pweights are allowed for the fixed-effects model. iweights, fweights, and pweights are allowed for the population-averaged model. iweights are allowed for the maximum-likelihood random-effects (MLE) model. See [U] **11.1.6 weight**. Weights must be constant within panel.

See [U] **20 Estimation and postestimation commands** for more capabilities of estimation commands.

Description

xtreg fits regression models to panel data. In particular, xtreg with the be option fits random-effects models by using the between regression estimator; with the fe option, it fits fixed-effects models (by using the within regression estimator); and with the re option, it fits random-effects models by using the GLS estimator (producing a matrix-weighted average of the between and within results). See [XT] **xtdata** for a faster way to fit fixed- and random-effects models.

Options for RE model

┌─── Model ──┐

re, the default, requests the GLS random-effects estimator.

sa specifies that the small-sample Swamy–Arora estimator individual-level variance component be used instead of the default consistent estimator. See the *Methods and Formulas* section for details.

┌─── SE/Robust ──┐

vce(*vcetype*) specifies the type of standard error reported, which includes types that are derived from asymptotic theory, that are robust to some kinds of misspecification, that allow for intragroup correlation, and that use bootstrap or jackknife methods; see [XT] *vce_options*.

vce(conventional), the default, uses the conventionally derived variance estimator for generalized least-squares regression.

nonest removes the check that the panels are nested within clusters.

┌─── Reporting ──┐

level(*#*); see [XT] **estimation options**.

theta, used with xtreg, re only, specifies that the output include the estimated value of θ used in combining the between and fixed estimators. For balanced data, this is a constant, and for unbalanced data, a summary of the values is presented in the header of the output.

Options for BE model

┌─── Model ──┐

be requests the between regression estimator.

wls specifies that, for unbalanced data, weighted least squares be used rather than the default OLS. Both methods produce consistent estimates. The true variance of the between-effects residual is $\sigma_\nu^2 + T_i \sigma_\epsilon^2$ (see *Methods and Formulas* below). WLS produces a "stabilized" variance of $\sigma_\nu^2/T_i + \sigma_\epsilon^2$, which is also not constant. Thus the choice between OLS and WLS amounts to which is more stable.

Comment: xtreg, be is rarely used anyway, but between estimates are an ingredient in the random-effects estimate. Our implementation of xtreg, re uses the OLS estimates for this ingredient, based on our judgment that σ_ν^2 is large relative to σ_ϵ^2 in most models. Formally, only a consistent estimate of the between estimates is required.

┌─── SE ───┐

vce(*vcetype*) specifies the type of standard error reported, which includes types that are derived from asymptotic theory and that use bootstrap or jackknife methods; see [XT] *vce_options*.

vce(conventional), the default, uses the conventionally derived variance estimator for generalized least-squares regression.

┌─── Reporting ──┐

level(*#*); see [XT] **estimation options**.

Options for FE model

Model

fe requests the fixed-effects (within) regression estimator.

SE/Robust

vce(_vcetype_) specifies the type of standard error reported, which includes types that are derived from asymptotic theory, that are robust to some kinds of misspecification, that allow for intragroup correlation, and that use bootstrap or jackknife methods; see [XT] **vce_options**.

vce(conventional), the default, uses the conventionally derived variance estimator for generalized least-squares regression.

nonest removes the check that the panels are nested within clusters. The cluster–robust–VCE estimator generally assumes that the panels are nested within the clusters or that there are many observations per panel.

dfadj adjusts the cluster–robust–VCE estimator for the within transform. dfadj will produce a conservative VCE when panels are not nested within clusters, even when there are only a few observations per panel.

Reporting

level(_#_); see [XT] **estimation options**.

Options for MLE model

Model

noconstant; see [XT] **estimation options**.

mle requests the maximum-likelihood random-effects estimator.

_SE_

vce(_vcetype_) specifies the type of standard error reported, which includes types that are derived from asymptotic theory and that use bootstrap or jackknife methods; see [XT] **vce_options**.

Reporting

level(_#_); see [XT] **estimation options**.

Max options

_maximize_options_: iterate(_#_), [no]log, trace, tolerance(_#_), ltolerance(_#_), from(_init_specs_); see [R] **maximize**. These options are seldom used.

Options for PA model

Model

noconstant; see [XT] **estimation options**.

pa requests the population-averaged estimator. For linear regression, this is the same as a random-effects estimator (both interpretations hold).

xtreg, pa is equivalent to xtgee, family(gaussian) link(id) corr(exchangeable), which are the defaults for the xtgee command. xtreg, pa allows all the relevant xtgee options such as vce(robust). Whether you use xtreg, pa or xtgee makes no difference. See [XT] **xtgee**.

offset(*varname*); see [XT] **estimation options**.

⌐ Correlation ⌐

corr(*correlation*), force; see [XT] **estimation options**.

⌐ SE/Robust ⌐

vce(*vcetype*) specifies the type of standard error reported, which includes types that are derived from asymptotic theory, that are robust to some kinds of misspecification, and that use bootstrap or jackknife methods; see [XT] *vce_options*.

vce(conventional), the default, uses the conventionally derived variance estimator for generalized least-squares regression.

nmp; see [XT] *vce_options*.

rgf specifies that the robust variance estimate is multiplied by $(N - 1)/(N - P)$, where N is the total number of observations and P is the number of coefficients estimated. This option can be used with family(gaussian) only when vce(robust) is either specified or implied by the use of pweights. Using this option implies that the robust variance estimate is not invariant to the scale of any weights used.

scale(x2 | dev | phi | #); see [XT] *vce_options*.

⌐ Reporting ⌐

level(#); see [XT] **estimation options**.

⌐ Opt options ⌐

optimize_options control the iterative optimization process. These options are seldom used.

iterate(#) specifies the maximum number of iterations. When the number of iterations equals #, the optimization stops and presents the current results, even if convergence has not been reached. The default is iterate(100).

tolerance(#) specifies the tolerance for the coefficient vector. When the relative change in the coefficient vector from one iteration to the next is less than or equal to #, the optimization process is stopped. tolerance(1e-6) is the default.

nolog suppresses display of the iteration log.

trace specifies that the current estimates be printed at each iteration.

Remarks

If you have not read [XT] **xt**, please do so.

See Baltagi (2005, chap. 2) and Wooldridge (2002, chap. 10) for good overviews of fixed-effects and random-effects models.

Consider fitting models of the form

$$y_{it} = \alpha + \mathbf{x}_{it}\boldsymbol{\beta} + \nu_i + \epsilon_{it} \tag{1}$$

In this model, $\nu_i + \epsilon_{it}$ is the residual in that we have little interest in it; we want estimates of $\boldsymbol{\beta}$. ν_i is the unit-specific residual; it differs between units, but for any particular unit, its value is constant. In the pulmonary data of [XT] **xt**, a person who exercises less would presumably have a lower FEV year after year and so would have a negative ν_i.

ϵ_{it} is the "usual" residual with the usual properties (mean 0, uncorrelated with itself, uncorrelated with $\mathbf{x}$, uncorrelated with ν, and homoskedastic), although in a more thorough development, we could decompose $\epsilon_{it} = \upsilon_t + \omega_{it}$, assume that ω_{it} is a standard residual, and better describe υ_t.

Before making the assumptions necessary for estimation, let us perform some useful algebra on (1). Whatever the properties of ν_i and ϵ_{it}, if (1) is true, it must also be true that

$$\overline{y}_i = \alpha + \overline{\mathbf{x}}_i\boldsymbol{\beta} + \nu_i + \overline{\epsilon}_i \tag{2}$$

where $\overline{y}_i = \sum_t y_{it}/T_i$, $\overline{\mathbf{x}}_i = \sum_t \mathbf{x}_{it}/T_i$, and $\overline{\epsilon}_i = \sum_t \epsilon_{it}/T_i$. Subtracting (2) from (1), it must be equally true that

$$(y_{it} - \overline{y}_i) = (\mathbf{x}_{it} - \overline{\mathbf{x}}_i)\boldsymbol{\beta} + (\epsilon_{it} - \overline{\epsilon}_i) \tag{3}$$

These three equations provide the basis for estimating $\boldsymbol{\beta}$. In particular, xtreg, fe provides what is known as the fixed-effects estimator—also known as the within estimator—and amounts to using OLS to perform the estimation of (3). xtreg, be provides what is known as the between estimator and amounts to using OLS to perform the estimation of (2). xtreg, re provides the random-effects estimator and is a (matrix) weighted average of the estimates produced by the between and within estimators. In particular, the random-effects estimator turns out to be equivalent to estimation of

$$(y_{it} - \theta\overline{y}_i) = (1 - \theta)\alpha + (\mathbf{x}_{it} - \theta\overline{\mathbf{x}}_i)\boldsymbol{\beta} + \{(1 - \theta)\nu_i + (\epsilon_{it} - \theta\overline{\epsilon}_i)\} \tag{4}$$

where θ is a function of σ_ν^2 and σ_ϵ^2. If $\sigma_\nu^2 = 0$, meaning that ν_i is always 0, $\theta = 0$ and (1) can be estimated by OLS directly. Alternatively, if $\sigma_\epsilon^2 = 0$, meaning that ϵ_{it} is 0, $\theta = 1$ and the within estimator returns all the information available (which will, in fact, be a regression with an R^2 of 1).

For more reasonable cases, few assumptions are required to justify the fixed-effects estimator of (3). The estimates are, however, conditional on the sample in that the ν_i are not assumed to have a distribution but are instead treated as fixed and estimable. This statistical fine point can lead to difficulty when making out-of-sample predictions, but that aside, the fixed-effects estimator has much to recommend it.

More is required to justify the between estimator of (2), but the conditioning on the sample is not assumed since $\nu_i + \overline{\epsilon}_i$ is treated as a residual. Newly required is that we assume that ν_i and $\overline{\mathbf{x}}_i$ are uncorrelated. This follows from the assumptions of the OLS estimator but is also transparent: were ν_i and $\overline{\mathbf{x}}_i$ correlated, the estimator could not determine how much of the change in $\overline{y}_i$, associated with an increase in $\overline{\mathbf{x}}_i$, to assign to $\boldsymbol{\beta}$ versus how much to attribute to the unknown correlation. (This, of course, suggests the use of an instrumental-variable estimator, $\overline{\mathbf{z}}_i$, which is correlated with $\overline{\mathbf{x}}_i$ but uncorrelated with ν_i, though that approach is not implemented here.)

The random-effects estimator of (4) requires the same no-correlation assumption. In comparison with the between estimator, the random-effects estimator produces more efficient results, albeit ones with unknown small-sample properties. The between estimator is less efficient because it discards the over-time information in the data in favor of simple means; the random-effects estimator uses both the within and the between information.

All this would seem to leave the between estimator of (2) with no role (except for a minor, technical part it plays in helping to estimate σ_ν^2 and σ_ϵ^2, which are used in the calculation of θ, on which the random-effects estimates depend). Let us, however, consider a variation on (1):

$$y_{it} = \alpha + \overline{\mathbf{x}}_i \boldsymbol{\beta}_1 + (\mathbf{x}_{it} - \overline{\mathbf{x}}_i)\boldsymbol{\beta}_2 + \nu_i + \epsilon_{it} \tag{1$'$}$$

In this model, we postulate that changes in the average value of $\mathbf{x}$ for an individual have a different effect from temporary departures from the average. In an economic situation, y might be purchases of some item and $\mathbf{x}$ income; a change in average income should have more effect than a transitory change. In a clinical situation, y might be a physical response and $\mathbf{x}$ the level of a chemical in the brain; the model allows a different response to permanent rather than transitory changes.

The variations of (2) and (3) corresponding to (1$'$) are

$$\overline{y}_i = \alpha + \overline{\mathbf{x}}_i \boldsymbol{\beta}_1 + \nu_i + \overline{\epsilon}_i \tag{2$'$}$$
$$(y_{it} - \overline{y}_i) = (\mathbf{x}_{it} - \overline{\mathbf{x}}_i)\boldsymbol{\beta}_2 + (\epsilon_{it} - \overline{\epsilon}_i) \tag{3$'$}$$

That is, the between estimator estimates β_1 and the within β_2, and neither estimates the other. Thus even when estimating equations like (1), it is worth comparing the within and between estimators. Differences in results can suggest models like (1$'$), or at the least some other specification error.

Finally, it is worth understanding the role of the between and within estimators with regressors that are constant over time or constant over units. Consider the model

$$y_{it} = \alpha + \mathbf{x}_{it} \boldsymbol{\beta}_1 + \mathbf{s}_i \boldsymbol{\beta}_2 + \mathbf{z}_t \boldsymbol{\beta}_3 + \nu_i + \epsilon_{it} \tag{1$''$}$$

This model is the same as (1), except that we explicitly identify the variables that vary over both time and i ($\mathbf{x}_{it}$, such as output or FEV); variables that are constant over time ($\mathbf{s}_i$, such as race or sex); and variables that vary solely over time ($\mathbf{z}_t$, such as the consumer price index or age in a cohort study). The corresponding between and within equations are

$$\overline{y}_i = \alpha + \overline{\mathbf{x}}_i \boldsymbol{\beta}_1 + \mathbf{s}_i \boldsymbol{\beta}_2 + \overline{\mathbf{z}} \boldsymbol{\beta}_3 + \nu_i + \overline{\epsilon}_i \tag{2$''$}$$
$$(y_{it} - \overline{y}_i) = (\mathbf{x}_{it} - \overline{\mathbf{x}}_i)\boldsymbol{\beta}_1 + (\mathbf{z}_t - \overline{\mathbf{z}})\boldsymbol{\beta}_3 + (\epsilon_{it} - \overline{\epsilon}_i) \tag{3$''$}$$

In the between estimator of (2$''$), no estimate of β_3 is possible because $\overline{\mathbf{z}}$ is a constant across the i observations; the regression-estimated intercept will be an estimate of $\alpha + \overline{\mathbf{z}}\beta_3$. On the other hand, it can provide estimates of β_1 and β_2. It can estimate effects of factors that are constant over time, such as race and sex, but to do so it must assume that ν_i is uncorrelated with those factors.

The within estimator of (3$''$), like the between estimator, provides an estimate of β_1 but provides no estimate of β_2 for time-invariant factors. Instead, it provides an estimate of β_3, the effects of the time-varying factors. The between estimator can also provide estimates u_i for ν_i. More correctly, the estimator u_i is an estimator of $\nu_i + \mathbf{s}_i \beta_2$. Thus u_i is an estimator of ν_i only if there are no time-invariant variables in the model. If there are time-invariant variables, u_i is an estimate of ν_i plus the effects of the time-invariant variables.

Assessing goodness of fit

R^2 is a popular measure of goodness of fit in ordinary regression. In our case, given $\widehat{\alpha}$ and $\widehat{\beta}$ estimates of α and β, we can assess the goodness of fit with respect to (1), (2), or (3). The prediction equations are, respectively,

$$\widehat{y}_{it} = \widehat{\alpha} + \mathbf{x}_{it}\widehat{\beta} \tag{1'''}$$

$$\widehat{\overline{y}}_i = \widehat{\alpha} + \overline{\mathbf{x}}_i\widehat{\beta} \tag{2'''}$$

$$\widehat{\widetilde{y}}_{it} = (\widehat{y}_{it} - \widehat{\overline{y}}_i) = (\mathbf{x}_{it} - \overline{\mathbf{x}}_i)\widehat{\beta} \tag{3'''}$$

xtreg reports "R-squares" corresponding to these three equations. R-squares is in quotes because the R-squares reported do not have all the properties of the OLS R^2.

The ordinary properties of R^2 include being equal to the squared correlation between $\widehat{y}$ and y and being equal to the fraction of the variation in y explained by $\widehat{y}$—formally defined as $\mathrm{Var}(\widehat{y})/\mathrm{Var}(y)$. The identity of the definitions is from a special property of the OLS estimates; in general, given a prediction $\widehat{y}$ for y, the squared correlation is not equal to the ratio of the variances, and the ratio of the variances is not required to be less than 1.

xtreg reports R^2 values calculated as correlations squared, calling them R^2 overall, corresponding to (1'''); R^2 between, corresponding to (2'''); and R^2 within, corresponding to (3'''). In fact, you can think of each of these three numbers as having all the properties of ordinary R^2s if you bear in mind that the prediction being judged is not $\widehat{y}_{it}$, $\widehat{\overline{y}}_i$, and $\widehat{\widetilde{y}}_{it}$, but $\gamma_1\widehat{y}_{it}$ from the regression $y_{it} = \gamma_1\widehat{y}_{it}$; $\gamma_2\widehat{\overline{y}}_i$ from the regression $\overline{y}_i = \gamma_2\widehat{\overline{y}}_i$; and $\gamma_3\widehat{\widetilde{y}}_{it}$ from $\widetilde{y}_{it} = \gamma_3\widehat{\widetilde{y}}_{it}$.

In particular, xtreg, be obtains its estimates by performing OLS on (2), and therefore its reported R^2 between is an ordinary R^2. The other two reported R^2s are merely correlations squared, or, if you prefer, R^2s from the second-round regressions $y_{it} = \gamma_{11}\widehat{y}_{it}$ and $\widetilde{y}_{it} = \gamma_{13}\widehat{\widetilde{y}}_{it}$.

xtreg, fe obtains its estimates by performing OLS on (3), so its reported R^2 within is an ordinary R^2. As with be, the other R^2s are correlations squared, or, if you prefer, R^2s from the second-round regressions $\overline{y}_i = \gamma_{22}\widehat{\overline{y}}_i$ and, as with be, $\widetilde{y}_{it} = \gamma_{23}\widehat{\widetilde{y}}_{it}$.

xtreg, re obtains its estimates by performing OLS on (4); none of the R^2s corresponding to (1'''), (2'''), or (3''') correspond directly to this estimator (the "relevant" R^2 is the one corresponding to (4)). All three reported R^2s are correlations squared, or, if you prefer, from second-round regressions.

xtreg and associated commands

▷ Example 1: Between-effects model

Using nlswork.dta described in [XT] **xt**, we will model ln_wage in terms of completed years of schooling (grade), current age and age squared, current years worked (experience) and experience squared, current years of tenure on the current job and tenure squared, whether black, whether residing in an area not designated an SMSA (standard metropolitan statistical area), and whether residing in the South. Most of these variables are in the data, but we need to construct a few:

```
. use http://www.stata-press.com/data/r10/nlswork
(National Longitudinal Survey.  Young Women 14-26 years of age in 1968)

. generate age2 = age^2
(24 missing values generated)

. generate ttl_exp2 = ttl_exp^2
```

```
. generate tenure2 = tenure^2
(433 missing values generated)
. generate byte black = race==2
```

To obtain the between-effects estimates, we use xtreg, be. nlswork.dta has previously been xtset idcode year because that is what is true of the data, but for running xtreg, it would have been sufficient to have xtset idcode by itself.

```
. xtreg ln_w grade age* ttl_exp* tenure* black not_smsa south, be

Between regression (regression on group means)     Number of obs      =       28091
Group variable: idcode                             Number of groups   =        4697

R-sq:  within  = 0.1591                             Obs per group: min =           1
       between = 0.4900                                            avg =         6.0
       overall = 0.3695                                            max =          15

                                                   F(10,4686)         =      450.23
sd(u_i + avg(e_i.))=  .3036114                      Prob > F           =      0.0000
```

ln_wage	Coef.	Std. Err.	t	P>|t|	[95% Conf. Interval]	
grade	.0607602	.0020006	30.37	0.000	.0568382	.0646822
age	.0323158	.0087251	3.70	0.000	.0152105	.0494211
age2	-.0005997	.0001429	-4.20	0.000	-.0008799	-.0003194
ttl_exp	.0138853	.0056749	2.45	0.014	.0027598	.0250108
ttl exp2	.0007342	.0003267	2.25	0.025	.0000936	.0013747
tenure	.0698419	.0060729	11.50	0.000	.0579361	.0817476
tenure2	-.0028756	.0004098	-7.02	0.000	-.0036789	-.0020722
black	-.0564167	.0105131	-5.37	0.000	-.0770272	-.0358061
not_smsa	-.1860406	.0112495	-16.54	0.000	-.2080949	-.1639862
south	-.0993378	.010136	-9.80	0.000	-.1192091	-.0794665
_cons	.3339113	.1210434	2.76	0.006	.0966093	.5712133

The between-effects regression is estimated on person-averages, so the "n = 4697" result is relevant. xtreg, be reports the "number of observations" and group-size information: describe in [XT] **xt** showed that we have 28,534 "observations"—person-years, really—of data. If we take the subsample that has no missing values in ln_wage, grade, ..., south leaves us with 28,091 observations on person-years, reflecting 4,697 persons, each observed for an average of 5.98 years.

For goodness of fit, the R^2 between is directly relevant; our R^2 is .4900. If, however, we use these estimates to predict the within model, we have an R^2 of .1591. If we use these estimates to fit the overall data, our R^2 is .3695.

The F statistic tests that the coefficients on the regressors grade, age, ..., south are all jointly zero. Our model is significant.

The root mean squared error of the fitted regression, which is an estimate of the standard deviation of $\nu_i + \bar{\epsilon}_i$, is .3036.

For our coefficients, each year of schooling increases hourly wages by 6.1%; age increases wages up to age 26.9 and thereafter decreases them (because the quadratic $ax^2 + bx + c$ turns over at $x = -b/2a$, which for our age and age2 coefficients is $.0323158/(2 \times .0005997) \approx 26.9$); total experience increases wages at an increasing rate (which is surprising and bothersome); tenure on the current job increases wages up to a tenure of 12.1 years and thereafter decreases them; wages of blacks are, these things held constant, (approximately) 5.6% below that of nonblacks (approximately because black is an indicator variable); residing in a non-SMSA (rural area) reduces wages by 18.6%; and residing in the South reduces wages by 9.9%.

◁

▷ Example 2: Fixed-effects model

To fit the same model with the fixed-effects estimator, we specify the fe option.

```
. xtreg ln_w grade age* ttl_exp* tenure* black not_smsa south, fe
```

Fixed-effects (within) regression   Number of obs   =   28091
Group variable: idcode   Number of groups   =   4697

R-sq: within = 0.1727   Obs per group: min =   1
       between = 0.3505   avg =   6.0
       overall = 0.2625   max =   15

                                           F(8,23386)   =   610.12
corr(u_i, Xb) = 0.1936   Prob > F   =   0.0000

ln_wage	Coef.	Std. Err.	t	P>|t|	[95% Conf. Interval]	
grade	(dropped)					
age	.0359987	.0033864	10.63	0.000	.0293611	.0426362
age2	-.000723	.0000533	-13.58	0.000	-.0008274	-.0006186
ttl_exp	.0334668	.0029653	11.29	0.000	.0276545	.039279
ttl_exp2	.0002163	.0001277	1.69	0.090	-.0000341	.0004666
tenure	.0357539	.0018487	19.34	0.000	.0321303	.0393775
tenure2	-.0019701	.000125	-15.76	0.000	-.0022151	-.0017251
black	(dropped)					
not_smsa	-.0890108	.0095316	-9.34	0.000	-.1076933	-.0703282
south	-.0606309	.0109319	-5.55	0.000	-.0820582	-.0392036
_cons	1.03732	.0485546	21.36	0.000	.9421497	1.13249
sigma_u	.35562203					
sigma_e	.29068923					
rho	.59946283	(fraction of variance due to u_i)				

F test that all u_i=0:   F(4696,23386) =   5.13   Prob > F = 0.0000

The observation summary at the top is the same as for the between-effects model, although this time it is the "Number of obs" that is relevant.

Our three R^2s are not too different from those reported previously; the R^2 within is slightly higher (.1727 versus .1591), and the R^2 between is a little lower (.3505 versus .4900), as expected, since the between estimator maximizes R^2 between and the within estimator R^2 within. In terms of overall fit, these estimates are somewhat worse (.2625 versus .3695).

xtreg, fe can estimate σ_ν and σ_ϵ, although how you interpret these estimates depends on whether you are using xtreg to fit a fixed-effects model or random-effects model. To clarify this fine point, in the fixed-effects model, ν_i are formally fixed—they have no distribution. If you subscribe to this view, think of the reported $\hat{\sigma}_\nu$ as merely an arithmetic way to describe the range of the estimated but fixed ν_i. If, however, you are using the fixed-effects estimator of the random-effects model, .355622 is an estimate of σ_ν or would be if there were no dropped variables.

Here both grade and black were dropped from the model because they do not vary over time. Since grade and race are time invariant, our estimate u_i is an estimate of ν_i plus the effects of grade and race, so our estimate of the standard deviation is based on the variation in ν_i, grade, and race. On the other hand, had race and grade been dropped merely because they were collinear with the other regressors in our model, u_i would be an estimate of ν_i, and .3556 would be an estimate of σ_ν. (xtsum and xttab allow you to determine whether a variable is time invariant; see [XT] **xtsum** and [XT] **xttab**.)

Regardless of the status of u_i, our estimate of the standard deviation of ϵ_{it} is valid (and, in fact, is the estimate that would be used by the random-effects estimator to produce its results).

Our estimate of the correlation of u_i with $\mathbf{x}_{it}$ suffers from the problem of what u_i measures. We find correlation but cannot say whether this is correlation of ν_i with $\mathbf{x}_{it}$ or merely correlation of grade and race with $\mathbf{x}_{it}$. In any case, the fixed-effects estimator is robust to such a correlation, and the other estimates it produces are unbiased.

So, although this estimator produces no estimates of the effects of grade and race, it does predict that age has a positive effect on wages up to age 24.9 years (compared with 26.9 years estimated by the between estimator); that total experience still increases wages at an increasing rate (which is still bothersome); that tenure increases wages up to 9.1 years (compared with 12.1); that living in a non-SMSA reduces wages by 8.9% (compared with a more drastic 18.6%); and that living in the South reduces wages by 6.1% (as compared with 9.9%).

◁

▷ Example 3: Fixed-effects models with robust standard errors

If we suspect that there is heteroskedasticity in the idiosyncratic error term ϵ_{it}, we could specify the vce(robust) option:

```
. xtreg ln_w grade age* ttl_exp* tenure* black not_smsa south, fe vce(robust)
Fixed-effects (within) regression              Number of obs      =     28091
Group variable: idcode                         Number of groups   =      4697

R-sq:  within  = 0.1727                         Obs per group: min =         1
       between = 0.3505                                        avg =       6.0
       overall = 0.2625                                        max =        15

                                                F(8,23386)         =    553.03
corr(u_i, Xb)  = 0.1936                         Prob > F           =    0.0000
```

ln_wage	Coef.	Robust Std. Err.	t	P>|t|	[95% Conf. Interval]	
grade	(dropped)					
age	.0359987	.0039755	9.06	0.000	.0282064	.0437909
age2	-.000723	.0000634	-11.40	0.000	-.0008473	-.0005987
ttl_exp	.0334668	.003215	10.41	0.000	.0271652	.0397684
ttl_exp2	.0002163	.000141	1.53	0.125	-.0000601	.0004926
tenure	.0357539	.0019756	18.10	0.000	.0318817	.0396261
tenure2	-.0019701	.0001362	-14.47	0.000	-.002237	-.0017032
black	(dropped)					
not_smsa	-.0890108	.0113004	-7.88	0.000	-.1111603	-.0668613
south	-.0606309	.013096	-4.63	0.000	-.0863	-.0349618
_cons	1.03732	.0564117	18.39	0.000	.9267494	1.14789
sigma_u	.35562203					
sigma_e	.29068923					
rho	.59946283	(fraction of variance due to u_i)				

Although the estimated coefficients are the same with and without the vce(robust) option, the robust estimator produced larger standard errors and a p-value for ttl_exp2 above the conventional 10%. The F test of $\nu_i = 0$ is suppressed because it is too difficult to compute the robust form of the statistic when there are more than a few panels.

◁

❑ Technical Note

Clustering on the panel variable produces an estimator of the VCE that is robust to cross-sectional heteroskedasticity and within-panel (serial) correlation that is asymptotically equivalent to that proposed by Arellano (1987). Although the example above applies the fixed-effects estimator, the robust and cluster–robust VCE estimators are also available for the random-effects estimator. Wooldridge (2002) and Arellano (2003) discuss these robust and cluster–robust VCE estimators for the fixed-effects and random-effects estimators. More details are available in *Methods and Formulas*.

❑

▷ Example 4: Random-effects model

Refitting our log-wage model with the random-effects estimator, we obtain

. xtreg ln_w grade age* ttl_exp* tenure* black not_smsa south, re theta

| Random-effects GLS regression | | Number of obs | = | 28091 |
| Group variable: idcode | | Number of groups | = | 4697 |

R-sq: within = 0.1715	Obs per group: min =	1
between = 0.4784	avg =	6.0
overall = 0.3708	max =	15

| Random effects u_i ~ Gaussian | Wald chi2(10) | = | 9244.87 |
| corr(u_i, X)   = 0 (assumed) | Prob > chi2 | = | 0.0000 |

| ──────── theta ──────── |
| min | 5% | median | 95% | max |
| 0.2520 | 0.2520 | 0.5499 | 0.7016 | 0.7206 |

ln_wage	Coef.	Std. Err.	z	P>|z|	[95% Conf. Interval]
grade	.0646499	.0017811	36.30	0.000	.0611589	.0681408
age	.036806	.0031195	11.80	0.000	.0306918	.0429201
age2	-.0007133	.00005	-14.27	0.000	-.0008113	-.0006153
ttl_exp	.0290207	.0024219	11.98	0.000	.0242737	.0337676
ttl_exp2	.0003049	.0001162	2.62	0.009	.000077	.0005327
tenure	.039252	.0017555	22.36	0.000	.0358114	.0426927
tenure2	-.0020035	.0001193	-16.80	0.000	-.0022373	-.0017697
black	-.0530532	.0099924	-5.31	0.000	-.0726379	-.0334685
not_smsa	-.1308263	.0071751	-18.23	0.000	-.1448891	-.1167634
south	-.0868927	.0073031	-11.90	0.000	-.1012066	-.0725788
_cons	.2387209	.0494688	4.83	0.000	.1417639	.335678

sigma_u	.25790313
sigma_e	.29069544
rho	.44043812	(fraction of variance due to u_i)

According to the R^2s, this estimator performs worse within than the within fixed-effects estimator and worse between than the between estimator, as it must, and slightly better overall.

We estimate that σ_ν is .2579 and σ_ϵ is .2907 and, by assertion, assume that the correlation of ν and x is zero.

All that is known about the random-effects estimator is its asymptotic properties, so rather than reporting an F statistic for overall significance, xtreg, re reports a χ^2. Taken jointly, our coefficients are significant.

xtreg, re also reports a summary of the distribution of θ_i, an ingredient in the estimation of (4). θ is not a constant here because we observe women for unequal periods.

We estimate that schooling has a rate of return of 6.5% (compared with 6.1% between and no estimate within); that the increase of wages with age turns around at 25.8 years (compared with 26.9 between and 24.9 within); that total experience yet again increases wages increasingly; that the effect of job tenure turns around at 9.8 years (compared with 12.1 between and 9.1 within); that being black reduces wages by 5.3% (compared with 5.6% between and no estimate within); that living in a non-SMSA reduces wages 13.1% (compared with 18.6% between and 8.9% within); and that living in the South reduces wages 8.7% (compared with 9.9% between and 6.1% within).

◁

▷ Example 5: Random-effects model fitted using ML

We could also have fitted this random-effects model with the maximum likelihood estimator:

```
. xtreg ln_w grade age* ttl_exp* tenure* black not_smsa south, mle
Fitting constant-only model:
Iteration 0:   log likelihood = -13690.161
Iteration 1:   log likelihood = -12819.317
Iteration 2:   log likelihood = -12662.039
Iteration 3:   log likelihood = -12649.744
Iteration 4:   log likelihood = -12649.614

Fitting full model:
Iteration 0:   log likelihood =  -8922.145
Iteration 1:   log likelihood = -8853.6409
Iteration 2:   log likelihood = -8853.4255
Iteration 3:   log likelihood = -8853.4254
```

Random-effects ML regression	Number of obs	=	28091
Group variable: idcode	Number of groups	=	4697
Random effects u_i ~ Gaussian	Obs per group: min =		1
	avg =		6.0
	max =		15
	LR chi2(10)	=	7592.38
Log likelihood = -8853.4254	Prob > chi2	=	0.0000

ln_wage	Coef.	Std. Err.	z	P>|z|	[95% Conf. Interval]	
grade	.0646093	.0017372	37.19	0.000	.0612044	.0680142
age	.0368531	.0031226	11.80	0.000	.030733	.0429732
age2	-.0007132	.0000501	-14.24	0.000	-.0008113	-.000615
ttl_exp	.0288196	.0024143	11.94	0.000	.0240877	.0335515
ttl_exp2	.000309	.0001163	2.66	0.008	.0000811	.0005369
tenure	.0394371	.0017604	22.40	0.000	.0359868	.0428875
tenure2	-.0020052	.0001195	-16.77	0.000	-.0022395	-.0017709
black	-.0533394	.0097338	-5.48	0.000	-.0724172	-.0342615
not_smsa	-.1323433	.0071322	-18.56	0.000	-.1463221	-.1183644
south	-.0875599	.0072143	-12.14	0.000	-.1016998	-.0734201
_cons	.2390837	.0491902	4.86	0.000	.1426727	.3354947
/sigma_u	.2485556	.0035017			.2417863	.2555144
/sigma_e	.2918458	.001352			.289208	.2945076
rho	.4204033	.0074828			.4057959	.4351212

Likelihood-ratio test of sigma_u=0: chibar2(01)= 7339.84 Prob>=chibar2 = 0.000

The estimates are nearly the same as those produced by xtreg, re—the GLS estimator. For instance, xtreg, re estimated the coefficient on grade to be .0646499, xtreg, mle estimated .0646093, and the ratio is .0646499/.0646093 = 1.001 to three decimal places. Similarly, the standard errors are nearly equal: .0017812/.0017372 = 1.025. Below we compare all 11 coefficients:

Estimator	Coefficient ratio			SE ratio		
	mean	min.	max.	mean	min.	max.
xtreg, mle (ML)	1.	1.	1.	1.	1.	1.
xtreg, re (GLS)	.997	.987	1.007	1.006	.997	1.027

◁

▷ Example 6: Population-averaged model

We could also have fitted this model with the population-averaged estimator:

```
. xtreg ln_w grade age* ttl_exp* tenure* black not_smsa south, pa

Iteration 1: tolerance = .0310561
Iteration 2: tolerance = .00074898
Iteration 3: tolerance = .0000147
Iteration 4: tolerance = 2.880e-07
```

```
GEE population-averaged model          Number of obs      =      28091
Group variable:                idcode   Number of groups   =       4697
Link:                        identity   Obs per group: min =          1
Family:                      Gaussian                  avg =        6.0
Correlation:              exchangeable                  max =         15
                                        Wald chi2(10)      =    9598.89
Scale parameter:              .1436709   Prob > chi2        =     0.0000
```

ln_wage	Coef.	Std. Err.	z	P>|z|	[95% Conf. Interval]	
grade	.0645427	.0016829	38.35	0.000	.0612442	.0678412
age	.036932	.0031509	11.72	0.000	.0307564	.0431076
age2	-.0007129	.0000506	-14.10	0.000	-.0008121	-.0006138
ttl_exp	.0284878	.0024169	11.79	0.000	.0237508	.0332248
ttl_exp2	.0003158	.0001172	2.69	0.007	.000086	.0005456
tenure	.0397468	.0017779	22.36	0.000	.0362621	.0432315
tenure2	-.002008	.0001209	-16.61	0.000	-.0022449	-.0017711
black	-.0538314	.0094086	-5.72	0.000	-.072272	-.0353909
not_smsa	-.1347788	.0070543	-19.11	0.000	-.1486049	-.1209526
south	-.0885969	.0071132	-12.46	0.000	-.1025386	-.0746552
_cons	.2396286	.0491465	4.88	0.000	.1433034	.3359539

These results differ from those produced by xtreg, re and xtreg, mle. Coefficients are larger and standard errors smaller. xtreg, pa is simply another way to run the xtgee command. That is, we would have obtained the same output had we typed

```
. xtgee ln_w grade age* ttl_exp* tenure* black not_smsa south
```
(output omitted because it is the same as above)

See [XT] **xtgee**. In the language of xtgee, the random-effects model corresponds to an exchangeable correlation structure and identity link, and xtgee also allows other correlation structures. Let us stay with the random-effects model, however. xtgee will also produce robust estimates of variance, and we refit this model that way by typing

```
. xtgee ln_w grade age* ttl_exp* tenure* black not_smsa south, vce(robust)
```
(output omitted, coefficients the same, standard errors different)

In the previous example, we presented a table comparing xtreg, re with xtreg, mle. Below we add the results from the estimates shown and the ones we did with xtgee, vce(robust):

		Coefficient ratio			SE ratio		
Estimator		mean	min.	max.	mean	min.	max.
xtreg, mle	(ML)	1.	1.	1.	1.	1.	1.
xtreg, re	(GLS)	.997	.987	1.007	1.006	.997	1.027
xtreg, pa	(PA)	1.060	.847	1.317	.853	.626	.986
xtgee, vce(robust)	(PA)	1.060	.847	1.317	1.306	.957	1.545

So, which are right? This is a real dataset, and we do not know. However, in example 2 in [XT] **xtreg postestimation**, we will present evidence that the assumptions underlying the xtreg, re and xtreg, mle results are not met.

◁

Acknowledgments

We thank Richard Goldstein, who wrote the first draft of the routine that fits random-effects regressions, and Badi Baltagi of Syracuse University and Manuelita Ureta of Texas A&M University, who assisted us in working our way through the literature.

Saved Results

xtreg, re saves the following in e():

Scalars

e(N)	number of observations	e(r2_b)	R-squared for between model
e(N_g)	number of groups	e(sigma)	ancillary parameter (gamma, lnormal)
e(df_m)	model degrees of freedom	e(sigma_u)	panel-level standard deviation
e(g_max)	largest group size	e(sigma_e)	standard deviation of ϵ_{it}
e(g_min)	smallest group size	e(rmse)	root mean squared error of GLS
e(g_avg)	average group size		regression
e(chi2)	χ^2	e(thta_min)	minimum θ
e(rho)	ρ	e(thta_5)	θ, 5th percentile
e(Tbar)	harmonic mean of group sizes	e(thta_50)	θ, 50th percentile
e(Tcon)	1 if T is constant	e(thta_95)	θ, 95th percentile
e(r2_w)	R-squared for within model	e(thta_max)	maximum θ
e(r2_o)	R-squared for overall model	e(N_clust)	number of clusters

Macros

e(cmd)	xtreg	e(vcetype)	title used to label Std. Err.
e(cmdline)	command as typed	e(chi2type)	Wald; type of model χ^2 test
e(depvar)	name of dependent variable	e(sa)	Swamy–Arora estimator of the variance
e(model)	re		components (sa only)
e(ivar)	variable denoting groups	e(properties)	b V
e(clustvar)	name of cluster variable	e(predict)	program used to implement predict
e(vce)	*vcetype* specified in vce()		

Matrices

e(b)	coefficient vector	e(Vf)	VCE for fixed-effects model
e(theta)	θ	e(bf)	coefficient vector for fixed-effects model
e(V)	variance–covariance matrix of the estimators		

Functions

e(sample)	marks estimation sample

`xtreg, be` saves the following in `e()`:

Scalars

`e(N)`	number of observations	`e(ll)`	log likelihood
`e(N_g)`	number of groups	`e(ll_0)`	log likelihood, constant-only model
`e(mss)`	model sum of squares	`e(g_max)`	largest group size
`e(df_m)`	model degrees of freedom	`e(g_min)`	smallest group size
`e(rss)`	residual sum of squares	`e(g_avg)`	average group size
`e(df_r)`	residual degrees of freedom	`e(Tbar)`	harmonic mean of group sizes
`e(r2)`	R-squared	`e(Tcon)`	1 if T is constant
`e(r2_a)`	adjusted R-squared	`e(r2_w)`	R-squared for within model
`e(F)`	F statistic	`e(r2_o)`	R-squared for overall model
`e(rmse)`	root mean squared error	`e(r2_b)`	R-squared for between model

Macros

`e(cmd)`	xtreg	`e(ivar)`	variable denoting groups
`e(cmdline)`	command as typed	`e(vce)`	*vcetype* specified in vce()
`e(depvar)`	name of dependent variable	`e(vcetype)`	title used to label Std. Err.
`e(title)`	title in estimation output	`e(properties)`	b V
`e(model)`	be	`e(predict)`	program used to implement predict

Matrices

`e(b)`	coefficient vector	`e(V)`	variance–covariance matrix of the estimators

Functions

`e(sample)`	marks estimation sample

`xtreg, fe` saves the following in `e()`:

Scalars

e(N)	number of observations	e(F)	F statistic
e(N_g)	number of groups	e(g_max)	largest group size
e(mss)	model sum of squares	e(g_min)	smallest group size
e(tss)	total sum of squares	e(g_avg)	average group size
e(df_m)	model degrees of freedom	e(rho)	ρ
e(rss)	residual sum of squares	e(Tbar)	harmonic mean of group sizes
e(df_r)	residual degrees of freedom	e(Tcon)	1 if T is constant
e(r2)	R-squared	e(r2_w)	R-squared for within model
e(r2_a)	adjusted R-squared	e(r2_o)	R-squared for overall model
e(sigma)	ancillary parameter (gamma, lnormal)	e(r2_b)	R-squared for between model
e(rmse)	root mean squared error	e(N_clust)	number of clusters
e(ll)	log likelihood	e(corr)	corr(u_i, Xb)
e(ll_0)	log likelihood, constant-only model	e(sigma_u)	panel-level standard deviation
e(df_a)	degrees of freedom for absorbed effect	e(sigma_e)	standard deviation of ϵ_{it}
e(df_b)	numerator degrees of freedom for F statistic	e(F_f)	F for $u_i=0$

Macros

e(cmd)	xtreg	e(wexp)	weight expression
e(cmdline)	command as typed	e(vce)	*vcetype* specified in vce()
e(depvar)	name of dependent variable	e(vcetype)	title used to label Std. Err.
e(model)	fe	e(properties)	b V
e(ivar)	variable denoting groups	e(predict)	program used to implement predict
e(clustvar)	name of cluster variable		
e(wtype)	weight type		

Matrices

e(b)	coefficient vector	e(V)	variance–covariance matrix of the estimators

Functions

e(sample)	marks estimation sample

(Continued on next page)

`xtreg, mle` saves the following in `e()`:

Scalars

e(N)	number of observations	e(g_min)	smallest group size
e(N_g)	number of groups	e(g_avg)	average group size
e(df_m)	model degrees of freedom	e(chi2)	χ^2
e(ll)	log likelihood	e(chi2_c)	χ^2 for comparison test
e(ll_0)	log likelihood, constant-only model	e(rho)	ρ
e(ll_c)	log likelihood, comparison model	e(sigma_u)	panel-level standard deviation
e(g_max)	largest group size	e(sigma_e)	standard deviation of ϵ_{it}

Macros

e(cmd)	xtreg	e(vcetype)	title used to label Std. Err.
e(cmdline)	command as typed	e(chi2type)	Wald or LR; type of model χ^2 test
e(depvar)	name of dependent variable	e(chi2_ct)	Wald or LR; type of model χ^2 test
e(model)	ml		corresponding to e(chi2_c)
e(ivar)	variable denoting groups	e(distrib)	Gaussian; the distribution of the RE
e(wtype)	weight type	e(crittype)	optimization criterion
e(wexp)	weight expression	e(properties)	b V
e(title)	title in estimation output	e(predict)	program used to implement predict
e(vce)	*vcetype* specified in vce()		

Matrices

e(b)	coefficient vector	e(V)	variance–covariance matrix of the estimators

Functions

e(sample)	marks estimation sample

xtreg, pa saves the following in e():

Scalars

e(N)	number of observations		e(df_pear)	degrees of freedom for Pearson χ^2
e(N_g)	number of groups		e(deviance)	deviance
e(df_m)	model degrees of freedom		e(chi2_dev)	χ^2 test of deviance
e(g_max)	largest group size		e(dispers)	deviance dispersion
e(g_min)	smallest group size		e(chi2_dis)	χ^2 test of deviance dispersion
e(g_avg)	average group size		e(tol)	target tolerance
e(rc)	return code		e(dif)	achieved tolerance
e(chi2)	χ^2		e(phi)	scale parameter

Macros

e(cmd)	xtgee		e(scale)	x2, dev, phi, or #; scale parameter
e(cmd2)	xtreg		e(ivar)	variable denoting groups
e(cmdline)	command as typed		e(vce)	*vcetype* specified in vce()
e(depvar)	name of dependent variable		e(vcetype)	title used to label Std. Err.
e(model)	pa		e(chi2type)	Wald; type of model χ^2 test
e(wtype)	weight type		e(disp)	deviance dispersion
e(wexp)	weight expression		e(offset)	offset
e(family)	Gaussian		e(crittype)	optimization criterion
e(link)	identity; link function		e(properties)	b V
e(corr)	correlation structure		e(predict)	program used to implement predict

Matrices

e(b)	coefficient vector		e(V)	variance–covariance matrix of the
e(R)	estimated working correlation matrix			estimators

Functions

e(sample)	marks estimation sample

Methods and Formulas

The model to be fitted is

$$y_{it} = \alpha + \mathbf{x}_{it}\boldsymbol{\beta} + \nu_i + \epsilon_{it}$$

for $i = 1, \ldots, n$ and, for each i, $t = 1, \ldots, T$, of which T_i periods are actually observed.

xtreg, fe

xtreg, fe produces estimates by running OLS on

$$(y_{it} - \overline{y}_i + \overline{\overline{y}}) = \alpha + (\mathbf{x}_{it} - \overline{\mathbf{x}}_i + \overline{\overline{\mathbf{x}}})\boldsymbol{\beta} + (\epsilon_{it} - \overline{\epsilon}_i + \overline{\nu}) + \overline{\overline{\epsilon}}$$

where $\overline{y}_i = \sum_{t=1}^{T_i} y_{it}/T_i$, and similarly, $\overline{\overline{y}} = \sum_i \sum_t y_{it}/(nT_i)$. The conventional covariance matrix of the estimators is adjusted for the extra $n - 1$ estimated means, so results are the same as using OLS on (1) to estimate ν_i directly. Specifying vce(robust) or vce(cluster *clustvar*) causes the Huber/White/sandwich VCE estimator to be calculated for the coefficients estimated in this regression. See [U] **20.15 Obtaining robust variance estimates** and [P] **_robust** for details. Wooldridge (2002) and Arellano (2003) discuss this application of the Huber/White/sandwich VCE estimator.

Clustering on the panel variable produces a consistent VCE estimator when the disturbances are correlated within panels and not identically distributed over the panels. The most common example is within-panel serial-correlation and cross-panel heteroskedasticity.

The cluster–robust–VCE estimator requires that there are many clusters and the disturbances are uncorrelated across the clusters. Usually, the panel variable must be nested within the cluster variable because of the within-panel correlation induced by the within transform.

Care should be taken in using `nonest`, which removes the restriction that the panel variable be nested within the clusters. When using this option with `xtreg, fe`, you will need many observations per panel so that the within-panel correlation caused by the within transform becomes negligible.

The `dfadj` option adjusts the cluster–robust–VCE estimator for the n degrees-of-freedom used in the within transform. Although this option usually causes the standard errors to be too large, it may be useful when the panels are not nested within the clusters and there are few observations per panel.

From the estimates $\widehat{\alpha}$ and $\widehat{\beta}$, estimates u_i of ν_i are obtained as $u_i = \overline{y}_i - \widehat{\alpha} - \overline{\mathbf{x}}_i\widehat{\beta}$. Reported from the calculated u_i are its standard deviation and its correlation with $\overline{\mathbf{x}}_i\widehat{\beta}$. Reported as the standard deviation of e_{it} is the regression's estimated root mean squared error, s, which is adjusted (as previously stated) for the $n - 1$ estimated means.

Reported as R^2 within is the R^2 from the mean-deviated regression.

Reported as R^2 between is $\operatorname{corr}(\overline{\mathbf{x}}_i\widehat{\beta}, \overline{y}_i)^2$.

Reported as R^2 overall is $\operatorname{corr}(\mathbf{x}_{it}\widehat{\beta}, y_{it})^2$.

xtreg, be

`xtreg, be` fits the following model:

$$\overline{y}_i = \alpha + \overline{\mathbf{x}}_i\boldsymbol{\beta} + \nu_i + \overline{\epsilon}_i$$

Estimation is via OLS unless T_i is not constant and the `wls` option is specified. Otherwise, the estimation is performed via WLS. The estimates and conventional VCE are obtained from `regress` for both cases, but for WLS, `[aweight=`T_i`]` is specified.

Reported as R^2 between is the R^2 from the fitted regression.

Reported as R^2 within is $\operatorname{corr}\left\{(\mathbf{x}_{it} - \overline{\mathbf{x}}_i)\widehat{\beta}, y_{it} - \overline{y}_i\right\}^2$.

Reported as R^2 overall is $\operatorname{corr}(\mathbf{x}_{it}\widehat{\beta}, y_{it})^2$.

xtreg, re

The key to the random-effects estimator is the GLS transform. Given estimates of the idiosyncratic component, $\widehat{\sigma}_e^2$, and the individual component, $\widehat{\sigma}_u^2$, the GLS transform of a variable z for the random-effects model is

$$z_{it}^* = z_{it} - \widehat{\theta}_i\overline{z}_i$$

where $\overline{z}_i = \frac{1}{T_i}\sum_t^{T_i} z_{it}$ and

$$\widehat{\theta}_i = 1 - \sqrt{\frac{\widehat{\sigma}_e^2}{T_i\widehat{\sigma}_u^2 + \widehat{\sigma}_e^2}}$$

Given an estimate of $\widehat{\theta}_i$, one transforms the dependent and independent variables, and then the coefficient estimates and the conventional variance–covariance matrix come from an OLS regression of y_{it}^* on $\mathbf{x}_{it}^*$ and the transformed constant $1 - \widehat{\theta}_i$. Specifying `vce(robust)` or `vce(cluster `*clustvar*`)` causes the Huber/White/sandwich VCE estimator to be calculated for the coefficients estimated in this regression. See [U] **20.15 Obtaining robust variance estimates** and [P] **_robust** for details. Wooldridge (2002) and Arellano (2003) discuss this application of the Huber/White/sandwich VCE estimator.

Stata has two implementations of the Swamy–Arora method for estimating the variance components. They produce the same results in balanced panels and share the same estimator of σ_e^2. However, the two methods differ in their estimator of σ_u^2 in unbalanced panels. We call the first $\widehat{\sigma}_{u\overline{T}}^2$ and the second $\widehat{\sigma}_{\mathrm{uSA}}^2$. Both estimators are consistent; however, $\widehat{\sigma}_{\mathrm{uSA}}^2$ has a more elaborate adjustment for small samples than $\widehat{\sigma}_{u\overline{T}}^2$. (See Baltagi [2005], Baltagi and Chang [1994], and Swamy and Arora [1972] for derivations of these methods.)

Both methods use the same function of within residuals to estimate the idiosyncratic error component σ_e. Specifically,

$$\widehat{\sigma}_e^2 = \frac{\sum_i^n \sum_t^{T_i} e_{it}^2}{N - n - K + 1}$$

where

$$e_{it} = (y_{it} - \overline{y}_i + \overline{\overline{y}}) - \widehat{\alpha}_w - (\mathbf{x}_{it} - \overline{\mathbf{x}}_i + \overline{\overline{\mathbf{x}}})\widehat{\boldsymbol{\beta}}_w$$

and $\widehat{\alpha}_w$ and $\widehat{\boldsymbol{\beta}}_w$ are the within estimates of the coefficients and $N - \sum_i^n T_i$. After passing the within residuals through the within transform, only the idiosyncratic errors are left.

The default method for estimating σ_u^2 is

$$\widehat{\sigma}_{u\overline{T}}^2 = \max\left\{0, \frac{SSR_b}{n - K} - \frac{\widehat{\sigma}_e^2}{\overline{T}}\right\}$$

where

$$SSR_b = \sum_i^n T_i \left(\overline{y}_i - \widehat{\alpha}_b - \overline{\mathbf{x}}_i\widehat{\boldsymbol{\beta}}_b\right)^2$$

$\widehat{\alpha}_b$ and $\widehat{\boldsymbol{\beta}}_b$ are coefficient estimates from the between regression and $\overline{T}$ is the harmonic mean of T_i:

$$\overline{T} = \frac{n}{\sum_i^n \frac{1}{T_i}}$$

This estimator is consistent for σ_u^2 and is computationally less expensive than the second method. The sum of squared residuals from the between model estimate a function of both the idiosyncratic component and the individual component. Using our estimator of σ_e^2, we can remove the idiosyncratic component, leaving only the desired individual component.

The second method is the Swamy–Arora method for unbalanced panels derived by Baltagi and Chang (1994), which has a more precise small-sample adjustment. Using this method,

$$\ddot{\sigma}_{\mathrm{uSA}}^2 = \max\left\{0, \frac{SSR_b - (n - K)\widehat{\sigma}_e^2}{N - tr}\right\}$$

where

$$tr = \text{trace} \left\{ (\mathbf{X}'\mathbf{P}\mathbf{X})^{-1} \mathbf{X}'\mathbf{Z}\mathbf{Z}'\mathbf{X} \right\}$$

$$\mathbf{P} = \text{diag} \left\{ \left(\frac{1}{T_i} \right) \iota_{T_i} \iota'_{T_i} \right\}$$

$$\mathbf{Z} = \text{diag} \left[\iota_{T_i} \right]$$

$\mathbf{X}$ is the $N \times K$ matrix of covariates, including the constant, and ι_{T_i} is a $T_i \times 1$ vector of ones.

The estimated coefficients $(\widehat{\alpha}_r, \widehat{\beta}_r)$ and their covariance matrix $\mathbf{V}_r$ are reported together with the previously calculated quantities $\widehat{\sigma}_e$ and $\widehat{\sigma}_u$. The standard deviation of $\nu_i + e_{it}$ is calculated as $\sqrt{\widehat{\sigma}_e^2 + \widehat{\sigma}_u^2}$.

Reported as R^2 between is $\text{corr}(\overline{\mathbf{x}}_i \widehat{\beta}, \overline{y}_i)^2$.

Reported as R^2 within is $\text{corr}\{ (\mathbf{x}_{it} - \overline{\mathbf{x}}_i)\widehat{\beta}, y_{it} - \overline{y}_i \}^2$.

Reported as R^2 overall is $\text{corr}(\mathbf{x}_{it}\widehat{\beta}, y_{it})^2$.

xtreg, mle

The log likelihood for the ith unit is

$$l_i = -\frac{1}{2} \left(\frac{1}{\sigma_e^2} \left[\sum_{t=1}^{T_i} (y_{it} - \mathbf{x}_{it}\beta)^2 - \frac{\sigma_u^2}{T_i \sigma_u^2 + \sigma_e^2} \left\{ \sum_{t=1}^{T_i} (y_{it} - \mathbf{x}_{it}\beta) \right\}^2 \right] \right.$$
$$\left. + \ln\left(T_i \frac{\sigma_u^2}{\sigma_e^2} + 1 \right) + T_i \ln(2\pi\sigma_e^2) \right)$$

The `mle` and `re` options yield essentially the same results, except when total $N = \sum_i T_i$ is small (200 or less) and the data are unbalanced.

xtreg, pa

See [XT] **xtgee** for details on the methods and formulas used to calculate the population-averaged model using a generalized estimating equations approach.

References

Andrews, M., T. Schank, and R. Upward. 2006. Practical fixed-effects estimation methods for the three-way error-components model. *Stata Journal* 6: 461–481.

Arellano, M. 1987. Computing robust standard errors for within-groups estimators. *Oxford Bulletin of Economics and Statistics* 49: 431–434.

——. 2003. *Panel Data Econometrics.* New York: Oxford University Press.

Baltagi, B. H. 1985. Pooling cross-sections with unequal time-series lengths. *Economics Letters* 18: 133–136.

——. 2005. *Econometric Analysis of Panel Data.* 3rd ed. New York: Wiley.

Baltagi, B. H., and Y. Chang. 1994. Incomplete panels: A comparative study of alternative estimators for the unbalanced one-way error component regression model. *Journal of Econometrics* 62: 67–89.

Baum, C. F. 2001. Residual diagnostics for cross-section time series regression models. *Stata Journal* 1: 101–104.

Blackwell, J. L., III. 2005. Estimation and testing of fixed-effect panel-data systems. *Stata Journal* 5: 202–207.

Bottai, M., and N. Orsini. 2004. Confidence intervals for the variance component of random-effects linear models. *Stata Journal* 4: 429–435.

Bruno, G. S. F. 2005. Estimation and inference in dynamic unbalanced panel-data models with a small number of individuals. *Stata Journal* 5: 473–500.

Dwyer, J., and M. Feinleib. 1992. Introduction to statistical models for longitudinal observation. In *Statistical Models for Longitudinal Studies of Health*, ed. J. Dwyer, M. Feinleib, P. Lippert, and H. Hoffmeister, 3–48. New York: Oxford University Press.

Greene, W. H. 1983. Simultaneous estimation of factor substitution, economies of scale, and non-neutral technical change. In *Econometric Analyses of Productivity*, ed. A. Dogramaci. Boston: Kluwer.

——. 2003. *Econometric Analysis*. 5th ed. Upper Saddle River, NJ: Prentice Hall.

Hoyos, R. E. De, and V. Sarafidis. 2006. Testing for cross-sectional dependence in panel-data models. *Stata Journal* 6: 482–496.

Judge, G. G., W. E. Griffiths, R. C. Hill, H. Lütkepohl, and T.-C. Lee. 1985. *The Theory and Practice of Econometrics*. 2nd ed. New York: Wiley.

Lee, L., and W. Griffiths. 1979. The prior likelihood and best linear unbiased prediction in stochastic coefficient linear models. University of New England Working Papers in Econometrics and Applied Statistics No. 1, Armidale, Australia.

Rabe-Hesketh, S., A. Pickles, and C. Taylor. 2000. sg129: Generalized linear latent and mixed models. *Stata Technical Bulletin* 53: 47–57. Reprinted in *Stata Technical Bulletin Reprints*, vol. 9, pp. 293–307.

Sosa-Escudero, W., and A. K. Bera. 2001. sg164: Specification tests for linear panel data models. *Stata Technical Bulletin* 61: 18–21. Reprinted in *Stata Technical Bulletin Reprints*, vol. 10, pp. 307–311.

Swamy, P. A. V. B., and S. S. Arora. 1972. The exact finite sample properties of the estimators of coefficients in the error components regression models. *Econometrica* 40: 643–657.

Taub, A. J. 1979. Prediction in the context of the variance-components model. *Journal of Econometrics* 10: 103–108.

Twisk, J. W. R. 2003. *Applied Longitudinal Data Analysis for Epidemiology: A Practical Guide*. Cambridge: Cambridge University Press.

Wooldridge, J. M. 2002. *Econometric Analysis of Cross Section and Panel Data*. Cambridge, MA: MIT Press.

Also See

Title

> **xtreg postestimation** — Postestimation tools for xtreg

Description

The following postestimation commands are of special interest after `xtreg`:

command	description
xttest0	Breusch and Pagan LM test for random effects

For information about this command, see below.

The following standard postestimation commands are also available:

command	description
adjust[1]	adjusted predictions of $\mathbf{x}\boldsymbol{\beta}$
*estat	AIC, BIC, VCE, and estimation sample summary
estimates	cataloging estimation results
hausman	Hausman's specification test
lincom	point estimates, standard errors, testing, and inference for linear combinations of coefficients
lrtest	likelihood-ratio test
mfx	marginal effects or elasticities
nlcom	point estimates, standard errors, testing, and inference for nonlinear combinations of coefficients
predict	predictions, residuals, influence statistics, and other diagnostic measures
predictnl	point estimates, standard errors, testing, and inference for generalized predictions
test	Wald tests for simple and composite linear hypotheses
testnl	Wald tests of nonlinear hypotheses

[1] adjust is not appropriate with time-series operators.

*estat ic is not appropriate after `xtreg` with the be, pa, or re options.

See the corresponding entries in the *Stata Base Reference Manual* for details.

Special-interest postestimation commands

`xttest0`, for use after `xtreg, re`, presents the Breusch and Pagan (1980) Lagrange multiplier test for random effects, a test that $\mathrm{Var}(\nu_i) = 0$.

Syntax for predict

For all but the population-averaged model

> predict [*type*] *newvar* [*if*] [*in*] [, *statistic* <u>nooff</u>set]

Population-averaged model

> predict [*type*] *newvar* [*if*] [*in*] [, *PA_statistic* <u>nooff</u>set]

statistic	description
Main	
xb	$\mathbf{x}_j\mathbf{b}$, fitted values; the default
stdp	standard error of the fitted values
ue	$u_i + e_{it}$, the combined residual
*xbu	$\mathbf{x}_j\mathbf{b} + u_i$, prediction including effect
*u	u_i, the fixed- or random-error component
*e	e_{it}, the overall error component

Unstarred statistics are available both in and out of sample; type predict ... if e(sample) ... if wanted only for the estimation sample. Starred statistics are calculated only for the estimation sample, even when if e(sample) is not specified.

PA_statistic	description
Main	
mu	predicted probability of *depvar*; considers the offset()
rate	predicted probability of *depvar*
xb	linear prediction
stdp	standard error of the linear prediction
<u>sc</u>ore	first derivative of the log likelihood with respect to $\mathbf{x}_j\beta$

These statistics are available both in and out of sample; type predict ... if e(sample) ... if wanted only for the estimation sample.

Options for predict

> ┌─ **Main** ───

xb calculates the linear prediction, that is, $a + \mathbf{b}\mathbf{x}_{it}$. This is the default for all except the population-averaged model.

stdp calculates the standard error of the linear prediction. For the fixed-effects model, this excludes the variance due to uncertainty about the estimate of u_i.

mu and rate both calculate the predicted probability of *depvar*. mu takes into account the offset(), and rate ignores those adjustments. mu and rate are equivalent if you did not specify offset(). mu is the default for the population-averaged model.

ue calculates the prediction of $u_i + e_{it}$.

xbu calculates the prediction of $a + \mathbf{b}\mathbf{x}_{it} + u_i$, the prediction including the fixed or random component.

u calculates the prediction of u_i, the estimated fixed or random effect.

e calculates the prediction of e_{it}.

score calculates the equation-level score, $u_j = \partial \ln L_j(\mathbf{x}_j\beta)/\partial(\mathbf{x}_j\beta)$.

nooffset is relevant only if you specified offset(*varname*) for xtreg, pa. It modifies the calculations made by predict so that they ignore the offset variable; the linear prediction is treated as $\mathbf{x}_{it}\mathbf{b}$ rather than $\mathbf{x}_{it}\mathbf{b} + \text{offset}_{it}$.

Syntax for xttest0

```
xttest0
```

Remarks

▷ Example 1

Continuing with our xtreg, re estimation example (example 4) in xtreg, we can see that xttest0 will report a test of $\nu_i = 0$. In case we have any doubts, we could type

```
. xtreg ln_w grade age* ttl_exp* tenure* black not_smsa south, re theta
(output omitted)
. xttest0
Breusch and Pagan Lagrangian multiplier test for random effects
        ln_wage[idcode,t] = Xb + u[idcode] + e[idcode,t]

        Estimated results:
                        |     Var       sd = sqrt(Var)
              ----------+-------------------------------
               ln_wage  |  .2283326        .4778416
                     e  |  .0845038        .2906954
                     u  |   .066514        .2579031

        Test:   Var(u) = 0
                               chi2(1) =  14779.98
                           Prob > chi2 =     0.0000
```

◁

▷ Example 2

More importantly, after xtreg, re estimation, hausman will perform the Hausman specification test. If our model is correctly specified, and if ν_i is uncorrelated with $\mathbf{x}_{it}$, the (subset of) coefficients that are estimated by the fixed-effects estimator and the same coefficients that are estimated here should not statistically differ:

```
. xtreg ln_w grade age* ttl_exp* tenure* black not_smsa south, re
(output omitted)
. estimates store random_effects
. xtreg ln_w grade age* ttl_exp* tenure* black not_smsa south, fe
(output omitted)
```

```
. hausman . random_effects
```

	——— Coefficients ——— (b) .	(B) random_eff~s	(b-B) Difference	sqrt(diag(V_b-V_B)) S.E.
age	.0359987	.036806	-.0008073	.0013177
age2	-.000723	-.0007133	-9.68e-06	.0000184
ttl_exp	.0334668	.0290207	.0044461	.001711
ttl_exp2	.0002163	.0003049	-.0000886	.000053
tenure	.0357539	.039252	-.0034981	.0005797
tenure2	-.0019701	-.0020035	.0000334	.0000373
not_smsa	-.0890108	-.1308263	.0418155	.0062745
south	-.0606309	-.0868927	.0262618	.0081346

```
                      b = consistent under Ho and Ha; obtained from xtreg
             B = inconsistent under Ha, efficient under Ho; obtained from xtreg
    Test:   Ho:  difference in coefficients not systematic

               chi2(8) = (b-B)'[(V_b-V_B)^(-1)](b-B)
                       =       149.44
               Prob>chi2 =      0.0000
```

We can reject the hypothesis that the coefficients are the same. Before turning to what this means, note that `hausman` listed the coefficients estimated by the two models. It did not, however, list `grade` and `race`. `hausman` did not make a mistake; in the Hausman test, we compare only the coefficients estimated by both techniques.

What does this mean? We have an unpleasant choice: we can admit that our model is misspecified—that we have not parameterized it correctly—or we can hold that our specification is correct, in which case the observed differences must be due to the zero correlation of ν_i and the $\mathbf{x}_{it}$ assumption.

◁

❏ Technical Note

We can also mechanically explore the underpinnings of the test's dissatisfaction. In the comparison table from `hausman`, it is the coefficients on `not_smsa` and `south` that exhibit the largest differences. In equation $(1')$ of [XT] **xtreg**, we showed how to decompose a model into within and between effects. Let us do that with these two variables, assuming that changes in the average have one effect, whereas transitional changes have another:

```
. egen avgnsmsa = mean(not_smsa), by(idcode)
. generate devnsma = not_smsa -avgnsmsa
(8 missing values generated)
. egen avgsouth = mean(south), by(idcode)
. generate devsouth = south - avgsouth
(8 missing values generated)
```

(Continued on next page)

```
. xtreg ln_w grade age* ttl_exp* tenure* black avgnsm devnsm avgsou devsou
```

Random-effects GLS regression   Number of obs   =   28091
Group variable: idcode   Number of groups   =   4697

R-sq: within   = 0.1723   Obs per group: min =   1
       between = 0.4809   avg =   6.0
       overall = 0.3737   max =   15

Random effects u_i ~ Gaussian   Wald chi2(12)   =   9319.69
corr(u_i, X)   = 0 (assumed)   Prob > chi2   =   0.0000

ln_wage	Coef.	Std. Err.	z	P>|z|	[95% Conf. Interval]	
grade	.0631716	.0017903	35.29	0.000	.0596627	.0666805
age	.0375196	.0031186	12.03	0.000	.0314072	.043632
age2	−.0007248	.00005	−14.50	0.000	−.0008228	−.0006269
ttl_exp	.0286542	.0024207	11.84	0.000	.0239097	.0333987
ttl_exp2	.0003222	.0001162	2.77	0.006	.0000945	.0005499
tenure	.0394424	.001754	22.49	0.000	.0360045	.0428803
tenure2	−.0020081	.0001192	−16.85	0.000	−.0022417	−.0017746
black	−.0545938	.0102099	−5.35	0.000	−.0746048	−.0345827
avgnsmsa	−.1833238	.0109337	−16.77	0.000	−.2047533	−.1618942
devnsma	−.0887596	.0095071	−9.34	0.000	−.1073932	−.070126
avgsouth	−.1011235	.0098787	−10.24	0.000	−.1204855	−.0817616
devsouth	−.0598538	.0109054	−5.49	0.000	−.081228	−.0384796
_cons	.268298	.0495776	5.41	0.000	.1711277	.3654683
sigma_u	.25791607					
sigma_e	.29069544					
rho	.44046285	(fraction of variance due to u_i)				

We will leave the reinterpretation of this model to you, except that if we were really going to sell this model, we would have to explain why the between and within effects are different. Focusing on residence in a non-SMSA, we might tell a story about rural people being paid less and continuing to get paid less when they move to the SMSA. Given our panel data, we could create variables to measure this (an indicator for moved from non-SMSA to SMSA) and to measure the effects. In our assessment of this model, we should think about women in the cities moving to the country and their relative productivity in a bucolic setting.

In any case, the Hausman test now is

```
. estimates store new_random_effects

. xtreg ln_w grade age* ttl_exp* tenure* black avgnsm devnsm avgsou devsou, fe
(output omitted)

. hausman . new_random_effects
```

| | ———— Coefficients ———— | | | |
	(b)	(B) new_random~s	(b-B) Difference	sqrt(diag(V_b-V_B)) S.E.
age	.0359987	.0375196	-.001521	.0013198
age2	-.000723	-.0007248	1.84e-06	.0000184
ttl_exp	.0334668	.0286542	.0048126	.0017127
ttl_exp2	.0002163	.0003222	-.0001059	.0000531
tenure	.0357539	.0394424	-.0036885	.0005839
tenure2	-.0019701	-.0020081	.000038	.0000377
devnsma	-.0890108	-.0887596	-.0002512	.0006826
devsouth	-.0606309	-.0598538	-.0007771	.0007612

```
                   b = consistent under Ho and Ha; obtained from xtreg
        B = inconsistent under Ha, efficient under Ho; obtained from xtreg
  Test:  Ho:  difference in coefficients not systematic
              chi2(8) = (b-B)'[(V_b-V_B)^(-1)](b-B)
                      =      92.52
            Prob>chi2 =     0.0000
```

We have mechanically succeeded in greatly reducing the χ^2, but not by enough. The major differences now are in the age, experience, and tenure effects. We already knew this problem existed because of the ever-increasing effect of experience. More careful parameterization work rather than simply including squares needs to be done.

❑

Methods and Formulas

All postestimation commands listed above are implemented as ado-files.

xttest0

xttest0 reports the Lagrange multiplier test for random effects developed by Breusch and Pagan (1980) and as modified by Baltagi and Li (1990). The model

$$y_{it} = \alpha + \mathbf{x}_{it}\boldsymbol{\beta} + \nu_{it}$$

is fitted via OLS, and then the quantity

$$\lambda_{\text{LM}} = \frac{(n\overline{T})^2}{2}\left(\frac{A_1^2}{(\sum_i T_i^2) - n\overline{\overline{T}}}\right)$$

is calculated, where

$$A_1 = 1 - \frac{\sum_{i=1}^{n}(\sum_{t=1}^{T_i} v_{it})^2}{\sum_i \sum_t v_{it}^2}$$

The Baltagi and Li modification allows for unbalanced data and reduces to the standard formula

$$\lambda_{\text{LM}} = \frac{nT}{2(T-1)} \left\{ \frac{\sum_i (\sum_t v_{it})^2}{\sum_i \sum_t v_{it}^2} - 1 \right\}^2$$

when $T_i = T$ (balanced data). Under the null hypothesis, λ_{LM} is distributed $\chi^2(1)$.

Reference

Baltagi, B. H., and Q. Li. 1990. A Lagrange multiplier test for the error components model with incomplete panels. *Econometric Reviews* 9: 103–107.

Breusch, T. S., and A. R. Pagan. 1980. The Lagrange multiplier test and its applications to model specification in econometrics. *Review of Economic Studies* 47: 239–253.

Hausman, J. A. 1978. Specification tests in econometrics. *Econometrica* 46: 1251–1271.

Also See

[XT] **xtreg** — Fixed-, between-, and random-effects, and population-averaged linear models

[U] **20 Estimation and postestimation commands**

Title

> **xtregar** — Fixed- and random-effects linear models with an AR(1) disturbance

Syntax

Random-effects (RE) model

> xtregar *depvar* $\begin{bmatrix} indepvars \end{bmatrix}$ $\begin{bmatrix} if \end{bmatrix}$ $\begin{bmatrix} in \end{bmatrix}$ $\begin{bmatrix} , & \texttt{re} & options \end{bmatrix}$

Fixed-effects (FE) model

> xtregar *depvar* $\begin{bmatrix} indepvars \end{bmatrix}$ $\begin{bmatrix} if \end{bmatrix}$ $\begin{bmatrix} in \end{bmatrix}$ $\begin{bmatrix} weight \end{bmatrix}$, fe $\begin{bmatrix} options \end{bmatrix}$

options	description
Model	
re	use random-effects estimator; the default
fe	use fixed-effects estimator
<u>rhot</u>ype(*rhomethod*)	specify method to compute autocorrelation; see *Options* for details; seldom used
rhof(*#*)	use # for ρ and do not estimate ρ
<u>two</u>step	perform two-step estimate of correlation
Reporting	
<u>level</u>(*#*)	set confidence level; default is level(95)
lbi	perform Baltagi–Wu LBI test

A panel variable and a time variable must be specified; use xtset; see [XT] **xtset**.
depvar and *indepvars* may contain time-series operators; see [U] **11.4.3 Time-series varlists**.
by, statsby, and xi are allowed; see [U] **11.1.10 Prefix commands**.
fweights and aweights are allowed for the fixed-effects model with rhotype(regress) or rhotype(freg),
    or with a fixed rho; see [U] **11.1.6 weight**. Weights must be constant within panel.
See [U] **20 Estimation and postestimation commands** for more capabilities of estimation commands.

Description

    xtregar fits cross-sectional time-series regression models when the disturbance term is first-order autoregressive. **xtregar** offers a within estimator for fixed-effects models and a GLS estimator for random-effects models. Consider the model

$$y_{it} = \alpha + \mathbf{x}_{it}\boldsymbol{\beta} + \nu_i + \epsilon_{it} \qquad i = 1, \ldots, N; \quad t = 1, \ldots, T_i, \tag{1}$$

where

$$\epsilon_{it} = \rho \epsilon_{i,t-1} + \eta_{it} \tag{2}$$

421

and where $|\rho| < 1$ and η_{it} is independent and identically distributed (i.i.d.) with mean 0 and variance σ_η^2. If ν_i are assumed to be fixed parameters, the model is a fixed-effects model. If ν_i are assumed to be realizations of an i.i.d. process with mean 0 and variance σ_ν^2, it is a random-effects model. Whereas in the fixed-effects model, the ν_i may be correlated with the covariates x_{it}, in the random-effects model the ν_i are assumed to be independent of the x_{it}. On the other hand, any x_{it} that do not vary over t are collinear with the ν_i and will be dropped from the fixed-effects model. In contrast, the random-effects model can accommodate covariates that are constant over time.

xtregar can accommodate unbalanced panels whose observations are unequally spaced over time. xtregar implements the methods derived in Baltagi and Wu (1999).

Options

    ⌐ Model ⌐

re requests the GLS estimator of the random-effects model, which is the default.

fe requests the within estimator of the fixed-effects model.

rhotype(*rhomethod*) allows the user to specify any of the following estimators of ρ:

dw	$\rho_{\mathrm{dw}} = 1 - d/2$, where d is the Durbin–Watson d statistic
regress	$\rho_{\mathrm{reg}} = \beta$ from the residual regression $\epsilon_t = \beta\epsilon_{t-1}$
freg	$\rho_{\mathrm{freg}} = \beta$ from the residual regression $\epsilon_t = \beta\epsilon_{t+1}$
tscorr	$\rho_{\mathrm{tscorr}} = \epsilon'\epsilon_{t-1}/\epsilon'\epsilon$, where ϵ is the vector of residuals and ϵ_{t-1} is the vector of lagged residuals
theil	$\rho_{\mathrm{theil}} = \rho_{\mathrm{tscorr}}(N-k)/N$
nagar	$\rho_{\mathrm{nagar}} = (\rho_{\mathrm{dw}}N^2 + k^2)/(N^2 - k^2)$
onestep	$\rho_{\mathrm{onestep}} = (n/m_c)(\epsilon'\epsilon_{t-1}/\epsilon'\epsilon)$, where ϵ is the vector of residuals, n is the number of observations, and m_c is the number of consecutive pairs of residuals

dw is the default method. Except for onestep, the details of these methods are given in [TS] **prais**. prais handles unequally spaced data. onestep is the one-step method proposed by Baltagi and Wu (1999). More details on this method are available below in *Methods and Formulas*.

rhof(#) specifies that the given number be used for ρ and that ρ not be estimated.

twostep requests that a two-step implementation of the *rhomethod* estimator of ρ be used. Unless a fixed value of ρ is specified, ρ is estimated by running prais on the de-meaned data. When twostep is specified, prais will stop on the first iteration after the equation is transformed by ρ—the two-step efficient estimator. Although it is customary to iterate these estimators to convergence, they are efficient at each step. When twostep is not specified, the FGLS process iterates to convergence as described in [TS] **prais**.

    ⌐ Reporting ⌐

level(#); see [XT] **estimation options**.

lbi requests that the Baltagi–Wu (1999) locally best invariant (LBI) test statistic that $\rho = 0$ and a modified version of the Bhargava et al. (1982) Durbin–Watson statistic be calculated and reported. The default is not to report them. p-values are not reported for either statistic. Although Bhargava et al. (1982) published critical values for their statistic, no tables are currently available for the Baltagi–Wu LBI. Baltagi and Wu (1999) derive a normalized version of their statistic, but this statistic cannot be computed for datasets of moderate size. You can also specify these options upon replay.

Remarks

Remarks are presented under the following headings:

> Introduction
> The fixed-effects model
> The random-effects model

Introduction

If you have not read [XT] **xt**, please do so.

Consider a linear panel-data model described by (1) and (2). In the fixed-effects model, the ν_i are a set of fixed parameters to be estimated. Alternatively, the ν_i may be random and correlated with the other covariates, with inference conditional on the ν_i in the sample; see Mundlak (1978) and Hsiao (2003). In the random-effects model, also known as the variance-components model, the ν_i are assumed to be realizations of an i.i.d. process with mean 0 and variance σ_ν^2. **xtregar** offers a within estimator for the fixed-effect model and the Baltagi–Wu (1999) GLS estimator of the random-effects model. The Baltagi–Wu (1999) GLS estimator extends the balanced panel estimator in Baltagi and Li (1991) to a case of exogenously unbalanced panels with unequally spaced observations. Both these estimators offer several estimators of ρ.

The data can be unbalanced and unequally spaced. Specifically, the dataset contains observations on individual i at times t_{ij} for $j = 1, \ldots, n_i$. The difference $t_{ij} - t_{i,j-1}$ plays an integral role in the estimation techniques used by **xtregar**. For this reason, you must **xtset** your data before using **xtregar**. For instance, if you have quarterly data, the "time" difference between the third and fourth quarter must be 1 month, not 3.

The fixed-effects model

Let's examine the fixed-effect model first. The basic approach is common to all fixed-effects models. The ν_i are treated as nuisance parameters. We use a transformation of the model that removes the nuisance parameters and leaves behind the parameters of interest in an estimable form. Subtracting the group means from (1) removes the ν_i from the model

$$y_{it_{ij}} - \overline{y}_i = \left(\overline{\mathbf{x}}_{it_{ij}} - \overline{\mathbf{x}}_i\right)\boldsymbol{\beta} + \epsilon_{it_{ij}} - \overline{\epsilon}_i \tag{3}$$

where

$$\overline{y}_i = \frac{1}{n_i}\sum_{j=1}^{n_i} y_{it_{ij}} \qquad \overline{\mathbf{x}}_i = \frac{1}{n_i}\sum_{j=1}^{n_i} \mathbf{x}_{it_{ij}} \qquad \overline{\epsilon}_i = \frac{1}{n_i}\sum_{j=1}^{n_i} \epsilon_{it_{ij}}$$

After the transformation, (3) is a linear AR(1) model, potentially with unequally spaced observations. (3) can be used to estimate ρ. Given an estimate of ρ, we must do a Cochrane–Orcutt transformation on each panel and then remove the within-panel means and add back the overall mean for each variable. OLS on the transformed data will produce the within estimates of α and $\boldsymbol{\beta}$.

▷ Example 1

Let's use the Grunfeld investment dataset to illustrate how **xtregar** can be used to fit the fixed-effects model. This dataset contains information on 10 firms' investment, market value, and the value of their capital stocks. The data were collected annually between 1935 and 1954. The following output shows that we have **xtset** our data and gives the results of running a fixed-effects model with investment as a function of market value and the capital stock.

```
. use http://www.stata-press.com/data/r10/grunfeld
. xtset
      panel variable:  company (strongly balanced)
       time variable:  year, 1935 to 1954
              delta:  1 year
. xtregar invest mvalue kstock, fe
```

| FE (within) regression with AR(1) disturbances | Number of obs | = | 190 |
| Group variable: company | Number of groups | = | 10 |

R-sq: within = 0.5927	Obs per group: min =	19
between = 0.7989	avg =	19.0
overall = 0.7904	max =	19

| | F(2,178) | = | 129.49 |
| corr(u_i, Xb) = -0.0454 | Prob > F | = | 0.0000 |

invest	Coef.	Std. Err.	t	P>|t|	[95% Conf. Interval]
mvalue	.0949999	.0091377	10.40	0.000	.0769677	.113032
kstock	.350161	.0293747	11.92	0.000	.2921935	.4081286
_cons	-63.22022	5.648271	-11.19	0.000	-74.36641	-52.07402

rho_ar	.67210608	
sigma_u	91.507609	
sigma_e	40.992469	
rho_fov	.8328647	(fraction of variance due to u_i)

```
F test that all u_i=0:     F(9,178) =     11.53              Prob > F = 0.0000
```

Since there are 10 groups, the panel-by-panel Cochrane–Orcutt method decreases the number of available observations from 200 to 190. The above example used the default dw estimator of ρ. Using the tscorr estimator of ρ yields

```
. xtregar invest mvalue kstock, fe rhotype(tscorr)
```

| FE (within) regression with AR(1) disturbances | Number of obs | = | 190 |
| Group variable: company | Number of groups | = | 10 |

R-sq: within = 0.6583	Obs per group: min =	19
between = 0.8024	avg =	19.0
overall = 0.7933	max =	19

| | F(2,178) | = | 171.47 |
| corr(u_i, Xb) = -0.0709 | Prob > F | = | 0.0000 |

invest	Coef.	Std. Err.	t	P>|t|	[95% Conf. Interval]
mvalue	.0978364	.0096786	10.11	0.000	.0787369	.1169359
kstock	.346097	.0242248	14.29	0.000	.2982922	.3939018
_cons	-61.84403	6.621354	-9.34	0.000	-74.91049	-48.77758

rho_ar	.54131231	
sigma_u	90.893572	
sigma_e	41.592151	
rho_fov	.82686297	(fraction of variance due to u_i)

```
F test that all u_i=0:     F(9,178) =     19.73              Prob > F = 0.0000
```
◁

❏ Technical Note

The `tscorr` estimator of ρ is bounded in $[-1, 1]$. The other estimators of ρ are not. In samples with short panels, the estimates of ρ produced by the other estimators of ρ may be outside $[-1, 1]$. If this happens, use the `tscorr` estimator. However, simulations have shown that the `tscorr` estimator is biased toward zero. `dw` is the default because it performs well in Monte Carlo simulations. In the example above, the estimate of ρ produced by `tscorr` is much smaller than the one produced by `dw`.

❏

▷ Example 2

`xtregar` will complain if you try to run `xtregar` on a dataset that has not been `xtset`:

```
. xtset, clear
. xtregar invest mvalue kstock, fe
must specify panelvar and timevar; use xtset
r(459);
```

You must `xtset` your data to ensure that `xtregar` understands the nature of your time variable. Suppose that our observations were taken quarterly instead of annually. We will get the same results with the quarterly variable `t2` that we did with the annual variable `year`.

```
. generate t = year - 1934
. generate t2 = tq(1934q4) + t
. format t2 %tq
. list year t2 in 1/5
```

	year	t2
1.	1935	1935q1
2.	1936	1935q2
3.	1937	1935q3
4.	1938	1935q4
5.	1939	1936q1

```
. xtset company t2
       panel variable:  company (strongly balanced)
        time variable:  t2, 1935q1 to 1939q4
                delta:  1 quarter
```

(Continued on next page)

```
. xtregar invest mvalue kstock, fe

FE (within) regression with AR(1) disturbances   Number of obs      =        190
Group variable: company                          Number of groups   =         10

R-sq:  within  = 0.5927                           Obs per group: min =         19
       between = 0.7989                                          avg =       19.0
       overall = 0.7904                                          max =         19

                                                  F(2,178)           =     129.49
corr(u_i, Xb)  = -0.0454                           Prob > F           =     0.0000
```

invest	Coef.	Std. Err.	t	P>|t|	[95% Conf. Interval]	
mvalue	.0949999	.0091377	10.40	0.000	.0769677	.113032
kstock	.350161	.0293747	11.92	0.000	.2921935	.4081286
_cons	-63.22022	5.648271	-11.19	0.000	-74.36641	-52.07402

rho_ar	.67210608	
sigma_u	91.507609	
sigma_e	40.992469	
rho_fov	.8328647	(fraction of variance due to u_i)

```
F test that all u_i=0:     F(9,178) =     11.53              Prob > F = 0.0000
```

◁

In all the examples thus far, we have assumed that ϵ_{it} is first-order autoregressive. Testing the hypothesis of $\rho = 0$ in a first-order autoregressive process produces test statistics with extremely complicated distributions. Bhargava et al. (1982) extended the Durbin–Watson statistic to the case of balanced, equally spaced panel datasets. Baltagi and Wu (1999) modify their statistic to account for unbalanced panels with unequally spaced data. In the same article, Baltagi and Wu (1999) derive the locally best invariant test statistic of $\rho = 0$. Both these test statistics have extremely complicated distributions, although Bhargava et al. (1982) did publish some critical values in their article. Specifying the lbi option to xtregar causes Stata to calculate and report the modified Bhargava et al. Durbin–Watson and the Baltagi–Wu LBI.

▷ Example 3

In this example, we calculate the modified Bhargava et al. Durbin–Watson statistic and the Baltagi–Wu LBI. We exclude periods 9 and 10 from the sample, thereby reproducing the results of Baltagi and Wu (1999, 822). p-values are not reported for either statistic. Although Bhargava et al. (1982) published critical values for their statistic, no tables are currently available for the Baltagi–Wu (LBI). Baltagi and Wu (1999) did derive a normalized version of their statistic, but this statistic cannot be computed for datasets of moderate size.

```
. xtregar invest mvalue kstock if year !=1934 & year !=1944, fe lbi
```

| FE (within) regression with AR(1) disturbances | Number of obs | = | 180 |
| Group variable: company | Number of groups | = | 10 |

R-sq: within = 0.5954	Obs per group: min =	18
between = 0.7952	avg =	18.0
overall = 0.7889	max =	18

| | F(2,168) | = | 123.63 |
| corr(u_i, Xb) = -0.0516 | Prob > F | = | 0.0000 |

invest	Coef.	Std. Err.	t	P>|t|	[95% Conf. Interval]
mvalue	.0941122	.0090926	10.35	0.000	.0761617	.1120627
kstock	.3535872	.0303562	11.65	0.000	.2936584	.4135161
_cons	-64.82534	5.946885	-10.90	0.000	-76.56559	-53.08509

rho_ar	.6697198	
sigma_u	93.320452	
sigma_e	41.580712	
rho_fov	.83435413	(fraction of variance due to u_i)

```
F test that all u_i=0:     F(9,168) =    11.55           Prob > F = 0.0000
modified Bhargava et al. Durbin-Watson = .71380994
Baltagi-Wu LBI = 1.0134522
```

◁

The random-effects model

In the random-effects model, the ν_i are assumed to be realizations of an i.i.d. process with mean 0 and variance σ_ν^2. Furthermore, the ν_i are assumed to be independent of both the ϵ_{it} and the covariates $\mathbf{x}_{it}$. The latter of these assumptions can be strong, but inference is not conditional on the particular realizations of the ν_i in the sample. See Mundlak (1978) for a discussion of this point.

▷ Example 4

By specifying the **re** option, we obtain the Baltagi–Wu GLS estimator of the random-effects model. This estimator can accommodate unbalanced panels and unequally spaced data. We run this model on the Grunfeld dataset:

(Continued on next page)

```
. xtregar invest mvalue kstock if year!=1934 & year !=1944, re lbi
```

```
RE GLS regression with AR(1) disturbances          Number of obs      =        190
Group variable: company                            Number of groups   =         10

R-sq:  within  = 0.7707                             Obs per group: min =         19
       between = 0.8039                                            avg =       19.0
       overall = 0.7958                                            max =         19

                                                   Wald chi2(3)       =     351.37
corr(u_i, Xb)       = 0 (assumed)                  Prob > chi2        =     0.0000
```

invest	Coef.	Std. Err.	z	P>|z|	[95% Conf. Interval]	
mvalue	.0947714	.0083691	11.32	0.000	.0783683	.1111746
kstock	.3223932	.0263226	12.25	0.000	.2708019	.3739845
_cons	-45.21427	27.12492	-1.67	0.096	-98.37814	7.949603

rho_ar	.6697198	(estimated autocorrelation coefficient)
sigma_u	74.662876	
sigma_e	42.253042	
rho_fov	.75742494	(fraction of variance due to u_i)
theta	.66973313	

```
modified Bhargava et al. Durbin-Watson = .71380994
Baltagi-Wu LBI = 1.0134522
```

The modified Bhargava et al. Durbin–Watson and the Baltagi–Wu LBI are the same as those reported for the fixed-effects model because the formulas for these statistics do not depend on fitting the fixed-effects model or the random-effects model.

◁

Saved Results

xtregar, re saves the following in e():

Scalars

e(d1)	Bhargava et al. Durbin–Watson	e(LBI)	Baltagi–Wu LBI statistic
e(ds)	centered Baltagi–Wu LBI	e(N_LBI)	number of obs used in e(LBI)
e(N)	number of observations	e(r2_o)	R-squared for overall model
e(N_g)	number of groups	e(r2_b)	R-squared for between model
e(df_m)	model degrees of freedom	e(rho_ar)	autocorrelation coefficient
e(g_max)	largest group size	e(sigma_u)	panel-level standard deviation
e(g_min)	smallest group size	e(sigma_e)	standard deviation of ϵ_{it}
e(g_avg)	average group size	e(thta_min)	minimum θ
e(chi2)	χ^2	e(thta_5)	θ, 5th percentile
e(rho_fov)	u_i fraction of variance	e(thta_50)	θ, 50th percentile
e(Tbar)	harmonic mean of group sizes	e(thta_95)	θ, 95th percentile
e(Tcon)	1 if T is constant	e(thta_max)	maximum θ
e(r2_w)	R-squared for within model		

Macros

e(cmd)	xtregar	e(ivar)	variable denoting groups
e(cmdline)	command as typed	e(tvar)	time variable
e(depvar)	name of dependent variable	e(chi2type)	Wald; type of model χ^2 test
e(model)	re	e(properties)	b V
e(rhotype)	method of estimating ρ_{ar}	e(predict)	program used to implement predict
e(dw)	LBI, if requested		

Matrices

e(b)	coefficient vector	e(V)	VCE for random-effects model

Functions

e(sample)	marks estimation sample

(*Continued on next page*)

`xtregar, fe` saves the following in `e()`:

Scalars

e(d1)	Bhargava et al. Durbin–Watson	e(LBI)	Baltagi–Wu LBI statistic
e(ds)	centered Baltagi–Wu LBI	e(N_LBI)	number of obs used in e(LBI)
e(N)	number of observations	e(g_max)	largest group size
e(N_g)	number of groups	e(g_min)	smallest group size
e(mss)	model sum of squares	e(g_avg)	average group size
e(tss)	total sum of squares	e(rho_fov)	u_i fraction of variance
e(df_m)	model degrees of freedom	e(Tbar)	harmonic mean of group sizes
e(rss)	residual sum of squares	e(Tcon)	1 if T is constant
e(df_r)	residual degrees of freedom	e(r2_w)	R-squared for within model
e(r2)	R-squared	e(r2_o)	R-squared for overall model
e(r2_a)	adjusted R-squared	e(r2_b)	R-squared for between model
e(F)	F statistic	e(rho_ar)	autocorrelation coefficient
e(rmse)	root mean squared error	e(corr)	corr(u_i, Xb)
e(ll)	log likelihood	e(sigma_u)	panel-level standard deviation
e(ll_0)	log likelihood, constant-only model	e(sigma_e)	standard deviation of ϵ_{it}
e(df_a)	degrees of freedom for absorbed effect	e(F_f)	F for $u_i{=}0$
e(df_b)	numerator degrees of freedom for F statistic		

Macros

e(cmd)	xtregar	e(ivar)	variable denoting groups
e(cmdline)	command as typed	e(tvar)	time variable
e(depvar)	name of dependent variable	e(wtype)	weight type
e(model)	fe	e(wexp)	weight expression
e(rhotype)	method of estimating ρ_{ar}	e(properties)	b V
e(dw)	LBI, if requested	e(predict)	program used to implement predict

Matrices

e(b)	coefficient vector	e(V)	variance–covariance matrix of the estimators

Functions

e(sample)	marks estimation sample

Methods and Formulas

Consider a linear panel-data model described by (1) and (2). The data can be unbalanced and unequally spaced. Specifically, the dataset contains observations on individual i at times t_{ij} for $j = 1, \ldots, n_i$.

Estimating ρ

The estimate of ρ is always obtained after removing the group means. Let $\widetilde{y}_{it} = y_{it} - \overline{y}_i$, let $\widetilde{x}_{it} = x_{it} - \overline{x}_i$, and let $\widetilde{\epsilon}_{it} = \epsilon_{it} - \overline{\epsilon}_i$.

Then except for the `onestep` method, all the estimates of ρ are obtained by running Stata's `prais` on

$$\widetilde{y}_{it} = \widetilde{x}_{it}\beta + \widetilde{\epsilon}_{it}$$

See [TS] **prais** for the formulas for each of the methods.

When `onestep` is specified, a regression is run on the above equation, and the residuals are obtained. Let $e_{it_{ij}}$ be the residual used to estimate the error $\widetilde{\epsilon}_{it_{ij}}$. If $t_{ij} - t_{i,j-1} > 1$, $e_{it_{ij}}$ is set to zero. Given this series of residuals

$$\widehat{\rho}_{\text{onestep}} = \frac{n}{m_c} \frac{\sum_{i=1}^{N} \sum_{t=2}^{T} e_{it} e_{i,t-1}}{\sum_{i=1}^{N} \sum_{t=1}^{T} e_{it}^2}$$

where n is the number of nonzero elements in e and m_c is the number of consecutive pairs of nonzero e_{it}s.

Transforming the data to remove the AR(1) component

After estimating ρ, Baltagi and Wu (1999) derive a transformation of the data that removes the AR(1) component. Their $C_i(\rho)$ can be written as

$$y_{it_{ij}}^{\star} = \begin{cases} (1-\rho^2)^{1/2} y_{it_{ij}} & \text{if } t_{ij} = 1 \\[2ex] (1-\rho^2)^{1/2} \left[y_{i,t_{ij}} \left\{ \frac{1}{1-\rho^{2(t_{ij}-t_{i,j-1})}} \right\}^{1/2} - y_{i,t_{i,j-1}} \left\{ \frac{\rho^{2(t_{ij}-t_{i,j-1})}}{1-\rho^{2(t_{i,j}-t_{i,j-1})}} \right\}^{1/2} \right] & \text{if } t_{ij} > 1 \end{cases}$$

Using the analogous transform on the independent variables generates transformed data without the AR(1) component. Performing simple OLS on the transformed data leaves behind the residuals μ^*.

The within estimator of the fixed-effects model

To obtain the within estimator, we must transform the data that come from the AR(1) transform. For the within transform to remove the fixed effects, the first observation of each panel must be dropped. Specifically, let

$$\breve{y}_{it_{ij}} = y_{it_{ij}}^* - \overline{y}_i^* + \overline{\overline{y}}^* \qquad \forall j > 1$$

$$\breve{\mathbf{x}}_{it_{ij}} = \mathbf{x}_{it_{ij}}^* - \overline{\mathbf{x}}_i^* + \overline{\overline{\mathbf{x}}}^* \qquad \forall j > 1$$

$$\breve{\epsilon}_{it_{ij}} = \epsilon_{it_{ij}}^* - \overline{\epsilon}_i^* + \overline{\overline{\epsilon}}^* \qquad \forall j > 1$$

(Continued on next page)

where

$$\overline{y}_i^* = \frac{\sum_{j=2}^{n_i-1} y_{it_{ij}}^*}{n_i - 1}$$

$$\overline{\overline{y}}^* = \frac{\sum_{i=1}^{N} \sum_{j=2}^{n_i-1} y_{it_{ij}}^*}{\sum_{i=1}^{N} n_i - 1}$$

$$\overline{\mathbf{x}}_i^* = \frac{\sum_{j=2}^{n_i-1} \mathbf{x}_{it_{ij}}^*}{n_i - 1}$$

$$\overline{\overline{\mathbf{x}}}^* = \frac{\sum_{i=1}^{N} \sum_{j=2}^{n_i-1} \mathbf{x}_{it_{ij}}^*}{\sum_{i=1}^{N} n_i - 1}$$

$$\overline{\epsilon}_i^* = \frac{\sum_{j=2}^{n_i-1} \epsilon_{it_{ij}}^*}{n_i - 1}$$

$$\overline{\overline{\epsilon}}^* = \frac{\sum_{i=1}^{N} \sum_{j=2}^{n_i-1} \epsilon_{it_{ij}}^*}{\sum_{i=1}^{N} n_i - 1}$$

The within estimator of the fixed-effects model is then obtained by running OLS on

$$\breve{y}_{it_{ij}} = \alpha + \breve{\mathbf{x}}_{it_{ij}} \boldsymbol{\beta} + \breve{\epsilon}_{it_{ij}}$$

Reported as R^2 within is the R^2 from the above regression.

Reported as R^2 between is $\left\{ \mathrm{corr}(\overline{\mathbf{x}}_i \widehat{\boldsymbol{\beta}}, \overline{y}_i) \right\}^2$.

Reported as R^2 overall is $\left\{ \mathrm{corr}(\mathbf{x}_{it} \widehat{\boldsymbol{\beta}}, y_{it}) \right\}^2$.

The Baltagi–Wu GLS estimator

The residuals μ^* can be used to estimate the variance components. Translating the matrix formulas given in Baltagi and Wu (1999) into summations yields the following variance-components estimators:

$$\widehat{\sigma}_\omega^2 = \sum_{i=1}^{N} \frac{(\mu_i^{*\prime} g_i)^2}{(g_i' g_i)}$$

$$\widehat{\sigma}_\epsilon^2 = \frac{\left[\sum_{i=1}^{N} (\mu_i^{*\prime} \mu_i^*) - \sum_{i=1}^{N} \left\{ \frac{(\mu_i^{*\prime} g_i)^2}{(g_i' g_i)} \right\} \right]}{\sum_{i=1}^{N} (n_i - 1)}$$

$$\widehat{\sigma}_\mu^2 = \frac{\left[\sum_{i=1}^{N} \left\{ \frac{(\mu_i^{*\prime} g_i)^2}{(g_i' g_i)} \right\} - N \widehat{\sigma}_\epsilon^2 \right]}{\sum_{i=1}^{N} (g_i' g_i)}$$

where

$$g_i = \left[1, \frac{\left\{1 - \rho^{(t_{i,2}-t_{i,1})}\right\}}{\left\{1 - \rho^{2(t_{i,2}-t_{i,1})}\right\}^{\frac{1}{2}}}, \ldots, \frac{\left\{1 - \rho^{(t_{i,n_i}-t_{i,n_i-1})}\right\}}{\left\{1 - \rho^{2(t_{i,n_i}-t_{i,n_i-1})}\right\}^{\frac{1}{2}}} \right]'$$

and μ_i^* is the $n_i \times 1$ vector of residuals from μ^* that correspond to person i.

Then

$$\widehat{\theta}_i = 1 - \left(\frac{\widehat{\sigma}_\mu}{\widehat{\omega}_i}\right)$$

where

$$\widehat{\omega}_i^2 = g_i' g_i \widehat{\sigma}_\mu^2 + \widehat{\sigma}_\epsilon^2$$

With these estimates in hand, we can transform the data via

$$z_{it_{ij}}^{**} = z_{it_{ij}}^* - \widehat{\theta}_i g_{ij} \frac{\sum_{s=1}^{n_i} g_{is} z_{it_{is}}^*}{\sum_{s=1}^{n_i} g_{is}^2}$$

for $z \in \{y, \mathbf{x}\}$.

Running OLS on the transformed data $y^{**}, \mathbf{x}^{**}$ yields the feasible GLS estimator of α and β.

Reported as R^2 between is $\left\{\mathrm{corr}(\overline{\mathbf{x}}_i \widehat{\boldsymbol{\beta}}, \overline{y}_i)\right\}^2$.

Reported as R^2 within is $\left\{\mathrm{corr}\{(\mathbf{x}_{it} - \overline{\mathbf{x}}_i)\widehat{\boldsymbol{\beta}}, y_{it} - \overline{y}_i\}\right\}^2$.

Reported as R^2 overall is $\left\{\mathrm{corr}(\mathbf{x}_{it}\widehat{\boldsymbol{\beta}}, y_{it})\right\}^2$.

The test statistics

The Baltagi–Wu LBI is the sum of terms

$$d_* = d_1 + d_2 + d_3 + d_4$$

where

$$d_1 = \frac{\sum_{i=1}^{N} \sum_{j=1}^{n_i} \{\widetilde{z}_{it_{i,j-1}} - \widetilde{z}_{it_{ij}} I(t_{ij} - t_{i,j-1} = 1)\}^2}{\sum_{i=1}^{N} \sum_{j=1}^{n_i} \widetilde{z}_{it_{ij}}^2}$$

$$d_2 = \frac{\sum_{i=1}^{N} \sum_{j=1}^{n_i-1} \widetilde{z}_{it_{i,j-1}}^2 \{1 - I(t_{ij} - t_{i,j-1} = 1)\}^2}{\sum_{i=1}^{N} \sum_{j=1}^{n_i} \widetilde{z}_{it_{ij}}^2}$$

$$d_3 = \frac{\sum_{i=1}^{N} \widetilde{z}_{it_{i1}}^2}{\sum_{i=1}^{N} \sum_{j=1}^{n_i} \widetilde{z}_{it_{ij}}^2}$$

$$d_4 = \frac{\sum_{i=1}^{N} \widetilde{z}_{it_{in_i}}^2}{\sum_{i=1}^{N} \sum_{j=1}^{n_i} \widetilde{z}_{it_{ij}}^2}$$

$I()$ is the indicator function that takes the value of 1 if the condition is true and 0 otherwise. The $\widetilde{z}_{it_{i,j-1}}$ are residuals from the within estimator.

Baltagi and Wu (1999) also show that d_1 is the Bhargava et al. Durbin–Watson statistic modified to handle cases of unbalanced panels and unequally spaced data.

Acknowledgment

We thank Badi Baltagi, Department of Economics, Syracuse University, for his helpful comments.

References

Baltagi, B. H. 2005. *Econometric Analysis of Panel Data*. 3rd ed. New York: Wiley.

Baltagi, B. H., and Q. Li. 1991. A transformation that will circumvent the problem of autocorrelation in an error component model. *Journal of Econometrics* 48: 385–393.

Baltagi, B. H., and P. X. Wu. 1999. Unequally spaced panel data regressions with AR(1) disturbances. *Econometric Theory* 15: 814–823.

Bhargava, A., L. Franzini, and W. Narendranathan. 1982. Serial correlation and the fixed effects model. *Review of Economic Studies* 49: 533–549.

Drukker, D. M. 2003. Testing for serial correlation in linear panel-data models. *Stata Journal* 3: 168–177.

Hsiao, C. 2003. *Analysis of Panel Data*. 2nd ed. New York: Cambridge University Press.

Mundlak, Y. 1978. On the pooling of time series and cross section data. *Econometrica* 46: 69–85.

Also See

[XT] **xtregar postestimation** — Postestimation tools for xtregar

[XT] **xtset** — Declare data to be panel data

[XT] **xtgee** — Fit population-averaged panel-data models by using GEE

[XT] **xtgls** — Fit panel-data models by using GLS

[XT] **xtreg** — Fixed-, between-, and random-effects, and population-averaged linear models

[TS] **newey** — Regression with Newey–West standard errors

[TS] **prais** — Prais–Winsten and Cochrane–Orcutt regression

[U] **20 Estimation and postestimation commands**

Title

> **xtregar postestimation** — Postestimation tools for xtregar

Description

The following postestimation commands are available for xtregar:

command	description
adjust[1]	adjusted predictions of $\mathbf{x}\beta$ or $\exp(\mathbf{x}\beta)$
*estat	AIC, BIC, VCE, and estimation sample summary
estimates	cataloging estimation results
hausman	Hausman's specification test
lincom	point estimates, standard errors, testing, and inference for linear combinations of coefficients
mfx	marginal effects or elasticities
nlcom	point estimates, standard errors, testing, and inference for nonlinear combinations of coefficients
predict	predictions, residuals, influence statistics, and other diagnostic measures
predictnl	point estimates, standard errors, testing, and inference for generalized predictions
test	Wald tests for simple and composite linear hypotheses
testnl	Wald tests of nonlinear hypotheses

[1] adjust is not appropriate with time-series operators.

* estat ic is not appropriate after xtregar, re.

See the corresponding entries in the *Stata Base Reference Manual* for details.

Syntax for predict

> predict [*type*] *newvar* [*if*] [*in*] [, *statistic*]

statistic	description
Main	
xb	$\mathbf{x}_{it}\mathbf{b}$, linear prediction; the default
ue	$u_i + e_{it}$, the combined residual
*u	u_i, the fixed- or random-error component
*e	e_{it}, the overall error component

u and e are available only for the fixed-effects estimator. Unstarred statistics are available both in and out of sample; type predict ... if e(sample) ... if wanted only for the estimation sample. Starred statistics are calculated only for the estimation sample, even when if e(sample) is not specified.

Options for predict

___Main___

xb, the default, calculates the linear prediction, $\mathbf{x}_{it}\boldsymbol{\beta}$.

ue calculates the prediction of $u_i + e_{it}$.

u calculates the prediction of u_i, the estimated fixed or random effect.

e calculates the prediction of e_{it}.

Methods and Formulas

All postestimation commands listed above are implemented as ado-files.

Also See

[XT] **xtregar** — Fixed- and random-effects linear models with an AR(1) disturbance

[U] **20 Estimation and postestimation commands**

Title

> **xtset** — Declare data to be panel data

Syntax

Declare data to be panel

    xtset *panelvar*

    xtset *panelvar timevar* [, *tsoptions*]

Display how data are currently xtset

    xtset

Clear xt settings

    xtset, clear

In the declare syntax, *panelvar* identifies the panels and the optional *timevar* identifies the times within panels. *tsoptions* concern *timevar*.

tsoptions	description
unitoptions	specify units of *timevar*
deltaoption	specify periodicity of *timevar*

unitoptions	description
(*default*)	*timevar*'s units to be obtained from *timevar*'s display format
<u>c</u>locktime	*timevar* is %tc: 0 = 1jan1960 00:00:00.000, 1 = 1jan1960 00:00:00.001, ...
<u>d</u>aily	*timevar* is %td: 0 = 1jan1960, 1 = 2jan1960, ...
<u>w</u>eekly	*timevar* is %tw: 0 = 1960w1, 1 = 1960w2, ...
<u>m</u>onthly	*timevar* is %tm: 0 = 1960m1, 1 = 1960m2, ...
<u>q</u>uarterly	*timevar* is %tq: 0 = 1960q1, 1 = 1960q2,...
<u>h</u>alfyearly	*timevar* is %th: 0 = 1960h1, 1 = 1960h2,...
<u>y</u>early	*timevar* is %ty: 1960 = 1960, 1961 = 1961, ...
<u>g</u>eneric	*timevar* is %tg: 0 = ?, 1 = ?, ...
<u>f</u>ormat(%*fmt*)	specify *timevar*'s format and then apply default rule

In all cases, negative *timevar* values are allowed.

deltaoption specifies the period between observations in *timevar* units and may be specified as

deltaoption	example
<u>del</u>ta(*#*)	delta(1) or delta(2)
<u>del</u>ta((*exp*))	delta((7*24))
<u>del</u>ta(*# units*)	delta(7 days) or delta(15 minutes) or delta(7 days 15 minutes)
<u>del</u>ta((*exp*) *units*)	delta((2+3) weeks)

Allowed units for %tc and %tC *timevars* are

seconds	secs	sec
minutes	mins	min
hours	hour	
days	day	
weeks	week	

and for all other %t *timevars* are

days	day
weeks	week

Description

xtset declares the data in memory to be a panel. You must xtset your data before you can use the other xt commands. If you save your data after xtset, the data will be remembered to be a panel and you will not have to xtset again.

There are two syntaxes for setting the data:

> xtset *panelvar*
> xtset *panelvar* *timevar*

In the first syntax—xtset *panelvar*—the data are set to be a panel and the order of the observations within panel is considered to be irrelevant. For instance, *panelvar* might be country and the observations within be city.

In the second syntax—xtset *panelvar* *timevar*—the data are to be a panel and the order of observations within panel are considered ordered by *timevar*. For instance, in data collected from repeated surveying of the same people over various years, *panelvar* might be person and *timevar*, year. When you specify *timevar*, you may then use Stata's time-series operators such as L. and F. (lag and lead) in other commands. The operators will be interpreted as lagged and lead values within panel.

xtset without arguments—xtset—displays how the data are currently xtset. If the data are set with a *panelvar* and a *timevar*, xtset also sorts the data by *panelvar* *timevar*. If the data are set with a *panelvar* only, the sort order is not changed.

xtset, clear is a rarely used programmer's command to declare that the data are no longer to be considered a panel.

Options

unitoptions clocktime, daily, weekly, monthly, quarterly, halfyearly, yearly, generic, and format(%*fmt*) specify the units in which *timevar* is recorded, if *timevar* is specified.

timevar will often simply be a variable that counts 1, 2, ..., and is to be interpreted as first year of survey, second year, ..., or first month of treatment, second month, ... In these cases, you do not need to specify a *unitoption*.

In other cases, *timevar* will be a year variable or the like such as 2001, 2002, ..., and is to be interpreted as year of survey or the like. In those cases, you do not need to specify a *unitoption*.

In still other, more complicated cases, *timevar* will be a full-blown %t variable; see [D] **dates and times**. If *timevar* already has a %t display format assigned to it, you do not need to specify a *unitoption*; xtset will obtain the units from the format. If you have not yet bothered to assign the appropriate %t format to the %t variable, however, you can use the *unitoptions* to tell xtset the units. Then xtset will set *timevar*'s display format for you. Thus, the *unitoptions* are convenience options; they allow you to skip formatting the time variable. The following all have the same net result:

Alternative 1	Alternative 2	Alternative 3
`format t %td`	*(t not formatted)*	*(t not formatted)*
`xtset pid t`	`xtset pid t, daily`	`xtset pid t, format(%td)`

Understand that *timevar* is not required to be a %t variable; it can be any variable of your own concocting so long as it takes on integer values. When you xtset a time variable that is not %t, the display format does not change unless you specify the *unitoption* generic or use the format() option.

delta() specifies the periodicity of *timevar* and is commonly used when *timevar* is %tc. delta() is only sometimes used with the other %t formats or with generic time variables.

If delta() is not specified, delta(1) is assumed. This means that at *timevar* = 5, the previous time is *timevar* = 5 − 1 = 4 and the next time would be *timevar* = 5 + 1 = 6. Lag and lead operators, for instance, would work this way. This would be assumed regardless of the units of *timevar*.

If you specified delta(2), then at *timevar* = 5, the previous time would be *timevar* = 5 − 2 = 3 and the next time would be *timevar* = 5 + 2 = 7. Lag and lead operators would work this way. In the observation with *timevar* = 5, L.income would be the value of income in the observation for which *timevar* = 3 and F.income would be the value of income in the observation for which *timevar* = 7. If you then add an observation with *timevar* = 4, the operators will still work appropriately; i.e., at *timevar* = 5, L.income will still have the value of income at *timevar* = 3.

There are two aspects of *timevar*: its units and its periodicity. The *unitoptions* set the units. delta() sets the periodicity. You are not required to specify one to specify the other. You might have a generic *timevar* but it counts in 12: 0, 12, 24, ... You would skip specifying *unitoptions* but would specify delta(12).

We mentioned that delta() is commonly used with %tc *timevars* because Stata's %tc variables have units of milliseconds. If delta() is not specified and in some model you refer to L.bp, you will be referring to the value of bp 1 ms ago. Few people have data with periodicity of a millisecond. Perhaps your data are hourly. You could specify delta(3600000). Or you could specify delta((60*60*1000)), because delta() will allow expressions if you include an extra pair of parentheses. Or you could specify delta(1 hour). They all mean the same thing: *timevar* has periodicity of 3,600,000 ms. In an observation for which *timevar* = 1,489,572,000,000 (corresponding to 15mar2007 10:00:00), L.bp would be the observation for which *timevar* = 1,489,572,000,000 − 3,600,000 = 1,489,568,400,000 (corresponding to 15mar2007 9:00:00).

When you xtset the data and specify delta(), xtset verifies that all the observations follow the specified periodicity. For instance, if you specified delta(2), then *timevar* could contain any subset of {. . . , −4, −2, 0, 2, 4, . . . } or it could contain any subset of {. . . , −3, −1, 1, 3, . . . }. If *timevar* contained a mix of values, xtset would issue an error message. The check is made on each panel independently, so one panel might contain *timevar* values from one set and the next, another, and that would be fine.

clear—used in xtset, clear—makes Stata forget that the data ever were xtset. This is a rarely used programmer's option.

Remarks

xtset declares the dataset in memory to be panel data. You need to do this before you can use the other xt commands. The storage types of both *panelvar* and *timevar* must be numeric, and both variables must contain integers only.

❑ Technical Note

In previous versions of Stata there was no xtset command. The other xt commands instead had options i(*panelvar*) and t(*timevar*). Older commands still have those options, but they are no longer documented and, if you specify them, they just perform the xtset for you. Thus, do-files that you previously wrote will continue to work. Modern usage, however, is to xtset the data first.

❑

❑ Technical Note

xtset is related to the tsset command, which declares data to be time series. One of the syntaxes of tsset is tsset *panelvar timevar*, which is identical to one of xtset's syntaxes, namely, xtset *panelvar timevar*. Here they are in fact the same command, meaning that xtsetting your data is sufficient to allow you to use the ts commands and tssetting your data is sufficient to allow you to use the xt commands. You do not need to set both, but it will not matter if you do.

xtset and tsset are different, however, when you set just a *panelvar*—you type xtset *panelvar*—or when you set just a *timevar*—you type tsset *panelvar*.

❑

▷ Example 1

Many panel datasets contain a variable identifying panels but do not contain a time variable. For example, you may have a dataset where each panel is a family, and the observations within panel are family members, or you may have a dataset in which each person made a decision multiple times but the ordering of those decisions is unimportant and perhaps unknown. In this latter case, if the time of the decision were known, we would advise you to xtset it. The other xt statistical commands do not do something different because *timevar* has been set—they will ignore *timevar* if *timevar* is irrelevant to the statistical method that you are using. You should always set everything that is true about the data.

In any case, let's consider the case where there is no *timevar*. We have data on U.S. states and cities within states:

```
. list state city in 1/10, sepby(state)
```

	state	city
1.	Alabama	Birmingham
2.	Alabama	Mobile
3.	Alabama	Montgomery
4.	Alabama	Huntsville
5.	Alaska	Anchorage
6.	Alaska	Fairbanks
7.	Arizona	Phoenix
8.	Arizona	Tucson
9.	Arkansas	Fayetteville
10.	Arkansas	Fort Smith

Here we do not type `xtset state city` because city is not a time variable. Instead, we type `xtset state`:

```
. xtset state
varlist:  state:  string variable not allowed
r(109);
```

You cannot `xtset` a string variable. We must make a numeric variable from our string variable and `xtset` that. One alternative is

```
. egen statenum = group(state)
. list state statenum in 1/10, sepby(state)
```

	state	statenum
1.	Alabama	1
2.	Alabama	1
3.	Alabama	1
4.	Alabama	1
5.	Alaska	2
6.	Alaska	2
7.	Arizona	3
8.	Arizona	3
9.	Arkansas	4
10.	Arkansas	4

```
. xtset statenum
        panel variable:  statenum (unbalanced)
```

(*Continued on next page*)

Perhaps a better alternative is

```
. encode state, gen(st)
. list state st in 1/10, sepby(state)
```

```
        +-----------------------+
        |    state           st |
        |-----------------------|
   1.   |  Alabama      Alabama |
   2.   |  Alabama      Alabama |
   3.   |  Alabama      Alabama |
   4.   |  Alabama      Alabama |
        |-----------------------|
   5.   |   Alaska       Alaska |
   6.   |   Alaska       Alaska |
        |-----------------------|
   7.   |  Arizona      Arizona |
   8.   |  Arizona      Arizona |
        |-----------------------|
   9.   | Arkansas     Arkansas |
  10.   | Arkansas     Arkansas |
        +-----------------------+
```

encode (see [D] **encode**) produces a numerical variable with a value label, so when we list the result, new variable st looks just like our original. It is, however, numeric:

```
. list state st in 1/10, nolabel sepby(state)
```

```
        +----------------+
        |    state    st |
        |----------------|
   1.   |  Alabama     1 |
   2.   |  Alabama     1 |
   3.   |  Alabama     1 |
   4.   |  Alabama     1 |
        |----------------|
   5.   |   Alaska     2 |
   6.   |   Alaska     2 |
        |----------------|
   7.   |  Arizona     3 |
   8.   |  Arizona     3 |
        |----------------|
   9.   | Arkansas     4 |
  10.   | Arkansas     4 |
        +----------------+
```

We can xtset new variable st:

```
. xtset st
       panel variable:  st (unbalanced)
```

◁

▷ Example 2

Some panel datasets do contain a time variable. Dataset abdata.dta contains labor demand data from a panel of firms in the United Kingdom. Here are wage data for the first two firms in the dataset:

```
. use http://www.stata-press.com/data/r10/abdata, clear

. list id year wage if id==1 | id==2, sepby(id)
```

	id	year	wage
1.	1	1977	13.1516
2.	1	1978	12.3018
3.	1	1979	12.8395
4.	1	1980	13.8039
5.	1	1981	14.2897
6.	1	1982	14.8681
7.	1	1983	13.7784
8.	2	1977	14.7909
9.	2	1978	14.1036
10.	2	1979	14.9534
11.	2	1980	15.491
12.	2	1981	16.1969
13.	2	1982	16.1314
14.	2	1983	16.3051

To declare this dataset as a panel dataset, you type

```
. xtset id year, yearly
        panel variable:  id (unbalanced)
         time variable:  year, 1976 to 1984
                 delta:  1 year
```

The output from `list` shows that the last observations for these two firms are for 1983, but `xtset` shows that for some firms data are available for 1984 as well. If one or more panels contain data for nonconsecutive periods, `xtset` will report that gaps exist in the time variable. For example, if we did not have data for firm 1 for 1980 but did have data for 1979 and 1981, `xtset` would indicate that our data have a gap.

For yearly data, we could omit the `yearly` option and just type `xtset id year` because years are stored and listed just like regular integers.

Having declared our data to be a panel dataset, we can use time-series operators to obtain lags:

```
. list id year wage L.wage if id==1 | id==2, sepby(id)
```

	id	year	wage	L.wage
1.	1	1977	13.1516	.
2.	1	1978	12.3018	13.1516
			(*output omitted*)	
6.	1	1982	14.8681	14.2897
7.	1	1983	13.7784	14.8681
8.	2	1977	14.7909	.
9.	2	1978	14.1036	14.7909
			(*output omitted*)	
13.	2	1982	16.1314	16.1969
14.	2	1983	16.3051	16.1314

`L.wage` is missing for 1977 in both panels because we have no wage data for 1976. In observation 8, the lag operator did not incorrectly reach back into the previous panel.

◁

❑ Technical Note

The terms *balanced* and *unbalanced* are often used to describe whether a panel dataset is missing some observations. If a dataset does not contain a time variable, then panels are considered *balanced* if each panel contains the same number of observations; otherwise, the panels are *unbalanced*.

When the dataset contains a time variable, panels are said to be *strongly balanced* if each panel contains the same time points, *weakly balanced* if each panel contains the same number of observations but not the same time points, and *unbalanced* otherwise.

❑

▷ Example 3

If our data are observed more than once per year, applying time-series formats to the time variable can improve readability.

We have a dataset consisting of individuals who joined a gym's weight-loss program that began in January 2005 and ended in December 2005. Each participant's weight was recorded once per month. Some participants did not show up for all the monthly weigh-ins, so we do not have all 12 months' records for each person. The first two people's data are

```
. use http://www.stata-press.com/data/r10/gymdata
. list id month wt if id==1 | id==2, sepby(id)
```

	id	month	wt
1.	1	1	145
2.	1	2	144
	(output omitted)		
11.	1	11	124
12.	1	12	120
13.	2	1	144
14.	2	2	143
	(output omitted)		
23.	2	11	122
24.	2	12	118

To set this data, we can type

```
. xtset id month
       panel variable:  id (unbalanced)
        time variable:  month, 1 to 12, but with gaps
               delta:  1 unit
```

The note "but with gaps" above is no cause for concern. It merely warns us that, within some panels, some time values are missing. We already knew that about our data—some participants did not show up for the monthly weigh-ins.

The rest of this example concerns making output more readable. Month numbers such as 1, 2, ..., 12 are perfectly readable here. In another dataset, where month numbers went to, say 127, they would not be so readable. In such cases, we can make a more readable date—2005m1, 2005m2, ...—by using Stata's %t variables. For a discussion, see [D] **dates and times**. We will go quickly here. One of the %t formats is %tm—monthly—and it says that 1 means 1960m1. Thus, we need to recode our `month` variable so that, rather than taking on values from 1 to 12, it takes on values from 540 to 551. Then we can put a %tm format on that variable. Working out 540–551 is subject to mistakes. Stata function `tm(2005m1)` tells us the %tm month corresponding to January of 2005, so we can type

```
. generate month2 = month + tm(2005m1) - 1
. format month2 %tm
```

New variable `month2` will work just as well as the original `month` in an `xtset`, and even a little better, because output will be a little more readable:

```
. xtset id month2
        panel variable:  id (unbalanced)
         time variable:  month2, 2005m1 to 2005m12, but with gaps
                 delta:  1 month
```

By the way, we could have omitted typing `format month2 %tm` and then, rather than typing `xtset id month2`, we would have typed `xtset id month2, monthly`. Option `monthly` specifies that the time variable is `%tm`. When we did not specify the option, `xtset` determined that it was monthly from the display format we had set.

◁

▷ Example 4: Clock times

We have data from a large hotel in Las Vegas that changes the reservation prices for its room reservations hourly. A piece of the data looks like

```
. list in 1/5
```

	roomtype	time	price
1.	1	02.13.2007 08:00	140
2.	1	02.13.2007 09:00	155
3.	1	02.13.2007 10:00	160
4.	1	02.13.2007 11:00	155
5.	1	02.13.2007 12:00	160

The panel variable is `roomtype` and, although you cannot see it from the output above, it takes on 1, 2, ..., 20. Variable `time` is a string variable. The first step in making this dataset `xt` is to translate the string to a numeric variable:

```
. generate double t = clock(time, "MDY hm")
. list in 1/5
```

	roomtype	time	price	t
1.	1	02.13.2007 08:00	140	1.487e+12
2.	1	02.13.2007 09:00	155	1.487e+12
3.	1	02.13.2007 10:00	160	1.487e+12
4.	1	02.13.2007 11:00	155	1.487e+12
5.	1	02.13.2007 12:00	160	1.487e+12

See [D] **dates and times** for an explanation of what is going on here. `clock()` is the function that converts strings to date–time (`%tc`) values. We typed `clock(time, "MDY hm")` to convert string variable `time`, and we told clock that the values in `time` were in the order month, day, year, hour, and minute. We stored new variable `t` as a `double` because time values are large and that is required to prevent rounding. Even so, the resulting values 1.487e+12 look rounded, but that is only because of the default display format for new variables. We can see the values better if we change the format:

```
. format t %20.0gc
. list in 1/5
```

	roomtype	time	price	t
1.	1	02.13.2007 08:00	140	1,486,972,800,000
2.	1	02.13.2007 09:00	155	1,486,976,400,000
3.	1	02.13.2007 10:00	160	1,486,980,000,000
4.	1	02.13.2007 11:00	155	1,486,983,600,000
5.	1	02.13.2007 12:00	160	1,486,987,200,000

Even better, however, would be to change the format to %tc—Stata's clock-time format:

```
. format t %tc
. list in 1/5
```

	roomtype	time	price	t
1.	1	02.13.2007 08:00	140	13feb2007 08:00:00
2.	1	02.13.2007 09:00	155	13feb2007 09:00:00
3.	1	02.13.2007 10:00	160	13feb2007 10:00:00
4.	1	02.13.2007 11:00	155	13feb2007 11:00:00
5.	1	02.13.2007 12:00	160	13feb2007 12:00:00

We could now drop variable time. New variable t contains the same information as time and t is better because it is a Stata time variable, the most important property of which being that it is numeric rather than string. We can xtset it. Here, however, we also need to specify the periodicity with xtset's delta() option. Stata's time variables are numeric, but they record milliseconds since 01jan1960 00:00:00. By default, xtset uses delta(1), and that means the time-series operators would not work as we want them to work. For instance, L.price would look back only 1 ms (and find nothing). We want L.price to look back 1 hour (3,600,000 ms):

```
. xtset roomtype t, delta(1 hour)
       panel variable:  roomtype (strongly balanced)
        time variable:  t,
                        13feb2007 08:00:00 to 31mar2007 18:00:00,
                        but with gaps
                delta:  1 hour
. list t price l.price in 1/5
```

	t	price	L.price
1.	13feb2007 08:00:00	140	.
2.	13feb2007 09:00:00	155	140
3.	13feb2007 10:00:00	160	155
4.	13feb2007 11:00:00	155	160
5.	13feb2007 12:00:00	160	155

◁

▷ Example 5: Clock times must be double

In the previous example, it was of vital importance that when we generated the %tc variable t,

```
. generate double t = clock(time, "MDY hm")
```

we generated it as a double. Let's see what would have happened had we forgotten and just typed generate t = clock(time, "MDY hm"). Let's go back and start with the same original data:

```
. list in 1/5
```

	roomtype	time	price
1.	1	02.13.2007 08:00	140
2.	1	02.13.2007 09:00	155
3.	1	02.13.2007 10:00	160
4.	1	02.13.2007 11:00	155
5.	1	02.13.2007 12:00	160

Remember, variable time is a string variable, and we need to translate it to numeric. So we translate, but this time we forget to make the new variable a double:

```
. generate t = clock(time, "MDY hm")
. list in 1/5
```

	roomtype	time	price	t
1.	1	02.13.2007 08:00	140	1.49e+12
2.	1	02.13.2007 09:00	155	1.49e+12
3.	1	02.13.2007 10:00	160	1.49e+12
4.	1	02.13.2007 11:00	155	1.49e+12
5.	1	02.13.2007 12:00	160	1.49e+12

We see the first difference—t now lists as 1.49e+12 rather than 1.487e+12 as it did previously—but this is nothing that would catch our attention. We would not even know that the value is different. Let's continue.

We next put a %20.0gc format on t to better see the numerical values. In fact, that is not something we would usually do in an analysis. We did that in the example to emphasize to you that the t values were really big numbers. We will repeat the exercise just to be complete, but in real analysis, we would not bother.

```
. format t %20.0gc
. list in 1/5
```

	roomtype	time	price	t
1.	1	02.13.2007 08:00	140	1,486,972,780,544
2.	1	02.13.2007 09:00	155	1,486,976,450,560
3.	1	02.13.2007 10:00	160	1,486,979,989,504
4.	1	02.13.2007 11:00	155	1,486,983,659,520
5.	1	02.13.2007 12:00	160	1,486,987,198,464

Okay, we see big numbers in t. Let's continue.

Next we put a %tc format on t, and that is something we would usually do, and you should always do. You should also list a bit of the data, as we did:

```
. format t %tc
. list in 1/5
```

	roomtype	time	price	t
1.	1	02.13.2007 08:00	140	13feb2007 07:59:40
2.	1	02.13.2007 09:00	155	13feb2007 09:00:50
3.	1	02.13.2007 10:00	160	13feb2007 09:59:49
4.	1	02.13.2007 11:00	155	13feb2007 11:00:59
5.	1	02.13.2007 12:00	160	13feb2007 11:59:58

By now, you should see a problem: the translated date–time values are off by a second or two. That was caused by rounding. Dates and times should be the same, not approximately the same, and when you see a difference like this, you should say to yourself, "The translation is off a little. Why is that?" and then you should think, "Of course, rounding. I bet that I did not create t as a double."

Let us assume, however, that you do not do this. You instead plow ahead:

```
. xtset roomtype t, delta(1 hour)
time values with periodicity less than delta() found
r(451);
```

And that is what will happen when you forget to create t as a double. The rounding will cause uneven periodicity, and xtset will complain.

By the way, it is important only that clock times (%tc and %tC variables) be stored as doubles. The other date values %td, %tw, %tm, %tq, %th, and %ty are small enough that they can safely be stored as floats, although forgetting and storing them as doubles does no harm.

◁

❏ Technical Note

Stata provides two clock-time formats, %tc and %tC. %tC provides a clock with leap seconds. Leap seconds are occasionally inserted to account for randomness of the earth's rotation, which gradually slows. Unlike the extra day inserted in leap years, the timing of when leap seconds will be inserted cannot be foretold. The authorities in charge of such matters announce a leap second approximately 6 months before insertion. Leap seconds are inserted at the end of the day, and the leap second is called 23:59:60 (i.e., 11:59:60 pm), which is then followed by the usual 00:00:00 (12:00:00 am). Most nonastronomers find these leap seconds vexing. The added seconds cause problems because of their lack of predictability—knowing how many seconds there will be between 01jan2012 and 01jan2013 is not possible—and because there are not necessarily 24 hours in a day. If you use a leap second–adjusted clock, most days have 24 hours, but a few have 24 hours and 1 second. You must look at a table to find out.

From a time-series analysis point of view, the nonconstant day causes the most problems. Let's say that you have data on blood pressure for a set of patients, taken hourly at 1:00, 2:00, ..., and that you have xtset your data with delta(1 hour). On most days, L24.bp would be blood pressure at the same time yesterday. If the previous day had a leap second, however, and your data were recorded using a leap second–adjusted clock, there would be no observation L24.bp because 86,400 seconds before the current reading does not correspond to an on-the-hour time; 86,401 seconds before the current reading corresponds to yesterday's time. Thus, whenever possible, using Stata's %tc encoding rather than %tC is better.

When times are recorded by computers using leap second–adjusted clocks, however, avoiding %tC is not possible. For performing most time-series analysis, the recommended procedure is to map the

%tC values to %tc and then xtset those. You must ask yourself whether the process you are studying is based on the clock—the nurse does something at 2 o'clock every day—or the true passage of time—the emitter spits out an electron every 86,400,000 ms.

When dealing with computer-recorded times, first find out whether the computer (and its time-recording software) use a leap second–adjusted clock. If it does, translate that to a %tC value. Then use function cofC() to convert to a %tc value and xtset that. If variable T contains the %tC value,

```
. gen double t = cofC(T)
. format t %tc
. xtset panelvar t, delta(...)
```

Function cofC() moves leap seconds forward: 23:59:60 becomes 00:00:00 of the next day.

❏

Saved Results

xtset saves the following in r():

Scalars

r(imin)	minimum panel ID
r(imax)	maximum panel ID
r(tmin)	minimum time
r(tmax)	maximum time
r(tdelta)	delta

Macros

r(panelvar)	name of panel variable
r(timevar)	name of time variable
r(tdeltas)	formatted delta
r(tmins)	formatted minimum time
r(tmaxs)	formatted maximum time
r(tsfmt)	%fmt of time variable
r(unit)	units of time variable: Clock, clock, daily, weekly, monthly, quarterly, halfyearly, yearly, or generic
r(unit1)	units of time variable: C, c, d, w, m, q, h, y, or ""
r(balanced)	unbalanced, weakly balanced, or strongly balanced; a set of panels are strongly balanced if they all have the same time values, otherwise balanced if same number of time values, otherwise unbalanced

Methods and Formulas

xtset is implemented as an ado-file.

Also See

[XT] **xtdescribe** — Describe pattern of xt data

[XT] **xtsum** — Summarize xt data

[TS] **tsset** — Declare data to be time-series data

[TS] **tsfill** — Fill in gaps in time variable

Title

> **xtsum** — Summarize xt data

Syntax

> xtsum [*varlist*] [*if*]

A panel variable must be specified; use xtset; see [XT] **xtset**.

varlist may contain time-series operators; see [U] **11.4.3 Time-series varlists**.

by is allowed; see [D] **by**.

Description

xtsum, a generalization of summarize, reports means and standard deviations for panel data; it differs from summarize in that it decomposes the standard deviation into between and within components.

Remarks

If you have not read [XT] **xt**, please do so.

xtsum provides an alternative to summarize. For instance, in the nlswork dataset described in [XT] **xt**, hours contains the number of hours worked last week:

```
. use http://www.stata-press.com/data/r10/nlswork
(National Longitudinal Survey.  Young Women 14-26 years of age in 1968)

. summarize hours
    Variable |      Obs        Mean    Std. Dev.       Min        Max

       hours |    28467    36.55956    9.869623         1        168

. xtsum hours
    Variable |            Mean    Std. Dev.       Min        Max |    Observations

hours   overall |      36.55956    9.869623         1        168 | N =      28467
        between |                   7.846585         1       83.5 | n =       4710
        within  |                   7.520712   -2.154726   130.0596 | T-bar = 6.04395
```

xtsum provides the same information as summarize and more. It decomposes the variable x_{it} into a between ($\overline{x}_i$) and within ($x_{it} - \overline{x}_i + \overline{\overline{x}}$, the global mean $\overline{\overline{x}}$ being added back in make results comparable). The overall and within are calculated over 28,467 person-years of data. The between is calculated over 4,710 persons, and the average number of years a person was observed in the hours data is 6.

xtsum also reports minimums and maximums. Hours worked last week varied between 1 and (unbelievably) 168. Average hours worked last week for each woman varied between 1 and 83.5. "Hours worked within" varied between −2.15 and 130.1, which is not to say that any woman actually worked negative hours. The within number refers to the deviation from each individual's average, and naturally, some of those deviations must be negative. Then the negative value is not disturbing but the positive value is. Did some woman really deviate from her average by +130.1 hours? No. In our definition of within, we add back in the global average of 36.6 hours. Some woman did deviate from her average by $130.1 - 36.6 = 93.5$ hours, which is still large.

450

The reported standard deviations tell us something that may surprise you. They say that the variation in hours worked last week across women is nearly equal to that observed within a woman over time. That is, if you were to draw two women randomly from our data, the difference in hours worked is expected to be nearly equal to the difference for the same woman in two randomly selected years.

If a variable does not vary over time, its within standard deviation will be zero:

```
. xtsum birth_yr
    Variable   |       Mean   Std. Dev.        Min        Max |    Observations
-------------+--------------------------------------------+----------------
birth_yr overall |   48.08509   3.012837         41         54 | N  =     28534
         between |              3.051795         41         54 | n  =      4711
          within |                     0   48.08509   48.08509 | T-bar = 6.05689
```

Also See

[XT] **xtdescribe** — Describe pattern of xt data

[XT] **xttab** — Tabulate xt data

Title

xttab — Tabulate xt data

Syntax

xttab *varname* [*if*]

xttrans *varname* [*if*] [, <u>freq</u>]

A panel variable must be specified; use xtset; see [XT] **xtset**.
by is allowed with xttab and xttrans; see [D] **by**.

Description

xttab, a generalization of tabulate, performs one-way tabulations and decomposes counts into between and within components in panel data.

xttrans, another generalization of tabulate, reports transition probabilities (the change in one categorical variable over time).

Option

   Main

freq, allowed with xttrans only, specifies that frequencies as well as transition probabilities be displayed.

Remarks

If you have not read [XT] **xt**, please do so.

▷ Example 1: xttab

Using the nlswork dataset described in [XT] **xt**, variable msp is 1 if a woman is married and her spouse resides with her, and 0 otherwise:

```
. use http://www.stata-press.com/data/r10/nlswork
(National Longitudinal Survey.  Young Women 14-26 years of age in 1968)

. xttab msp
```

	Overall Freq.	Overall Percent	Between Freq.	Between Percent	Within Percent
0	11324	39.71	3113	66.08	55.06
1	17194	60.29	3643	77.33	71.90
Total	28518	100.00	6756	143.41	64.14

(n = 4711)

The overall part of the table summarizes results in terms of person-years. We have 11,324 person-years of data in which msp is 0 and 17,194 in which it is 1—in 60.3% of our data, the woman is married with her spouse present. Between repeats the breakdown, but this time in terms of women rather than person-years; 3,113 of our women ever had msp 0 and 3,643 ever had msp 1, for a grand total of 6,756 ever having either. We have in our data, however, only 4,711 women. This means that there are women who sometimes have msp 0 and at other times have msp 1.

The within percent tells us the fraction of the time a woman has the specified value of msp. If we take the first line, conditional on a woman ever having msp 0, 55.1% of her observations have msp 0. Similarly, conditional on a woman ever having msp 1, 71.9% of her observations have msp 1. These two numbers are a measure of the stability of the msp values, and, in fact, msp 1 is more stable among these younger women than msp 0, meaning that they tend to marry more than they divorce. The total within of 64.14% is the normalized between weighted average of the within percents, that is, $(3113 \times 55.06 + 3643 \times 71.90)/6756$. It is a measure of the overall stability of the msp variable.

A time-invariant variable will have a tabulation with within percents of 100:

```
. xttab race
```

	Overall		Between		Within
race	Freq.	Percent	Freq.	Percent	Percent
1	20180	70.72	3329	70.66	100.00
2	8051	28.22	1325	28.13	100.00
3	303	1.06	57	1.21	100.00
Total	28534	100.00	4711	100.00	100.00

$$(n = 4711)$$

◁

▷ Example 2: xttrans

xttrans shows the transition probabilities. In cross-sectional time-series data, we can estimate the probability that $x_{i,t+1} = v_2$ given that $x_{it} = v_1$ by counting transitions. For instance

```
. xttrans msp
```

1 if married, spouse present	1 if married, spouse present		Total
	0	1	
0	80.49	19.51	100.00
1	7.96	92.04	100.00
Total	37.11	62.89	100.00

The rows reflect the initial values, and the columns reflect the final values. Each year, some 80% of the msp 0 persons in the data remained msp 0 in the next year; the remaining 20% became msp 1. Although msp 0 had a 20% chance of becoming msp 1 in each year, the msp 1 had only an 8% chance of becoming (or returning to) msp 0. The freq option displays the frequencies that go into the calculation:

```
. xttrans msp, freq
```

1 if married, spouse present	1 if married, spouse present		Total
	0	1	
0	7,697	1,866	9,563
	80.49	19.51	100.00
1	1,133	13,100	14,233
	7.96	92.04	100.00
Total	8,830	14,966	23,796
	37.11	62.89	100.00

◁

❏ Technical Note

The transition probabilities reported by xttrans are not necessarily the transition probabilities in a Markov sense. xttrans counts transitions from each observation to the next once the observations have been put in t order within i. It does not normalize for missing periods. xttrans does pay attention to missing values of the variable being tabulated, however, and does not count transitions from nonmissing to missing or from missing to nonmissing. Thus if the data are fully rectangularized, xttrans produces (inefficient) estimates of the Markov transition matrix. fillin will rectangularize datasets; see [D] **fillin**. Thus the Markov transition matrix could be estimated by typing

```
. fillin idcode year
. xttrans msp
  (output omitted )
```

❏

Also See

[XT] **xtdescribe** — Describe pattern of xt data

[XT] **xtsum** — Summarize xt data

Title

> **xttobit** — Random-effects tobit models

Syntax

xttobit *depvar* [*indepvars*] [*if*] [*in*] [*weight*] [, *options*]

options	description
Model	
<u>nocon</u>stant	suppress constant term
ll(*varname* | #)	left-censoring variable/limit
ul(*varname* | #)	right-censoring variable/limit
<u>off</u>set(*varname*)	include *varname* in model with coefficient constrained to 1
<u>constraints</u>(*constraints*)	apply specified linear constraints
<u>col</u>linear	keep collinear variables
SE	
vce(*vcetype*)	*vcetype* may be oim, <u>boot</u>strap, or <u>jack</u>knife
Reporting	
<u>level</u>(#)	set confidence level; default is level(95)
tobit	perform likelihood ratio test comparing against pooled tobit model
noskip	perform overall model test as a likelihood-ratio test
Int opts (RE)	
<u>intm</u>ethod(*intmethod*)	integration method; *intmethod* may be <u>mvag</u>hermite, <u>ag</u>hermite, or <u>g</u>hermite; default is intmethod(mvaghermite)
<u>intp</u>oints(#)	use # quadrature points; default is intpoints(12)
Max options	
maximize_options	control maximization process; see [R] **maximize**

A panel variable must be specified; use xtset; see [XT] **xtset**.
depvar and *indepvars* may contain time-series operators; see [U] **11.4.3 Time-series varlists**.
by, statsby, and xi are allowed; see [U] **11.1.10 Prefix commands**.
iweights are allowed; see [U] **11.1.6 weight**. Weights must be constant within panel.
See [U] **20 Estimation and postestimation commands** for more capabilities of estimation commands.

Description

xttobit fits random-effects tobit models. There is no command for a parametric conditional fixed-effects model, as there does not exist a sufficient statistic allowing the fixed effects to be conditioned out of the likelihood. Honoré (1992) has developed a semiparametric estimator for fixed-effect tobit models. Unconditional fixed-effects tobit models may be fitted with the tobit command with indicator variables for the panels. The appropriate indicator variables can be generated using tabulate or xi. However, unconditional fixed-effects estimates are biased.

xttobit is slow because the likelihood function is calculated by adaptive Gauss–Hermite quadrature; see *Methods and Formulas*. Computation time is roughly proportional to the number of points used for the quadrature. The default is intpoints(12). Increasing the number of quadrature points can improve the quadrature approximation. See [XT] **quadchk**.

Options

___Model___

noconstant; see [XT] **estimation options**.

ll(*varname*|*#*) and ul(*varname*|*#*) indicate the censoring points. You may specify one or both. ll() indicates the lower limit for left-censoring. Observations with *depvar* $\leq$ ll() are left-censored, observations with *depvar* $\geq$ ul() are right-censored, and remaining observations are not censored.

offset(*varname*), constraints(*constraints*), collinear; see [XT] **estimation options**.

___SE___

vce(*vcetype*) specifies the type of standard error reported, which includes types that are derived from asymptotic theory and that use bootstrap or jackknife methods; see [XT] *vce_options*.

___Reporting___

level(*#*); see [XT] **estimation options**.

tobit specifies that a likelihood-ratio test comparing the random-effects model with the pooled (tobit) model be included in the output.

noskip; see [XT] **estimation options**.

___Int opts (RE)___

intmethod(*intmethod*), intpoints(*#*); see [XT] **estimation options**.

___Max options___

maximize_options: difficult, technique(*algorithm_spec*), iterate(*#*), [no]log, trace, gradient, showstep, hessian, shownrtolerance, tolerance(*#*), ltolerance(*#*), gtolerance(*#*), nrtolerance(*#*), nonrtolerance, from(*init_specs*); see [R] **maximize**. Some of these options are not available if intmethod(ghermite) is specified. These options are seldom used.

Remarks

Consider the linear regression model with panel-level random effects

$$y_{it} = \mathbf{x}_{it}\boldsymbol{\beta} + \nu_i + \epsilon_{it}$$

for $i = 1, \ldots, n$ panels, where $t = 1, \ldots, n_i$. The random effects, ν_i, are i.i.d., $N(0, \sigma_\nu^2)$, and ϵ_{it} are i.i.d. $N(0, \sigma_\epsilon^2)$ independently of ν_i.

The observed data, y_{it}^o, represent possibly censored versions of y_{it}. If they are left-censored, all that is known is that $y_{it} \leq y_{it}^o$. If they are right-censored, all that is known is that $y_{it} \geq y_{it}^o$. If they are uncensored, $y_{it} = y_{it}^o$. If they are left-censored, y_{it}^o is determined by ll(). If they are right-censored, y_{it}^o is determined by ul(). If they are uncensored, y_{it}^o is determined by *depvar*.

▷ Example 1

Using the nlswork data described in [XT] **xt**, we fit a random-effects tobit model of adjusted (log) wages. We use the ul() option to impose an upper limit on the recorded log of wages. We use the intpoints(25) option to increase the number of integration points to 25 from 12, which aids convergence of this model.

```
. use http://www.stata-press.com/data/r10/nlswork3
(National Longitudinal Survey.  Young Women 14-26 years of age in 1968)
. xttobit ln_wage union age grade not_smsa south southXt, ul(1.9) intpoints(25)
> tobit
```

(output omitted)

```
Random-effects tobit regression             Number of obs      =       19224
Group variable: idcode                      Number of groups   =        4148

Random effects u_i ~ Gaussian               Obs per group: min =           1
                                                           avg =         4.6
                                                           max =          12

                                            Wald chi2(6)       =     2925.06
Log likelihood  = -6814.5655                Prob > chi2        =      0.0000
```

ln_wage	Coef.	Std. Err.	z	P>|z|	[95% Conf. Interval]	
union	.1430786	.0069719	20.52	0.000	.1294139	.1567432
age	.0091626	.0005452	16.81	0.000	.0080941	.0102311
grade	.078454	.0022756	34.48	0.000	.0739938	.0829141
not_smsa	-.1340719	.0092048	-14.57	0.000	-.152113	-.1160309
south	-.1263125	.0124581	-10.14	0.000	-.15073	-.1018951
southXt	.0031133	.0008419	3.70	0.000	.0014633	.0047633
_cons	.4674631	.0339875	13.75	0.000	.4008489	.5340773
/sigma_u	.3045975	.0048337	63.02	0.000	.2951236	.3140713
/sigma_e	.2488754	.0018254	136.34	0.000	.2452977	.2524531
rho	.599667	.0084081			.5831034	.6160533

```
Likelihood-ratio test of sigma_u=0: chibar2(01)= 6660.01 Prob>=chibar2 = 0.000
        Observation summary:          0  left-censored observations
                                  12334      uncensored observations
                                   6890 right-censored observations
```

The output includes the overall and panel-level variance components (labeled sigma_e and sigma_u, respectively) together with ρ (labeled rho)

$$\rho = \frac{\sigma_\nu^2}{\sigma_\epsilon^2 + \sigma_\nu^2}$$

which is the percent contribution to the total variance of the panel-level variance component.

When rho is zero, the panel-level variance component is unimportant, and the panel estimator is not different from the pooled estimator. A likelihood-ratio test of this is included at the bottom of the output. This test formally compares the pooled estimator (tobit) with the panel estimator.   ◁

❏ Technical Note

The random-effects model is calculated using quadrature. As the panel sizes (or ρ) increase, the quadrature approximation can become less accurate. We can use the quadchk command to see if changing the number of quadrature points affects the results. If the results do change, the quadrature approximation is not accurate, and the results of the model should not be interpreted. See [XT] **quadchk** for details and [XT] **xtprobit** for an example.

❏

Saved Results

xttobit saves the following in e():

Scalars

e(N)	# of observations	e(rho)	ρ
e(N_g)	# of groups	e(sigma_u)	panel-level standard deviation
e(N_unc)	# of uncensored observations	e(sigma_e)	standard deviation of ϵ_{it}
e(N_lc)	# of left-censored observations	e(n_quad)	# of quadrature points
e(N_rc)	# of right-censored observations	e(k)	# of parameters
e(N_int)	# of interval observations	e(k_eq)	# of equations
e(N_cd)	# of completely determined obs.	e(k_eq_model)	# of equations in model Wald test
e(df_m)	model degrees of freedom	e(k_dv)	# of dependent variables
e(ll)	log likelihood	e(p)	significance
e(ll_0)	log likelihood, constant-only model	e(rank)	rank of e(V)
e(g_max)	largest group size	e(rank0)	rank of e(V) for constant-only model
e(g_min)	smallest group size	e(ic)	# of iterations
e(g_avg)	average group size	e(rc)	return code
e(chi2)	χ^2	e(converged)	1 if converged, 0 otherwise
e(chi2_c)	χ^2 for comparison test		

Macros

e(cmd)	xttobit	e(distrib)	Gaussian; the distribution of the random effect
e(cmdline)	command as typed		
e(depvar)	names of dependent variables	e(intmethod)	integration method
e(ivar)	variable denoting groups	e(vce)	*vcetype* specified in vce()
e(wtype)	weight type	e(vcetype)	title used to label Std. Err.
e(wexp)	weight expression	e(opt)	type of optimization
e(title)	title in estimation output	e(ml_method)	type of ml method
e(llopt)	contents of ll(), if specified	e(user)	name of likelihood-evaluator program
e(ulopt)	contents of ul(), if specified	e(technique)	maximization technique
e(offset1)	offset	e(crittype)	optimization criterion
e(chi2type)	Wald or LR; type of model χ^2 test	e(properties)	b V
e(chi2_ct)	Wald or LR; type of model χ^2 test corresponding to e(chi2_c)	e(predict)	program used to implement predict

Matrices

e(b)	coefficient vector	e(ilog)	iteration log
e(V)	variance–covariance matrix of the estimator	e(gradient)	gradient vector

Functions

e(sample)	marks estimation sample

Methods and Formulas

`xttobit` is implemented as an ado-file.

Assuming a normal distribution, $N(0, \sigma_\nu^2)$, for the random effects ν_i, we have the joint (unconditional of ν_i) density of the observed data from the ith panel

$$f(y_{i1}^o, \ldots, y_{in_i}^o | \mathbf{x}_{i1}, \ldots, \mathbf{x}_{in_i}) = \int_{-\infty}^{\infty} \frac{e^{-\nu_i^2/2\sigma_\nu^2}}{\sqrt{2\pi}\sigma_\nu} \left\{ \prod_{t=1}^{n_i} F(y_{it}^o, \mathbf{x}_{it}\boldsymbol{\beta} + \nu_i) \right\} d\nu_i$$

where

$$F(y_{it}^o, \Delta_{it}) = \begin{cases} \left(\sqrt{2\pi}\sigma_\epsilon\right)^{-1} e^{-(y_{it}^o - \Delta_{it})^2/(2\sigma_\epsilon^2)} & \text{if } y_{it}^o \in C \\ \Phi\left(\frac{y_{it}^o - \Delta_{it}}{\sigma_\epsilon}\right) & \text{if } y_{it}^o \in L \\ 1 - \Phi\left(\frac{y_{it}^o - \Delta_{it}}{\sigma_\epsilon}\right) & \text{if } y_{it}^o \in R \end{cases}$$

where C is the set of noncensored observations, L is the set of left-censored observations, R is the set of right-censored observations, and $\Phi()$ is the cumulative normal distribution.

The panel level likelihood l_i is given by

$$l_i = \int_{-\infty}^{\infty} \frac{e^{-\nu_i^2/2\sigma_\nu^2}}{\sqrt{2\pi}\sigma_\nu} \left\{ \prod_{t=1}^{n_i} F(y_{it}^o, \mathbf{x}_{it}\boldsymbol{\beta} + \nu_i) \right\} d\nu_i$$

$$\equiv \int_{-\infty}^{\infty} g(y_{it}^o, x_{it}, \nu_i) d\nu_i$$

This integral can be approximated with M-point Gauss–Hermite quadrature

$$\int_{-\infty}^{\infty} e^{-x^2} h(x) dx \approx \sum_{m=1}^{M} w_m^* h(a_m^*)$$

This is equivalent to

$$\int_{-\infty}^{\infty} f(x) dx \approx \sum_{m=1}^{M} w_m^* \exp\left\{(a_m^*)^2\right\} f(a_m^*)$$

where the w_m^* denote the quadrature weights and the a_m^* denote the quadrature abscissas. The log likelihood, L, is the sum of the logs of the panel level likelihoods l_i.

The default approximation of the log likelihood is by adaptive Gauss–Hermite quadrature, which approximates the panel level likelihood with

$$l_i \approx \sqrt{2}\widehat{\sigma}_i \sum_{m=1}^{M} w_m^* \exp\left\{(a_m^*)^2\right\} g(y_{it}^o, x_{it}, \sqrt{2}\widehat{\sigma}_i a_m^* + \widehat{\mu}_i)$$

where $\widehat{\sigma}_i$ and $\widehat{\mu}_i$ are the adaptive parameters for panel i. Therefore, with the definition of $g(y_{it}^o, x_{it}, \nu_i)$, the total log likelihood is approximated by

$$L \approx \sum_{i=1}^{n} w_i \log \left[\sqrt{2}\widehat{\sigma}_i \sum_{m=1}^{M} w_m^* \exp\{(a_m^*)^2\} \frac{\exp\{-(\sqrt{2}\widehat{\sigma}_i a_m^* + \widehat{\mu}_i)^2 / 2\sigma_\nu^2\}}{\sqrt{2\pi}\sigma_\nu} \right.$$

$$\left. \prod_{t=1}^{n_i} F(y_{it}^o, x_{it}\boldsymbol{\beta} + \sqrt{2}\widehat{\sigma}_i a_m^* + \widehat{\mu}_i) \right]$$

where w_i is the user-specified weight for panel i; if no weights are specified, $w_i = 1$.

The default method of adaptive Gauss–Hermite quadrature is to calculate the posterior mean and variance and use those parameters for $\widehat{\mu}_i$ and $\widehat{\sigma}_i$ by following the method of Naylor and Smith (1982), further discussed in Skrondal and Rabe-Hesketh (2004). We start with $\widehat{\sigma}_{i,0} = 1$ and $\widehat{\mu}_{i,0} = 0$, and the posterior means and variances are updated in the kth iteration. That is, at the kth iteration of the optimization for l_i we use

$$l_{i,k} \approx \sum_{m=1}^{M} \sqrt{2}\widehat{\sigma}_{i,k-1} w_m^* \exp\{a_m^*\}^2\} g(y_{it}^o, x_{it}, \sqrt{2}\widehat{\sigma}_{i,k-1} a_m^* + \widehat{\mu}_{i,k-1})$$

Letting

$$\tau_{i,m,k-1} = \sqrt{2}\widehat{\sigma}_{i,k-1} a_m^* + \widehat{\mu}_{i,k-1}$$

$$\widehat{\mu}_{i,k} = \sum_{m=1}^{M} (\tau_{i,m,k-1}) \frac{\sqrt{2}\widehat{\sigma}_{i,k-1} w_m^* \exp\{(a_m^*)^2\} g(y_{it}^o, x_{it}, \tau_{i,m,k-1})}{l_{i,k}}$$

and

$$\widehat{\sigma}_{i,k} = \sum_{m=1}^{M} (\tau_{i,m,k-1})^2 \frac{\sqrt{2}\widehat{\sigma}_{i,k-1} w_m^* \exp\{(a_m^*)^2\} g(y_{it}^o, x_{it}, \tau_{i,m,k-1})}{l_{i,k}} - (\widehat{\mu}_{i,k})^2$$

and this is repeated until $\widehat{\mu}_{i,k}$ and $\widehat{\sigma}_{i,k}$ have converged for this iteration of the maximization algorithm. This adaptation is applied on every iteration until the log-likelihood change from the preceding iteration is less than a relative difference of 1e–6; after this, the quadrature parameters are fixed.

One can instead use the adaptive quadrature method of Liu and Pierce (1994), option `intmethod(aghermite)`, which uses the mode and curvature of the mode as approximations for the mean and variance. We take the integrand

$$g(y_{it}^o, x_{it}, \nu_i) = \frac{e^{-\nu_i^2/2\sigma_\nu^2}}{\sqrt{2\pi}\sigma_\nu} \left\{ \prod_{t=1}^{n_i} F(y_{it}^o, \mathbf{x}_{it}\boldsymbol{\beta} + \nu_i) \right\}$$

and find α_i the mode of $g(y_{it}^o, x_{it}, \nu_i)$. We calculate

$$\gamma_i = -\frac{\partial^2}{\partial \nu_i^2} \log\{g(y_{it}^o, x_{it}, \nu_i)\}\Big|_{\nu_i = \alpha_i}$$

Then

$$\int_{-\infty}^{\infty} g(y_{it}^o, x_{it}, \nu_i) d\nu_i \approx \left(\frac{2}{\gamma_i}\right)^{1/2} \sum_{m=1}^{M} w_m^* \exp\{(a_m^*)^2\} g\left\{ y_{it}^o, x_{it}, \left(\frac{2}{\gamma_i}\right)^{1/2} a_m^* + \alpha_i \right\}$$

This adaptation is performed on the first iteration only; that is, the α_i and γ_i are calculated once at the first iteration and then held constant throughout later iterations.

The log likelihood can also be calculated by nonadaptive Gauss–Hermite quadrature, option `intmethod(ghermite)`:

$$
L = \sum_{i=1}^{n} w_i \log \left\{ \Pr(y_{i1}, \ldots, y_{in_i} | \mathbf{x}_{i1}, \ldots, \mathbf{x}_{in_i}) \right\}
$$

$$
\approx \sum_{i=1}^{n} w_i \log \left[\frac{1}{\sqrt{\pi}} \sum_{m=1}^{M} w_m^* \prod_{t=1}^{n_i} F \left\{ y_{it}^o, \mathbf{x}_{it}\boldsymbol{\beta} + \sqrt{2}\sigma_\nu a_m^* \right\} \right]
$$

All three quadrature formulas require that the integrated function be well approximated by a polynomial of degree equal to the number of quadrature points. The number of periods (panel size) can affect whether

$$
\prod_{t=1}^{n_i} F(y_{it}^o, \mathbf{x}_{it}\boldsymbol{\beta} + \nu_i)
$$

is well approximated by a polynomial. As panel size and ρ increase, the quadrature approximation can become less accurate. For large ρ, the random-effects model can also become unidentified. Adaptive quadrature gives better results for correlated data and large panels than nonadaptive quadrature; however, we recommend that you use the `quadchk` command to verify the quadrature approximation used in this command, whichever approximation you choose.

References

Honoré, B. 1992. Trimmed LAD and least squares estimation of truncated and censored regression models with fixed effects. *Econometrica* 60: 533–565.

Liu, Q., and D. A. Pierce. 1994. A note on Gauss–Hermite quadrature. *Biometrika* 81: 624–629.

Naylor, J. C., and A. F. M. Smith. 1982. Applications of a method for the efficient computation of posterior distributions. *Journal of the Royal Statistical Society, Series C* 31: 214–225.

Neuhaus, J. M. 1992. Statistical methods for longitudinal and clustered designs with binary responses. *Statistical Methods in Medical Research* 1: 249–273.

Pendergast, J. F., S. J. Gange, M. A. Newton, M. J. Lindstrom, M. Palta, and M. R. Fisher. 1996. A survey of methods for analyzing clustered binary response data. *International Statistical Review* 64: 89–118.

Skrondal, A., and S. Rabe-Hesketh. 2004. *Generalized Latent Variable Modeling: Multilevel, Longitudinal, and Structural Equation Models*. Boca Raton, FL: Chapman & Hall/CRC.

Also See

[XT] **xttobit postestimation** — Postestimation tools for xttobit

[XT] **quadchk** — Check sensitivity of quadrature approximation

[R] **constraint** — Define and list constraints

[XT] **xtintreg** — Random-effects interval-data regression models

[XT] **xtreg** — Fixed-, between-, and random-effects, and population-averaged linear models

[R] **tobit** — Tobit regression

[U] **20 Estimation and postestimation commands**

Title

> **xttobit postestimation** — Postestimation tools for xttobit

Description

The following postestimation commands are available for `xttobit`:

command	description
adjust[1]	adjusted predictions of $\mathbf{x}\beta$
estat	AIC, BIC, VCE, and estimation sample summary
estimates	cataloging estimation results
lincom	point estimates, standard errors, testing, and inference for linear combinations of coefficients
lrtest	likelihood-ratio test
mfx	marginal effects or elasticities
nlcom	point estimates, standard errors, testing, and inference for nonlinear combinations of coefficients
predict	predictions, residuals, influence statistics, and other diagnostic measures
predictnl	point estimates, standard errors, testing, and inference for generalized predictions
test	Wald tests for simple and composite linear hypotheses
testnl	Wald tests of nonlinear hypotheses

[1] `adjust` is not appropriate with time-series operators.

See the corresponding entries in the *Stata Base Reference Manual* for details.

Syntax for predict

> predict [*type*] *newvar* [*if*] [*in*] [, *statistic* <u>nooff</u>set]

statistic	description
Main	
xb	linear prediction assuming $\nu_i = 0$, the default
stdp	standard error of the linear prediction
stdf	standard error of the linear forecast
<u>pr</u>0(*a*,*b*)	$\Pr(a < y < b)$ assuming $\nu_i = 0$
<u>e</u>0(*a*,*b*)	$E(y \mid a < y < b)$ assuming $\nu_i = 0$
<u>ystar</u>0(*a*,*b*)	$E(y^*)$, $y^* = \max\{a, \min(y, b)\}$ assuming $\nu_i = 0$

These statistics are available both in and out of sample; type `predict ... if e(sample) ...` if wanted only for the estimation sample.

where a and b may be numbers or variables; a missing ($a \geq .$) means $-\infty$, and b missing ($b \geq .$) means $+\infty$; see [U] **12.2.1 Missing values**.

Options for predict

Main

xb, the default, calculates the linear prediction.

stdp calculates the standard error of the prediction. It can be thought of as the standard error of the predicted expected value or mean for the observation's covariate pattern. The standard error of the prediction is also referred to as the standard error of the fitted value.

stdf calculates the standard error of the forecast. This is the standard error of the point prediction for 1 observation. It is commonly referred to as the standard error of the future or forecast value. By construction, the standard errors produced by stdf are always larger than those produced by stdp; see [R] **regress** *Methods and Formulas*.

pr0(a,b) calculates estimates of $\Pr(a < y < b \mid \mathbf{x} = \mathbf{x}_{it}, \nu_i = 0)$, which is the probability that y would be observed in the interval (a, b), given the current values of the predictors, $\mathbf{x}_{it}$, and given a zero random effect; see *Remarks*. In the discussion that follows, these two conditions are implied.

a and b may be specified as numbers or variable names; *lb* and *ub* are variable names;
pr0(20,30) calculates $\Pr(20 < y < 30)$;
pr0(*lb*,*ub*) calculates $\Pr(lb < y < ub)$; and
pr0(20,*ub*) calculates $\Pr(20 < y < ub)$.

a missing ($a \geq .$) means $-\infty$; pr0(.,30) calculates $\Pr(-\infty < y < 30)$;
pr0(*lb*,30) calculates $\Pr(-\infty < y < 30)$ in observations for which $lb \geq .$
(and calculates $\Pr(lb < y < 30)$ elsewhere).

b missing ($b \geq .$) means $+\infty$; pr0(20,.) calculates $\Pr(+\infty > y > 20)$;
pr0(20,*ub*) calculates $\Pr(+\infty > y > 20)$ in observations for which $ub \geq .$
(and calculates $\Pr(20 < y < ub)$ elsewhere).

e0(a,b) calculates estimates of $E(y \mid a < y < b, \mathbf{x} = \mathbf{x}_{it}, \nu_i = 0)$, which is the expected value of y conditional on y being in the interval (a, b), meaning that y is censored. a and b are specified as they are for pr0().

ystar0(a,b) calculates estimates of $E(y^* \mid \mathbf{x} = \mathbf{x}_{it}, \nu_i = 0)$, where $y^* = a$ if $y \leq a$, $y^* = b$ if $y \geq b$, and $y^* = y$ otherwise, meaning that y^* is the truncated version of y. a and b are specified as they are for pr0().

nooffset is relevant only if you specify offset(*varname*) for xttobit. It modifies the calculations made by predict so that they ignore the offset variable; the linear prediction is treated as $\mathbf{x}_{it}\beta$ rather than $\mathbf{x}_{it}\beta + \text{offset}_{it}$.

Methods and Formulas

All postestimation commands listed above are implemented as ado-files.

Also See

Glossary

Arellano–Bond estimator. The Arellano–Bond estimator is a generalized method-of-moments (GMM) estimator for linear dynamic panel-data models that uses lagged levels of the endogenous variables as well as first differences of the exogenous variables as instruments. The Arellano–Bond estimator removes the panel-specific heterogeneity by first-differencing the regression equation.

autoregressive process. In autoregressive processes, the current value of a variable is a linear function of its own past values and a white-noise error term. For panel data, a first-order autoregressive process, denoted as an AR(1) process, is $y_{it} = \rho y_{i,t-1} + \epsilon_{it}$, where i denotes panels, t denotes time, and ϵ_{it} is white noise.

balanced data. A longitudinal or panel dataset is said to be balanced if each panel has the same number of observations. See *weakly balanced* and *strongly balanced*.

between estimator. The between estimator is a panel-data estimator that obtains its estimates by running OLS on the panel-level means of the variables. This estimator uses only the between-panel variation in the data to identify the parameters, ignoring any within-panel variation. For it to be consistent, the between estimator requires that the panel-level means of the regressors be uncorrelated with the panel-specific heterogeneity terms.

BLUPs. BLUPs are best linear unbiased predictions of either random effects or linear combinations of random effects. In linear models containing random effects, these effects are not estimated directly but instead are integrated out of the estimation. Once the fixed effects and variance components have been estimated, you can use these estimates to predict group-specific random effects. These predictions are called BLUPs because they are unbiased and have minimal mean squared error among all linear functions of the response.

canonical link. Corresponding to each family of distributions in a generalized linear model is a canonical link function for which there is a sufficient statistic with the same dimension as the number of parameters in the linear predictor. The use of canonical link functions provides the GLM with desirable statistical properties, especially when the sample size is small.

conditional fixed-effects model. In general, including panel-specific dummies to control for fixed effects in nonlinear models results in inconsistent estimates. For some nonlinear models, the fixed-effect term can be removed from the likelihood function by conditioning on a sufficient statistic. For example, the conditional fixed-effect logit model conditions on the number of positive outcomes within each panel.

correlation structure. A correlation structure is a set of assumptions imposed on the within-panel variance–covariance matrix of the errors in a panel-data model. See [XT] **xtgee** for examples of different correlation structures.

crossed-effects model. A crossed-effects model is a mixed model in which the levels of random effects are not nested. A simple crossed-effects model for cross-sectional time-series data would contain a random effect to control for panel-specific variation and a second random effect to control for time-specific random variation. Rather than being nested within panel, in this model a random effect due to a given time is the same for all panels.

cross-sectional data. Cross-sectional data refers to data collected over a set of individuals, such as households, firms, or countries sampled from a population at a given point in time.

cross-sectional time-series data. Cross-sectional time-series data is another name for panel data. The term *cross-sectional time-series data* is sometimes reserved for datasets in which a relatively small number of panels were observed over many periods. See *panel data*.

disturbance term. The disturbance term encompasses any shocks that occur to the dependent variable that cannot be explained by the conditional (or deterministic) portion of the model.

dynamic model. A dynamic model is one in which prior values of the dependent variable or disturbance term affect the current value of the dependent variable.

endogenous variable. An endogenous variable is a regressor that is correlated with the unobservable error term. Equivalently, an endogenous variable is one whose values are determined by the equilibrium or outcome of a structural model.

error-components model. The error-components model is another name for the random-effects model. See *random-effects model*.

exogenous variable. An exogenous variable is a regressor that is not correlated with any of the error terms in the model. Equivalently, an exogenous variable is one whose values change independently of the other variables in a structural model.

fixed-effects model. The fixed-effects model is a model for panel data in which the panel-specific errors are treated as fixed parameters. These parameters are panel-specific intercepts and therefore allow the conditional mean of the dependent variable to vary across panels. The linear fixed-effects estimator is consistent, even if the regressors are correlated with the fixed effects. See also *random-effects model*.

generalized estimating equations (GEE). The method of generalized estimating equations is used to fit population-averaged panel-data models. GEE extends the GLM method by allowing the user to specify a variety of different within-panel correlation structures.

generalized linear model (GLM). The generalized linear model is an estimation framework in which the user specifies a distributional family for the dependent variable and a link function that relates the dependent variable to a linear combination of the regressors. The distribution must be a member of the exponential family of distributions. GLM encompasses many common models, including linear, probit, and Poisson regression.

hierarchical model. A hierarchical model is one in which successively more narrowly defined groups are nested within larger groups. For example, in a hierarchical model, patients may be nested within doctors who are in turn nested within the hospital at which they practice.

idiosyncratic error term. In longitudinal or panel-data models, the idiosyncratic error term refers to the observation-specific zero-mean random-error term. It is analogous to the random-error term of cross-sectional regression analysis.

instrumental variables. Instrumental variables are exogenous variables that are correlated with one or more of the endogenous variables in a structural model. The term *instrumental variable* is often reserved for those exogenous variables that are not included as regressors in the model.

instrumental-variables (IV) estimator. An instrumental variables estimator uses instrumental variables to produce consistent parameter estimates in models that contain endogenous variables. IV estimators can also be used to control for measurement error.

interval data. Interval data are data in which the true value of the dependent variable is not observed. Instead, all that is known is that the value lies within a given interval.

link function. In a GLM, the link function relates a linear combination of predictors to the expected value of the dependent variable. In a linear regression model, the link function is simply the identity function.

longitudinal data. Longitudinal data is another term for panel data. See *panel data*.

mixed model. A mixed model contains both fixed and random effects. The fixed effects are estimated directly, whereas the random effects are summarized according to their (co)variances. Mixed models are used primarily to perform estimation and inference on the regression coefficients in the presence of complicated within-panel correlation structures induced by multiple levels of grouping.

negative binomial regression model. The negative binomial regression model is for applications in which the dependent variable represents the number of times an event occurs. The negative binomial regression model is an alternative to the Poisson model for use when the dependent variable is overdispersed, meaning that the variance of the dependent variable is greater than its mean.

one-level model. A one-level mixed model is a mixed model with one level of random variation. Suppose that you have a panel dataset consisting of patients at hospitals; a one-level model would contain a set of random effects "at the hospital level" to control for hospital-specific random variation.

overidentifying restrictions. The order condition for model identification requires that the number of exogenous variables excluded from the model be at least as great as the number of endogenous regressors. When the number of excluded exogenous variables exceeds the number of endogenous regressors, the model is overidentified, and the validity of the instruments can then be checked via a test of overidentifying restrictions.

panel-corrected standard errors (PCSEs). The term *panel-corrected standard errors* refers to a class of estimators for the variance–covariance matrix of the OLS estimator when there are relatively few panels with many observations per panel. PCSEs account for heteroskedasticity, autocorrelation, or cross-sectional correlation.

panel data. Panel data are data in which the same units were observed over multiple periods. The units, called panels, are often firms, households, or patients who were observed at several points in time. In a typical panel dataset, the number of panels is large, and the number of observations per panel is relatively small.

Poisson model. The Poisson regression model is used when the dependent variable represents the number of times an event occurs. In the Poisson model, the variance of the dependent variable is equal to the conditional mean.

pooled estimator. A pooled estimator ignores the longitudinal or panel aspect of a dataset and treats the observations as if they were cross-sectional.

population-averaged model. A population-averaged model is used for panel data in which the parameters measure the effects of the regressors on the outcome for the average individual in the population. The panel-specific errors are treated as uncorrelated random variables drawn from a population with zero mean and constant variance, and the parameters measure the effects of the regressors on the dependent variable after integrating over the distribution of the random effects.

predetermined variable. A predetermined variable is a regressor in which its contemporaneous and future values are not correlated with the unobservable error term but past values are correlated with the error term.

production function. A production function describes the maximum amount of a good that can be produced, given specified levels of the inputs.

quadrature. Quadrature is a set of numerical methods to evaluate an integral. Two types of quadrature commonly used in fitting panel-data models are Gaussian and Gauss–Hermite quadrature.

random-coefficients model. A random-coefficients model is a panel-data model in which group-specific heterogeneity is introduced by assuming that each group has its own parameter vector, which is drawn from a population common to all panels.

random-effects model. A random-effects model for panel data treats the panel-specific errors as uncorrelated random variables drawn from a population with zero mean and constant variance. The regressors must be uncorrelated with the random effects for the estimates to be consistent.

strongly balanced. A longitudinal or panel dataset is said to be strongly balanced if each panel has the same number of observations, and the observations for different panels were all made at the same times.

two-level model. A two-level mixed model is a mixed model with two levels of random variation. Suppose that you have a dataset consisting of patients overseen by doctors at hospitals, and each doctor practices at one hospital. Then a two-level model would contain a set of random effects to control for hospital-specific variation and a second set of random effects to control for doctor-specific random variation.

unbalanced data. A longitudinal or panel dataset is said to be unbalanced if each panel does not have the same number of observations. See *weakly balanced* and *strongly balanced*.

variance components. In a mixed model, the variance components refer to the variances and covariances of the various random effects.

weakly balanced. A longitudinal or panel dataset is said to be weakly balanced if each panel has the same number of observations but the observations for different panels were not all made at the same times.

within estimator. The within estimator is a panel-data estimator that removes the panel-specific heterogeneity by subtracting the panel-level means from each variable and then performing ordinary least squares on the demeaned data. The within estimator is used in fitting the linear fixed-effects model.

Subject and author index

This is the subject and author index for the *Stata Longitudinal/Panel-Data Reference Manual*. Readers interested in topics other than cross-sectional time-series should see the combined subject index (and the combined author index) in the *Stata Quick Reference and Index*. The combined index indexes the *Getting Started* manuals, the *User's Guide*, and all the Reference manuals except the *Mata Reference Manual*.

Semicolons set off the most important entries from the rest. Sometimes no entry will be set off with semicolons, meaning that all entries are equally important.

A

abond, estat subcommand, [XT] **xtabond postestimation**, [XT] **xtdpd postestimation**, [XT] **xtdpdsys postestimation**

Abramowitz, M., [XT] **xtmelogit**, [XT] **xtmepoisson**

Aigner, D. J., [XT] **xtfrontier**

Albert, P. S., [XT] **xtgee**

Alvarez, J., [XT] **xtabond**

Amemiya, T., [XT] **xthtaylor**, [XT] **xtivreg**

Anderson, T. W., [XT] **xtabond**, [XT] **xtdpd**, [XT] **xtdpdsys**, [XT] **xtivreg**

Andrews, M., [XT] **xtmelogit**, [XT] **xtmepoisson**, [XT] **xtmixed**, [XT] **xtreg**

Arellano–Bond
  estimator, [XT] **xtabond**
  postestimation, [XT] **xtabond postestimation**, [XT] **xtdpd postestimation**, [XT] **xtdpdsys postestimation**

Arellano–Bover estimator, [XT] **xtdpd**, [XT] **xtdpdsys**

Arellano, M., [XT] **xtabond**, [XT] **xtdpd**, [XT] **xtdpd postestimation**, [XT] **xtdpdsys**, [XT] **xtdpdsys postestimation**, [XT] **xtreg**

Arora, S. S., [XT] **xtivreg**, [XT] **xtreg**

autocorrelation, [XT] **xtabond**, [XT] **xtgee**, [XT] **xtgls**, [XT] **xtpcse**, [XT] **xtregar**

autoregressive model, [XT] **xtabond**, [XT] **xtdpd**, [XT] **xtdpdsys**

B

Balestra, P., [XT] **xtivreg**

Baltagi, B. H., [XT] **xt**, [XT] **xtabond**, [XT] **xtdpd**, [XT] **xtdpdsys**, [XT] **xthtaylor**, [XT] **xtivreg**, [XT] **xtmixed**, [XT] **xtreg**, [XT] **xtreg postestimation**, [XT] **xtregar**

Basford, K. E., [XT] **xtmelogit**, [XT] **xtmepoisson**, [XT] **xtmixed**

Bates, D. M., [XT] **xtmelogit**, [XT] **xtmepoisson**, [XT] **xtmixed**

Battese–Coelli parameterization, [XT] **xtfrontier**

Battese, G. E., [XT] **xtfrontier**

Baum, C. F., [XT] **xtgls**, [XT] **xtreg**

Beck, N., [XT] **xtgls**, [XT] **xtpcse**

Bentham, G., [XT] **xtmepoisson**

Bera, A. K., [XT] **xtreg**

between-cell means and variances, [XT] **xtdescribe**, [XT] **xtsum**

between estimators, [XT] **xtivreg**, [XT] **xtreg**

Bhargava, A., [XT] **xtregar**

Blackwell, J. L., III, [XT] **xtgls**, [XT] **xtpcse**, [XT] **xtreg**

Blundell–Bond estimator, [XT] **xtdpd**, [XT] **xtdpdsys**

Blundell, R., [XT] **xtdpd**, [XT] **xtdpdsys**

Bond, S., [XT] **xtabond**, [XT] **xtdpd**, [XT] **xtdpd postestimation**, [XT] **xtdpdsys**, [XT] **xtdpdsys postestimation**

bootstrap standard errors, [XT] *vce_options*

Bottai, M., [XT] **xtreg**

Bover, O., [XT] **xtdpd**, [XT] **xtdpdsys**

Boyle, P., [XT] **xtmepoisson**

Breslow, N. E., [XT] **xtmelogit**, [XT] **xtmepoisson**

Breusch–Pagan Lagrange multiplier test, [XT] **xtreg postestimation**

Breusch, T. S., [XT] **xtreg postestimation**

Bruno, G. S. F., [XT] **xtabond**, [XT] **xtdpd**, [XT] **xtdpdsys**, [XT] **xtreg**

Bryk, A. S., [XT] **xtmelogit**, [XT] **xtmepoisson**, [XT] **xtmixed**

C

Cameron, A. C., [XT] **xtnbreg**, [XT] **xtpoisson**

Carpenter, J. R., [XT] **xtmelogit**

Carroll, R. J., [XT] **xtmixed**

Carter, S. L., [XT] **xt**, [XT] **xtmelogit**, [XT] **xtmepoisson**, [XT] **xtmixed**

Casella, G., [XT] **xtmixed**

Caudill, S. B., [XT] **xtfrontier**

Center for Human Resource Research, [XT] **xt**

Chang, Y., [XT] **xtivreg**, [XT] **xtreg**

Chao, E. C., [XT] **xtmelogit**, [XT] **xtmelogit postestimation**, [XT] **xtmepoisson**, [XT] **xtmepoisson postestimation**

Clayton, D. G., [XT] **xtmelogit**, [XT] **xtmepoisson**

Cleland, J., [XT] **xtmelogit**

cluster estimator of variance, [XT] *vce_options*
  fit population-averaged panel-data models by using GEE, [XT] **xtgee**
  fixed- and random-effects linear models, [XT] **xtreg**
  population-averaged cloglog models, [XT] **xtcloglog**
  population-averaged logit models, [XT] **xtlogit**
  population-averaged negative binomial models, [XT] **xtnbreg**
  population-averaged Poisson models, [XT] **xtpoisson**
  population-averaged probit models, [XT] **xtprobit**

Coelli, T. J., [XT] **xtfrontier**

complementary log-log
  postestimation, [XT] **xtcloglog postestimation**
  regression, [XT] **xtcloglog**, [XT] **xtgee**

conditional logistic regression, [XT] **xtlogit**

constrained estimation, [XT] **estimation options**
  random- and fixed-effects logit models, [XT] **xtlogit**

Q

Qaqish, B., [XT] **xtgee**
quadchk command, [XT] **quadchk**
qualitative dependent variables, [XT] **xtcloglog**,
[XT] **xtgee**, [XT] **xtlogit**, [XT] **xtnbreg**,
[XT] **xtpoisson**, [XT] **xtprobit**

R

Rabe-Hesketh, S., [XT] **xtcloglog**, [XT] **xtgee**,
[XT] **xtintreg**, [XT] **xtlogit**, [XT] **xtmelogit**,
[XT] **xtmelogit postestimation**,
[XT] **xtmepoisson**, [XT] **xtmepoisson**
postestimation, [XT] **xtmixed**, [XT] **xtpoisson**,
[XT] **xtprobit**, [XT] **xtreg**, [XT] **xttobit**
random-coefficients
linear regression, [XT] **xtrc**
postestimation, [XT] **xtrc postestimation**
random-effects model, [XT] **xtabond**, [XT] **xtcloglog**,
[XT] **xtdpd**, [XT] **xtdpdsys**, [XT] **xtgee**,
[XT] **xthtaylor**, [XT] **xtintreg**, [XT] **xtivreg**,
[XT] **xtlogit**, [XT] **xtnbreg**, [XT] **xtpoisson**,
[XT] **xtprobit**, [XT] **xtreg**, [XT] **xtregar**,
[XT] **xttobit**
range of data, [XT] **xtsum**
Rao, C. R., [XT] **xtmixed**
Rao, D. S. P., [XT] **xtfrontier**
Rasbash, J., [XT] **xtmelogit**
Raudenbush, S. W., [XT] **xtmelogit**, [XT] **xtmepoisson**,
[XT] **xtmixed**
recovariance, estat subcommand, [XT] **xtmelogit**
postestimation, [XT] **xtmepoisson**
postestimation, [XT] **xtmixed postestimation**
regression (in generic sense),
dummy variables, with, [XT] **xtreg**
fixed-effects, [XT] **xtreg**
instrumental variables, [XT] **xtabond**, [XT] **xtdpd**,
[XT] **xtdpdsys**, [XT] **xthtaylor**, [XT] **xtivreg**
random-effects, [XT] **xtgee**, [XT] **xtreg**
Revankar, N., [XT] **xtfrontier**
robust, Huber/White/sandwich estimator of variance,
[XT] **vce_options**
fit population-averaged panel-data models by using
GEE, [XT] **xtgee**
fixed- and random-effects linear models, [XT] **xtreg**
linear dynamic panel-data estimation, [XT] **xtabond**,
[XT] **xtdpd**, [XT] **xtdpdsys**
population-averaged cloglog models, [XT] **xtcloglog**
population-averaged logit models, [XT] **xtlogit**
population-averaged negative binomial models,
[XT] **xtnbreg**
population-averaged Poisson models, [XT] **xtpoisson**
population-averaged probit models, [XT] **xtprobit**
Rodríguez, G., [XT] **xtmelogit**
Roodman, D., [XT] **xtdpd**, [XT] **xtdpdsys**
Rosen, H. S., [XT] **xtabond**, [XT] **xtdpd**,
[XT] **xtdpdsys**

Rubin, D. B., [XT] **xtmixed**
Ruppert, D., [XT] **xtmixed**

S

Sarafidis, V., [XT] **xtreg**
sargan, estat subcommand, [XT] **xtabond**
postestimation, [XT] **xtdpd postestimation**,
[XT] **xtdpdsys postestimation**
Sargan test, [XT] **xtabond postestimation**, [XT] **xtdpd**
postestimation, [XT] **xtdpdsys postestimation**
Schank, T., [XT] **xtmelogit**, [XT] **xtmepoisson**,
[XT] **xtmixed**, [XT] **xtreg**
Schmidt, P., [XT] **xtfrontier**
Searle, S. R., [XT] **xtmelogit**, [XT] **xtmepoisson**,
[XT] **xtmixed**
Self, S. G., [XT] **xtmelogit**, [XT] **xtmepoisson**,
[XT] **xtmixed**
Skrondal, A., [XT] **xtcloglog**, [XT] **xtgee**,
[XT] **xtintreg**, [XT] **xtlogit**, [XT] **xtmelogit**,
[XT] **xtmelogit postestimation**,
[XT] **xtmepoisson**, [XT] **xtmepoisson**
postestimation, [XT] **xtmixed**, [XT] **xtpoisson**,
[XT] **xtprobit**, [XT] **xttobit**
Smans, M., [XT] **xtmepoisson**
Smith, A. F. M., [XT] **xtcloglog**, [XT] **xtintreg**,
[XT] **xtlogit**, [XT] **xtmelogit**, [XT] **xtmepoisson**,
[XT] **xtpoisson**, [XT] **xtprobit**, [XT] **xttobit**
Song, S. H., [XT] **xtmixed**
Sosa-Escudero, W., [XT] **xtreg**
specification test, [XT] **xtreg postestimation**
Sribney, W. M., [XT] **xtfrontier**
standard deviations, displaying, [XT] **xtsum**
standard errors, panel-corrected, [XT] **xtpcse**
Stegun, I., [XT] **xtmelogit**, [XT] **xtmepoisson**
Stewart, M., [XT] **xtprobit**
stochastic frontier
model, [XT] **xtfrontier**
postestimation, [XT] **xtfrontier postestimation**
Stock, J. H., [XT] **xthtaylor**
Stram, D. O., [XT] **xtmixed**
Stroup, W. W., [XT] **xtmelogit**
summarizing data, [XT] **xtsum**
survival analysis, [XT] **xtnbreg**, [XT] **xtpoisson**
survival-time data, see survival analysis
Swamy, P. A. V. B., [XT] **xtivreg**, [XT] **xtrc**,
[XT] **xtreg**

T

table, frequency, see frequency table
Taub, A. J., [XT] **xtreg**
Taylor, C., [XT] **xtgee**, [XT] **xtreg**
Taylor, W. E., [XT] **xthtaylor**
test,
Breusch–Pagan Lagrange multiplier, see Breusch–
Pagan Lagrange multiplier test